MANAGERIAL ECONOMICS

TEXT, PROBLEMS, AND SHORT CASES

MANAGERIAL ECONOMICS

TEXT, PROBLEMS, AND SHORT CASES

SEVENTH EDITION

K. K. SEO

Professor of Financial Economics and Institutions
University of Hawaii at Manoa

Homewood, IL 60430
Boston, MA 02116

© RICHARD D. IRWIN, INC., 1959, 1964, 1968, 1975, 1979, 1984, and 1991

Sponsoring editor: Gary L. Nelson
Project editor: Karen Murphy
Production manager: Ann Cassady
Designer: Stuart Patterson
Compositor: Publication Services, Inc.
Typeface: 10/12 Times Roman
Printer: R. R. Donnelley & Sons Company

Library of Congress Cataloging-in-Publication Data

Seo, K. K.
　　Managerial economics : text, problems, and short-cases / K.K. Seo.
　— 7th ed.
　　　　p.　　cm.
　　Includes bibliographies and index.
　　ISBN 0-256-05662-5
　　1. Managerial economics.　2. Industrial management. 3. Decision-making.　I. Title.
　　HD30.22.S46　1991
　　338.5—dc20

　　　　　　　　　　　　　　　　　　　　　　　　　　　90–4605

To my family:
Katherine,
Darius, Margaret, Judith,
Charlie, Alex, and Maki

E D I T O R ' S N O T E

Revising a successful textbook requires the right compromise between continuity and innovation. An author must account for the steady march of theory and empirical evidence that often outpaces the present curricula. Even more difficult is developing text and problems that capture students' interest while maintaining appropriate standards of rigor. Such an effort requires patient, motivated prose born from countless hours in the classroom and at the word processor. K.K. Seo rose to this challenge to produce an outstanding vehicle for teaching modern managerial economics.

The seventh edition of *Managerial Economics* offers instructors and students modern, carefully developed tools of analysis for a rapidly changing world. This text has benefited from careful market research, numerous manuscript reviews, classroom testing by a dozen instructors and over 300 students, and careful editing, problem checking, and proofreading. This edition brings to the student a global, managerial perspective and integrates risk and uncertainty very early in the text. In all, the book provides students with an analytical foundation to help them solve the problems of the future, not to just recreate the analyses of the past.

We are grateful to the large number of instructors who have decided to let *Managerial Economics* enhance their students' education. Hundreds of thousands of students have used *Managerial Economics* since it was first published. Please note the highlights outlined in the Preface. We challenge you to let this edition of *Managerial Economics* work for you!

Using *Manager* Software to Solve Homework Problems in *Managerial Economics, Seventh Edition*

MANAGER Software can assist or solve numerous homework problems in your text. It can provide equations, numerical answers, and graphics. Following is a list of problems where *MANAGER* can be of use, and where appropriate, hints for transforming the information in the homework problem into a form allowing you to apply the tools in the software. All references are to the "Use Your Own Data" component of the software.

CHAPTER 10

CHAPTER 11

CHAPTER 12

CHAPTER 13

CHAPTER 15

PREFACE

The business environment has experienced two major changes since the previous edition of this text was published. First, there has been an acceleration of technological change, and second, national economies are being rapidly submerged into a global economy that is less and less sensitive to national policies. These developments have resulted in changes in the scope and context of managerial decision making, creating an environment in which economic analysis and its application assume even greater importance than before in both private and public sectors.

Like the previous edition, this seventh edition of *Managerial Economics* is designed to integrate economic theory with management science and other disciplines to provide a practical approach to managerial decision making in both the private and public sectors of the economy.

Although numerous changes have been made in the basic framework of this book as well as in its contents, the book continues to emphasize microeconomic analysis and tools for practical application of economic theory to the solution of real-life problems. Quantitative tools are provided to help the student gain greater insight into the methods of economic analysis as well as to facilitate the practical use of economics in decision making and problem solving. The text is intended for upper-division undergraduates, MBA candidates, graduate students in economics, and students in professional schools such as those in engineering, public administration, and public health.

Organization of the Text

The seventh edition contains 18 chapters that cover eight major topics, as follows:

1. The Nature of Managerial Economics and Behavior of the Firm (Chapters 1–2). These chapters discuss the nature of managerial economics and its relationship with other disciplines. Then they introduce the theory of the firm in alternative models, including a Japanese model, and show how models are used to explain and predict a firm's behavior. The present value concept is introduced as a tool for measurement of owners' wealth in terms of the present value of an anticipated future stream of income.

2. Optimization Techniques in the Decision Environment (Chapters 3–4). These chapters introduce utility theory and the decision environments of certainty, risk, and uncertainty. They then explain the techniques for optimal decision making under each of the three environments. Linear programming is covered in an appendix to Chapter 3.

3. Demand (Chapters 5–9). These five chapters analyze the sources and nature of demand, the measurement of demand, and the forecasting of demand. Separate chapters deal with consumer behavior (Chapter 5), demand functions and the elasticities of demand (Chapter 6), empirical estimation of demand using simple linear regression (Chapter 7), multiple linear regression (Chapter 8), and the forecasting of demand (Chapter 9).

4. Production and Cost (Chapters 10–13). These chapters present the theory and measurement of production and cost, with emphasis on empirical development of production and cost functions. Problems in measurement of input and output are discussed.

5. Profit Planning and Control (Chapter 14). This chapter deals with the use of budgets for profit planning and control and introduces break-even analysis as a profit-planning tool. The chapter also discusses problems of evaluating divisional performance in a decentralized firm.

6. Output and Pricing Decisions in Different Market Structures (Chapters 15–16). These chapters introduce the market structures of perfect competition, pure monopoly, monopolistic competition, and oligopoly and describe various methods of pricing that are actually practiced by firms operating in the different market structures.

7. The Economic Role of Government (Chapter 17). This chapter deals with economic externalities, government regulation of industry, antitrust laws and their enforcement, and the current trend of deregulation and privatization of public services.

8. Capital Budgeting (Chapter 18). This final chapter covers the estimation of the cost of capital, estimation of cash flows, and evaluation of investment proposals.

Unique Features

1. Internationalization of Text Materials. This text recognizes the increasing importance of the internationalization of the business curriculum. Wherever appropriate, this edition places the text, illustrative cases, examples, and end-of-chapter problems in an international business setting and the Japanese model of the firm is introduced. This emphasis is intended to remind students to approach decision making in a global context.

2. Flexibility of Coverage. Flexibility has been achieved for instructors in at least three different ways:

a. Chapters are largely self-contained, so they may be taken up in various orders to suit the instructor.

b. Appendixes containing fuller explanation or more rigorous analyses of material in the chapter have been added to some chapters.

c. Students with differing backgrounds are accommodated by separating chapters covering fundamentals from chapters containing additional rigorous material. For example, the general topic of demand analysis is covered by five chapters. For fundamental treatment, three chapters cover the specific topics of utility theory and consumer behavior, the elasticities of demand, and the elementary techniques of demand estimation. For more advanced treatment, the other two chapters cover multiple linear regression and forecasting. (Detailed suggestions for use of the text in undergraduate and graduate courses are contained in the Instructor's Manual.)

3. Illustrative problems and short cases. The theoretical material in each chapter is supported by illustrative problems designed to enhance understanding of the theory by showing its practical application. More rigorous application of the theory is reinforced by end-of-chapter problems and short cases.

4. Appropriate level of discourse. The seventh edition presupposes only that the student has completed courses in college algebra and typical introductory courses in micro- and macroeconomics. Although some calculus is used in the text, the student needs only to understand how to take a derivative. A complete set of formulas for taking derivatives is contained in Table I of the Appendix at the end of this book, although only the first three of these formulas is used in the text. In-depth discussions of the full range of optimization techniques using calculus are presented in chapter appendices.

Chapter Organization

All chapters have been reorganized into a standard format designed for clear presentation and ready reference. Each chapter of this edition is written in the following format:

1. Brief overview.
2. Chapter outline, briefly stating the contents of each major section of the chapter.
3. Text with illustrative problems and cases.
4. Chapter summary.
5. Problems and short cases.
6. References.
7. Appendixes, if any.

For better comprehension, illustrative problems are set off from the text with special typography to emphasize the application of theory.

Major Changes from the Previous Edition

In addition to updating textual materials to reflect the changing business environment, outdated materials have been deleted and new materials have been added. The layout of the chapters in this edition has been reorganized to emphasize application of managerial economics to problem solving. The comments of students and critiques by instructors who adopted the previous edition have been carefully reviewed and many of their suggestions have been incorporated in this edition. Major changes include the following:

1. Reorganization of the text:

   a. Chapter 1 of the sixth edition has been divided into two chapters in order to give each of the two chapters a clear identification with its contents. This has caused renumbering of Chapters 2 through 12 of the sixth edition into Chapters 3 through 13 of the seventh edition. Chapter 13, *Profit: Concepts and Measurement*, and Chapter 14, *Profit: Planning and Control*, in the sixth edition have become the seventh edition's Chapter 14, *Profit: Concepts, Measurement, Planning, and Control.* Chapter 18, *Capital Budgeting: Investment Selection,* and Chapter 19, *Capital Budgeting: Financial Policy,* in the sixth edition have been become the new Chapter 18 of the seventh edition, entitled *Capital Budgeting.* Altogether, the total number of chapters has been reduced from 19 in the sixth edition to 18 in the seventh edition.

    b. Eight new chapter appendixes have been added, and one has been deleted. The end-of-chapter appendixes cover new materials, illustrative cases, or materials that are either especially difficult (because of somewhat rigorous or sophisticated mathematics) or primarily of interest to advanced students.

    c. Material that has become obsolete since the previous edition has been deleted and about 40 percent of the remaining material has been rewritten for clarity and easier understanding. Whenever appropriate, old material has been expanded for better coverage of the topic.

    d. The end-of-chapter problems and short cases have been reworked to ensure that they are directly related to the text. Problems failing this test have been discarded and new problems have been created to provide emphasis on the internationalization of business. More than 30 percent of the end-of-chapter problems have been replaced and more than 25 percent of those retained have been rewritten.

        The end-of-chapter problems now include discussion questions that the instructor can use to clarify and reinforce the student's understanding of the theoretical material in the chapter. Short cases that extend the concepts and tools discussed in the text are also included for each chapter.

2. Major new materials:

    a. The agency model of managerial behavior (Chapter 2)

    b. The value-added maximization model (Japanese model) of the firm (Chapter 2)

    c. Derivation of the discount formula (Appendix 2A)

    d. An empirical study of value-added maximizing behavior by Japanese automakers (Appendix 2B)

    e. Linear programming, covering graphical solution, the simplex method, the dual, and sensitivity analysis (Appendix 3B)

    f. Probability distribution of cash flows (Appendix 4B)

    g. Mathematics of consumer equilibrium (Appendix 5A)

    h. Returns to scale and the firm's expansion path for expansion of production (Chapter 10)

    i. The effect of wage increases on jobs (Appendix 10A)

    j. Quadratic and cubic curve fitting (Appendix 11A)

    k. Cost behavior and managerial strategy (Chapter 12), which includes:

        (1) Minimum efficient scale

        (2) The learning curve and its application

    l. Rewards and costs of innovation (Chapter 14)

    m. Market-share model of oligopoly (Chapter 15)

    n. Deregulation and privatization trends (Chapter 17)

    o. Current capital-budgeting practices by major American firms (Chapter 18)

Ancillary Publications

For the Student

Updated Student Study Guide and Workbook.   Like the previous edition, the seventh edition is accompanied by a study guide under separate cover. The study guide is designed to enable the student to grasp the material in the text with a minimum of instruction. It consists of two parts. Part I contains for each chapter (1) a chapter outline, (2) a glossary of important terminology, and (3) a self-test consisting of true-false and multiple-choice questions and problems. Answers to the questions and solutions to the problems are also provided so students can check their grasp of the material in the chapter.

Part II of the Study Guide contains test material similar to Part I, but without answers and solutions. Part II thus can be assigned as graded homework. Answers and solutions are contained in the Instructor's Manual. The Study Guide will:

a. Emphasize the important concepts that the student must grasp.
b. Help the student solve end-of-chapter problems by providing similar examples.
c. Provide practice in the application of economic theory to practical problems.
d. Help the student to prepare for course exams.

For the Instructor

Instructor's Manual.   The Instructor's Manual is designed to give as much assistance as possible to an instructor who is using this text to teach a course in managerial economics. It consists of three parts. Part I contains the answers to the end-of-chapter problems in the text. Part II contains a large test bank of true-false and multiple-choice questions that the instructor may use to prepare examinations. Part III contains the answers to the questions and problems contained in Part II of the Study Guide.

Acknowledgments

In preparing this edition, I was fortunate to receive many helpful suggestions and comments from students and professors who have used the previous edition, and I have also benefited from comments and suggestions from many other colleagues. For their reviews of text material, I am particularly grateful to Professor James V. Koch, Old Dominion University; Dr. Kazukiyo Kurosawa,Tokyo Institute of Technology (Tokyo); Richard E. Peterson, Jack P. Suyderhoud, Russell A. Taussig, and Reginald G. Worthley of the University of Hawaii; Professor Barbara Beliveau, University of Connecticut; Professor Edward Heinze, Valparaiso University; Professor V. N. Krishnan, Bowling Green State University; Professor Gaines Liner, University of North Carolina at Charlotte; and Professor Joseph Maddalena, St. Thomas Aquinas College. For case material contribution and review, my thanks go to Professor Han Fenglin, Beijing Institute of Chemical Engineering (Beijing); Mr. C. K. Kim, Daelim Industrial Company (Seoul); Dr. George Shen, *Hong Kong Economic Journal* (Hong Kong); and Mr. Shunsei Tazoe, Seiso Bussan Company (Tokyo). Also, I want to express my deep appreciation to Dr. David H.

Bess, Dean of the College of Business Administration at the University of Hawaii, for his encouragement and support.

My special thanks go to Professor William A. Long, University of Hawaii, and Steven Schoen, Hawaiian Telephone Company. Mr. Schoen's painstaking editorial review of the manuscript greatly improved its readability. Professor Long, who taught me the subtleties of the English language and has been my colleague and dear friend for the past two decades, assisted me at every stage of the book's development and has agreed to co-author the Instructor's Manual and Study Guide.

I was also very fortunate to have able assistants who patiently and cheerfully performed many tasks related to preparation of my manuscript. They are Pauline Abe, David Kang, Jan Yamamoto, and Darcie Yoshinaga, all of the College of Business Administration of the University of Hawaii. Finally, I would like to thank the editorial staff at Richard D. Irwin for their invaluable assistance and especially for their choice of five reviewers, who gave my first manuscript a thorough critique and offered many valuable criticisms and suggestions that were incorporated into the final version of this text.

Although every effort has been made to eliminate errors in the text, some may have slipped through. If so, I accept full responsibility for them.

K.K. Seo

CONTENTS

MANAGERIAL ECONOMICS

TEXT, PROBLEMS, AND SHORT CASES

INTRODUCTION TO MANAGERIAL ECONOMICS

The application of economic theory and its stock of analytical tools to everyday activities is no easy matter, as many frustrated students of economics have found out. "The economic theory is very neat," they say, "and I understand the tools, but how do I apply them to real-life problems?"

Because this is a legitimate question for which there are no easy answers, the branch of economic study called **managerial economics** emerged in the 1940s to bridge the gap between theory and practice. Managerial economics today is an integral part of both undergraduate and graduate programs in business administration. It is also a popular offering in the curricula of other professional schools, such as those in engineering, public administration, public health, law, medicine, and urban and regional planning. This is because the principles and techniques of managerial economics apply not only to profit-seeking organizations, but to any organization that wants to optimize the use of its resources, whether that organization is domestic or international.

The Nature of Managerial Economics

To some, managerial economics is the application of economic theory (particularly microeconomic theory) to problems concerning the optimal allocation of economic resources. Other scholars view managerial economics as applied microeconomics, an approach requiring the integration of principles and practices from other functional areas such as accounting, finance, marketing, and management. Still other scholars regard managerial economics as a link between economic theory and decision science. Its purpose in this capacity is to contribute to sound decision making not only in business but also in government agencies and nonprofit organizations. Where alternative allocation strategies are available, managerial economics provides the tools to help identify the best alternative.

Actually, all of these views are correct, for managerial economics is all of these things. We need not choose among them, for certain common elements are readily apparent in all of these definitions. These common elements are:

1. Managerial economics is an application of economic theory, particularly microeconomic theory, to practical problem solving.
2. Managerial economics can be used to make better management decisions.
3. Managerial economics pertains to decision making about the optimal allocation of scarce resources to competing activities in both the private and public sectors.

Economic Theory and Managerial Economics

Economic theory traditionally is divided into two broad subfields: (1) microeconomics, which deals with economic behavior in the marketplace where buyers and sellers interact, and (2) macroeconomics, which deals with the behavior of economic aggregates such as the gross national product, national income, national employment, and national consumption. Macroeconomics focuses on the collective results of millions of individual economic decisions, while microeconomics focuses on the behavior of individual decision makers within the macroeconomic environment.

Since microeconomic theory deals with topics that are more closely associated with the firm's behavior in resource allocation (namely, consumer behavior, demand theory, production and cost analysis, market structure and pricing, profit planning, capital budgeting, and finance), it makes a major contribution to managerial economics. The individual firm, however, does not operate in a vacuum. Its environment is the general economy in a global setting, which both affects and is affected by the activities of billions of individuals who are producers and consumers all over the world.

The national and international economic climate, over which the individual firm has no control, largely influences the availability and price of the economic resources that the firm buys. These resources include such things as labor, materials, supplies, machinery, and equipment. The national and international economic climates also affect the availability and cost of financing, especially interest rates. On the revenue side, the national and international economic climates strongly influence the firm's ability to sell its products. Thus macroeconomics does make important contributions to managerial economics, even though managerial economics draws more heavily from the microeconomic side of economic theory.

Although a combination of microeconomic and macroeconomic theory is brought to bear on economic problem solving, effective decision making depends on more than economic theory. As illustrated in Exhibit 1–1, managerial economics also relies on economic methodology, analytical tools, and the principles of accounting, finance, marketing, personnel administration, and production.

EXHIBIT 1–1   The Nature of Managerial Economics

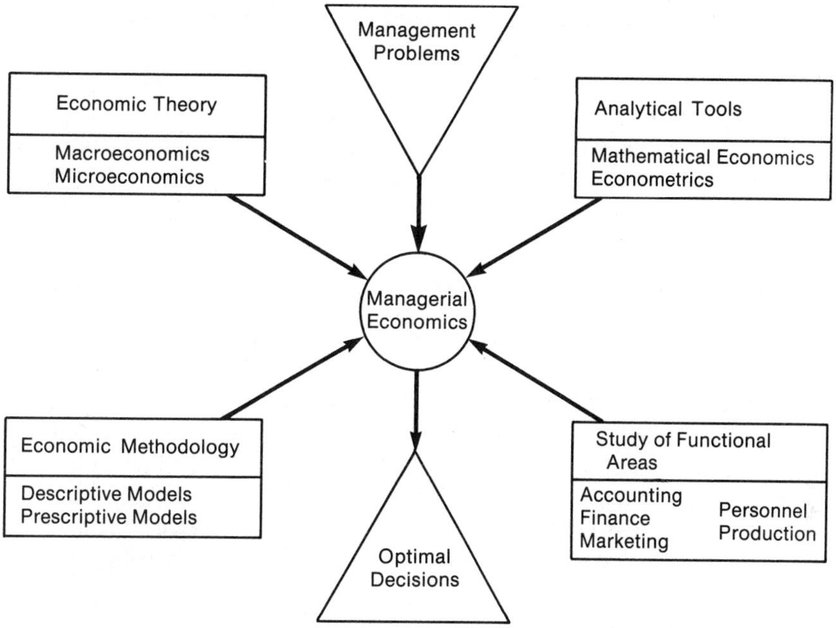

As the exhibit shows, there are two broad approaches to economic methodology, both of which involve the use of models that may be *descriptive* or *prescriptive*.[1] The two types may be used separately or in conjunction with each other.

Descriptive models are based upon empirical observations. They attempt to describe and explain economic relationships as they exist in the real world, but in a simplified, abstract way. Simplification is achieved through the aggregation of details, and often through necessary simplifying assumptions that may not correspond perfectly to facts in the real world. A good example of such a model is the model of perfect competition. It assumes perfect knowledge of the market by all concerned, which is manifestly impossible. Nevertheless, the model has been highly successful in explaining and predicting the general behavior of price movements in the real world. It is used as a norm, or benchmark, which can help us to explain the imperfections that actually occur in the real world. The fact that the model does not accurately describe real life in every respect does not prevent it from achieving its purpose, which is to *explain* and *predict* pricing behavior.

Prescriptive models are also called *normative* or *optimizing* models. An optimizing model enables a decision maker to find the most efficient way to reach a stated objective.

---

[1] A model is a simplified, abstract representation or generalization of reality whose purpose is to explain or predict the phenomenon being modeled. Since it is a generalization, it does not always explain individual phenomena.

An optimizing model defines an *objective function* in operational terms. It characterizes the set of *alternative strategies* that can achieve the objective within *specified constraints*. Finally, it prescribes the procedure(s) by which the decision maker can determine the optimal strategy, given those constraints.

Since business decisions are usually related to the optimization of some function, prescriptive models are the principal tools of managerial economics. However, descriptive models are often helpful in the development of such optimizing models. Our interest lies not so much in the classification of a model as in its ability to explain and predict the phenomenon under study.

Analytical Tools: Mathematical Economics and Econometrics

In mathematical economics, economic relationships are expressed in mathematical form, thereby rendering them amenable to empirical testing or other modeling techniques. In addition to making the search for solutions easier, mathematical representations often permit insights into problems that would easily be missed in a purely descriptive approach. Moreover, mathematical modeling often defines the limits of analysis and pinpoints infeasible alternatives.

Econometrics uses statistical techniques to test economic models developed to explain quantitative economic relationships. For example, statistical techniques may be used to determine the relationship between demand for a company's product and such factors as the product's price, the price of related products, consumer income, expenditures on advertising, and the number of potential consumers. Econometric methods can (1) help to identify the factors that influence demand, (2) determine how demand is impacted as those factors vary and/or interact, and (3) assist in accurate measurement of (1) and (2). Such information is very useful for making good decisions.

Managerial Economics in an International Setting

In recognition of the growing internationalization of the marketplaces of the world, this edition of *Managerial Economics* takes a global approach, using examples and cases from both domestic and international environments.

To be effective in the private or public sector today, managers need to be aware of the increasing internationalization of the marketplace. U.S. organizations doing business outside of the United States are finding that they must adapt management style, marketing strategy, and product development to different social, cultural, and political settings. This is to be expected, but even those businesses operating strictly within national boundaries increasingly are being affected by international trade and investment. For example, when the Soviet Union purchased a large quantity of wheat at less than the world market price, the price of flour for small bakeries in the United States rose by about 20 percent. Small and not-so-small businesses in the United States may find their competition coming from a foreign-owned firm. Companies anywhere in the world that find their labor costs are too high may elect to move production to another country where labor costs are lower. We can expect more integration of the world economy during the remainder of this century. Companies that want to grow and prosper will need to adapt their decision making to this worldwide market. Further, in this rapidly changing global setting, rigorous analysis is more necessary than ever for good decision making. This makes the analytical tools of managerial economics more valuable than ever before.

Summary

Managerial economics is a branch of economic study that bridges the gap between economic theory and practice. It is studied largely for its contribution to sound decision making, not only in profit-seeking businesses, but also in nonprofit organizations and government agencies.

Managerial economics incorporates elements of both micro- and macroeconomics. It uses both descriptive and prescriptive models and the analytical tools of mathematical economics and econometrics. The rapid internationalization of the marketplace makes the decision-making tools of managerial economics more valuable than ever before.

References

Cairncross, Sir Alec. "Economics in Theory and Practice." *American Economic Review* (May 1985), pp. 1–14.

Dean, Joel. *Managerial Economics*. Englewood Cliffs, N.J.: Prentice-Hall, 1951.

Harris, Robert G. "The Values of Economic Theory in Management Education." *AEA Papers and Proceedings* (May 1984), pp. 122–126.

McKinnon, Ronald I.; Christopher Radcliffe; Kong-Yam Tan; Arthur D. Warga; and Thomas D. Willett. "International Influences on the U. S. Economy: Summary of an Exchange." *American Economic Review* (December 1984), pp. 1132–1134.

C H A P T E R

2

THE FIRM AND
ITS BEHAVIOR

To understand the behavior of business organizations in the marketplace, it is useful first to examine (1) the role of the firm in society and (2) the goals and objectives of the business organization. Understanding these issues helps us to understand the firm's decision-making process with regard to production, cost control, and pricing in the marketplace—subjects that will be covered in subsequent chapters.

CHAPTER OUTLINE

This chapter will begin with a brief discussion of the firm's role in society and then introduce a number of models that have been advanced from time to time to explain the behavior of the firm. Accordingly, the chapter is divided into two sections and two appendixes:

1. **The Role of the Firm in Society.** This section briefly discusses the firm's relationship to society and the environment in which the firm must do business.
2. **Alternative Models of the Firm's Behavior.** This section discusses the motives that govern a firm's decision making and presents several models that have been advanced to explain a firm's behavior in the marketplace.
3. **Appendix 2A: Derivation of the Discount Formula.** This appendix shows how to derive the discount formula used for calculating the present value of a uniform stream of future payments.
4. **Appendix 2B: Empirical Study of Value-Added Behavior by Japanese Automakers.** This appendix describes an empirical study of the value-added behavior of Toyota, Nissan, Mazda, and Honda.

The Role of the Firm in Society

One of the major concerns of managerial economics is the way that profit-seeking businesses interact with the society in which they operate. To understand the firm's role in society, we might begin with the elementary proposition that raw materials are worthless until combined with labor and capital in an effective process of transformation. The role of the firm is to marshal the resources of capital and labor, allocate these scarce resources to competing activities, direct the transformation process so that useful goods and services are produced, and distribute these products to members of society in the marketplace, where competitive forces reward efficiency.

When the firm effectively serves society's desires for goods and services, the firm is rewarded with the profit that it seeks. This reward—profit—is in a certain sense the engine that drives the economic system for the benefit of all—workers, managers, investors, and consumers. Society relies upon the profit-seeking firm not only to produce goods or services it desires, but also to provide employment, pay taxes, and allocate scarce resources in an efficient manner.

The firm's operations in the marketplace, however, do not always coincide with society's demands for goods and services. To meet consumers' tastes and preferences, which often change, the firm must make correct decisions with regard to volume, price, quality, and timely production. The firm may not always have all of the information that it needs for such decisions, but nevertheless must operate in spite of the uncertainties of the marketplace. In the face of uncertainty, the firm must have good planning and effective strategies in order to survive and prosper.

Private firms operating in the competitive environment of a free market are best able to allocate scarce resources in an efficient and effective manner. Increasing awareness of this fact has led the U.S. government to deregulate some industries, such as airlines and financial institutions, including commercial banks. This awareness is emerging worldwide—even many socialist and communist countries have loosened government controls in recent years in the hope that movement toward a market economy will improve productivity and the utilization of resources for production of consumer goods. The trend toward further deregulation, in the United States and elsewhere, is likely to increase the demand for professional managers who are well versed in the principles and techniques of managerial economics.

Alternative Models of the Firm's Behavior

A number of models have been advanced to explain the behavior of business organizations and their managers in terms of their goals and objectives. These models include the profit-maximization model, the sales-maximization model, the growth-maximization model, three managerial-behavior models, and the Japanese model, which seeks to maximize value added by the firm.

The Profit-Maximization Model

It has long been customary for economists to assume that the primary goal of any type of organization is to maximize the benefits provided by the organization's operations in relation to its costs. In the case of a business organization, the benefits it seeks are profits. Since our economic system permits firms in unregulated industries to earn all they can, it was originally proposed that the firm is best described by a profit-maximization model derived from the theory of the firm set forth in microeconomic studies.

Earlier versions of the profit-maximization model concentrated on decision making to maximize short-run profits; that is, to maximize short-run total revenue minus total cost. In later versions of the model, the goal of the firm is assumed to be the maximization of the value of the firm in the long run. Since the firm's value in the long run depends upon a stream of future profits that may or may not actually materialize as expected, the model has been expanded to include the time value of money (the present value of future profits) and the concepts of risk. To understand the model, the student must have a clear understanding of the concept of present value.

Present Value. The concept of present value is based upon the principle of compound interest. Suppose that \$1 is invested today at i percent interest per annum; then one year from today the accumulated amount A_1, which is principal plus interest, will be

$$A_1 = \$1 + (\$1 \times i)$$

or

$$A_1 = \$1(1 + i) \tag{1}$$

and the accumulated amount two years from now, call it A_2, will be

$$A_2 = \$1(1 + i)(1 + i) = \$1(1 + i)^2. \tag{2}$$

The reverse of compounding is called discounting. If we expect A_2 to equal $\$1(1 + i)^2$ two years from now, it is worth \$1 now when discounted at i percent; that is

$$\frac{\$1(1 + i)^2}{(1 + i)^2} = \$1 \quad \text{or} \quad \frac{A_2}{(1 + i)^2} = \$1. \tag{3}$$

In general terms, the concept of the present value (PV) of future profits, π, is expressed by

$$PV = \frac{\pi}{(1 + i)^n} \tag{4}$$

where PV represents the present value of the future profit, π, available at the end of n discount periods in the future, with the risk-free periodic discount rate i expressed in decimal form. That is to say, if the future return is certain, the risk-free discount rate i is appropriate. If the future return is not certain, we use the risky discount rate r, where r equals i plus a **risk premium** to compensate for the risk involved. The magnitude of r reflects the degree of risk. It is the firm's **capitalization rate** or **cost of capital**, that is, the rate of return required by an investor after giving due consideration to the firm's business and financial risk.

Whether we use i or r, the model attempts to maximize the present value of the discounted flow of profits. When a stream of profits of differing magnitudes is expected over a period of years, the equation can be expanded as below, where π_1, π_2, π_3, and π_n represent profits expected to be realized in the first, second, third, and nth years and r is the risky discount rate or required rate of return:

$$PV = \frac{\pi_1}{(1 + r)} + \frac{\pi_2}{(1 + r)^2} + \frac{\pi_3}{(1 + r)^3} + \cdots + \frac{\pi_n}{(1 + r)^n}. \tag{5}$$

If the same amount of profit is expected every year, the problem of maximizing the stream of profits reduces simply to the problem of maximizing π. The present value of a stream of *equal* payments may be calculated by Equation 5, but is more easily calculated by the formula

$$PV = \pi \left[\frac{1 - (1 + r)^{-n}}{r} \right] \tag{6}$$

where p = the periodic payment, r = the periodic risky discount rate, and n = the number of periods. The expression in brackets is called the discount factor. Its derivation is explained in Appendix 2A at the end of this chapter, while discount factors for various annual discount rates are contained in Table A in the Appendix at the end of this book.

In a dynamic situation, where fluctuating values for π are projected, the problem of maximizing is more complicated, and Equation 5 must be used. However, as a practical approach to the problem, it is often useful to estimate a uniform annual profit in perpetuity and to project this into the future until a change in conditions (such as installation of a new plant) calls for a new projection.

If the flow of expected uniform annual profit, U, is projected for an indefinite period of time (i.e., into perpetuity), the following equation defines the present value, PV, of this income sequence:

$$PV = \frac{U}{r} \tag{7}$$

where r is the appropriate capitalization rate that reflects the business and financial risk of the firm.[1]

Illustrative Problem

John M., a recent graduate of a college of business administration, has inherited $100,000 in cash from his grandfather. He is considering three different proposals of equal risk for investment of his inheritance. Each alternative requires an initial investment of $100,000. Expected returns are:

Year	Proposal 1	Proposal 2	Proposal 3
1	$ 30,000	$ 50,000	$—0—
2	30,000	50,000	30,000
3	30,000	30,000	60,000
4	30,000	20,000	60,000
5	30,000	—0—	—0—
Total	$150,000	$150,000	$150,000

---

[1] The formula may be derived from Equation 6: $PV = U[1 - \frac{1}{(1+r)^n}/r] = \frac{U}{r} - \frac{U}{r(1+r)^n}$. As n approaches infinity, $\frac{U}{r(1+r)^n}$ approaches zero. Hence $PV = \frac{U}{r}$.

Questions:

a. What is the net present value (i.e., discounted cash inflows minus discounted cash outflows) of each proposal at a discount rate of 12 percent?
b. What is the effect on present value of the timing of cash flows?

Solutions:

a. *Proposal 1:* $PV = 30,000 \left[\dfrac{1 - (1.12)^{-5}}{0.12} \right] - \$100,000 = \$8,143$

   Proposal 2: $PV = \dfrac{\$50,000}{1.12} + \dfrac{\$50,000}{(1.12)^2} + \dfrac{\$30,000}{(1.12)^3} + \dfrac{\$20,000}{(1.12)^4} - \$100,000 = \$18,566$

   Proposal 3: $PV = \dfrac{\$30,000}{(1.12)^2} + \dfrac{\$60,000}{(1.12)^3} + \dfrac{\$60,000}{(1.12)^4} - \$100,000 = \$4,754$

b. The longer the cash return is postponed, the less it is worth. Thus Proposal 2, which receives its largest cash inflows in the earlier years, is worth more than either Proposal 1 or Proposal 3. Proposal 3, which receives larger annual sums than either Proposal 1 or Proposal 2, but gets those sums in the later years, is worth the least.

Maximization of Owners' Wealth.   The measure of owners' wealth is the per-share valuation of the firm. Therefore the profit-maximization model includes the firm's attempt to maximize the market value per-share of its stock. The fundamental approach to per-share valuation may be expressed as

$$V = \frac{E}{r}$$

where

   V = the capitalized value per share
   E = the expected yield per share, that is, profit (total revenue − total cost) divided by the number of shares outstanding. (This is not the same as the dividend per share unless all of the company's earnings are distributed as dividends, which is usually not the case.)
   r = the stockholder's capitalization rate, or required rate of return.

This approach is employed universally in the valuation of stocks by investors who multiply estimated earnings by a factor variously known as the **price–earnings ratio, times–earnings ratio,** or **price–earnings multiplier** to arrive at an estimated value for the stock in question. The price–earnings ratio is simply the reciprocal of the capitalization rate, r (i.e., $1/r$).

The firm's decision-making process greatly depends upon the interrelationship between the earnings per share, E, and the required rate of return, r, where r reflects the risk perceived by the firm to be inherent in a particular investment proposal. For example, suppose a firm's cost of capital is such that the owners require a 20 percent rate of return on their investment. If the firm's annual earnings are $1 per share, the capitalized value of the firm is

$$V = \frac{\$1.00}{0.20} = \$5 \text{ per share.}$$

Now suppose that the firm has an opportunity to invest in a project that will increase earnings by 20 cents per share but will also increase its risk to the point where a prudent investor would demand a 25 percent return. The increased earnings might be very tempting to management until they consider the effect on the capitalized value of the common stock. Because of the increased risk, the capitalized value of the common stock would decrease to

$$V = \frac{\$1.20}{0.25} = \$4.80.$$

The decision criterion should be clear—the proposed project would increase earnings by 20 percent, but the required rate of return has increased by 25 percent (from 0.20 to 0.25). Consequently, the owners' wealth, as measured by the value of the stock, has declined. This is why it is axiomatic in business that the higher the risk, the higher the required profit. Otherwise, riskier projects would not be undertaken.

The present value of future profits represents the value of the firm at any given level of risk, the level of risk being incorporated in the discount rate, r. Therefore, maximizing the present value of future profits is the same as maximizing owners' wealth. The profit-maximization model thus holds that a firm's management seeks to maximize the present value of future profits subject to a given level of risk.

Illustrative Problem

American Sports, Inc. (ASI) exports American-made ski equipment for sale in Japan. The capitalized value of ASI's common stock is $45 per share and current earnings are $4.50 per share. ASI has been offered the distributorship for a line of American-made sportswear, which may increase earnings by about $1.25 per share. However, ASI would have to borrow additional working capital in order to maintain an adequate stock for immediate shipment upon receipt of an order. Also, ASI's management notes that the rate of exchange between the U.S. dollar and the Japanese yen is unstable, and predicting the tastes of Japanese consumers is no easy matter. After evaluating the business risk involved in marketing a new line, the financial risk of an unpredictable exchange rate, and other factors, ASI's management concludes that in order to take on the new line, it must be assured of a return on investment of 19 percent.

Questions:

a. Find the present rate of return on investment.
b. Should ASI market the new line of sportswear in Japan?

Solutions:

a.

$$V = \frac{E}{r}, \text{ hence } r = \frac{E}{V}$$

$$r = \frac{\$4.50}{\$45} = 0.10 \text{ or } 10\%$$

b.

$$V = \frac{4.50 + 1.25}{0.19} = \frac{5.75}{0.19} = \$30.26$$

or

$$r = \frac{\$5.75}{\$45} = 0.1277 \approx 12.8\%$$

If ASI accepts the offer, the capitalized value of its stock will decrease from $45.00 to $30.26. Alternatively, we note that the return on stock capitalized at $45 is less than the required 19 percent. Both solutions indicate that ASI should not accept the offer.

Limitations of the Profit-Maximization Model.   The principles governing the profit-maximization model may tell us much about how firms would like to behave, how they would like to make investment decisions, and how they would prefer to time their activities. In a world in which the timing of investments is crucial to success, the profit-maximization model can give important insights into the probable behavior of firms. But the profit-maximization model, like all models, is a simplified, abstract version of reality. In the real world, there are a number of complexities that limit its descriptive adequacy. This is because in addition to a lack of complete information, (1) it requires the firm to predict accurately the magnitude and timing of a stream of profits to be realized in the future—something that is difficult to do under the best of circumstances and impossible under the worst—and (2) there are many legal, ethical, and social constraints that limit a firm's all-out pursuit of profit. Within this network of constraints, the firm seeks optimal profit.

This means that firms do not necessarily seek maximum profits but instead seek to balance their desire for profit with other goals and objectives—short-run and long-run, economic and noneconomic. Achievement of these other goals as well as profits provides maximization of benefits, and this is not necessarily the same as maximization of profit.

Recognition of this fact has led to a number of alternative models that state that the motivation of the firm is something other than maximization of profit. These models, which are of considerable importance to the understanding of the behavior of firms, can be grouped into four general classes:[2]

- Sales-maximization models
- Growth-maximization models
- Managerial-behavior models
- Value-added–maximization models.

---

[2] There are also "realism-in-process" models (developed by behavioral scientists) and game-theory models (developed by operations-research analysts). For more detailed discussion, see James Koch, *Industrial Organization and Price Level*, 2nd ed. (Englewood Cliffs, N.J.: Prentice-Hall, 1980), chap. 3, and other references at the end of this chapter.

Sales-Maximization Model

The sales-maximization model is probably the best known alternative to the profit-maximization model. This is because it is easily understood and because it can be supported by intuitively appealing anecdotal examples. Rigorous empirical tests, however, have failed to support the strict sales-maximization hypothesis, particularly in terms of the long-run objectives of the firm.

Scholars have cited a number of reasons why firms might give first consideration to sales revenues:

1. A change in sales will bring about larger changes in sales techniques and production technology than an equivalent change in profits.
2. The firm's management may feel that lack of growth in sales will impair the company's reputation and dealings with its customers, distributors, financial institutions, and employees.
3. The firm's management may feel that lack of growth in sales will reduce the company's influence in the marketplace and make it more vulnerable to competitors.
4. Because of the separation of management from ownership, corporate-management performance is more apt to be judged by the level of sales than by the level of profits (as long as a satisfactory profit is maintained).

The proponents of sales maximization recognize that some minimum level of profit is necessary, but they hold that the sales-maximizing firm is willing to sacrifice some or all profit above this minimum in order to increase sales. Casual observations often have been made of this type of behavior. Japanese firms, in particular, have drawn considerable attention to their efforts to increase their share of the world market by allegedly "dumping" (i.e., selling their product abroad at prices lower than those charged in their own country), a tactic that is objectionable to the United States. Japanese makers of computer chips, for example, have been accused of dumping their products either directly in the United States or through an intermediary such as Hong Kong. While dumping may be an effective way to increase market share, it is illegal in the United States.

Another example arose in the latter half of the 1980s when the U.S. dollar depreciated in value against the Japanese yen. Japanese automakers would have been forced to raise their prices in the United States if they had wanted to maintain their profit margins. Instead, they chose to hold the line on dollar prices, thus accepting lower profits in order to preserve their market shares. Such behavior is an important factor in international trade. However, the nature of the evidence suggests that such firms may be sacrificing some short-run profits in order to maximize profits in the long run. Sales maximization is part of their strategy to secure an advantageous competitive position that will produce more profit in the long run.

Growth-Maximization Model

In any company, growth is apt to be the cornerstone of corporate strategy. Growth and growth potential are the yardsticks used to measure corporate success in annual reports, in the financial pages of the press, and by financial analysts and investors. Under the conventional profit-maximization model, however, once the firm finds an equilibrium level of output that will maximize its profits, output will remain constant as long as costs and demand remain constant. There is no reason for the firm to expand production and sales any further.

In reality, of course, demands and costs do not remain constant, and firms do want to grow for many of the same reasons that motivate them to maximize sales. Growth, however, must be financed either from retained earnings or from borrowing, usually from both. A prudent management seeks to maintain a debt/asset ratio high enough to stimulate growth, but not high enough to indicate an imprudent level of risk.

The long-run growth of the firm depends upon the continued availability of a large stream of profits. It seems clear, then, that whatever differences may exist in the short-run interests of growth-maximizing, sales-maximizing, or profit-maximizing firms, their long-run interests and decisions are virtually the same. The decision to maximize growth is necessarily a decision to maximize profit in the long run.

Managerial-Behavior Models

Managerial-behavior models are concerned with the separation between owners and managers that is inherent in publicly held corporations. Managerial-behavior models include the *managerial-utility model*, the *managerial-discretion model*, and the *agency model*. All of these models make two basic assumptions: (1) both the owners (stockholders) and the managers are rational beings who attempt to maximize their own personal utilities and (2) there is an inherent contradiction between the interests of the owners and the interests of the managers such that when managers try to maximize their utility, they diminish the utility of the owners.

The Managerial-Utility Model. This model is based on the proposition that the separation of ownership and management in modern corporations results in economically important behavior. It argues that owners (stockholders) want to maximize the value of the firm and are therefore interested in maximizing profits. Managers, the model says, have a different set of goals, motives, needs, and desires, and are more interested in satisfying these interests for their own personal benefit than in maximizing the firm's value for its owners. The model asserts that (1) profit rates are lower in manager-controlled firms than in owner-controlled firms because management ignores the profit-maximizing interests of the owners and (2) professional managers have no personal interest in maximizing profits. Neither of these propositions has stood up under rigorous empirical investigation, according to researchers in this area.

Empirical studies by a number of scholars have demonstrated that salaries are only part of total executive compensation. The remainder takes the form of valuable perquisites, bonuses, stock options, and profit sharing, all of which depend upon profits. The empirical evidence suggests, then, that professional managers do have a direct and personal interest in maximizing profits.

The Managerial-Discretion Model.   A more useful theory of the firm based upon managerial behavior is found in the managerial-discretion model. In this model, managers are free to pursue their own self-interests once they have achieved a level of profit that will pay satisfactory dividends to stockholders and still provide funds for growth. The manager's self-interest depends upon many things besides salary. These include other forms of compensation, the number and type of people supervised, non-income perquisites, and the amount of discretion exercisable in spending or investing the firm's money. When the firm is prospering, managers tend to extract nonessential perquisites from the firm (such as chauffeured limousines). Behaviorists call these nonessential items **management slack**.

The general hypothesis of the managerial-discretion model is that firms led by a utility-maximizing manager spend more on staff and exhibit more organizational slack than a profit-maximizing firm. The empirical evidence offered to support this model is only mildly supportive and suffers from several deficiencies. Most notably, the measure of compensation does not give sufficient weight to compensation other than salary. Consequently, it may seriously underestimate the profit-maximizing behavior of managers in the real world.

The Agency Model.   The agency model is concerned with contractual relationships between the **principals** (stockholders) and their **agents** (the managers). In order for the managers to function, the stockholders, acting through their board of directors, must delegate decision-making authority to a chief executive officer (CEO). The CEO's authority will include the right to further delegate decision-making power to other executives of the firm.

There are a number of things that executives might do in pursuit of their own interests rather than maximization of the owners' wealth. For example, managers might enact highly visible policies that make themselves look good and thus insure promotions. Dishonest managers might make decisions to enhance their personal wealth at company expense, such as buying from higher-cost suppliers who give kickbacks. Managers might be more interested in expensive perquisites (perks), such as beautifully decorated offices, luxury automobiles, and memberships in exclusive country clubs, than in reducing costs. Managers might tend to avoid decisions with elements of risk that might threaten their jobs, or that might lead to stress and conflict inside the company or in the marketplace, without regard to maximization of profits.

The problem is that the stockholders have no way of knowing whether or not managers are doing their best to maximize the owners' wealth. Stockholders can observe the *results* of top management activities (the bottom line). But unless the stockholders are also the managers (as in a closely held corporation), they are not in a position to observe the day-to-day process of company management.

If the results are unsatisfactory, the owners, acting through their board of directors, have the power to discipline managers by denying them salary increases or bonuses, or even by firing and replacing them. But even when results are satisfactory, stockholders are not able to determine if the results actually represent the managers' best efforts in their behalf.

It is theoretically possible for stockholders to evaluate the managers' efforts by establishing an elaborate and costly intelligence system to monitor the managers' actions. In reality, of course, the stockholders' interests lie in avoiding such costs, and some agency theorists hold that monitoring management action is unnecessary. They point to empirical data that show a strong relationship between a company's profitability and executive compensation and offer these data as proof that market dynamics are sufficient to lead managers to give their best effort.

Other theorists argue that some costs to the stockholders are inevitable and are best incurred in the form of incentives for managers to give their best efforts for maximization of the owners' wealth. This usually takes the form of an employment contract that provides for an annual bonus directly related to the firm's profits. The bonus may be related to the current year's profits or to the firm's performance over several years in the immediate past.

Of course, this type of profit sharing does not guarantee peak performance because managers still have more knowledge than stockholders about the firm's operation. Despite the bonus, they can still put out less than maximum effort or still seek expensive perks. In recognition of this fact, stockholders may seek to share the risks of ownership with managers by granting them stock options. The effect is to more nearly align the managers' interests with the owners' interests.

The agency model described previously may not apply to firms outside the United States. In other countries, executive salaries are much lower than in the United States and perquisites are more generous. Also laws of other countries may forbid such devices as stock options. In Germany, for example, onerous tax laws make stock options impracticable. In Japan, executives are forbidden to own stock in their company. Further, the basic assumption of conflict between the interests of owners and managers does not hold in the value-added–maximization behavior of Japanese companies, which is described next.

Value-Added–Maximization Model (Japanese Model)

Although the profit-maximization model can be applied either short-run or long-run, in reality U.S. firms tend to concentrate on short-run profits. To satisfy stockholders and financiers, earnings are reported quarterly, semiannually, and annually. Emphasis is on financial aspects such as earnings per share during these short-run periods, rather than on the long-run concepts of improving productive resources or organization.

The concentration on short-run profits to satisfy stockholders is a simplistic concept that largely ignores the interests of the firm's most important productive resource—the employees who make the firm's earnings possible. Management often tries to improve the firm's financial picture by holding down wages to reduce costs, while labor unions keep pressing their own interests such as higher wages and expanded fringe benefits. Thus the emphasis on short-run profits is in large measure responsible for the adversarial relationship between American management and rank-and-file workers.

In contrast, very few Japanese firms use a short-run approach, such as maximizing the current quarter's earnings per share, as a guide for managing the firm. Instead they attempt to maximize **value added** by their productive activities. The company buys raw materials (goods and services) from suppliers outside the company. Value is added to these raw materials by the coordinated activities of managers and workers who use the assets of the company to convert the raw materials into the company's product. Value added can be calculated as sales minus the cost of goods and services purchased from suppliers outside of the company. Thus value added includes labor, management, capital costs, and profits.

The value-added model is a long-range concept that seeks to provide maximum benefits for all concerned—management, workers, suppliers, and stockholders. The underlying philosophy is that private corporations exist primarily to reward their employees, both management and ordinary workers. Rewards include not only expanding wages, salaries, and fringe benefits, but also the satisfaction that comes from making a high-quality product. The salaries of management, the wages of workers, and other personnel expenses are all integral parts of the total value added. Thus management and labor are not adversaries; rather, they are partners in pursuit of the same goal—maximization of value added.

When maximizing value added is the goal, both managers and workers become keenly aware that each one's personal interests are inseparably linked to the ability of their firm to compete in global markets. They all pull together to cut costs and increase sales. Together they seek ways to improve the productivity of their labor and of the firm's investment in capital goods (fixed assets). Together they design and produce innovative products for the world's markets.

Every employee and stockholder of a value-added–maximizing firm is aware that continued investments in plant and equipment, in research and development, and in market development must be given the highest priority, regardless of economic conditions. If need be, necessary and agreed-upon investments are financed by temporary restraint of salaries, wages, and stock dividends. If employee compensation must be reduced, top management salaries are cut first. This is how the Japanese automakers and other Japanese manufacturers have managed to increase their value-added targets year after year regardless of general economic conditions.

American Difficulties with the Japanese Model

The Japanese model is rooted in their culture, which stresses harmonious and cooperative relationships within the family, between workers and management, and between government and business. (It is not clear, however, that such relationships extend across international boundaries.) This cultural value seems to be exhibited in steadfast devotion to the practice of maximizing value added. It also helps to explain the success of Japanese firms in coordinating the major functions of manufacturing, research and development, and marketing. Such coordination requires a corporate environment that fosters learning, camaraderie, and a strong commitment to the corporate goal by all employees.

Unfortunately, despite notable exceptions, many American executives equate corporate leadership with personal power. They see themselves as "king of the hill" in their respective companies, with decision-making authority extending from the top down. All too often, management is exercised in American companies by pitting one profit or cost center against another or one individual against another. Often each segment of the company has its own budget that has to be met without thought of consequences to the firm as a whole. Production managers may be told to cut production costs any way they can. As a result, one American firm after another has moved production from the United States into countries with lower wage rates. This may be a simple solution in the short run, but it is not a good solution for the industry in the long run because it tends to destroy the manufacturing base for a strong economy.

In some American firms, financing decisions come before strategic investment decisions. Emphasis may be placed on financial controls that enable the firm to achieve budgeted short-run profits. In contrast, Japanese firms put investment decisions ahead of financing decisions, and this gives them the ability to make rapid adjustments to technological and marketing changes. When a profit-maximizing firm meets a value-added–maximizing firm in head-on competition in the international marketplace, the odds are that the profit-maximizing firm will be the loser.

Evaluation: Why We Use a Profit-Maximizing Model

Each of the models discussed in this chapter is based upon a different premise with respect to the objective of the firm. Our ability to explain and predict managerial-behavior patterns and decision-making processes depends upon which model we choose. The harmonious corporate organization embodied in the value-added–maximization model (Japanese model) seems to offer a competitive edge in the international marketplace and is worthy of serious consideration by American firms. However, we use the profit-maximization model in this text because of all the models discussed, it is best able to explain and predict the behavior of the vast majority of American firms. Even so, the profit-maximization model has many critics. The main arguments offered by the critics may be summarized as follows:

- Profit maximization is not a rational action for managers to take.
- In the real world of uncertainty, managers do not have the knowledge of demand, costs, and future events that is necessary for profit maximization.
- In the modern firm, managers pursue many goals besides profit.
- The separation of ownership and management in a modern corporation diverts managers' interests from maximizing profits to maximizing their own welfare.
- Policies that tend to maximize profits cause increased risk and instability, which managers fear. Therefore, risk-averse managers avoid a policy of profit maximization.

Defenders of the profit-maximization model respond with three major counterarguments:

- There is very little empirical evidence to support *any* of the models discussed in this chapter, including the profit-maximization model.
- Regardless of what managers may say about their motivation, if they act as if they are attempting to maximize profits, then the profit-maximization model is valid.
- When vigorous competition exists, the firm that does not maximize profits does not survive.

We can expand these arguments into at least five good reasons why we should persist in using the profit-maximization model:

1. *Survival against competition requires profits.* Consider the strong competition that a firm encounters, not only in the markets where it sells its goods, but also in the financial markets where it must obtain its working capital. Such competition forces management to pay close attention to profits. The larger its profits, the easier it is for the firm to succeed in both markets. Hence, the tendency is to pursue maximum profits.

2. *Managerial compensation is closely related to profitability.* Recent studies reveal that the gap between managers' and owners' interests is more apparent than real, and managers do have a strong incentive to maximize profits. Furthermore, about 40 percent of corporate stock is held by financial institutions, and this share is growing. These institutions have the potential to intervene in corporate management. Top managers of publicly held corporations are well aware of this potential and thus have a powerful incentive to maximize profits.

3. *The profit-maximizing model best explains and predicts the firm's behavior.* The assumption of profit-maximizing behavior by business managers may be an oversimplification of the firm's multifaceted objectives. This doesn't matter as long as the resulting model enables us to understand and predict the behavior of business firms.

4. *The profit-maximization model explicitly provides for necessary cost analyses.* Before management can arrive at a decision as to whether to maximize profits or to settle for something else, it must consider costs as well as benefits.

5. *The profit-maximization model provides an insight into the relative costs and benefits of long-range versus short-range planning.* This issue is particularly apparent when social responsibilities are considered. A firm's pursuit of profit is often tempered by its social responsibilities. Most of these responsibilities are imposed by government, but in some cases a firm's management assumes social responsibilities on its own initiative. There is, however, a question: How far can a firm be expected to go in bearing the costs of social-responsibility programs without receiving commensurate benefits—especially in the short run?

Some farsighted firms, without abandoning their goal of profit optimization, have already initiated programs designed to create long-run benefits for themselves as well as for society. Such firms are willing, within limits, to sacrifice a certain amount of short-run profit to obtain a long-run benefit.

Summary

Managerial economics shows that the profit-seeking firm enjoys a mutually beneficial relationship with the society in which it exists. The firm provides employment, taxes, and goods or services by allocating scarce resources in an efficient manner. In exchange for these benefits, the firm is rewarded with profits. Profit, then, is the engine that powers our economic system.

The profit-maximization model will be used throughout this book to explain and predict the behavior of business organizations in the United States despite legal, moral, and social constraints. There are a number of other models, however, that postulate objectives other than the maximization of profits. These objectives include maximization of sales and maximization of growth. A close examination of these models reveals that although they differ from the profit-maximization model with respect to short-run objectives, they share with the profit-maximization model the long-run objective of maximizing profit.

Another model stresses the effect of the separation between owners and managers. It holds that managers seek to maximize their own welfare. However, close scrutiny reveals that a manager's welfare is more closely tied to the company's profits than to anything else.

The value-added maximization (Japanese) model emphasizes decision making for the long term and best explains the behavior of many firms in Japan. It holds that the firm exists for the long-run welfare of all persons involved with the corporation—employees, managers, suppliers, and stockholders. The firm's objective is to increase the value added to the goods and services purchased from outside suppliers. This objective is pursued regardless of economic cycles. In bad times, the firm increases its bank loans and may temporarily reduce dividends to stockholders and compensation to its employees; in good times, higher earnings are used to increase its equity in total assets. Thus the firm's behavior is characterized by continuous emphasis on technological improvement and production flexibility.

Although the Japanese model is based upon their cultural values, some Japanese manufacturers, such as Honda, have established plants in the United States where they are practicing the Japanese style of management with remarkable success. This seems to indicate that the Japanese approach to harmonious labor-management relations is worth some concentrated study by American managers.

Problems

1. In *Time* magazine David B. Tinnan wrote, "It is historical irony that in the United States, the stronghold of world capitalism, so few citizens understand that profits provide the basis for the prosperity on which rests the well-being of both individuals and the nation."

   a. Explain the crucial function that economic profit performs in a market-enterprise system such as our own.

   b. Telephone companies, electric-power companies, and other utilities are examples of government-regulated industries. Inasmuch as profit is such a strong incentive, why does the government continue to regulate them?

   c. Does the deregulation of the airline, trucking, and banking industries show that Americans are

   learning to understand the role of profit in the economy? Explain.

2. Some economists have advanced a theory of the firm that postulates that firms seek to maximize sales rather than profits or the value of the firm.

   a. Explain what the motivation of managers might be in seeking to maximize sales rather than profits.

   b. Explain the reasons why we retain the theory of the firm in terms of value maximization rather than sales maximization.

3. Another model advanced as an alternative to the value-maximization model of the firm postulates that with the advent of the modern corporation and the resulting separation of management from ownership, managers are more interested in maximizing their own utility than corporate profits.

a. Indicate how you would measure managers' utility.

b. Explain the reason why this theory cannot supplant our theory of the firm in terms of value maximization.

4. Almost all successful business firms desire to grow and do grow, but there is a limit to the size to which they can grow. Explain why this is so.

5. Johnson & Johnson, the maker of Tylenol, had its share of the pain-reliever market threatened when someone poisoned some Tylenol capsules in their containers. Removing all Tylenol capsules from the shelves, conducting hundreds of tests, and running a costly promotional campaign resulted in a tremendous drop in profits. Because of these drastic measures, however, Johnson & Johnson has managed to save a large portion of its market.

a. What profit theory was Johnson & Johnson following?

b. Why do companies focus on market share?

c. Why didn't Johnson & Johnson simply change the Tylenol brand name?

6. A few years ago, after congressional hearings on the problems of stockholder control, Senator Howard Metzenbaum (Dem-Ohio), said, "Too often the individual shareholders have little or no say about how that money is actually spent."

His view is strongly shared by Carl Icahn, chairman of Icahn & Company, a member of the New York Stock Exchange, who says the directors and chief executive officers of publicly held American companies "are for the most part answerable to no one." Corporate democracy, he lamented, "does not work because there is no real corporate democracy. Annual corporate elections have become a travesty."

Although an estimated 30 million individuals own stock in U.S. corporations, there has been an almost total void in organizing shareholders. There have been some sporadic efforts in the past to unite stockholders to protect their own interests, but they remain among the nation's most docile minority groups.

Suggest how stockholders might make their voices heard by top management.

7. Some economists warn that lavish raises for corporate executives could spark an upsurge of inflation because rank-and-file workers can exploit such salary jumps to justify higher wages for themselves. And that, in turn, would make the United States even less competitive with foreign producers than it is now.

From 1979 to 1989, annual compensation for the nation's major business executives has increased 12 to 16 percent each year, with the 25 highest-paid receiving from more than $3 million up to $18 million in salary, bonuses, stock options, and other compensation.

In 1984, Clayton Yuetter, President Reagan's chief trade representative, was so indignant over such high compensation that he threatened to remove the pressure on Japan for another year of voluntary quotas on auto exports to the United States. Japanese executives are paid only about one fifth of what their American counterparts get.

a. In your opinion, are American executives really worth the compensation they are getting?

b. Does the compensation that American executives receive impair their firms' abilities to compete in the world market?

8. What effect would the following situations have on the capital value of a firm's stock?

a. Interest rates rise substantially.

b. The firm develops a time-saving technological breakthrough.

c. The union wins a labor dispute resulting in a 20 percent pay hike.

9. Global Inc. has a current capitalized value of $25 per share and current annual earnings of $3 per share. Global has been offered a lucrative investment that would increase earnings by 95 cents per share but at the same time would increase the company's business risk so as to require a 15 percent return on investment.

a. What is Global's present rate of return on investment?

b. Should Global accept the new investment?

c. Explain the correlation between risk and return.

d. What is Global's major problem when making investment decisions for the future?

10. A firm is contemplating an advertising campaign that promises to yield $115 in increased profits one year from now for every $100 spent now.

Should the firm give up $100 of current profits to make $115 one year from now?

11. A firm has three proposals under consideration. As shown in the following table, the first proposal promises a cash inflow of $10,000 per year for 10 years. The second proposal offers a return of $75,000, all of which comes in the first four years. The third proposal offers a return of $115,000. Receipts don't start until the fourth year, but they are fully realized within the following five years.

Timing of Cash Flow

Year	Proposal 1	Proposal 2	Proposal 3
1	$ 10,000	$30,000	—0—
2	10,000	20,000	—0—
3	10,000	15,000	—0—
4	10,000	10,000	$ 10,000
5	10,000	—0—	15,000
6	10,000	—0—	20,000
7	10,000	—0—	30,000
8	10,000	—0—	40,000
9	10,000	—0—	—0—
10	10,000	—0—	—0—
Totals	$100,000	$75,000	$115,000

a. What is the present value of each proposal at discount rates of 8, 12, and 18 percent?

b. What effect does the timing of the cash flows have on the present value of the proposals?

12. Nonesuch Goodies is a small but profitable bakery owned by a single proprietor who wants to retire. Two employees want to buy the bakery, but neither has any immediate cash. However, each knows that the payback period of this investment would be only a few years.

Employee A offers a price of $150,000 on an agreement of sale calling for interest only at 12 percent per annum for eight years, with a balloon payment of $150,000 at the end of eight years.

Employee B offers a price of $125,000 to be paid at the end of five years and also agrees to pay interest at the rate of 12 percent per annum for the five years.

Before the proprietor can decide between these two offers, another bakery owner offers a price of $120,000 with $30,000 down and the remainder at the end of four years. This offer also stipulates

to pay 12 percent interest on the balance due for the four years.

a. Which is the best offer?

b. If the interest rate were 8 percent instead of 12 percent, would it make a difference in the relative net values of the offers?

13. You are in the process of buying a new car. You have bargained with the dealer to obtain a price of $11,895. You have enough cash to pay for licensing, insurance, and a down payment of $500. Your credit union will finance the balance for three years at an interest rate of 12 percent per annum, but will reduce the interest rate to 11 percent if you finance for only two years.

a. What is your monthly payment if you finance the car for three years?

b. What is your monthly payment if you finance the car for two years?

c. How much will you save by financing for two years instead of three?

Case Problem: Big Business Objective— Public Good or Corporate Profit?

14. American big-business firms, such as Exxon, GM, AT&T, and IBM, are admired for their size and industrial muscle. Production of goods and services by such industrial giants has led to better jobs, which in turn have raised the U.S. standard of living. The U.S. per capita disposable income in real terms rose from $2,073 in 1934 to over $13,850 in 1988—almost a sevenfold increase. Not only has business raised incomes but also, while competing for profits, it has built the United States into a consumer paradise unmatched in both the variety of its products and services and their prices relative to consumer income.

Of course, the large growth of business in the United States has produced some undesirable side effects. For example, social costs are imposed when wastes are dumped into the air and water or when the earth is defaced by strip mining. In addition, there is a tendency for power to become more centralized in the hands of giant corporations. Because of the increasing number of mergers and takeovers the past few years, moreover, some people fear big business's power and are skeptical and distrustful of corporate America. These people feel that business is profit-mad and will stop at nothing in its pursuit of money. They feel that business is not working for the public good; instead, business seeks only to maximize profits.

Questions:

a. Does business perform a public service when it attempts to maximize profits, or should its main goal instead be some form of social responsibility?

b. Professor Milton Friedman, Nobel prize economist, stresses profit maximization, "so long as it (business) stays within legal and moral rules of the game established by society."

What are the rules of the game? Where do you draw the line, for example, when a business pollutes the environment while maximizing profits?

c. What is the government's role in business? Could government, through the use of tax incentives and other measures, make profit maximization and the maximization of social good one and the same? (Consider, for example, President Reagan's proposal for inner-city economic zones.)

d. Should business be allowed to make as much profit as possible? What do you think about the windfall tax that was levied on U.S. oil companies after OPEC increased the price of oil? Was it fair? Was it wise from an economic standpoint?

References

Aupperle, Kenneth E.; Archie B. Carroll; and John D. Hatfield. "An Empirical Examination of the Relationship Between Corporate Social Responsibility and Profitability." *Academy of Management Journal* (June 1985), pp. 446–63.

Bailey, Duncan, and Stanley E. Boyle. "Sales Revenue Maximization: An Empirical Vindication." *Industrial Organization Review* 5, no. 1 (1977), pp. 46–55.

Baumol, William J. *Business Behavior, Value and Growth*, Rev. ed. New York: Harcourt Brace Jovanovich, 1967.

Byrne, John A.; Ronald Grover; and Todd Vogel. "Is the Boss Getting Paid Too Much?" *Business Week*, no. 3103 (May 1, 1989), pp. 46–93.

Cubbin, John, and Dennis Leach. "Growth versus Profit Maximization: A Simultaneous Equations Approach to Testing the Marris Model." *Managerial and Decision Economics* (June 1986), pp. 123–31.

Dyl, Edward A. "Corporate Control and Management Compensation: Evidence on the Agency Problem." *Managerial and Decision Economics* 9 (1988), pp. 21–25.

Fama, E. F. "Agency Problems and the Theory of the Firm." *Journal of Political Economy* (April 1980), pp. 272–84.

Fama, E. F., and Michael C. Jensen. "Separation of Ownership and Control." *Journal of Law and Economics* (June 1983), pp. 301–25.

Lewellen, Wilbur G., and Blaine Huntsman. "Managerial Pay and Corporate Performance." *American Economic Review* (September 1970), pp. 710–20.

Murphy, Kevin J. "Top Executives Are Worth Every Nickel They Get." *Harvard Business Review* (March-April 1986), pp. 125–32.

Palmer, John P. "The Separation of Ownership from Control in Large U.S. Industrial Corporations." *Quarterly Review of Economics and Business* (Autumn 1972), pp. 55–62.

Tsurumi, Y., and H. Tsurumi. "Value-Added Maximizing Behavior of Japanese Firms and Role of Corporate Investment and Finance." *Columbia Journal of World Business* (Spring 1985), pp. 29–35.

Welch, P. J. "On the Compatibility of Profit Maximization and the Other Goals of the Firm." *Review of Social Economics* (April 1980), pp. 65–74.

Williamson, J. "Profit, Growth, and Sales Maximization." *Economica* 33, no. 29 (1966), pp 1–16.

APPENDIX 2A   Derivation of the Discount Formula

The discount formula is derived as follows:

The sum of \$1 per year for *n* years, discounted by *r*, is

$$\sum_{i=0}^{-n}(1+r)^{-i} = (1+r)^{-1} + (1+r)^{-2} + (1+r)^{-3} + \cdots + (1+r)^{-n}. \quad (1)$$

Multiply Equation 1 by $(1+r)$:

$$(1+r)\sum_{i=0}^{-n}(1+r)^{-i} = 1 + (1+r)^{-1} + (1+r)^{-2} + \cdots + (1+r)^{-(n-1)}. \quad (2)$$

Subtract Equation 1 from Equation 2:

$$\sum_{i=0}^{-n}(1+r)^{-i} + r\sum_{i=0}^{-n}(1+r)^{-i} = 1 + (1+r)^{-1} + (1+r)^{-2}$$
$$+ \cdots + (1+r)^{-(n-1)} \quad (2)$$

$$\sum_{i=0}^{-n}(1+r)^{-i} = (1+r)^{-1} + (1+r)^{-2}$$
$$+ \cdots + (1+r)^{-(n-1)} + (1+r)^{-n} \quad (1)$$

$$r\sum_{i=0}^{-n}(1+r)^{-i} = 1 + 0 + 0 + \ldots + 0 - (1+r)^{-n}. \quad (3)$$

Hence the present value of \$1 per year for *n* years, discounted by *r*, is

$$\sum_{i=0}^{-n}(1+r)^{-i} = \frac{1 - (1+r)^{-n}}{r}. \quad (4)$$

Equation 4 is called the discount factor, and the present value of $A per year for *n* years, discounted by *r*, is A times the discount factor. That is,

$$PV = A \left[\frac{1 - (1 + r)^{-n}}{r} \right]$$

The discount rate *r* is assumed to be the capitalization rate or required annual rate of return. However, the formula can be used for shorter periods. For example, to determine the monthly payments on the purchase of a car, let *r* equal the annual rate of interest divided by 12, while *n* equals the number of monthly payments. Let *PV* equal the amount financed, and solve for *A*, which is the monthly payment to the lender, including principal and interest.

APPENDIX 2B   Empirical Study of Value-Added Behavior by Japanese Automakers

A convincing empirical study of value-added behavior in Japanese production of automobiles has been performed by Yoshi and Hiroki Tsurumi.[1] Their seminal study covered Japanese production of passenger automobiles from 1970 to 1983. In the course of this study, they developed two financial and three productivity indexes for four different manufacturers (Toyota, Nissan, Mazda, and Honda):

- Earnings before interest and taxes (EBIT)/total assets
- Equity/total assets
- Value added/total assets
- Value added/fixed assets
- Value added/number of employees.

EBIT/Total Assets

The ratio of earnings before interest and taxes to total assets is a conventional measure of a firm's profitability. It was chosen because it affords a meaningful profitability comparison among firms in different countries—particularly between Japanese and American firms. This ratio fluctuated widely during the years studied, changing as much as 50 percent from one year to the next.

Equity/Total Assets

The ratio of equity to total assets was chosen as the most reasonable estimate of a Japanese firm's debt/equity ratio because in Japan ostensible short-term bank loans have a way of becoming actual long-term loans with floating and adjustable rates of interest.

---

[1] Yoshi Tsurumi and Hiroki Tsurumi, "Value-Added Maximizing Behavior of Japanese Firms and Roles of Corporate Investment and Finance," *Columbia Journal of World Business* (Spring 1985), pp. 29–35.

This ratio showed a steadily increasing trend during the 14 years studied as the Japanese firms used their profits to pay off debt.

Value Added/Total Assets

The ratio of value added to total assets is a measure of the productivity of a firm as a whole. The higher the ratio, the more efficient the firm. This ratio showed a steadily increasing trend during the 14 years studied.

Value Added/Fixed Assets

The ratio of value added to fixed assets is a measure of the productivity of a firm's technology. Like the other two productivity measures, this ratio also showed a steadily increasing trend during the 14 years studied.

Value Added/Number of Employees

The ratio of value added to the number of employees is a measure of the productivity of a firm's personnel. It is important to note that this measure makes no distinction between top management and rank-and-file workers. All are members of the firm and all share the long-term goal of competing successfully in the marketplaces of the whole world. Like the other two productivity measures, this ratio also showed a steadily increasing trend during the 14 years studied.

The five ratios just cited support several conclusions about the results of maximizing value added.

1. Japanese automakers have learned that maximizing value added increases annual cash flows needed for financing investments and market development. They use productivity ratios to guide their decisions about marketing and financial planning.

2. In order to increase both the productivity of their technology, as measured by the value-added/fixed-assets ratio, and the productivity of their people, as measured by the value-added/number of employees ratio, the firms had to increase their ratio of fixed assets per employee.[2] They did so by means of heavy investment in automation and other innovative labor-saving improvements. By 1979, Mazda, for example, was able to produce one well-made subcompact with just 47 labor hours. In contrast, Ford was taking 112 hours to produce one car of comparable size. By reducing the labor component of their products, Japanese automakers now lead the worldwide market, producing a half-million more units than the United States in 1986.

3. As firms increase production capacity, they must minimize the possibility of being stuck with expensive human and physical assets during sudden economic downturns. One way to do this is to increase the equity proportion and reduce the debt proportion of their financial structures. This reduces the fixed cost of debt service, thereby lowering

---

[2] This ratio is easily calculated by dividing the value-added/number of employees ratio by the value-added/fixed-assets ratio, as follows: $\frac{v.a.}{e} \div \frac{v.a.}{f.a.} = \frac{v.a.}{e} \frac{f.a.}{v.a.} = \frac{f.a.}{e}$.

the firm's breakeven sales figure. Therefore, all firms attempt to increase their equity bases as much as possible.

4. Japanese automakers faced several periods of depressed economic conditions from 1970 to 1983. First came the recession of 1974–1976, which was caused by the oil crisis engineered by the OPEC cartel. In 1979, there was another recession. Finally, 1981–1983 exports to the United States were voluntarily curtailed in response to political pressure from the U.S. government. Although the automakers' profitability fluctuated widely during these 14 years, their productivity ratios showed a clear trend upward throughout the period. During the down years, the firms obtained cash for continued productivity improvement by increasing both short-term and long-term borrowing. When cash flows improved as a result of increasing productivity and sales of new products, surplus earnings were retained to improve ratios of equity to total assets.

5. Even during economic downturns, Japanese automakers continued to expand their investments in newer production facilities and product development. From 1970 to 1983, Japan's big four automakers' real fixed assets (adjusted for inflation) increased three- to fivefold.

The behavior of the Japanese automakers supports the value-added model described in this chapter, and similar emphasis on continuous modernization of production facilities can be observed in many other Japanese industries. For example, Kawasaki Steel's continuous push to increase the value added per employee had reduced its personnel costs in 1984 to about 25 percent of value added without decreasing workers' wages. This may be contrasted with Inland Steel Corporation, a U.S. firm with similar scales of production and product mix. In the same year, more than 75 percent of value added by Inland Steel went for personnel costs.

C H A P T E R

3

DECISION ENVIRONMENTS AND DECISION MAKING UNDER THE CONDITION OF CERTAINTY

The ability to make good decisions is the key to success in any line of endeavor. Nevertheless, decision making is a human activity. It is not surprising, therefore, that it is often subjective, depending upon the personality, temperament, and experience of the decision maker as well as the environment in which the decision must be made. Yet even within the framework of subjective decision making, we have analytical tools that can provide some objectivity in the decision-making process when they are accompanied by disciplined and logical thinking.

For example, a physician's diagnosis and treatment of a patient's illness is analogous to the decision-making process in business and government. The physician's problem is to identify the illness, its cause, and its treatment. Data are gathered about the patient's problem by physical examination and questioning of the patient. After gathering and evaluating sufficient data, the physician makes a diagnosis, considers ways of treating the problem, and ends up prescribing what seems to be the best treatment. This may be a subjective judgment, but it is either tempered by or based upon objective data.

The decision-making procedure is the same whether it is conducted in medicine, profit-seeking business, nonprofit organizations, or government agencies. In each case, the effective decision maker must:

1. Define the problem and establish objectives.
2. Identify all pertinent factors, constraints, and relationships.

3. Collect as much relevant data as possible within constraints of time and cost.
4. Analyze the data.
5. Specify alternative solutions and evaluate them in terms of benefits and costs.
6. Choose the best solution.

Thus we see that effective decision making is the art of making the best choice from all available alternatives. This choice must be made under one of three states of knowledge: certainty, risk, or uncertainty. In this chapter, we define the three states of knowledge that constitute the decision-making environment; we then describe some tools and procedures for decision making under the condition of certainty. Decision making under risk and uncertainty will be discussed in the next chapter.

CHAPTER OUTLINE

This chapter is divided into two main sections and two appendixes:

1. **Decision Environments.**   This section discusses the states of knowledge in which a decision must be made. These states may be classified as *certainty*, *risk*, or *uncertainty*. Each of these conditions calls for a different set of decision-making tools and techniques.
2. **Decision Making under Certainty.**   This section discusses the three major tools available to the decision maker for optimization of objectives under conditions of certainty. These tools are *marginal analysis*, *incremental profit analysis*, and *linear programming*.
3. **Appendix 3A: Marginal Analysis.**   This appendix explains the tabular method and the use of differential calculus to find the marginal value of a function. It also explains the use of a Lagrangian multiplier for optimization of constrained nonlinear functions.
4. **Appendix 3B: Linear Programming.**   This appendix explains the graphic and simplex methods of linear programming for optimization of a constrained linear function, and it presents a brief explanation of "the dual."

Decision Environments

Business decisions usually consist of choices between courses of action or **strategies.** Frequently those choices must be made in an environment over which the decision maker exercises limited control or perhaps no control. We use the general term **states of nature** to designate such conditions. The decision hinges, therefore, on the decision maker's knowledge of the possible states of nature and how each contemplated strategy might fare under each possible state of nature. As stated already, the decision maker's knowledge can be classified as a state of *certainty*, *risk*, or *uncertainty*.

The distinctions among certainty, risk, and uncertainty reflect differences in the degree of knowledge enjoyed by the decision maker. If we conceive of one's state of knowledge as a continuum, then certainty (complete knowledge) would occupy one end, while uncertainty (complete lack of knowledge) would occupy the other. Risk (partial knowledge) would occupy the middle. The continuum thus would represent degrees of certainty (or uncertainty, if you prefer).

The Concept of Certainty

Certainty is defined as a state of knowledge in which the decision maker knows in advance the specific outcome to which each alternative will invariably lead. In other words, the decision maker has perfect knowledge of the environment and the result of whatever decision he might make.

How realistic is this concept? At first glance this state may appear to be merely theoretical and impractical—and therefore of academic interest only. Actually, however, the opposite is true. There are many short-run situations in which the decision maker has complete knowledge. Many business decisions require only a knowledge of current prices, terms, and quantities demanded, and these can be ascertained with certainty in the short run. For example, suppose a firm borrows $100,000 on a short-term note that still has 30 days to maturity. The interest rate on the note is 3 percent more than the yield on Treasury bills. If the firm generates $100,000 in surplus cash, management can determine with certainty that it is better off to prepay the loan than to invest in a Treasury bill.

Decision making under certainty includes most of the problems pertaining to theories of choice that arise in economics and the behavioral sciences. Certainty may be found in classical applications of calculus and algebra as well as in many types of optimization models such as linear and nonlinear programming. These models are used to find the allocation of resources that yields the highest value of some index (such as profits or utility) or the lowest value of some other index (such as costs), given specified constraints.

In reality, however, few things remain certain for very long. The outcome of a long-range investment, for example, is really impossible to predict when we consider the dynamic interaction of many unknown variables, such as the general economic situation, national and international competition, consumer tastes, the political climate in various countries, and technological advances. Thus, most *strategic* decisions are made under conditions of less than perfect knowledge. That is, they are made under conditions of either *risk* or *uncertainty*.

The Concept of Risk

Risk is defined as a state of knowledge in which each alternative leads to one of a set of specific outcomes, with each outcome occurring with a probability that is known objectively to the decision maker. Under conditions of risk, the decision maker possesses some *objective* knowledge of the environment and is able to predict *objectively* the probability of the possible states of nature and the outcome or payoff of each contemplated strategy. The most common criterion for evaluation of each strategy is *expected value*, as discussed in the next chapter.

The Concept of Uncertainty

Uncertainty is a state in which one or more alternatives result in a set of possible specific outcomes whose probabilities are either not known or not meaningful. Unlike risk, therefore, uncertainty is a *subjective* phenomenon. No two individuals who view the same event will necessarily formulate the same quantitative opinion. This is not only because they may differ in degree of knowledge, but also because of differences in temperament and outlook. Uncertainty also is often caused by rapid changes in the structural variables and market phenomena that determine the economic and social environments in which the firm operates.

Decision making under uncertainty and methods for dealing with uncertainty are discussed in the next chapter.

Decision Making under Certainty: Optimization Analysis

Under conditions of certainty, the decision maker has complete knowledge of the various states of nature that are relevant to the decision and knows which one will occur. The decision maker simply chooses the strategy, course of action, or project that yields the greatest payoff.

In general, decision making under certainty requires that we find the largest payoff either by maximizing benefits (such as revenue, profit, or utility) or by minimizing costs. We can refer to these activities as optimization analysis. We shall discuss three optimization techniques available to the decision maker for this purpose. They are *marginal analysis*, *linear programming*, and *incremental profit analysis*.

Marginal Analysis

Under conditions of certainty, revenues and costs are known for each level of production and sales. The objective is to find the level of output and sales that will maximize profit. Marginal analysis is a tool that can be used to find this optimal relationship. Marginal analysis utilizes the concepts of marginal revenue and marginal cost, as illustrated by Exhibit 3–1. The exhibit shows typical revenue, cost, and profit curves of microeconomic theory, with revenue, cost, and profit scaled in dollars on the vertical axis, and output (quantity produced and sold) scaled on the horizontal axis.

Marginal revenue (*MR*) is defined as the additional revenue (change in total revenue) gained from the sale of one more unit of the product. It is graphed as the slope of the total revenue (*TR*) curve.

Marginal cost (*MC*) is defined as the additional cost (change in total cost) of acquiring or producing one more unit. It is graphed as the slope of the total cost (*TC*) curve. We also note the following:

1. At output levels Q_1 and Q_4, *TR* is just equal to *TC*, so profit is zero. Outputs below Q_1 or above Q_4 result in a loss (negative profit).
2. When the output level is greater than Q_1 and less than Q_4, positive profits result.
3. Marginal analysis shows that as long as *MR* exceeds *MC*, the production and sale of one more unit will increase profit. *Profit, therefore, is maximized at the level of output where* $MR = MC$.

EXHIBIT 3-1   Revenue, Cost, and Profit Functions

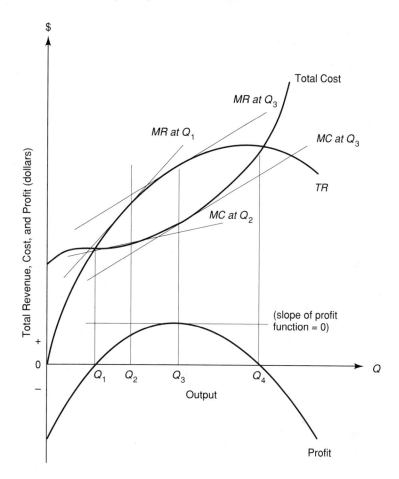

$MR = MC$ occurs at Q_3. At this level of output, if we draw a line tangent to the *TR* curve and another line tangent to the *TC* curve, it can be seen that these lines are parallel; that is to say, the slopes of the two curves are equal. This means that at Q_3 units of output, $MR = MC$. At this level of output, the slope of the profit function, or marginal profit (*MP*), is zero.

Illustrative Problem

The Black Star coal mine is a family-operated enterprise that sells its product in a purely competitive market in which the market sets the price. The Black Star's cost function is

$$TC = 1,000 - 5Q + 0.05Q^2$$

where

Q = tons of coal per week
TC = total cost per week.

The market price for coal is $20 per ton.

Questions:

a. What is Black Star's profit-maximizing output?

b. What is Black Star's maximum profit?

Solutions:

a. Profit is maximized when $MR = MC$. MR is the first derivative of the TR function. MC is the first derivative of the TC function.[1]

$$TR = 20Q \qquad\qquad MR = 20$$

$$TC = 1,000 - 5Q + 0.05Q^2 \qquad MC = -5 + 0.10Q$$

At optimum,

$$MC = MR$$
$$0.10Q - 5 = 20$$
$$0.10Q = 25$$
$$Q* = 250 \text{ tons per week.}[2]$$

The same result can be obtained by taking the derivative of the profit function, setting it equal to zero, and solving for $Q*$.

$$\pi = TR - TC = PQ - TC = 20Q - 1,000 + 5Q - 0.05Q^2$$

$$= -1,000 + 25Q - 0.05Q^2$$

$$\frac{d\pi}{dQ} = 25 - 0.10Q = 0$$

$$Q* = 250, \text{ as before.}$$

b.

$$\pi = TR - TC = PQ - TC$$

$$= 20(250) - 1,000 + 5(250) - 0.05(250)^2 = \$2,125/\text{week.}$$

Instead of specifying the precise degree of resource utilization necessary for profit maximization, we can build some realistic complexities into the model by indicating that certain resource limitations exist. Suppose that a scarcity of resources or perhaps a lack of demand limits production to Q_2 units. (See Exhibit 3–1.) The decision maker must then find out whether the output that maximizes profit under limited production is Q_2 units, or whether it is some other output to the left of (less than) Q_2. This becomes a difficult problem with a general solution that may involve restrictions on availability of resources, restrictions on or requirements for the use of resources, and/or restrictions on or requirements for output. When such limitations exist under the right conditions, **linear programming**, which is an extension of marginal analysis, offers a powerful alternative procedure.

---

[1] The calculus used in this text requires no more than the ability to take a first derivative or partial derivative of a function. The formulas for these operations are contained in Table I of the Appendix at the end of this book.

[2] The asterisk indicates that this particular value of Q is optimal.

Linear Programming

Consider the well-known nursery rhyme:

> *Jack Sprat could eat no fat,*
> *His wife could eat no lean,*
> *And so you see between the two*
> *They licked the platter clean.*

Although most people learned this ditty in their childhood, how many are familiar with the fact that it can serve as the basis for some fundamental problems in linear programming?

For example, suppose that the Sprats' weekly dietary requirement is such that Mr. Sprat needs at least eight pounds of lean meat and Mrs. Sprat needs at least two pounds of fat. If beef selling for $4.50 a pound contains 75 percent lean meat and 25 percent fat, and pork at $2.00 a pound contains 60 percent lean meat and 40 percent fat, what should the Sprats' total weekly consumption of beef and pork be in order to minimize the cost? What would the answer be if pork costs $4 per pound? Questions of this nature are typical of some types of problems that can be resolved by linear programming when complete information is available to the decision maker.

What is linear programming? It is a form of mathematical modeling that deals with the optimal allocation of scarce resources among competing activities. Any economic problem that is concerned with maximizing or minimizing (i.e., optimizing) a linear objective function (e.g., profit, revenue, total cost, or a similar economic quantity) and that is subject to a set of linear inequalities in the form of constraints (e.g., limitations of personnel, materials, capital, or other resources) is a linear programming problem. Linear programming has been used with great success to solve a variety of business problems, such as:

1. *Determining a product mix that meets certain established specifications at minimum cost.* Examples are found in the blending of gasolines and in obtaining feed mixes that satisfy specified nutritional requirements.
2. *Determining optimal product lines and production processes.* Examples are found wherever capacity limitations exist (e.g., factory size, warehouse space, and machine time) and where decisions must be made about which products to produce, given such scarce resources.
3. *Determining optimal transportation routes.* Examples occur among firms whose plants and warehouses are scattered and whose objective is to minimize transportation costs from factories to warehouses.

These are a few of the common types of problems that are routinely handled by linear-programming methods. In terms of actual application, it is perhaps the most successful and widely used approach for solution of resource allocation problems.[3] Its usage closely parallels growth in computer technology, because a complicated linear-programming problem has enormous computational requirements that only a computer can handle efficiently. For most business managers, what is really required is to be able to recog-

---

[3] Techniques of nonlinear programming also exist.

nize a linear programming problem and then communicate its essentials to the technical personnel who will input that data to a computer program for linear programming.[4] The communication is easier and less susceptible to error if the data are assembled in the good form illustrated in the following example.

Illustrative Example

Suppose that a chemical plant receives an order for 5,000 pounds of a special mixture of three ingredients, the composition of which is constrained as follows:

Ingredient 1, costing $5 per pound, not to exceed 1,500 pounds.
Ingredient 2, costing $6 per pound, not less than 750 pounds.
Ingredient 3, costing $7 per pound, not less than 1,000 pounds.

How much of each ingredient should be used in order to minimize the cost? The problem is set up in good form as follows:

Let

$$x_1 = \text{pounds of Ingredient 1} \tag{1}$$
$$x_2 = \text{pounds of Ingredient 2} \tag{2}$$
$$x_3 = \text{pounds of Ingredient 3} \tag{3}$$

Objective

$$\text{Minimize } Z = 5x_1 + 6x_2 + 7x_3 \tag{4}$$

subject to

$$x_1 + x_2 + x_3 \geq 5,000 \tag{5}$$
$$x_1 \leq 1,500 \tag{6}$$
$$x_2 \geq 750 \tag{7}$$
$$x_3 \geq 1,000 \tag{8}$$
$$x_1, x_2, x_3 \geq 0. \tag{9}$$

Equations 1, 2, and 3 simply define variables x_1, x_2, and x_3 in terms of quantities of Ingredients 1, 2, and 3, respectively. These quantities, of course, cannot be less than zero.[5]

Equation 4 states that the objective is the minimization of the total cost of the ingredients. (The cost of an ingredient is calculated by multiplying the quantity of that ingredient by its respective unit cost. Summing the costs of all the ingredients produces the total cost.)

Equation 5 says that the total mixture must weigh at least 5,000 pounds.

Equation 6 says that no more than 1,500 pounds of Ingredient 1 may be used.

Equation 7 says that at least 750 pounds of Ingredient 2 must be used.

Equation 8 says that at least 1,000 pounds of Ingredient 3 must be used.

Equation 9 formally states that the variables are nonnegative.

---

[4] Computer programs for the execution of linear programming have many names, usually in some form of acronym. Consult with your computer-lab personnel to find one that suits your requirements.

[5] Students often confuse the variable, which is always a quantity, with the thing it is measuring. Thus x_1 in *not* ingredient 1, but *pounds* of Ingredient 1. Another common error is to confuse variables with constants. The first step in any linear-programming problem is to identify the variables.

The problem setup illustrated here conforms to the format required by computer packages for linear programming. When the data are entered, they are processed by the computer program, and the solution to the problem appears in the output. For this problem, the solution is

$$x_1 = 1,500, \qquad x_2 = 2,500, \qquad x_3 = 1,000.$$

This means that the objective of minimizing cost is satisfied by using 1,500 pounds of Ingredient 1; 2,500 pounds of Ingredient 2; and 1,000 pounds of Ingredient 3. Note that these values also satisfy each of the constraints, as they must.

Linear programming is applicable only to problems that display all four of the following characteristics:

1. A set of nonnegative, independent variables.
2. One and only one objective that is a function of the variables, such as cost minimization or profit maximization.
3. Constraints that limit the attainment of the objective. These usually take the form of upper or lower limits on combinations of the variables.
4. Linearity of all quantitative relationships.

The preceding illustrative example had three variables, so the problem had to be solved by the *simplex method*. The simplex method can be performed by hand, but is best performed by a computer. But if only two variables are involved, a graphing technique may be used. Both the graphing technique and the simplex method are explained in Appendix 3B at the end of this chapter.

Incremental Profit Analysis (A Short-Run Concept)

Marginal analysis, it will be recalled, is concerned with changing values of related but unchanging functions. In the real world, however, demand, revenue, production, and cost functions cannot be known with much precision and are subject to change. Nevertheless, these problems can be largely overcome by incremental profit analysis, a practical application of the marginal analysis concept, but broader in scope.

Incremental profit analysis is concerned with *any* and *all* changes in revenues, costs, and consequent profits that result from a particular decision. Thus the concept of incremental analysis includes changes in the functions themselves as well as changes in their values. The basic decision rule is to accept any proposal that will increase profits and reject any proposal that will not.

Since incremental decision making is concerned only with variables that can change, then fixed costs (such as insurance and depreciation) are irrelevant to the decision. Hence, incremental decision making is a short-run concept. Unfortunately, many managers do not think in incremental terms; rather, they make decisions based on average values of total costs, including both fixed and variable costs (fully allocated costs). Almost invariably, short-run decisions based on average fully allocated cost will be wrong if the firm's objective is to maximize profit.

Illustrative Example

Suppose a tire manufacturer is currently producing and selling 100,000 tires per month at a price of $24 each. Variable cost is $14 per tire, and fixed cost is $600,000; hence the fully absorbed cost is $20 per tire.

Now suppose that a large discount store (not a current customer) offers to contract for 25,000 tires per month at a price of $18 each. In order to make the additional 25,000 tires, the manufacturer would have to work overtime, which would add $2 to the variable cost of the additional 25,000 tires. The average fully allocated cost per tire then would be:

Variable cost of first 100,000 tires at $14	$1,400,000
Variable cost of next 25,000 tires at $16	400,000
Fixed cost	600,000
Total cost of 125,000 tires	$2,400,000
Average cost per tire	$19.20

If the firm based its decision on average cost, the order would be rejected on the grounds that the cost is greater than the offered price. But if incremental costs are calculated, the incremental cost of the last 25,000 tires is $16 each, while the incremental revenue offered is $18 each. Thus the proposed contract would bring in profits of $50,000 that the firm would not earn otherwise.

Does incremental profit analysis provide the last word in this decision? Not necessarily, since other (nonquantifiable) considerations might outweigh the results of the incremental profit analysis (e.g., reactions of current customers if they find out about this deal, or even the legality of this type of price discrimination). Nevertheless, incremental profit analysis provides a powerful and relatively easy-to-use tool for the decision maker.

Summary

Good decision making follows the same general procedure whether it takes place in a profit-seeking business, a nonprofit organization, or a government agency. The decision maker must define the problem, establish objectives, identify all relevant factors, gather and evaluate relevant information, specify alternatives, and finally evaluate alternatives in order to choose the best solution to the problem.

Decisions are made within the context of a decision maker's state of knowledge. Under conditions of certainty, the decision maker can calculate in advance the specific outcome to which each available strategy invariably leads. Risk is defined as a state of knowledge in which each alternative leads to one of a set of specific outcomes with objectively determined probabilities. Uncertainty is defined as a state of knowledge in which one or more alternatives result in a set of possible outcomes whose probabilities are either unknown or meaningless. Each of these conditions calls for a different set of decision making tools and techniques.

Conditions of certainty prevail in many short-run operating problems in which the decision maker needs no more than a knowledge of current prices, terms, and quantities demanded. The condition of certainty is often associated with optimizing models.

Three major tools are available for decision making under conditions of certainty. They are: (1) marginal analysis, (2) linear programming, and (3) incremental profit analysis.

Under marginal analysis, profit is maximized when marginal revenue equals marginal cost.

Linear programming is a mathematical modeling technique that deals with the optimal allocation of scarce resources among competing activities. It can be used only when all quantitative relationships are linear. It finds the values of a set of variables that will either maximize or minimize a single stated objective.

Incremental profit analysis is a practical application of marginal analysis in the short run, but it is broader in scope. It considers only the changes in revenues, costs, and profits that will result from each particular decision. Revenues and costs that will not be changed by the decision are not considered, because they are irrelevant to the decision.

Problems

1. Classify each of the following situations as decision making under certainty, risk, or uncertainty, and explain your answers.

    a. A farmer in Illinois must decide how many acres to plant in corn and how many in soybeans.

    b. In very hot weather at the baseball stadium, ice cream is the big seller, with hot dogs a poor second. But if the weather is moderate or cool, the opposite occurs. Sanitary regulations do not permit the concessionaire to store either hot dogs or ice cream for more than two days. Because the concessionaire's orders are so large, suppliers require orders seven days in advance or else they cannot guarantee delivery. Therefore, the concessionaire must decide now what to order for next week's big game.

    c. Quality standards used by a maker of animal feeds set minimum percentages of protein, fat, and carbohydrates and a maximum percentage of inert ingredients in the final mixture. Three basic ingredients are available for mixing, each with different proportions of protein, fat, carbohydrate, and inert matter, and each has a different cost. The feed maker desires to meet or better the quality standards at minimum cost and must decide what proportions of the basic ingredients to use in the final mixture.

2. The Friendly Electric Company has petitioned its state's public-utility commission for permission to practice "time-of-day" pricing. This means that electricity consumed at certain hours of the day (late at night, for example) would be priced lower than a like amount consumed during periods of peak demand. The company argues that this kind of pricing would enable it to charge lower rates overall. Evaluate this proposal in terms of marginal cost.

3. A small manufacturer makes two grades of surfboards for which we have the following information:

	Surfmaster	Wavemaster
Selling price	$250	$200
Cost of styrofoam per board	8	10
Cost of resin per board	20	15
Cost of labor per board at $10/hr.	120	80

We also have the following data:

Available styrofoam	$80 worth per day
Available resin	$150 worth per day
Available production labor	96 hours per day
Fixed costs	$250 per day

Assuming that the company's objective is to maximize profits, and that all boards manufactured will eventually be sold, how many of each board should be manufactured per day? Set up the problem in good form for linear programming and solve by the graphic method. (The graphic method is explained in Appendix 3B of this chapter.)

4. The EasTenn Furniture Makers, Inc., of Knoxville, Tennessee, manufactures dining room tables, upholstered dining chairs, and Lazyman reclining chairs. The three main input resources are wood, upholstery cloth, and labor. The resources required per unit and total available per week are as follows:

	Wood (lbs.)	Fabric (sq. yds.)	Labor (hrs.)
Tables	20	—	10
Chairs	5	3	5
Recliners	6	7	8
Available	3,000	1,000	400

The furniture is produced on a weekly basis and stored in the company's warehouse until sold. The warehouse can hold a total of 750 pieces of furniture of all types.

The company earns a profit of $250 on each table sold, $150 on each dining chair, and $200 on each recliner. The company's objective is to maximize profits.

a. Set up a linear programming model to determine the optimal output of each product.

b. Use a computer to solve the problem (if one is available).

Case Problem: Changeroyl, Inc.

5. Changeroyl, Inc., is a 15-minute oil-change–and–lube station. In addition to brand-name motor oil in quart cans, Changeroyl dispenses bulk motor oil from 55-gallon drums. The bulk oil is priced by the gallon, but the customer is charged only for the exact amount pumped into the car's engine.

The station's average hourly revenue from the bulk oil is expressed by the equation $TR = 12Q - 0.9Q^2$, where TR = total revenue and Q = the number of gallons sold per hour.

The total cost of buying, storing, and dispensing the oil is expressed by the equation $TC = 12 + 2Q - 0.7Q2 + 0.08Q^3$, where TC = total cost and Q = the number of gallons sold per hour.

Questions

a. What is the station's maximum hourly revenue from bulk oil? What price will bring in maximum revenue?

b. What is the station's maximum hourly profit from bulk oil? What price will bring maximum profit?

c. Create a table showing price, total revenue, total cost, and profit for sales from 0 to 10 gallons per hour in increments of one gallon. Also include fractional quantities bringing maximum profit and maximum revenue.

d. Graph total revenue, total cost, and profit in a manner similar to Exhibit 3–1. Then add lines representing marginal revenue and marginal cost to the upper graph, and show that profit is maximized when $MR = MC$.

References

Baumol, W. J. *Economic Theory and Operations Analysis*, 4th ed., chaps. 18, 19. Englewood Cliffs, N.J.: Prentice-Hall, 1977.

Gordon, G., and I. Pressman. *Quantitative Decision Making for Business*, chaps. 3,4. Englewood Cliffs, N.J.: Prentice-Hall, 1978.

Horowitz, I. *Decision Making and the Theory of the Firm*. New York: Holt, Rinehart & Winston, 1970.

Simon, H. "Rational Decision Making in Business Organizations." *American Economic Review, 69*, (September 1979), pp. 493–513.

APPENDIX 3A   Marginal Analysis

Two methods may be used to find the marginal value of a function. One is the tabular method, which can be used whether or not the function is known. The other is differential calculus, which can be used only when the function is known and continuous.

The marginal value of a function is rigorously defined as the change in the dependent variable caused by a one-unit change in a single independent variable while all other independent variables (if any) are held constant. This definition explicitly specifies that the selected values of the independent variable must be discrete numbers in increments of 1.0. By this strict definition, if $\Delta X = 1$, the marginal value is the slope, $\Delta Y/\Delta X$, of the secant line between the two points P_1 and P_2, as shown in Exhibit 3A–1.

When the tabular method is used in actual practice (usually because the function is unknown), discrete values of the independent variable are used, but the requirement that $\Delta X = 1$ is relaxed. The marginal value is taken to be $\Delta Y/\Delta X$, whatever ΔX may be. If the function is linear, this causes no problem, since the slope of the line is constant. But if the function is not linear, large values of ΔX will introduce error. The amount of error will depend upon the slope of the curve as well as the magnitude of ΔX.

If the function is known and continuous, common practice is to approximate the marginal value by taking the first derivative. This means that the marginal value is measured as the slope of a line tangent to the curve precisely at some point on the curve. It can be seen on Exhibit 3A–1 (page 42) that if the function is not linear, the slope of the curve at P_1 is not equal to the slope of the secant between P_1 and P_2, nor is it equal to the slope at P_2. Consequently, some error is introduced when the derivative is used as the marginal value of a nonlinear function, but the error is inconsequential and therefore ignored in actual practice.

Of course, to find the marginal value as the slope of a curve, one must be able to take a derivative (i.e., differentiate the function). This requires no more than becoming familiar with standard notation and understanding a few simple rules, which are provided in Table I of the Appendix at the end of this book. As for notation, if we have the function $Y = f(X)$, the first derivative may be written as $f'(X)$ (read "f-prime of X") or dY/dX (read "the derivative of Y with respect to X"). The first derivative is also a function of X and can be differentiated to obtain the second derivative, which is written as $f''(X)$ or d^2Y/dX^2.

Optimization of a Function

When a function is at a maximum or minimum, the slope of its curve is zero; therefore, the first derivative is zero at that point. The maximum or minimum points on the curve can be located by the following procedure:

Step 1. Find the first derivative of the function and set it equal to zero.

Step 2. Solve the resulting equation for the critical value or values of X, that is, the value(s) of X at which the function is maximum or minimum.

Step 3. Find the second derivative of the function, that is, the derivative of the first derivative.

EXHIBIT 3A–1   Marginal Value

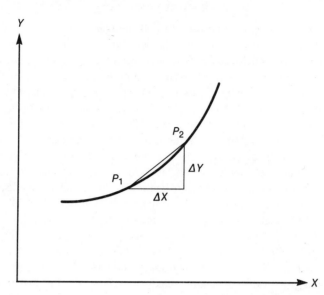

Step 4. Insert each of the critical values into the second derivative. If the result is a positive number, the function is at a minimum. If the result is negative, the function is at a maximum.

The technique for marginal analysis of multivariate functions is an extension of the calculus method. The underlying concept is this: To study the effect on a multivariate function of changes in one of the independent variables, we must hold all other independent variables constant. We carry this concept into calculus when we take a partial derivative. The same rules of differentiation are followed to take the derivative with respect to one variable while all other variables are treated as constants.[1]

A Case Illustration

Suppose that a firm has developed a new product. During its first year on the market, the firm has sold 500 units at a price of $300 per unit. Its production function is linear, with variable costs of a constant $100 per unit, and fixed overhead allocated to the product is $40,000. These costs are not expected to change during the coming year.

The firm has engaged an advertising agency to promote the product. The agency recommends an advertising campaign featuring full-page ads in two nationally circulated magazines, *Medium One* and *Medium Two*. A full-page ad in *Medium One* costs $6,000. *Medium Two*, which has a smaller circulation, charges $4,000 for a full page.

After conducting appropriate market research, the advertising agency advises the firm that the effectiveness of the campaign will depend upon the number of ads run, according to the demand equation

---

[1] The scope of this discussion of optimization is necessarily limited. Students who desire a more comprehensive explanation should consult a standard text on differential calculus.

$$Q = 500 + 100A - 5A^2,$$

where Q represents the number of units that will be sold at a price of $300 if A units of advertising are used. A unit of advertising consists of one page in *Medium One* and one page in *Medium Two*, at a total cost of $10,000.

The firm has a choice between two marketing strategies: one that will maximize profits (in the short run) and one that will maximize sales (which will give them a larger share of the market and may thus improve profits in the long run). The question facing management is how much to budget for advertising under each of the two strategies.

The first step in solving this problem is to identify all of the factors (constants and variables) that are relevant:

A = number of units of advertising at $10,000 each (independent variable)
P = price of the product (constant $300)
Q = number of units of the product to be produced and sold (dependent variable)
TVC = total variable cost at a given level of advertising, calculated as the cost of production plus the cost of advertising (variable)
TFC = total fixed cost (constant)
TC = total cost ($TFC + TVC$, a variable)
TR = total revenue from sale of Q units (variable)
TCP = total contribution profit ($TR - TVC$, a variable)
π = operating income or profit, a dependent variable

The next step is to express the relationships among the factors in a set of equations:

$$Q = 500 + 100A - 5A^2 \tag{1}$$

$$TR = PQ = 300(500 + 100A - 5A^2)$$
$$= 150,000 + 30,000A - 1,500A^2 \tag{2}$$

$$TVC = 100Q + 10,000A$$
$$= 100(500 + 100A - 5A^2) + 10,000A$$
$$= 50,000 + 20,000A - 500A^2 \tag{3}$$

$$TCP = TR - TVC = 150,000 + 30,000A - 1,500A^2$$
$$- (50,000 + 20,000A - 500A^2)$$
$$= 100,000 + 10,000A - 1,000A^2 \tag{4}$$

$$TC = TFC + TVC = 40,000 + 50,000 + 20,000A - 500A^2$$
$$= 90,000 - 20,000A + 500A^2 \tag{5}$$

$$\pi = TR - TC = 150,000 + 30,000A - 1,500A^2$$
$$- (90,000 - 20,000A + 500A^2)$$
$$= 60,000 + 10,000A - 1,000A^2. \tag{6}$$

At this stage, two methods are available for solving the problem. One is to construct a table in which the crucial relationships are revealed. The other method is to use the maximization technique of calculus. Using calculus is faster and easier, but the tabular method perhaps gives more insight into the true relationships of the variables and the concept of marginal analysis. Both methods are demonstrated next.

Exhibit 3A–2   **Revenues, Variable Costs, and Contribution Profits as Functions of Advertising**

(1) Advertising Purchased (units)	(2) Total Revenue ($000)	(3) Marginal Revenue ($000)	(4) Variable Costs ($000)	(5) Marginal Costs ($000)	(6) Contribution Profit ($000)	(7) Marginal Profit ($000)
0	150.0		50.0		100.0	
		28.5		19.5		9.0
1	178.5		69.5		109.0	
		25.5		18.5		7.0
2	204.0		88.0		116.0	
		22.5		17.5		5.0
3	226.5		105.5		121.0	
		19.5		16.5		3.0
4	246.0		122.0		124.0	
		16.5		15.5		1.0
5	262.5		137.5		125.0	
		13.5		14.5		−1.0
6	276.0		152.0		124.0	
		10.5		13.5		−3.0
7	286.5		165.5		121.0	
		7.5		12.5		−5.0
8	294.0		178.0		116.0	
		4.5		11.5		−7.0
9	298.5		189.5		109.0	
		1.5		10.5		−9.0
10	300.0		200.0		100.0	
		−1.5		9.5		−11.0
11	298.5		209.5		89.0	
		−4.5		8.5		−13.0
12	294.0		218.0		76.0	

Tabular Method

The tabular method of marginal analysis requires the construction of a table such as that in Exhibit 3A–2.

The first step in constructing the table is to select the desired values of the independent variable, in this case, advertising purchased. Note that the selected values of the independent variable must be discrete numbers in increments of 1.0. This is because marginal value is defined as the change in the function that results from a one-unit change in the independent variable.

Each of the selected values of the independent variable is then substituted into the appropriate equation to obtain corresponding functional values. In this case, Equations 2, 3, and 4 are used to obtain total revenue, variable costs, and contribution profit, respectively, for each selected number of units of advertising purchased.

Exhibit 3A–3 presents the histograms of the functional values shown on Exhibit 3A–2. We shall use these histograms to gain a better understanding of the concepts of marginality.

Note in Exhibit 3A–3 that the columns are centered on the discrete values of the independent variable, and that the margins or boundaries of the columns have been

EXHIBIT 3A–3   **Histograms of Total Revenue, Variable Costs, and Contribution Profit versus Units of Advertising**

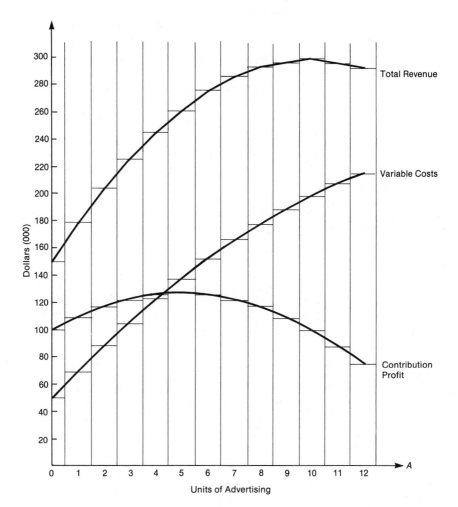

extended upward to aid our visualization. Note also that the midpoints of the upper ends of adjacent columns have been joined by straight lines. For ease of reference, we will call these *lines of change*.

When the independent variable changes from one value to the next, we travel to the new functional value along the line of change. In making this movement, we are traveling ΔX units in a horizontal direction and ΔY units in a vertical direction. The slope of the line of change is the ratio $\Delta Y/\Delta X$. Since the line of change is a straight line, its slope is the same everywhere, including the point where it crosses the margin between $f(X_1)$ and $f(X_2)$. Since we have restricted ΔX to a value of 1.0, the marginal value by definition is equal to ΔY.

Taking total revenue in Exhibit 3A–2 as an example, we see that at the margin between 0 and 1 unit of advertising, the marginal revenue is $178.5 - 150.0 = 28.5$; between 1 and 2 units, marginal revenue is $204.0 - 178.5 = 25.5$; and so on.

When we examine all of the data in the total-revenue column, we find that total revenue is at a maximum when 10 units of advertising are purchased. We note on Exhibit 3A-2 that the marginal revenue at the left-hand margin (between 9 and 10 units) is $+1.5$ while at the right-hand margin (between 10 and 11 units) it is -1.5. Looking at Exhibit 3A–3, we see that the change of slope from positive to negative takes place in the center of the top of the histogram column for 10 units of advertising. Similarly, we note on Exhibit 3A–2 that maximum contribution profit occurs when 5 units of advertising are purchased. Marginal profit on the left is $+1.0$ and on the right is -1.0.

Note that in developing marginal-profit data, fixed costs and the resulting operating income are ignored. This is because fixed costs do not affect marginal profits, as we can see by referring again to Exhibit 3A–3. If we were to deduct fixed costs from the contribution-profit data, we would merely reduce the height of each column by the same amount. The slopes of the lines of change would be exactly the same as before, hence the marginal profit would be the same.

The Calculus Method

Referring again to Exhibit 3A–3, we see that although the lines of change are straight lines, when joined together they come very close to forming the smooth curve that we associate with a continuous function. This is the basis for using differential calculus to find marginal values. We assume that the function is continuous even if it is not, so that instead of many lines of change, we have just one smooth, continuous curve.

The calculus method is far more powerful than the tabular method for two reasons:

1. Because we know that a function is optimal[2] when the slope of its graph is zero, we can find the optimal value of the independent variable simply by taking the first derivative of the function, setting it equal to zero, and solving for X. For example, Equation 2 says:

$$TR = 150,000 + 30,000A - 1,500A^2$$

$$\frac{d(TR)}{dA} = 30,000 - 3,000A = 0$$

$$A = 10$$

as we have seen before.

2. Calculus enables us to handle multivariate functions that would be very difficult, perhaps impossible to handle by the tabular method. The technique for the marginal analysis of multivariate functions is an extension of the calculus method previously discussed. A partial derivative is taken for each independent variable, holding all other independent variables constant. All partial derivatives are then set equal to zero. The result is a system of equations in which the number of variables is equal to the number of equations and hence can be solved for the value of each variable. We shall demonstrate the technique by continuing with our case illustration.

---

[2] Of course, optimization also covers minimization. In order to determine whether the function is at a maximum or a minimum, certain conditions concerning *second* derivatives must be met, as previously discussed.

Marginal Analysis of Multivariate Functions

Suppose after some experience with the firm's advertising campaign, the advertising agency acquires new information that reveals the specific impact of ads in each of the two magazines. It now says that the demand equation is

$$Q = 500 + 66M_1 - 3M_1^2 + 34M_2 - 2M_2^2 \qquad (7)$$

where M_1 represents the number of full-page ads placed in *Medium One* and M_2 represents the number of full-page ads in *Medium Two*.

In the light of this additional information, what should the advertising budget be for each of the two magazines? To answer this question, we take the partial derivatives of Equation 7:

$$\frac{\partial Q}{\partial M_1} = 66 - 6M_1 \qquad (8)$$

$$\frac{\partial Q}{\partial M_2} = 34 - 4M_2 \qquad (9)$$

Optimal Input Factors.   Equation 8 says that demand (output) for the product will change by $(66 - 6M_1)$ units per unit change in M_1 when M_2 is held constant. Equation 9 says that demand will change by $(34 - 4M_2)$ units per unit change in M_2 when M_1 is held constant. These functions are the marginal products of M_1 and M_2, respectively.

We can now apply the theory of marginal productivity to determine the optimal mix of M_1 and M_2. Marginal-productivity theory says that the optimal allocation of the factors of production occurs when the ratio of the marginal product *MP* of the factor to its price *P* is the same for all input factors; that is, when

$$\frac{MP_A}{P_A} = \frac{MP_B}{P_B} = \cdots = \frac{MP_N}{P_N}.$$

Applying this rule, allocation is optimal when

$$\frac{66 - 6M_1}{\$6000} = \frac{34 - 4M_2}{\$4000}.$$

Upon solving this equation, we find that $M_1 = M_2 + 2.5$; that is to say, we should always place 2.5 more ads in *Medium One* than in *Medium Two*. This does not tell us how many ads are optimal—it simply says that at any level of output, we will get the most output for our money by following the indicated allocation.

Optimal Output.   If by "optimal" we mean a maximum of sales, we can get our answer simply by setting Equations 8 and 9 equal to zero. We learn from this that M_1 should be 11 and M_2 should be 8.5. Although this agrees with our conclusion regarding the optimal mix of ads in *Medium One* and *Medium Two*, it requires us to buy one half-page ad in *Medium Two*. This is contrary to the stated condition that we would run full-page ads only. Can it be that our assumption of continuity of the demand function has led us astray?

Technically, the answer is yes, but as a practical matter the error is inconsequential. If we substitute the values $M_1 = 11$ and $M_2 = 8.0$, 8.5, or 9.0, we get the following results:

M_1	M_2	Q
11	8.0	1,007.0
11	8.5	1,007.5
11	9.0	1,007.0

Buying a half-page ad could have unpredictable results, and making and selling half a product may be impossible (depending on the product), so it does not take long to decide to run 11 full-page ads in *Medium One* and 8 full-page ads in *Medium Two*.

Does this advertising budget improve our performance? Under the previous 1:1 allocation, our optimum production was 1,000 units, worth $300,000 in sales, at an advertising cost of $100,000. With the new allocation, our optimum production is 1,007 units with a sales value of $302,100, at an advertising cost of $98,000. This improves our profit by $4,100.

Optimal Profits. If by "optimal" we mean maximum profits, we must first use Equation 7 to develop new equations for total revenue, total variable cost, and contribution profit. The new functions are

$$Q = 500 + 66M_1 - 3M_1^2 + 34M_2 - 2M_2^2 \qquad \textbf{(7 repeated)}$$
$$TR = 300Q = 150,000 + 19,800M_1 - 900M_1^2 + 10,200M_2 - 600M_2^2 \qquad \textbf{(10)}$$
$$TVC = 100Q + 6,000M_1 + 4,000M_2$$
$$= 50,000 + 12,600M_1 - 300M_1^2 + 7,400M_2 - 200M_2^2 \qquad \textbf{(11)}$$
$$TCP = TR - TVC = 100,000 + 7,200M_1 - 600M_1^2 + 2,800M^2 - 400M_2^2 \qquad \textbf{(12)}$$

To determine the allocation of advertising to secure maximum profits, we take the partial derivatives of Equation 12 and set them equal to zero:

$$\frac{\partial(TCP)}{\partial M_1} = 7,200 - 1,200M_1 = 0; \; M_1 = 6 \qquad \textbf{(13)}$$

$$\frac{\partial(TCP)}{\partial M_2} = 2,800 - 800M_2 = 0; \; M_2 = 3.5 \qquad \textbf{(14)}$$

The optimal expenditure on advertising in the two magazines would be

$$6(\$6,000) + 3(\$4,000) = \$48,000.$$

At this level of advertising expenditure, sales will be

$$Q = 500 + 66M_1 - 3M_1^2 + 34M_2 - 2M_2^2$$
$$= 500 + 66(6) - 3(36) + 34(3) - 2(9) = 872 \text{ units,}$$

on which the contribution profit will be

$$TCP = 100,000 + 7,200M_1 - 600M_1^2 + 2,800M_2 - 400M_2^2$$
$$= 100,000 + 7,200(6) - 600(36) + 2,800(3) - 400(9) = \$126,400$$

Constrained Optima

In the preceding discussion, we made the implicit assumption that unlimited resources were available. No limits were placed on plant capacity or the amount of working capital that could be spent on advertising. In real life, however, planners are not able to work under such ideal conditions. All planners must make trade-offs in the allocation of scarce resources in order to do the best they can within the limitations imposed by management decisions or simply the hard facts of business life. Fortunately, marginal analysis via differential calculus can come to the rescue.

Once again, we shall use our case to illustrate the point. We have shown that profits will be maximized if we place six ads in *Medium One* and three ads in *Medium Two* at a total cost of $48,000. But suppose we can spend only $40,000 on advertising—how shall we spend it to maximize profits?

Application of Marginal Productivity. From our previous maximization of sales without any constraint on advertising, we obtained the optimal mix equation:

$$M_1 = M_2 + 2.5 \qquad (15)$$

If we can spend only $40,000 on advertising, we know that

$$\$6,000M_1 + \$4,000M_2 = \$40,000 \qquad (16)$$

Substituting Equation 15 into Equation 16 we get

$$6,000(M_2 + 2.5) + 4,000M_2 = 40,000$$
$$10,000M_2 + 15,000 = 40,000$$
$$M_2 = 2.5$$
$$M_1 = 5$$

The conclusion is that we should buy five ads in *Medium One* for $30,000 and two ads in *Medium Two* for $8,000, a total expenditure of $38,000. Sales at this level of advertising, calculated from Equation 7, are:

$$Q = 500 + 66(5) - 3(25) + 34(2) - 2(4) = 815 \text{ units.}$$

The contribution profit would be

$$TCP = \$200(815) - 38,000 = \$125,000.$$

Lagrangian Multiplier. An even more powerful tool for optimizing any multivariate function subject to one or more constraints is the Lagrangian multiplier. A Lagrangian multiplier is an artificial variable usually symbolized by the Greek letter lambda (λ). It can be more easily explained by use of the same example, in which we have the demand function

$$Q = (M_1, M_2) = 500 + 66M_1 - 3M_1^2 + 34M_2 - 2M_2^2 \qquad (17)$$

and the constraint equation

$$6,000M_1 + 4,000M_2 = 40,000. \qquad (18)$$

The demand function will be maximized when we set both the constraint Equation 18 and the partial derivatives of Equation 17 to zero and solve for M_1 and M_2. We can set the constraint equation to zero by rewriting it as

$$6,000M_1 + 4,000M_2 - 40,000 = 0, \qquad (19)$$

but when we take the partial derivatives of Equation 17, we end up with a system of three equations with only two variables, for which there is no solution.

The way out of our dilemma is to multiply Equation 19 by the artificial variable and add it to Equation 17. Now we have a function of three variables:

$$Q = f(M_1, M_2, \lambda) = 500 + 66M_1 - 3M_1^2 + 34M_2 - 2M_2^2$$
$$+ 6{,}000\lambda M_1 + 4{,}000\lambda M_2 - 40{,}000\lambda.$$

When we take the partial derivatives of this function, we obtain three equations in three variables, which we can solve:

$$\frac{\partial f}{\partial M_1} = 66 - 6M_1 + 6{,}000\lambda = 0$$

$$\frac{\partial f}{\partial M_2} = 34 - 4M_2 + 4{,}000\lambda = 0$$

$$\frac{\partial f}{\partial \lambda} = 6{,}000M_1 + 4{,}000M_2 - 40{,}000 = 0.$$

Notice that the partial derivative with respect to λ is just the constraint equation, as it always is. When we solve the system, we get

$$M_1 = 5.0; \quad M_2 = 2.5; \quad \lambda = -0.006.$$

Observe that the values of M_1 and M_2 are the same as we got from the application of the theory of marginal productivity. The value of λ, however, gives us additional information that we can get in no other way. The minus sign tells us that the value of the function will be increased if we reduce the restraining effect of the constraint equation. How much will it be improved? In this instance, by approximately 0.006 unit for each dollar added to the advertising budget. Since each unit sold contributes \$200 to profit, the marginal profit for this level of advertising expenditure is $\$200 \times 0.006 = \$1.20$. Since the profit function is not linear, the marginal profit will decrease as the advertising expenditure increases and will become negative when advertising expenditure exceeds \$48,000.

In real life, of course, we often have multivariate functions with multiple constraints. To solve such problems, we merely introduce one additional artificial variable for each additional constraint equation. It should be noted that the Lagrangian multipliers in nonlinear-programming problems such as this example are analogous to the dual variables in linear-programming problems, as discussed in Appendix 3B. Both the dual variables and the Lagrangian multipliers express the change in the objective function that can be expected from a one-unit change in the right-hand side of the constraint equation.

APPENDIX 3B   Linear Programming

In terms of actual application, linear programming is the most successful and widely used approach for solving resource-allocation problems. It is a post–World War II development and its usage has closely paralleled growth in the computer industry due to the enormous computational requirements of most of its applications.

Linear programming may be formally defined as a method of optimizing (i.e., maximizing or minimizing) a linear function of several variables subject to a set of linear constraints. Linear-programming problems are solved by using the row operations of matrix algebra in a technique known as the simplex method. Because the relationships are linear, a problem with only two variables can also be solved graphically.[1] The graphic method is impractical for solving realistic linear-programming problems, but it is quite useful for explaining the basic concepts and techniques and the elementary geometry of linear programming. Therefore, before presenting the algebraic technique of the simplex method, we will solve a two-variable model graphically.

Graphic Illustration:
Linear-Programming Problem with Two Variables

The Wayside Pottery makes two types of clay pots. One is a plain clay pot with a reinforced rim. The other is a smaller but fancier urn with handles and rope-like decoration on its sides. Making the plain clay pot requires four pounds of clay and one hour of labor. It brings in a profit of $4 per unit. The fancier urn is smaller, so it uses only three pounds of clay, but requires two hours of labor. It brings in a profit of $5 per unit. The firm employs one potter who works a 40-hour week and is supplied with 120 pounds of clay per week. How many plain pots and how many urns should she make in order to maximize the company's profits?

Solution

First we will set up the linear-programming model in good form. Then we will solve the problem twice, first by graphing and then by the simplex method.

Step 1. Define the variables.

Let

x_1 = number of plain clay pots produced each day
x_2 = number of urns produced each day.

Step 2. Define the objective function.   Each pot brings in a profit of $4 and each urn brings in a profit of $5. The objective, Z, is to maximize profits, which is expressed as:

Objective:

Maximize $Z = 4x_1 + 5x_2$.

Step 3. Define the constraints.

a. *Labor constraint:* Whether working on pots or on urns, the potter will work a maximum of 40 hours per week. She could work less but not more. Each pot requires one hour of labor and each urn requires two hours. Therefore

$$x_1 + 2x_2 \leq 40.$$

---

[1] It is also possible but very difficult to graph a set of three variables, and models with four variables or more cannot be graphed at all.

b. *Materials constraint:* The potter has a maximum of 120 pounds of clay per week for construction of both pots and urns. Each pot takes four pounds and each urn takes three pounds. Therefore

$$4x_1 + 3x_2 \leq 120.$$

Step 4.   State the nonnegativity constraints.   It is physically impossible to produce a negative quantity of either pots or urns. Therefore

$$x_1, x_2 \geq 0.$$

Step 5.   Draw the horizontal and vertical axes of the graph.   Label the horizontal axis x_1 and the vertical axis x_2. These axes are the boundaries of the nonnegativity constraints. All points that lie above the horizontal axis and to the right of the vertical axis will satisfy the nonnegativity constraints, as shown by the shaded area of Exhibit 3B–1.

Step 6.   Draw a line representing the first constraint.   The labor constraint is the inequality $x_1 + 2x_2 \leq 40$. If $x_2 = 0$, then $x_1 \leq 40$, and $x_1 = 40$ is the X-intercept. If $x_1 = 0$, then $x_2 \leq 20$, and $x_2 = 20$ is the Y-intercept. The line $x_1 + 2x_2 = 40$ drawn between the intercepts is the upper boundary of the shaded area on Exhibit 3B–2. All points in this area, including those on the line, satisfy the labor constraint.

Step 7.   Draw a line representing the second constraint.   The second constraint is the materials constraint $4x_1 + 3x_2 \leq 120$. If $x_2 = 0$, then $x_1 \leq 30$, and $x_1 = 30$ is the X-intercept. If $X_1 = 0$, then $x_2 \leq 40$, and $x_2 = 40$ is the Y-intercept. We draw the line $4x_1 + 3x_2 = 120$ between the intercepts, as shown on Exhibit 3B–3.

After completing Step 7, the materials-constraint line crosses the labor-constraint line at the coordinates (24,8), as shown in the exhibit. These coordinates may be found by solving the two equations simultaneously:

$$(x_1 + 2x_2 = 40) \times 3 = 3x_1 + 6x_2 = 120$$
$$(4x_1 + 3x_2 = 120) \times 2 = 8x_1 + 6x_2 = 240$$
$$-5x_1 = -120$$
$$x_1 = 24$$
$$x_1 + 2x_2 = 40$$
$$24 + 2x_2 = 40$$
$$2x_2 = 16$$
$$x_2 = 8.$$

The shaded area in Exhibit 3B–3 (page 54) is called the feasible solutions area, since it contains all combinations of the variables that satisfy all of the constraints. Obviously, there are a great many such combinations—an infinite number, in fact. Fortunately, we do not have to consider any combination within the shaded area, since the optimal combination will occur at one of the corners or extreme points of its boundaries.

Exhibit 3B–4 (page 54) illustrates graphically the basic principle of linear programming by placing parallel lines representing various levels of the objective function $Z = 4x_1 + 5x_2$ at the corners of the feasible-solutions region.

EXHIBIT 3B–1   The Nonnegativity Constraints

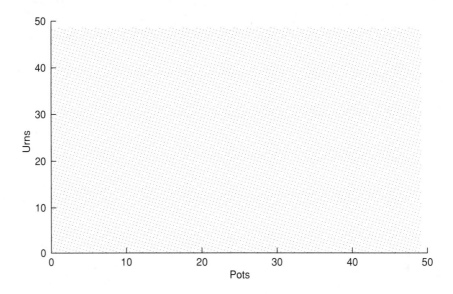

EXHIBIT 3B–2   The Labor Constraint

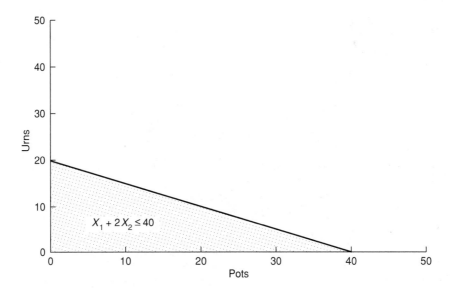

EXHIBIT 3B–3   Area of Feasible Solutions That Will Satisfy All Constraints

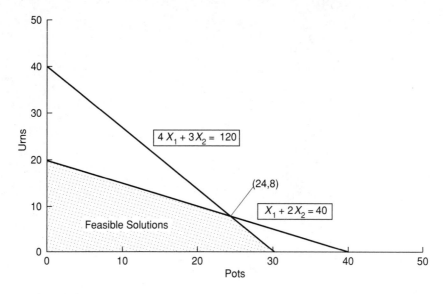

EXHIBIT 3B–4   Possible Solutions

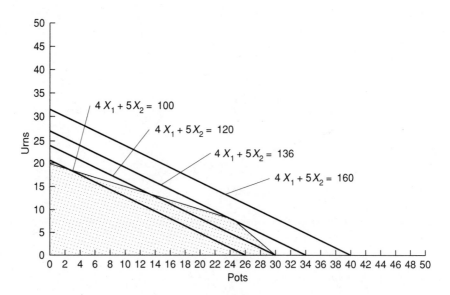

At the origin (0,0), all of the constraints are satisfied, but the value of the objective function is zero. As we move the objective-function line away from the origin in a parallel manner, the profits grow larger. At the corner (0,20), all constraints are satisfied and profits are $100. This can be improved by moving to the corner (30,0). Again all constraints are satisfied and profits improve to $120. This is still not optimal, for profits can be increased by moving to the corner (24,8) where the two constraint boundaries intersect. Here the profits are $136 and this is the maximum. If we move any farther away from the origin, the constraints will no longer be satisfied; that is, no part of the objective function line will lie within or upon the feasible region. This is illustrated by the line $4x_1 + 5x_2 = 160$.

It should be noted that a linear-programming problem does not necessarily have a single solution. If the objective-function line is parallel to one of the constraint boundaries, then every point along that boundary is optimal, giving an infinite number of solutions. At the other extreme, it may be that there is no solution for the problem as formulated. For example, if a minimum quantity of output is required but the constraints on resources are such that the minimum quantity cannot be produced, there will be no solution to the problem. The simplex method incorporates a way of identifying problems with an infinite number of solutions and problems with no solution, as explained next.

The Simplex Method

Whether obtained by hand or by computer, algebraic solution of linear-programming problems by the **simplex method** offers two main advantages: (1) it permits solution of problems with three or more variables, since algebra is not restricted by three-dimensional space and (2) values of the slack variables in the final solution provide very useful information for decision-making purposes.

Since the method is the same no matter how many variables are in the problem, we will use the two-variable model previously graphed to explain the simplex method. First, we make a slight change in the way the nonnegativity constraints are stated:

$$\text{Objective: Maximize } Z = 4x_1 + 5x_2$$

$$\begin{aligned}
\text{Subject to: } x_1 + 2x_2 &\le 40 \\
4x_1 + 3x_2 &\le 120 \\
x_1 + 0x_2 &\ge 0 \\
0x_1 + x_2 &\ge 0.
\end{aligned}$$

The first step in solving this problem is to convert the inequalities to equations. The transformation is achieved by introducing additional nonnegative variables whose sole purpose is to take up the difference or *slack* between the inequality and the equation. If the constraint provides an *upper* limit (inequality sign is $\le$), each **slack variable** represents the quantity of the available resource that is *not* being used and is introduced with a coefficient of $+1$. If the constraint provides a *lower* limit (inequality sign is $\ge$), each slack variable represents the amount by which use of the available resource may exceed the constraint, and is introduced with a coefficient of -1. For our example, only the nonnegativity constraints represent lower limits, so the introduction of slack variables gives the following arrangement:

$$
\begin{aligned}
x_1 + 2x_2 + s_1 \qquad\qquad\qquad &= \quad 40 \\
4x_1 + 3x_2 \quad\; + s_2 \qquad\qquad\; &= \; 120 \\
x_1 + 0x_2 \qquad\quad - s_3 \qquad\quad &= \quad\; 0 \\
0x_1 + \; x_2 \qquad\qquad\quad - s_4 &= \quad\; 0.
\end{aligned}
$$

In order for us to get started, the simplex method requires a canonical arrangement of the $n \times n$ matrix of the slack variables, where n equals the number of constraint equations.[2] In this case we have a 4×4 matrix of the slack variables, but it is not canonical because two of the coefficients are negative. The solution to this problem is to introduce an artificial variable into each of these equations with a coefficient of $+1$:

$$
\begin{aligned}
x_1 + 2x_2 + s_1 \qquad\qquad\qquad\qquad &= \quad 40 \\
4x_1 + 3x_2 \quad\; + s_2 \qquad\qquad\qquad\;\; &= \; 120 \\
x_1 + 0x_2 - s_3 \qquad + A_1 \qquad\quad\;\; &= \quad\; 0 \\
0x_1 + 0x_2 \qquad\; - s_4 \qquad + A_2 &= \quad\; 0.
\end{aligned}
$$

We now have the necessary canonical arrangement. Besides the constraint matrix, the artificial variables are also *added* to the objective function if we are *minimizing* it or *subtracted* from it if we are *maximizing* it. In either case they are given the value M, which is an unspecified but very large number. The modified objective function becomes

$$
Z = 4x_1 + 5x_2 - MA_1 - MA_2.
$$

We now have an undetermined system of four equations in eight variables; that is, $x_1, x_2, s_1, s_2, s_3, s_4, A_1, A_2$. The difference between the number of variables and the number of equations makes direct simultaneous solution impossible. Whether performed by a computer or by hand, the simplex method handles this problem by evaluating a combination of n variables at a time, where n equals the number of constraints. Each time the combination is changed by replacing one variable with another, it is called an **iteration**. Each iteration must constitute a **basic feasible solution**, which is one that satisfies *all* of the constraints and also satisfies the requirement that the solution shall have no more positive variables than the number of constraint equations.

The simplex method changes the basic feasible solutions by means of row operations in a tabular format called a tableau. In order to get started, the simplex algorithm assigns the value of zero to the functional variables, x_i, to obtain an initial basic feasible solution. The initial tableau (Iteration 0) appears as shown by Exhibit 3B–5.

Explanation of the Initial Tableau.   The second row contains column headings that include all of the variables in the problem. The C_j row contains the coefficients of the variables in the objective function. These will remain constant during all iterations. The coefficients of the constraint variables are carried in the cells of an $n \times m$ matrix where n equals the number of constraints (four rows in this case) and m equals the total number of variables, including the functional variables, the slack variables, and the artificial variables (eight columns in this case). Each cell in the matrix may be identified as a_{ij}, where the subscript i indicates the row and j indicates the column. To the right of the matrix is the column labeled b_i. It contains the right-hand sides of the constraint equations. The column labeled b_i / a_{ie} will be explained later.

---

[2] A canonical arrangement is one in which each number in the principal diagonal of an $n \times n$ matrix is $+1$.

EXHIBIT 3B–5 **Initial Simplex Tableau (Iteration 0)**

	C_j	4	5	0	0	0	0	$-M$	$-M$		
C_b	Basis	x_1	x_2	s_1	s_2	s_3	s_4	A_1	A_2	b_i	b_i/a_{ie}
0	s_1	1	2	1	0	0	0	0	0	40	
0	s_2	4	3	0	1	0	0	0	0	120	
$-M$	A_1	1	0	0	0	-1	0	1	0	0	
$-M$	A_2	0	1	0	0	0	-1	0	1	0	
	Z_j	$-M$	$-M$	0	0	M	M	$-M$	$-M$	0	
	C_j-Z_j	$M+4$	$M+5$	0	0	$-M$	$-M$	0	0		

The "Basis" column shows which basic variables are in the current basic feasible solution, and each basic variable will have the coefficient 1 in its column. To the left of the "Basis" column is the C_b column in which are entered the coefficients of the basic variables contained in the objective function. For the slack variables, this value is always zero. For the artificial variables, it is plus or minus M, depending on whether we are maximizing or minimizing the objective function. In this case we are maximizing, so the sign is negative.

Each cell of the Z_j row contains the change in the objective function that will result from the introduction of one unit of the variable identified by the column header. It is computed as

$$Z_j = \sum_{i=1}^{n} C_b a_{ij}.$$

In the initial tableau, Z_1 is computed as $0(1) + 0(4) + (-M)(1) + (-M)(0) = -M$; Z_2 is computed as $0(2) + 0(3) + (-M)(0) + (-M)(1) = -M$. The remaining columns, including the b_i column, are computed in the same manner. The Z-value in the b_i column is the current value of the objective function. In the initial tableau, this value is zero because all of the functional variables are set to zero.

The $C_j - Z_j$ row contains the criteria by which we will determine whether or not we have arrived at an optimal solution. If we are maximizing the objective function, the solution is optimal when all $C_j - Z_j$ are zero or *negative*. If we are minimizing, the solution is optimal when all $C_j - Z_j$ are zero or *positive*. In this example, we are maximizing and there are two positive values in the $C_j - Z_j$ row. This means we are not optimal and must therefore select a new basis.

Selecting a New Basis. A new basis is selected by replacing one of the present basic variables with a presently nonbasic variable; that is, one variable enters and one variable leaves the basis. The entering variable is chosen first, and it should be the one that increases Z at the fastest rate. It is identified by the largest positive number in the $C_j - Z_j$

EXHIBIT 3B–6   **Choosing the Entering and Leaving Variables**

	C_j	4	5	0	0	0	0	−M	−M		
C_b	Basis	x_1	x_2	s_1	s_2	s_3	s_4	A_1	A_2	b_i	b_i/a_{ie}
0	s_1	1	2	1	0	0	0	0	0	40	20
0	s_2	4	3	0	1	0	0	0	0	120	40
−M	A_1	1	0	0	0	−1	0	1	0	0	∞
−M	A_2	0	1	0	0	0	−1	0	1	0	⇐ 0
	Z_j	−M	−M	0	0	M	M	−M	−M	0	
	$C_j−Z_j$	M+4	M+5	0	0	−M	−M	0	0		

⇑

row. In our example, this is in the x_2 column, as indicated by the vertical arrow in Exhibit 3B–6.

The amount that Z can be increased by the entering variable is limited by the value of the leaving variable, which must decrease to zero but may not go negative. The limit of the increase from the entering variable is just the ratio of b_i to the coefficient of the entering variable, a_ie, where the subscript e indicates the column of the entering variable. This ratio is called the **min-ratio**. If a_{ie} is zero, the min-ratio is undefined. If a_{ie} is negative, the min-ratio is negative even if it is zero. There is one min-ratio for each row. For the purpose of this illustration, the min-ratio is posted in the b/a_{ie} column as shown in Exhibit 3B–6, but it might not be printed out by a computer program.

The leaving variable is indicated by the smallest positive min-ratio. In this example, it is A_2 as indicated by the horizontal arrow. The element at the intersection of the x_2 column and the A_2 row is called the *pivot element*. Since we want to enter one unit of the entering variable, x_2, the pivot element must be changed to 1. This is done by dividing all elements in the row by the pivot element's value. All other elements in the pivot element's column must then be changed to zero by row operations, as follows:

In the s_1 row, the value in the x_2 column is 2. In order to change that number to 0, we multiply the new x_2 row by 2 and subtract it from the s_1 row.

For the s_2 row, we multiply the new x_2 row by 3 and subtract it from the s_2 row.

In the A_1 row, the value in the x_2 column is already zero, so we need not make any change if we are solving the problem by hand. The computer, of course, would multiply the new x_2 row by 0 and subtract it from the A_1 row.

The new tableau after these row operations is shown as Exhibit 3B–7. This tableau also shows that the C_b value for the x_2 row is 5, which is the coefficient of x_2 in the objective function. It has been used to calculate new values for the Z_j and $C_j − Z_j$ rows, as shown. The b_i column shows that Z is still zero, meaning no improvement in the objective function, but the $C_j − Z_j$ row shows that one of the artificial variables has been driven to zero. This effectively removes that artificial variable from the objective function, which we want to do as quickly as possible. That is the reason why the

EXHIBIT 3B–7   **Tableau after One Iteration**

	C_j	4	5	0	0	0	0	$-M$	$-M$		
C_b	Basis	x_1	x_2	s_1	s_2	s_3	s_4	A_1	A_2	b_i	b_i/a_{ie}
0	s_1	1	0	0	1	2	0	0	-2	40	40
0	s_2	4	0	1	0	3	0	0	-3	120	30
$-M$	A_1	1	0	0	0	0	-1	1	0	0	$\Leftarrow 0$
5	x_2	0	1	0	0	0	-1	0	1	0	∞
	Z_j	$-M$	5	0	0	-5	M	$-M$	5	0	
	$C_j - Z_j$	$M+4$	0	0	0	5	$-M$	0	$-M-5$		

⇑

artificial variables were given the value M, with M being a very large number. The $C_j - Z_j$ value of the second artificial variable will be driven to zero in the next iteration.

The vertical arrow identifies x_1 as the entering variable for the next iteration, since it has the largest value in the $C_j - Z_j$ row. When the min-ratio values are calculated, they point to A_1 as the leaving variable. The second iteration then appears as shown by Exhibit 3B–8 (page 60).

For the third iteration, s_3 enters and s_1 leaves, with the results shown in Exhibit 3B–9 (page 60).

For the next iteration, s_4 enters and s_2 leaves. The results are shown in Exhibit 3B–10 (page 61).

Since all values in the $C_j - Z_j$ row are zero or negative, the optimal solution has been reached, with a Z-value of 136. The values of the variables in the basic solution can be read from b_i column. The value of all other variables not in the basic solution is zero. Hence the solution is $[x_1, x_2, s_1, s_2, s_3, s_4, A_1, A_2] = [24, 8, 0, 0, 8, 24, 0, 0]$. This can be interpreted to mean that all available labor and all available clay will be used to produce 24 pots and 8 urns for a total profit of $136.

Complications and Their Resolution

The following discussion covers a number of problems that can be encountered in the simplex process and the ways in which they can be resolved.

Minimization.   Minimizing an objective function is equivalent to maximizing its negative. For example, minimizing $Z = 3x_1 + 5x_2$ is equivalent to maximizing $Z' = -3x_1 - 5x_2$. There are two ways to handle the algorithm, either of which may be built into a particular computer program:

1. Reverse the optimality criteria to select the variable with the most negative $C_j - Z_j$ value as the entering variable and quit when all $C_j - Z_j$ values are either zero or positive.

2. Change the objective function from Z to Z', that is, reverse the signs of the C_j and proceed as usual.

EXHIBIT 3B–8   **Tableau after Two Iterations**

C_j		4	5	0	0	0	0	$-M$	$-M$		
C_b	Basis	x_1	x_2	s_1	s_2	s_3	s_4	A_1	A_2	b_i	b_i/a_{ie}
0	s_1	0	0	0	1	2	1	-1	-2	40	⇐20
0	s_2	0	0	1	0	3	4	-4	-3	120	40
4	x_1	1	0	0	0	0	-1	1	0	0	∞
5	x_2	0	1	0	0	-1	0	0	1	0	-0
	Z_j	4	5	0	0	-5	-4	4	5	0	
	C_j-Z_j	0	0	0	0	5	4	$-M-4$	$-M-5$		

⇑

EXHIBIT 3B–9   **Tableau after Three Iterations**

C_j		4	5	0	0	0	0	$-M$	$-M$		
C_b	Basis	x_1	x_2	s_1	s_2	s_3	s_4	A_1	A_2	b_i	b_i/a_{ie}
0	s_3	0	0	0	0.5	1	0.5	-0.5	-1	20	40
0	s_2	0	0	1	-1.5	0	2.5	-2.5	0	60	⇐24
4	x_1	1	0	0	0	0	-1	1	0	0	-0
5	x_2	0	1	0	0.5	0	0.5	-0.5	0	20	40
	Z_j	4	5	0	2.5	0	-1.5	1.5	0	100	
	C_j-Z_j	0	0	0	-2.5	0	1.5	$-M-1.5$	$-M$		

⇑

Equalities.   The problem with an original constraint that is already an equality is that it has no slack, hence no slack variable is added to the constraint equation. Therefore there is no obvious basic feasible solution with which to begin. The remedy is the same as when the constraint inequality is $\geq$, that is, add an artificial variable with a coefficient of 1 and a value of $-M$ for the C_j row if maximizing or $+M$ if minimizing the objective function.

Variable Unconstrained in Sign.   Sometimes it is physically possible to have a variable that may be either positive or negative, but the simplex algorithm requires that all variables be nonnegative. A variable that is unconstrained in sign (i.e., can be either positive or negative) can always be expressed as the difference between two nonnegative variables. If $u \geq 0$ and $v \geq 0$, then x can be expressed as $x = u - v$.

EXHIBIT 3B–10   **Tableau after Four Iterations**

	C_j	4	5	0	0	0	0	$-M$	$-M$		
C_b	Basis	x_1	x_2	s_1	s_2	s_3	s_4	A_1	A_2	b_i	b_i/a_{ie}
0	s_3	0	0	-0.2	0.8	1	0	0	-1	8	
0	s_4	0	0	0.4	-0.6	0	1	-1	0	24	
4	x_1	1	0	0.4	-0.6	0	0	0	0	24	
5	x_2	0	1	-0.2	0.8	0	0	0	0	8	
	Z_j	4	5	0.6	1.6	0	0	0	0	136	
	C_j-Z_j	0	0	-0.6	-1.6	0	0	$-M$	$-M$		

If x is positive, let $u = x$ and $v = 0$, then $u - v \geq 0$. For example, suppose $x = 18$. Let $u = 18$ and $v = 0$; then $18 - 0 = 18$, which is positive.

If x is negative, let $v = x$ and $u = 0$, then $u - v \geq 0$. For example, suppose $x = -5$. Let $v = -5$ and $u = 0$; then $0 - (-5) = 5$, a positive number.

Since the simplex method examines only the extreme points of the feasible-solutions space, either u or v or both will always be set to zero. If $u_j - v_j$ is substituted for x_j in the objective function and in all constraints, the simplex algorithm can handle it. If more than one variable can be either positive or negative, let $v = $ the largest negative variable and use this same v for all cases; i.e., $v = $ maximum $(-x_j)$ and $x_j = u_j - v$.

Tie for Entering Basic Variable.   If the maximum $C_j - Z_j$ value should be the same for two or more variables, pick any one of them as the entering variable. It will make no difference in the final outcome of the simplex solution.

Tie for Leaving Basic Variable.   A tie for the leaving variable leads immediately to a degenerate basic feasible solution, that is, one in which one of the variables is zero. Although theoretically the simplex algorithm could go into an endless loop, this has never actually happened, so the selection of a leaving variable can be made arbitrarily whenever a tie occurs.

Multiple Solutions.   If there are multiple solutions to a linear programming problem, the simplex algorithm will stop when it reaches the first of the multiple solutions. How then can we tell if there are other solutions?

The way to tell is to examine the $C_j - Z_j$ row of the last iteration, keeping in mind that the $C_j - Z_j$ value indicates the change in Z that will take place if one more unit of that variable is entered. If there is only one solution, the $C_j - Z_j$ value for each of the basic variables in the solution will be zero and all others will be nonzero (i.e., negative if we are maximizing or positive if we are minimizing). If we find a nonbasic variable with a $C_j - Z_j$ value of zero, this indicates that there are other optimal solutions. If we select that variable as the entering variable and run another iteration,[3] it will yield another solution but will make no difference in the value of Z. Hence that solution will also be optimal. In fact, it will be the other end of a line along which all solutions would be optimal. This may be a fact of great interest to the manager, since there may be qualitative factors that would make one solution more desirable than another.

No Feasible Solution.   If the problem actually has no feasible solution, the simplex algorithm will stop with an ostensibly feasible solution. However, one of the artificial variables, which were supposed to be driven to zero, will appear in the solution.

Unbounded Variables.   Lack of restrictions may permit a variable to increase without bound. When an unbounded variable is selected as an entering variable, there will be no leaving variable available by the min-ratio test. The simplex algorithm will then stop without a solution.

The Dual Problem

Every linear programming problem has two forms: a **primal** and a **dual**. The original model of the problem is the primal form. The dual of the maximization problem presented previously is a counterpart that addresses the question: What is the value to the Wayside Pottery of additional units of resources? The dual represents the marginal value of the constraining resources, hence the dual solution is commonly called **shadow prices**.

The primal and the dual are complementary to each other in such a way that the simplex algorithm automatically solves both problems simultaneously. Hence either problem may be designated as primal and the other will be solved as the dual. The computer program will not show a tableau for the dual; rather, it will simply print out the shadow prices.[4] The shadow prices for our example are:

Constraint Number	Value
1	0.600
2	1.600
3	0.000
4	0.000

Going back to Exhibit 3B–10, which presents the final tableau in the solution of this problem, we see that the shadow prices are entered for each of the constraint variables in the Z_j row, and this will be generally true. That is, in any linear programming problem, the final tableau will hold the marginal values of the constraining elements in the Z_j row.

---

[3] It would have to be done by hand, since the computer will be programmed to stop when the first optimal solution is found.

[4] A full explanation of the relationship between the primal and the dual is beyond the scope of this book, but may be obtained from a standard text on management science or operations research.

In this example, the primal solution says that profit will be maximum when 24 pots and 8 urns are produced, and this level of production uses up all available resources of labor and clay. (The final values of s_1 and s_2 are zero.) The shadow prices of zero for the slack variables s_3 and s_4 indicate that changing the right-hand side of the indicated constraint equations will make no difference in profits. The shadow prices for s_1 and s_2 indicate that adding one more hour of labor would increase profit by $0.60 and adding one more pound of clay would increase profit by $1.60.

The importance of the dual to a manager is the information it gives about the use of resources. For example, production managers' first concern is the control of the resources at their disposal. Information about the value of those resources with respect to profit is needed for decisions about acquiring more of those resources and how much the firm can afford to pay for them.

Sensitivity Analysis

The preceding model of a linear-programming problem was formulated as if the exact parameters of the model were known with certainty. In most real-life problems, however, some parameters may be known with certainty, but most are best estimates or educated guesses and therefore subject to change. The analysis of parameter changes and their effect on the model's solution is called **sensitivity analysis**.

The most obvious way to determine the effect of changes in the parameters is to reformulate the model and solve it again. Fortunately, this time-consuming and costly procedure is unnecessary, since the final tableau of the primal solution can be worked to give such information.[5] The computer program will do this automatically and print out results such as shown in Exhibit 3B–11 (page 64).

Changes in Objective-Function Coefficients.   A change in one of the coefficients in the objective function can change the optimal solution if the change is large enough. Sensitivity analysis determines the range of values within which the optimal solution will not change. The upper table shows that daily production of 24 pots and 8 urns will remain optimum:

1. If the price of pots is changed to provide a profit of any amount between $2.50 and $6.67, inclusive.

2. If the price of urns is changed to provide a profit of any amount between $3 and $8, inclusive.

It is important to note that these ranges apply to a change in the price of pots *or* a change in the price of urns, but *not* to changes in both.

Changes in Constraint Quantities.   A change in the right-hand side of a constraint equation can change the boundaries of the feasible area. Sensitivity analysis determines the range of right-hand–side values over which the solution basis will remain feasible.

---

[5] The technique of sensitivity analysis is beyond the scope of this book, but may be obtained from a standard text on management science or operations research.

EXHIBIT 3B–11   **Typical Computer Printout of Sensitivity Analysis**

```
********************
SENSITIVITY ANALYSIS
********************
```

	Objective Function Coefficient Ranges		
Variable	Lower Limit	Current Value	Upper Limit
X1	2.50	4.00	6.67
X2	3.00	5.00	8.00

	Right-Hand--Side Ranges		
Constraint Number	Lower Limit	RHS Value	Upper Limit
1	30.00	40.00	80.00
2	60.00	120.00	160.00
3	No limit	0.00	24.00
4	No limit	0.00	8.00

The lower table in Exhibit 3B–11 shows that the solution basis $[x_1, x_2, s_1, s_2]$ will remain feasible:

1. If the quantity of labor available is changed to any amount between 30 hours and 80 hours, inclusive.

2. If the quantity of clay available is changed to any amount between 60 pounds and 160 pounds, inclusive.

3. If the nonnegativity constraint on x_1 is changed to any number between 0 and 24 pots, inclusive.

4. If the nonnegativity constraint on x_2 is changed to any number between 0 and 8 urns, inclusive.

These ranges apply to a change in the right-hand side of just one constraint equation. If the right-hand side of more than one constraint equation is changed, a whole new problem is created. It is also important to note that while the variables in the basis remain intact throughout these ranges, the quantities of those variables may be changed.

References

Bernhard, Richard H. "Mathematical Programming Models for Capital Budgeting—A Survey, Generalization, and Critique." *Journal of Financial and Quantitative Analysis 4* (June 1969), pp. 111–58. This is an excellent review of mathematical modeling in the field of finance.

Dantzig, George B. *Linear Programming and Extensions.* Princeton, N.J.: Princeton University Press, 1963.

Lee, Sang M. *Goal Programming for Decision Analysis*. Philadelphia: Auerback, 1972.

Myers, Stewart C. "A Note on Linear Programming and Capital Budgeting." *Journal of Finance* 27 (March 1972), pp. 89–92.

Plane, Donald R., and Gary A. Kochenberger. *Operations Research for Managerial Decisions,* 3d. ed. Homewood, Ill.: Richard D. Irwin, 1976.

Taylor, Bernard W. *Introduction to Management Science*. Dubuque, Iowa: William C. Brown, 1982.

C H A P T E R·

4

DECISION MAKING UNDER RISK AND UNCERTAINTY

As discussed in the preceding chapter, many short-run managerial decisions involve no more than choosing the best of a set of alternatives whose outcomes are known with certainty. Other short-run decisions, however, and virtually all long-run decisions are made under conditions of risk or uncertainty where managers must select a course of action from perceived alternatives with less than perfect knowledge about the occurrence of events that will affect the outcome. This chapter presents tools and techniques that may be used to make decisions under such conditions.

CHAPTER OUTLINE

This chapter is divided into three sections and two appendixes:

1. **The Decision Matrix**. This section introduces the decision matrix, also known as the payoff matrix, which is a model of decision possibilities for a typically complex decision problem.
2. **Decision Making under Risk**. This section discusses risk measurement, expected value, risk–return trade-offs, risk and utilities, and risk adjustment. It also introduces the decision tree, a useful tool in sequential decision analysis.
3. **Decision Making under Uncertainty**. This section discusses subjective decision making using four major criteria: the Wald criterion (also called the maximin

criterion), the Hurwicz alpha criterion, the Savage criterion (also called the minimax regret criterion), and the Laplace criterion (also called the Bayes criterion).

4. **Appendix 4A: Summary of the Laws of Probability**. This appendix defines probability and shows how to calculate joint and conditional probabilities.

5. **Appendix 4B: Probability Distribution of Cash Flows**. This appendix shows how to calculate and evaluate the present value of a series of net cash flows expected in the future.

The Decision Matrix

Under conditions of risk or uncertainty, the typical decision problem is sufficiently complex to permit a number of possible outcomes or payoffs for each strategy—outcomes that are often a function of conditions beyond the control of the decision maker. A decision matrix, also called a payoff matrix, provides a useful tool for the presentation and analysis of these outcomes. The decision matrix helps the decision maker to conceptualize and formalize the decision process into

1. A statement of objectives,
2. The selection of payoffs, and
3. The evaluation and selection of alternative strategies.

An example of a payoff matrix is shown in Exhibit 4–1, in which the decision maker's five alternative strategies or courses of action are listed at the left as S_1 through S_5. The decision maker also envisions four possible states of nature (conditions or events), which are marked off along the top as N_1 through N_4. The numbers in the matrix cells represent the resulting payoffs or outcomes for each strategy and associated state of nature.

In this example, the strategies might be different advertising campaigns, and the states of nature could be economic conditions of boom, stability, recession, or depression. The payoffs represent the decision maker's best estimate of outcomes for each combination of strategy and state of nature, expressed in the most meaningful terms. Conceptually, the most meaningful terms might be quantities, such as units of output sold, dollar volume of sales, dollars of profits, or any other number that makes sense to the decision maker.[1]

Under a condition of certainty, there can be only one state of nature, and the payoff matrix would be reduced to a single column. The decision maker knows what the payoff will be if a particular strategy is followed, and needs only to select the strategy with the greatest payoff.

Under a condition of risk, the probability of each state of nature and its associated payoffs can be developed *objectively* from empirical evidence, from company records, or from experimentation.

---

[1] In this illustration, the payoffs would have to represent some function of profit, since it is not possible to have negative output or sales.

EXHIBIT 4–1   Decision Matrix

Alternative Strategies	States of Nature			
	N_1	N_2	N_3	N_4
S_1	6	6	6	4
S_2	25	7	7	-15
S_3	20	20	7	-1
S_4	19	16	9	-2
S_5	20	15	15	-3

Under a condition of uncertainty, the probabilities of the states of nature and their associated payoffs must be developed *subjectively* according to the decision maker's best information and belief. This, of course, requires that decision makers assume some knowledge of the possible states of nature and associated payoffs. If decision makers decide that their knowledge is insufficient to assign subjective probabilities, they can always fall back on the Bayesian postulate that the probabilities are equal.

Decision Making under Risk

As noted in the preceding chapter, risk exists when the decision maker does not know in advance the specific outcome of a decision but is able to establish an objective probability distribution of the possible states of nature and their associated payoffs or outcomes.

Methods of Estimating Risk

There are two basic approaches to objective measurement of probability (degree of risk). One is **a priori**, by deduction; the other is **a posteriori**, by statistical analysis of empirical data.

The a priori method.   In the a priori method, the decision maker is able to determine the probability of an outcome without experimentation or analysis of past experience. Instead, probabilities are determined deductively on the basis of assumed principles, provided that the characteristics of the eventuality are known in advance. For example, we know a coin has only two sides. Because of this, a tossed coin must come up with either a head or a tail. Assuming the coin is evenly balanced, we can deduce that there is an equal probability of getting a head or a tail on any one toss. Thus it is not necessary to toss a coin a large number of times to discover that the relative frequency of a head (or tail) approaches $\frac{1}{2}$, or one out of every two tosses. By the same reasoning, it is not necessary to continuously draw cards from a deck containing 52 cards to conclude that the probability of drawing any particular card is 1/52.

Are these probability statements intended to predict a particular outcome? Certainly not. They merely state that in a sufficiently large number of trials a particular outcome will be realized. It follows then that habitual gamblers, entertained with organized games of chance, face a condition of risk, not of uncertainty. The only thing that is nearly certain is that they will lose and the house will win in the long run.

The a priori method of estimating risk is appropriate whenever the decision maker can compute the probability of an outcome without relying upon experimentation, sampling, or past experience. When this is not possible, the decision maker must fall back on the a posteriori method. In the a priori method, we proceed from cause to effect. In the a posteriori method, we observe the effect by means of empirical measurement and then seek to establish the cause.

The a posteriori method.   The a posteriori method assumes that past performances were typical and will continue in the future. In order to establish a probability measure, the decision makers begin by observing the number of times that each event of interest has occurred and the distribution of these frequencies over the total number of observations. For example, suppose that for a number of years an international airline has scheduled extra flights between Honolulu and Hong Kong to handle the surge of travel over the Christmas and New Year holidays. Now the firm must decide whether or not to schedule extra flights this year. First, it should gather data on how many seats were filled (load factor) on each of the past flights. The number of times that each particular load factor was reached is that load factor's frequency. When the frequencies are arranged in ascending or descending order, they become a **frequency distribution.**

Statistical theory requires that frequency data satisfy three technical conditions:

1. The data must provide enough cases or observations to exhibit stability.
2. The observations must be repeated in the population of observations.
3. The observations must be independent.[2]

If these conditions are satisfied, the frequency distribution can be converted to a **probability distribution**. Note, however, that there is a distinction between frequency distribution and probability distribution. A frequency distribution is a tabulation of how many times certain events have occurred in the past. A probability distribution is a tabulation of the percentage of time that they are likely to occur in the future.

If the decision maker is willing to assume that past performances were typical and will continue in the future, the simplest way to construct a probability distribution is to make a direct conversion of the frequency distribution. For example, if a certain load factor occurred during 20 of the past 50 flights, we might say that the expected frequency, and hence the probability, of occurrence on the next flight is 20/50 = 0.4, or 40 percent.

The decision maker, of course, is not required to accept a direct conversion of the frequency distribution. The probability distribution can be modified to recognize the presence of new factors that might have important bearing upon later economic behavior, or to correct for past controls not continuing in the future.

If conditions are such that the statistical probability of an event can be computed objectively, then the likelihood of that outcome can be classified as a risk. Thus, insurance companies can predict with a high degree of accuracy the probabilities of deaths, accidents, and fire losses. These probabilities enable them to make decisions about pre-

---

[2] Independence means that the observations are drawn at random, and thus the magnitude of any particular random variable is not affected by the magnitude of another random variable drawn from the same population.

mium levels and rates. Although they cannot establish the probability that a particular individual will die or that a particular house will burn, they can predict with small error how many people in a given age group will die next year or how many houses of a given type and general location will burn.

When faced with eventualities or outcomes that involve risks, a primary task of professional decision makers (e.g., managers) is to develop techniques that will enable them to calculate and subsequently minimize the risks inherent in a particular problem. One method used to accomplish this is to calculate the probability distribution of possible outcomes from a set of sample observations, and then compute an *expected value*.

Expected Value

Under conditions of risk, the primary decision criterion is expected value, which is computed as

$$E(X) = P_1X_1 + P_2X_2 + \ldots + P_nX_n = \sum_{i=1}^{n} P_iX_i \tag{1}$$

where

X_i = value of the ith payoff

P_i = probability of the ith payoff (which is equal to the probability of the ith state of nature).

From Equation 1 we see that the expected value of a strategy is a weighted mean value, using the probabilities of the payoffs as weights. That is to say, if the strategy were to be executed many times under similar states of nature, we could expect to receive an *average* payoff equal to the expected value.

Suppose a number of strategies with the same cost of investment are being evaluated. Expected value serves as a yardstick for comparison among these alternatives. When comparing two or more strategies, the one with the highest expected value will be the decision maker's choice.

To illustrate, suppose we consider again the decision matrix in Exhibit 4–1, which has four possible states of nature. Let us say that N_1 = boom times, N_2 = stable times, N_3 = recession, and N_4 = depression. Let us assume also that the decision maker, by careful research, is able to assign objective probabilities of 20 percent to N_1, 65 percent to N_2, 10 percent to N_3, and 5 percent to N_4, as shown in Exhibit 4–2 (page 72). Note that the probabilities add up to 100 percent—this must always be the case. The expected value of each strategy is calculated as follows:

$$
\begin{aligned}
E(S_1) &= 0.20(6) + 0.65(6) + 0.10(6) + 0.05(4) &&= 5.90 \\
E(S_2) &= 0.20(25) + 0.65(7) + 0.10(7) + 0.05(-15) &&= 9.50 \\
E(S_3) &= 0.20(20) + 0.65(20) + 0.10(7) + 0.05(-1) &&= 17.65 \\
E(S_4) &= 0.20(19) + 0.65(16) + 0.10(9) + 0.05(-2) &&= 15.00 \\
E(S_5) &= 0.20(20) + 0.65(15) + 0.10(15) + 0.05(-3) &&= 15.10.
\end{aligned}
$$

To make a decision, the strategy with the highest expected value is chosen. In this example, there is a clear decision in favor of strategy S_3. But suppose that the expected values of alternative strategies are the same, as illustrated by Exhibit 4–3—then what?

EXHIBIT 4–2   Expected Value Calculation

		States of Nature			
Alternative Strategies	N_1 $(p = .20)$	N_2 $(p = .65)$	N_3 $(p = .10)$	N_4 $(p = .05)$	*Expected Value E(S)*
S_1	6	6	6	4	5.90
S_2	25	7	7	−15	9.50
S_3	20	20	7	−1	17.65[a]
S_4	19	16	9	−2	15.00
S_5	20	15	15	−3	15.10

[a] Best strategy.

Exhibit 4–3 shows a decision matrix with a probability of 0.25 for N_1, 0.50 for N_2, and 0.25 for N_3. Included also are the payoffs for three different strategies or projects. The expected values are calculated as follows:

$$E(S_1) = 0.25(20) + 0.50(10) + 0.25(20) = 15.0$$
$$E(S_2) = 0.25(40) + 0.50(10) + 0.25(0) = 15.0$$
$$E(S_3) = 0.25(10) + 0.50(10) + 0.25(10) = 10.0.$$

Clearly, either S_1 or S_2 is preferable to S_3. But in order to choose between S_1 and S_2, which have the same expected value, we must use some other yardstick. The yardstick to use is **degree of risk**. Since expected value is a measure of central tendency, the degree of risk can be measured as the degree to which possible payoffs deviate from the expected value. Degree of risk thus is considered to be a secondary or auxiliary measure of expected value.

Measurement of Risk: Range and Standard Deviation

Looking at Exhibit 4–3, we see that although S_1 and S_2 have the same expected value of 15, S_1 will actually pay off either 20 or 10, while S_2 could pay either 40, 10, or 0. Intuitively, we sense that the farther away from the mean the actual payoff can be, the riskier the project. Hence, one way of measuring risk is to calculate the **range**, which is the difference between the most extreme payoff values. In our example, the range of S_1 is 10 (from a low of 10 to a high of 20) while the range of S_2 is 40 (from a low of 0 to a high of 40).

The range is a useful preliminary evaluation, but it considers only the most extreme values and gives no weight to values in between. If we assume a normal probability distribution, a more common and more accurate measurement of risk is the statistic called the **standard deviation**, σ (the Greek letter sigma), which is a measurement of the variation of payoffs from the expected value. The standard deviation measures the tightness of the probability distribution. The higher the standard deviation, the greater the variation of possible payoffs, and, therefore, the greater the risk.

EXHIBIT 4–3   Expected Value of Three Projects

Alternative Strategies	States of Nature			Expected Value E(S)
	N_1 (p = .25)	N_2 (p = .50)	N_3 (p = .25)	
S_1	20	10	20	15
S_2	40	10	0	15
S_3	10	10	10	10

Calculation of the standard deviation may proceed in four steps, as follows:

Step 1. Calculate the expected value (weighted arithmetic mean) of the distribution

$$E(X) = \sum_{i=1}^{n} X_i P_i \qquad (2)$$

where

X_i = The ith payoff or outcome

P_i = The probability of the ith payoff

$E(X)$ = The expected value, or weighted mean outcome, with probabilities as the weights.

Step 2. Subtract the expected value from each outcome to obtain a set of deviations from the expected value, that is,

$$d_i = X_i - E(X_i). \qquad (3)$$

Step 3. Square each deviation, then multiply the squared deviation by the probability of its related outcome. Then sum those products to obtain the mean squared deviation, or **variance**, σ^2, of the probability distribution:

$$\sigma^2 = \sum_{i=1}^{n} [X_i - E(X)]^2 P_i. \qquad (4)$$

Step 4. Take the square root of the variance to obtain the *standard deviation*, σ:

$$\sigma = \sqrt{\sum_{i=1}^{n} [X_i - E(X)]^2 P_i}. \qquad (5)$$

Equation 5 may also be written as

$$\sigma = \sqrt{\sum_{i=1}^{n} (X_i - \mu_x)^2 P_i} \qquad (6)$$

since the arithmetic mean of the distribution, μ_x (read mu of X), is the expected value. The notation in Equation 6 is less cumbersome than that in Equation 5.

Exhibit 4–4 (page 74) shows the calculations of standard deviations for the strategies shown in Exhibit 4–3. Exhibit 4–4 shows that S_2, with a standard deviation of 15, is three times

EXHIBIT 4–4   Calculation of Standard Deviation

Strategy	$(X_i - \mu)$	$(X_i - \mu)^2$	P_i	$(X_i - \mu)^2 P_i$	
S_1	5	25	0.25	6.25	
	−5	25	0.50	12.50	
	5	25	0.25	6.25	
				$\sigma_1^2 = 25.00$	$\sigma_1 = 5$
S_2	25	625	0.25	156.25	
	−5	25	0.50	12.50	
	−15	225	0.25	56.25	
				$\sigma_2^2 = 225.00$	$\sigma_2 = 15$
S_3	0	0	0.25	0.0	
	0	0	0.50	0.0	
	0	0	0.25	0.0	
				$\sigma_3^2 = 0.0$	$\sigma_3 = 0$

as risky as S_1, with a standard deviation of 5; while S_3, with a standard deviation of zero, offers no risk at all.

For any normal distribution, the probability-distribution curve is symmetric about the mean. The area under the curve represents a total probability of 1.0, divided into two equal parts. Thus the probability (area) to the left of the mean is 0.5 and to the right is 0.5. Exhibit 4–5 illustrates the concept. The figure is drawn to the **standard** or **Z-scale**, which has a mean of zero and a standard deviation of ± 1.0.

If we consult a table of normal distribution (such as Table E in the Appendix at the end of this book), we find that a Z-value of 1.0 (meaning one standard deviation away from the mean) corresponds to an area of .3413. Hence, the area between $Z = -1.0$ and $Z = +1.0$ is .6826. In other words, there is a 68.26 percent probability that the actual outcome will lie within one standard deviation of the mean (in either direction). Using the same procedure, the area within ± 2 standard deviations of the mean is .9544, or 95.44 percent, and the area within ± 3 standard deviations is 99.73 percent, as shown in the exhibit.

Returning to our earlier comparisons of strategies S_1 and S_2, Exhibit 4–6 shows the probability distributions for each strategy, as well as the mean and standard deviation of each. In Exhibit 4–6, the zone of 68 percent probability, (that is, $\mu \pm 1\sigma$) is shown as a shaded area. For the probability distribution of S_1, this is a narrow band between payoffs of 10 and 20. For the probability distribution of S_2, there is a much wider band ranging from 0 to 40. Clearly, the absolute variation of possible payoffs is much greater for S_2 than for S_1. The greater variation indicates S_2 is riskier than S_1, since the two alternatives have the same expected value.

Measurement of Relative Risk: Coefficient of Variation

Suppose a firm has an opportunity to invest in two different projects. One has an expected value of $500,000 with a standard deviation of $5,000. The other has an expected value of $100,000 with a standard deviation of $2,000. Which is riskier?

EXHIBIT 4–5   Probability Range for a Normal Distribution

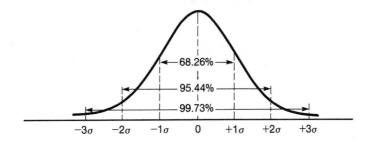

EXHIBIT 4–6   Probability Distribution of Two Strategies with the Same Expected Value

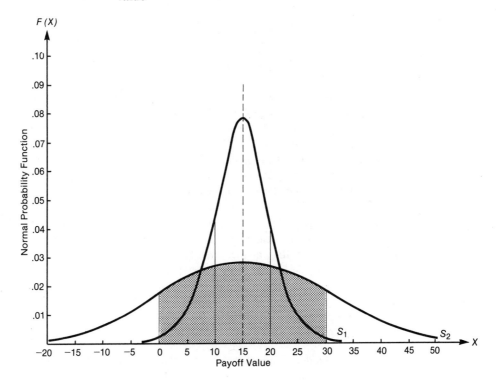

If we use standard deviation as a measure of risk, we would have to conclude that the larger project is riskier. But considering the standard deviation in relation to the size of the project, the relative risk is smaller for the larger project. Clearly, in order to compare the riskiness of projects with widely differing magnitudes of investments, payoffs, and expected values, a *relative* rather than an absolute measurement is necessary. **Relative standard deviation** (more commonly called the **coefficient of variation**) is such a measurement.

The coefficient of variation is the ratio of the standard deviation to the expected value, or mean. When calculated as a percentage, it provides an index of the risk per dollar of return, and thus makes possible a comparison of the relative risk of strategies or projects of widely differing magnitude. The formula is

$$C = \frac{\sigma}{\mu}(100) \qquad (7)$$

where

σ = standard deviation and

μ = the expected value (mean value).

In continuing the example outlined in Exhibits 4–3 and 4–4, the calculations for the coefficient of variation for each strategy are as follows:

For S_1: $\quad C_1 = \left(\frac{5}{15}\right)(100) = 33$

For S_2: $\quad C_2 = \left(\frac{15}{15}\right)(100) = 100$

For S_3: $\quad C_3 = \left(\frac{0}{10}\right)(100) = 0.$

In this case, using the coefficient of variation leads to the same conclusion that was reached when the standard deviation was used to measure risk. But this may not happen when the expected values are different. For example, suppose we are contemplating two projects and there are three possible states of nature: N_1, N_2, and N_3, with probabilities of 0.20, 0.70, and 0.10, respectively. Two projects, S_4 and S_5, offer the payoffs shown by Exhibit 4–7, which also shows the expected value, $E(S_i)$, standard deviation, σ_{Si}, and coefficient of variation, C, for each project.

In Exhibit 4–7, we see that S_5 clearly is a much larger project than S_4, with a larger expected value for which there is a larger standard deviation. The larger standard deviation indicates a greater *absolute* risk. But the *relative* risk (that is, the *risk per dollar of expected value*, as measured by the coefficient of variation) is roughly half as much for S_5 as it is for S_4. Since the expected value of S_5 is also greater than that for S_4, we can conclude that S_5 is a more desirable project.

Risk–Return Trade-Offs

What strategy a decision maker chooses depends on one's attitude toward risk in relation to the payoff, as well as on other considerations, such as one's general financial position. To illustrate, Exhibit 4–8 shows the expected return and relative risk for S_1, S_2, and S_3, the three strategies or projects presented earlier in Exhibit 4–3.

The horizontal axis of Exhibit 4–8 represents absolute risk (which is measured by the standard deviation, σ) and the relative risk (which is measured by the coefficient of variation, C). The vertical axis represents the expected mean payoff of a strategy or project, in dollars. The intersections of return and risk for the three strategies are plotted as the points S_1, S_2, and S_3.

EXHIBIT 4–7   Analysis of Risk for Two Projects

Project	N_1 (P = .20)	N_2 (P = .70)	N_3 (P = .10)	$E(S_i)$	σ_{Si}	C_{Si}
S_4	20	10	5	11.5	4.5	39
S_5	150	100	75	107.5	22.5	21

EXHIBIT 4–8   A Risk–Return Diagram

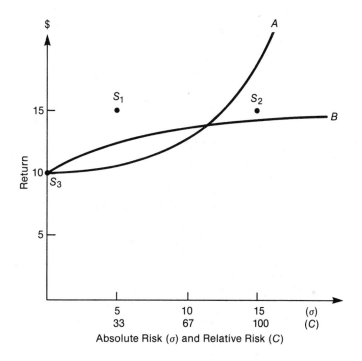

Absolute Risk (σ) and Relative Risk (C)

Curves A and B represent **risk–return functions** of Decision Maker A and Decision Maker B, respectively. These curves are plots of required return as a function of risk and are also called **market-indifference curves**. Curve A reflects risk aversion because as risk increases, the required return increases at an increasing rate. Curve B reflects the attitude of a risk seeker. As risk increases, the required return also increases, but at a decreasing rate.

The desirability of an expected return is measured by its vertical distance and direction from the decision maker's risk–return trade-off curve. Decision Maker A would not consider S_2 because it is below her curve. She would choose S_1 over S_3, even though S_3 is risk-free, because the expected return of S_1 is greater than the return she requires after due consideration of risk. Decision Maker B would consider all three strategies to be acceptable, but would also choose S_1 because it promises the greatest return in excess of requirements.

Utility, Risk Aversion, and Risk Premiums

Across the vast sea of human personalities, there are undoubtedly some who seek risk and some who are indifferent to it. But both common sense and empirical observation reveal that most investors and business managers are risk avoiders. Why? A number of theories attempt to explain this fact about human behavior, but the most satisfactory explanation lies in utility theory.

Utility and Decision Making.   Suppose two engineering firms are invited to submit design specifications for a large construction project. Company *A*, with assets of $50 million, is considerably larger than Company *B*, whose assets amount to only $10 million. However, the cost of preparing the bid, $1 million, is the same for both companies, and it cannot be recovered by the firm whose design is not accepted. On the other hand, the company that wins the competition can expect a profit of $25 million on the subsequent work.

The management of each company feels that it has an even chance of winning the competition.[3] The alternatives are: (1) compete and (2) do not compete. If both companies compete, the expected value for each is (in millions of dollars):

$$E(\text{profit}) = 0.5(-1) + 0.5(25) = 12.$$

Despite the fact that the expected value of competing is $12 million, the smaller firm may elect not to compete. Why?

The reason is that $12 million is only the theoretical average return from many trials. In reality, however, there is only one trial in which the company will either win $25 million or lose $1 million. If such a loss would put the firm into bankruptcy, the firm would not risk its survival no matter how great the potential reward. On the other hand, if the company is in a position to absorb a million-dollar loss, it might be inclined to assume the risk.

The conclusion to be drawn is that a transformation of dollar payoffs into some other reward structure may be necessary before a proper analysis can be made. If dollar values do not adequately reflect the decision maker's feelings or attitude toward gain or loss, the dollar values must be converted into a more meaningful measurement.

Utility is such a measurement, and it can be expressed in conceptual units called "**utils**." Unfortunately, no one has been able to establish a standard util by which one can perform a cardinal measurement of utility. Nevertheless, the concept is useful. Decision makers intuitively use this concept when arranging alternatives in order of preference; that is, the highest level of utility is first preference, the next highest is the next preference, and so forth. Thus, a quite practical ordinal measurement of utility is based upon the concept of cardinal measurement even if a cardinal measurement is not actually possible.

Risk and Diminishing Marginal Utility.   At this point, it is necessary to explain the relationship between risk and utility in a formal manner. To do so, profit and loss must be

---

[3] If the two firms have entered similar competitions in the past, management's belief might be based on experience, in which case it is applying objective probabilities under conditions of risk. But if it has no empirical data on which to base an opinion, the probabilities applied are subjective estimates formed under conditions of uncertainty (here, according to the Bayesian postulate of equal probability).

EXHIBIT 4–9 **Utility of Income**

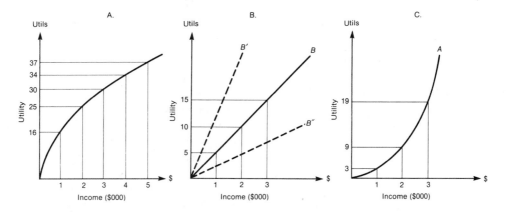

measured in terms of marginal utility rather than absolute dollar values. Marginal utility is defined as the change in total utility that takes place when one more unit of money is gained or lost. In the preceding example, if the company cannot afford to take a $1 million loss, it places a higher marginal utility on the dollars lost than on the dollars gained.

The three ways in which utility may theoretically relate to income are depicted in Exhibit 4–9. The three panels in the exhibit depict behavior of different types of investors when investment yield or income is increased by equal increments. The horizontal axes represent income measured in dollars. The vertical axes represent utility of dollars gained, measured in utils. Each curve represents utility as a function of income. The slope of each curve represents marginal utility, which is where our interest lies.

The most common investor, whose risk–return behavior is depicted in Panel A, is a risk avoider. The reason for risk aversion is **diminishing marginal utility.** Panel A shows that with no investment there is, of course, no return. Upon receipt of the first $1,000, total utility increases by 16 utils as the investor satisfies immediate needs. The second $1,000, while no doubt welcome, is not needed as badly as the first $1,000. Consequently, total utility rises by only 9 utils. That is, marginal utility for the second $1,000 is 9 utils, as compared to 16 for the first $1,000. When the third $1,000 is received, total utility rises to 30 utils, but marginal utility falls to 5 utils. Clearly, marginal utility diminishes as the return or income increases. This is a basic explanation of risk and has a decisive effect upon the investor's behavior.

For example, suppose that the investor has a choice between a risk-free investment in government bonds that will yield $30,000 and an investment in the stock of a new electronics firm that will yield $40,000 if all goes well, but only $10,000 if it does not go as well as expected. Suppose also that a thorough investigation convinces the investor that there is a probability of 0.75 that the new product will do well. The expected dollar values of the two projects are as follows:

$$E(\text{government bond}) = (1.0)(\$30,000) = \$30,000$$
$$E(\text{new venture}) = 0.75(\$40,000) + 0.25(\$10,000) = \$32,500.$$

The expected utility values of the two projects are (from panel A, Exhibit 4–9), in utils:

$$E(\text{government bond}) = (1.0)(30) = 30$$
$$E(\text{new venture}) = (.75)(34) + (.25)(16) = 29.5.$$

Thus we see that the expected monetary yield is greater for the new venture in the electronics firm, but the expected utility is greater for the risk-free government bond. The risk-averse investor will therefore prefer to buy the government bond.

The straight lines of panel B have constant slopes, characterizing a person indifferent to risk, for whom the marginal utility of a dollar lost is equal to that of a dollar gained. Indifference to risk, however, is not the same as indifference to profit. The individual represented in B' places a higher utility value on a dollar gained or lost than does B, and B gets more utility out of a dollar than does B''.

In panel C, marginal utility grows larger as income rises. This reflects the case of the compulsive gambler, who places higher utility on dollars won than dollars lost. The rising curve thus describes risk seekers' behavior—the more they win, the more important winning becomes.

It is conceivable that human behavior may follow any of the curves on Exhibit 4–9, or even some entirely different curve. There may be a few compulsive gamblers (panel-C types) who actually succeed in business. There may also be some managers who are indifferent to risk (panel-B types), perhaps because they are unaware of risk or do not understand its significance. If such managers exist, they certainly are in a minority. Most managers are panel-A types, keenly aware of business risk. They get more pain from losing a dollar than pleasure from gaining one. Hence, the utility function of most business managers exhibits diminishing marginal utility. Indeed, so prevalent is this behavior that the assumption of diminishing marginal utility is one of the two great cornerstones of economic theory.[4]

Risk Premiums.   Aversion to risk by managers and investors is manifested in many ways. Grade AA bonds sell for a higher price than grade B bonds. Investors diversify either by creating individual portfolios or by investing in mutual funds. People deposit their money in federally insured savings accounts at low rates of interest rather than in bonds that may earn substantially more interest. And people buy all kinds of casualty and life insurance.

Why, then, if investors are averse to risk, do they put their money into common stocks, commodities, precious metals, collectibles, and other risky investments? The answer is that they do not do so unless they receive a *risk premium*. The investor wants to be compensated not only for the use of his or her money, but also for the risk that it may be lost. In other words, the investor demands a higher rate of return when risk is involved.

To illustrate the concept of risk premium, suppose a woman has a utility function like the one in Exhibit 4–10 and is asked to bet $1,000 on the flip of a coin at even odds; that is, the probability of winning is 0.5 and the probability of losing is also 0.5. Thus

---

[4] The other is the *law of diminishing marginal returns* that applies to the input factors of production, as described in Chapter 10.

EXHIBIT 4–10   Utility of a Bet with No Risk Premium

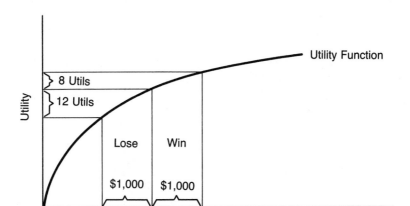

if she wins she gets $1,000 and if she loses she pays $1,000. Should she take the bet? To get the answer, let us look at Exhibit 4–10, which illustrates an investment without a risk premium.

If the investor wins $1,000, she gains 8 utils of utility; but if she loses, she sacrifices 12 utils. Since the probability of winning or losing is the same, the expected value in utils is $0.5(8) + 0.5(-12) = -2$. Since the expected value is negative, it is clear that the investor should not take this bet.

Now let us suppose that the same investor is offered a premium if she will take the bet. If she loses, she loses $1,000; but if she wins, she wins $1,800. Again the odds are 50-50. Should she take the bet? Let us look at Exhibit 4–11 (page 82).

Again the answer depends upon the investor's utility function. As the curve is drawn in Exhibit 4–11, a loss of $1,000 will bring a utility loss of 12 utils, while a win of $1,800 will provide a utility gain of 12 utils. The expected value of the bet then is $0.5(-12) + 0.5(+12) = 0$, meaning that the investor may be indifferent to the bet; that is, she may accept the bet, but probably will not. If the risk premium is increased, she will accept the bet; but if the risk premium is decreased, she definitely will not accept.

Now let us suppose that the same investor is offered another bet for $500, again on the flip of a coin. Will she also require an $800 premium on the $500 bet? This time we look at Exhibit 4–12 (page 82), which shows that the loss of $500 for this investor involves the loss of five utils. In order to win five utils, the investor requires a risk premium of $100. But this $100 is only one eighth of the $800 risk premium required for the $1,000 bet. That is to say that when the bet is doubled, the risk premium demanded is increased eight times. How can this be?

The answer, of course, lies in the shape of the investor's utility function or curve. The risk is measured by the dispersion of possible outcomes. Since the dispersion of ±$1,000 is twice as great as the dispersion of ±$500, it would seem that the risk should be twice as great. But we have seen in Exhibits 4–11 and 4–12 that when a risk premium is added to the winning side of the bet, the dispersion of the possible outcomes is changed, hence the risk is also changed.

EXHIBIT 4–11   **Utility of a Bet with a Risk Premium**

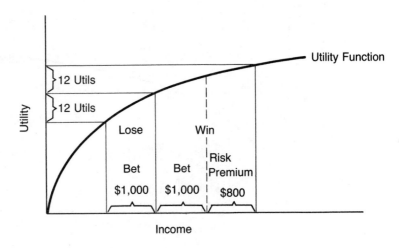

EXHIBIT 4–12   **Risk Premium for a Smaller Bet**

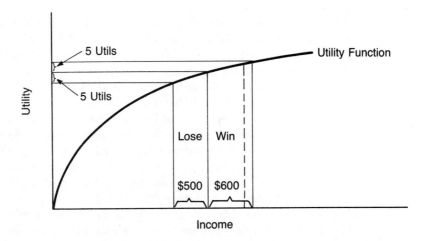

Two well-known scholars—Milton Friedman and Leonard J. Savage—were troubled with the traditional-marginal utility approach we have outlined because it does not explain why an individual might exhibit both risk-seeking and risk-avoiding behavior at the same time. For example, a person who gambles (risk-seeking behavior) will most likely drive to the casino in an insured car and live in an insured home (risk-avoiding behavior). Friedman and Savage attempted to explain such behavior by hypothesizing a utility function that rises initially but then decreases, as shown on Exhibit 4–13.[5]

---

[5] See Milton Friedman and Leonard J. Savage, "The Utility Analysis of Choices Involving Risk," *Journal of Political Economy*, August 1948, pp. 279–304.

EXHIBIT 4–13   The Friedman-Savage Utility Function

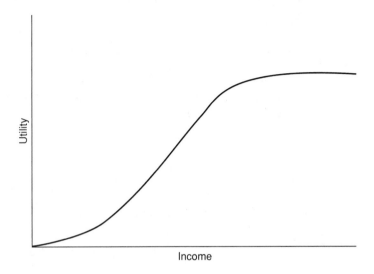

Investors' attitudes toward risk depend first of all upon the shape of their utility curves, which in turn depend upon the investors' personalities; and second upon each one's current position on the curve, which is determined by current income. If current income is low, marginal utility of income (measured by the slope of the curve) is high, and one will accept risk for a much lower premium than when income is higher. Or, as Friedman and Savage hypothesized, at low levels of income one might even seek risk.

Business Risk and Financial Risk.   For a firm, the risk premium may be viewed as having two components: a *business risk* and a *financial risk*. **Business risk** is associated with the investment decisions of a firm. It is defined as the relative dispersion of the net operating income of the firm and can be measured by the coefficient of variation, which was discussed earlier in this chapter.

Business risk is always present to some degree, since no business is guaranteed success. The degree of risk depends upon the nature of the business and the demonstrated skill of its management. Certain types of businesses are inherently more risky than others. Within any type of business, an investor would usually perceive more business risk in a newly established firm than in one with a longer record of earnings. On the other hand, a long-established firm whose products or business methods have become outdated may present a high degree of business risk.

Financial risk is separate and distinct from business risk. Whereas business risk is determined by the investment decisions of a firm, financial risk is determined by the firm's financing decisions. Financial risk has two broad aspects: (1) the risk of possible insolvency and (2) variability in the earnings available to the common stockholders.

Whenever a firm includes long-term debt in its capital structure, financial risk must be added to business risk to determine the total risk incurred by the firm. This is because earnings must go first to payment of debt service (payments to principal and interest).

The higher the debt, the higher the probability that cash earnings will be insufficient to service the debt. If the firm is unable to make the required payments, it may be forced into bankruptcy. To a lesser degree, financial risk is also incurred by the sale of preferred-stock, since preferred-stock dividends must be paid after debt service, but before equity investors can receive any return on their investments.

In any case, the more the firm must pay out of its earnings to debt service, the less will be available for distribution to the stockholders. If a probability distribution can be determined for the earnings available to the stockholders, financial risk can also be measured by the coefficient of variation.

Risk Adjustment

In estimating the payoffs for a particular strategy, the decision maker must consider both the present value of future returns and the degree of risk. Both considerations are incorporated in the following valuation model:

$$NPV_I = \sum_{t=1}^{n} \frac{R_t}{(1 + r)^t} - I_0 \tag{8}$$

where

NPV_I = the net present value of the cash flows related to an investment

R_t = the expected return (cash flow) in time period t for $t = 1, 2, \ldots, n$ after all expenses for the period have been paid

r = the required rate of return considering the level of business and financial risk involved

n = the number of time periods considered

I_0 = the amount of the initial investment, which is a cash outflow (negative number) at $t = 0$.

Several ways to adjust the valuation model for risk are discussed in the literature of finance. Two of the most commonly used methods are the *risk-adjusted discount rate* and the *certainty-equivalent approach*.

The Risk-Adjusted Discount Rate.   We may define the **risk-adjusted discount rate** as the required rate of return from a proposed investment after due consideration of the risk involved. As discussed earlier, every firm has a required rate of return reflecting its perception of its normal risk (normal business risk plus financial risk). If the level of risk of a proposed project or investment seems to be no greater than the firm's normal risk, then the value of r in Equation 8 will be firm's normal required rate of return. But if the proposal's assumed or expected risk is greater than the firm's normal risk, a higher value of r will be used in Equation 8 to compensate for the greater risk.

For example, suppose a firm's normal business and financial risk requires a 20 percent rate of return. The firm is considering an investment strategy that initially costs $100,000 and is expected to yield $50,000 cash inflow per year for the next three years.

At a discount rate of 20 percent, the net present value of the investment and its returns is

$$NPV_I = \frac{\$50,000}{(1.20)} + \frac{\$50,000}{(1.20)^2} + \frac{\$50,000}{(1.20)^3} - \$100,000 = \$5,324.$$

The net present value is positive; therefore the project is acceptable. It promises to yield a net present value of a 20 percent return on the investment, plus \$5,324. But suppose the risk were such that management feels it should get a 25 percent return. Then the net present value would be

$$NPV_I = \frac{\$50,000}{(1.25)} + \frac{\$50,000}{(1.25)^2} + \frac{\$50,000}{(1.25)^3} - \$100,000 = -\$2,400.$$

Now the net present value is negative. The proposal will fail to provide a 25 percent discounted return by a deficit of \$2,400, and should be rejected.

Thus we see that in the risk-adjusted discount-rate approach to evaluation of proposed investments, risk is wholly reflected by the discount rate and discounting process. There are, however, at least three limitations to this approach to incorporation of risk:

1. How do we determine the appropriate discount rate? Clearly, the introduction of a new product is riskier than buying government bonds—but how much riskier? It is very difficult to resolve this question consistently and objectively, particularly when there is no historical evidence on which to base an estimate.
2. This method does not consider the probability distribution of future cash flows—information that could be of great value.
3. The risk-adjusted discount rate does not offer any consistent method for evaluation of risk, an evaluation that may be quite subjective. This limitation may be overcome by the *certainty-equivalent approach*.

The Certainty-Equivalent Approach. The risk-adjusted discount-rate approach discussed in the preceding section accounts for risk by simply modifying the discount rate, r, in the denominator of the valuation model. In contrast, the **certainty-equivalent approach** accounts for risk in the numerator of the valuation model and uses a risk-free discount rate, i (such as the rate of return on government bonds) in the denominator to account for the time value of money. The degree of risk is reflected in the numerator by multiplying the expected risky return, R_t, by a certainty-equivalent coefficient, α, to obtain a risk-free equivalent sum, R_t^*. That is,

$$\alpha_t R_t = R_t^*, \tag{9}$$

hence

$$\alpha_t = \frac{R_t^*}{R_t}. \tag{10}$$

Equation 10 says that

$$\alpha_t = \frac{\text{Equivalent expected return without risk in the } t^{\text{th}} \text{ time period}}{\text{Expected return subject to risk in the } t^{\text{th}} \text{ time period}}.$$

This changes the valuation model to

$$NPV_I = \sum_{t=1}^{n} \frac{\alpha_t R_t}{(1+i)^t} - I_0 = \sum_{t=1}^{n} \frac{R_t^*}{(1+i)^t} - I_0 \tag{11}$$

where

NPV_I = the net present value of the cash flows related to an investment
α_t = the certainty-equivalent coefficient for the tth time period
R_t = the expected cash flow in time period t that is subject to risk
R_t^* = the risk-free equivalent cash flow in time period t
i = the risk-free rate of return or interest rate
n = the number of time periods considered
I_0 = the amount of the initial investment, which is a cash outflow (negative number) at $t = 0$.

The certainty-equivalent coefficient, α, is a number between 0 and 1 that reflects the decision maker's risk function. It varies inversely with the degree of risk; that is, the higher the risk, the smaller α will be. A value of 0 means the decision maker feels the project is too risky to offer any effective return. A value of 1 means that the decision maker sees the project as risk-free. Thus α and the related R_t^* serve as benchmarks for the decision maker's assessment of risk.

To illustrate, suppose a firm that is considering an investment of $100,000 that is expected to yield a cash inflow (at risk) of $50,000 per year for three years. Suppose also that management's perception of risk is such that it considers risk-free returns of $45,000 in the first year, $40,000 in the second year, and $35,000 in the third year to be equivalent to the risky return of $50,000 for each year. Then the certainty-equivalent coefficients would be

$$\alpha_1 = \frac{\$45,000}{\$50,000} = 0.90 \text{ or } 90\%$$

$$\alpha_2 = \frac{\$40,000}{\$50,000} = 0.80 \text{ or } 80\%$$

$$\alpha_3 = \frac{\$35,000}{\$50,000} = 0.70 \text{ or } 70\%.$$

Now suppose that the interest rate on Treasury bills is 12 percent. If we accept that rate of return as risk-free, the net present value of the investment is

$$NPV = \frac{0.9(\$50,000)}{1.12} + \frac{0.8(\$50,000)}{(1.12)^2} + \frac{0.7(\$50,000)}{(1.12)^3} - \$100,000 = -\$3,021.$$

The proposal would be rejected because the negative *NPV* indicates that the return from the investment would not be commensurate with the management's perception of the risk involved.

Certainty-Equivalent Approach versus Risk-Adjusted Discount Approach.   In both approaches, management determines the degree of risk in a proposed investment and then incorporates this risk into the valuation model. The risk-adjusted discount approach accounts for risk by adding a risk premium to the risk-free rate, i, to get the risky rate of return, r, which is then used to discount the periodic cash flows. The certainty-equivalent approach accounts for risk in the valuation of the certainty-equivalent coefficient, α, and uses the risk-free discount rate to calculate the time-value of money. If both approaches assume the same risky cash flow, R_t, in each time period and further assume a constant discount rate (which is the required rate of return, r, for the risk-adjusted discount approach and the risk-free rate of return, i, for the certainty-equivalent approach), then the two approaches should yield the same present value of the cash flow, R_t, for any particular time period, that is,

$$\frac{\alpha_t R_t}{(1 + i)^t} = \frac{R_t}{(1 + r)^t}. \tag{12}$$

Dividing both sides by R_t and multiplying both sides by $(1 + i)^t$, we get an equivalent αt of:

$$\alpha_t = \frac{(1 + i)^t}{(1 + r)^t}. \tag{13}$$

Illustrative Problem

Suppose a firm's required rate of return is 20 percent because of business and financial risk, while the rate on Treasury bills is 8 percent. The firm is considering an investment of $500,000 in a venture that promises to yield $150,000 per year for the next five years.

Questions:

a. Calculate the net present value of the proposed venture by the risk-adjusted discount method.
b. Calculate equivalent values of α_t that will cause the certainty-equivalent approach to yield the same result.
c. Prove that the α_t calculated in (b) will cause the certainty-equivalent approach to yield the same results as the risk-adjusted discount-rate method.

Solutions:

a. According to risk-adjusted discount-rate method,

$$NPV = \$150,000 \left[\frac{(1 - 1.20)^{-5}}{0.20} \right] - \$500,000 = -\$51,408.18.$$

b. Under the certainty-equivalent approach, the equivalent value for α would be

$$\text{Year 1}: \alpha = \frac{1.08}{1.20} = 0.900$$

$$\text{Year 2}: \alpha = \frac{(1.08)^2}{(1.20)^2} = 0.810$$

$$\text{Year 3}: \alpha = \frac{(1.08)^3}{(1.20)^3} = 0.729$$

$$\text{Year 4}: \alpha = \frac{(1.08)^4}{(1.20)^4} = 0.6561$$

$$\text{Year 5}: \alpha = \frac{(1.08)^5}{(1.20)^5} = 0.59049.$$

c. Using these equivalent values for α, we get

$$NPV = \frac{0.90(\$150,000)}{1.08} + \frac{0.81(\$150,000)}{(1.08)^2} + \frac{0.729(\$150,000)}{(1.08)^3}$$

$$+ \frac{0.6561(\$150,000)}{(1.08)^4} + \frac{0.59049(\$150,000)}{(1.08)^5} - \$500,000$$

$$= -\$51,408.18.$$

Clearly, as long as the two approaches remain equivalent, the equivalent α_t grows smaller as t increases. Thus the constant discount rate, r, implies decreasing equivalent α_t and increasing risk as we go farther into the future. It can also be shown that the equivalent α_t decreases and risk increases over time at a constant rate. In addition, it should also be clear from Equation 13 that the greater the difference between the risk-adjusted discount rate, r, and the risk-free rate, i, the greater will be the effect on the decrease in α and the increase in risk as time goes by.

If the perceived risk in every period of the periodic cash flow is such that the certainty-equivalent approach and the risk-adjusted discount approach yield the same discounted cash flow, there is no point in using the certainty-equaivalent approach, since the risk-adjusted discount approach will provide the same answer with less computation. If, however, there are any time periods in which perceived risk is more or less than what is represented by the risk-adjusted discount rate, then the certainty-equivalent approach can provide a better estimate of the net present value of a proposed investment.

For example, the return from an investment for the introduction of a new product might be more uncertain (riskier) in its earlier years, while the firm is struggling for product recognition and market share, than in later years when the product's market has become established. The certainty-equivalent approach can easily handle this situation during the process of establishing α_t for each separate time period. That is to say, the certainty-equivalent approach enables management to specify directly the degree of risk for each specific future time period and then discount the cash flow for that period by the time value of money as expressed by the risk-free interest rate. For this reason, the certainty-equivalent approach is considered to be superior to the risk-adjusted discount rate.

Illustrative Case: East-West Trading Company

The East-West Trading Company has an opportunity to establish a manufacturing operation in Hong Kong, with operations planned to start at the beginning of 1991. The initial investment would be $1.5 million, from which the expected return would be no less than $500,000 per year for at least 11 years. The company's cost of capital is 15 percent, which is 7 percent more that the current interest rate on Treasury bills. The business and financial risk for the new enterprise is comparable to the firm's current position. However, in assessing the risk involved, the firm's controller notes that Hong Kong, which is now a British crown colony, will be turned over to the Peoples' Republic of China in 1997. Although the Chinese have promised no change in Hong Kong's free-enterprise economic system for 50 years, there is considerable doubt that this will actually be the case, particularly after the events in Tiananmen Square on June 4, 1989.

In discussing the matter with the controller, the president remarked that it is quite possible that the Chinese would demand a share of the venture's returns after 1997.

"Suppose," he said, "the Chinese want more and more of our returns, like 50 percent in 1997 and 10 percent more each year after that until they take over the whole business. How would that affect our investment?"

"Out of the expected returns of $500,000 per year, that would leave for us $250,000 in 1997, $200,000 in 1998, $150,000 in 1999, $100,000 in 2000, $50,000 in 2001, and nothing after that," answered the controller. "If you could obtain those amounts, would you be satisfied?"

"I wouldn't like it," said the president, "but after we have recovered our investment, whatever we make is profit. I would like for you to determine (1) when our investment will be fully recovered, (2) the net present value of this venture from 1991 through the year 2001 if the Chinese do not interfere, and (3) the net present value of this venture through the year 2001 if the Chinese gradually take over the business as discussed today."

Later in the day, the controller sent the president the following memo:

In answer to your first question: Assuming that we achieve a minimum cash inflow of $500,000 per year, our investment will be fully recovered in no more than 4.3 years. My calculations follow:

Let n = the number of years and set the present value equation (in $million) equal to the initial investment of $1.5 million.

$$1.5 = 0.5 \left[\frac{1 - (1.15)^{-n}}{0.15} \right] = 0.5 \left[\frac{1 - \frac{1}{(1.15)^n}}{0.15} \right]$$

$$0.15(1.5) = 0.5 - \frac{0.5}{(1.15)^n} = \frac{0.5(1.15)^n - 0.5}{(1.15)^n}$$

$$0.225(1.15)^n = 0.5(1.15)^n - 0.5$$
$$0.275(1.15)^n = 0.5$$
$$(1.15)^n = 1.8181818\ldots$$
$$n(\log 1.15) = \log 1.8181818$$
$$(0.06069784)n = 0.259637306$$
$$n = 4.2775 \approx 4.3 \text{ years.}$$

In answer to your second question:

$$NPV = \$500,000 \left[\frac{1 - (1.15)^{-11}}{0.15} \right] - \$1,500,000 = \$1,116,856$$

In order to answer your third question, I have assumed that the Chinese will reduce our expected returns of $500,000 per year to the amounts discussed in your office today, that is, $250,000 in 1997, $200,000 in 1998, $150,000 in 1999, $100,000 in 2000, and $50,000 in 2001. If I treat these amounts as risk-free equivalents of the risky $500,000 and discount by the risk-free interest rate on government bonds, the net present value becomes

$$NPV = \$500,000 \left[\frac{1 - (1.15)^{-6}}{0.15} \right] + \frac{250,000}{(1.08)^7} + \frac{200,000}{(1.08)^8} + \frac{150,000}{(1.08)^9}$$

$$+ \frac{100,000}{(1.08)^{10}} + \frac{50,000}{(1.08)^{11}} - \$1,500,000 = \$788,969.$$

This seems to be an excellent opportunity, no matter what the Chinese decide to do in 1997.

EXHIBIT 4–14   **A Decision Tree Depicting the Consequences of Marketing a New Product**

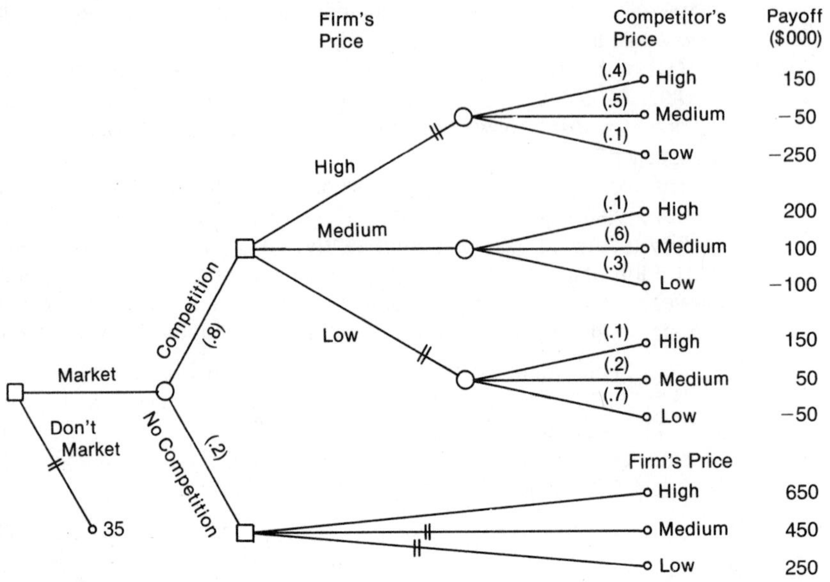

	Firm's Price		Competitor's Price	Payoff ($000)

Sequential Decision Analysis Using Decision Trees

A decision tree is a graphic device that shows a sequence of strategic decisions and the expected consequences under each possible set of circumstances. The construction and analysis of a decision tree is appropriate whenever a sequential series of conditional decisions must be made under conditions of risk. By conditional decision, we mean a decision that depends upon circumstances or options that will occur at a later time.

Construction of the decision tree begins with the first or earliest decision and proceeds forward in time through a series of subsequent events and decisions. At each decision or event the tree branches out to show each possible course of action, until finally all logical consequences and the resulting payoffs are depicted. Exhibit 4–14 is an example of a decision tree. The exhibit describes a problem faced by a firm that must decide whether to spend $350,000 to market a new product or to invest the money elsewhere for a 10 percent return. Taking the sequence of events from left to right, the first decision (symbolized by a square) is whether or not to market the product. If the product isn't marketed, the payoff will be $35,000 from the alternative investment.

If the firm markets the product, the next event (a noncontrollable situation, symbolized by a large circle) may be the entry of a competitor into the market. The probability of competition (0.8) and the probability of no competition (0.2) are entered in parentheses beside the appropriate branches.

It is important to note that in the construction of a decision tree, the branches out of squares represent strategies and the branches out of large circles represent states of nature. Since the decision maker has full control over which strategy is chosen, the

EXHIBIT 4–15 **Analysis of the Decision Tree Depicting the Consequences of Marketing a New Product**

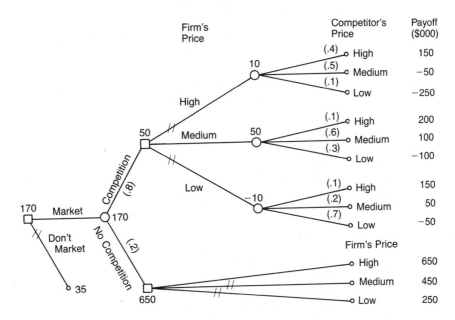

branches out of squares do not have probabilities. But the decision maker has no control over states of nature. Therefore, the branches out of large circles have probabilities and the probabilities for all branches coming from any one circle must add up to 1.0. In this example, the probabilities of competition (0.8) and no competition (0.2) add up to 1.0, since one or the other must happen.

If there is no competition, the only remaining decision is whether to charge a high, midrange, or low price. The three branches are drawn and labeled (high, medium, low) and the payoff for each is noted at the end of each branch. If there is competition, the same three branches are appropriate. However, each branch divides again to reflect the competitor's options to price high, midrange, or low. The competitor's options are states of nature, so they proceed out of a circle. Each of these final branches is marked with a probability, and the payoff is noted at the end of each one. Once again, the probabilities add up to 1.0 for each circle, since the competitor is certain to charge either a high, midrange, or low price.

The decision tree thus depicts in graphic form the expectation that the price a competitor charges depends upon the price the firm sets. At the same time, the firm's consequent profits depend upon what price the competitor charges. Since each decision depends upon the evaluation of events taking place at a later time, the analysis of a decision tree begins at the end of the sequence and works backward. Exhibit 4–15 depicts the analysis for our example.

Beginning in the upper right of the exhibit, the analyst calculates the expected value if the firm's price is high and there is competition. The expected value is $(150 \times 0.4) + (-50 \times 0.5) + (-250 \times 0.1) = 10$. This expected value is noted in or above the event circle. The expected values of midrange (medium) and low prices are computed and noted in a similar manner. Since the medium price gives the highest expected value, that value is noted in the decision box, and the other two branches are slashed to indicate they are nonoptimal.

In the alternative state of no competition, the only question is whether to charge a high, midrange, or low price. The payoffs indicate that a high price is optimal, and the other two branches are marked out.

At the first event point (introduction of a competitive product) the expected value is $(50 \times 0.8) + (650 \times 0.2) = 170$. The firm is now ready to make a decision. If it does not market, it gets $35,000. If it does market its product, there is an expected return of $170,000. Clearly, then, the firm should enter the market.

The diagram also gives a clear indication of the most profitable pricing strategy. The product should be initially marketed at a high price. If competition develops—and there is an 80 percent probability that it will—the price should then be lowered to a midrange price in order to maximize the expected return.

Risk Planning and the Cost of Risk

In its capacity as decision maker and planner, management's activities are essentially forward-looking. Plans are made in the present in expectation of the future. Since it is a characteristic of risk that the probabilities of outcomes can be estimated statistically, the expected gains or losses can be incorporated in advance into the firm's cost structure. This is true whether the risk is of an intrafirm or interfirm nature.

Intrafirm risk refers to possible losses that a firm chooses to absorb as costs rather than purchase insurance against such losses from sources outside the company. When the number of occurrences within the firm is large enough to be predicted with known error, management can establish the probability of loss and add it to other known costs.

For example, suppose that a factory's experience shows that 2 parts of every 100 will break during installation. Instead of seeking insurance against breakage, the factory will add the probable cost of the broken parts to the standard cost for those parts. In other words, where the mean expected loss for the company can be predicted for the coming period, the loss can be self-insured by treating it as a cost of doing business. No insurance from outside sources to cover the loss is necessary.

The probability of such losses may also become a part of the firm's planning by the establishment of loss or contingency reserves. Thus, small-loan companies expect a certain number of defaults, banks regularly write off bad loans, and it is common accounting practice to set up an allowance for uncollectible accounts for any business that has accounts receivable on its books.

Interfirm risk occurs when the number of observations or cases is not large enough within any one firm for management to feel that it can predict the loss with reasonable confidence. When many firms are considered, however, the number of observations becomes large enough to exhibit the necessary stability for prediction. Examples of such risks are fires, floods, storms, and other "acts of God." Since managers are unable to predict such losses for themselves, they shift the burden to insurance companies.

The insurance companies establish the probability of such losses based on a large number of cases. Probability of loss cannot be established for a particular firm, but the probability of loss covering many firms can be predicted with small error. The insurance company assumes the aggregate risk of all firms that it insures and spreads the cost of the aggregate expected loss by charging each firm a fee called a **premium**. The insurance premiums then become part of the insured firm's cost structure.

The insurance company will decide what premium to charge on the basis of the expected loss payouts plus administrative costs and profit. The risk-avoiding manager, however, can decide whether or not to buy the insurance on the basis of the expected value of the firm's operation and its utility function.

Illustrative Problem

Suppose that a firm has the utility function $TU = X - 0.0002X^2$, where $X =$ thousands of dollars, as shown by Exhibit 4–16 (page 94). Let us further suppose that this firm is engaged in a manufacturing operation that requires the use of flammable solvents and welding operations in the same building. Suppose also that an insurance company has determined that this is a type of high-risk operation in which a fire would result in total destruction of the building and the industry-wide probability of fire is 20 percent. The firm's building would cost $400,000 to replace if it should burn down. The firm can reasonably expect operating income of $500,000 per year. The insurance company requires premiums 25 percent above losses to cover administrative costs and profit.

Questions:

a. How much would the firm be willing to pay for a fire-insurance policy providing for replacement of the building if it should burn down?
b. What would be the premium for a fire-insurance policy covering losses up to $400,000?
c. Should the firm buy the insurance?

Solutions:

a. The firm's anticipated operating income of $500,000 has a utility value of $TU = 500 - 0.0002(500)^2 = 450$. If the firm has no insurance and a fire occurs, its operating income would be reduced to $500,000 - $400,000 = $100,000. The utility value of $100,000 is $TU = 100 - 0.0002(100)^2 = 98$.

Although the insurance company has established the probability of fire as 0.2 *for the industry*, the firm has no idea of what the probability of fire might be *for the firm*. Therefore the firm might assume equal probability for fire or no fire. The expected value of next year's operation (in thousands of dollars) thus is

$$E(X) = 0.5(\$100) + 0.5(\$500) = \$300$$

and its expected utility is

$$E(U) = 0.5(98) + 0.5(450) = 274.$$

Thus the expected utility for this *uncertain* prospect of $300,000 of operating income is 274. But a *certain* prospect of $291,000 would also generate a utility of 274, according to the firm's utility functions, $TU = 291 - .0002(291)^2 = 274$. Hence a risk-averse,

EXHIBIT 4–16 Risk-Avoiding Firm's Utility Function

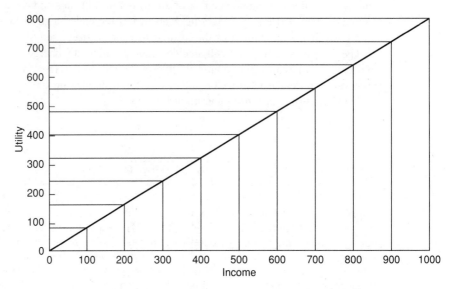

profit-maximizing manager might be willing to pay a premium up to $500,000 − $291,000 = $209,000 for fire insurance. Why? Because it would guarantee $291,000 operating income whether or not the building burns down.

b. The insurance premium is determined by the probability of loss, which is 0.2 for the industry. Therefore, $400,000 × 0.20 = $80,000. To this is added 25 percent for overhead and profit for a total premium of $80,000 × 1.25 = $100,000.

c. Buying an insurance policy for a premium of $100,000 guarantees an operating income of at least $400,000, whether or not the building burns down. This sum has a utility of 368. Clearly, the utility of 368 is to be preferred to the utility of 274.

In a different approach, the firm's management might use a decision matrix to consider four possible payoffs:

1. Fire loss fully covered by insurance, premium = $100,000
   Operating income = $500,000 − $100,000 = $400,000
   $TU = 400 − 0.0002(400)^2 = 368$
2. Fire loss, with no insurance, loss = $400,000
   Operating income = $500,000 − $400,000 = $100,000
   $TU = 100 − 0.0002(100)^2 = 98$
3. No fire loss, insured, premium = $100,000
   Operating income = $500,000 − $100,000 = $400,000
   $TU = 400 − 0.0002(400)^2 = 368$
4. No fire loss, no insurance
   Operating income = $500,000
   $TU = 500 − 0.0002(500)^2 = 450.$

The utility payoffs can be placed in a decision matrix, as follows:

	Fire (p = 0.5)	No fire (p = 0.5)	Expected Utility
Insure	368	368	368
Don't insure	98	450	274

The decision matrix confirms that the firm will be better off buying the insurance.

Decision Making under Uncertainty

Uncertainty is defined as the state of knowledge in which one or more alternatives result in a set of possible specific outcomes whose probabilities are unknown. This is usually because no reliable data are available from which objective probabilities can be derived a posteriori, nor is there any way of deducing probabilities a priori. This means that *decision making under uncertainty is always subjective*.

Degree of Uncertainty

Since expectations are subjective, there will be degrees of uncertainty on the part of decision makers. For example, two persons may view the same event, but each will establish personal expectations with greater or less confidence than the other. The procedure for making a decision may depend upon the degree of uncertainty perceived by the decision maker.

Two basic approaches to decision making under uncertainty are available:

1. The decision maker may use the best available information and his or her own personal judgment and experience to (1) identify and assign subjective probabilities to the possible states of nature and (2) estimate the resulting payoffs for each available strategy under each state of nature. This effectively makes the condition of uncertainty similar to a condition of risk, and the decision-making procedures previously discussed for conditions of risk are followed.

2. If the degree of uncertainty is so great that the decision maker prefers to make no assumptions about the probabilities of the various states of nature, the decision maker may either disregard probabilities or treat them as equal, which amounts to the same thing. When this approach is taken, four decision criteria are available for evaluation of proposed strategies:

   a. The *Wald* decision criterion, also called *maximin*
   b. The *Hurwicz alpha* decision criterion
   c. The *Savage* decision criterion, also called *minimax regret*
   d. The *Laplace* decision criterion, also called the *Bayes* decision criterion.

Perhaps the most difficult task for the decision maker is choosing the one criterion most appropriate to the problem at hand. The choice of a criterion should be both

---

EXHIBIT 4–17   **Application of Maximin and Maximax Criteria**

| | States of Nature | | | | Criterion | |
Strategy	N_1	N_2	N_3	N_4	Maximin	Maximax
S_1	6	6	6	4	4^a	6
S_2	25	7	7	−15	−15	25^a
S_3	20	20	7	−1	−1	20
S_4	19	16	9	−2	−2	19
S_5	20	15	15	−3	−3	20

a Best strategy under indicated criterion.

---

logical under the circumstances and also consistent with management's philosophy and temperament. Is the current management outlook optimistic or pessimistic? Conservative or adventurous?

The Wald Decision Criterion

The **Wald**, or **maximin**, **decision criterion** is the criterion of conservatism, and an attempt to maximize the security level. It envisions nature as perverse and malevolent and assumes that Murphy's law is fully operational.[6] Therefore, the criterion says, determine the worst possible outcome of each strategy and then pick the strategy yielding the best of the worst results.

The maximin criterion can be illustrated by applying it to the example first shown in Exhibit 4–1, for which we shall assume that the probabilities of the various states of nature are unknown. As shown in Exhibit 4–17, the most dismal payoff from each row is chosen as the minimal security level associated with the strategy. The largest of these, a value of +4, implies that strategy S_1 is the best strategy under this criterion.

Is this a good choice? It all depends upon what you mean by "good." Note that if state of nature N_4 should occur, S_1 is the only strategy that avoids a loss. On the other hand, should any other state of nature occur, strategy S_1 repeatedly results in the poorest return. Is such a situation inconsistent with reality? Perhaps, but perhaps not. S_1 simply represents the most conservative strategy—it involves the smallest risks but at the same time promises the smallest returns. It is up to the firm to decide just how a minimal level of return is to be weighted in the decision-making process and how much it can afford to risk if things turn for the worse. Because the criterion is fiscally conservative, it is particularly well suited to small business firms whose survival depends upon avoiding losses.

Added to Exhibit 4–17 is the antithesis of maximin, called the **maximax criterion**. Here the decision maker is completely optimistic and therefore chooses the maximum payoff for each strategy as a yardstick. The strategy that offers the best of the best is then chosen as optimal. This, of course, is nonsense. We have included it because maximax and maximin represent the extremes of alpha in the Hurwicz alpha decision criterion, which will be discussed next.

---

[6] Murphy's law is the wry jest that if anything *can* go wrong, it *will*.

EXHIBIT 4–18   Hurwicz Alpha Solution to Decision Problem

Strategy	M	α	αM	m	$(1 - \alpha)$	$(1 - \alpha)m$	d
S_1	6	0.7	4.2	4	0.3	1.2	5.4
S_2	25	0.7	17.5	−15	0.3	−4.5	13.0
S_3	20	0.7	14.0	−1	0.3	−0.3	13.7[a]
S_4	19	0.7	13.3	−2	0.3	−0.6	12.7
S_5	20	0.7	14.0	−3	0.3	−0.9	13.1

[a] Best strategy.

The Hurwicz Alpha Decision Criterion

The **Hurwicz alpha decision criterion** proposes to create a decision index, d, for each strategy, which is a weighted average of its extreme payoffs. The weighting factors are a **coefficient of optimism**, α, which is applied to the maximum payoff, M, and its complement, $1 - \alpha$, which is applied to the minimum payoff, m. The value of each strategy is thus

$$d_i = \alpha M_i + (1 - \alpha)m_i. \qquad (13)$$

The strategy with the highest value for d_i is chosen as optimal.

The coefficient of optimism ranges from 0 to 1, enabling the decision maker to express his attitude toward risk-taking as a subjective degree of optimism. If the decision maker is completely pessimistic, he may decide that $\alpha = 0$. The result is the same as the maximin criterion. If the decision maker is an incurable optimist, he may decide that $\alpha = 1$. The result would be the same as the maximax criterion.

Actually, the Hurwicz alpha criterion was advanced to enable the decision maker to look at both the worst and the best payoffs for a particular strategy and to assign a subjective probability to each. Suppose, for example, that the decision maker is on the optimistic side and decides that $\alpha = 0.7$. His analysis of the current decision problem would be as shown in Exhibit 4–18. It can be seen that the highest weighted-average payoff results from selecting strategy S_3.

The decision indicated by the Hurwicz alpha criterion depends on the value of α, which in turn depends on the decision maker's own attitude toward risk.[7] It is suitable for use by business firms; but if the decision maker's degree of optimism proves unfounded, substantial losses are likely. Therefore, due caution is advised.

---

[7] The decision will tend toward maximax as α increases and toward maximin as α decreases. You should verify this by finding the value at which the decision is changed in our example. Hint: One shift point occurs when $d_1 = d_3$. Perhaps another advantage of α is that it forces the decision maker to be consistent from one decision to another. If the decision maker believes one α value is appropriate for one decision while another value is used in a second decision, perhaps he knows more about the decision than was initially believed. If so, this information should be brought into the decision making.

EXHIBIT 4–19   Construction of a Regret Matrix

	Decision Matrix				Regret Matrix				Maximum Regret
Strategy	N_1	N_2	N_3	N_4	N_1	N_2	N_3	N_4	
S_1	6	6	6	4	19	14	9	0	19
S_2	25	7	7	-15	0	13	8	19	19
S_3	20	20	7	-1	5	0	8	5	8
S_4	19	16	9	-2	6	4	6	6	6^a
S_5	20	15	15	-3	5	5	0	7	7

^{a} Best strategy.

The Savage Decision Criterion

The **Savage decision criterion**, sometimes called the **minimax regret criterion**, examines "regrets," which are the opportunity costs of incorrect decisions. Regret is measured as the absolute difference between the payoff for a given strategy and the payoff for the most effective strategy within the same state of nature.

The rationale for measurement of regret is quite simple. If any particular state of nature occurs in the future and we have chosen the strategy that yields the maximum payoff for that state of nature, then we have no regret. But if we choose any other strategy, regret is the difference between what actually occurs and what we could have earned had we made the optimal decision.

A regret matrix is needed to calculate regrets, and it is constructed by modifying the payoff matrix. Within each column (state of nature) the largest payoff is subtracted from each payoff number in the column (including itself). The absolute difference between them (ignore the sign) is the measurement of regret. From our example in Exhibit 4–1, we construct the regret matrix in Exhibit 4–19.

This exhibit shows that when the state of nature turns out to be N_1 and the decision maker has chosen S_2, there is no regret, because the right strategy was chosen. However, if S_1 was chosen, the regret is measured as $|6 - 25| = 19$; if S_3 was chosen, the regret would be $|20 - 25| = 5$; and so forth.

After completing the regret matrix, the maximum regret for each strategy is noted. Then the strategy with the smallest maximum regret is chosen. From Exhibit 4–19, the correct strategy is seen to be S_4 because it minimizes the maximum penalty for an incorrect guess about the state of nature.

Note that the decision maker who uses the Savage criterion explicitly abandons attempts to maximize payoff in favor of a strategy to achieve a satisfactory payoff with less risk. The Savage criterion is therefore particularly useful for evaluating a series of projects over a long span of time.

The Laplace Decision Criterion

There is a Bayesian postulate that if the probabilities of occurrences are unknown, they should be assumed equal. The **Laplace decision criterion** uses this postulate to calculate the expected value of each strategy; hence the Laplace criterion is also called the "Bayes criterion." The strategy selected is the one with the greatest expected value resulting from the assumed equal probabilities.

For strategies S_1, S_2, S_3, S_4, and S_5 from our example, the expected values are 22/4, 24/4, 46/4, 42/4, and 47/4, respectively, and strategy S_5 would be selected.[8] The effect of assuming an equal probability for each of the states of nature is to make the decision problem under uncertainty like one under risk, so the previous discussion of the decision criterion under risk applies.

The Laplace criterion is a criterion of rationality, completely insensitive to the decision maker's attitude. It is extremely sensitive, however, to the decision maker's definition of the states of nature. For example, suppose the states of nature are hot, warm, and cool weather. In the absence of any weather forecast, the Bayesian probability of cool weather would be one third. But suppose the states of nature are warm and cool. Now the probability of cool weather has changed to one half. In reality, of course, equiprobability of all states of nature is unlikely, particularly in the short run. Thus the Laplace criterion is more suitable to long-run forecasts by larger firms.

To conclude, the process of decision making under uncertainty is essentially one of choosing a criterion and then performing the calculations necessary to establish a choice within that criterion. We have also seen that the four decision criteria discussed, when applied to the same decision matrix, can lead to four different strategy selections.

Which criterion is "best"? There is no universally correct answer. Each of the criteria is logically defensible under particular circumstances, and each can be criticized on one ground or another. The choice will often depend on personal considerations. In view of this, of what use is the notion of a payoff matrix? Perhaps the best answer is that it provides a useful tool for conceptualizing and formalizing the decision process. At this point it should be noted that there are other, nonquantitative methods of dealing with uncertainty.

Other Methods of Dealing with Uncertainty

It is rarely possible to insure against uncertainty or to incorporate uncertainty into a firm's cost structures and forecasts. There are a number of approaches, however, that knowledgeable business executives commonly use to reduce the perils of uncertainty. Among these are hedging, flexible investments, diversification of the firm's interests, acquisition of additional information, modification of goals, referral to authority for guidance, and control of the environment.

Hedging. Hedging is one of the most widespread methods by which business executives can replace future uncertainty with the security of a present contract. Hedging takes many forms, but it emerges most commonly in the writing of contracts for goods and services and in the trading of futures at commodity exchanges. Contracts for the supply of goods and services, especially in the construction industry, usually contain protective

---

[8] Note that the decision is based on the values of the numerators of the fractions, which are just the summations of each row of payoffs.

clauses for both the buyer and the contractor. Buyers are protected by clauses that spell out penalties against contractors for late delivery or nondelivery. Contractors are protected by escape clauses that excuse late delivery or nondelivery caused by conditions beyond their control, such as labor disputes, natural disaster, or civil disorder.

In the commodity exchange, futures market trading is predicated on a series of spot (current) prices and a series of future (forward) prices for various commodities. These markets perform two vital functions besides facilitating actual exchanges of commodities: (1) they provide an opportunity for both buyers and sellers to guarantee the future market price of the goods they are exchanging and (2) they provide an opportunity for speculators to enter the market.

Flexible Investments.   The wise manager knows change is inevitable and thus doesn't get locked into investments in specialized capital assets unless it is clear that the requirement for such specialized assets will exist over the life of the investment. For example, a general-purpose machine costs more than a specialized machine, but the general-purpose machine permits rapid changeover from one line of goods to another. Flexibility is particularly important for long-term investments such as land and buildings. While it may cost more to erect a general-purpose building than one tailored to the firm's current business, this flexibility will pay off if conditions change and the building must be sold or leased to another business.

Diversification of the Firm's Interests.   Diversification is closely related to flexibility. This approach is summed up by the old adage, "Don't put all your eggs in one basket." Diversification stresses stability and a long-run point of view. In the short run, maximum profit would result from concentration on the most profitable product. However, such a policy might well lead to a firm's demise if the market for that one product diminishes or disappears. Diversification of the product line may dampen fluctuations in the firm's profit function by stabilizing production and earnings. It helps insure survival of the firm and may even maximize profits in the long run. The manufacturer who produces a varied line of products, the investor who buys a diversified portfolio or stock in a mutual fund, and the conglomerate corporation all are examples of diversification to reduce uncertainty.

Acquisition of Additional Information.   Reliable, relevant information is the key to successful decision making. Obviously, the more information you gather about the future, the less uncertain the future will be. But after some point, the law of diminishing marginal utility takes over. The collection of information is a costly business, and the benefits to be derived from additional information must be weighed against the additional cost of obtaining it. Moreover, time is of the essence in most decisions. A hasty decision made before sufficient information is gathered can be very costly. On the other hand, a decision delayed too long in the pursuit of information may put the firm in the position of "too little, too late." Both the timing of the decision and the amount of information to be gathered are important concerns for the decision maker.

Modification of Goals.   In the face of complete uncertainty, an optimal decision might be impossible. However, if the decision maker is willing to settle for something less than the maximum, the problem is reduced to more manageable proportions. For example, break-even analysis[9] can be used to establish a sales goal that will provide a satisfactory return on investment. Although some uncertainty remains as to whether or not the goal can be met, the higher degree of uncertainty (with reference to maximization) becomes less relevant to the decision. Thus, pricing objectives are commonly established to achieve a target return on investment, to realize a target market share, or to meet competition.[10]

Referral to Authority for Guidance. Perhaps the most pragmatic approach to the reduction of uncertainty, and unquestionably a very common one, is to let an authority make the decision. In some cases, there is a literal authority (such as the Securities and Exchange Commission or the National Labor Relations Board) that dictates the choice of behavior whether the business executive wants it or not. But there are also figurative authorities, such as tradition, rule of thumb, convention, peer-group pressure, professional ethics, or simply what others are doing.

Control of the Environment. A more sophisticated approach to the reduction of uncertainty than referral to authority is the attempt to gain some control over the business environment. This approach usually takes the form of attempts to gain a monopoly by means of patents, copyrights, exclusive dealerships, or just being the first to "fill a hole" in the market. As with referral to authority, this approach works, if at all, only in the short run. Government casts a jaundiced eye on any reduction of competition, to say nothing of outright monopoly. In addition, if the market is profitable, competitors may be quick to enter despite patents or copyrights.

Illustrative Case

Tropical Products, Inc., with headquarters in Hawaii, is one of the world's largest producers of canned and fresh pineapple. In recent years, the company has also moved into the production of macadamia nuts, which are native to Australia, but do well in Hawaii. Up to now, Tropical Products has sold its macadamia nuts in the local market. The product, because of its high quality, has been very popular among tourists. This has led the company to believe that a national—perhaps international—market exists for its product. It has enlarged its plantations to support its envisioned market expansion, so additional production will soon be available for national marketing.

The firm's marketing division has proposed two alternative strategies for its national promotion of macadamia nuts, each of which will cost $3 million:

1. *Strategy 1 (S₁):* National television promotion consisting of sixteen 15-second prime-time spots on a nationwide network over a period of four weeks.
2. *Strategy 2 (S₂):* Distribution of samples to Hawaii-bound passengers on all flights of American, Continental, Delta, TWA, and United airlines for one year.

The marketing division proposes to price the product to yield a profit margin of 30 percent of the sales dollar, out of which the promotional expenses will be paid. At that price,

---

[9] Break-even analysis is discussed in Chapter 13.
[10] Pricing objectives and methods are discussed in Chapter 16.

EXHIBIT 4–20 **Estimated Sales in Millions of Dollars**

Strategy	Highly Successful ($p=0.30$)	Moderately Successful ($p=0.40$)	Not Successful ($p=0.30$)
S_1	80	45	15
S_2	45	35	30

EXHIBIT 4–21 **Assumed Utility Function**

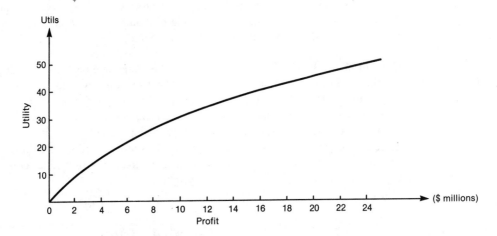

marketing has estimated revenues for each strategy under highly successful, moderately successful, and unsuccessful sales campaigns, using subjective probabilities as shown in Exhibit 4–20.

The company's financial vice president believes that the firm's utility function with respect to profit is as shown by Exhibit 4–21.

The financial vice president also notes that:

- The current yield on government bonds is 10 percent.
- The company's cost of capital is 15 percent.
- The riskinesses of S_1 and S_2 are such that risk premiums of 20 percent rate of return for S_1 and 8 percent rate of return for S_2 are required.

All of the foregoing information was turned over to a financial analyst, who was instructed to prepare a briefing, complete with charts, from which top management may be able to choose between the two proposed strategies: S_1 and S_2. Imagine that you are the analyst and proceed as follows:

1. Convert the matrix of expected sales into a matrix of expected net profit after deducting the cost of promotion, as shown in Exhibit 4–22.

EXHIBIT 4–22   Estimated Net Profit on Sales after Deducting Cost of Promotion, in Millions of Dollars

Strategy	N_1 $(p=0.3)$	N_2 $(p=0.4)$	N_3 $(p=0.3)$
S_1	$21.0[a]$	$15.0	$1.5
S_2	$10.5	$11.0	$6.0

[a] Example of calculation: $(0.3)80 - 3 = 21.0$.

EXHIBIT 4–23   Expected Net Profit (in $ Millions) and Relative Risk When Expected Values of Net Profit Are Discounted by Risk-Adjusted Discount Rates

Strategy	N_1 $(p=0.3)$	N_2 $(p=0.4)$	N_3 $(p=0.3)$	$E(S_i)$	σ_{S_i}	C_{S_i}
S_1	$15.556[a]$	$11.111	$1.111	$9.444	$5.758	61.0%
S_2	$8.537	$8.943	$4.878	$7.602	$3.208	42.2%

[a] Example of calculation: $\dfrac{21}{1 + 0.15 + 0.20} = 15.556$.

EXHIBIT 4–24   Utility Values of Estimated Risk-Adjusted Net Profit and Relative Risk of Two Strategies

Strategy	N_1 $(p=0.3)$	N_2 $(p=0.4)$	N_3 $(p=0.3)$	$E(S_i)$	σ_{S_i}	C_{S_i}
S_1	41.0	30.0	5.0	25.8	14.4	55.7%
S_2	29.0	30.0	19.0	26.4	4.9	18.4%

2. For each strategy, calculate the net profit discounted by the risk-adjusted discount rate. Then calculate the expected value, standard deviation, and coefficient of variation for each strategy. First, note that S_1 requires a risk premium of 20 percent in addition to the 15 percent cost of capital, for a total required return of 35 percent. For S_2, the risk premium is 8 percent in addition to the cost of capital, for a total required return of 23 percent. The risk-adjusted payoffs are as shown in Exhibit 4–23.

3. It seems clear that S_1 promises a greater return even after adjustment for risk, but it remains about one and a half times as risky as S_2. One task remains, and that is to evaluate the payoffs in terms of utility rather than dollars. Although it is very difficult to make a precise measurement from Exhibit 4–21, the approximate utility values are shown in Exhibit 4–24. This exhibit shows that S_1 and S_2 are very close in terms of expected utility of profits, but S_1 is approximately three times as risky.

Summary

This chapter has dealt with methods and approaches to decision making under conditions of risk and uncertainty. A useful model of the decision problem is a decision matrix in which rows represent strategies, columns represent states of nature, and the cells of the matrix contain the estimated payoffs from each strategy under each state of nature.

Under the condition of risk, the primary decision criterion for selecting the optimum strategy is *expected value*. The degree of risk is indicated by the *standard deviation*. Standard deviation by itself, however, cannot be used to compare risks. Such comparisons require the *relative standard deviation*, commonly called the *coefficient of variation*.

How decision makers choose to deal with risk depends upon their attitudes. Some may try to seek risk, some may be indifferent toward it, but most businesspeople try to avoid risk. Their attitudes are based upon utility functions in which increasing increments of income (profits) bring decreasing increments of satisfaction (utility).

A risk-averse decision maker will accept risk only if there is a commensurate risk premium. Every business firm and individual investor has in mind some required rate of return that reflects the perceived risk. As the degree of risk increases, the required rate of return also increases along a market-indifference curve that depicts the investor's risk-return trade-off function.

The profit-maximization model can be simultaneously adjusted for both risk and the true value of money by several techniques. Two of the most common are the *risk-adjusted discount rate* and the *certainty-equivalent approach*.

When a sequential series of conditional decisions are to be made under risk, a *decision tree* enables the decision maker to visualize and evaluate all possible options for action. Construction of the decision tree begins with the earliest decision and proceeds forward in time through a series of subsequent events and decisions. At each decision or event, the tree branches out to show each possible course of action, until finally all logical consequences and the resulting payoffs are depicted.

What decision makers under risk actually decide depends largely upon their attitudes toward risk. These may be expressed by *risk–return functions* or *market-indifference curves*. The net present value of the payoff must lie on or above a decision maker's market indifference curve for it to be acceptable.

Under conditions of uncertainty, if the decision maker is unable or unwilling to assign subjective probabilities to the possible states of nature, there still are four criteria that may be used for decision making:

1. The *Wald* or *maximin* criterion, by which the strategy that yields the best of the worst results is chosen.
2. The *Hurwicz alpha* criterion, which allows the decision maker to inject optimism or pessimism into the decision process.
3. The *Savage* or *minimax* regret criterion, which seeks to minimize the opportunity cost of an incorrect decision.
4. The *Laplace* or *Bayes* criterion, which gives equal probability to each state of nature.

There are also methods for dealing with uncertainty in a nonquantitative way. These include hedging, flexible investments, diversification, acquisition of additional information, modification of goals, referral to authority for guidance, and attempts to control the environment.

Whatever method of dealing with uncertainty decision makers may choose, they should strive for as much objectivity as possible. Poor decisions result when decision makers allow their emotions and personal prejudices to overrule good judgment and common sense. Good decision makers temper subjectivity with education, knowledge, experience, and stable temperaments.

Problems

1. In researching a new product, a marketing consultant comes up with four alternative brand names, five possible package designs, and three different advertising campaigns.

   a. How many strategies must management consider?

   b. What are the states of nature and how might they affect management's choice? Give examples.

   c. How can management take into account the reaction of competitors?

2. Explain how measures of dispersion such as the range, variance, and standard deviation can be used to indicate the degree of risk in decision making. What is the coefficient of variation used for?

3. Most businesspeople are considered to be risk averters or risk avoiders. Why is this so? What are the factors that influence the risk–return functions of decision makers?

4. Under what circumstances would expected value alone be insufficient to reach a decision? What other measures might be necessary?

5. Summarize a logical sequence of actions for making decisions under conditions of risk and under conditions of uncertainty.

6. Explain why the certainty-equivalent approach to risk adjustment is considered to be superior to the risk-adjusted discount approach.

7. Suppose that you have before you an urn containing nine red balls, eight white balls, and seven green balls. If you shake the urn in such a way that the balls are thoroughly mixed and then draw out one ball, what is the probability that it will be green? Is this an a priori or an a posteriori probability? Why?

8. Smith, who recently retired from running a successful business with a net worth of about $1 million, has just purchased a house in Greenville, South Carolina, for $120,000. Fire insurance on the property will cost $500 per year. Since Smith has substantial assets that could easily be converted to cash in an emergency, he is uncertain as to whether or not he should purchase the fire insurance, especially since a friend who is an actuary has informed him that the probability of a fire that would completely destroy his house is only 0.002.

   a. Should Smith purchase the fire insurance? If you were Smith, would you purchase the insurance?

   b. Suppose that Smith is a real-estate investor with 500 $120,000 homes located throughout the United States. Given the same probability of fire in each house, should each one be insured?

9. After receiving her MBA degree, Susan K. obtained an excellent position with an international accounting firm. During her first year of employment, Susan managed to save $6,000, which she tucked away in a money-market fund. At the present time, she is investigating two investment opportunities.

   For Project A, the probability of a return with net present value of $3,000 is 0.20, the probability of a return with net present value of $10,000 is 0.10, and the probability of a return with net present value of $7,000 is 0.70.

For Project B, the probability of return with net present value of $4,000 is 0.35, the probability of a return with net present value of $6,500 is 0.40, and the probability of a return with net present value of $8,000 is 0.25.

a. What is the expected present value for each investment?

b. Find the standard deviation and coefficient of variation for each investment. Which investment should be chosen?

c. Suppose that Susan's marginal utility of income can be expressed by the equation $MU = 25 - 3X$, where X is in thousands of dollars of present value? Which investment should she choose? Why?

10. Suppose a firm has an opportunity to invest in two different projects. Using the accompanying matrix, find the expected values of both investments and their standard deviations. By using the coefficient of variation, indicate which investment is riskier, and explain why.

	Probabilities		
Project	1/3	1/3	1/3
#1	80	60	20
#2	75	65	30

11. The Europe and Far East Parcel Service is planning to establish a door-to-door pickup and delivery service for small high-value packages between London and Hong Kong, with extensions to the Chinese cities of Guangchou, Shanghai, and Beijing. They will use commercial airlines for transportation and will guarantee two-day delivery. The firm is considering five different marketing strategies and has identified four possible conditions over which they have no control. Since it is a new venture, they are unable to determine objective probabilities for these four states of nature, but they can estimate revenues for each strategy under each state of nature, in units of £100,000, as shown on the accompanying payoff matrix. Before deciding upon which strategy to follow, the firm wants to find out which is the best strategy under each of the four criteria we have discussed: Laplace, Hurwicz (with $\alpha = 0.6$), Savage, and Wald. They have asked you to provide this information.

	States of Nature			
Strategy	N_1	N_2	N_3	N_4
A	11	15	9	6
B	13	4	14	7
C	10	10	10	10
D	9	11	15	13
E	8	3	7	5

12. The Grand Slalom Ski Company of Ogden, Utah, is contemplating three new lines of downhill racing skis. The cost schedule for the three designs is as follows:

Skis	Fixed Costs	Variable Cost per Pair
A	$50,000	$75
B	75,000	60
C	90,000	30

Three probable sales levels are estimated to be 2,000 pairs, 4,000 pairs, and 6,000 pairs, with probabilities of 0.30, 0.45, and 0.25, respectively. The selling price will be $400 per pair.

a. Construct an appropriate payoff matrix. Which design should be chosen?

b. Now suppose that the firm has no knowledge of probabilities of the three sales levels.
   (1) Which line would be chosen under the Bayes criterion?
   (2) Construct a regret matrix and determine which line would be chosen under the Savage criterion.

13. You are the traffic manager of a firm that makes computer-controlled robots for manufacturing operations. Late one afternoon, the director of customer services informs you that the failure of a certain component has caused a good customer to shut down his assembly line. An emergency shipment of a replacement is required, and the customer has offered a bonus of $15,000 if the shipment reaches his plant by 6 A.M. tomorrow.

After considering ground-transportation times at both ends of the route, you conclude that there is no chance of making the 6 A.M. delivery using scheduled flights. A local air-freight line has two types of small cargo planes available for charter:

jet and turboprop. The cost of chartering the jet is $10,000, while chartering the turboprop aircraft will cost $7,000. Because of the difference in flying time, you estimate the probability of making the delivery on time is 0.8 for the jet and 0.3 for the turboprop.

a. Construct a decision tree that includes all pertinent data relative to the decision to be made.

b. What is the expected return for shipment by jet? By turboprop?

c. Which alternative would you choose? Why?

14. The Trans-Atlantic Corporation has recently completed production facilities for its new model of a fax machine. The company has already completed studies to choose the best strategy by which to promote its new product. After the field of possible marketing strategies was narrowed down, two alternatives remained. Management must now decide between those two alternatives

Strategy A calls for promoting the fax machine by media advertising aimed at potential end users of the product. Strategy B requires vigorous sales calls on distributors by Trans-Atlantic executives to persuade the distributors to push their product.

As a part of their analysis, the Trans-Atlantic planners have considered the likelihood of four possible sales volumes under Strategy A and three under Strategy B. These possibilities together with their estimated probabilities are shown in the accompanying table. The probabilities are subjective, representing management's best guesses about the future of this new product.

a. If Trans-Atlantic has a 40 percent profit margin on sales, what are the expected profits under each strategy?

Strategy A (Consumer Emphasis)	
Estimated Sales	Probability
$100,000	0.2
250,000	0.3
300,000	0.3
450,000	0.2

Strategy B (Distributor Emphasis)	
Estimated Sales	Probability
$200,000	0.3
250,000	0.3
300,000	0.4

b. Construct a bar graph of profits under each strategy. By visual inspection of the two graphs, which strategy appears to be riskier?

c. Calculate the standard deviation of profit distribution for each strategy. Which seems to have more risk?

d. Suppose the firm's utility function is as shown here. Which strategy would the marketing manager recommend to the top management of the company?

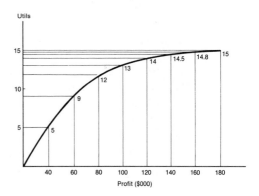

Case Problem: JB Foundry

15. The JB Foundry is a small foundry specializing in custom castings. The firm is having trouble with its old arc furnace, which has been completely depreciated for accounting purposes but can be sold for $6,000. An immediate decision must be made either to modify the old machine or to buy a current model, offering many desirable features that cannot be included in modification of the old machine. The decision is complicated by the general opinion in the industry that a breakthrough in furnace technology is coming within three years.

The best estimate the owners can get is that there is a 40 percent chance of a radically improved furnace in about three years. If the new furnace actually appears, the probability that it will make all current models noncompetitive is 0.9; the probability that it will amount to no more than a minor improvement is 0.1.

The cost of modifying the old furnace is $8,000, and the cost of a current model is

$25,000. In either case, the furnace will be used for eight years and then sold. The accompanying table gives the expected annual savings and the salvage value under three conditions (states of nature):

N_1: No technological breakthrough.

N_2: New furnace developed that makes all current furnaces obsolete.

N_3: New furnace developed, but provides only minor savings.

The table is based on a study period and life of eight years for both furnaces. The sharp decreases in savings and salvage value in states N_2 and N_3 occur because the development of a radically different or even an improved furnace would probably cut into the foundry's demand and its general competitive position.

	Buy New Furnace		Modify Old Furnace	
State	Annual Savings	Salvage Value	Annual Savings	Salvage Value
N_1	$6,000	$8,000	$2,000	$4,000
N_2	2,000	2,000	1,000	2,000
N_3	3,000	4,000	1,000	3,000

Another alternative exists for the foundry. If the new type of furnace is developed in three years, the modified old furnace could be sold at that time for $9,000 and the radical new furnace purchased for an estimated $45,000. There is 0.9 probability of state N_2, in which case the new furnace would save $13,000 annually and be worth $20,000 at the end of five years; and a 0.1 probability of state N_3, in which case the new furnace would save only $8,000 a year and would be worth only $15,000 after five years. If a new furnace is purchased now, however, it will be used for eight years, regardless of new developments.

Use a decision tree to determine whether the old furnace should be modified or a new, current model should be purchased. (Ignore the time value of money.)

Case Problem: Pan-Pacific Corporation

16. Pan-Pacific Corporation is a major producer of athletic equipment for schools, professional athletes, and the Olympic games. The corporation was quite successful from 1970 to 1985, reach-

ing a sales volume near $300 million with profits of about $15 million annually. In the latter part of the 1980s, however, the market was flooded with cheap imports, causing Pan-Pacific to suffer severe losses, first from falling sales, then from a profit squeeze as it cut prices to meet the competition. Losses over a three-year period amounted to $40 million, as the accompanying table shows.

	1987	1988	1989
Sales ($ millions)	250	270	300
Loss	(10)	(10)	(20)

In an effort to deal with the problem, Pan-Pacific has researched the possibilities of entering new market segments and of producing other products that would be more profitable. After evaluating the staff's research, the Board of Directors has decided that Pan-Pacific should follow a strategy of producing and marketing one of the following new products:

S_1: CB radios, selling for $100 each

S_2: Facsimile (fax) machines, selling for $800 each

S_3: Personal computers, selling for $1,000 each.

The firm's managers estimate that the needed initial investment in plant and equipment will be $10 million, whichever product they decide to produce. Sales volume will depend upon which of three states of the economy occurs: boom, stability, or recession. Fully allocated unit cost will vary with sales volume, as shown in Table 1.

The estimated annual cash flow is shown in Table 2.

If the net cash inflows in Table 2 are realized in each of the three years (1991, 1992, and 1993), the present value of the net cash inflows, discounted at 10 percent, would be those shown in Table 3.

Pan-Pacific's managers are uncertain about which state of the economy will prevail over the next three years. Therefore, they have constructed a payoff matrix using present values of the three-year cash inflows as payoffs. When the decision criteria for decision making under uncertainty are applied, the results are as shown in Tables 4, 5, and 6.

TABLE 1   Estimated Average Annual Unit Sales and Unit Costs, 1991–1993

	Product	State of Economy	Unit Sales	Unit Cost of Production
S_1:	CB radios	Boom	950,000	$84.56
		Stability	900,000	84.57
		Recession	860,000	84.75
S_2:	Fax machines	Boom	280,000	629.75
		Stability	240,000	646.30
		Recession	200,000	653.80
S_3:	Computers	Boom	120,000	720.40
		Stability	90,000	725.75
		Recession	75,000	767.80

TABLE 2   Estimated Annual Cash Flow, 1991–1993

	Product	State of Economy	Unit Sales (000)	Gross Revenue ($ millions)	Production Costs ($ millions)	Net Cash Inflow ($ millions)
S_1:	CB radios	Boom	950	95	80.332	14.668
		Stability	900	90	76.113	13.887
		Recession	860	86	72.885	13.115
S_2:	Fax machines	Boom	280	224	176.330	47.670
		Stability	240	192	155.112	36.888
		Recession	200	160	130.760	29.240
S_3:	Computers	Boom	120	120	86.448	33.552
		Stability	90	90	65.318	24.682
		Recession	75	75	51.585	17.415

TABLE 3   Present Value of Three-Year Cash Inflow Discounted at 10 Percent

	Product	State of Economy	Average Annual Net Cash Inflow ($ millions)	Present Value of Three-Year Net Inflow ($ millions)	Initial Outlay ($ millions)	Present Value of Three-Year Net Profit ($ millions)
S_1:	CB radios	Boom	14.668	36.447	10.0	26.447
		Stability	13.887	34.535	10.0	24.535
		Recession	13.115	32.615	10.0	22.615
S_2:	Fax machines	Boom	47.670	118.548	10.0	108.548
		Stability	36.888	91.735	10.0	81.735
		Recession	29.240	72.716	10.0	62.716
S_3:	Computers	Boom	33.552	83.439	10.0	73.439
		Stability	24.682	61.380	10.0	51.380
		Recession	17.415	43.309	10.0	33.309

TABLE 4   Application of Maximin and Hurwicz Alpha Criteria

		State of Economy			Criteria	
					Wald	Hurwicz
	Product	Boom	Stability	Recession	Maximin	$\alpha = 0.5$
S_1:	CB radios	26.447	24.535	22.615	22.615	24.531
S_2:	Fax machines	108.548	81.735	62.716	62.716[a]	85.632[a]
S_3:	Computers	73.439	51.380	33.309	33.309	53.374

[a] Best choice under stated criterion.

TABLE 5   Application of the Minimax Regret (Savage) Criterion

		State of Economy			Regret Matrix			Maximum
	Product	Boom	Stability	Recession	Boom	Stability	Recession	Regret
S_1:	CB radios	26.447	24.535	22.615	82.101	57.200	40.101	82.101
S_2:	Fax machines	108.548	81.735	62.716	0	0	0	0[a]
S_3:	Computers	73.439	51.380	33.309	35.109	30.355	29.407	35.109

[a] Best choice under stated criterion.

TABLE 6   Application of the Laplace Criterion

		State of Economy					
		Boom	Stability	Recession	Expected	Standard	Coefficient
	Product	$p = 1/3$	$p = 1/3$	$p = 1/3$	Value	Deviation	of Variation
S_1:	CB radios	26.447	24.535	22.615	24.532	1.564	6.38
S_2:	Fax machines	108.548	81.735	62.716	84.333[a]	18.800	22.29
S_3:	Computers	73.439	51.380	33.309	52.709	16.410	31.13

[a] Best choice under stated criterion.

TABLE 7   Annual Cash Flows Adjusted for Different Degrees of Risk

			Average Annual	Present Value of Three-Year	Initial	Present Value
		State of	Cash Inflow	Cash Inflow	Outlay	of Net Profit
	Product	Economy	($ millions)	($ millions)	($ millions)	($ millions)
S_1:	CB radios	Boom	14.668	35.230	10.0	25.230
		Stability	13.887	33.354	10.0	23.354
		Recession	13.115	31.500	10.0	21.500
S_2:	Fax machines	Boom	47.670	108.840	10.0	98.840
		Stability	36.888	84.224	10.0	74.224
		Recession	29.240	66.762	10.0	56.762
S_3:	Computers	Boom	33.552	70.677	10.0	60.677
		Stability	24.682	51.992	10.0	41.992
		Recession	17.415	36.684	10.0	26.684

The coefficients of variation in Table 6 show that the three proposals have different degrees of risk. Pan-Pacific's management believes, therefore, that the discount rate should be adjusted to reflect the different degrees of risk, as follows:

Product	Risk-Adjusted Discount Rate
CB radios	12%
Fax machines	15
Computers	20

This will change the present value of the net cash flows, as shown in Table 7.

Questions:

a. Which product should management choose? Why?

b. Evaluate the estimation of sales and profits. What are the assumptions in computing the present values of net profits?

c. How may you improve decision making involving various risk-analysis criteria?

d. Do you think Pan-Pacific should stop producing athletic equipment? Why?

References

Arrow, Kenneth J. "Risk Perception in Psychology and Economics." *Economic Inquiry*, xx (January 1982), pp. 1–8.

Barron, F. Hutton. "Payoff Matrices Pay Off at Hallmark." *Interfaces* 15 (July–August 1985), pp. 20–25.

Brunk, Gregory G. "A Test of the Friedman-Savage Gambling Model." *Quarterly Journal of Economics* (May 1981), pp. 341–48.

Cozzolino, John M. "A New Method for Risk Analysis." *Sloan Management Review* (Spring 1979), pp. 53–65.

Einhorn, Hillel J., and Robin M. Hogarth. "Decision Making: Going Forward in Reverse." *Harvard Business Review* 1 (January–February 1987), p. 66.

Friedman, D. "Why There Are No Risk Preferrers." *Journal of Political Economy* 89 (June 1981), p. 600.

Gay, Gerald D., and Steven Manaster. "Hedging against Commodity Price Inflation: Stocks and Bills as Substitutes for Futures Contracts." *Journal of Business* (July 1982), pp. 317–44.

Graham, Daniel. "Cost–Benefit Analysis Under Uncertainty." *American Economic Review* (September 1981), pp. 715–21.

Huber, G. P. *Managerial Decision Making*. Glenview, Ill.: Scott, Foresman, 1980.

Loomes, G., and R. Sugden. "Regret Theory: An Alternate Theory of Rational Choice under Uncertainty." *Economic Journal* 92 (December 1982), pp. 805–24.

Machina, Mark J. "Decision Making in the Presence of Risk." *Science* 236 (May 1, 1987), pp. 537–43.

Magee, J. F. "Decision Trees for Decision-Making." *Harvard Business Review* 42 (July-August 1964), pp. 126–36.

Peterson, Richard, and K. K. Seo. "Public Administration Planning in Developing Countries: A Bayesian Decision Theory Approach." *Policy Sciences* (September 1972), pp. 371–78.

Schlaifer, R. *Analysis of Decisions Under Uncertainty*. New York: McGraw-Hill, (reprinted 1978.)

Slovic, Paul. "Perception of Risk." *Science* 236 (April 17, 1987), pp. 280–85.

Szpiro, George G. "Measuring Risk Aversion: An Alternative Approach." *Review of Economics and Statistics* 68 (February 1986), pp. 156–59.

Wilson, Richard; and E. A. C. Crouch. "Risk Assessment and Comparison: An Introduction." *Science* 236 (April 17, 1987), pp. 267–70.

APPENDIX 4A   Summary of the Laws of Probability

Definition

The probability of any event is a positive real number between zero and one, inclusive. A probability of zero means that the event can never happen. (The event is impossible.) A probability of one means that the event is sure to happen. (It is 100 percent certain.)

Joint Probability (Logical AND)

If A and B are not independent (one can influence the other), then:

$$P(A \text{ AND } B) = P(B)\,P(A|B) = P(A)\,P(B|A). \tag{1}$$

If A and B are independent (one does *not* influence the other), then

$$P(A|B) = P(A) \text{ and } P(B|A) = P(B). \tag{2}$$

Therefore, by Equation 1,

$$P(A \text{ AND } B) = P(A)\,P(B). \tag{3}$$

Conditional Probability

If the probability of B is not zero, then the conditional probability of A given B is

$$P(A|B) = \frac{(P(A \text{ AND } B))}{P(B)}. \tag{4}$$

Logical OR

If the events A and B are mutually exclusive (if one happens, the other cannot happen), then

$$P(A \text{ OR } B) = P(A) + P(B). \tag{5}$$

If events A and B are not mutually exclusive (both can happen at the same time), then

$$P(A \text{ OR } B) = P(A) + P(B) - P(A \text{ AND } B). \tag{6}$$

Illustrative Example

Suppose a large corporation employs 10,000 people who can be classified by age group and sex as shown on Exhibit 4A–1.

The Totals row at the bottom of Exhibit 4A–1 shows that the firm's 10,000 employees are 70 percent male (Event B_1) and 30 percent female (Event B_2). The Totals column at the far right of the exhibit shows that 30 percent of all employees are under 34 (Event A_1), 60 percent are between 34 and 54, inclusive (Event A_2), and 10 percent are 55 or older (Event A_3).

Now suppose that we reach into the firm's personnel files and select one folder at random.

EXHIBIT 4A–1   Distribution of Employees by Age Group and Sex

Event⇒		B_1	B_2	
Event ⇓	Age	Male	Female	Totals
A_1	Under 34	2,100 (0.21)	900 (0.09)	3,000 (0.30)
A_2	34–54	4,200 (0.42)	1,800 (0.18)	6,000 (0.60)
A_3	55 or over	700 (0.07)	300 (0.03)	1,000 (0.10)
	Totals	7,000 (0.70)	3,000 (0.30)	10,000 (1.00)

Question: What is the probability that the employee will be either under 34, or 34–54, or 55 or older? What is the probability that the employee will be male or female?

Answer: Because of the way that the age groups are defined, an individual employee must belong to one of the three groups. Also, because there are only two sexes, an individual employee must be either male or female. In the language of probability, Events A_1, A_2, and A_3 are disjointed (mutually exclusive), and so are Events B_1 and B_2. Furthermore, the A events and the B events are independent. (One's sex does not affect one's age and vice versa.) Therefore,

$$P(A_1 \text{ OR } A_2 \text{ OR } A_3) = P(A_1) + P(A_2) + P(A_3) = 0.30 + 0.60 + 0.10 = 1.0$$
$$P(B_1 \text{ OR } B_2) = P(B_1) + P(B_2) = 0.70 + 0.30 = 1.0.$$

Question: What are the joint probabilities between age group and sex?

Answer: Joint probability—that is, $P(A \text{ AND } B)$—is formed by dividing the joint frequency by the total frequency. Since the two events are independent, the joint probability can also be calculated as

$$P(A \text{ AND } B) = P(A)P(B).$$
$$\text{Example}: P(\text{Male } 55+) = P(\text{Male})P(55+) = (.7)(.1) = .07.$$

Question: Suppose the personnel records for men and women are kept in separate files. If we select one record at random from the women's file, what is the probability that she will be between 34 and 54 years of age?

Answer: This is a question of conditional probability, with the condition being that the employee is female, that is, $P(A_2|B_2)$. Since the events are independent, the conditional probability is

$$P(A_2|B_2) = \frac{P(A_2 \text{ AND } B_2)}{P(B_2)} = \frac{P(A_2)P(B_2)}{P(B_2)} = P(A_2) = 0.60.$$

Now suppose that the firm may be divided into three major departments (production, administration, and sales) and that all of the employees are assigned to one of the three departments, as shown in Exhibit 4A–2.

Question: Does an employee's sex have anything to do with where the employee is assigned to work?

Answer: $P(A_1)P(B_1) = (0.70)(0.75) = 0.525$. From the table, however, we see that the joint probability is 0.60. Therefore, we conclude that the events are *not* independent, and one's sex does influence where one is assigned to work.

EXHIBIT 4A–2   Distribution of Employees by Sex and Department

Event ⇒		B₁	B₂	B₃	
Event ⇓	Sex	Production	Administration	Sales	Totals
A₁	Male	6,000 (0.60)	700 (0.07)	300 (0.03)	7,000 (0.70)
A₂	Female	1,500 (0.15)	1,300 (0.13)	200 (0.02)	3,000 (0.30)
	Totals	7,500 (0.75)	2,000 (0.20)	500 (0.05)	10,000 (1.00)

APPENDIX 4B   Probability Distribution of Cash Flows

In adjusting the profit-maximization model for risk, the risk-adjusted discount-rate approach and the certainty-equivalent approach view the income received at future times as given sums. In reality these sums are more apt to be expected values of probability distributions. Hence the net present value will be the present value of a series of expected values. The elements of the series may or may not be independent; that is to say, the outcome in time period t may or may not depend upon what the outcome was in time period $t - 1$. If the outcomes are independent, then the net present value is

$$NPV = \sum_{t=0}^{n} \frac{E_t}{(1 + i)^t} \qquad (1)$$

where E_t is the expected value of the outcome in time period t, and i is the risk-free interest rate.[1] The standard deviation of the probability distribution of possible net present values is

$$s = \sqrt{\sum_{t=0}^{n} \frac{s_t^2}{(1 + i)^t}}$$

where s_t^2 is the variance of the probability distribution of net cash flows in time period t, calculated as

$$s_t^2 = \sum_{t=1}^{n} (Ax_t - E_t)^2 Px_t$$

where Ax_t is the xth possible net cash flow in time period t, Px_t is the probability of its occurrence, and E_t is the expected value of the outcome in time period t. To illustrate

---

[1] Since we are using the dispersion of the probability distribution of possible net present values to measure risk, we must use the risk-free interest rate to avoid accounting twice for the same risk.

EXHIBIT 4B–1   **Probability Distribution of Possible Cash Flows**

Period 1		Period 2		Period 3	
Net Cash Flow ($000)	Proba-bility	Net Cash Flow ($000)	Proba-bility	Net Cash Flow ($000)	Proba-bility
10	0.05	10	0.10	10	0.20
20	0.15	20	0.20	20	0.20
30	0.40	30	0.30	30	0.20
40	0.25	40	0.25	40	0.20
50	0.15	50	0.15	50	0.20

this method, suppose that the risk-free interest rate is 12 percent, and we have possible cash flows for the next three years as shown in Exhibit 4B–1.[2]

For this example, the first step is to calculate the expected value and variance for each time period, as follows:

Period 1:

$$E_1(X) = 0.05(10) + 0.15(20) + 0.40(30) + 0.25(40) + 0.15(50) = 33$$
$$\sigma_1^2 = (10 - 33)^2(0.05) + (20 - 33)^2(0.15) + (30 - 33)^2(0.40)$$
$$+ (40 - 33)^2(0.25) + (50 - 33)^2(0.15) = 111.$$

Period 2:

$$E_2(X) = 0.10(10) + 0.20(20) + 0.30(30) + 0.25(40) + 0.15(50) = 31.5$$
$$\sigma_2^2 = (10 - 31.5)^2(0.10) + (20 - 31.5)^2(0.20) + (30 - 31.5)^2(0.30)$$
$$+ (40 - 31.5)^2(0.25) + (50 - 31.5)^2(0.15) = 142.75.$$

Period 3:

$$E_3(X) = 0.20(10) + 0.20(20) + 0.20(30) + 0.20(40) + 0.20(50) = 30$$
$$\sigma_3^2 = (10 - 30)^2(0.20) = (20 - 30)^2(0.20) + (30 - 30)^2(0.20)$$
$$+ (40 - 30)^2(0.20) + (50 - 30)^2(0.20) = 200.$$

The net present value and standard deviation for the three periods are:

$$NPV = \frac{33.0}{1.12} + \frac{31.5}{(1.12)^2} + \frac{30.0}{(1.12)^3} = 75.929$$

$$\sigma = \sqrt{\frac{111.0}{(1.12)^2} + \frac{142.75}{(1.12)^4} + \frac{200.0}{(1.12)^6}} = \sqrt{280.53} = 16.749.$$

Evaluation of the Probability Distribution

If the distribution of possible net present values is normal (which it usually will be), the normal distribution table in the Appendix at the back of this book (or in any statistics

---

[2] Note that more or less objective probabilities have been developed for Periods 1 and 2. For the third period, however, the decision maker apparently has resorted to Bayesian analysis under uncertainty, giving all payoffs the same probability.

text) can be used to determine the probability that the actual net present value is greater or less than any given amount.

For example, suppose we want to know the probability that the net present value of the cash flows of Exhibit 4B–1 will be less than zero. The first step is to determine the number of standard deviations between zero and the mean. This can be determined by computing the Z-value for $X = 0$ using the formula

$$Z = \frac{X - \mu}{\sigma}.$$

In our example,

$$Z = \frac{0 - 75.929}{16.749} = -4.53.$$

In a table of normal distribution areas,[3] we find that for a Z-value that large, the corresponding area is in excess of 0.49997. The area remaining to the left of Z therefore is too small to measure. For all practical purposes, therefore, there is no chance that our actual return will be less than zero.

Dependent Cash Flows

The relatively simple technique discussed in the preceding section assumes independent cash flows. In reality the cash flow realized in one period often depends on the cash flow realized in the preceding period. Under these circumstances, the calculation of the net present value of the possible cash flows is much more complicated. In some cases, it may require full-scale simulation on a computer. A full discussion of the equations and techniques used is beyond the scope of this book, but may be obtained from many finance texts.

---

[3] Table E of the Appendix at the end of this book.

C H A P T E R

5

DEMAND ANALYSIS
AND CONSUMER
BEHAVIOR

Demand analysis provides the basic information needed to guide some of the firm's most crucial activities. These include

1. Sales forecasting
2. Production planning
3. Cost analysis and financial planning
4. Pricing and the manipulation of other demand variables such as advertising and promotion
5. Resource and inventory management
6. Profit planning.

From a managerial viewpoint, the main objectives of demand analysis are the discovery and measurement of the variables that affect product sales. For a profit-seeking firm, therefore, the study of demand is an essential part of business planning. Moreover, the firm cannot be content with a purely descriptive investigation. It must understand the dynamics of the forces that affect demand, and it must determine whether and how these forces can be manipulated to improve profitability.

Since demand analysis is a prerequisite for successful business operations, a thorough discussion of demand analysis and measurement will be presented in this and the following three chapters:

Chapter 5: Demand Analysis and Consumer Behavior
Chapter 6: Demand Functions and Elasticities of Demand
Chapter 7: Demand Estimation: Elementary Techniques
Chapter 8: Demand Estimation: Multiple-Regression Analysis.

CHAPTER OUTLINE

The main thrust of this chapter is to provide a framework for analysis of demand for goods and services by individual consumers.[1] We begin with the ultimate determinant of all demand—the consumer—because all demand functions are related to the manner in which consumers are both *willing* and *able* to act. Therefore, it is necessary to understand consumer behavior in order to understand the forces that determine demand for any commodity. (We shall use the word **commodity** to designate any economic good or service.) In order to understand consumer behavior, we shall construct a model of *consumer equilibrium.*

This chapter is divided into two sections and an appendix:

1. **The Cardinal Approach to Consumer Equilibrium.** This section describes the construction of the consumer-equilibrium model using the cardinal approach, which requires cardinal measurement of utility.
2. **The Ordinal Approach to Consumer Equilibrium.** This section shows how the same model of consumer-equilibrium can be derived by the ordinal approach, which requires only that commodities be ranked in order of preference.
3. **Appendix 5A: The Mathematics of Consumer Equilibrium.** This appendix shows the mathematical derivation of the consumer-equilibrium equation under the cardinal approach.

The Cardinal Approach to Consumer Equilibrium

Why do you purchase goods or services? Obviously, your decision to buy is based upon two considerations: (1) the **utility** that you derive from the commodity and (2) your ability to pay for it.

The economist defines utility as the pleasure or satisfaction associated with having, using, or consuming goods or services (commodities). Utility has many sources or causes. It may have objective features (for example, any building is objectively useful as a shelter), but it is mostly subjective. This is because utility is a function of individual tastes, preferences, perceptions, personality, state of mind, and background. Furthermore, utility is not an absolute value. Rather, it varies from person to person. Also, even for a single individual, it varies from time to time and from place to place. At the time of the purchase decision, however, each consumer evaluates the utility of a commodity and bases the decision to buy or not to buy upon that perception.

Utility Function: Marginal Utility

Conceptually, utility can be measured in units called *utils.* The problem, however, is that nobody can define a util, so it is actually impossible to measure utility in this way.

---

[1] *Market* demand, which is the aggregate of all individual demands, is discussed in the next three chapters.

Nevertheless, it is analytically useful to pretend that we can, in order to establish the *law of diminishing marginal utility*. This law says that the consumer's marginal utility decreases as consumption increases. Marginal utility is defined as the change in total utility that results from a one-unit change in consumption, that is,

$$MU_X = \frac{\Delta TU_X}{\Delta Q_X} \tag{1}$$

where

MU_X = The marginal utility of commodity X
ΔTU_X = The change in total utility of commodity X
ΔQ_X = The change in the quantity of commodity X consumed per time period.

In actual practice, this rigorous definition of marginal utility is relaxed a bit to permit its application to continuous functions. For a continuous utility function, marginal utility is defined as the slope of the utility function's curve at some specific level of utility. It can be measured at any particular point on the curve by taking the first derivative of the function at that point, that is,

$$MU_X = \frac{dTU_X}{dQ_X}. \tag{2}$$

To illustrate, suppose we let $TU = 20Q_X - 2Q_X^2$. This is a quadratic function for which marginal utility is the linear function $MU_X = 20 - 4Q_X$. The values for TU and MU are plotted in Exhibit 5–1 (page 120), which shows the total utility function on the upper panel and the corresponding marginal-utility function on the lower panel.

Since marginal utility is measured as the slope of the total-utility curve, the saturation point at which total utility is maximum is easily determined as the point where marginal utility equals zero. This point corresponds to the consumption of five units of X per time period. If more than five units are consumed, disutility sets in as the marginal utility becomes negative and the total utility decreases.

An intuitive analysis of our own consumption patterns fits in well with the total-utility and marginal-utility functions depicted in Exhibit 5–1. For example, suppose Commodity X is a Danish sweet roll. If we are very hungry, we might get great satisfaction from eating one Danish— 18 utils worth, according to the utility function $TU_X = 20(1) - 2(1)^2 = 18$. If we were to eat more of the sweet rolls, the total satisfaction would increase up to the consumption of five, but the additional pleasure (marginal utility) from each additional consumption would continuously diminish. When the fifth roll is consumed, total satisfaction reaches a peak of 50 utils $[TU_X = 20(5) - 2(25) = 50]$. The marginal utility at this point is zero $[MU_X = 20 - 4(5) = 0]$, which tells us that there is no more satisfaction to be gained from eating more. Even partial consumption of a sixth roll would create negative marginal utility, meaning that total utility is decreasing instead of increasing. Disutility has set in; for example, a sixth roll might make us sick.

This steadily decreasing marginal utility is called the *law of diminishing marginal utility*. This law's usefulness is not vitiated by the current lack of a definition of a util or a cardinal scale for measuring it. It is an accepted principle because of its predictive and explanatory value. This assumption of diminishing marginal utility is one of the most important cornerstones of economic theory.

EXHIBIT 5–1   Total and Marginal-Utility Functions

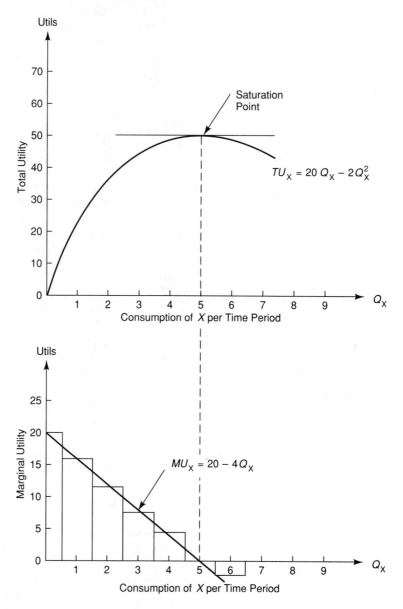

Consumer Equilibrium at Maximum Utility

The consumer's total income will be either spent or saved (held in money). The question is: How does a consumer decide what to buy?

Suppose a homemaker goes to the supermarket with $100 to spend on groceries. Will she spend it all on chicken, all on beef, or all on bread? Not very likely. She might spend some on meat, some on bread, some on milk, some on fresh vegetables, some on canned goods, and so on. In real life, of course, consumers spend their incomes on many different commodities, but *they always try to get the most for their money*.

Now let us try to create a model of consumer behavior that assumes this common-sense principle. In the analysis of consumer behavior, as with many other aspects of economics, it is helpful to think of maximum utility as a position of equilibrium. A consumer in equilibrium will balance the cost of consumption (the utility of money) against the utility to be gained from purchasable goods and services. In order to construct a model of such behavior, a few simplifying assumptions are necessary:

1. Consumers are free to spend their incomes as they please.
2. Consumers have perfect knowledge of all factors that may affect their decision, such as income, prices of other commodities, and the utility of each commodity.
3. The sales units of all commodities are divisible. This assumption is necessary to establish a *continuous* function such that total utility depends upon the quantity consumed per period of time.
4. The consumer's tastes and preferences are so well established that no difficulty exists in choosing between one bundle of commodities and another in a consistent manner.
5. The marginal utility of each commodity diminishes for the consumer as the quantity consumed increases.
6. *More* is better than *less*. (Useless or nuisance items are either disregarded or redefined.)
7. Finally, consumers always attempt to maximize utility while either spending or saving their entire incomes.

Each commodity purchased provides utility that diminishes as consumption increases, and each can be purchased at a particular price. The marginal utility of each commodity is associated with the last unit purchased or the last dollar spent. If we divide the marginal utility of that transaction by the price of the commodity, the resulting ratio, MU_X/P_X, is the marginal utility of commodity X per dollar. This ratio enables us to compare the relative satisfaction gained from purchasing many different commodities with widely differing prices, such as bread and automobiles.

Now suppose a consumer has a fixed amount of money, all of which will be spent to buy apples and oranges. If the last dollar spent on apples yields more marginal utility than the last dollar spent on oranges, the consumer will buy more apples and fewer oranges. But as more apples are consumed, their marginal utility diminishes. As fewer oranges are consumed, their marginal utility increases. Eventually, the marginal utility per dollar equalizes for apples and oranges. At this point the consumer can no longer increase total utility by buying more or less of either. The consumer is in equilibrium, because

$$\frac{MU_{\text{apples}}}{P_{\text{apples}}} = \frac{MU_{\text{oranges}}}{P_{\text{oranges}}}.$$

The same procedure can be used to establish equilibrium in the consumption of other commodities. Further, by treating money as a commodity whose price is always $1 per dollar saved or kept on hand, we can state a general rule for consumer equilibrium: *The consumer achieves maximum total utility at the point of equilibrium where the marginal utility per last dollar spent is equal for all commodities, including savings*, that is,

$$\frac{MU_A}{P_A} = \frac{MU_B}{P_B} = \cdots = \frac{MU_N}{P_N} = MU_M. \tag{3}$$

This equation is the utility model for maximizing consumer satisfaction, including the satisfaction of holding or saving money.[2]

How realistic is this model, considering that most consumers have never heard of it? Does it *explain* and *predict* real-world consumer behavior? Yes, if we keep in mind that utility is personal and variable, as previously mentioned. All the model really says is that most people most of the time try to get the most for their money. Failure to do so is usually due to lack of information.

Some observers contend that consumers are not rational economic persons, as assumed by the model. To support such views, they cite such attributes of consumer behavior as habit, loyalty, whim, impulse, inertia, and reluctance to change. However, it can be argued that these attributes are simply aspects of each consumer's unique individual utility function. Common sense tells us that if, *at the moment of decision*, consumers know how to get more for the money, they will do so.

There are many superficial events or conditions, of course, that might influence one particular consumer's decision about a particular purchase at a particular time. But underlying these superficial variations is a sustained and consistent pattern of consumer behavior in which the consumer attempts to obtain maximum utility from a limited income. The consumer does this by allocating income to expenditures on various commodities according to a personal perception of marginal utility per dollar. That is to say, the consumer achieves efficiency in purchasing various commodities by equalizing at the marginal level and maximizing at the total level of utility.

Effects of Advertising and Promotion

The model of consumer behavior depicted by Equation 3 shows that a consumer's purchases are regulated by the ratio of marginal utility to price. This ratio fluctuates when either marginal utility or price is changed. For example, suppose beef sales are rising at the expense of pork sales. The implication is that there is an imbalance in the equation such that

$$\frac{MU_{beef}}{P_{beef}} > \frac{MU_{pork}}{P_{pork}}$$

This inequality shows that the consumer receives more utility per dollar from beef than from pork. As a homemaker buys more beef and less pork, the marginal utility of beef will decline and the marginal utility of pork will rise until the ratios are equal.

In these circumstances, how can the producers of pork halt the decline of their sales? They have two options: (1) reduce the price of pork to equalize the ratios, or (2) change

---

[2] See Appendix 5A for the derivation of Equation 3.

EXHIBIT 5–2   Calculation of Price from Information on Marginal Utility of Commodity *X* and Marginal Utility of Money

Q_X	MU_X	MU_M	$P_X = \dfrac{MU_X}{MU_M}$
0	200	2	100
5	180	2	90
10	160	2	80
15	140	2	70
20	120	2	60
25	100	2	50
30	80	2	40
35	60	2	30
40	40	2	20
45	20	2	10
50	0	2	0

the marginal utility of pork. Since the utility of any commodity exists *only in the consumer's mind*, marginal utility may be changed by persuasive advertising and promotion. Promotion may include point-of-sale displays, distribution of recipes for pork dishes, or anything that will enhance the image of pork as a desirable food.

Marginal Utility and Demand Curves

A consumer's demand curve can be derived from marginal utility data. As we have seen, when the consumer is at equilibrium, the marginal utility per dollar for any particular commodity is equal to the marginal utility of money, that is,

$$\frac{MU_X}{P_X} = \frac{MU_M}{\$1} = MU_M \tag{4}$$

where

MU_M = the marginal utility of money
MU_X = the marginal utility of commodity X
P_X = the price per unit of commodity X.

Cross-multiplying,

$$P_X MU_M = MU_X. \tag{5}$$

Hence

$$P_X = \frac{MU_X}{MU_M}. \tag{6}$$

Let's assume that the marginal utility of money is constant, say $MU_M = 2$, and the marginal utility of commodity X is $MU_X = 200 - 4Q_X$. Using this information along with Equation 6, we can set up the schedule shown by Exhibit 5–2.

When the quantity, Q_X, and the price, P_X, are graphed, the result is the linear demand curve shown on Exhibit 5–3. The downward slope of the demand curve is the direct result of the law of diminishing marginal utility. As the quantity consumed increases by one

EXHIBIT 5–3   **Linear Demand Curve Derived from Information on Marginal Utility of Commodity X and Marginal Utility of Money**

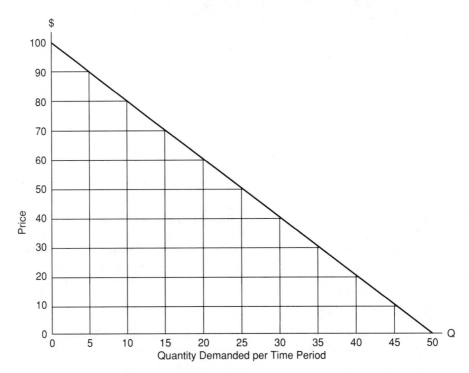

unit, the marginal utility is reduced, even though the total utility may be increased. The consumer is not willing to exchange the same amount of money for an additional unit that has less utility. Hence the price must fall if consumption is to rise.[3]

Marginal Utility and Consumer Surplus

The downward sloping demand curve in Exhibit 5–3 shows that at a price of $100, the consumer will not buy any of the product. The consumer is willing to pay $98 for the first product unit,[4] $96 for the second product unit, $94 for the third product unit, and so on, with the consumer willing to buy one more product unit for each $2 reduction in price. The consumer will take a maximum of 50 product units if the commodity is given

---

[3] In the case of the individual consumer, it does not necessarily follow that if the price is reduced, consumption will increase. For example, people who have just bought new automobiles are not likely to rush out and buy more just because the price has been reduced. In the total market, however, where market demand is the aggregate of all consumers' demand, a reduction in price will attract other buyers who have not just bought new cars.

[4] We intend to make a distinction in this discussion between a product unit, which is the producer's unit of output, and a sales unit, which may consist of one or more product units. For example, ballpoint pens are often sold in packages of 10 and priced by the package rather than by the pen.

EXHIBIT 5–4 **Price to Consumer of 30 Product Units Sold in Sales Units of Five Product Units Each**

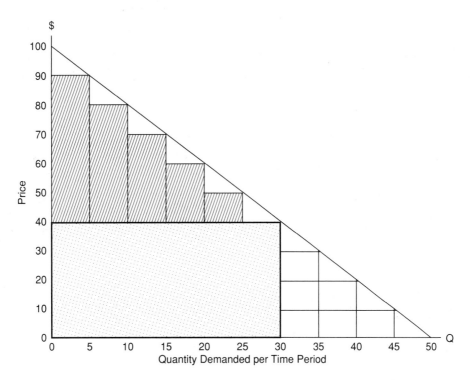

away free, because at that level of consumption marginal utility is zero and any further consumption would cause disutility to set in.

Although this may explain the theory of a demand curve, we know that products are not priced this way. Instead, a single price is set for all units demanded at that price, as shown by Exhibit 5–4. The exhibit shows that in order to sell $Q_i = 30$ units to this particular consumer, the price P_i is set at $40 per unit for all 30 units. Total revenue to the seller is $30 \times \$40 = \$1,200$, which is represented by the shaded area below the horizontal line $P = \$40$. But the diagram shows that this consumer is willing to pay $90 for each of the first five units, $80 for each of the second five, $70 for each of the third five, $60 for each of the fourth five, and $50 for each of the fifth five units. The difference between what the consumer is willing to pay and what is actually paid is called **consumer surplus**. It is represented by the cross-hatched area above the horizontal line $P = \$40$.

The exact amount of consumer surplus is the summation for all sales units of the difference between the sales-unit price the consumer is willing to pay and the price actually paid. The sales-unit price is the product-unit price multiplied by the number of product units in the sales unit. Since the price the consumer is willing to pay for the last sales unit is the same as the price charged, the last sales unit is omitted from the summation. The formula thus is

EXHIBIT 5–5   Consumer Surplus on Sales of 30 Product Units When One Sales Unit = One Product Unit

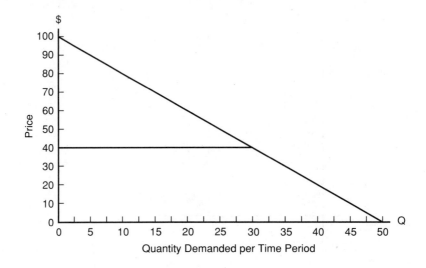

Quantity Demanded per Time Period

$$CS = \sum_{i=1}^{n-1}(P_{wi} - P_i)S_i \tag{7}$$

where

CS = consumer surplus
n = number of sales units purchased
P_{wi} = price consumer is willing to pay for the ith product unit
P_i = price actually paid for the ith product unit
S_i = number of product units in the ith sales unit.

In this case 30 product units are purchased, but the sales unit is a bundle of five units of the product, so $n = 6$. From Equation 7, the consumer surplus is:

$$
\begin{array}{ll}
(90 - 40)5 = & \$250 \\
(80 - 40)5 = & 200 \\
(70 - 40)5 = & 150 \\
(60 - 40)5 = & 100 \\
(50 - 40)5 = & \underline{50} \\
& \$750
\end{array}
$$

In this case, the limit of consumer surplus is the area bounded by the triangle above the horizontal line $P = \$40$ and in general by the triangle above any price line $P = P_i$. In theory, this limit can never be reached because it would require an infinite number of units on the X-axis between the origin and the X-intercept. As a practical matter, however, consumer surplus is approximately equal to the area of the triangle above the price line if a large number of units are sold. For example, suppose the 30 product units sold in the example in Exhibit 5–4 were sold in sales units of one product unit each instead of five. The result is shown in Exhibit 5–5.

Exhibits 5–4 and 5–5 represent the same quantity sold at the same price under the same demand function. In both exhibits, the area of the triangle above the price line $P = \$40$ represents the maximum consumer surplus possible and is measured as $[(30)(100-40)]/2 = \$900$. In Exhibit 5–4, the consumer surplus is held to $750 (83.3 percent of the maximum) because the sales unit consists of five product units. In Exhibit 5–5, the sales unit is one product unit and the consumer surplus of $870 is 96.7 percent of the maximum.

The question arises: Why doesn't the seller raise the price and thus recover the consumer surplus? The answer is: Because at a higher price, the quantity now being sold would not be sold. There is, however, a way of recovering some of the consumer surplus by volume-discount pricing, which is discussed in a later chapter. The point we are making here is that *as long as there is a single price for a commodity, that price will be established by the marginal utility of the last (or least valuable) unit sold.* Thus we may define consumer surplus as the extra utility that consumers get but do not pay for because they are required to pay only the price set by the marginal utility of the last unit purchased.

This principle explains why some commodities, such as gems and precious metals, are very expensive while other commodities, such as water, are low priced. In most places, water is so plentiful that the last gallon, which we are willing to pour upon the ground, is not worth much. Thus when water is abundant, it is a product whose marginal utility becomes very low even when its total utility is very high. An even more striking example is the air we breathe. Its total utility is the value of life itself. But the supply of air is so plentiful that the price of the last cubic foot that we breathe is zero. Therefore, we pay nothing for the first precious life-sustaining breath.

Illustrative Problem

After graduating from the university in the spring, Peter M. is hired by a local investment company as a financial analyst. The new job requires that he dress more formally than in his student days. In particular, he must now wear dress shirts instead of T-shirts. Suppose that Peter's utility function for dress shirts is

$$TU_X = 80Q_X - 2Q_X^2.$$

Questions:

a. If Peter buys five dress shirts, what is his total and marginal utility at that level of consumption?
b. How many dress shirts should Peter buy in order to maximize his total utility?
c. Assume that Peter's marginal utility of money is a constant two utils per dollar.
   (1) Construct Peter's demand schedule for dress shirts.
   (2) Find Peter's demand equation.
   (3) Plot Peter's demand curve.
d. Suppose Peter decides to buy eight dress shirts. According to his demand schedule, what price would he pay and how much would be his consumer surplus?

Solutions:

a.
$$TU_X = 80Q_X - 2Q_X^2$$

$$MU_X = \frac{dTU_X}{dQ_X} = 80 - 4Q_X.$$

When $Q_X = 5$, $TU_X = 80(5) - 2(5)^2 = 350$ utils.

$$MU_X = 80 - 4(5) = 60 \text{ utils.}$$

b. Total utility is maximum when marginal utility is zero:

$$MU_X = 80 - 4Q_X = 0$$

$$Q_X = 20.$$

c. (1) Peter's demand schedule is:

Q_X	MU_X	MU_M	$P_X = \dfrac{MU_X}{MU_M}$
0	80	2	40
1	76	2	38
2	72	2	36
3	68	2	34
4	64	2	32
5	60	2	30
6	56	2	28
7	52	2	26
8	48	2	24
9	44	2	22
10	40	2	20
11	36	2	18
12	32	2	16
13	28	2	14
14	24	2	12
15	20	2	10
16	16	2	8
17	12	2	6
18	8	2	4
19	4	2	2
20	0	2	0

(2) To find Peter's demand function, select any two (Q, P) points from the demand schedule and plug them into the standard formula for the equation of a straight line. Taking the end points (0,40) and (20,0), we get

$$Q_X = Q_{X_1} + \frac{Q_{X_2} - Q_{X_1}}{P_{X_2} - P_{X_1}} (P_X - P_{X_1})$$

$$= 0 + \frac{20 - 0}{0 - 40} (PX - 40) = -0.5P_X + 20; \text{ that is,}$$

$$Q_X = 20 - 0.5P_X \text{ and } P_X = 40 - 2Q_X.$$

(3) The plot of Peter's demand curve is:

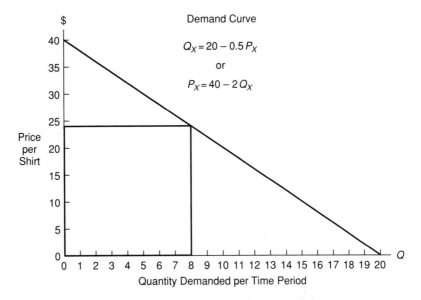

Demand Curve

$$Q_X = 20 - 0.5 P_X$$

or

$$P_X = 40 - 2 Q_X$$

d. When $Q_X = 8$, $P_X = 40 - 2Q_X = 40 - 16 = \$24$. According to his demand schedule, Peter would have been willing to pay $\$38 + \$36 + \$34 + \$32 + \$30 + \$28 + \$26 + \$24 = \$248$ for the first through the eighth shirt. However, the eight shirts actually cost him only $8 \times \$24 = \$192$. His consumer surplus is $\$248 - \$192 = \$56$.

As we have illustrated, consumers' efforts to get the most for their money are reflected in their individual demand functions. Market-demand curves are simply the aggregates of all individual consumer-demand curves. Since utility is based on individual taste and preferences, each market-demand curve reflects the aggregate market preferences of all consumers in that market. Therefore, a market-demand curve is a powerful signal to producers about what and how much to produce.

The Ordinal Approach to Consumer Equilibrium

Although the cardinal-utility approach is conceptually sound and offers useful insights into consumer behavior, it is difficult to connect consumer preferences, which are *subjective*, to changes in prices, incomes, and other variables in the marketplace, which are *objective*. Consequently, economists have developed an alternative model that we call the **ordinal approach**. The ordinal approach requires only that combinations of commodities be ranked in order of preference.

The ordinal approach to demand analysis uses the same basic assumptions as those used with the cardinal approach. In addition, it is assumed that consumers are able to rank all conceivable bundles of commodities; that is, when confronted with two or more bundles of goods and services, consumers can determine an order of preference among them.

Order of preference does not require consumers to estimate how much utility will be attained from a bundle of commodities. Only the ability to rank is fundamental. For example, when a homemaker goes to the supermarket, she doesn't count utils for each commodity. She simply chooses the preferred commodities that she thinks will give her the most satisfaction for her money. Furthermore, the degree of preference is irrelevant. It is quite enough for the consumer to think, subjectively and idiosyncratically, that one commodity or bundle of commodities is better than another.

In more precise terms, we assume that the consumer's preference pattern possesses the following characteristics:

1. Given three bundles of goods (*A*, *B*, and *C*), if an individual prefers *A* to *B* and *B* to *C*, he must prefer *A* to *C*. Similarly, if an individual is indifferent between *A* and *B* and between *B* and *C*, he must be indifferent between *A* and *C*. Finally, if he is indifferent between *A* and *B* and prefers *B* to *C*, he must prefer *A* to *C*. This assumption obviously can be carried over to four or more different bundles.
2. If an individual can rank any pair of bundles chosen at random from all conceivable bundles, he can rank all conceivable bundles.
3. If bundle *A* contains at least as many units of each commodity as bundle *B*, and more units of at least one commodity, *A* must be preferred to *B*.

Now that we understand our basic assumptions and the consumer's preference pattern, we are ready to consider the analytical tools used in the ordinal approach to derive the same consumer-equilibrium model that is obtained by the cardinal approach.

Indifference Curves

Consumers purchase and use varying quantities of many different commodities, a fact captured by the total utility function *TU*:

$$TU = f(X_1, X_2, \ldots, X_n) \tag{8}$$

where $(X_1, X_2, \ldots, X_n)$ represents the quantities consumed per period of time of a set of commodities. Fortunately for our analysis, we need to consider only two commodities at a time. Suppose *X* represents the quantities consumed per period of time of one commodity and *Y* the quantity consumed per period of time of another commodity or bundle of commodities. Then Equation 8 reduces to

$$TU = f(X, Y). \tag{9}$$

This equation describes the surface of a three-dimensional figure, an example of which is shown in Exhibit 5–6. The diagrams in the exhibit have two horizontal axes in the base plane (*XY*-plane). Along the *X*-axis is scaled consumption of Commodity *X* per period of time and along the *Y*-axis is scaled consumption of Commodity *Y* per period of time. Both *X* and *Y* are scaled in a positive direction only. Total utility is measured vertically. There is one utility value, $TU_{X,Y}$, for each combination of *X* and *Y*. Since an infinite number of combinations is possible, there is also an infinite number of utility values, each represented by a point in space. Taken together, these points form a smooth utility surface.

EXHIBIT 5–6 **Utility Surface—Total Utility Gained from Consumption of Various Combinations of Commodities *X* and *Y***

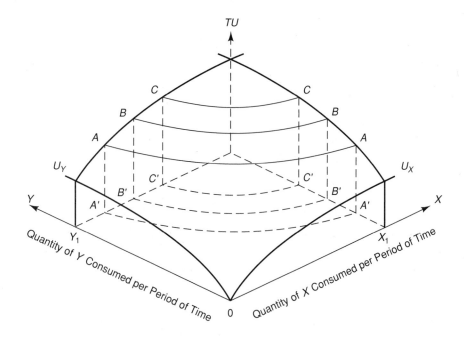

A utility surface may be viewed as a hill, with greater utility represented by greater height of the surface. Utility is increased as we move up the hill. This is done by increasing consumption of one or the other of the commodities, or of both at the same time.

If a plane is passed through the utility surface, it will leave a *trace* upon the surface. If the plane is passed 90° to the base and parallel to one axis, the resulting trace will reflect the utility function of that commodity. Thus in the exhibit, if the quantity of input *Y* is held constant at 0, while input *X* is allowed to vary, a vertical slice upon the *X*-axis produces the trace U_X on the utility surface. Similarly, if the quantity of input *X* is held constant at 0, a vertical slice upon the *Y*-axis will produce the trace U_Y.

These traces, or surface lines, are simply utility-function curves. Each expresses a relationship between total utility and consumption of one commodity, while consumption of the other commodity is held constant at some specified level. Obviously, since infinitely many vertical slices can be made, infinitely many utility curves can be drawn. The slopes of the individual utility curves indicate the marginal utilities of the variable consumption of the commodities.

By repeatedly passing a plane horizontally through the figure in Exhibit 5–6, thus keeping it parallel to the base, level curves such as *AA*, *BB*, and *CC* are traced on the surface. Each such trace represents the loci of all possible combinations of *X* and *Y* that yield equal utility. For example, at the left end of the curve *AA*, the combination of Y_1 units of commodity *Y* and *A'* units of commodity *X* yields *A* utils of total utility, whatever a util may be. At the right end of the line, the combination of X_1 units of *X* and

EXHIBIT 5–7   Typical Indifference Map

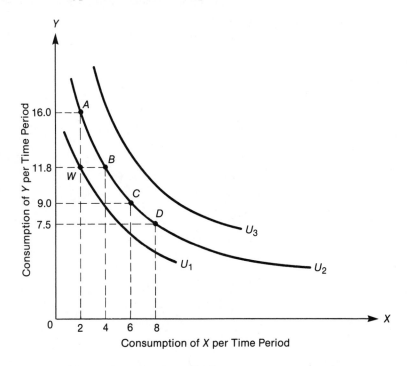

A' units of Y also yields A utils of utility. The curve AA represents all combinations of X and Y that yield A utils of utility. Logically, the consumer would be indifferent as to which of these combinations is consumed. Consumers would not be indifferent, however, as to which level of utility is reached, since we assume that consumers always seek the highest level of utility their incomes will allow.

When these level curves are projected onto the X–Y base of the figure, the result is a set of indifference curves on an indifference map, such as A'A', B'B', and C'C' in Exhibit 5–6. The X–Y base on which the indifference map is drawn is called the **commodity space.**

> *Definition: An **indifference curve** is the set of all combinations of commodities X and Y that yield the same level of total utility or satisfaction. An **indifference map** is a graph that shows a set of indifference curves.*

Exhibit 5–7 shows a typical indifference map on which the curves U_1, U_2, and U_3 represent three of the many possible utility levels derived from the consumption of various combinations of X and Y during the same period of time. Since all points along any one curve represent equal levels of satisfaction, the consumer would have no preference among positions A, B, C, or D in the figure. But any of these points would be preferable to position W, which lies on a lower curve.

Characteristics of Indifference Curves.   Indifference curves have five basic properties:

1. They are infinite in number and every point in the commodity space lies on an indifference curve.
2. They are continuous and downward-sloping.
3. They are concave from above (convex to the origin).
4. The farther away from the origin an indifference curve is, the higher the level of utility it represents.
5. They cannot intersect, since each curve represents a different and unique level of utility.

Curves that do not exhibit all of the properties just described are excluded from our analysis.[5]

Marginal Rate of Substitution

In the preceding discussion, it was seen that indifference curves are concave from above and downward-sloping. These characteristics arise from the assumption of diminishing marginal utility that was built into the utility surface from which the indifference curves were derived. Since diminishing marginal utility plays such a crucial role in the consumer-behavior model, it must be thoroughly understood.

As previously noted, different combinations of commodities can provide equal levels of total utility. When a consumer remains on a particular indifference curve, one commodity can be substituted for the other so that the consumer remains as well off as before. The rate at which a consumer is willing to make such a substitution is a matter of great interest and importance. We call it the **marginal rate of substitution**, X for Y, defined as follows:

> *Definition: The marginal rate of substitution, X for Y, (written MRS_{XY}) indicates the number of units of Y that must be given up to acquire one additional unit of X while satisfying the condition of constant total utility.*

The MRS_{XY} is a rate of change. It is measured as the slope of the indifference curve, which is different at each point along the curve.[6] Since each point represents a different combination of commodities X and Y, it follows that each combination has a different MRS_{XY}.

Relationship between MU and MRS.   Is there a relationship between marginal utility and the marginal rate of substitution? Indeed there is, since the slope of the indifference curve is the direct result of the law of diminishing marginal utility.

---

[5] Excluded curves include those for perfect substitutes, those for perfect complements, and those for situations where one commodity is good but the other is not desirable. Students may consult a standard price-theory text for further explanation.

[6] To find the slope at a particular point P, draw a line tangent to the curve at P. Using a segment of this line as a hypotenuse, complete a right triangle with base ΔX and height ΔY. The slope of the tangent line is $\Delta Y/\Delta X$, and this is the slope of the curve at P.

To understand the relationship, consider what happens when we move down the indifference curve between any two points. Consumption of Y is reduced by ΔY units, causing a loss of utility of $-\Delta Y \cdot MU_Y$ utils. But since total utility is unchanged as we move down the curve, the loss of utility from consuming less Y is precisely offset by a gain from consuming more X, that is,

$$-\Delta Y \cdot MU_Y = \Delta X \cdot MU_X. \tag{10}$$

Dividing both sides by $-\Delta X \cdot MU_Y$, we get

$$\frac{-\Delta Y \cdot MU_Y}{-\Delta X \cdot MU_Y} = \frac{\Delta X \cdot MU_X}{-\Delta X \cdot MU_Y} \tag{11}$$

so that the slope of the curve is

$$\frac{\Delta Y}{\Delta X} = -\frac{MU_X}{MU_Y}. \tag{12}$$

To illustrate, let us return to Exhibit 5–7, which is drawn so that the consumption of X increases in increments of two units. All points on the indifference curve U_2 yield the same level of total utility; but as we move down the curve, successively smaller increments of Y are given up in order to increase X by two units without changing total utility.

At point A, the consumer is using 16 units of Y and 2 units of X to gain a certain level of total utility represented by the indifference curve U_2. Now suppose that 4.2 units of Y are taken away, forcing the consumer to point W on the lower indifference curve, U_1. The change in utility from this move is

$$\Delta U_Y = -\Delta Y \cdot MU_Y = -4.2 MU_Y$$

where MU_Y means the marginal utility of Y and the minus sign indicates a loss of total utility. But the lost utility can be restored by substituting two more units of X. This moves the consumer back onto the indifference curve U_2 at point B. The utility gained from two more units of X is

$$\Delta U_X = \Delta X \cdot MU_X = 2 MU_X.$$

Since total utility at point B is equal to total utility at point A, then

$$2 MU_X = -4.2 MU_Y;$$

hence

$$\frac{MU_X}{MU_Y} = \frac{-4.2}{2} = -2.1,$$

indicating a negative slope.

Now, as we go from point B to point C, we have

$$MRS_{XY} = \frac{MU_X}{MU_Y} = \frac{-2.8}{2} = -1.4;$$

then, from point C to point D, we have

$$MRS_{XY} = \frac{MU_X}{MU_Y} = \frac{-1.5}{2} = -0.75.$$

The pattern is clear: The more of X consumed, the less its marginal utility in relation to the marginal utility of Y; that is to say, the MRS_{XY} declines as more X is consumed.

This explains why the indifference curve is concave from above. Only such a curve can satisfy the condition of a continuously declining slope.

MRS and the Exchange of Goods.   The continuously-declining *MRS* is the logical result of the assumption that the marginal utility of a commodity decreases as we obtain more of it. It follows, then, that the more of a commodity one has, the more willing one is to trade it for another commodity. For example, a person with 10 shirts and one pair of shoes might be willing to trade 3 shirts for another pair of shoes. But if he had 3 pairs of shoes and only 5 shirts he might be willing to trade only one shirt for another pair of shoes.

This willingness to exchange what we value less for what we value more is true whether the owners of the commodities are individuals, firms, or nations. Thus the marginal rate of substitution governs both domestic and foreign trade.

Illustrative Example

Two computer manufacturers, JCOR in Japan and USCOR in the United States, each produce and use microchips Q and Z. JCOR has a marginal rate of substitution between Q-chips and Z-chips equal to 6 Q-chips for 5 Z-chips. USCOR has a marginal rate of substitution between Q-chips and Z-chips of 13 Q-chips for 10 Z-chips.

Question:

Does it make sense for the corporations to swap microchips? If a trade is desirable, what would be traded, and why?

Solution:

Because of their different rates of marginal substitution between microchips Q and Z, a trade between the corporations can be mutually beneficial. Suppose JCOR trades 20 Z-chips for 25 Q-chips. JCOR gives up the equivalent of 24 Q-chips, but gets 25 in exchange. USCOR receives the equivalent of 26 Q-chips, but gives up only 25. The trade is desirable because both parties benefit from the exchange.

The Budget Line

Indifference curves reflect the consumer's personal feelings and the relative values regarding the consumption of various combinations of any two commodities. They show what combinations of *X* and *Y* the consumer is willing to accept as equally satisfactory and they are totally independent of the consumer's income and market prices. Income and market prices determine what a consumer is ***able*** to do, whereas indifference curves show what the consumer is ***willing*** to do.

The consumer's ability to buy Commodities X and Y is determined by the **budget constraint**, which can be expressed graphically as the budget line or line of attainable combinations. To illustrate, suppose a consumer has a limited amount of money to spend on Commodities X and Y. Let us also suppose that he will spend all of this amount on X and Y. The budget equation then is

$$B = Q_X P_X + Q_Y P_Y \tag{13}$$

where

B = consumer budget (income) available for the purchase of X and Y, all of which will be spent

Q_X = quantity of Commodity X purchased during some period of time

Q_Y = quantity of Commodity Y purchased during the same period of time

P_X = price of Commodity X

P_Y = price of Commodity Y

To explain the budget line, suppose a consumer has $25 to spend on X and Y, each of which costs $5 per unit. As illustrated in Exhibit 5–8, if the entire budget were spent on Y, the consumer could purchase five units of Y. Hence the Y-intercept is at $(0,5)$. Likewise, if the entire budget were spent on X, the consumer could purchase five units of X. Hence the X-intercept is at $(5,0)$. The budget line is represented by the straight line B_1 between the two intercepts.

> *Definition: The **budget line** or **line of attainable combinations** is the set of all combinations of commodities X and Y that can be purchased when all available income is spent on X and Y.*

Exhibit 5–8 also shows a family of budget lines for three levels of income. With the price of X and Y remaining constant at $5 per unit, line B_2 represents a budget of $50, and line B_3 represents a budget of $75. The lines are parallel because the prices have not changed. Line B_4, however, has a different slope because the prices have changed to $7 per unit for X and $3 per unit for Y, applied to a $50 budget.

For any budget line, the Y intercept is at B/P_Y and the X intercept is at B/P_X. If we move down the line from the Y-intercept to the X-intercept, the change in Y is $-B/P_Y$ units and the change in X is B/P_X units. Therefore the slope of the line is

$$\frac{\Delta Y}{\Delta X} = \frac{-B/P_Y}{B/P_X} = \frac{-BP_X}{BP_Y} = -\frac{P_X}{P_Y}. \tag{14}$$

The equation states that the slope of the budget line is the negative of the ratio of the price of X to the price of Y.

Consumer Equilibrium

The principal assumption upon which the theory of consumer behavior rests is that consumers attempt to allocate their limited money incomes to purchase available goods and services so as to maximize their satisfaction (utility). In other words, consumers

EXHIBIT 5–8   A Family of Budget Lines

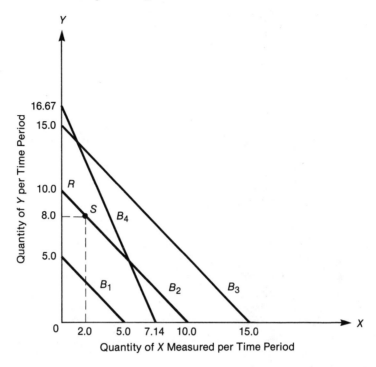

attempt to achieve an equilibrium at the highest possible level of satisfaction between what they are *willing* to purchase and what they are *able* to purchase.

As illustrated in Exhibit 5–9 (page 138), the point of equilibrium can be located by drawing the budget line on the indifference map for commodities X and Y. Since the number of indifference curves upon the indifference map is infinite, one curve will be tangent to the budget line regardless of where the budget line lies. The point of tangency is the point of equilibrium, representing the attainable combination of X and Y that gives the highest level of utility.

Exhibit 5–9 illustrates that the budget line is tangent to the indifference curve, U_2, at point M, where the consumer acquires nine units of Y and six units of X. Since indifference curves may not intersect, it is clear that U_2 represents the highest level of utility that can be obtained with the budget available. An indifference curve representing a higher level would not touch the budget line, and an indifference curve representing a lower level would intersect the budget line at two places. It should not be difficult to see why point M is preferable to any other point on the budget line. For example, point L also exhausts the income, but it clearly offers less utility than point M because it lies on a lower indifference curve.

At the point of tangency between the indifference curve and the budget line, the slope of the indifference curve equals the slope of the budget line, that is,

$$-\frac{MU_X}{MU_Y} = -\frac{P_X}{P_Y} \tag{15}$$

EXHIBIT 5–9   Illustration of Consumer Equilibrium

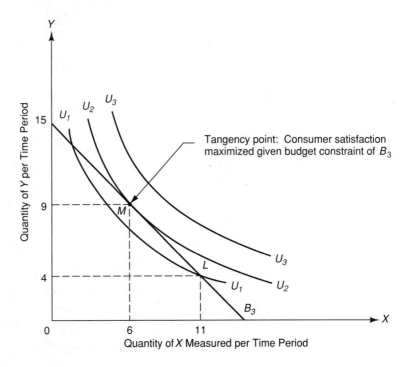

which is easily manipulated to give

$$\frac{MU_X}{P_X} = \frac{MU_Y}{P_Y}.$$ (16)

The conclusion from this two-commodity case can be extended to cover all possible goods the consumer might purchase, including future consumption. This leads to the general equation for achieving an optimal allocation of income among all commodities, which is

$$\frac{MU_A}{P_A} = \frac{MU_B}{P_B} = \cdots = \frac{MU_N}{P_N}.$$ (17)

This is the same model as provided by the cardinal approach. The model states that total utility from consumption is maximized when the consumer's income is allocated in such a way that the marginal utility per dollar expenditure on each commodity is equal. As before, this model treats money held in savings or otherwise unspent as a commodity with a price of $1 per dollar held.

Illustrative Problem

A certain consumer has $100 to spend on beef, chicken, and fish. Suppose that his utility functions are

$$TU_B = 400Q_B - 10Q_B^2$$
$$TU_C = 550Q_C - 20Q_C^2$$
$$TU_F = 200Q_F - 5Q_F^2$$

where the subscripts B, C, and F indicate beef, chicken, and fish, respectively. Also suppose that the average prices are

$$P_B = \$4.00 \text{ per pound}$$
$$P_C = \$2.50 \text{ per pound}$$
$$P_F = \$4.00 \text{ per pound.}$$

Question:

How will this consumer's $100 be spent to maximize total utility?

Solution:

The marginal utilities of beef, chicken, and fish are the first derivatives of the respective total-utility functions

$$MU_B = 400 - 20Q_B$$
$$MU_C = 550 - 40Q_C$$
$$MU_F = 200 - 10Q_F.$$

Total utility is maximum when

$$\frac{MU_B}{P_B} = \frac{MU_C}{P_C} = \frac{MU_F}{P_F}.$$

Taking the first pair of commodities, beef and chicken

$$\frac{MU_B}{P_B} = \frac{400 - 20Q_B}{4.00} = \frac{550 - 40Q_C}{2.50} = \frac{MU_C}{P_C}.$$

Cross-multiplying,

$$1,000 - 50Q_B = 2,200 - 160Q_C$$
$$-50Q_B = 1,200 - 160Q_C \qquad (18)$$
$$Q_B = -24 + 3.2Q_C.$$

Taking the second pair of commodities, chicken and fish,

$$\frac{MU_C}{P_C} = \frac{550 - 40Q_C}{2.50} = \frac{200 - 10Q_F}{4.00} = \frac{MU_F}{P_F}.$$

Cross-multiplying,

$$2,200 - 160Q_C = 500 - 25Q_F$$
$$-160Q_C = -1,700 - 25Q_F \qquad (19)$$
$$Q_C = 10.625 + 0.15625Q_F.$$

Total expenditure is

$$4.00Q_B + 2.50Q_C + 4.00Q_F = 100$$
$$4.00Q_B = 100 - 2.50Q_C - 4.00Q_F \qquad (20)$$
$$Q_B = 25 - 0.625Q_C - Q_F.$$

Substituting Equation 19 into Equation 20, we get

$$\begin{aligned} Q_B &= 25 - 0.625Q_C - Q_F \\ &= 25 - 0.625(10.625 + 0.15625Q_F) - Q_F \\ &= 25 - 6.640625 - 0.09765625Q_F - Q_F \\ &= 18.359375 - 1.09765625Q_F. \end{aligned} \qquad (21)$$

Substituting Equation 19 into Equation 18, we get

$$Q_B = -24 + 3.2Q_C = -24 + 3.2(10.625 + 0.15625Q_F)$$
$$Q_B = -24 + 34 + 0.5Q_F = 10 + 0.5Q_F. \tag{22}$$

Setting Equation 20 equal to Equation 22, we get

$$18.359375 - 1.09765625Q_F = 10 + 0.5Q_F$$
$$-1.59765625Q_F = -8.359375$$
$$Q_F = 5.232273839 \approx 5.23 \text{ lbs. of fish.}$$

Substituting Q_F into Equation 19, we get

$$Q_C = 10.625 + 0.15625Q_F = 10.625 + 0.15625(5.232273839)$$
$$= 11.44254279 \approx 11.44 \text{ lbs. of chicken.}$$

Substituting Q_F into Equation 22, we get

$$Q_B = 10 + 0.5Q_F = 10 + 0.5(5.232273839)$$
$$= 12.61613692 \approx 12.62 \text{ lbs. of beef.}$$

The consumer's $100 would be spent as follows:

12.62 lbs. of beef @ $4.00 per lb. =	$ 50.48
11.44 lbs. of chicken @ $2.50 per lb. =	28.60
5.23 lbs. of fish @ $4.00 per lb. =	20.92
	$100.00

Summary

Consumer behavior is best explained in terms of *utility*, which is defined as the satisfaction gained from having, using, or consuming goods or services. Conceptually, utility can be measured in cardinal units called utils, even though we are unable to define a util.

Marginal utility is defined as the change in total utility caused by a one-unit increase in consumption of some commodity (good or service). Thinking of total utility as a function of consumption enables us to establish the law of diminishing marginal utility. This law says that marginal utility decreases as consumption increases and becomes zero at the saturation point where total utility is maximum. Further consumption will cause disutility to set in, with marginal utility becoming negative and total utility falling.

Maximum total utility from all commodities combined occurs when the marginal utility per dollar is the same for all commodities, including money (savings), that is, when

$$\frac{MU_A}{P_A} = \frac{MU_B}{P_B} = \cdots = \frac{MU_N}{P_N} = MU_M.$$

When this equation prevails, the consumer is said to be in equilibrium, receiving the most satisfaction for the money spent or held. The consumer may be thrown out of equilibrium by a change in price or by a change in the consumer's perception of marginal utility.

The consumer's demand curve for a particular commodity is directly related to the marginal utility of that commodity. The downward-sloping demand curve is due to the law of diminishing marginal utility.

The demand curve indicates that there is a different price for each successive unit or fraction of a unit demanded. In reality, however, a price is set and the entire quantity demanded at that price is sold at that price. The price will be established by the marginal utility of the last, least-valuable unit sold. Since some customers are willing to pay a higher price, a consumer surplus is said to exist.

The equation for consumer equilibrium can also be reached by an ordinal approach, which requires only that consumers be able to rank commodities in order of preference. When such an order has been established, pairs of commodities can be combined in an infinite number of combinations that yield the same level of total satisfaction. Graphing these combinations results in an indifference curve upon an indifference map.

The slope of an indifference curve is called the marginal rate of substitution, X for Y (MRS_{XY}) and is equal to the negative of MU_X/MU_Y. It represents the amount of one commodity, Y, that must be given up to obtain one more unit of the other commodity, X, without changing the total utility derived from X and Y together. As we move down the indifference curve, the MRS_{XY} diminishes as a direct result of the law of diminishing marginal utility.

Indifference curves portray what a consumer is *willing* to do. What the consumer is *able* to do is portrayed by a budget line (line of attainable combinations). The budget line is defined as the loci of all combinations of X and Y that can be purchased by full expenditure of a given income or budget. The slope of the budget line is the negative of the ratio of commodity prices, $-P_X/P_Y$.

When the budget line is drawn upon an indifference map, it will be just tangent to some indifference curve at a particular point representing some combination of X and Y. This is the maximum total utility obtainable within the constraint of the budget and is the point of consumer equilibrium. At this point, the slope of the indifference curve and the slope of the budget line are the same; that is,

$$-\frac{MU_X}{MU_Y} = -\frac{P_X}{P_Y}.$$

Therefore,

$$\frac{MU_X}{P_X} = \frac{MU_Y}{P_Y}.$$

More generally, the equation or model for consumer equilibrium in the allocation of income to all commodities, including savings, is

$$\frac{MU_A}{P_A} = \frac{MU_B}{P_B} = \cdots = \frac{MU_N}{P_N} = MU_M.$$

Problems

1. Explain why water, which is essential to life, is so inexpensive while gem-quality diamonds, which we really don't need, are so very costly.

2. In order to construct a model of consumer behavior, is it necessary to assume that one is able to measure the degree of satisfaction obtained from consumption of one more unit? Why or why not?

3. Betty G., mother of three, takes pride in feeding her family of five on a limited grocery budget that includes $150 per month for meat. One month, the Safeway supermarket runs a special on chicken at $1 per pound. Betty buys 150 pounds and stores the chicken in her freezer. Unfortunately, this exhausts her meat budget for the month, so the family has to eat chicken every day for a month.

   a. How would her family react to her "bargain" purchase?

   b. What guiding principle would you suggest that Betty follow in her future shopping? Explain in detail.

4. If a consumer is in equilibrium and the marginal utility of the last unit of X consumed is twice the marginal utility of the last unit of Y consumed, what is the relationship between the price of X and the price of Y?

5. Express mathematically the condition for equilibrium in the utility approach to consumer theory and the condition for equilibrium in the indifference-curve approach. Show that if a cardinal measure of utility exists, the conditions for consumer equilibrium in the two approaches are equivalent.

6. Ernest P., a recent graduate of a large midwestern university, has secured a position with an international firm that requires him to travel a lot in Europe and the Far East, where his company's employees are expected to dress well. Ernest has discovered that packing enough neckties in his luggage so that he can wear a different tie each day helps to create the impression of the well-dressed young executive that he wants to make. He estimates his utility function for neckwear as $TU_N = 160Q_N - 4Q_N^2$ and his marginal utility of money as 2.5.

   a. How many neckties should Ernest buy in order to maximize his satisfaction?

   b. Construct Ernest's demand schedule for neckwear.

   c. If the price of neckties is $12.90 each, how many will Ernest be willing to purchase and what is his consumer surplus?

7. A budget line on an indifference map is depicted here. Assume that X costs $8 per unit.

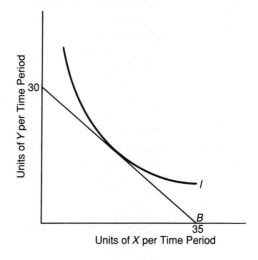

   a. What is the price of Y?

   b. Calculate the equation for the budget line.

   c. Draw a new budget line with the price of X going to $12 per unit and the price of Y unchanged. Use the indifference map to determine whether total utility will increase or decrease.

   d. Assume the following: $P_X = 8, $P_Y = 5, budget $= 200. Draw a new budget line.

8. Suppose a shopper is equally satisfied by the following combinations of apples and oranges:

Oranges	Apples
3	9
5	7
7	5
9	3
11	1

a. What is the marginal rate of substitution between oranges and apples? Does it vary?

b. In the shopper's opinion, which has the greater utility: oranges or apples?

c. Is this a realistic situation? Explain.

9. Suppose a consumer has an indifference map with two budget lines, *M* and *N*, as shown here. The price of commodity *Y* is $5.

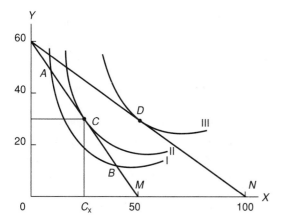

a. Consider budget line *M*:
   (1) How much is the consumer's budget for *X* and *Y*?
   (2) What is the price of *X*?
   (3) Write the equation for budget line *M*.
   (4) What is the optimal combination of *X* and *Y*, and what is the marginal rate of substitution at that equilibrium point?
   (5) Explain in terms of the *MRS* why the consumer would not choose the combinations of *X* and *Y* designated by point *A* or point *B*.

b. Let the budget line shift to *N* with the budget (money income) remaining constant.
   (1) What is the new price of *X*?
   (2) What is the equation of the new budget line?
   (3) What is the optimal combination of *X* and *Y*?
   (4) What is the *MRS* at the new point of equilibrium?

10. India and Indonesia both produce cotton and linen cloth. The Indian market has a marginal rate of substitution between cotton and linen equal to 40 yards of cotton for 10 yards of linen. The Indonesian market has a marginal rate of substitution between cotton and linen of 120 yards of cotton for 20 yards of linen. Does it make sense for the two nations to trade cotton and linen fabrics? If so, what might be traded?

11. Suppose that a person who has just received a windfall of $20,000 is facing the following disequilibrium:

$$\frac{MU_{\text{savings}}}{P_{\text{savings}}} < \frac{MU_{\text{new car}}}{P_{\text{new car}}}.$$

a. Which will this person do: put the money into a money-market fund or buy a new car?

b. Suppose the price of a new car goes up. Will this change the consumer's decision?

c. Suppose money-market rates go up. What will be the result?

12. Assume that the following data describe the preferences and opportunities of Jane Jackson, who has $54 to spend on *X* and *Y*:

$$MU_X = 60 - 2X \qquad P_X = \$2$$
$$MU_Y = 48 - Y \qquad P_Y = \$4$$

What combination of *X* and *Y* will Ms. Jackson consume in order to maximize her utility?

13. Executive compensation often includes perquisites and fringe benefits such as free travel, company cars, and stock options.

a. In a progressive tax system, why would tax-free fringe benefits and perquisites have more utility than higher salaries?

b. What was the effect on the utility of tax-free fringe benefits when the maximum income-tax rate was reduced from 50 to 33 percent?

c. What would be the effect of a flat income tax of 20 percent?

14. Jack Miller hopes to get into a school of engineering next semester. For acceptance, he must raise his grade-point average by 0.15. Today is the last day of classes, so Jack has five days left to prepare for final exams. In desperation, Jack asks you, a distinguished economics major, to advise him how to spend his study hours so as to maximize his grade-point average. Jack's final exam in chemistry represents 35 percent of his final grade; in calculus, 35 percent; and in mechanical analy-

sis, 30 percent. Since mechanical analysis is a major requirement, the grade in that course is twice as important as the others for admittance to the school of engineering.

If Jack plans to study for seven hours each day, how many hours should he spend in preparation for each final exam?

References

Baumol, W. J. *Economic Theory and Operations Analysis*, 4th ed., chap. 9. Englewood Cliffs, N.J.: Prentice-Hall, 1977.

Hausman, Jerry A. "Exact Consumer's Surplus and Deadweight Loss." *American Economic Review*, 71, no. 4 (September 1981), pp. 662–76.

Haveman, Robert H.; Mary Gabay; and James Andreoni. "Exact Consumer's Surplus and Deadweight Loss: A Correction." *American Economic Review*, 77, no. 3 (June 1987), p. 494.

Hull, J.; P. G. Moore; and H. Thomas. "Utility and Its Measurement." *Royal Statistical Society Journal* 136, part 2 (1973), pp. 226–47.

Hyman, David N. *Modern Microeconomics*, 2nd ed. Homewood, Ill.: Richard D. Irwin, 1988.

Schoemaker, P. J. H. "The Expected Utility Model: Its Variants, Purposes, Evidence and Limitations." *Journal of Economic Literature*, 20 (June 1982), pp. 529–63.

Willig, R. "Consumer's Surplus without Apology." *American Economic Review*, 66 (September 1976), pp. 589–97.

APPENDIX 5A   The Mathematics of Consumer Equilibrium

A consumer will spend or save her entire income, so that

$$I = P_1X_1 + P_2X_2 + \cdots + P_nX_n \tag{1}$$

where

$$I = \text{Consumer's income}$$
$$X_1, X_2, \ldots, X_n = \text{Quantities of } n \text{ commodities, one of which is savings}$$
$$P_1, P_2, \ldots, P_n = \text{Respective prices of the } n \text{ commodities.}$$

The consumer wants to maximize

$$TU = f(X_1, X_2, \ldots, X_n) \tag{2}$$

subject to the constraint of Equation 1.

Equation 2 is maximized when each of its partial derivatives and the constraint equation is equal to zero. However, this gives a system of $n + 1$ equations with only n variables, which cannot be solved. Therefore, an artificial variable known as the Lagrangian multiplier must be introduced. The Greek letter lambda (λ) usually is used as the symbol for the Lagrangian multiplier.

After setting the constraint equation equal to zero, multiply it by λ and add the result to Equation 2. This gives

$$TU = f(X_1, X_2, \ldots, X_n) + \lambda(I - P_1X_1 - P_2X_2 - \cdots - P_nX_n). \tag{3}$$

The marginal utility of each commodity is its own partial derivative. Taking the partial derivatives of Equation 3, we get

$$\frac{\partial TU}{\partial X_1} = MU_{X_1} - \lambda P_1 = 0 \tag{4}$$

$$\frac{\partial TU}{\partial X_2} = MU_{X_2} - \lambda P_2 = 0 \tag{5}$$

$$\frac{\partial TU}{\partial X_n} = MU_{X_n} - \lambda P_n = 0 \tag{6}$$

$$\frac{\partial TU}{\partial \lambda} = I - P_1 X_1 - P_2 X_2 - \cdots - P_n X_n = 0. \tag{7}$$

Equation 7 says that the entire income is spent (or saved) when total utility is at a maximum. Dividing Equations 4, 5, and 6 by $P_1, P_2, \ldots, P_n$, respectively, we get

$$\frac{MU_{X_1}}{P_{X_1}} = \lambda; \quad \frac{MU_{X_2}}{P_{X_2}} = \lambda; \quad \frac{MU_{X_n}}{P_{X_n}} = \lambda. \tag{8}$$

Things equal to the same thing are also equal to each other. Since money is one of the commodities, we conclude that total utility is at a maximum when the marginal utility of the last dollar spent or saved is the same for all commodities, that is,

$$\frac{MU_{X_1}}{P_{X_1}} = \frac{MU_{X_2}}{P_{X_2}} = \cdots = \frac{MU_{X_n}}{P_{X_n}}. \tag{9}$$

C H A P T E R

6

DEMAND FUNCTIONS AND ELASTICITIES OF DEMAND

To a professional economist, the term *demand* has a specific meaning. It refers to the number of units of a particular commodity (good or service) that consumers are willing and able to buy under explicitly stated conditions of time, place, price, and so forth. Thus demand is a function of a number of independent variables or demand determinants; it can be expressed as an algebraic equation or by a graph or table.

The sensitivity of the quantity demanded to changes in the demand determinants is called the **elasticity** of demand. Measurements of elasticity with respect to changes in price, income, or prices of other products can help business managers to understand the market characteristics of the goods or services they are selling, and thus can help them in planning their marketing strategies, especially the pricing of their products.

CHAPTER OUTLINE

This chapter is divided into two main sections.

1. **Market-Demand Functions.** In this first section, we examine the concept of the market-demand function. In a very real sense, market demand is the market manifestation of the variables derived from consumer-behavior theory, which was discussed in the preceding chapter. Management controls some of these variables, such as the price and quality of the product, customer service, and the advertising budget. Other variables, such as consumer tastes, preferences, and expectations, cannot be controlled by the firm, but they can be influenced by skillful advertising and promotion. Still other variables, such as consumer income,

prices of related products, the range of goods and services available, the number of potential consumers, and interest rates, are completely beyond management's control. Regardless of the degree of control a firm exercises over particular demand variables, their effects on demand must be measured in order to develop a successful marketing strategy.

2. **Elasticities of Demand.** The second section of the chapter discusses price elasticity, which is the measurement of the sensitivity of demand to a change in price. It also discusses three more demand elasticities that are commonly encountered in economic analysis as well as in marketing, finance, and other disciplines. They are income elasticity of demand, cross elasticity of demand, and advertising elasticity. Three ways of measuring elasticity (point elasticity, arc elasticity, and graphical measurement) are illustrated. This section also explains the relationships of elasticity to total revenue (*TR*) and marginal revenue (*MR*), and shows how knowledge of these relationships can help the firm to develop an effective pricing strategy for its product.

Market-Demand Functions

Business managers know that the demand for most products is affected by many factors other than price. The basic demand function, therefore, sets forth the relationship between the quantity demanded and all of the variables that affect demand. Nevertheless, it is the effect of *price* on the quantity demanded when all other variables are held constant, that is of most concern in demand analysis. In notational shorthand,

$$Q_d = f(P|X_1, X_2, \ldots, X_n)$$

where Q_d = quantity demanded, P = price, and $X_1, X_2, \ldots, X_n$ are all other demand determinants, which are held constant, as indicated by the vertical line.

Market Demand versus Firm's Demand Function

In the preceding chapter, we saw that demand is created by the behavior of individual customers. Individual **consumer-demand functions** reveal the quantity of a particular commodity that a consumer is willing and able to purchase at each price within some range of prices at a particular time and place, assuming that all demand variables other than price are held constant. The **market-demand function** is the summation of all consumer-demand functions in that market. That is, individual quantities demanded at a given price are combined to get the market demand for the product at that price. When repeated for all prices, these summations result in the market demand.

It is essential to understand the nature of the relationship between market demand and the individual firm's demand function.

1. All markets are alike in that they consist of buyers and sellers, with third parties such as brokers or agents occasionally providing auxiliary services to bring buyers and sellers together. Within that framework, however, market demand and markets vary tremendously in size, arrangement, and dynamics. For example, the United States as a

whole is the market for a wide range of household products, whereas only those states with heavy winter snowfalls form the domestic market for such goods as snowmobiles. On the other hand, the market for collectibles, such as rare coins, paintings, and stamps, consists of relatively few customers scattered all over the world.

2. Clearly, demand for a firm's product is some fraction of the total market demand for that type of product. This does not mean, however, that the firm's demand function is a scaled-down version of the market-demand function. The many factors other than price that influence demand are not necessarily the same for the firm as they are for the market.

3. A basic relationship between a firm's demand function and market demand is established by *market structure*.[1] In a market structure of pure competition, the firm's demand curve is a horizontal line even though the market-demand curve is downward-sloping. In market structures where competition exists between producers, such as in monopolistic competition and oligopoly, the firm's demand is influenced by competitors' activities that may have little or no influence upon the total market demand. In a monopoly, the firm's demand *is* the market demand.

Regardless of the market structure, it is the demand curve facing the firm that is most important to the firm's decisions with respect to pricing, output, and promotion of its product.

Quantity Demanded versus Change in Demand

The student must be careful to distinguish changes in the quantity demanded from changes in demand. When the price changes while all other variables are held constant, the result is a change in the quantity demanded, as illustrated in panel A of Exhibit 6–1 (page 150). Lowering the price from P_{X_1} to P_{X_2} causes movement along the demand curve from point A to point B as the quantity demanded changes from X_1 to X_2.

Panel B of Exhibit 6–1 illustrates the effect of changing income on the demand for a normal good. A **normal good** is defined as a good whose consumption increases as income rises, in contrast to an **inferior good**, that is, one whose consumption decreases when income rises. In this exhibit, starting with the demand curve D_1, an increase in income causes the whole curve to shift outward to D_2. Thus a larger quantity is demanded at all price levels. Conversely, a decrease in income reduces the quantity demanded at all price levels, and the entire curve shifts to D_3.

This is the meaning of the term "change in demand." In the case of an inferior good, an increase in income will cause the demand curve to shift in the opposite direction, that is, toward the origin. The point is that a change in income causes the demand curve to shift one way or the other, depending upon the type of commodity. Furthermore, a shift in the demand curve will be caused not only by a change in income, *but also by a change in any variable other than price.*

---

[1] The way in which prices, output quantities, and competitive strategies are determined in different market structures is the subject matter of Chapter 15.

EXHIBIT 6–1   Change in Quantity Demanded versus Change in Demand

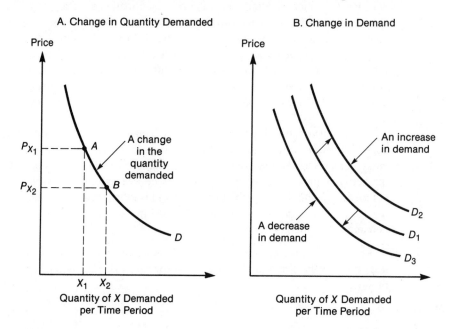

A. Change in Quantity Demanded

B. Change in Demand

The Nature of the Demand Function

When an economist speaks of market demand or the demand curve, these terms refer to demand as a function of price alone, with all other variables held constant. Of course, demand can also be expressed as a function of any other single variable with all other variables held constant, using the same analysis that leads to demand as a function of price, and it can also be expressed as a function of a number of variables.

To illustrate, suppose that a large food processor has identified the multivariate demand function for a brand of Swiss cheese it markets on a national basis. The function is

$$Q_X = 5 - 10P_X + 15P_Y - 25P_Z + 0.001I \tag{1}$$

where

Q_X = Annual consumption per family of Brand X Swiss cheese, in pounds
P_X = Price per pound of Brand X Swiss cheese
P_Y = Price per pound of competing brands of Swiss cheese
P_Z = Price index of 10-ounce packages of snack-type crackers
I = Median annual family income

Equation 1 may have been obtained by linear regression of data obtained either from the firm's own records or from secondary sources of published statistics.[2] In any case, the estimation of the demand function is essentially a matter of estimating its parameters

---

[2] The techniques of linear regression are explained in Chapters 7 and 8.

from data about its variables.[3] The parameters of Equation 1 show the effect of each variable upon the overall demand when all other variables are held constant, as follows:

- $-10P_X$ indicates that a \$1 increase in the price of Brand X Swiss cheese will cause a 10-pound decrease in its annual consumption per family.
- $15P_Y$ indicates that a \$1 increase in the price of competing brands will cause a 15-pound increase in consumption of Brand X Swiss cheese.
- $-25P_Z$ indicates that a 100 percent increase in the price of complementary snack-type crackers will cause a 25-pound decrease in the consumption of Brand X Swiss cheese.
- $0.001I$ indicates that a \$1,000 increase in median family income will cause a one-pound increase in consumption of Brand X Swiss cheese.

Now let us assume the following values of the variables for the upcoming year:

$$P_X = \$2.50$$
$$P_Y = \$3.00$$
$$P_Z = \$1.00$$
$$I = \$30,000.$$

As shown by Exhibit 6–2, the expected sales next year of Brand X Swiss cheese would be 30 pounds per family.

The demand equation for Q_X as a function of price when all other variables are held constant at the values given by Exhibit 6–2 can be calculated as follows:

$$Q_X = (5 + 45 - 25 + 30) - 10P_X$$
$$Q_X = 55 - 10P_X.$$

When $P_X = \$2.50$, as shown in Column 2 of the exhibit, then

$$Q_X = 55 - 10(2.5) = 30.$$

Price is the only independent variable in this equation, but that does not mean that the quantity demanded is influenced only by price. The other variables, such as the price of other products and the consumer's income, are not being ignored—they are just being held constant while price is allowed to vary.

In a similar fashion, we can use the data in Exhibit 6–2 to develop demand equations in terms of each of the other independent variables:

$$Q_X = (5 - 25 - 25 + 30) + 15P_Y$$
$$Q_X = -15 + 15P_Y$$

$$Q_X = (5 - 25 + 45 + 30) - 25P_Z$$
$$Q_X = 55 - 25P_Z$$

$$Q_X = (5 - 25 + 45 - 25) + 0.001I$$
$$Q_X = 0 + 0.001I.$$

The point we are making here is that the coefficient of each variable in a demand equation indicates the effect of that variable upon the quantity demanded when all other variables are held constant.

---

[3] A parameter is a constant whose value is determined at the time of its use. Equation 1, which is of the form $Y = b_0 + b_1X_1 + b_2X_2 + b_3X_3 + b_4X_4$, has four variables and the five parameters labeled b_0 through b_4.

EXHIBIT 6–2   Demand Function: Estimate of the Sales of Brand *X* Swiss Cheese

Independent Variable	Expected Value of Independent Variable	Value of Parameter in Demand Equation	Total Effect (2) × (3)
(1)	*(2)*	*(3)*	*(4)*
Constant term			+5.0
P_x	$2.50	−10.0	−25.0
P_y	$3.00	+15.0	+45.0
P_z	1.00	−25.0	−25.0
I	$30,000.00	+0.001	+30.0
Expected Sales			+30.0

Elasticities of Demand

If we lower a product's price, we know that sales will increase, but by how much? And what will happen to total revenue? What will happen to sales if consumers' disposable income increases? What will happen to sales if the advertising budget is increased? Will a change in the price of butter affect the sales of margarine? If so, by how much? These are important questions in the business world, and they all can be answered by understanding the concept and measurement of *elasticity*.

In general, the elasticity of any function is defined as the percentage change in the dependent variable *Y* that is caused by a one percent (or relatively small) change in the independent variable *X* while all other independent variables are held constant. This general concept of elasticity is applicable to *any* function. For example, in Chapter 10 we shall be particularly interested in the elasticity of production. In theory, the demand function has an elasticity for each of its many independent variables. However, we shall confine our discussion to the four demand elasticities that are most widely discussed in the literature of demand theory. These are:

1. **Price elasticity of demand**, which measures the responsiveness of sales to changes in price.
2. **Income elasticity of demand**, which measures the responsiveness of sales to changes in consumer income.
3. **Cross elasticity of demand**, which measures the responsiveness of sales of one commodity to changes in price of another commodity.
4. **Advertising elasticity**, which measures the responsiveness of sales to changes in the amount spent on advertising and promotion.

Price Elasticity of Demand

Price elasticity is defined as the percentage change in the quantity demanded that is caused by a one percent change in price while all other variables are held constant. The general equation for the measurement of price elasticity is

$$\text{Elasticity} = \frac{\text{Percentage change in the quantity demanded}}{\text{Percentage change in the price of the product}}.$$

In symbols,

$$\epsilon_D = \frac{\Delta Q_X/Q_X}{\Delta P_X/P_X} = \frac{\Delta Q_X}{Q_X} \cdot \frac{P_X}{\Delta P_X} = \frac{\Delta Q_X}{\Delta P_X} \cdot \frac{P}{Q} \tag{2}$$

where

ϵ_D = price elasticity of demand

Q_X = quantity of the product X that is demanded

P_X = price of product X with all other variables held constant.

Thus the elasticity of the demand function is simply the rate of change, $\Delta Q_X/\Delta P_X$, combined with a multiplicative factor, P_X/Q_X, which makes the elasticity independent of the units used in its calculation.

There are two types of elasticity measurement. One is direct measurement at a particular point, using the **point-elasticity** formula. The other is the measurement of the average elasticity over an arc or segment of the demand curve, using the **arc-elasticity** formula. The arc-elasticity formula applies to most empirical measurements of the price elasticity of demand.

Point Elasticity (Calculus Method). Point elasticity is a marginal concept in that it measures the elasticity at a specific point on the demand curve. In the general definition of elasticity previously given as Equation 1, the term $\Delta Q_X/\Delta P_X$ approximates the slope of a curvilinear demand curve in the neighborhood of point (P_X, Q_X) if ΔP_X is sufficiently small. If we want the precise slope at that point, we call on differential calculus and let ΔP_X approach the limit of zero. Hence we have the condition $\lim_{\Delta P_X \to 0} (\Delta Q_X/\Delta P_X)$, which is the definition of the derivative dQ_X/dP_X. Consequently, we may define point elasticity as

$$\epsilon_D = \frac{dQ_X}{dP_X} \cdot \frac{P_X}{Q_X}. \tag{3}$$

To illustrate, consider the demand function $Q_X = 30 - 2P_X$, where Q_X represents the quantity demanded and P_X represents the price of commodity X. What is the price elasticity at the point on the demand curve where $P_X = 6$?

By Equation 2, we get

$$\epsilon_D = \frac{dQ_X}{dP_X} \cdot \frac{P_X}{Q_X} = (-2)\frac{6}{30 - (2 \times 6)} = (-2)\frac{6}{18} = -0.67.$$

This may be interpreted to mean that when the price is $6, a one percent change in price will cause a 0.67 percent change in quantity demanded. The minus sign indicates that the variables move in opposite directions.

If a demand curve is linear, its slope is constant so that $(dQ_x/dP_X) = (\Delta Q_X/\Delta P_X)$ everywhere along the line. The ratio (P/Q), however, is different at each point along the line. Therefore elasticity is different at each point on the line, whether or not the curve is linear.

If there are a number of independent variables in a demand function, the point elasticity of each variable, X_i, can be found by taking partial derivatives, that is, $\Delta Q/\Delta X_i = \partial Q/\partial X_i$. If the demand function is linear, the partial derivatives turn out to be the coefficients of the respective variables.

Arc Elasticity.   As previously discussed, the point formula of Equation 3 reflects a *marginal* concept, and is valid only for very small movements from point to point along a demand curve. Furthermore, Equation 3 requires that the precise change in Q_X generated by a very small change in P_X be known, which requires that the demand function be known. There are many instances, however, when we are interested in measuring elasticity when the demand function is not known or when our interest lies in a larger segment of the demand curve. For this, we need the formula for arc elasticity, which calculates the average elasticity between two points on the demand curve.

To explain the rationale of the arc formula, suppose the price of papayas (tropical fruit) in the Safeway supermarkets in Honolulu is reduced from $0.50 per pound to $0.38 per pound, and this causes the average sales of papayas to increase from 300 pounds to 450 pounds per day, that is,

P_X (cents per pound)	Q_X (pounds)
50	300
38	450

These data locate two points along a demand curve whose equation we do not know. What is the average elasticity between these two points?

If we use the upper point (50,300) as our base point, then

$$\text{Price elasticity} = \frac{\text{Percentage change in } Q_X}{\text{Percentage change in } P_X}$$

$$= \frac{\dfrac{450 - 300}{300}}{\dfrac{38 - 50}{50}} = \frac{450 - 300}{300} \times \frac{50}{38 - 50} = \frac{150}{300} \times \frac{50}{-12} = -2.08.$$

If we use the lower point (38,450) as our base point and move up the curve, the price elasticity becomes

$$\text{Price elasticity} = \frac{\dfrac{300 - 450}{450}}{\dfrac{50 - 38}{38}} = \frac{300 - 450}{450} \times \frac{38}{50 - 38} = \frac{-150}{450} \times \frac{38}{12} = -1.06.$$

We see, then, that the price elasticity of papayas is quite different at the upper and lower ends of this segment of the demand curve.

What to do? The solution is to find an average elasticity for this increment of changing demand. To do this, we must change our base for calculating elasticity to an average between the two bases (P_1, Q_1) and (P_2, Q_2) at the ends of the arc. The average price is $(P_2 + P_1)/2$ and the average quantity demanded is $(Q_2 + Q_1)/2$. These average coordinates designate a point halfway between them along a straight line. We then modify the basic definition of elasticity to get the arc formula, using the average coordinates of P and Q. The change in P and Q is the change between the end points, that is, $\Delta P = P_2 - P_1$ and $\Delta Q = Q_2 - Q_1$. We designate the arc formula E_D rather than ϵ_D in order to distinguish arc elasticity from point elasticity. The arc formula is

$$E_D = \frac{\frac{\Delta Q_X}{Q_X}}{\frac{\Delta P_X}{P_X}} = \frac{\frac{Q_2 - Q_1}{Q_2 + Q_1}}{\frac{P_2 - P_1}{P_2 + P_1}} = \frac{\frac{2(Q_2 - Q_1)}{Q_2 + Q_1}}{\frac{2(P_2 - P_1)}{P_2 + P_1}} = \frac{(Q_2 - Q_1)(P_2 + P_1)}{(Q_2 + Q_1)(P_2 - P_1)}. \tag{4}$$

Applying the arc formula to our example, we get

$$E_D = \frac{(450 - 300)(38 + 50)}{(450 + 300)(38 - 50)} = \frac{(150)(88)}{(750)(-12)} = \frac{13,200}{-9,000} = -1.47.$$

We interpret this to mean that on the average within the range of prices from 50 cents to 38 cents per pound, the quantity demanded will change by 1.47 percent for each one percent change in the price of papayas.

To sum up this discussion, we emphasize once again that point elasticity is a marginal concept because it measures elasticity at a particular point on a demand curve. It can be properly used only for analysis of the effect of very small changes in price. The broader concept of arc elasticity enables the measurement of average elasticity over a broader range of price changes. Arc elasticity thus is more apt to be the appropriate tool for analysis of empirical data about prices and quantities demanded.

Illustrative Problem

Assume a demand function of $Q_X = 100 - 5P_X$.

Questions:

a. What is the price elasticity of demand at the point where the price is $5 if the price increases to $7? What is the price elasticity at the point where the price is $7 if the price decreases to $5?
b. What is the average elasticity between these two points?

Solutions:

a. If $P_X = \$5, Q_X = 100 - 5(5) = 75$.

If $P_X = \$7, Q_X = 100 - 5(7) = 65$.

The elasticities at the end points of the arc are:
at the point (5,75),

$$\epsilon_D = \frac{dQ_X}{dP_X} \cdot \frac{P_X}{Q_X} = -5\left(\frac{5}{75}\right) \approx -0.33;$$

at the point (7,65),

$$\epsilon_D = \frac{dQ_X}{dP_X} \cdot \frac{P_X}{Q_X} = -5\left(\frac{7}{65}\right) \approx -0.54.$$

b. The average elasticity is calculated by the arc formula:

$$E_D = \frac{(Q2 - Q1)(P2 + P1)}{(Q2 + Q1)(P2 - P1)} = \frac{(65 - 75)(7 + 5)}{(65 + 75)(7 - 5)} = \frac{(-10)(12)}{(140)(2)} \approx -0.43.$$

CAUTION: It should also be noted that the average elasticity at the midpoint of the arc is *not* an average between the elasticities of the end points; that is,

$$\frac{(-0.33) + (-0.54)}{2} \approx -0.44 \neq -0.43.$$

The correct arc elasticity can be obtained only by use of the arc formula.

Elastic versus Inelastic.   The coefficient of price elasticity (determined by either the point or arc formula) consists of two components: sign and magnitude. The sign indicates the relative direction of movement between the two variables. If the sign is negative, they move in opposite directions. If it is positive, they move in the same direction. The magnitude (absolute value) of the coefficient indicates the degree of sensitivity of the quantity demanded to change in price; that is,

- If $|\epsilon| = 1.0$, the function is **unit elastic**, meaning that a 1.0 percent change in price will cause a 1.0 percent change in the quantity demanded.
- If $|\epsilon| > 1.0$, the function is *elastic*, meaning that a 1.0 percent change in price will cause a greater than 1.0 percent change in the quantity demanded.
- If $|\epsilon| < 1.0$, the function is inelastic, meaning that a 1.0 percent change in price will cause a less than 1 percent change in the quantity demanded.

Graphical Measurement of Point Elasticity

Suppose we have constructed a graph of the demand curve from a demand schedule. Is there a way to estimate price elasticity by visual inspection of the curve?

The answer is yes. For example, suppose we have the linear demand curve AC, as shown in Exhibit 6–3. Point B is located at the midpoint of AC, and we want to find the elasticity at this point.

First, note that triangles AOC, AP_1B, BFE, BQ_1C, and EQ_2C are all similar, since all of their corresponding angles are the same. Therefore, their corresponding sides are proportional. Since point B is placed such that $AB = BC$, this means that $OQ_1 = Q_1C$ and $OP_1 = P_1A$.

Next, take the similar triangles BFE and BQ_1C. Suppose we let the price decrease a very small amount—say, from P_1 to P_2, that is,

$$\Delta P = P_1P_2 = BF.$$

This causes the quantity demanded to increase from Q_1 to Q_2, that is,

$$\Delta Q = Q_1Q_2 = FE.$$

At point B, the price P is OP_1 dollars, and the quantity Q is OQ_1 units. Therefore,

$$\epsilon_D = \frac{\Delta Q}{\Delta P} \cdot \frac{P}{Q} = \frac{FE}{BF} \cdot \frac{OP_1}{OQ_1}. \tag{5}$$

By triangular similarity,

$$\frac{\Delta Q}{\Delta P} = \frac{FE}{BF} = \frac{Q_1C}{BQ_1}. \tag{6}$$

EXHIBIT 6–3   Graphical Measurement of Point Elasticity

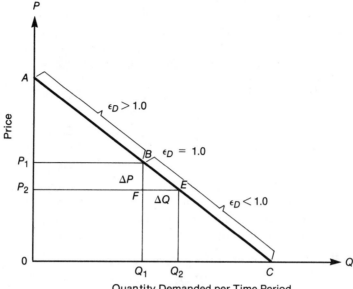

Quantity Demanded per Time Period

Since $BQ_1 = OP_1$,

$$\frac{\Delta Q}{\Delta P} = \frac{Q_1 C}{BQ_1} = \frac{Q_1 C}{OP_1}. \tag{7}$$

By substitution into Equation 4,

$$\epsilon_D = \frac{\Delta Q}{\Delta P} \cdot \frac{P}{Q} = \frac{Q_1 C}{OP_1} \cdot \frac{OP_1}{OQ_1}. \tag{8}$$

Hence,

$$\epsilon_D = \frac{Q_1 C}{OQ_1} = \frac{BC}{BA} \tag{9}$$

by triangular similarity.

Since we have located B at the midpoint of the line AC (i.e., $BC = BA$), we conclude that the linear-demand function is unit elastic at the midpoint of AC. It follows that given any point $B_{(Q,P)}$ on a linear-demand curve with a P-intercept at A and a Q-intercept at C,

If $BC = BA$, or $OP = PA$, or $QC = QO$, then $\epsilon_D = 1.0$

If $BC > BA$, or $OP > PA$, or $QC > QO$, then $\epsilon_D > 1.0$

If $BC < BA$, or $OP < PA$, or $QC < QO$, then $\epsilon_D < 1.0$.

To find price elasticity at a point, B, on the graph of a curvilinear demand function, we simply draw a line between the axes and tangent to the demand curve at point B. If we designate the Y-intercept of the straight line as A and the X-intercept as C, then elasticity is the ratio BC/BA, as we have shown.

The graphical measurement of elasticity can help us to see the relationship between total revenue, marginal revenue, and elasticity, all of which are affected by a change in price.

Demand, Revenue, and Price Elasticity

First, we note that the demand function may be written to show that the quantity demanded is a function of the price charged; that is, $Q_X = f(P_X)$. However, in theoretical demand analysis, we can also use the inverse form $P_X = f(Q_X)$, which is mathematically equivalent. The function $P_X = f(Q_X)$ makes it easier to explain the relationships of total revenue and marginal revenue to changes in demand, as well as cost–price relationships under various market structures.

Taking our previous example of the demand function for Brand X Swiss cheese, we can write

$$Q_X = 55 - 10P_X \tag{10}$$

or we can write

$$P_X = 5.5 - 0.1Q_X, \tag{11}$$

which is the mathematically equivalent inverse of Equation 10. We use it to obtain the marginal-revenue function.

Using Equation 10, total revenue may be expressed as

$$TR_X = P_XQ_X = P_X(55 - 10P_X) = 55P_X - 10P_X^2. \tag{12}$$

Using Equation 11, total revenue can be expressed as

$$TR_X = P_XQ_X = (5.5 - 0.1Q_X)Q_X = 5.5Q_X - 0.1Q_X^2 \tag{13}$$

and the answer in dollars will be the same. But the derivatives of Equations 12 and 13 are *not* the same. Since marginal revenue is defined as the change in total revenue when *one more unit* is sold, marginal revenue, MR_X, is taken to be the derivative of Equation 13, that is, with respect to Q_X:

$$MR_X = \frac{dTR}{dQX} = 5.5 - 0.2Q_X. \tag{14}$$

Total revenue is maximum when marginal revenue is zero:

$$MR_X = 5.5 - 0.2Q_X = 0$$
$$0.2Q_X = 5.5$$
$$Q_X = 27.5 \text{ units.}$$

Therefore, the price at which total revenue is maximum is

$$P_X = 5.5 - 0.1Q_X = 5.5 - 0.1(27.5) = \$2.75.$$

At this price,

$$TR = PQ = 2.75(27.5) = \$75.63.$$

Price elasticity, total revenue, and marginal revenue are all functionally related to the demand curve. These relationships are depicted in Exhibit 6–4.

Total Revenue and Price Elasticity. Exhibit 6–4 shows that on the upper portion of the demand curve (where price is higher), the magnitude (absolute value) of the elasticity coefficient is greater than 1.0, hence demand is said to be elastic. In the lower portion of the curve, the magnitude of the elasticity coeffecient is less than 1.0, hence demand is said to be inelastic. At the center of the curve, where price is $2.75, the magnitude of the elasticity coefficient equals 1.0, hence demand is said to be unit elastic.

EXHIBIT 6–4   **Relationship of the Demand Function $Q_X = 55 - 10P_X$ to Total Revenue (TR_X), Marginal Revenue (MR_X), and Price Elasticity (ϵ_X)**

Current MacBooks

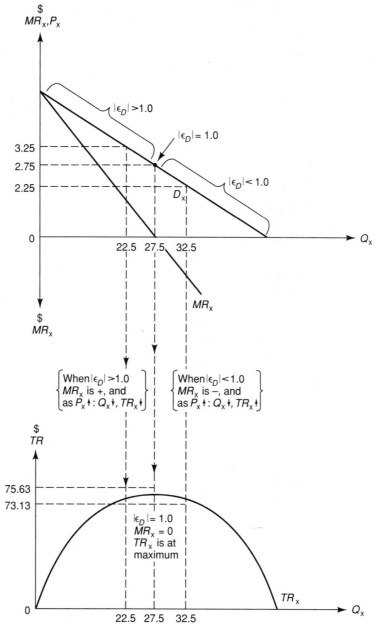

The exhibit shows that when demand is elastic, reducing the price causes total revenue to rise. Why? Because a magnitude of elasticity greater than 1.0 means that if the price is cut by some percentage, the quantity demanded will rise by a greater percentage. The increase in the number of units sold will more than make up for the lower price, and total revenue will increase. By the same reasoning, when demand is inelastic, a price increase will cause total revenue to rise, even though fewer units will be sold.

Maximum revenue occurs when the magnitude of elasticity equals 1.0, as shown in Exhibit 6–4. At this point, any change in price in either direction will cause a reduction in total revenue.

The relationships between price changes, elasticity, and total revenue may be summarized as follows:

1. If demand is *elastic* ($|\epsilon_D| > 1.0$):
    Total revenue rises when price falls; total revenue falls when price rises.
2. If demand is *inelastic* ($|\epsilon_D| < 1.0$):
    Total revenue rises when price rises; total revenue falls when price falls.
3. If demand is *unit elastic* ($|\epsilon_D| = 1.0$):
    Total revenue is maximum. Any change in price (up or down) will cause total revenue to fall.

CAUTION: Do not confuse maximum *revenue* with maximum *profit*. The calculation of profit requires consideration of cost as well as revenue.

Marginal Revenue and Price Elasticity.   As we have noted, marginal revenue may be derived from Equation 13 as

$$MR_X = (\frac{dTR}{dQ_X}) = 5.5 - 0.2Q_X. \tag{15}$$

Going back to the demand function of Equation 11, $P_X = 5.5 - 0.1Q_X$, we see that the slope of the related marginal-revenue function in Equation 15 is just twice as steep. It follows that the MR_X curve will lie exactly halfway between the demand curve and the vertical axis; that is, the X-intercept of the MR curve will be halfway between the origin and the X-intercept of the demand curve, as shown in Exhibit 6–4. This is characteristic of all linear-demand functions.

Since marginal revenue is derived from total revenue, it is also related to price elasticity of demand, as illustrated by Exhibit 6–4. It shows that as the price decreases, the quantity sold increases and

1. Marginal revenue continuously decreases as the quantity sold increases (because the price is decreasing).
2. In the elastic range of the demand function, marginal revenue is positive and total revenue increases as the quantity sold increases.
3. When the function is unit elastic, marginal revenue is zero and total revenue is at a maximum.
4. In the inelastic range of the demand function, marginal revenue is negative and total revenue decreases as the quantity sold increases.

The relationships depicted in this demand curve can be generalized for all linear-demand curves. Finally, there is a formula that links together price, price elasticity, and marginal revenue:

$$MR_X = P_X\left(1 - \frac{1}{|\epsilon P|}\right). \tag{16}$$

This formula says that when the magnitude (absolute value) of the elasticity coefficient is greater then 1.0, the marginal revenue will be positive. Conversely, when the magnitude of the elasticity coefficient is less than 1.0, the marginal revenue will be negative. When the magnitude of the elasticity coefficient is equal to 1.0, the marginal revenue will be zero.

Illustrative Problem

Digimill, Inc., is a U.S. manufacturer of digital controls for milling machines. The firm has been exporting its least expensive model, which sells for US$1,500, to Mexico, where the demand has proved to be

$$Q = 3,500 - 2P,$$

where Q = quantity demanded and P = price. Digimill wants to break into the South American markets in Brazil, Argentina, and Chile.

Question:

If the demand in each of these countries is the same as in Mexico,
a. How many machines can Digimill expect to sell in all three countries?
b. At a price of $1,500, what will be the total revenue, *TR*, from sales in all three countries?
c. What is the price elasticity of demand in each country when the price is $1,500? Would a price increase of 10 percent increase total revenue?
d. If the price is $1,500, what will be the marginal revenue, *MR*, in each country?
e. How many units must Digimill sell in each country in order to maximize revenue? What would be the price?
f. Show that price elasticity equals −1.0 when total revenue is maximum.

Solutions:

a. If $P = \$1,500$, then $Q = 3,500 - 2P = 3,500 - 2(1,500) = 500$ units in each country, or 1,500 units altogether.

b. $Q = 3,500 - 2P$; hence $P = 1,750 - 0.5Q$
$\quad TR = PQ = (1,750 - 0.5Q)Q = 1,750Q - 0.5Q^2$
$\qquad = 1,750(500) - 0.5(500)^2 = \$750,000$ in each country
$\quad \$750,000 \times 3$ countries $= \$2,250,000$

c. $\epsilon_D = \dfrac{dQ}{dP} \cdot \dfrac{P}{Q} = -2\left(\dfrac{1,500}{500}\right) = -6.0,$

meaning that a 10 percent increase in price would trigger a 60 percent decrease in sales. At a price of ($1,500 \times 1.10) = \$1,650$, sales would be

$$Q = 3,500 - 2(1,650) = 200,$$

which is a reduction of 300 units per country. Total revenue would be

$$TR = PQ = (1,650)(200) = \$330,000,$$

which is a reduction in total revenue of $750,000 - $330,000, = $420,000 in each country. Obviously, a price increase is not advisable.

d.
$$MR = \frac{dTR}{dQ} = \frac{d(1,750Q - 0.5Q^2)}{dQ} = 1,750 - Q$$
$$= 1,750 - 500 = \$1,250$$

e. Total revenue is maximum when marginal revenue is zero. Hence,

$$MR = 1,750 - Q = 0$$
$$Q = 1,750$$
$$P = 1,750 - 0.5(1,750) = \$875.$$

f.
$$Q = 3,500 - 2P$$
$$\epsilon_D = \frac{dQ}{dP} \cdot \frac{P}{Q} = -2\left(\frac{875}{1750}\right) = -1.0$$

or

$$MR_X = P_X\left(1 - \frac{1}{|\epsilon|}\right)$$

$$0 = 875\left(1 - \frac{1}{|\epsilon|}\right) = 875|\epsilon| - 875$$

$$875|\epsilon| = 875$$
$$|\epsilon| = 1.0$$
$$\epsilon = -1.0, \text{ since price elasticity is always negative.}$$

Factors That Affect Price Elasticity

In order to develop pricing and marketing strategies, decision makers need to be aware not only of the relationships among price, price elasticity, total revenue, and marginal revenue, but also of the reasons why different products have different price elasticities. There are many such reasons, but they can be generally lumped into four categories: availability of substitues, relative size of expenditure, consumer's perceptions of necessities versus luxuries, and the time period to which the demand curve pertains.

Availability of Substitutes. The more substitutes there are for a product, the more price elastic it is apt to be. In contrast, when the price of a complementary good changes, demand is affected for both that commodity and its complement. Since complementary commodities, in effect, share the price change, they tend to be less price elastic. Closely related to the substitution effect is the effect of multiple uses of a product. If a product has only one use or a very limited number of uses, then the effect of a change in price is relatively limited. But if there are many ways in which the product can be used, then

EXHIBIT 6–5 **Summary of Product Characteristics with Respect to Price Elasticity**

Tendency of Product Characteristic

⇐ *More elastic*	*Less elastic* ⇒
Substitutes	Complementary goods
Multiple uses	Limited uses
Large outlays	Small outlays
Durables	Nondurables
Luxuries	Necessities
Long time frame	Short time frame

the effect of a price change is more profound. Therefore, products with many uses are apt to be more price elastic than single-use products, as shown in Exhibit 6–5.

Relative Size of Expenditure. Exhibit 6–5 also shows that price elasticity is affected by the cost of the commodity relative to the consumer's total budget. For example, a price increase for pencils or chewing gum tends to have little effect on the demand for these goods because expenditure on them represents such a small portion of the consumer's total income. In general, the demand for nondurable goods, unless they are luxuries, tends to be less elastic than the demand for durable goods. Big-ticket durable items such as large appliances, solar water-heating systems, wall-to-wall carpeting, automobiles, and houses tend to be very price elastic, not only because of the relative size of the expenditure involved, but also because such purchases can be postponed.

Consumers' Perceptions of Necessities versus Luxuries. One of the most important determinants of elasticity is the consumer's perception of a product as a necessity or as a luxury. Consumers will continue to buy almost the same quantity of a necessity even when the price goes up. Consequently, demand for necessities tends to be less elastic. Some examples are prescription medicines and food staples such as bread, milk, and salt. In contrast, luxuries are commodities that consumers buy when they can afford them. Since what they can afford with any given income is determined by price, the demand for luxuries tends to be more price elastic.[4]

Time Period to Which the Demand Curve Pertains. Over a long period of time, consumers can either adjust their budgets to a price change in a particular commodity or find a substitute for it. Given enough time, a substitute can be found for almost any product. Consequently, there can be substantial differences between long-run and short-run elasticity, as shown in Exhibit 6–6. For example, this exhibit shows that gasoline is inelastic in the short run, with a price elasticity of −0.40. When gasoline prices almost doubled in the mid-1970s, from $0.35 per gallon in mid-1973 to $0.60 per gallon

---

[4] Please note that we did not say that necessities are price inelastic and luxuries are price elastic. The demand functions for all commodities have both elastic ($|\epsilon| > 1.0$) and inelastic ($|\epsilon| < 1.0$) ranges.

EXHIBIT 6–6   **Examples of Short-Run and Long-Run Price Elasticity of Demand**

	Estimated Price Elasticity	
Commodity	Short-Run	Long-Run
Automobiles and parts	-1.87	-2.24
China, glassware, tableware	-1.54	-2.55
Electricity, household	-0.13	-1.89
Foreign travel by U.S. residents	-0.14	-1.77
Gasoline	-0.40	-1.50
Housing	-0.30	-1.88
Intercity rail travel	-1.40	-3.19
Jewelry and watches	-0.41	-0.67
Motion pictures	-0.87	-3.67
Radio and TV repair	-0.47	-3.84
Stationery	-0.47	-0.56
Tires and tubes	-0.86	-1.19
Tobacco products	-0.46	-1.89
Toilet articles and preparations	-0.20	-3.04

Source: Hendrik S. Houthakker and Lester D. Taylor, *Consumer Demand in the United States, 1929–1970: Analysis and Projections* (Cambridge, Mass.: Harvard University Press, 1970), pp. 166–67. The short-run gasoline figure is from Robert Archibald and Robert Gillingham, "The Review of the Short-Run Consumer Demand for Gasoline Using Household Survey Data," *Review of Economics and Statistics* 62 (November 1980), pp. 622–28. The long-run gasoline figure is from J. M. Griffin, *Energy Conservation in the OECD, 1980–2000* (Cambridge, Mass.: Ballinger, 1979).

in mid-1974, motorists complained but continued to drive much as they did before the price went up. But as the price of gasoline continued to rise in the late 1970s and early 1980s, motorists turned to smaller cars and drove less in order to consume less of the high-priced gasoline. Such behavior reflects the higher long-run price elasticity of gasoline and indicates that any further price increases in the future will encounter higher elasticity and, therefore, even more consumer resistance.

Applications of Price Elasticity

Price-elasticity measurements have many uses in managerial decision making. Three examples are in setting prices in general and in price setting after deregulation of the air-transportation and oil industries.

Price Elasticity as a Guide for Setting Prices.   Price elasticity is especially useful as a guide for setting prices. Price elasticities can be used to answer questions such as

- What will happen to sales if we raise the price by 5 percent?
- How much should we reduce the price in order to obtain a 10 percent increase in sales?

As we saw in Exhibit 6–4, marginal revenue is negative throughout the inelastic portion of a firm's demand curve, where the price elasticity magnitude is less than 1.0. This means that a one percent increase in price will decrease sales by less than one percent; consequently, total revenue will rise. Conversely, a one percent decrease in price will result in less than a one percent increase in sales; consequently, total revenue will fall.

Does this mean that a firm that finds itself operating in the inelastic portion of its demand curve should increase its price? Not necessarily; remember that the firm's objective is to maximize profits, not revenues. In order to maximize profits, costs must be considered. It may be that by decreasing its price, the firm can gain a level of production at which large economies of scale can be achieved. If this lowers costs more than it lowers revenues, the firm's profits might be improved.

Price Elasticity after Deregulation of Air Transportation. In the airline industry, deregulation led to widespread discounting of fares amid a shuffling of routes among the carriers. Airline managements had to decide whether to keep or drop old routes, whether or not to enter new markets, and how to price their services in the face of vigorous competition in the market. Price elasticity of demand played a key role in such decisions as airline executives tried to determine whether lower fares would increase total revenue.

Total revenue is a crucial factor in determining airline strategy, first because the aircraft have fixed capacities, and second because the airline's product (transportation) cannot be inventoried. Once the aircraft departs with empty seats, the revenue from those seats is lost forever. This is why the airlines have a number of different fares, each appealing to a different segment of the market with a different price elasticity. Very low standby fares represent the airline's last-ditch effort to fill all its seats on every flight. These fares appeal to travelers with the highest price elasticity of demand for air travel.

Price Elasticity after Deregulation of Oil Prices. Price elasticity of demand has been a key element in the establishment of national policy toward deregulation of oil and natural-gas prices. Debates about the advisability of deregulation have often centered on the question of price elasticity. During the Arab oil embargo of 1973, for example, government officials believed that oil consumption would have to be reduced by 20–30 percent. To reduce the quantity demanded, officials had to decide either to raise prices or to resort to rationing. Some economists believed the demand for gasoline was so inelastic that enormous, politically unacceptable price increases would be required to reduce demand as required. Others felt that demand was sufficiently elastic that acceptable price increases could do the job.

As it turned out, the government deregulated oil prices, and then supply, demand, and prices soon stabilized—prices actually declined in 1982. This behavior of gasoline prices is consistent with the short-run (-0.4) and long-run (-1.5) price elasticities previously noted in Exhibit 6–6. In the short run, the demand for gasoline was price-inelastic, but in the long run conservation measures reduced the demand for gasoline to the point where price decreases were necessary to maintain revenues.

Other Demand Elasticities

Conceptually, every factor that affects demand has an elasticity. However, the natures of some factors (such as tastes and preferences as well as consumer expectations) are such that it is impossible, or at least extremely difficult, to quantify or measure elasticity. The variables that are readily quantified are income, the prices of other products, and the level of advertising expenditures. Each of these variables thus has its own elasticity, as we discuss next.

Income Elasticity of Demand.   Income elasticity of demand measures the sensitivity of the quantity demanded to changes in income. The point-elasticity formula for income elasticity is

$$\epsilon_I = \frac{dQ_X}{dI} \times \frac{I}{Q_X} \tag{17}$$

where I = income and Q_X = quantity of commodity X demanded when price and all other variables are held constant. The arc formula is

$$E_I = \frac{Q_{X2} - Q_{X1}}{Q_{X2} + Q_{X1}} \times \frac{I_2 + I_1}{I_2 - I_1}. \tag{18}$$

Demand with respect to income may be elastic or inelastic, depending upon whether the magnitude of the income-elasticity coefficient is greater or less than 1.0. But unlike price elasticity, which is always negative, the sign of the income-elasticity coefficient may be either plus or minus. A plus sign indicates a normal good, while a negative sign indicates an inferior good.

Income elasticities for 14 products, all normal goods, are shown in Exhibit 6–7. Most of these normal goods show long-run income elasticities greater than short-run elasticities, as we might expect. As noted by the asterisks in Exhibit 6–7, automobiles, furniture, and household appliances (all durable goods) are exceptions whose long-run income elasticities are substantially less than the short-run elasticities. This may be attributed to the fact that consumers do not always replace such items when their incomes increase.

Applications of Income Elasticity.   Income elasticity of demand is applicable to a broad range of market-planning and strategy problems. Some examples are long-range planning of the firm's growth, developing marketing strategies, and forecasting housing requirements.

Long-range Planning of the Firm's Growth.   Over the long run, we expect consumer income to rise. Consequently, prospects for long-run growth in sales are much brighter for luxury goods because of their higher income elasticities. On the other hand, higher income elasticities mean greater sales volatility in the short run, which is not desirable. For example, Exhibit 6–7 shows the short-run income elasticity of demand for automobiles to be 5.5. No doubt this high value can partially explain why new car sales fall so drastically during recessions and then rebound so vigorously during recoveries.

Companies whose products have high income elasticities can look forward to growth in a generally growing economy, but they will be much more vulnerable to recession. On the other hand, companies whose products have low income elasticities are virtually recession-proof, but they cannot expect to share in a growing economy when times are good. Such firms may find it necessary to diversify into different products or even a different industry in order to achieve healthy growth.

EXHIBIT 6–7   **Estimated Income Elasticity of Demand for Selected Commodities**

	Income Elasticity	
Commodity	*Short-Run*	*Long-Run*
Automobiles	5.50	1.07*
China, glassware, tableware	0.47	0.77
Clothing	0.95	1.17
Dental services	0.38	1.00
Foreign travel by U.S. citizens	0.24	3.09
Furniture	2.60	0.53*
Gasoline and oil	0.55	1.36
Household appliances	2.72	1.40*
Housing, owner-occupied	0.07	2.45
Jewelry and watches	1.00	1.60
Physician services	0.28	1.15
Shoes	0.90	1.50
Spectator sports	0.46	1.07
Toilet articles and preparations	0.25	3.74

Source: Hendrik S. Houthakker and Lester D. Taylor, *Consumer Demand in the United States, 1929–1970: Analysis and Projections* (Cambridge, Mass.: Harvard University Press, 1970), pp. 166–67.

Developing Marketing Strategies.   The income elasticity of demand influences decisions on the location and nature of sales outlets as well as the extent and focus of advertising and promotional activities. For example, vendors of luxury goods typically direct their advertising to rising young professionals whose incomes can be expected to grow substantially.

Forecasting Housing Requirements.   A particularly interesting application of income elasticity is in the area of housing. An estimated range of income elasticity of demand for housing can be combined with forecasted growth in real income to provide forecasts of demand for both owner-occupied and rental housing.

> ## Illustrative Problem

Suppose that the annual growth in real income in the United Kingdom is expected to be between 2 and 3 percent. Suppose further that income elasticity of demand for housing in London is estimated to be between 0.8 and 1.0 for rental units and between 0.7 and 1.5 for owner-occupied housing.

Questions:

a.   What will be the growth in demand for rental units over the next 10 years?
b.   What will be the growth in demand for owner-occupied units over the next 10 years?

EXHIBIT 6–8   Forecasted Growth in Demand for Rental Units over 10 Years

Income Elasticity of Demand	Growth in Demand for Rental Units if Real Income Grows 2% per Annum		Growth in Demand for Rental Units if Real Income Grows 3% per Annum
0.8	$0.8 \times 21.9\% = 17.5\%$	$\Rightarrow$	$0.8 \times 34.4\% = 27.5\%$
$\Downarrow$			$\Downarrow$
1.0	$1.0 \times 21.9\% = 21.9\%$	$\Rightarrow$	$1.0 \times 34.4\% = 34.4\%$

Solutions:

a. If the annual growth in real income is 2 percent, the compounded growth in 10 years would be $(1.02)^{10} = 1.219$, an increase of 21.9 percent. At 3 percent, the compounded growth in 10 years would be $(1.03)^{10} = 1.344$, an increase of 34.4 percent. Forecasts of the growth of demand for rental units corresponding to income elasticities of 0.8 and 1.0 are shown in Exhibit 6–8. The exhibit shows that in 10 years the growth in demand for *rental* housing units due to growth of income could range from a low of 17.5 percent to a high of 34.4 percent.

b. The growth of demand for *owner-occupied* units is shown in Exhibit 6–9. The exhibit shows that growth in demand for owner-occupied housing units is even greater than that for rental units, that is, from a low of 15.3 percent to a high of 51.6 percent. It must be emphasized that this growth in demand is due solely to increased income. No doubt it would be offset to a greater or lesser extent by a decrease in demand due to higher prices.

Cross Elasticity of Demand.   Several different measures of elasticity may be developed for interpreting the economic effects and interactions of substitute and complementary products. The most important of these measures is the *cross elasticity of demand*. Suppose we let P_X and P_Y denote the prices of commodity X and commodity Y, respectively, while Q_X and Q_Y denote the respective quantities demanded. The cross elasticity of demand measures the percentage change in the quantity of X demanded relative to a slight percentage change in the price of Y. The point formula is

$$\epsilon_C = \frac{dQ_X}{dP_Y} \times \frac{P_Y}{Q_X}. \tag{19}$$

The arc formula is

$$E_C = \frac{Q_{X2} - Q_{X1}}{Q_{X2} + Q_{X1}} \times \frac{P_{X2} + P_{X1}}{P_{X2} - P_{X1}}. \tag{20}$$

The cross elasticity can be positive, negative, or zero. It will be positive if the products are substitutes. Thus, other things remaining the same, if the price of butter increases,

EXHIBIT 6–9   Forecasted Growth in Demand for Owner-Occupied Housing Units over 10 Years

Income Elasticity of Demand	Growth in Demand for Owner-Occupied Units if Real Income Grows 2% per Annum		Growth in Demand for Owner-Occupied Units if Real Income Grows 3% per Annum
0.7	$0.7 \times 21.9\% = 15.3\%$	$\Rightarrow$	$0.87 \times 34.4\% = 24.1\%$
$\Downarrow$			$\Downarrow$
1.5	$1.5 \times 21.9\% = 32.9\%$	$\Rightarrow$	$1.5 \times 34.4\% = 51.6\%$

the consumption of butter will fall, but the consumption of margarine should increase to substitute for the decrease in butter consumption. Thus the price of butter and the consumption of margarine move in the same direction, up or down, so the sign of the cross elasticity coefficient is plus.

On the other hand, when commodities are complementary, their cross elasticities are negative. Increases in the prices of gasoline, for example, would decrease the quantity of gas-guzzling automobiles demanded. Presumably, this will result in fewer purchases of large cars, again assuming a constancy of other factors. The price of gasoline and the number of large cars demanded move in opposite directions, up or down; hence the sign of the cross elasticity coefficient is minus.

Finally, a small or zero cross elasticity would indicate that the products (or the markets in which they are sold) are effectively independent of each other, since variations in the price of one produce no appreciable changes in purchases of the other.

In a well-known study, Herman Wold estimated cross elasticities between beef and pork and between butter and margarine. His results are shown in Exhibit 6–10 (page 170). These cross elasticities show that if the price of pork rises by one percent, the quantity of beef demanded will rise by 0.28 percent. But if the price of beef is raised one percent, the quantity of pork demanded is increased by only 0.14 percent. Thus the sensitivity of the demand for beef to changes in pork prices is twice as great as the sensitivity of the demand for pork to changes in the price of beef, but the demand for neither reacts strongly to changes in the price of the other. Their cross inelasticity indicates that they are not very close substitutes for each other.

Cross elasticities are somewhat higher between butter and margarine, but the demands are still cross-inelastic. Apparently, consumers who like butter are inclined to ignore changes in the price of margarine, since a one percent change in the price of margarine produces only a 0.67 percent change in the consumption of butter. Users of margarine are slightly more sensitive to changes in the price of butter, since a one percent change in the price of butter produces a 0.81 percent change in the consumption of margarine.

The concept of cross elasticity of demand is particularly useful not only for decision making by the firm, but also for measurement of interrelationships among industries.

At the level of the firm, cross elasticities help in the formulation of marketing strategy. For example, the firm needs to know how the demand for its products will react to price

EXHIBIT 6–10   **Cross-Elasticities of Demand for Two Pairs of Commodities**

Commodity	*Substitute*	*Cross Elasticity*
Beef	Pork	+0.28
Pork	Beef	+0.14
Butter	Margarine	+0.67
Margarine	Butter	+0.81

Source: H. Wold, *Demand Analysis*, New York: John Wiley & Sons, 1953, pp. 282, 285.

changes in either substitute or complementary goods offered by a competitor. In many cases, the competition exists "in house"; that is, a firm will produce a number of related products that may be either substitutes or complements to each other. For example, Procter & Gamble makes at least five different hand soaps and four different household cleaning products, all competing against each other. Cross elasticities of these products will assist in pricing strategies that yield maximum profit for the firm as a whole. Gillette makes both safety razors and razor blades. Since these products are complementary, Gillette needs to know how a price change in razors will affect the demand for blades, and vice versa, so that both products can be priced to yield maximum profit.

At the industry level, the cross elasticity of demand indicates whether or not a substitute exists for the industry's product. For example, when the price of imported oil became too high, extraction of oil from shale became economically feasible and attractive. But when OPEC prices fell in response to a worldwide glut of oil, development of shale-oil extraction was halted because shale oil no longer was a viable substitute for Middle Eastern oil. Demand for coal is also responding to changes in the price of oil, and demand for oil can be expected to respond to changes in the price of natural gas.

In some cases, cross elasticity studies show that what seems to be a monopoly is actually vulnerable to competition from the product of a different industry. For example, in cities where both natural gas and electricity are available from lines in the street, gas can be substituted for electricity or else electricity can be substituted for gas for cooking, heating water, and heating buildings. Each utility has a monopoly on its product, but must be very careful about pricing.

One important use of cross elasticity is in the definition of industries. Cross elasticity studies can define the boundaries of an industry as including all firms whose products are close substitutes as determined by high positive cross elasticities. Firms whose products exhibit negative or very small cross elasticities would be excluded as belonging to some other industry. Definition of an industry is an important consideration in antitrust cases and even more important in statistical studies. The validity of a study of an industry will depend in large part upon how the industry is defined.

Advertising Elasticity of Demand.   Advertising elasticity of demand measures the sensitivity of sales (quantity demanded) to changes in expenditure for advertising and promotion. Like the other elasticities discussed so far, formulas for advertising elasticity may be adapted from the general formula,

$$\epsilon = \frac{dY}{dX} \times \frac{X}{Y}. \tag{21}$$

If we assume that sales are a function of advertising expenditure, the point formula is

$$_A\epsilon_S = \frac{dS}{dA} \times \frac{A}{S} \tag{22}$$

where S equals the quantity sold or total revenue from sales and A equals units of advertising expenditure. Arc elasticity is measured as

$$_A\epsilon_S = \frac{S_2 - S_1}{S_2 + S_1} \times \frac{A_2 + A_1}{A_2 - A_1}. \tag{23}$$

In treating sales as a function of advertising expenditure, the analyst must recognize that the effect of the advertising budget is clouded by a number of factors, such as

1. The stage of the product's market development.
2. The extent to which competitors react to the company's advertising, either with their own advertising campaigns or by increased merchandising.
3. The quality and quantity of the company's past and present advertising compared to that of competitors, since variations in qualitative factors (e.g., choice of media) obscure the effects of differences in advertising outlays.
4. The importance of nonadvertising demand determinants (such as growth trends, prices, and incomes) and the extent to which these can be filtered out of the analysis.
5. The time that elapses between advertising outlays and a sales response to these outlays, which is difficult to ascertain because such intervals depend in part on the type of product, type of advertisement, and so forth.
6. The influence of the "investment effect" of the company's past advertising and the extent to which this may affect current and future sales through delayed and cumulative buying. (The investment effect is the realization of sales as a result of advertising expenditure, but long after the period in which the advertising expenditure was made.)

All of these factors must be considered when reckoning sales as a function of advertising. In order to do this, the methods of measurement must be devised to allow for and compensate for the complexities just mentioned. As one might imagine, this is no easy task. Indeed, it may prove to be exceptionally difficult, but the usefulness of advertising elasticity depends on the successful accomplishment of this task.

Illustrative Problem

At a vacation resort area, a local airline provides once-a-day passenger service to and from Paradise Island, a one-way distance of about 150 miles. The airline's controller has estimated its demand function to be

$$Q = 20 - 5P + 0.2A + 0.01I$$

where

Q = average number of one-way passengers per day

P = price of a one-way ticket

A = advertising expenditure per month

I = per capita income in the airline's market.

Question:

At the present time, P = \$50, A = \$1,000, and I = \$12,000. Find the price elasticity of demand, the income elasticity of demand, and the advertising elasticity.

Solution:

$$Q = 20 - 5P + 0.2A + 0.01I$$
$$= 20 - 5(\$50) + 0.2(\$1,000) + 0.01(\$12,000) = 90.$$

$$\text{Price elasticity } = \epsilon_D = \frac{\partial Q}{\partial P} \times \frac{P}{Q} = (-5)\frac{50}{90} = -2.78,$$

which means that a one percent increase (decrease) in price, with all other variables held constant, will produce a 2.78 percent decrease (increase) in the number of tickets sold.

$$\text{Income elasticity } = \epsilon_I = \frac{\partial Q}{\partial I} \times \frac{I}{Q} = (0.01)\frac{12,000}{90} = +1.33,$$

which means that a one percent change in potential passengers' income, up or down, with all other variables held constant, will generate a 1.33 percent change, up or down, in the number of tickets sold.

$$\text{Advertising elasticity } = {}_A\epsilon_S = \frac{\partial S}{\partial A} \times \frac{A}{S} = (0.2)\frac{1,000}{90} = +2.22,$$

which means that a one percent change in advertising, up or down, with all other variables held constant, will generate a 2.22 percent change, up or down, in the number of tickets sold.

Combined Effect of Demand Elasticities.   As we said at the beginning of this section, every factor that affects demand has an elasticity. When all factors are allowed to change and interact as they will, their combined influence on demand is simply the sum of the effects of their individual elasticities. For example, if both price and income will be changing, the quantity demanded next year, Q_1, will be the current demand, Q_0, plus the change caused by the price increase, plus the change caused by the rise in income. The change caused by the price increase is equal to the current demand $\times$ the percentage change in price $\times$ the price elasticity of demand. The change caused by the rise in income is equal to the current demand $\times$ the percentage change in income $\times$ the income elasticity of demand. In symbols,

$$Q_1 = Q_0 + Q_0\left(\frac{\Delta P}{P}\right)\epsilon_D + Q_0\left(\frac{\Delta I}{I}\right)\epsilon_I = Q_0\left[1 + \frac{\Delta P}{P}\epsilon_D + \frac{\Delta I}{I}\epsilon_I\right] \quad (24)$$

where

Q_0 = Quantity demanded in Year 0 (current demand)

Q_1 = Quantity demanded in Year 1 (next year's demand)

$\Delta P/P$ = Percentage change in price, expressed as a decimal

ϵ_D = Price elasticity of demand

$\Delta I/I$ = Percentage change in income, expressed as a decimal

ϵ_I = Income elasticity of demand.

Illustrative Problem

Gotham Leather Goods, Inc., is producing a ladies' handbag with European styling. The firm enjoys annual sales of 100,000 units. Currently the sales price per unit is twice the direct cost of manufacture. The firm's management estimates that the price elasticity of demand for this product, ϵ_D, is about -1.3 and the income elasticity of demand for it, ϵ_I, is about 2.0. Economic forecasters expect real disposable income to increase by 6 percent in the coming year. The company has just signed a labor contract that will increase direct manufacturing costs next year by 10 percent.

Question:

If the company follows its current pricing policy next year, how many units can it expect to sell?

Solution:

Using Equation 24,

$$Q_1 = Q_0 + Q_0\left(\frac{\Delta P}{P}\right)\epsilon_D + Q_0\left(\frac{\Delta I}{I}\right)\epsilon_I = Q_0\left[1 + \frac{\Delta P}{P}\epsilon_D + \frac{\Delta I}{I}\epsilon_I\right]$$

$$= 100,000[1 + (0.10)(-1.3) + (0.06)(2.0)] = 99,000.$$

That is to say, the reduced sales caused by the price increase amount to $(0.1)(-1.3)$ $(100,000) = -13,000$. This reduction in sales will be partially offset by increased sales caused by the increase in income, amounting to $(0.06)(2.0)(100,000) = +12,000$. If we assume that all other factors, such as advertising and competitors' prices, remain the same, the result will be a net loss in sales of 1,000 units.

Summary

Elasticity is the most commonly used measurement of the sensitivity of demand to any of its determinants. In general, elasticity is defined as the percentage change in a dependent variable that is attributable to a one percent change in a single independent variable, holding all other variables constant. Elasticity may be measured at any point on the functional curve with the *point* formula,

$$\epsilon = \frac{dY}{dX} \times \frac{X}{Y}.$$

It may also be computed over a segment of the curve with the arc formula,

$$E = \frac{Y_2 - Y_1}{Y_2 + Y_1} \times \frac{X_2 + X_1}{X_2 - X_1}.$$

The result of either formula is an elasticity coefficient whose sign indicates the relative direction of movement between the two variables, and whose absolute value or magnitude indicates the degree of sensitivity. If the magnitude is less than 1.0, the function is said to be inelastic at the point of measure. If the magnitude is greater than 1.0, the function is elastic, and if it is equal to 1.0, the function is unit elastic at the point of measure.

Elasticity is a general concept that applies to any function. When applied to demand, four elasticities are of primary interest: (1) price elasticity of demand, (2) income elasticity of demand, (3) cross elasticity of demand, and (4) advertising elasticity of sales. These elasticities have wide application to decision making in both the public and private sectors. For example, price elasticity is a primary consideration in deciding to change prices, income elasticity may point to the proper location for a new facility, cross elasticity will govern reaction to competitors' activities, and advertising elasticity may determine the scope and magnitude of a new advertising campaign.

Price elasticity of demand measures the sensitivity of demand to changes in price. Its sign is always negative, indicating that an increase in price will reduce the quantity demanded, and vice versa. The demand function is unit elastic at the point where marginal revenue is zero and total revenue is at a maximum. Below this point, demand is inelastic, marginal revenue is negative, and a price increase will increase total revenue. Above this point, demand is elastic and the firm can increase total revenue by reducing price.

Income elasticity of demand measures the sensitivity of demand to changes in consumer income. Its sign will be plus for a normal good, minus for an inferior good. Income elasticity is an important consideration in long-range planning as well as in the formulation of short-run marketing strategy.

Cross elasticity measures the sensitivity of demand to changes in the price of some other commodity. The sign is plus if the two products are substitutes and minus if they are complements. For unrelated products, the coefficient will be zero or very close to zero. Cross elasticity is important for the development of marketing strategy of the firm, and for definition of industries as well as for the evaluation of the competitive position of entire industries.

Advertising elasticity of sales measures the responsiveness of demand (sales) to changes in advertising expenditure. This is a particularly difficult quantity to measure because of the many factors that interact with advertising.

Each factor that affects demand has its own elasticity. In reality, all of these factors act and interact more or less at the same time. The total effect on demand is the sum of their individual effects.

Problems

1. The J.P. Jackson Company, a department store, conducted a study of the demand for men's ties. It found that the average daily demand, Q, in terms of price, P, is given by the equation:

$$Q = 60 - 5P.$$

   a. How many ties per day can the store expect to sell at a price of $3 per tie?

   b. If the store wants to sell 20 ties per day, what price should it charge?

   c. What would be the demand if the store offered to give the ties away?

   d. What is the highest price that anyone would be willing to pay for these ties?

   e. Plot the demand curve.

2. "Demand elasticity measures percentage changes in quantity demanded relative to percentage changes in price. It follows that with 10 equal demanders for a product, the elasticity will be 10 times as great as it is for one." True or false? Explain.

3. "The elasticity of demand for a product usually increases with the length of time over which a price change persists. Thus, a one percent decrease in price may result at first in a less than one percent increase in quantity demanded, but eventually the quantity may increase by 2 percent, 5 percent, or even more." True or false? Explain.

4. The more narrowly a product is defined—"Toyota Tercel" versus "automobile," for example—the more elastic the demand. True or false? Explain.

5. Generally speaking, would you expect the cross elasticity of demand to be positive, negative, or zero for each of the following pairs of products? What general rule, if any, can you infer from your answers?

   a. Convertibles and sedans

   b. Coca-Cola and Pepsi-Cola

   c. Textbook sales and school enrollments

   d. Desks and chairs

   e. Chinese egg rolls and children's socks

6. Central City Meat Packers has noted that the demand, Q, for its smoked breakfast sausages is affected by changes in per capita personal income, I, in such a way that $Q = 1,000 + 0.2I$.

   a. Calculate the quantity demanded at each $1,000 of per capita income from $2,000 to $6,000.

   b. Calculate the income elasticity of demand if income changes from $3,000 to $5,000 and from $10,000 to $15,000.

   c. Judging from the behavior of income elasticity, are smoked breakfast sausages a luxury or a necessity?

7. Bruce Home Products manufactures a vacuum cleaner that it sells for $100 a unit. At this price, sales have been averaging about 2,000 units per month. The company has recently learned, however, that its major competitor intends to cut the price of its vacuum cleaner from $90 to $80. Management at Bruce Home Products believes the cross elasticity of demand between its product and that of the competitor is +0.8. Assuming no changes in other demand variables, calculate in units and dollars the sales loss to Bruce Home Products that can be expected from the competitor's price cut.

8. Consider the accompanying demand curve representing the demand function $Q = 60 - 5P$.

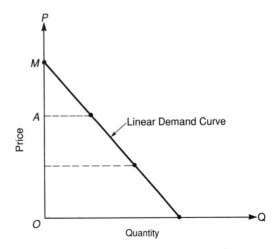

Using the geometric method of calculating price elasticity, we can determine that at a price of A dollars, the price elasticity is

$$\epsilon_D = \frac{A}{A - M} = \frac{OA}{AM}$$

and at a price of B dollars, the price elasticity is

$$\epsilon_D = \frac{B}{B - M} = \frac{OB}{BM}.$$

Now use this information and the formula $MR = P + \frac{1}{\epsilon}$ to fill in the following table.

P	Q	TR	ϵ	MR
12				
10				
8				
6				
4				
2				
0				

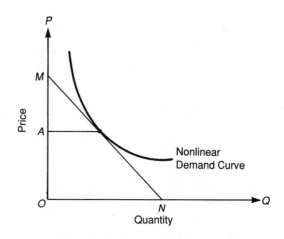

Now consider the demand curve $P = 20/Q$ and fill in the following table.

P	Q	TR	ϵ	MR
5				
4				
3				

9. Problem 8 illustrates a geometric technique for finding price elasticity and then applies it to a linear demand curve. However, the same approach can be used for estimating point price elasticities on nonlinear demand curves. For example, on the accompanying demand curve we are interested in determining price elasticity at the price A. The line MN is drawn tangent to the demand curve at price A and price elasticity is estimated as before: $\epsilon = A/(A - M)$.

10. The Upland Sears automotive center typically sells 300 deluxe five-year auto batteries every month for a list price of $75. However, sales declined last month to 225 units. The manager of the automotive department feels the decline in sales was the result of a sale on three-year batteries, whose price was reduced from $65 to $55.

   a. Calculate the cross elasticity between five-year and three-year auto batteries. (Use the arc formula.)

   b. Calculate the sales of five-year batteries if the price of three-year batteries were set at $60.

11. Freshbake and Dreambake both sell wedding cakes. Assume current wedding cake sales to be $Q_F = 1,650$ and $Q_D = 620$. The demand curves for the two competitors are:

Freshbake : $P_F = 750 - 0.3Q_F$
Dreambake : $P_D = 700 - 0.5Q_D$.

a. Calculate the point price elasticities for Freshbake and Dreambake.

b. Suppose Freshbake reduces the price of wedding cakes, thereby increasing sales from 1,650 to 1,734 units and reducing Dreambake's sales to 610 units. What is the cross elasticity between Freshbake and Dreambake wedding cakes?

c. What does the cross elasticity coefficient calculated in part (b) indicate about the substitutability of the two products?

d. Would the price reduction by Freshbake make sense with regard to revenue? Explain your answer.

12. *(Library research)* Obtain price and consumption data covering the most recent 10 or more years for any two competing or complementary products. (**Suggestion:** *Agricultural Statistics,* published annually by the U.S. Dept. of Agriculture, provides data for numerous agricultural products. Check the index of the most recent volume.) Examples of products that may be selected include *meat:* beef, veal, lamb, pork, ham; *dairy:* cheese, milk, ice cream; and *citrus:* oranges, lemons. A pair of products may be selected from different product groups, such as ham and eggs or meat and cheese, if it makes economic sense to do so. Of course, you may choose nonagricultural products from any source you can find. Analyze the data on the two products you select by estimating the arc measures for the cross elasticity of demand. Interpret your results.

Case Problem: Sparklife Industries

13. Sparklife Industries presently controls 4 percent of the spark-plug market. The sales manager at Sparklife is taking an aggressive position to increase the company's market share. At the most recent board meeting, he showed top management that after a price reduction from $1.10 to $1.00 made in January 1986, sales climbed from 2.2 million to 2.75 million units per year.

While this is a dramatic jump, members on the board were quick to point out other factors that may have influenced the situation: (1) the

consumer price index rose 4 percent; (2) per capita disposable income rose 3 percent; (3) a well-known auto parts manufacturer entered the market; (4) a composite index of auto, truck, and motorcycle manufacturers showed a 6 percent increase in sales; (5) other spark-plug producers exhibited stable prices; and (6) gas prices increased during the last three months of the year by 5 percent.

Questions

a. Calculate the price elasticity of demand with all other factors remaining constant.

b. Analyze each of the additional factors, explaining possible effects on your original measure of price elasticity.

c. Which of the additional factors are quantifiable?

d. Considering only the information given, would you advise a price reduction?

Case Problem: LRS Corporation

14. Video Magic is a retail distributor of new and used television sets. In 1980, Video Magic was purchased and became a wholly owned subsidiary of LRS Corporation, a holding company that owns several large hotels. Because of its hotel operations, LRS often makes large purchases of television sets, and this gives it increased operating leverage in the television-set market. Also, Video Magic provides an excellent sales outlet for LRS's used television sets. To develop more efficient ordering and pricing policies, a company accountant organized data for the past 10 years of operations, as shown in the table on page 178.

Questions

a. Economists predict further rises in disposable income. What plans should management make for future inventories?

b. An LRS hotel is scheduled for renovation, which includes replacing 1,050 four-year-old television sets. To get rid of the old sets, management is considering a sale at reduced prices on all used sets. What effect, if any, will a price reduction on used televisions have on new television sales?

c. Management is also evaluating pricing policies for its new television sets. What suggestions could you make?

(HINT: Each of these questions involves a form of elasticity. Remember that elasticity applies only when all other factors remain constant.)

Year	Price of New Televisions	Price of Used Televisions	Number of New Televisions Sold	Average per Capita Disposable Income
1981	$600	$150	2,000	$2,000
1982	650	150	1,900	2,000
1983	650	175	2,000	2,250
1984	650	200	2,100	2,250
1985	600	150	2,000	2,250
1986	600	175	2,100	2,250
1987	600	175	2,000	2,000
1988	700	175	2,100	2,250
1989	750	150	2,000	2,250
1990	800	150	1,900	2,250

References

Archibald, Robert, and Robert Gillingham. "Review of the Short-Run Consumer Demand for Gasoline Using Household Survey Data." *Review of Economics and Statistics* 62 (November 1980), pp. 622–28.

Barrett, W. B., and M. B. Slovin. "Economic Volatility and the Demand for Consumer Durables." *Applied Economics* 20, no. 6 (June 1988), p. 731.

Clarke, Darral G. "Sales-Advertising Cross-Elasticities and Advertising Competition." *Journal of Marketing Research* 10 (August 1973), pp. 250–61.

Dax, P. "Estimation of Income Elasticities from Cross-Section Data." *Applied Economics* 19, no. 11 (November 1987), p. 1471.

Gillingham, Robert, and Robert P. Hagemann. "Household Demand for Fuel Oil." *Applied Economics* 16 (1984), pp. 475–82.

Houthakker, Hendrik S., and Lester D. Taylor. *Consumer Demand in the United States: Analysis and Projections.* Cambridge, Mass.: Harvard University Press, 1970.

Hyman, David N. *Modern Microeconomics,* 2nd ed. Homewood, Ill: Richard D. Irwin, 1988.

Nevin, John R. "Laboratory Experiments for Estimating Consumer Demand: A Validation Study." *Journal of Marketing Research* 11 (August 1974), pp. 261–68.

Pouris, A. "The Price Elasticity of Electricity Demand in South Africa." *Applied Economics* 19, no. 9 (September 1987), p. 1269.

Simon, Herman. "Dynamics of Price Elasticity and Brand Life Cycles: An Empirical Study." *Journal of Marketing Research* 16 (November 1979), pp. 439–52.

Van Helden, G. J.; P. S. H. Leeflang; and E. Sterken. "Estimation of the Demand for Electricity." *Applied Economics* 19, no. 1 (January 1987), p. 69.

C H A P T E R

7

DEMAND
ESTIMATION:
ELEMENTARY
TECHNIQUES

The objective of demand analysis is to discover the forces that affect product sales and to establish the relationships between these controlling forces and sales. Two complementary and often overlapping approaches to demand analysis are discussed in this chapter: **statistical analysis** and **market research**. In the statistical-analysis approach, empirical data is analyzed statistically to determine the structural form and parameters of the demand function. When reliable data are not available or nonexistent (as for a new product), market research is required. This involves some degree of direct contact with the consumer through observation, surveys, or marketing experiments. Afterwards, statistical analysis may be brought to bear upon the collected data. Which approach is used (or whether both are used jointly) depends upon the availability and reliability of empirical data and the skills of the analyst. When sufficient reliable data are available, statistical analysis by itself is sufficient.

CHAPTER OUTLINE

The chapter is divided into two sections:

1. **Statistical Analysis.** This section discusses the use of time series and cross-sectional data for demand analysis. It includes necessary adjustments to the data, the least-squares method of simple linear regression, and the statistical measures and graphs that are used to test the validity of the regression equation.

2. **Market-Research Approach to Demand Estimation.** This section discusses three market-research techniques that may be used to investigate consumer buying habits.

Statistical Analysis

When adequate data are available, statistical analysis is the preferred approach to demand analysis on the grounds of reliability and cost. Statistical analysis involves the following major steps:

1. Gather, adjust, and evaluate the data to be analyzed.
2. Fit a curve to the data.
3. Test and evaluate the fitted curve.

Gathering the Data

Economists commonly use two different types of data for demand estimation: *time-series* data and *cross-sectional* data.

Time-Series Data. **Time-series data** record historical changes in quantities demanded of a particular good or service and the timely corresponding changes in price, income, population, and other independent variables that affect demand. In a simple regression analysis, we deal with one independent variable at a time, while attempting to hold all others constant. Unfortunately, over a period of time the variable we are interested in may be significantly influenced by some other variable. For example, monetary quantities such as prices, sales, costs, and incomes are always distorted over time by the changing value of the dollar because of inflation. Also, the quantities demanded are affected by the growth in population. Whenever we want to determine the effect of a single variable over a period of time, we must hold all other variables constant. Thus, in any study using time-series data, it is necessary to adjust the data to eliminate the effects of population growth and monetary inflation before attempting a regression analysis.

Population Adjustment. To neutralize the effects of population variation on product sales, aggregate income and demand quantities are adjusted to a per capita basis. This transformation is usually made, however, only when the data cover a long period of time, since population does not usually show sharp fluctuations from year to year. If the product being analyzed is a family-type good, such as an automobile or washing machine, a better demand estimate is often obtained by adjusting the relevant data to a per household or per family basis.

Deflation Adjustment. Over a number of years, the steady decrease in the purchasing power of money is reflected in rising prices. This makes it impossible to make valid comparisons of nominal dollar amounts of different time periods. That is to say, $100 in 1990 is definitely *not* equivalent to $100 in 1970.

The solution to this problem is to divide all nominal dollar amounts by an appropriate price index. The Consumer Price Index (CPI) is the index most commonly used in consumer demand studies. The CPI reflects the weighted average of prices paid by consumers for selected goods and services, relative to a previous base period. When the nominal dollars for each particular time period are divided by the CPI for that time period and multiplied by 100, this converts the time series from nominal dollars to "constant dollars" of the base period, which has a CPI equal to 100. For example, the May 1989 CPI on the base year 1967 was 370.8. This means that $1,000 in May 1989 was worth only $269.69 [$1,000 (100.0/370.8) = $269.69] in 1967 dollars. Or we could say that it took $370.80 to buy in May 1989 what $100.00 would have bought in 1967.

Other Adjustments. In addition to population and deflation adjustments in time-series data, other adjustments are sometimes made, such as the removal of trend, seasonal, and cyclical influences. Methods for making these adjustments are briefly discussed in Chapter 9.

Cross-Sectional Data. Time-series analysis is conducted to determine how a single variable changes over time. In contrast, **cross-sectional analysis** is concerned with differences in a variable or set of variables among a number of entities at some particular time.[1] For example, in order to measure the effect of income upon demand for a product, the variable could be sales of the product during the month of May 19*xx* and the entities could be income groups. Or the variable might be production of a particular product during the year 19*xx* and the entities could be firms in the industry that produces the product.

The choice between the time-series approach and the cross-sectional approach often depends upon the data already available and consideration of time and expense limitations. For these reasons, the time-series method is perhaps more commonly used in demand studies—the data being already available from published sources.

Fitting a Curve to the Data

In curve fitting, observed data are used to estimate the parameters of a selected demand function. This demand function can then be used to predict the value of the dependent variable when any value(s) of the independent variable(s) are given. There are two fundamental questions in curve fitting:

1. What sort of equation should be used?
2. How well does the curve fit and how well does the estimated function predict demand?

With respect to the first question, the choice of an equation to be fitted to the data will depend upon two considerations: (1) the number of independent variables involved and (2) the distribution of the data, that is, is the distribution linear or nonlinear?

---

[1] The time chosen could be a particular day, week, month, or year, depending upon the nature of the study. However, it would have to be a period short enough to avoid significant changes in economic variables.

If the trend of observed values of the dependent variable is approximately linear and there are multiple independent variables, then the estimating equation will be of the form

$$\hat{Q} = b_0 + b_1X_1 + b_2X_2 + \ldots + b_kX_k \tag{1}$$

where

$\hat{Q}$ = Estimated demand for the commodity under investigation
X_i = Quantity of the ith independent variable, $i = 1, 2, \ldots k$
b_0 = The constant term
b_i = Parameters or coefficients of the ith independent variable.

Mathematically, this equation describes the hyperplane[2] of *multiple regression* (to be discussed in the next chapter). If the data can be reduced to a single independent variable (such as price) and the trend of the dependent variable is approximately linear, then a **simple regression analysis** can be used to fit the equation of a line whose general form is

$$Q_x = a + bP_x \tag{2}$$

where

Q_x = The quantity of commodity X demanded per time period (the dependent variable)
P_x = Price per unit of commodity X (the independent variable)
a = The constant parameter (which is the Y-intercept on a graph of the function)
b = The regression parameter or regression coefficient for P_x (which is the slope of the line on a graph of the function).

If the trend of the dependent variable follows the nonlinear curve of a power function with a single independent variable, its general form will be

$$Q_x = aP_x^b. \tag{3}$$

This may be rewritten in its logarithmic form by taking the common logarithms of both sides of Equation 3:

$$\log Q_x = \log a + b \log P_X. \tag{4}$$

The logarithmic function is linear, and it can be estimated by simple regression analysis.

Simple Linear Regression

Most regression work today is done on computers by means of packaged regression programs. Simple regression analysis also can be done quickly and easily on many inexpensive hand-held electronic calculators, some of which have built-in regression

---

[2] A linear function fitted to two variables is called a *straight line*. If fitted to three variables, it is called a *plane*. If fitted to four or more variables, it is called a *hyperplane*.

EXHIBIT 7–1   **A Set of Observed Data Points in a Time Series**

Time Period	Observed X	Observed Y
1	12	47
2	10	38
3	15	55
4	14	49
5	19	60
6	17	56
7	20	66
8	25	80

programs. Still, even when these electronic tools are used, there is a need for routine analysis of the data before performing the linear regression plus a need for routine analysis and evaluation of the results. The problem should, therefore, be approached step by step as outlined next.

Step 1. Gather the data.   Before any method can be applied, we must gather the data to be used in the demand analysis. To demonstrate the analytic procedure, suppose that we have gathered the time-series data shown in Exhibit 7–1.[3] Our objective is to fit a regression line to these data.

Step 2. Plot the variables over time.   Plotting the variables over time, as illustrated in Exhibit 7–2, is necessary for two reasons: (1) a visual comparison of their fluctuations will uncover any leads and lags between the variables and a consequent need for adjustment and (2) the underlying trend will be revealed as linear or nonlinear so that an appropriate model for fitting a curve to the data may be chosen. A visual inspection of Exhibit 7–2 reveals the following:

1. There is a direct relationship between X and Y; that is, when X rises, Y rises, but when X falls, Y falls.
2. There is no apparent lead–lag relationship between the variables. If a lead–lag relationship were discovered, then the data could be adjusted by moving one series or the other forward or backward through time until the lead–lag relationship disappears.

---

[3] One of the first problems in performing studies of this sort is finding good sources of data. We are fortunate in the United States that many government agencies and private institutions publish data required for this type of demand analysis. These publications are usually available in college and public libraries. The *Statistical Abstract of the United States* is a good first source to consult, since it abstracts from many other sources and gives specific references to other publications that may also be of assistance. Other periodicals containing fairly extensive economic statistics are:
  1. *Economic Report to the President*, published annually by the Council of Economic Advisers.
  2. *Survey of Current Business* (monthly) and *Business Statistics* (biennially) published by the U.S. Dept. of Commerce.
  3. *Agricultural Statistics* (published yearly by the U.S. Dept. of Agriculture), an extremely useful general source for data relating to agriculture and the marketing of agricultural products.

EXHIBIT 7–2   Plotting the Variables over Time

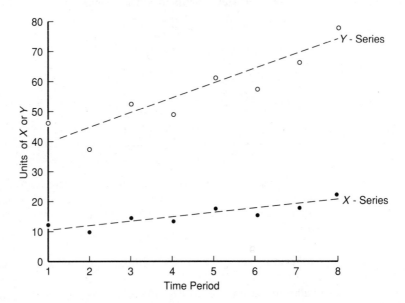

3. The underlying trend of each series appears to be linear, as indicated by the dotted line drawn through each series.

This information gives us a background for plotting the scatter diagram.

Step 3. Plot the scatter diagram.   The data base for a simple linear regression will be the set of ordered pairs, (X, Y), that are the observed values of X and Y per time period. If we hypothesize that the true underlying function, $Y = f(X)$, is linear, we must first determine whether or not that hypothesis is correct. In order to do this, we plot the data on a scatter diagram, as shown in Exhibit 7–3.

Since it was determined in the previous step that there was no lead or lag relationship between the variables, we can plot each year's Y-value against the same year's X-value, without having to shift one of the series forward or backward. Also, we have decided that the underlying trend of each series is linear. Therefore, the scatter diagram can be plotted on ordinary arithmetic scales. On the other hand, if the trends of the variables were approximately geometric, they could be plotted on logarithmic scales in order to express them more simply as linear relationships.

Exhibit 7–3 shows that $\overline{X}$ (read X-bar), the mean value of X, equals 16.5, and $\overline{Y}$ (read Y-bar), the mean value of Y, equals 56.375. The time period of each observation is also noted in the exhibit. Visual inspection confirms that the underlying function may be linear, as shown by the dotted line. Also plotted is the point of means, $(\overline{X}, \overline{Y})$.

It can be shown mathematically that the true regression line, which is based on the entire population of possible observations, must pass through the point of means.

EXHIBIT 7–3   Scatter Diagram of Observed Data Points

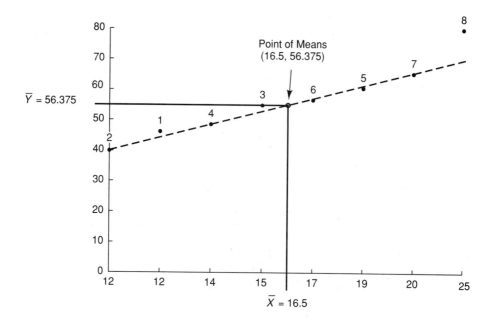

Our calculated regression line is based upon a sample of observations taken from the population of possible observations. The regression line that we fit to this sample is only an estimate of the true regression line, but it, too, will pass through the point of means.

Step 4. Estimate the regression line.   We shall use the least-squares method of regression analysis to fit a straight line to the data such that the sum of the squared deviations between the calculated and observed values of Y is minimized. If a straight line is drawn through the scatter of observed data points, some of the observed points will lie above the line, some will lie below, and perhaps some will lie upon the regression line. The vertical distances between locations of the observed data points and the fitted line are called **deviations** or **residuals**. The concept is illustrated by Exhibit 7–4 (page 186).

In order to estimate the true regression line, $Y_i = \alpha + \beta X_i$, the parameters a and b must be calculated for the estimated regression line:

$$\hat{Y}_i = a + bX_i \tag{5}$$

where

$X_i =$ the ith value of the independent variable
$\hat{Y}_i =$ the ith value of the dependent variable
$a =$ the Y-intercept of the regression line
$b =$ the slope of the regression line.

Differential calculus can be used to obtain equations for the regression coefficients or parameters a and b of the regression equation. Several equivalent versions of these

EXHIBIT 7–4   Typical Regression Line with Residuals

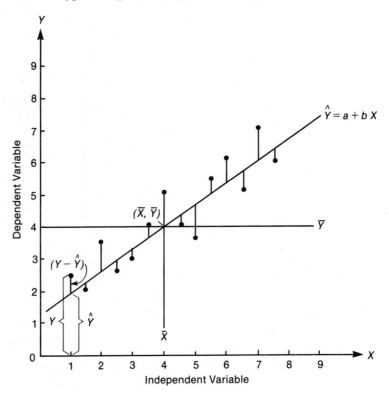

equations have been worked out. One version that is easy to use in manual calculation is the following,[4] in which n is the number of observed points:

$$b = \frac{n \sum X_i Y_i - \sum X_i \sum Y_i}{n \sum X_i^2 - (\sum X_i)^2} \tag{6}$$

and

$$a = \frac{\sum Y_i - b \sum X_i}{n}. \tag{7}$$

If we let $\overline{X}$ (read X-bar) denote the mean value of the independent variable X, and let $\overline{Y}$ (read Y-bar) denote the mean value of the dependent variable Y, then $\sum X_i = n\overline{X}$ and $\sum Y_i = n\overline{Y}$. Hence, Equation 6 can be rewritten as

$$b = \frac{n \sum X_i Y_i - \sum X_i \sum Y_i}{n \sum X_i^2 - (\sum X_i)^2} = \frac{n \sum X_i Y_i - n\overline{X}n\overline{Y}}{n \sum X_1^2 - (n\overline{X})^2} = \frac{n(\sum X_i Y_i - n\overline{XY})}{n(\sum X_i^2 - n\overline{X^2})}$$

---

[4] See a standard text on statistics for the derivation of Equations 6 and 7.

EXHIBIT 7–5   Sums Required by Least-Squares Method of Simple Linear Regression

Time Period	Observed X	Observed Y	XY	X^2	Y^2
1	12	47	564	144	2,209
2	10	38	380	100	1,444
3	15	55	825	225	3,025
4	14	49	686	196	2,401
5	19	60	1,140	361	3,600
6	17	56	952	289	3,136
7	20	66	1,320	400	4,356
8	25	80	2,000	625	6,400
Sums	132	451	7,867	2,340	26,571
Means	16.5	56.375			

$$= \frac{\sum X_i Y_i - n\overline{X}\,\overline{Y}}{\sum X_i^2 - n\overline{X}^2} \tag{8}$$

and Equation 7 can be rewritten as

$$a = \frac{\sum Y_i - b \sum X_i}{n} = \frac{\sum Y_i}{n} - \frac{b \sum X_i}{n} = \overline{Y} - b\overline{X}. \tag{9}$$

In order to calculate the regression line, we must first calculate the sums of X, Y, XY, and X^2. For later use in evaluating the regression equation, we shall also calculate the sum of Y^2, as shown on Exhibit 7–5. By Equation 6,

$$b = \frac{n \sum X_i Y_i - \sum X_i \sum Y_i}{n \sum X_i^2 - (\sum X_i^2)} = \frac{8(7,867) - (132)(451)}{8(2,340) - (132)^2} = \frac{3,404}{1,296}$$

$$= 2.6265.$$

Or by Equation 8,

$$b = \frac{\sum X_i Y_i - n\overline{X}\,\overline{Y}}{\sum X_i^2 - n\overline{X}^2} = \frac{7,867 - 8(16.5)(56.375)}{2,340 - 8(16.5)^2} = \frac{425.5}{162}$$

$$= 2.6265.$$

By Equation 7,

$$a = \frac{\sum Y_i - b \sum X_i}{n} = \frac{451 - 2.62654321(132)}{8} = 13.0370$$

Or by Equation 9,

$$a = \overline{Y} - b\overline{x} = 56.375 - 2.62654321(16.5) = 13.0370$$

Keeping in mind that the regression equation is only an estimate of the true regression, we round off a and b to avoid the impression of a degree of accuracy that does not really exist, and write the estimated regression equation as

$$\hat{Y}_i = 13 + 2.6X_i$$

EXHIBIT 7-6   Typical Computer Printout of Regression Analysis

```
-------------------- REGRESSION ANALYSIS ----------------------
HEADER DATA FOR: A:SEO    LABEL:
NUMBER OF CASES: 8    NUMBER OF VARIABLES: 2
----------------------------------------------------------------
INDEX       NAME              MEAN         STD.DEV.
   1          X              16.5000         4.8107
DEP. VAR.: y                 56.3750        12.7944
----------------------------------------------------------------
DEPENDENT VARIABLE: y
VAR.   REGRESSION COEFFICIENT    STD. ERROR   T(DF=  6)    PROB.
X               2.6265              .1706      15.398     .00000
CONSTANT       13.0370
STD. ERROR of EST. = 2.1711
r SQUARED = .9753
r = .9876


ANALYSIS OF VARIANCE TABLE
SOURCE        SUM OF SQUARES    D.F.   MEAN SQUARE   F RATIO PROB.
REGRESSION       1117.5941       1      1117.5941    237.106 4.742E-06
RESIDUAL           28.2809       6         4.7135
TOTAL            1145.8750       7
```

As illustrated above, the estimated regression equation can be obtained by manual calculation with the aid of a hand-held calculator. If a computer is available with a linear regression program, it is much easier and faster, of course, to use the computer to obtain not only the regression equation, but also other statistics which are used to evaluate the regression analysis. Exhibit 7–6 shows a computer solution to our example, using Microstat™ software.

The computer printout shown in Exhibit 7–6 begins with header data to identify the ensuing output and then states the number of cases (observations) and the number of variables that were input.[5] The next entry shows the names of the variables and the mean and standard deviation of their distributions (as input), and identifies the dependent variable. The next entry shows the regression coefficient for X, which is the b parameter in the estimated regression equation $\hat{Y}_i = a + bX_i$, and for the regression constant, a. Note that the values of these parameters agree with the manual calculation we previously performed.

The remainder of the printout is used in the evaluation of the regression analysis, as explained next.

Step 5. Compare calculated and actual values. How close are the calculated values of the dependent variable to the actual values? In other words, how well does our estimated

---

[5] The same computer program is used for either simple or multiple regression.

EXHIBIT 7–7   Observed and Calculated Values of $Y = f(X)$

Input X	Observed Y	Calculated $\hat{Y} = 13 + 2.6X$	Deviation
10	38	39.0	+1.0
12	47	44.2	−2.8
14	49	49.4	+0.4
15	55	52.0	−3.0
17	56	57.2	+1.2
19	60	62.4	+2.4
20	66	65.0	−1.0
25	80	78.0	−2.0

regression equation predict Y as a function of X? A visual answer to this question is obtained by first using the regression equation to calculate $\hat{Y}_i = 13 + 2.6X_i$ for each observation, and then comparing the actual Y_i and calculated Y_i values, as shown in Exhibit 7–7. Some computer programs will do this for you, either automatically or upon request.

The deviation of the observed Y values from the calculated $\hat{Y}$ values in this exhibit is a reflection of the fact that all of the observations did not fall on the regression line. For if they had, the variation in Y would be completely explained or accounted for by the variations in X, and all Y_i would equal $\hat{Y}_i$. The fact that the observations depart from the regression line indicates that forces other than X affect the value of Y.

Interpretation of the Parameters

The parameter a is a constant term that establishes the Y-intercept of the line when the function is graphed. It usually has no strict economic meaning in the demand equation $\hat{Q} = a + bP$ because it is unlikely that $P = 0$ will ever be within the range of observed data. Whether or not it has meaning in other functions will depend upon whether or not zero is within the range of observed values of the independent variable.

The parameter b is the slope of the regression line. It represents the marginal contribution of each unit of the independent variable to the value of the dependent variable. For example, in the regression equation $\hat{Y}_i = 13 + 2.6X_i$, each 1-unit increment of the independent variable X will change the value of the dependent variable Y by 2.6 units. The plus sign of the parameter b indicates that the variables move in the same direction, that is, up or down together.

Evaluating the Regression Equation

The primary purpose of linear-regression analysis is to establish a linear equation that can be used to predict the value of the dependent variable, Y, for any given value of the independent variable, X. The question then immediately arises: How meaningful or accurate is the predicted $\hat{Y}$?

For a simple regression analysis, two statistical measures are used to answer this question: (1) the standard error of estimate, S_e, and (2) the coefficient of determination, r^2, and its square root, r, which is called the coefficient of correlation.

The Standard Error of the Estimate. The standard error of the estimate, S_e, is simply the standard deviation of the normal probability distribution of the residuals, or deviations, of the observed data points from the estimated regression line. That is to say, S_e measures the spread of the possible observed values of Y in a normal distribution about the estimated $\hat{Y}$ for any given value of X. Therefore, the standard error of the estimate indicates the range within which Y can be predicted by the estimated regression equation with varying degrees of statistical confidence. It is calculated as

$$S_e = \sqrt{\frac{\sum (Y_i - \hat{Y}_i)^2}{n - k - 1}} \tag{10}$$

where

$$
\begin{aligned}
S_e &= \text{standard error of the estimate of the regression equation}^6 \\
Y_i &= \text{an observed } Y\text{-value at } X_i \\
\hat{Y}_i &= \text{calculated } Y\text{-value at } X_i \\
n &= \text{number of observations} \\
k &= \text{number of independent variables} \\
n - k - 1 &= \text{degrees of freedom.}^7
\end{aligned}
$$

Equation 10 says that the standard error of the estimate is the square root of the mean sum of the squared deviations or residuals. (The mean sum of the squared deviations is the sum of the squared deviations divided by $n - k - 1$ degrees of freedom.) In Exhibit 7–6, the standard error of the estimate is shown as 2.1711. The sum of the squared residuals is shown in the figure's Analysis of Variance Table as 28.2809 and the degrees of freedom (d.f.) are shown as 6. Thus

$$S_e = \sqrt{\frac{28.2809}{6}} = 2.1711,$$

as stated on the printout.

If $S_e = 0$, the estimating equation is a perfect fit; that is, all the observed points lie upon the regression line and there is no scatter around it. But if $S_e \neq 0$, then at least some of the observed points will lie above or below the regression line. The larger the standard error of the estimate, the wider will be the spread of the deviations. Therefore, the smaller the standard error of the estimate, the more reliable will be the estimates of Y that are calculated by the estimated regression equation for any given value of X.

---

[6] The symbol S_e indicates that we are talking about the standard deviation of a sample taken from a population of residuals whose standard deviation is σ_m. The notation may be made more specific by indicating the dependent and independent variables, in that order, as subscripts. For example, S_{Q*P} indicates the sampling distribution of residuals of Q as a function of P. This enables a distinction between the standard error, which refers to deviations from the regression line, and the standard deviations of the sample data from their mean values, which would be designated as S_P and S_Q.

[7] The term *degrees of freedom* refers to the fact that if we know n-1 terms of a sum, the nth term is automatically determined. To calculate the standard error of the estimate for a univariate function, we lose two degrees of freedom because the Y-value requires the parameters α and β, which are estimated by a and b in the regression equation $\hat{Y}_i = a + bX_i$. It should be noted also that there is a different t-distribution for each different degree of freedom.

As in any normal distribution, 95 percent of the possible values of Y can be expected to fall within ± 1.96 standard errors from the estimated $\hat{Y}$, and 99 percent can be expected to fall within ± 2.58 standard errors. In the case of our example, there is a 95 percent probability that an observed Y will fall within the range $\hat{Y} \pm (1.96)(2.1711) = \hat{Y} \pm 4.2554$; and there is a 99 percent probability that an observed Y will fall within the range $\hat{Y} \pm (2.58)(2.1711) = \hat{Y} \pm 5.6014$.

Standard Error of the Regression Coefficient

The standard error of the regression coefficient, S_b, measures the standard deviation of the distribution of the regression coefficient, b. It thus provides a measure of the reliability of the regression coefficient. It is calculated as

$$S_b = \frac{S_e}{\sqrt{\sum (X - \overline{X})^2}}. \tag{11}$$

Exhibit 7–6 shows the standard error of the regression coefficient on the same line as the regression coefficient, with a value of 0.1706. Following the standard error on the same line is the t-test ratio, which is calculated as the regression coefficient divided by the standard error of the regression coefficient. The t-test statistic is used to test the regression coefficient for statistical significance, as explained in the next chapter.

Coefficient of Determination, r^2

The coefficient of determination, r^2, is the statistic that tells how well the regression model explains variation in the dependent variable.[8] It is a test of the goodness of the fit of the regression line to the observed data, conceived in terms of explaining or accounting for the variation in the dependent variable.

The computer printout in Exhibit 7–6 shows "r SQUARED = .9753." This indicates that about 97.5 percent of the variation in the dependent variable, Y, is explained by variation in the independent variable, X. Values of r^2 can range from 0.0 to 1.0, or 0 to 100 percent. A magnitude of 0.0 indicates no relationship between the variables. A magnitude of 1.0 means that the regression line is a perfect fit, with all variation in Y explained by variation in X. That is to say, all observed points lie upon the regression line. This rarely, if ever, happens.

The coefficient of determination does *not* indicate cause and effect. It is merely a mathematical relationship between the dependent and independent variables that indicates the degree to which the two variables move together, although economic theory *may* postulate a cause-and-effect relationship.

The statistical concept of the coefficient of determination is illustrated by Exhibit 7–8. In the exhibit, $\overline{Y}$ is the mean of all observed Y-values on which the regression line is

---

[8] For a simple linear regression, the coefficient of determination is designated r^2. In multiple regression, the symbol R^2 is used for the coefficient of determination. In either case, the coefficient of determination indicates the proportion of variation in the dependent variable that is explained by the full set of independent variables included in the regression, acting together.

EXHIBIT 7–8   Explained, Unexplained, and Total Deviation

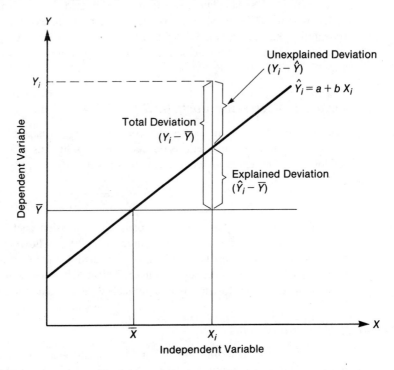

based, and (X_i, Y_i) is a particular observation. If $\overline{Y}$ were used to estimate Y_i, the *total deviation* would be $Y_i - \overline{Y}$. However, we can get a better estimate by using the regression line to estimate the Y-value. In so doing, we divide the total deviation $(Y_i - \overline{Y})$ into two parts. The deviation of the lower part, $(\hat{Y}_i - \overline{Y})$, is explained by the regression equation. The deviation of the upper part, $(Y_i - \hat{Y}_i)$, is not explained.

In a similar way, we can divide the total squared variation $\sum(Y_i - \overline{Y})^2$ into two parts, so that[9]

$$\sum(Y_i - \overline{Y})^2 = \sum(\hat{Y}_i - \overline{Y})^2 + \sum(Y_i - \hat{Y}_i)^2.$$

$$\underset{\text{variation}}{\text{Total}} = \underset{\text{variation}}{\text{Explained}} + \underset{\text{variation}}{\text{Unexplained}}$$

(12)

Hence

$$r^2 = \frac{\text{Explained variation}}{\text{Total variation}} = \frac{\sum(\hat{Y}_i - \overline{Y})^2}{\sum(Y_i - \overline{Y})^2},$$

(13)

---

[9] Some textbooks and computer programs use the terminology: "Total sum of squares = Regression sum of squares + Error sum of squares" or $SST = SSR + SSE$.

which is equivalent to

$$r^2 = 1 - \frac{\text{Unexplained variation}}{\text{Total variation}} = 1 - \frac{\sum (Y_i - \hat{Y}_i)^2}{\sum (Y_i - \overline{Y})^2}. \tag{14}$$

The form of Equation 14 leads to the following formula:

$$r^2 = 1 - \frac{\sum (Y_i - \hat{Y}_i)^2}{\sum Y_i^2 - [(\sum Y_i)^2/n]}. \tag{15}$$

The coefficient of determination can also be computed by the formula

$$r^2 = 1 - \left(\frac{S_e}{S_Y}\right)^2 \tag{16}$$

where

$$S_e = \text{the standard error of the estimate}$$
$$S_Y = \text{the standard error of the dependent variable.}$$

Both of these numbers are on the computer printout. Thus

$$r^2 = 1 - \left(\frac{S_e}{S_Y}\right)^2 = 1 - \left(\frac{2.1711}{12.7944}\right)^2 = 1 - 0.02879518 = 0.9712.$$

Coefficient of Correlation.   The square root of the coefficient of determination, r^2, is the coefficient of correlation, r, which is a measure of the degree of association between the variables. Since r^2 may range from 0 to 1, r will range from -1 to $+1$. In our example, $r = \sqrt{0.9753} = 0.9876$, as shown on the computer printout.

The *sign* of r indicates the relative direction of movement between the two variables. Since it may be either plus or minus, it must be chosen by the analyst to agree with the positive or negative slope of the regression line.

The *magnitude* of r indicates the degree of association between the variables. In our example, a very strong direct relationship is indicated between the independent variable X and the dependent variable Y.

Illustrative Problem

The chief of police of a certain city hypothesized a linear relationship between police coverage and accidents on the city's freeways. The city has compiled the following data for the past 12 months:

Police coverage in hundreds of labor hours per month	Number of accidents per month
64	625
53	750
67	560
52	690
82	515
59	680
67	630
90	510
50	800
77	550
88	550
71	525

Questions:

a. Calculate the hypothesized regression equation.
b. Calculate the standard error of the estimate, S_e.
c. Calculate the coefficient of determination, r^2.
d. According to the regression equation, how many labor hours of police coverage would be needed to reduce accidents to 500 per month?

Solutions:

a. Let X = labor hours of police coverage
   Y = number of accidents

X	Y	XY	X^2	Y^2
64	625	40,000	4,096	390,625
53	750	39,750	2,809	562,500
67	560	37,520	4,489	313,600
52	690	35,880	2,704	476,100
82	515	42,230	6,724	265,225
59	680	40,120	3,481	462,400
67	630	42,210	4,489	396,900
90	510	45,900	8,100	260,100
50	800	40,000	2.500	640,000
77	550	42,350	5,929	302,500
88	550	48,400	7,744	302,500
71	525	37,275	5,041	275,625
$\Sigma X =$ 820	$\Sigma Y =$ 7,385	$\Sigma XY =$ 491,635	$\Sigma X^2 =$ 58,106	$\Sigma Y^2 =$ 4,648,075

From Equation 6,

$$b = \frac{n \sum XY - \sum X \sum Y}{n \sum X^2 - (\sum X)^2} = \frac{(12)(491,635) - (820)(7,385)}{(12)(58,106) - (820)^2} = \frac{-156,080}{24,872}$$

$$\approx -6.27533.$$

From Equation 7,

$$a = \frac{\sum Y - b \sum X}{n} = \frac{7,385 - 6.275329688(820)}{12} = \frac{12,530.77034}{12}$$

$$\approx 1,044.231.$$

Hence, $\hat{Y} = 1,044 - 6.3X$.

b. Using the estimated regression $\hat{Y} = 1,044 - 6.3X$, we obtain the sum of the squared deviations:

X	Y	$\hat{Y}$	$(Y - \hat{Y})$	$(Y - \hat{Y})^2$
64	625	640.8	−15.8	249.64
53	750	710.1	39.9	1,592.01
67	560	621.9	−61.9	3,831.61
52	690	716.4	−26.4	696.96
82	515	527.4	−12.4	153.76
59	680	672.3	7.7	59.29
67	630	621.9	8.1	65.61
90	510	477.0	33	1,089.00
50	800	729.0	71	5.041.00
77	550	558.9	−8.9	79.21
88	550	489.6	60.4	3,648.16
71	525	596.7	−71.7	5,140.89

$$\Sigma(Y - \hat{Y})^2 = 21,647.14$$

By Equation 10,

$$S_e = \sqrt{\frac{\sum (Y_i - \hat{Y}_i)^2}{n - k - 1}} = \sqrt{\frac{21,647.14}{12 - 1 - 1}} = 46.53.$$

c. By Equation 15,

$$r^2 = 1 - \frac{\sum (Y_i - \hat{Y}_i)^2}{\sum Y_i^2 - [(\sum Y_i)^2/n]} = 1 - \frac{21,647.14}{4,648,075 - [(7,385)^2/12]}$$

$$= 0.7907 \approx 79.0\%.$$

This manual calculation is confirmed by the following computer printout:

```
--------------------- REGRESSION ANALYSIS ---------------------
HEADER DATA FOR: A:POLICE     LABEL:
NUMBER OF CASES: 12    NUMBER OF VARIABLES: 2
---------------------------------------------------------------
INDEX         NAME                 MEAN          STD.DEV.
1             laborhour            68.3333       13.7268
DEP. VAR.:    accident             615.4167      96.8705
---------------------------------------------------------------
```

```
DEPENDENT VARIABLE: accident
VAR.   REGRESSION COEFFICIENT      STD. ERROR    T(DF=  10)      PROB.
laborhour          -6.2753             1.0209       -6.147       .00011
CONSTANT         1044.2309
STD. ERROR OF EST. = 46.4777
r SQUARED = .7907
r = -.8892
ANALYSIS OF VARIANCE TABLE
SOURCE        SUM OF SQUARES    D.F.    MEAN SQUARE    F RATIO PROB.
REGRESSION       81621.1215      1       81621.1215     37.784 1.088E-04
RESIDUAL         21601.7952     10        2160.1795
TOTAL           103222.9167     11
```

d. $1044 - 6.3X = 500$

$6.3X = 544$

$X = 86.349$ hundreds of labor hours $\approx 8,635$ labor hours.

Testing the Basic Assumption

As previously shown, there is a residual or deviation between the estimated and observed values of the dependent variable, Y, for most values of the independent variable, X. Regression analysis assumes that the residuals for any given value of X constitute a random sample from an unknown population of residuals. Regression analysis makes three basic assumptions about the distribution of residuals related to each value of X:

1. Their distribution is *normal*.
2. They are *randomly* distributed about a mean value of zero.
3. Each distribution has the *same variance and standard deviation*. This assumption is necessary for a standard error of estimate that is the same for all values of X. If this assumption is not true, then the standard error at one point on the regression line would be different from the standard error at another point.

If any of these assumptions is violated, the validity of the regression analysis is questionable. We will discuss such problems in more detail in the next chapter, although we cannot go deeply into this complex part of econometrics. For detailed coverage of this topic, the student may consult any standard text on econometrics.

For our purposes in this chapter, a simple graphic method can be used to get some idea of whether or not the stated assumptions are being met in a particular study. Exhibit 7–9 shows a plot of residuals for a case in which the assumptions are being met, with the X-axis representing the regression line. When the residuals are plotted in their order of occurrence, there is no apparent pattern. That is, they seem to be randomly distributed about the regression line.

EXHIBIT 7–9 **Deviations from a Regression Equation Showing a Random Pattern**

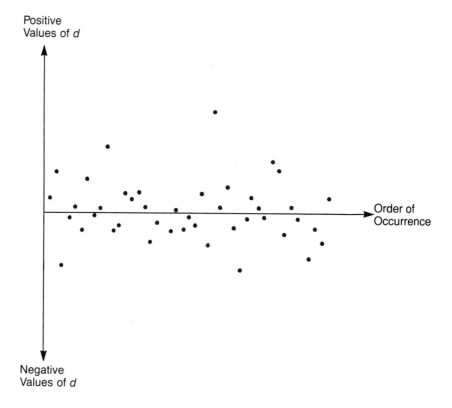

Exhibit 7–10 shows deviations for a case where the assumptions are not being met. It is a plot of residuals taken from a study of beef consumption over the years 1965 through 1979. In this example, the deviations follow a pattern of negative deviations in the earlier years, positive deviations in the middle years, and negative deviations in the later years. This pattern indicates the existence of trends in the variables and serves as a warning to the analyst that it might be better to work with "detrended" data.[10]

Market Research Approach to Demand Estimation

When sufficient reliable demand data for statistical analysis are not available, it first may be necessary to perform market research to obtain certain information directly from the consumer. Some of the reasons why direct approaches might be necessary or desirable are:

---

[10] There are several techniques for trend removal; some are discussed in Chapter 9. A very easy method is to use a multiple-regression model that has trend as one of the independent variables. Multiple regression is covered in the next chapter.

EXHIBIT 7–10 **Deviations from the Regression Equation in a Beef-Consumption Study**

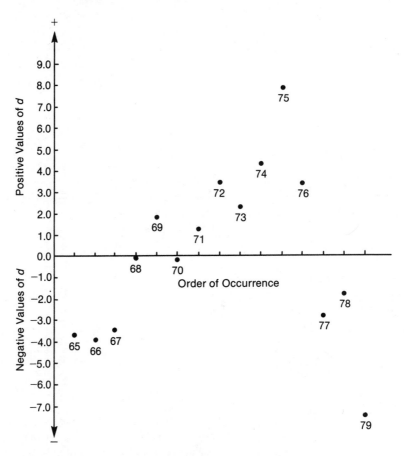

1. *A new product is being introduced:* A direct approach is necessary because no data exist for statistical analysis.
2. *Changes are suspected in qualitative variables, such as taste, preference, or consumer expectations:* Statistical data on variables such as price are analyzed on the assumption that such qualitative variables are constant. If they have changed, the statistical data are meaningless.
3. *Market experimentation is necessary:* In order to develop a pricing strategy, the firm needs to determine price elasticities in geographically separate markets.

This list is representative rather than exhaustive. Undoubtedly there are many other reasons why marketing managers would desire a direct approach to the consumer. The direct approaches most commonly discussed in the marketing literature are *consumer surveys, consumer clinics, and market experiments*.

Consumer Surveys

Consumer surveys are conducted by asking questions of a representative sample of present or potential buyers. Consumers are asked for their reactions to hypothetical changes in demand variables such as price, income, prices of other products, advertising expenditures, and other demand determinants. In theory, the analyst should be able to construct a demand relationship from consumers' responses to these questions. In practice, however, consumers may be either unable or unwilling to give accurate answers to such questions. For this reason, conclusions based on direct answers may be unreliable. Nevertheless, trained interviewers using properly designed questionnaires can gain useful information, indirectly, from the answers. For example, if people seem unaware of price differentials among competing goods, it may be a good indication of price inelasticity. The effectiveness of an advertising campaign may also be measured by the consumers' awareness of the ads.

Consumer surveys can be rather expensive, with survey costs being a function of sample size and the elaborateness of the analysis. However, they are essential for determination of at least one important demand variable, namely, consumer expectations (regarding future prices, inflation, income, and the availability of substitute goods), which can have a strong influence upon the demand function. The only way to find out what consumers expect is to ask them. Consumer interviews are also a good way to detect changes in tastes and preferences.

Consumer Clinics

Another method of observing consumer response to changes in demand variables is to conduct a controlled experiment called a **consumer clinic**. The participants in this experiment are given small amounts of money with which to buy certain items from the clinic. The clinic then manipulates demand variables such as product price or the price of competing goods. The consumers' reactions to these changes are observed and recorded.

The reliability of the data gained from such an experiment is often questioned on the grounds that participants know they are being watched, and therefore do not act naturally. In spite of such shortcomings, in some circumstances a consumer clinic can provide useful information about the demand for a product, particularly when the clinic is complemented by a consumer survey. For example, consumer clinics can detect differences in consumers' reactions in different geographical areas while avoiding the risks associated with market experiments (which are discussed next).

Market Experiments

Unlike the consumer clinic, which is conducted under laboratory conditions, a **market experiment** is performed under actual market conditions. The markets chosen for an experiment must be similar, yet segregated from one another. After the choice of markets has been made, the firm begins the experiment, varying one or more of the demand determinants in these markets and noting results. For example, the firm might charge different prices for the same product in different markets and compare results. With the help of demographic statistics developed by the U.S. Census Bureau, firms can perform experiments in several markets to determine how demand is affected by characteristics such as age, occupational classification, educational level, family size, and ethnic background.

Market experiments must be conducted on a scale sufficiently large to insure validity of the results, even though experimentation on a large scale is very expensive.

Market experiments can be quite risky. Consumers must be kept unaware that they are the subjects of an experiment lest they modify their behavior in response to being observed. Another risk: if customers are driven away by price increases or shifts in advertising emphasis, they may never come back.

If a controlled experiment is attempted, the cost goes even higher. If the experiment is not controlled, however, the firm is unable to distinguish the effects of experimental manipulation from those due to random disturbance factors such as strikes, bad weather, or unanticipated actions by competitors.

In spite of these problems, direct market experimentation can be quite useful. For example, if the firm is introducing a new product, no statistical data on it will exist. A market experiment may provide the best possible guidance for pricing the new product. A firm may also find market experiments useful for verifying the results of a statistical study before it commits itself to a particular marketing strategy.

Illustrative Example

Some years ago, researchers at the University of Florida chose Grand Rapids, Michigan, as the site for a market experiment to determine the effects of price competition on sales of three varieties of Valencia oranges.[11] One variety was from California, one from the Indian

---

EXHIBIT 7–11   Price Elasticities and Cross Elasticities of Three Varieties of Valencia Oranges

Variety Undergoing Price Change	Relative Change in Quantity Demanded		
	Florida Indian River	Florida Interior	California
Florida Indian River	**−3.07**	+1.56	+0.01
Florida Interior	+1.16	**−3.01**	+0.14
California	+0.18	+0.09	**−2.76**

---

[11] Reported by Marshal B. Godwin, W. Fred Chapman, Jr., and William T. Hanley in "Competition between Florida and California Valencia Oranges in the Fruit Market," Bulletin 704 (Gainesville, Fla.: Agricultural Experiment Stations, Institute of Food and Agricultural Services, University of Florida, in cooperation with the U.S. Dept. of Agriculture, Florida Citrus Commission, December 1965).

River district in Florida, and one from the interior district of Florida. The city of Grand Rapids was chosen as the site of the experiment because it was typical of midwestern markets in size, demographic characteristics, and economic base. Nine supermarkets located in various parts of the city participated in the experiment, which lasted 31 days.

Each day the price of each variety of orange was changed, and the quantity sold was recorded for each variety. The range of prices was 32 cents–16 cents above and below the going price when the study began. Recorded sales during the experiment exceeded 9,250 dozen oranges. Results of the study are summarized in the matrix of Exhibit 7–11. The **bold-face** entries in the exhibit show price elasticities; that is, the percent change in the quantity demanded of each variety as its own price changed. The remaining entries are cross elasticities of demand; that is, the percentage change in the quantity demanded of one variety when the price of another variety is changed by one percent. For example, Florida Indian River oranges (first column) have a price elasticity of −3.07, a cross elasticity of +1.16 with Florida-interior oranges, and a cross elasticity of +0.18 with California oranges.

The cross elasticities are particularly revealing. The two varieties of Florida oranges, with cross elasticities of +1.56 and +1.16, apparently are viewed by consumers as close substitutes. Consumers would readily switch from one to the other when prices changed. But California oranges seem to occupy a distinct market; that is, California and Florida oranges, with very low cross elasticities, were not viewed as close substitutes. This impression of two distinct markets is reinforced by the price elasticities in bold-face type. The Florida oranges are not only quite sensitive to price changes, but also exhibit almost the same price elasticity (−3.07 and −3.01). The California oranges were also highly price elastic at −2.76, but not as sensitive as the Florida fruit.

Two conditions were essential to the validity of this study. First, the time period was short enough to prevent changes in variables other than price, such as income, taste, population, and inflation. Second, experimenters were able to insure an adequate supply of each variety at each experimental price.

Summary

Demand estimation is an essential activity in any business concern. The method most often used for empirically measuring demand is linear regression. If the quantity demanded is considered to be a function of a single independent variable, then simple linear regression may be used. When two or more independent variables are involved, then multiple-regression analysis (to be discussed in the next chapter) is called for.

When adequate records are available, statistical analysis is the best method for demand measurement. The data base for statistical analysis may be one of two types:

1. *Time-series data*, which record movements of selected variables over a fairly long span of time. These data must be adjusted for population changes and inflation (or deflation) before they can be useful. It may also be necessary to remove trend, seasonal, and cyclical influences from them.

2. *Cross-sectional data*, which provide a snapshot of many variables at one particular point in time or during one particular time period. These data are not affected by changes in population or the real value of the dollar, but may require adjustment to get rid of other unwanted influences.

Finding an equation that explains the variation of the dependent variable in response to variation in the independent variable is accomplished by the least-squares method of curve fitting. This is best performed by a computer, but it can be performed manually with aid of a hand-held calculator. When a regression line is fitted to the data, the observed data points can be expected to lie above or below the line, and sometimes on it. The vertical distance between a data point and the line is called a deviation, or residual. Deviations exist because not all of a change in the dependent variable can be explained by a change in the independent variable. The least-squares method of fitting a regression line minimizes the sum of the squared deviations.

Regardless of the way it is obtained, a calculated regression line must be evaluated and tested for validity. Tests used for evaluation are:

1. The standard error of estimate
2. The coefficient of determination
3. The coefficient of correlation.

Of course, regression analysis cannot be performed unless an adequate statistical data base is available. If one is not available, then the consumer must be approached directly. Direct approaches may take the form of:

1. *Consumer surveys*, in which consumers are asked for their reactions to hypothetical changes in price, income, prices of other products, advertising, and other determinants of demand.
2. *Consumer clinics*, in which demand variables are manipulated and resulting consumer reactions are observed under controlled laboratory conditions.
3. *Market experiments*, in which prices or other variables are manipulated in single or multiple markets and resulting consumer reactions are observed.

Problems

1. Explain why a scatter diagram is an important first step in analyzing the relationship between dependent and independent variables.

2. Before generally introducing their product to the U. S. market, the French manufacturers of a new food processor conducted a market experiment in five American cities, with the following results:

City	Price	Unit Sales
Cincinnati, Ohio	$30	152
Memphis, Tennessee	35	142
St. Louis, Missouri	40	137
Kansas City, Missouri	45	125
Dallas, Texas	50	122

Data for Problem 4

Year	Company Sales ($millions)	Disposable Personal Income ($billions)	Population (millions)	Consumer Price Index
1983	$ 83.6	$1,551.2	222.6	195.4
1984	101.2	1,729.3	225.1	217.4
1985	111.1	1.918.0	227.8	246.8
1986	126.5	2,127.6	230.1	272.4
1987	143.0	2,261.4	232.5	289.1
1988	162.8	2.428.1	234.8	298.4
1989	212.3	2,670.6	237.0	311.1
1990	224.4	2,828.0	239.3	322.2

a. Assume that these five cities are typical of the American market. Use linear regression to find the demand function and estimate unit sales at a price of $47.50.

b. What is the price elasticity of demand at a price of $50?

c. What price will maximize total revenue?

3. The results of an empirical demand study are:

Regression equation: $\hat{Y} = 20 + 4X$

Mean values: $\overline{X} = 5$, $\overline{Y} = 40$

Standard error of the estimate: $S_e = 3.0$

Standard deviation of Y: $S_Y = 6.8$

Number of data points: $n = 60$.

a. Construct a scatter diagram of the data points as you imagine it might be.

b. What demand variable might X represent? Explain briefly.

c. Calculate r^2.

4. The Road Ranger Manufacturing Company makes conversion kits to transform ordinary pickups into recreational vehicles for camping. The company's management believes that sales of recreational vehicles are closely related to disposable income of the nation. The data shown above have been gleaned from the company's records and the *1987 Statistical Abstract of the United States*.

a. Make appropriate adjustments to the sales and income data.

b. Plot the variables over time. Are there any leads and lags in the data? What are the underlying trends?

c. Plot the scatter diagram.

d. Estimate the regression equation.

e. Plot the actual and calculated values of sales.

5. Given the three sets of data shown below:

Data for Problem 5

	A		B		C
Price P	Units Sold Q	Daily Average Temperature T	Admissions to Municipal Swimming Pool A	Number of Employees X	Monthly Contributions to IRA Accounts ($000) Y
$2.40	12,000	80.3	340	650	$ 82.8
3.13	5,700	69.4	210	100	5.0
2.65	8,000	83.1	410	520	59.3
3.03	6,400	85.7	480	960	148.7
2.52	8,900	82.3	400	210	15.2
2.43	11,300	79.8	320	740	100.6
3.74	4,800	76.4	280	140	8.3
2.60	9,000	73.7	250	360	34.0
2.62	9,300	80.6	330	1,050	110.1

a. Plot a scatter diagram for each of the three sets of data. What sort of curve seems to fit each set?

b. Using the least-squares method, calculate the regression equation for data set A and show that the calculated line passes through the point of means. CAUTION: Do not round off any numbers until you have completed the exercise.

c. Repeat part b for data set B.

6. A professor, hoping to encourage students to continue in higher education, assigned them to study the relationship between income and education. His students discovered the following data at the university library:

Average Number of Years of Education X	Average Annual Income ($000) Y
4	$12
5	14
6	16
7	18
8	22
10	24
12	30
14	42
15	60
17	80
20	90

a. Determine the regression equation.

b. What percentage of the variation of annual income is explained by the average number of years of education?

c. Critically evaluate the relationship between income and years of education. Can you suggest any other variables that should be included?

7. The sales manager of a large furniture store is attempting to measure the effectiveness of a newspaper advertising campaign. Over the past 13 weeks, varying amounts of space have been used to advertise sales of major appliances and other big-ticket items. Letting A represent column-inches of advertising space and Q the number of items sold in response to the ads, the data collected may be summarized as follows:

$$\Sigma A = 1.407 \qquad \Sigma Q = 403$$
$$\Sigma A^2 = 184,971 \qquad \Sigma Q^2 = 13,983$$
$$\Sigma AQ = 48,552$$

a. Calculate the regression equation.

b. Calculate the standard error of the estimate.

c. Calculate the coefficient of determination.

d. Evaluate the regression equation.

8. A New Zealand fuel-oil company has collected the following data to determine the relationship between average daily temperature and average daily fuel-oil consumption:

Average Daily Temperature (°C)	Average Daily Fuel-Oil Consumption (gallons)
−12	7.0
−8	6.7
−4	6.3
0	5.1
4	4.5
8	3.4
12	2.9
16	1.3

a. Calculate the estimated linear relationship and interpret the estimated intercept and slope. Do they both make sense?

b. Calculate the standard error of the estimate.

c. Predict the average daily fuel-oil consumption when the average daily temperature is 13 degrees Celsius.

d. In many cases, the parameter a in the regression equation has no economic significance. Is that true in this case? Explain your answer.

9. Since a major determinant of demand is per capita income, policymakers are always concerned about anything that will affect it. Of particular concern are fertility rates in developing countries. Suppose that data from 22 countries in Latin America and 26 countries in Africa have been used to develop the regression model

$$\hat{Y} = b_0 + b_1 X$$

where

Y = per capita income
X = percentage of the population under age 15.

Computer runs have produced the following results:
Latin America:

$b_0 = 2,170.7$ $SSR = 954,235$
$b_1 = -42.0$ $SSE = 33,402$
                         $SST = 987,637$

Africa:

$b_0 = 893.57$ $SSR = 153,785$
$b_1 = -17.28$ $SSE = 3,774$
                         $SST = 157,559$

where

SSR = regression sum of squares
SSE = error sum of squares
SST = total sum of squares.

a. What is the meaning of the slope coefficient in each model?

b. Compute and interpret the coefficient of determination for each model. Which one has a better fit? Why?

c. A Latin American manufacturer wants to know what the per capita income of a particular country might be if its population under age 15 is reduced to 12 percent of the total population. Can you tell him?

10. In an effort to determine the correct price for a new product, a company introduced the product in 10 similar markets with the same promotion but with 10 different prices. After gathering data on the first month's sales, the following regression equation was developed:

$$Q = 1,812.11 - 73.91P$$

for which the coefficient of correlation, r, is -0.519.

a. Given the value of the correlation coefficient, is there sufficient evidence to say that there is a negative linear relationship between price and the quantity demanded?

b. How strong is the relationship between price and quantity demanded? Discuss.

Case Problem: Midland State University

11. Midland State University is a state institution dedicated to the proposition that anyone who wants to should be able to get a college education. Consequently, the policy of the board of regents, with the backing of the state legislature, has been to keep tuition charges for state residents as low as possible. The last tuition increase occurred two years ago, and the present tuition of $600 per semester is one of the lowest in the United States. However, costs are such that the current tuition represents no more than 5 percent of the actual cost per student. It is clear that tuition should be increased still more; the question is: By how much?

In an effort to determine the effect of increased tuition charges on student enrollment, the chancellor of the university gave a questionnaire to a cross section of 1,000 students. Presented with five different tuition charges, each student was asked to choose one of the following responses as to whether he or she would remain in school for each of the tuition charges: (1) definitely not, (2) probably not, (3) perhaps, (4) probably, (5) very probably, and (6) definitely. In quantitative terms, these responses are equivalent to the following probabilities of remaining in school: (1) 0.0, (2) 0.2, (3) 0.4, (4) 0.6, (5) 0.8, and (6) 1.0. The results of the survey are as follows:

Tuition per Semester	Number of Students Responding in Category					
	(1)	*(2)*	*(3)*	*(4)*	*(5)*	*(6)*
$ 700	0	25	50	225	300	400
800	50	100	100	300	250	200
900	100	150	250	250	150	100
1,000	300	225	175	150	100	50
1,100	500	300	125	50	25	0

Questions:

a. How many students per 1,000 currently enrolled may be expected to remain in school at each tuition charge?

b. Plot the tuition changes and related enrollment expected and sketch the demand curve.

c. Perform linear regression analysis to estimate the true demand curve.

d. At what tuition charge will revenue be maximized?

Case Problem: Foodland Grocery Stores

12. Foodland is the largest grocery chain in Honolulu, operating nine stores in various locations. The marketing director observed the selling price and sales volume of milk for 10 randomly selected weeks during the year. The information has been organized and tabulated as follows:

	Milk Sales and Price	
	Sales (Q)	Price (P)
Week	(000 gallons)	($ per gallon)
1	11	$2.50
2	6	3.30
3	5	3.10
4	13	2.60
5	10	2.70
6	16	2.10
7	6	3.00
8	12	2.80
9	18	2.10
10	20	2.20

The marketing manager wants you to perform a linear regression with the aid of the university's computer and then present the results to the general manager. The general manager has little background in regression analysis, so you will have to explain the computer printout to him, taking care to define the statistical terminology you will be using in your discussion of the output. (If you do not have access to a linear-regression program on a computer, the problem can be solved using a handheld calculator.) You must include at least the following and add any other significant findings:

a. Regression equation
b. Intercept
c. Regression coefficient
d. Standard error of the estimate
e. r^2
f. Coefficient of correlation
g. Sum of squares deviation from regression
h. Sum of squares total
i. Residuals
j. Explained variation
k. Unexplained variation.

State your conclusion concerning the reliability of the regression equation.

References

Baumol, William J. *Economic Theory and Operations Analysis*, 4th ed. Englewood Cliffs, N.J.: Prentice-Hall, 1977.

Dean, Joel. *Managerial Economics*. Englewood Cliffs, N.J.: Prentice-Hall, 1960.

Eskin, Gerald J., and Penny H. Baron. "Effects of Price and Advertising in Test-Market Experiments." *Journal of Marketing Research* 14 (November 1987), pp. 499–508.

Godwin, M. B.; W. F. Chapman, Jr.; and W. T. Hanley. *Competition between Florida and Valencia Oranges in the Fruit Market*. Bulletin 704. Washington, D.C.: Economic Research Service, U.S. Dept. of Agriculture, December 1965.

Houthakker, H. S., and Lester D. Taylor. *Consumer Demand in the United States, 1929–1970: Analyses and Projections*. Cambridge, Mass: Harvard University Press, 1970.

Nevin, John R. "Laboratory Experiments for Estimating Consumer Demand: A Validation Study." *Journal of Marketing Research* 15 (August 1978), pp. 413–28.

Willis, Raymond E. *A Guide to Forecasting for Planners and Managers*. Englewood Cliffs, N.J.: Prentice-Hall, 1987.

C H A P T E R

8

DEMAND ESTIMATION: MULTIPLE-REGRESSION ANALYSIS

In the preceding chapter, we saw how simple linear regression can be used to analyze the relationship between a single independent variable that influences demand and the quantity demanded of some good or service. In some cases, variations in demand are explained satisfactorily by variations in a single independent variable, such as price. In other cases, however, we may want to examine the relationship between demand and two or more independent variables that may vary more or less simultaneously. This can be done by the method of **multiple-regression analysis**, a widely used and very important analytical tool in business and economics.

Multiple-regression analysis estimates the simultaneous relationship between a dependent variable, Y, and any number of independent variables, $X_1, X_2, X_3, \cdots, X_k$. Multiple-regression analysis is basically the estimation of the regression parameters, or coefficients, for each independent variable. Each parameter (or coefficient) is a measure of how much each independent variable influences the dependent variable when all other independent variables are held constant.

Because it is difficult to perform a multiple-regression by manual calculations, it is best left to a computer. Computer printouts of multiple-regression analysis are not standardized, but the differences, for the most part, lie only in the format, not in the content. If you become familiar with the computer printouts used in this chapter, you should have no difficulty in interpreting output presented in a different format.

Whatever the format, the computer output requires interpretation, testing, and validation before it is of any practical use. Therefore, this chapter will stress these subjects.

CHAPTER OUTLINE

This chapter covers three main topics:

1. **Construction of a Multivariate Demand Function.** This section shows how to identify the variables, collect and adjust the data, choose the best form of the equation, and interpret the output of a multiple-regression computer program.
2. **Testing and Evaluating the Results.** This section shows how to evaluate and test both the overall equation and its individual parameters.
3. **Assumptions and Special Problems of Multiple-Regression Analysis.** This section discusses the assumptions upon which the multiple-regression model is based and the special problems that arise when these assumptions are violated. In particular, the problems of multicollinearity, heteroscedasticity, and autocorrelation are discussed.

Construction of a Multivariate Demand Function

A multivariate demand equation must meet three very important requirements:

- It must represent as closely as possible the true relationships among the dependent and the independent variables.
- It must be a model that is reliable and easy to interpret.
- It must be feasible within given constraints of time and cost.

The technical aspects of multiple-regression models are explained in most standard statistics and econometrics textbooks. In addition to a working knowledge of these technical aspects of multiple regression, a skillful multiple-regression analysis requires sound economic reasoning, judgment, and imagination. To gain a better understanding of how regression analysis can be applied to the study of demand, we will take a step-by-step approach, beginning with the identification of the variables involved.

Step 1: Identification of the Variables

In Chapter 6, we learned that demand is a function of many variables, that is, $Q_D = f(X_1, X_2, \cdots, X_n)$. In any empirical study of demand, we need first to identify the independent variables and their relationship with the dependent variable. For example, a model of demand might be:

$$Q_D = f(P, T, I, P_r, E, R, N, A, O)$$

where

Q_D = quantity demanded of a particular commodity
P = market price of that commodity
T = consumer tastes and preferences
I = level of consumer income; that is, discretionary income plus credit
P_r = prices of related commodities (substitutes and complements)

E = consumer expectations about prices, income, and product availability

R = range of goods and services available

N = number of potential consumers

A = advertising and promotion

O = all other factors.

It is not enough, however, to determine the relationships of the demand variables with the quantity demanded (dependent variable). We must also determine whether or not the independent variables have relationships with each other. In the construction of a multivariate demand function, accurate estimates of the relationships between the quantity demanded and the independent variables that are determinants of demand are often difficult to obtain because of close interrelationships among the demand determinants and the fact that their values change more or less simultaneously. This latter problem is particularly vexing because it is hard to determine what effect any one variable has on demand when all are changing at the same time.

In the simple regression analysis discussed in Chapter 7, we assumed that the quantity demanded changed as a result of changes in price, with all other variables held constant, that is, $Q_D = f(P|T, I, P_r, E, R, N, A, O)$.[1] To establish the demand curve, therefore, all we needed was a series of observations of the quantity demanded at various prices.

We know that a market price is established at the intersection of a supply curve and a demand curve. As long as the supply and demand curves remain stable, the price will not change. Hence, if we see a change in market price, we know that either the supply curve or the demand curve has shifted, *or maybe both*.

If *only* the supply curve has shifted, the price–quantity plot points will follow a single demand curve, as shown in Exhibit 8–1 (page 210). If it can be determined that the condition depicted by the exhibit exists, then the demand curve can be closely approximated by a simple linear regression, as explained in the previous chapter.

A good example of the situation depicted by Exhibit 8–1 is the market for microprocessors, often called personal computers. Technological breakthroughs have rapidly lowered the cost of producing such machines. Consequently, producers have been willing to increase the supply at successively lower prices. This means that the supply curve has shifted successively farther to the right even if the demand curve has not changed. Thus the rapid increase in quantity demanded is mostly due to dramatic reductions in price that were made possible by reduced costs of production.

But suppose the variables other than price have not remained constant? Any change in an independent variable other than price will shift the demand curve. Exhibit 8–2 (page 211) illustrates a situation in which statistical data indicate that *both* supply and demand curves have shifted. At least three different equilibrium points have existed at the demand levels Q_1, Q_2, and Q_3. When these equilibrium points are connected by the line DD', we see that it slopes downward, thus seeming to conform with economic theory. But this is not enough to conclude that the line DD' in fact represents a single demand function. On the contrary, the diagram clearly shows that the line DD' rests upon three different demand functions.

---

[1] As discussed in Chapter 5, it is also possible to determine the quantity demanded as a function of any one of the variables, provided all others are held constant.

EXHIBIT 8–1   Equilibrium Points as Supply Curve Shifts

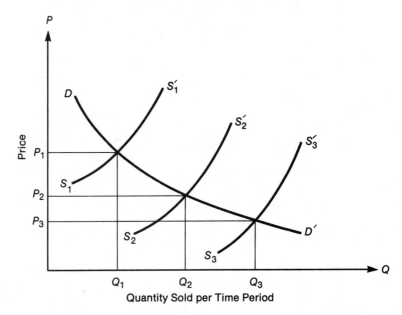

Quantity Sold per Time Period

Recall from Chapter 6 that a change in price causes movement along the demand curve, while a change in any other demand determinant causes the demand curve to shift position. (See Exhibit 6–1.) A valid analysis of demand requires that we have enough data to *identify* the interrelated functions that affect demand and distinguish between movement along the demand curve and shifts in the demand curve's position. Hence, the condition depicted by Exhibit 8–2 is known as the **identification problem**.

If the demand function is estimated from price and quantity data only, it may be impossible to separate the effect of price changes from the effect of all other factors, with serious consequences for the firm. For example, the line connecting the equilibrium points on Exhibit 8–2 has a shallower slope (is more elastic) than any of the true demand curves. If the firm were to mistake that line for its demand curve, it might cut price in expectation of substantially increased sales revenue. The true demand curves have a steeper slope (are less elastic), indicating that the hoped-for sales increase would not be realized.

The identification problem can be overcome by multiple regression, provided sufficient data are available. If sufficient data are not available, so that some of the variables that affect demand are omitted, or if a simple linear regression is performed, the result will be a misleading portrayal of the firm's demand function.

If analysis of time-series data is used to estimate the demand function, the analyst must be very aware of the identification problem, since substantial changes in variables other than price can be expected during a time period long enough for meaningful analysis. Quantitative variables, such as income and the prices of other products, are readily ascertained. Qualitative variables, such as consumer tastes, preferences, and expecta-

EXHIBIT 8–2   **A Series of Equilibrium Points as Both Supply and Demand Curves Shift**

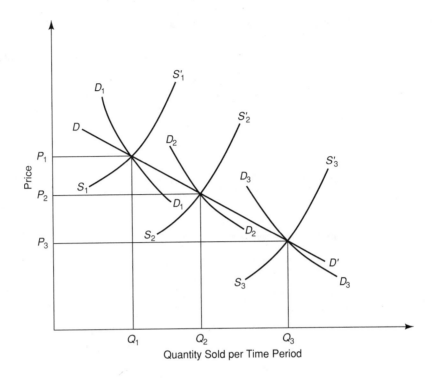

tions, are not directly quantifiable. The *degree* of change, however, can be represented numerically and therefore can be included in a multiple-regression analysis.

Step 2: Data Collection and Adjustment

Once the variables have been specified, data must be obtained. Sources for such data are highly dependent, of course, upon the model's requirements. As noted in Chapter 7, government publications such as the *Statistical Abstract of the United States*, the annual *Economic Report to the President, Business Statistics, Argricultural Statistics*, and the *Survey of Current Business* are usually good starting points. Other sources are the *Federal Reserve Bulletin*, and *U.S. Industry Outlook*. In gathering the data, two aspects must be considered: (1) data organization (i.e., whether to use monthly, quarterly, or annual data), and (2) the number of observations needed for good results.

Data Organization and Adjustment.   The question of whether to use monthly, quarterly, or annual data is often answered simply on the basis of availability. Many data sources do not publish economic series as often as researchers would desire, leaving researchers to do the best they can with annual data. If available, quarterly data are more desirable, since the larger number of observations permits greater statistical efficiency.

Time-series data must be adjusted for population and inflation variations, as discussed in the preceding chapter. Quarterly data may need adjustment for seasonality. Further, since many economic phenomena respond to changing conditions only after some delay, econometric models using quarterly data may be constructed with lagged, rather than current, variables. That is to say, one series or the other may be shifted in time to get the action and reaction to occur at the same time, as explained in Chapter 7.

Sample Size.   The question of how many observations are needed for good results is not easily answered. Perfect results might be expected if we could work with a census, which consists of the entire population. But it is rarely possible to work with a census. Usually, limitations on time and money available for data collection force us to use a sampling method. The size of the sample is a trade-off between the rising cost of data collection and the diminishing cost of sampling error as the sample size grows larger.

A good rule of thumb is that a properly specified model will require at least three to four times as many observations as independent variables.[2] After collecting and adjusting data, the next step is to choose the form of the regression equation.

Step 3: Choosing the Best Form of the Equation

Many demand functions are in fact linear over the range for which empirical data are available. If this is the case, then the appropriate form is an equation describing a regression plane above, below, or on which the observed data points lie. The estimating equation is

$$\hat{Q} = b_0 + b_1 X_1 + b_2 X_2 + \cdots + b_k X_k \tag{1}$$

where

$\hat{Q}$ = Estimate of the quantity demanded
X_i = Value of the ith independent variable
b_i = Estimated value of the ith regression parameter.

When the data indicate that the underlying function is clearly not linear, it is still possible to use linear regression to fit the logarithmic form of a power function to the data. If we postulate a power function of the form

$$\hat{Q} = b_0 X_1^{b_1} X_2^{b_2} \cdots X_k^{b_k} \tag{2}$$

the estimating linear-regression equation will describe a regression plane above, below, or on which the logarithms of the observed data points will lie. The estimating equation is

$$\log \hat{Q} = \log b_0 + b_1 \log X_1 + b_2 \log X_2 + \cdots + b_k \log X_k \tag{3}$$

There usually is no a priori reason to favor one form over another. When this is the case, it seems prudent to try both forms and then choose the one that best explains the relationship between the dependent and independent variables. Computer programs have made this very easy to do.

Functions in the multivariate power form have the useful property that the elasticity of each variable is equal to its respective exponent. Hence, in the logarithmic form, the

---

[2] If the model has been specified incorrectly, then no amount of data will yield good results.

coefficients of the independent variables are their respective elasticities. Also, if all independent variables of a power function are increased simultaneously by some proportion, k, then the proportionate increase in the dependent variable will be k multiplied by the sum of the exponents of the independent variables. That is to say, returns to scale are indicated by the sum of the exponents.[3]

In terms of analysis, multiple-linear regression is an extension of the least-squares method of simple linear regression that was explained in the preceding chapter. The method of least squares can be applied quickly and accurately by a computer program to estimate the regression coefficients, or parameters, of the regression equation. The computer printout not only provides values for all of the parameters of the regression equation, but also provides test data by which the validity of the model may be judged.

Step 4: Calculating the Regression Equation

To illustrate the calculation of a multivariate demand function, we shall use cross-sectional data for a marketing problem. Suppose that Pacific Traders imports black mushrooms from China. This oriental food specialty is then sold in 15 cities of the United States where there are concentrations of people of oriental ancestry. Since the price is the same in all 15 markets, Pacific Traders believes that the quantity sold is primarily influenced by two variables: (1) the size of the target population and (2) the per capita income in that population. The cross-sectional data are shown in Exhibit 8–3 (page 214).

The first step is to verify the linear relationship between the dependent variable and the independent variables. For cross-sectional data, this is done by plotting the dependent variable against each of the independent variables, as shown on Exhibit 8–4 (page 215).[4]

The plots in the exhibit indicate that the relationships of the independent variables with the dependent variable are linear in both cases; therefore we can perform multiple regression with no further treatment of the data. The selected demand function is

$$\hat{Q} = b_0 + b_1 X_1 + b_2 X_2 \tag{4}$$

where

$\hat{Q}$ = Estimated demand for black mushrooms, in number of cases per week
X_1 = Size of the target population (potential customers) in thousands of persons
X_2 = Per capita income (in dollars) of the target population
b_0, b_1, b_2 = Estimated parameters to be obtained by the regression analysis.

Input of the data to a multiple-regression computer package results in the typical output shown in Exhibit 8–5. (The output format may vary, depending on the software used, but the general content remains the same.[5])

---

[3] See Chapter 10 for discussion of returns to scale.

[4] If we were using time-series data, we would examine the data for each independent variable for linearity by plotting the X_i values over time, as explained in the preceding chapter. If any of the variables follows a curvilinear trend, then a logarithmic transformation may be necessary.

[5] Although the general content will be the same across regression packages, the specific content of the output may differ a bit because of the way in which rounding is handled. When there are many variables and some are highly correlated, rounding errors can accumulate into a serious problem. For this reason, it is wise to run a test problem for which the answers are known before adopting a particular program for use.

EXHIBIT 8–3 **Sales Data for Imported Chinese Black Mushrooms in 15 U.S. Cities**

City	Average Weekly Sales (cases) Q	Target Population (000) X_1	Annual Per Capita Income X_2
1	162	274	$2,450
2	120	180	3,254
3	223	375	3,802
4	131	205	2,838
5	67	86	2,347
6	169	265	3,782
7	81	98	3,008
8	192	330	2,450
9	116	195	2,137
10	55	53	2,560
11	252	430	4,020
12	232	372	4,427
13	144	236	2,660
14	103	157	2,088
15	212	370	2,605

In addition to the more or less standard output illustrated by Exhibit 8–5 (page 216), most programs will provide additional information upon request, such as the mean and standard deviation of the distribution of each variable, a correlation matrix, a variance–covariance matrix, and an analysis of the residuals. Thus, the computer program provides not only the regression equation, but also the data and the test statistics necessary to evaluate the regression analysis.

Step 5: Experimentation with the Regression Model

Generally, there are at least three different ways that analysts might experiment with a regression model:

1. Try different unit measurements for one or more particular variables. For example, labor can be measured by number of employees, by hours worked, or by wages paid.
2. Try both linear and nonlinear fits to the data.
3. Take out and put in various independent variables to see what happens to the regression equation.[6]

Because of the ease with which the regression equation can be manipulated by computer programs, it is extremely important for the analyst to have good a priori reasons

---

[6] In order to observe the effects of adding independent variables in a systematic way, the analyst may use a *stepwise multiple-regression program*. In such a program, the analyst inputs data for a set of independent variables. The computer program first selects the independent variable that results in the greatest reduction of unexplained variation and runs a simple regression. Then it performs successive regression analyses by adding one more variable to each run. The variable added is the one that offers the greatest additional reduction of the unexplained variation. The process continues until all variables in the set have been included, or until none of the remaining variables can make a significant reduction in the unexplained variation.

EXHIBIT 8–4   Testing Cross-Sectional Data for Linear Relationships

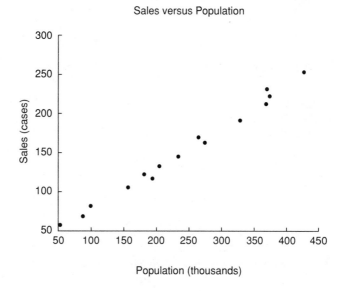

Sales versus Population

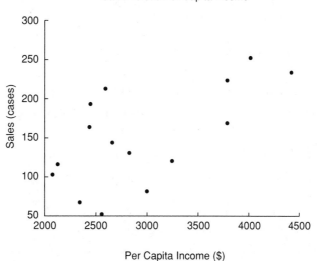

Sales versus Per Capita Income

for including each of the independent variables, keeping in mind that a strong correlation between the dependent variable and a particular independent variable does not
necessarily indicate cause and effect. For example, a strong correlation can probably
be shown between teachers' salaries and liquor sales. This does not mean that teachers
are drinking—it simply means that teachers' salaries and liquor sales are both related to
another variable, the general level of disposable income.

EXHIBIT 8–5   Typical Output of a Multiple-Regression Computer Program

```
VARIABLE #                 B            STD. ERROR     RATIO FOR THE T-TEST
0                    3.45301          2.43013              1.42091
1                     .496006         6.05316E-03          81.9416
2                    9.19890E-03      9.67909E-04          9.50389
ANALYSIS OF VARIANCE           SUM OF SQ.      MEAN SQ.      F. VALUE
REGRESSION                      53844.7        26922.4        5681.88
ERROR                           56.8594         4.73828
TOTAL                           53901.6
THE DEGREES OF FREEDOM FOR THE REGRESSION- 12
R-SQUARED=  .998945          R=  .999472
STANDARD ERROR OF THE ESTIMATE=  2.17676
THE DURBIN-WATSON STATISTIC=  2.70218
```

The analyst must also beware of discarding a variable simply because routine testing of its regression coefficient indicates that it is not statistically significant. If there are strong a priori economic reasons for believing that the variable affects demand, it probably is best to leave it in. The lack of significance, or even the presence of the wrong sign, may be the result of *multicollinearity*, which we shall discuss later.

In addition to the theoretical considerations previously mentioned, the analyst must also consider the availability of data. A mathematical characteristic of multiple regression is that the results can be improved by increasing the number of observations (sample size). It may or may not be improved by adding variables.

Step 6: Interpretation of the Computer Printout

On the output of Exhibit 8–5, "VARIABLE #" is the subscript of the coefficients (b_0, b_1, b_2) on the right side of the estimating equation,

$$\hat{Q} = b_0 + b_1 X_1 + b_2 X_2. \tag{5}$$

When suitably rounded, the estimating equation is calculated to be

$$\hat{Q} = 3.5 + 0.5 X_1 + 0.009 X_2. \tag{6}$$

This result may be interpreted as follows:

1. The regression constant, b_0, positions the regression plane in space. Theoretically, it represents the quantity demanded if all independent variables are zero. Mathematically, it can be negative. In reality, of course, it is impossible to have a negative demand, nor is it likely that all of the variables will ever be zero in the observed data. Hence, the parameter b_0 has no real economic meaning.

2. Each of the other parameters, b_i, indicates the direction and magnitude of change in the dependent variable, $\hat{Q}$, that is associated with a one-unit increase in the corresponding independent variable, X_i, when all the other independent variables are held constant. In this case:

a. The addition of 1,000 people to the target population while holding per capita income constant is estimated to increase expected demand by about one-half case per week.

b. An increase of $1,000 in per capita income while holding the population constant is estimated to increase expected demand by about nine cases per week.

Testing and Evaluating the Results

In multiple-regression analysis, the objectives are to estimate reliable parameters for independent variables on the basis of a sample; to draw statistical inferences about such parameters, both individually and collectively; and to test the validity of the estimated regression equation for demand forecasting. The computer printout illustrated by Exhibit 8–5 indicates such inferences and the results of statistical tests. The analyst must be aware, however, that the computer will accept whatever data are given to it as long as the data are in the correct format.

The computer merely follows a mathematical procedure specified by the program, and will indifferently crank out a regression analysis that has the correct form, whether or not it has any valid economic substance. Thus it is up to the analyst to determine whether or not the output is valid for predicting demand. In general, the overall assessment of the model may be obtained by seeking answers to two fundamental questions:

- Do the regression parameters bear the correct sign and are they of reasonable magnitude?
- How well are variations in demand explained by variations in the independent variables, both singly and collectively?

The first question tests the validity of the model by calling for answers based on economic theory and the analyst's judgment. The second question requires certain statistical tests leading to evaluation of the model as a whole as well as of each individual parameter.

Step 1: Testing the Validity of the Model

Signs of the Parameter.   Each regression coefficient (parameter) represents the marginal response of the demand variable to a unit change in the associated independent variable. The sign of the parameter indicates the direction of movement of the demand variable relative to the direction of movement of the independent variable when the independent variable changes. A plus means the demand variable moves in the same direction as the independent variable; a minus means that the two variables move in opposite directions. The analyst should check the sign of each parameter to see if it indicates the theoretically correct relative direction of movement between that variable and the demand variable.

Referring to the output in Exhibit 8–5, we expect increases in X_1 and X_2 to cause an increase in $\hat{Q}$. We note that the positive signs of b_1 and b_2 accord with this theory. If a sign is wrong, it may indicate that we have specified the model incorrectly by leaving out an important variable. In some cases, the wrong sign accompanies other symptoms of the statistical problem of multicollinearity.

Magnitude of the Parameter.   The test for reasonableness is clearly a test of judgment. Although there are no conventional limits, most economists have some ranges of values in mind that are associated with certain parameters. In other cases, a parameter may take a value that is clearly impossible. For example, suppose that we have modeled aggregate consumption demand in dollars as a function of price and disposable income:

$$C_d = b_0 + b_1 X_1 + b_2 X_2, \tag{7}$$

where X_1 = price and X_2 = disposable income.

Now suppose the signs of the parameters come out correctly, but b_2 assumes a value of 1.3. Does this make sense? Clearly not, since b_2 represents the aggregate marginal propensity to consume or, in more familiar language, the additional consumption that could be anticipated from a unit increase in income. Hence, the estimated value of 1.3 is clearly unreasonable because it states that the average consumer will spend $1.30 of the next $1 of incremental income.

Step 2: Statistical Tests and Evaluation

Test Data.   The typical linear-regression computer program prints out certain statistical results that answer the questions:

- How well do variations in the independent variables explain variation in the dependent variable when taken individually and when taken together as a whole?
- Are the independent variables statistically significant? That is to say, how reliable are the individual parameters for predicting the value of the dependent variable?

For the regression as a whole, the test measures are:

- The *multiple coefficient of determination*, R^2
- The corrected multiple coefficient of determination, R^{-2}
- The F-statistic for the regression
- The *standard error of the estimate* for the regression.

For the parameters of individual variables, the test measures are:

- The *standard error of the regression coefficient* for each statistic
- The *t-test* ratio for each parameter.

The ways in which each of these measures is interpreted and used are discussed in more detail in the following subsections.

Overall Tests

The Multiple Coefficient of Determination, R^2.   As noted already, the multiple regression describes a regression plane, and the observed data points lie above, below, or on this regression plane. The **multiple coefficient of determination** is a measure of how well the plane represented by the regression equation fits the observed data points. As we explained in the preceding chapter, the total variation[7] in the demand variable can be divided into two parts:

$$\begin{pmatrix} \text{Total} \\ \text{variation} \end{pmatrix} = \begin{pmatrix} \text{Explained} \\ \text{variation} \end{pmatrix} + \begin{pmatrix} \text{Unexplained} \\ \text{variation} \end{pmatrix}$$

that is,[8]

$$\Sigma(Q_i - \overline{Q})^2 = \Sigma(\hat{Q}_i - \overline{Q})^2 + \Sigma(Q_i - \hat{Q}_i)^2. \tag{8}$$

The multiple coefficient of determination, R^2, measures the proportion of total variation in the demand variable that is accounted for, or explained, by variations in the independent variables taken together in the equation of best fit. It is simply a mathematical relationship and it does not establish a cause-and-effect relationship. The formula for R^2 is

$$R^2 = \frac{\text{Total explained variation}}{\text{Total variation}} = \frac{\Sigma(\hat{Q}_i - \overline{Q})^2}{\Sigma(Q_i - \overline{Q})^2} \tag{9}$$

where

Q_i = the ith observed value of Q

$\hat{Q}_i$ = the ith estimated value of Q calculated by the regression equation

$\overline{Q}$ = the mean or average observed value of Q, i.e., $\Sigma Q/n$ where n is the number of observations.

This can be written as

$$R^2 = \frac{\text{Total variation} - \text{Total unexplained variation}}{\text{Total variation}}$$

$$= \frac{\Sigma(Q_i - \overline{Q})^2 - \Sigma(Q_i - \hat{Q}_i)^2}{\Sigma(Q_i - \overline{Q})^2}. \tag{10}$$

On the computer printout in Exhibit 8–5, we see under the heading "ANALYSIS OF VARIANCE" that the regression sum of squares, *SSR* (total explained variation), is 53,844.7, while the total sum of squares, *SST* (total variation), is 53,901.6. Thus R^2, which is printed farther down, is 53,844.7/53,901.6=0.9989, meaning that 99.89 percent of the variation in sales is explained by variation in the target population and per capita income acting together in the equation of best fit.

The value of R^2 may range from zero to one. A value of zero indicates that there is no relationship between demand and any of the independent variables. A value of one would mean that all of the variation in demand is explained by simultaneous variations in the independent variables.[9]

---

[7] Definitions of variation and variance are in order here. Variation is the sum of the squared deviations of the observed values from the value estimated by the regression line. Variance is the arithmetic mean of the variation.

[8] Computer programs often use the symbols *SST* = total sum of squares (i.e., total variation), *SSR* = regression sum of squares (i.e., explained variation), and SSE = error sum of squares (i.e., unexplained variation). Hence *SST* = *SSR* + *SSE*.

[9] If all variation in demand is explained, this would mean that all observed points lie on the regression plane with zero deviations. Hence *SST* = *SSR* and *SSE* = 0.

It is not unusual in empirical analysis to obtain a high R^2 accompanied by some regression coefficients that are statistically insignificant or have the wrong sign. Moreover, it is a mathematical property of the least-squares method of multiple linear regression that adding another independent variable will provide no decrease, and may provide an increase in R^2, whether or not that added variable is related to demand. Because of this characteristic, there may be a temptation to include as many variables as possible in order to achieve a high R^2. The temptation should be resisted, for not much can be said for a model that includes variables with little or no theoretical justification. We must remember that our objective is to develop reliable estimates of the true population parameters—not to develop a high R^2.

The Corrected Multiple Coefficient of Determination, $\overline{R}^2$. Another characteristic of R^2 is that it is sensitive to the number of observations that go into the regression. If the number of observations is just equal to the number of independent variables, then each observation will be placed exactly on the regression plane and the calculated $\hat{Q}$ will be equal to the observed Q. Therefore R^2 will be calculated as 1.0, but this indicates a lack of data rather than a good fit. To get a meaningful analysis, we must have enough observations so that the demand variable has some freedom to vary; that is, the degrees of freedom must be greater than zero.[10]

In order to give due consideration to the degrees of freedom allowed by the number of observations and the number of parameters, statisticians have developed the **corrected multiple coefficient of determination**, $\overline{R}^2$. Its formula is

$$\overline{R}^2 = R^2 - \left(\frac{k}{n - k - 1} \right) (1 - R^2) \tag{11}$$

where n = number of observations and k = number of independent variables.

What is an acceptable value for $\overline{R}^2$? This is largely a matter of individual judgment, and even this judgment varies according to the subject being studied. Cross-sectional analyses, which measure demographic relationships, tend to have lower $\overline{R}^2$ values than time-series studies, which measure historical relationships. In demand analysis using time-series data, $\overline{R}^2$ of .75 or more is generally considered to be acceptable, provided the number of observations is at least three or four times as large as the number of independent variables.

To find out whether or not a statistically significant portion of the total variation in the dependent variable is explained by the regression equation, we turn to the F-test for overall significance.

---

[10] The term *degrees of freedom* (or *df*) refers to the fact that if we know $n - 1$ terms of a sum, the nth term is automatically determined. For example, if we know that the sum of five numbers is 15, and we know that the first four numbers are 1, 2, 3, and 4, which add up to 10, then the fifth number has to be 5. It is not free to be anything else, hence $df = (5 - 1) = 4$.

If we have k independent variables in a regression equation, then we have $k + 1$ parameters, that is, one coefficient for each independent variable and one more for the intercept term. At least one observation is required for each parameter, and one degree of freedom is lost for each of the parameters. If we have n observations, then the number of degrees of freedom is $n - k - 1$. If the number of observations equals the number of parameters, then $df = 0$, and $R^2 = 1.0$, since the dependent variable has no room to vary. We can say, then, that R^2 approaches 1.0 as df approaches zero.

The *F*-Test for Overall Significance. The multiple coefficient of determination, R^2, and the corrected multiple coefficient of determination, $\overline{R}^2$, show whether the proportion of explained variation is high or low, but these measures do not tell us whether or not the explained variation is statistically significant. For that purpose, we use the ratio of variances known as the *F*-statistic. Like $\overline{R}^2$, the *F*-statistic is adjusted for degrees of freedom. It is calculated as

$$F = \frac{\text{(Total explained variation)}/(k)}{\text{(Total unexplained variation)}/(n-k-1)}$$

$$= \frac{\Sigma(\hat{Q}-\overline{Q})^2/k}{\Sigma(Q_i-\hat{Q}_i)^2/n-k-1} \tag{12}$$

where

F = the *F*-statistic
k = number of independent variables
n = number of observations.

The numerator of Equation 12 represents the variance of the dependent variable that is explained by variation of the independent variables. It is calculated as the regression sum of squares (explained variation) divided by the appropriate degrees of freedom, df. Since there is one chance of variation for each independent variable, $df = k$ in the numerator.

The denominator of Equation 12 represents the variance of the residuals, which is not explained by variation of the independent variables. It is calculated as the residual or error sum of squares (unexplained variation) divided by the appropriate degrees of freedom. In the denominator, the chances of variation depend upon the number of observations, n, reduced by the $(k+1)$ estimated parameters, $b_0, b_1, \ldots, b_k$. Hence $df = n-k-1$.

Since the *F*-statistic is intimately related to the coefficient of determination, R^2, it can also be calculated as[11]

$$F = \frac{R_2/k}{(1-R_2)/(n-k-1)}. \tag{13}$$

---

[11] Equation 13 is derived by first rewriting the denominator of Equation 12 as

$$\text{(Total unexplained variation)}/(n-k-1)$$

$$= \text{(Total variation} - \text{total explained variation)}/(n-k-1).$$

Then, dividing both numerator and denominator by total variation, we get

$$F = \frac{\frac{\text{Total explained variation}}{\text{(Total variation)}/k}}{\frac{\text{Total variation} - \text{Total explained variation}}{\text{(Total variation)}/(n-k-1)}}$$

$$= \frac{\frac{\text{Total explained variation}}{\text{(Total variation)}/k}}{\frac{\text{Total variation}}{\text{(Total variation)}/(n-k-1)} - \frac{\text{Total explained variation}}{\text{(Total variation)}/(n-k-1)}}.$$

In both the numerator and the denominator, we now have the expression (total explained variation/total variation), which we recognize as R^2 from Equation 9. Hence

$$F = \frac{R^2/k}{(1-R_2)/(n-k-1)}.$$

The *F*-test for overall significance is based on the fact that for the regression equation to be statistically significant, at least one of the true regression parameters must not be zero. A computed *F*-value is used to test the null hypothesis[12] that all of the true regression parameters are zero.

If this hypothesis is true, then there is no *actual* relationship between the dependent and independent variables. At the extreme, both R^2 and the *F*-statistic would be zero and in any case must be quite small. As the *F*-statistic increases, it will at some point become sufficiently large that we can reject the null hypothesis with some level of confidence. That particular *F*-value constitutes the upper limit of *F*-values that are possible if the null hypothesis is true, and is known as the critical value of the *F*-distribution.

Tables of critical values of the *F*-distribution have been constructed for various levels of statistical significance. Table G in the Appendix at the end of this book is a matrix of critical values of *F* at significance levels of .05 and .01, which correspond to confidence levels of 95 and 99 percent, respectively. To use the table, one must know the degrees of freedom, k, in the numerator and the degrees of freedom, $n - k - 1$, in the denominator of Equation 12 or Equation 13. For each combination of k and $n - k - 1$, a critical value of *F* is listed. For example, in the table for a significance level of .05, the critical value of *F* for 3 degrees of freedom in the numerator and 15 degrees of freedom in the denominator is 3.29. This means that if the null hypothesis is true, the probability of exceeding $F = 3.29$ is .05 or 5 percent. Stated another way, it means that if the computed *F* exceeds 3.29, we can be 95 percent confident that the regression coefficients are not actually all zeros. If we want to be 99 percent confident, we look up the critical value of *F* for a significance level of .01, and find it is 5.42 for the same degrees of freedom.

The computed *F*-value is determined by an analysis of variance, or ANOVA, as shown on the printout of Exhibit 8–5. For example, the printout reports a regression of two independent variables based on 15 observations. Therefore, the numerator has 2 degrees of freedom, while the denominator has $15 - 2 - 1 = 12$ degrees of freedom. Thus the computed *F*-value is

$$\frac{53,844.7 \div 2}{56.8594 \div 12} = \frac{26,922.35}{4.738283333} = 5,681.878458 \approx 5,681.88,$$

as shown on the printout. It means that the explained variance is 5,681.88 times as great as the unexplained variance.

The critical *F*-value from Table G for 2 *df* in the numerator and 12 *df* in the denominator at a significance level of .01 is 6.93. This means that if the null hypothesis (that all the regression parameters are zero) is true, the critical *F*-value of 6.93 will be exceeded only once in a hundred trials. Since the computed *F*-value is 5,681.88, we reject the null hypothesis and conclude that the regression *as a whole* is statistically significant at the .01 level.

This does not imply, however, that all of the independent variables are significant. The individual independent variables must be separately tested for statistical significance as

---

[12] In hypothesis testing, rejecting a null hypothesis when it is true is called a Type I error. Accepting a null hypothesis when it is false is called a Type II error. The level of significance is the maximum tolerable probability of a Type I error. There is a trade-off between Type I and Type II errors. The lower the level of significance, the higher the probability of a Type II error.

will be explained shortly when we take up the subject of testing individual parameters. First, however, we want to look at one more overall test statistic, called the standard error of the estimate.

The Standard Error of the Estimate. The **standard error of the estimate** measures the dispersion of the observed data points from the regression plane of best fit. Given the standard error of the estimate, S_e, we can calculate confidence intervals for the estimated value of the dependent variable for various levels of confidence. A confidence interval is the range of values that can be expected to contain the actual observation some given percentage of the time.

The standard error of the estimate is actually the estimated standard deviation of the probability distribution of the dependent variable when all of the independent variables are held constant. Thus it measures the dispersion of possible observed values of Q about the estimated $\hat{Q}$. For a multiple regression, it is calculated as the square root of the mean sum of the squared deviations (error mean square) by the formula:

$$S_e = \sqrt{\frac{\Sigma(Q_i - \hat{Q}_i)^2}{n - k - 1}} \tag{14}$$

where

$$S_e = \text{standard error of the estimate}$$
$$Q_i = \text{observed value of the dependent demand variable at the } i\text{th data point}$$
$$\hat{Q}_i = \text{estimated value of the dependent demand variable as calculated for the } i\text{th data point by the regression equation}$$
$$n = \text{number of data points observed}$$
$$k = \text{number of independent variables}$$
$$n - k - 1 = \text{degrees of freedom.}$$

On the computer printout in Exhibit 8–5, the error mean square is listed as 4.73828. Hence the standard error of the estimate is calculated as

$$S_e = \sqrt{4.73828} = 2.17676,$$

as shown on the printout.

Since we assume a normal distribution of the residuals about the plane of best fit, about 68 percent of all observed values of Q may be expected to fall within one standard error of the regression plane; about 95 percent may be expected within two standard errors; and practically all observations may be expected within three standard errors of the regression plane. Of course, the smaller the standard error, the closer the relationship between the dependent and independent variables and the better the fit of the regression equation to the observed data points.

Testing Individual Parameters

So far we have tested for the reliability and significance of the independent variables as a group when all are allowed to vary simultaneously. It is also necessary to perform a separate test for the reliability and significance of each independent variable while all others are held constant. For these tests we use the standard error of the regression coefficient and the *t*-test ratio, both of which are included on a typical computer printout.

Standard Error of the Regression Coefficient (SERC). Each regression coefficient, b_i, is the mean of a normal distribution of possible values. The **standard error of the regression coefficient (SERC)** measures the dispersion of values about the regression coefficient in the same way that standard deviation measures the dispersion of random variables about their mean. The computer program uses a complicated formula to calculate the SERC for each regression coefficient, and these values are routinely printed out.

The SERC indicates the reliability of that particular parameter. If the standard error is small relative to the estimated parameter, it indicates that the estimated parameter is near the true parameter. However, it still must be determined whether or not the true parameter might be zero. For this purpose, the regression coefficient is divided by its standard error to obtain the t-test ratio and the result is also printed as part of the standard output of the computer program. That is, the t-test ratio is the number of standard errors contained in the regression coefficient.[13] It is calculated as

$$t\text{-test ratio} = \frac{\text{Regression coefficient}}{\text{Standard error of the regression coefficient}} \tag{15}$$

and is used to test for statistical significance of each individual variable.

The t-Test for Individual Significance. If an individual variable is statistically significant, the true value of its parameter cannot be zero. Therefore, we must test the null hypothesis that the true parameter equals zero (i.e., $H_0 : \beta_i = 0$). If we can reject this hypothesis, we can infer that the independent variable does indeed have some effect on the dependent variable. We can test this hypothesis with the aid of the t-test ratio and an appropriate t-distribution.

The t-distribution. The t-distribution is a sampling distribution of small samples from an unknown population. Like the normal probability distribution, the t-distribution is symmetrical about a mean of zero, and the area under the curve represents a probability of 1.0. The exact shape of the curve depends upon the degrees of freedom, calculated as $n - k - 1$, where $k = $ the number of independent variables and $n = $ the number of observations in the sample. The t-distribution approaches the normal distribution as the sample size grows larger and for an infinite number of degrees of freedom, the t-distribution and normal distribution are precisely the same. The approach to this limit is quite rapid and there is a widely applied rule of thumb that the normal distribution is used when $n > 30$.

The t-test statistic and t-distribution are used to test for statistical significance at the level of α, where α is the probability of Type I error, usually taken to be .05 or .01. In order to perform the test, we divide the appropriate t-distribution into three parts, as illustrated by Exhibit 8–6. Exactly in the middle (i.e., centered on the mean), we carve out $(1 - \alpha)$ of the total probability, bounded on the left by $-t_{\alpha/2}$ and on the right by $+t_{\alpha/2}$. This leaves $\alpha/2$ probability in each tail. Alternatively (and not illustrated), all of α can be put in one tail, either right or left, bounded by plus or minus t_α.

---

[13] Since the standard error of the regression coefficient is always positive, the t-test ratio takes its sign from the regression coefficient. The sign is not important—we are concerned only with the magnitude.

EXHIBIT 8–6   Typical *t*-Distribution with Two-Tailed *t*-Test

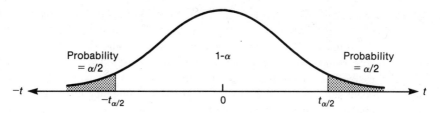

Note: α is the probability of Type 1 error, that is, rejecting the null hypothesis when it is true.

One-Tailed and Two-Tailed t-Tests.   A *t*-test is performed to test the null hypthesis that $\beta_i = 0$. If this hypothesis can be rejected at the α level of significance, we can conclude that the variable X_i is statistically significant at the α level.

In general, *t*-tests of hypotheses may be either one-tailed or two-tailed tests. In a one-tailed test, the decision maker is concerned about detecting departures from the null hypothesis in only one direction. For example, suppose a toy manufacturer wants to test a seller's claim that the mean life of a shipment of batteries is 10 continuous hours of use in one of the manufacturer's toys. In this case, the buyer does not care if the mean life is greater than 10 hours, but will reject the shipment if a random sample exhibits a mean life of less than 10 hours. The null hypothesis is $H_0 : \mu = 10$. The alternative hypothesis is $H_1 : \mu < 10$. The entire area of rejection of the null hypothesis is in the left-hand tail of the *t*-distribution.

For a multiple regression, a two-tailed test is used to test the null hypothesis that the true regression coefficient equals zero, that is, $H_0 : \beta_i = 0$. If we can reject this hypothesis, we can infer that the independent variable does indeed have some effect on the dependent variable. We can reject this hypothesis if the *t*-test ratio falls into either tail of the appropriate *t*-distribution.

A *t*-value indicates the number of standard deviations from the mean. The *t*-values $\pm t_{\alpha/2}$ (as shown in Exhibit 8–6) are called *critical values* of *t* for a two-tailed *t*-test. The *t*-value equal to $\pm t_\alpha$ (not shown by the exhibit) is the critical value of *t* for a one-tailed test. Critical values of *t* are published in tables such as Table F in the Appendix at the end of this book. Table F is a matrix with degrees of freedom as row heads and α-values as column heads. Each cell of the matrix contains a critical *t*-value corresponding to the combination of level of significance (represented by α) and degrees of freedom (which determines the *t*-distribution).

The column heads have two labels. The upper label equals $\alpha/2$ and the lower label equals α. The *t*-test for statistical significance of a regression coefficient requires only that we compare the *t*-test ratio with the critical *t*-value for our desired level of significance and the appropriate degrees of freedom. If the *t*-test ratio is larger, we can reject the null hypothesis that $\beta_i = 0$, and state that the variable X_i is statistically significant at the α level.

In our example on Exhibit 8–5, the *t*-test ratio for $X_1 = 81.942$ and for $X_2 = 9.504$. Suppose we want to test for significance at the .01 level. In Table F, we find the critical *t*-value for $\alpha/2 = .005$ and $df = 12$ is 3.055. Since both test ratios are many times greater than the critical value, we conclude that both variables are statistically significant at the .01 level of significance.

Confidence Intervals for the Regression Coefficients.   If the *t*-test for significance determines that the true parameter does not equal zero, we may still want to know, with some level of confidence, the interval in which the true parameter lies. This is easily determined from the regression coefficient b_i, the standard error of the regression coefficient, S_{bi} (which is calculated by the computer in the current example), and an appropriate *t*-value from Table F.

Having selected α (the probability of Type I error), the desired level of confidence is $1 - \alpha$ (the probability of no Type I error). The **confidence interval** for b_i is

$$b_i \pm t_{\alpha/2} S_{bi} \tag{16}$$

where

b_i = the *i*th regression coefficient

$t_{\alpha/2}$ = the critical value for the two-tailed *t*-statistic

S_{bi} = standard error of the *i*th regression coefficient.

For example, suppose we want a 95-percent confidence interval for the regression coefficients of Exhibit 8–5. The coefficients b_1 and b_2 are on the computer printout. The printout also contains S_{b1} and S_{b2}. Since the desired level of confidence is $1-\alpha$, α must be .05. From Table F, we obtain the *t*-statistic for $\alpha/2 = .025$ and $df = 12$. We find it is 2.179. Hence for $b_i = .496$, the 95-percent confidence interval is

$$.496 \pm (2.179)(.00605316) = .496 \pm .013189835.$$

For $b_2 = .0091989$, the 95-percent confidence interval is

$$.0091989 \pm (2.179)(.000967909) = .0091989 \pm .002109073.$$

These calculations tell us that we can be 95 percent certain that the true value of β_1 lies between .483 and .509, while the true value of β_2 lies between .007 and .011.

Assumptions and Special Problems of Multiple-Regression Analysis

Multiple regression is one of the most frequently used techniques in the empirical investigation not only of demand functions, but also of production functions, cost functions, and many others. It is a powerful technique, but it is also limited by its assumptions, which are quite specific. When any one of these assumptions is violated, a special problem arises. In particular, the problems of *multicollinearity, heteroscedasticity,* and *autocorrelation* may appear. A thorough discussion of these problems is beyond the scope of this book. Nevertheless, a brief explanation of the regression model's assumptions is in order, as well as a brief summary of the problems that arise when these assumptions are violated.

The validity of the regression model rests upon certain statistical assumptions that must be clearly understood. First of all, regression analysis requires that the analyst specify a set of independent variables $(X_1, X_2, \ldots X_k)$, each of which consists of a set of values. Although the X_i variables may actually be random variables, once their values have been selected (e.g., by observation), they do not change.

The observed value of the dependent variable is determined not only by the selected combination of values for the identified independent variables, but also by other independent variables that have not been identified and by variations due to chance. Consequently, for any given combination of values of the independent variables, many values of the dependent variable are possible. For example, suppose that we postulate the dependent variable Q as a function of two variables, that is,

$$Q = f(X_1, X_2)$$

where

Q = loaves of whole-wheat bread
X_1 = price of whole-wheat bread
X_2 = per capita income.

If we were to ask many households with the same per capita income how much whole-wheat bread they buy at a given price, we would expect to get many different answers. Of course, in actual practice, we would not attempt to limit our survey to households with the same per capita income or to bread with the same price. Instead, we would postulate many combinations of per capita income and price and observe the Q-value corresponding to each combination of X-values. The data would be input to a multiple-regression program to perform a multiple-regression analysis of the form

$$Q_j = \beta_0 + \beta_1 X_{1j} + \beta_2 X_{2j} + \mu_j \qquad (17)$$

where Q_j is the observed function of the jth combination of X_1 and X_2, and μ_j is the difference between Q_j and $\hat{Q}_j$. It should be emphasized that only Q is a random variable. This means that when the regression equation

$$\hat{Q}_j = b_0 + b_1 X_{1j} + b_2 X_{2j} \qquad (18)$$

is used to estimate Q, values of the independent variables are known precisely, but the estimated value of Q is subject to error. This may be because at least one other pertinent variable, the price of white bread, has been left out of the regression, and the estimate of Q is subject to random chance variations as well.

The value $\hat{Q}_j$ in Equation 18 is the mean, or expected value, of Q_j based on the regression equation and the given values of X_{1j} and X_{2j}; that is, $\hat{Q}_j$ is the mean of the probability distribution of the random variable Q in Equation 17. The distribution of Q is reflected in the error term, μ_j, which is a random disturbance or variation in Q_j that is not related to the specific independent variables used in the regression equation. It is with this error term that we account for the observed values of Q_j that lie above or below the regression plane rather than on it. Hence it is necessary to make certain assumptions about the error term:[14]

1. The random fluctuations in the observed Q are normally distributed with a mean of zero. That is, the deviations of Q_j from $\hat{Q}_j$ are both positive and negative and they cancel each other out.

---

[14] The first three assumptions pertain to both simple and multiple linear regression. The fourth assumption must be added for multiple-regression analysis.

2. The error-term distributions have constant variance. For each combination of X-values, there is a distribution of μ-values, and the variance is identical for all such distributions. This is the characteristic called *homoscedasticity*. (*Homo* means same; *scedasticity* means scatter.) If it is not true, the function is said to be *heteroscedastic*. (*Hetero* means different.)

3. The error terms are independent of (not influenced by) the values of the independent variables, X_{ij}, and of each other.

4. Independence means that there can be no strong linear relationships among the independent variables. For example, if X_{1j} is always three times X_{2j}, this assumption would be violated and the linear regression would be invalid.[15]

5. Another often stated assumption is that $E(\mu) = 0$. This implies that

$$E(Q) = \beta_0 + \sum_{i=1}^{k} \beta_i X_i,$$

which is linear.

With this understanding of the assumptions underlying regression analysis, we are now ready for a brief look at what happens when any of the assumptions is violated.

Multicollinearity

The fourth of our five previous basic assumptions is that the variables are not influenced by one another. Consequently no linear relationship exists between any independent variable and any other independent variable or linear combination of other independent variables. If this assumption is not true (i.e., if two or more independent variables are highly correlated), then **multicollinearity** exists.

Detection of multicollinearity is particularly important in multiple regressions in the fields of economics and business, where it is frequently encountered. For example, the independent variables "family income" and "family assets" would tend to be highly correlated, as would the independent variables "store sales" and "sales personnel." The clearest signs of multicollinearity are:

1. A high R^2 with individual variables that fail the t-test for significance
2. One or more of the regression coefficients having the wrong sign.

Another good test for multicollinearity is to examine the correlation matrix, which is provided routinely or optionally on the computer printout. Exhibit 8–7 (page 229) shows the correlation matrix for the linear regression previously depicted in Exhibit 8–5.

The rows and columns of the correlation matrix pertain to variables X_1, X_2, and $\hat{Q}$, respectively. Each number in the matrix is the coefficient of correlation between variables represented by row and column. Since each variable is perfectly correlated with itself, the principal diagonal consists of ones or numbers very, very close to 1.0. The matrix is symmetrical, so some printouts omit the coefficients above or below the principal diagonal.

---

[15] We should also note that it is necessary for the number of observations on data points to be greater than the number of independent variables plus one; that is, $n > k + 1$.

EXHIBIT 8–7 **Typical Correlation Matrix on a Computer Printout of Multiple-Regression Analysis**

	X1	X2	Q
X1	1	.56856	.995493
X2	.56856	.999999	.639301
Q	.995493	.639301	1.

Multicollinearity should be suspected if the coefficient of correlation between two independent variables is high. In this exhibit, the coefficient of correlation between X_1 and X_2 is 0.56856, so there is no reason to suspect multicollinearity. If multicollinearity seems to be present, the solution is to eliminate one of the variables from the regression analysis.

Heteroscedasticity

Our second basic assumption is that all of the distributions of the error terms have the same variance, σ^2. If this assumption of equal variance is violated, we have the situation of **heteroscedasticity**, as previously noted. The consequences of heteroscedasticity are exaggerated results of statistical significance tests. That is, the F-test is likely to exaggerate the statistical significance of the regression as a whole, and the t-tests of the individual parameters are very likely to exaggerate the statistical significance of each of the regression coefficients.[16]

Although it is easy to state the consequences of heteroscedasticity, it is not easy to determine that it exists. This is because we have no way of determining the actual variance of the error terms, which we have assumed to be the same for all distributions.

Sometimes the nature of the investigation indicates whether or not heteroscedasticity is likely. For example, suppose that small-, medium-, and large-sized firms are sampled together in a cross-sectional analysis of profits versus investment expenditures, sales, production costs, rates of interest, and other pertinent variables. Heteroscedasticity may be expected because the differences in the size of the firms might be expected to create differences in the distribution of data on most of these variables.

Residuals or squares of the residuals are routine or optional outputs of most multiple-regression computer programs, and there are several ways of detecting heteroscedasticity by working with them. These methods include a graphical method, the Park test, and the Spearman's rank correlation test. There are also remedial measures that can be taken when heteroscedasticity is discovered. Explanation of these tests and remedial measures is beyond the scope of this book, but may be found in textbooks on econometrics.[17]

---

[16] Exaggerated statistical significance may also result from autocorrelation, as discussed in the next section.

[17] An especially lucid discussion is contained in Damodar Gujarati, *Basic Econometrics* (New York: McGraw-Hill, 1978), pp. 200–206.

Autocorrelation

The third basic assumption is that the error terms are independent, that is, the error related to any one observation is not influenced by the error associated with any other observation. If we are dealing with time-series data, we assume that the events of the time t-1 do not influence the events of time t. If they do, then **autocorrelation** (also known as **serial correlation**) exists.[18] If autocorrelation exists, it leads to exaggerated values of the F-statistic and t-statistics. The F-test and t-tests used to evaluate the regression are no longer valid and can cause misleading conclusions.

There are a number of reasons why autocorrelation may exist in time-series data. Among these are:

1. *Inertia*. The movement of variables, up or down, leaves a built-in momentum that causes each successive observation to be influenced by the one before. For example, when recovery from a recession begins, increased employment in one time period leads to increased demand for goods and services, which leads to increased employment in the next period. The upward momentum continues until it becomes inhibited by developments such as a shortage of skilled labor, tight monetary policy to avoid inflation, shortages of critical raw materials, and so forth.

2. *Specification bias from excluded variables*. In attempting to improve a regression analysis, the analyst may exclude variables that should be left in. For example, suppose we have the demand model,

$$Q = \beta_0 + \beta_1 X_1 + \beta_2 X_2 + \beta_3 X_3 + \mu, \qquad (19)$$

where

Q = quantity of Cadillac automobiles demanded
X_1 = average price of a Cadillac
X_2 = per capita income
X_3 = average price of a Lincoln
μ = error term.

Suppose we run the regression

$$\hat{Q} = b_0 + b_1 X_1 + b_2 X_2 + \nu. \qquad (20)$$

If Equation 19 is correct, then by running Equation 20 we have let $\nu = \beta_3 X_3 + \mu$. To the extent that the price of Lincolns affects demand for Cadillacs, the term ν will follow a systematic pattern. This will create autocorrelation.

3. *Specification bias from incorrect functional form*. If a straight line is fitted to data that are actually curvilinear, autocorrelation will result. For example, suppose the quadratic curve

$$Q_i = \beta_0 + \beta_1 X_i + \beta_2 X_i^2 + \mu_i \qquad (21)$$

is fitted with the straight line

$$\hat{Q}_i = b_0 + b_1 X_1 + \nu_i. \qquad (22)$$

---

[18] We emphasize that autocorrelation is found only in time-series data, not in cross-sectional data.

In Equation 22 the term $v_i = \beta_2 X_i^2 + \mu_i$. As X_i increases, X_i^2 also increases systematically, and autocorrelation is generated.

4. *Cobweb phenomenon.* The dependent variable, such as supply, reacts to the independent variable, such as price, with a lag of one time period. This phenomenon is most common in agriculture, where the farmer's decision on how much to plant is greatly influenced by the price received for last year's crop. This causes the disturbance term, μ, to follow a regular pattern of up, down, up, down, as farmers overproduce one year and then decrease production the next.

5. *Other lagged influence on time-series data.* For example, in time-series regressions of demand as a function of income, the consumption expenditure (demand) in one time period is often influenced by the consumption expenditure of the previous period.

6. *Manipulation of data.* In empirical analysis, raw data are often manipulated by devices such as moving averages, or by interpolation or extrapolation. These devices amount to modification of current data by data from the past, which is a direct introduction of autocorrelation.

All of these things make lack of independence in residuals more common in time-series data than in cross-sectional data. Autocorrelation may be detected by the following tests:

1. Plot the residuals of a regression analysis to see if any regular pattern emerges, such as those shown in Exhibit 8–8 (page 232).

2. Another method of detecting autocorrelation is to make the Durbin-Watson *d*-test. The Durbin-Watson *d*-statistic is defined as

$$d = \frac{\sum_{t=2}^{n} (e_t - e_{t-1})^2}{\sum_{t=1}^{n} e_t^2} \tag{23}$$

where

e_t = the estimated residual of the regression, which is a proxy for the unknown disturbance term μ_t. The subscripts $t - 1$, t indicate successive residuals in a series.

d = the ratio of the sum of squared differences in successive residuals to the residual sum of squares. Note that the number of observations in the denominator is n, but in the numerator is $n - 1$, because one observation is lost in taking successive differences.

The Durbin-Watson statistic is calculated and printed out by most regression programs. It is used to test the null hypothesis that there is no first-order serial correlation (autocorrelation) in the disturbances, μ_i. Like the *F*-test and *t*-test discussed previously, the test is made by comparing the calculated *d*-value with a table of critical values. Unlike the *F*-test or *t*-test, however, there is no unique critical value by which to accept or reject the null hypothesis.

Exhibit 8–9 (page 233) shows that the maximum value of *d* is 4. In the middle of this spread lies a zone of decision to accept the null hypothesis. At the left end lies a zone of decision to reject the null hypothesis because positive autocorrelation is evident. At the

EXHIBIT 8–8   Patterns Indicating Autocorrelation

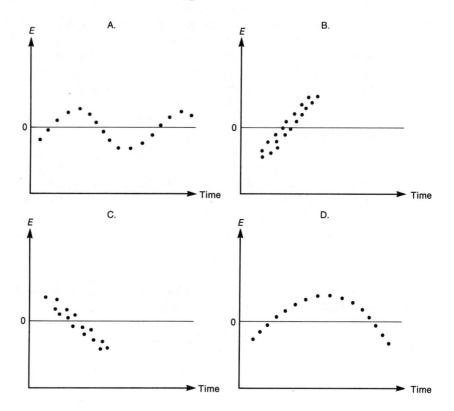

right end lies a zone of decision to reject the null hypothesis because negative auto-correlation is evident. But between these zones of acceptance or rejection lie zones of indecision where the *d*-test is inconclusive.

Durbin and Watson identified the lower limit of the left-most zone of indecision as d_L and its upper limit as d_U. The rightmost zone of indecision is bounded on the left by $4 - d_U$ and on the right by $4 - d_L$. The limits d_L and d_U depend only on the number of observations (which must be at least 15) and the number of explanatory variables. Durbin and Watson prepared a table of the critical lower (d_L) and upper (d_U) values for sample sizes from 15 through 100 and for 1 through 5 variables at a significance level of .05, with a similar table for the significance level of .01. These tables are reproduced as Table H in the Appendix at the end of this book.

The *d*-test is performed by comparing the computed Durbin-Watson statistic on the computer printout with the critical values listed in Table H. The test is made for either or both of the following hypotheses:

H_0 : No positive autocorrelation
H_0^* : No negative autocorrelation.

EXHIBIT 8–9   Decision Rules for the Durbin-Watson *d* Statistic

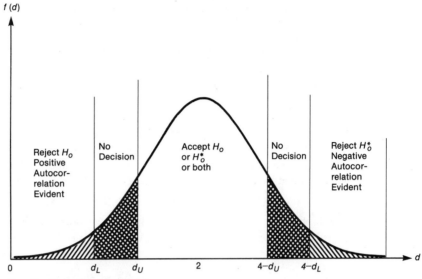

Key: H_0 : No positive autocorrelation
H_0^*: No negative autocorrelation

If the null hypothesis, H_0, is that there is no *positive* serial correlation, then if

$d < d_L$: reject H_0
$d > d_U$: accept H_0
$d_L \le d \le d_U$: the test is inconclusive.

If our null hypothesis, H_0^*, is that there is no *negative* serial correlation, then if

$d > 4 - d_L$: reject H_0^*
$d < 4 - d_U$: accept H_0^*
$4 - d_U \le d \le 4 - d_L$: the test is inconclusive.

Suppose we have run a regression analysis for which the sample size is 30 and the number of independent variables is 4. At the .05 level of significance, we find that $d_L = 1.14$ and $d_U = 1.74$. Our printout shows a Durbin-Watson statistic of 0.98. How do we interpret this?

The test statistic of 0.98 is less than d_L. Therefore we have reason to believe that positive autocorrelation exists.

Following is a brief overview of measures used to correct for autocorrelation. A thorough explanation of the procedure involved is beyond the scope of this book, but may be found in econometrics texts.[19]

When autocorrelation is detected, the first step is to run a simple linear regression on each variable to determine which ones yield autocorrelation and which do not. In

---

[19] See, for example, Gujarati, *Basic Econometrics*, pp. 239–45, from which this material has been extracted.

general, further corrective action requires transformation of the data to eliminate the spillover effects from one observation to the next. In practice, the usual assumption is that the error terms, μ_i, of the true regression equation

$$Y_t = \beta_0 + \beta_1 X_t + \mu_t \tag{24}$$

follow the first-order autoregressive scheme:

$$\mu_t = \rho\mu_{t-1} + \epsilon_t \tag{25}$$

where

ρ(rho) = the coefficient of autocorrelation

ϵ_t = the residuals of the regressive scheme.

Equation 25 assumes that the absolute value of ρ is less than 1 and that the ϵ_t have constant variance and zero expected value and are not autocorrelated. If ρ is known, the β_i can be found by linear regression of the *generalized difference equation*

$$(Y_t - \rho Y_{t-1}) = \beta_0(1 - \rho) + \beta_1(X_t - \rho X_{t-1}) + \epsilon_t. \tag{26}$$

The problem is that ρ is usually not known, so other methods had to be devised. One method is called the *first difference method*. The first difference method requires the assumption that $\rho = 1$. This reduces Equation 26 to

$$\Delta Y_t = \beta_1 \Delta X_t + \epsilon_t. \tag{27}$$

Equation 27 is easy to apply. All that is required is to calculate the first differences for both dependent and independent variables and use these values in the regression analysis. Unfortunately, however, if the assumption that $\rho = 1$ is wrong, the results of regressing Equation 27 will be farther off the mark than the original regression. A better procedure is to estimate ρ from the Durbin-Watson d-statistic as

$$\hat{\rho} = 1 - \frac{d}{2} \tag{28}$$

where

$\hat{\rho}$ = the estimate of ρ

d = the Durbin-Watson d-statistic.

Equation 28 is all right for large samples, but may not hold true for small samples. A better formulation has been suggested by Theil and Nagar[20] as

$$\hat{\rho} = \frac{N^2(1 - d/2) + k^2}{N^2 - k^2}. \tag{29}$$

When N is large, Equation 29 coincides with Equation 28. Once ρ has been estimated, the data can be transformed using the generalized difference equation, Equation 26. To avoid the loss of the first observation, the first observed values of X and Y are transformed by multiplying each of them by $\sqrt{1 - \rho^2}$. After transformation of all (X,Y) values, regression analysis may be performed on the transformed data.

---

[20] H. Thiel and A. L. Nagar, "Testing the Independence of Regression Disturbances," *Journal of the American Statistical Association* 56 (1961), pp. 793–806.

Summary

Multiple-regression analysis is a method of analyzing demand as a function of a number of independent variables acting more or less simultaneously. Because of the complexity and difficulty of the mathematical calculations in multiple-regression analysis, it is best performed by digital computers. Many programs are available for this purpose.

The statistical aspects of multiple-regression models are well explained in statistics and econometrics textbooks. The analyst, however, must apply economic thinking, judgment, and imagination when constructing a regression model and when interpreting and testing its results.

The basic economic variables that affect demand include demographic factors, buying-power factors, price factors, promotion factors, and qualitative factors. The regression model of demand is

$$Q_j = \beta_0 + \beta_1 X_{1j} + \beta_2 X_{2j} + \ldots + \beta_k X_{kj} + \mu_j$$

where

Q_j = quantity demanded in the jth observation
X_{ij} = the jth observed value of the ith independent determinant of demand
β_0 = regression constant
β_i = regression coefficient of the ith independent variable
μ_j = mean of the distribution of error terms of the jth observation (always assumed to be zero).

The computer output *estimates* the regression equation as

$$\hat{Q} = b_0 + b_1 X_1 + b_2 X_2 + \ldots + b_k X_k$$

where $\hat{Q}$ is the estimate of Q and each b_i is an estimate of the regression parameter β_i.

Data Collection.   Data collection involves a trade-off between sampling error and sampling cost. A rough rule of thumb is that the minimum sample size should be three or four times the number of independent variables. Because of the ease with which regression may be performed on a computer, the analyst must have good a priori reasons for including each of the independent variables.

Interpretation.   After running a multiple regression on a computer, the analyst must interpret and test the results. Testing the validity of the results involves three fundamental questions:

1. Do the regression parameters bear the correct sign and are they of reasonable magnitude?
2. How well are variations in demand explained by variations in the independent variables—both singly and collectively?
3. Are the regression coefficients, individually, and the regression equation as a whole statistically significant?

Evaluation.   The computer program prints out certain test data to aid in the evaluation. For the regression as a whole, these include:

- The multiple coefficient of determination[21] (R^2)
- The standard error of the estimate
- The *F*-statistic.

For evaluating individual variables and parameters, the printout includes:

- The standard error of each regression coefficient
- The *t*-test ratio for each regression coefficient
- The coefficient of correlation (r) of each variable with every other variable.

Assumptions and Special Problems with Multiple-Regression Analysis.   The validity of the regression rests upon certain assumptions about the input data. If any assumption is violated, special problems arise.

- *Multicollinearity* arises when two variables are not truly independent of one another. They move together so closely that the regression procedure is unable to distinguish between their effects upon Q. The solution for this problem is to eliminate one of the variables from the regression.
- *Heteroscedasticity* exists when there is a violation of the assumption that all distributions of the error terms have the same variance. The consequences are that the usual *t*- and *F*-tests will exaggerate the statistical significance of the regression coefficients. A number of methods for detecting this problem are discussed in econometrics texts, along with remedial measures. These methods include a graphical method, the Park test, and Spearman's rank-correlation test.
- *Autocorrelation*. If we are dealing with time-series data, a basic assumption is that events at time $t - 1$ do not influence events at time t. If this is not true, autocorrelation, or serial correlation, exists, and neither *F*-test for statistical significance of the regression nor the *t*-tests for statistical significance of the regression coefficients are valid. There are a number of reasons for autocorrelation, including inertia, specification bias, the cobweb phenomenon, other lags, and manipulation of the data in an attempt to correct other problems. Autocorrelation can be detected by plotting the residuals to detect a regular pattern, or by the Durbin-Watson *d*-test. Correction requires transformation of the input data to eliminate the spillover effects from one time period to the next.

Problems

1. Explain why the identification problem related to demand estimation is serious and often difficult to resolve.

2. You run a multiple-regression analysis of demand data on a computer and the printout indicates a high R^2 and high values for the *t*-statistics. Is this a good enough reason to believe that you have a good demand estimate? Explain why or why not.

3. Discuss tests for the detection of the following problems and methods for their remedy:

   (1) autocorrelation

   (2) multicollinearity

   (3) heteroscedasticity.

4. The Campus Bike Shop, located near the campus of a large university, sells and repairs bicycles of all

---

[21] Some computer programs also print out the corrected multiple coefficient of determination, $\overline{R}^2$.

types. The owner, who was only briefly exposed to a managerial-economics course during his college days, has been in the habit of ordering the same number of 10-speed bicycles each month. The result has been overstockage in some months and the loss of sales because of lack of inventory in other months. As a consultant, you propose to predict monthly sales by the linear-regression equation

$$\hat{Q} = b_0 + b_1X_1 + b_2X_2 + b_3X_3 + b_4X_4$$

where

$\hat{Q}$ = estimated monthly sales
X_1 = average selling price, in dollars
X_2 = average price of lead-free gasoline, in dollars
X_3 = 1 if fall semester, otherwise zero
X_4 = 1 if spring semester, otherwise zero. [22]

Using data from the past 15 months, you obtain the following results from a linear-regression program on a computer:

VARIABLE	COEFF	STD ERROR	T-VALUE
1	-0.604	1.33	-0.45
2	77.44	38.91	1.99
3	42.84	16.18	2.65
4	14.83	14.39	1.03
INTERCEPT	22.674	59.59	0.38

R-SQUARED = .636
STANDARD ERROR = 4.4
F-VALUE = 8.14

a. Write the estimated regression equation and interpret the estimated coefficients.

b. Test the regression equation for overall significance at the .05 level.

c. Interpret the coefficient of determination.

5. Referring to Problem 4:

a. Next month the average price of a 10-speed bicycle is expected to be $350 and the average price of lead-free gasoline is expected to be $1.35 per gallon. How many 10-speed bicycles can the Campus Bike Shop expect to sell?

b. Calculate a 95 percent confidence interval for your answer to (a).

c. Construct a 95 percent confidence interval for each of the parameters of the regression equation.

6. A land developer on the Kona coast of the island of Hawaii has constructed a linear-regression model to estimate the selling price of building lots as

$$\hat{P} = b_0 + b_1X_1 + b_2X_2 + b_3X_3$$

where

$\hat{P}$ = estimated selling price, in hundreds of dollars
X_1 = area of the lot, in square feet
X_2 = mean elevation of the lot, in feet above sea level
X_3 = mean slope of the lot, in degrees from horizontal.

The computer printout of a multiple-regression program provides the following information:

COEFFICIENTS:

VARIABLE	B	STD ERROR (B)
AREA	.099	.058
ELEVATION	.029	.006
SLOPE	.086	.031
CONSTANT	-2.491	1.011

SUMMARY STATS

MULTIPLE R	R-SQUARE
.8854	.7838

ANOVA

SOURCE	SUM OF SQUARES	DF	MEAN SQUARE	F
REGRESSION	21.409	3	7.136	19.339
RESIDUAL	5.903	16	.369	

a. Write the equation for $\hat{P}$.

b. Interpret the regression coefficients. Are their signs correct? Do they seem reasonable in magnitude?

c. Which of the explanatory variables are statistically significant at the .05 level?

d. Interpret the coefficient of determination. Considering its value, would you drop any insignificant variables from the model to try to improve it?

e. Interpret the F-value computed by the analysis of variance (ANOVA).

f. Do you consider this model to be acceptable? Why or why not?

---

[22] If X_3 and X_4 are both zero, it implies the summer term or vacation.

7. A market-research firm has collected data for 50 sales districts on the variation in sales with respect to income per household (INCOME) and advertising expenditures (ADVERT) by their client company. All figures were recorded in thousands of dollars and then input to a multiple-regression computer program. Part of the output was as follows:

```
                                      STAND.
COEFFICIENTS:  VARIABLE      B        ERROR
               INCOME      .0235      .00622
               ADVERT     1.234       .2894
               CONSTANT  55.016       .25678
ANOVA:         SOURCE        SS
               REGRESSION  729.028
               RESIDUAL     60.695
```

a. Write the regression equation for SALES.

b. Interpret the regression coefficients.

c. Test the regression coefficients for statistical significance at the .05 level.

d. Compute and interpret the multiple coefficient of determination.

e. Calculate and interpret the F-value.

8. What makes a good salesperson? The Sun Solar Company conducted a random survey of 16 full-time solar-system salespeople in an attempt to answer this question. First, salespeople were interviewed and given an aptitude test developed by the Maximum Sales Training Institute in Dallas, Texas. Then, an effort index was calculated on the basis of a salesperson's observed car mileage divided by the estimated mileage required to cover the assigned region satisfactorily. (Company cars have been provided by Sun Solar Company for salespeople.)

The data were analyzed by a young, newly hired college graduate from Denton University. She reported the following regression equation:

$$S = 18.0 + 0.75T + 22.4E$$
$$\quad\quad\;\; (0.08)\quad (2.05)$$

where

S = sales, in thousands of dollars
T = aptitude-test score
E = effort index

and the numbers in parentheses are standard errors of the regression coefficients. Further, she found that the standard error of the estimate was 3.82 and the standard deviation of sales was 18.2.

a. Interpret the regression coefficients of the variables.

b. Calculate and interpret R^2 and the F-statistic.

c. Estimate sales performance for Mr. Jones, who has an aptitude test score of 72 and an effort index of 0.65.

d. The Sun Solar Company would like to use this equation for predicting a salesperson's potential. What is the size of the 95 percent confidence interval for predicting S?

9. Fire Prevention Equipment Company (FPE) in Cincinnati, Ohio, produces smoke detectors and many other hardware items in the fire-prevention field, and these are sold through 26 retail outlets in midwestern states. Smoke-detector sales have been increasing at an annual rate of 8 percent and FPE's market share has been 22 percent in the region for the past three years. Since there is increasing competition, FPE is planning various means to compete better and thereby improve sales of its smoke detectors. The director of market research for FPE has performed a regression analysis of sales in the company's retail outlets and has obtained the following results:

$$\hat{Q} = 12.6 - 9.2P + 2.2A + 0.6D + 0.3H$$
$$\quad\;\;\; (7.2)\quad (2.1)\quad (1.2)\quad (0.24)\quad (0.12)$$

$$R^2 = .89 \quad\quad SEE = 7.6$$

where

$\hat{Q}$ = smoke-detector sales, in thousands of units
P = unit price of smoke detectors
A = advertising expenditure, in thousands of dollars
D = disposable income per household, in thousands of dollars
H = number of households, in hundreds
SEE = standard error of the estimate
$(n.n)$ = standard errors of the regression coefficients (printed under the regression coefficients).

a. Interpret R_2 and SEE.

b. Calculate the F-statistic.

c. Do sales depend more on the price of the smoke detector than on advertising expenditures?

d. Which independent variables have the most influence on sales?

e. Evansdale, Indiana, is a potential midwestern market with an economic environment and characteristics similar to the locations where FPE outlets are now located. In planning for the opening of a new outlet in Evansdale, the director of market research provided the following information for its first year: $A = 42; D = 22; H = 60$.

(i) Derive the demand equation for the Evansdale outlet.

(ii) Estimate the probability that the Evansdale outlet will generate at least $42,000 in revenue if the price of smoke detectors is $14 per unit.

Case Problem: Performance Auto Supplies

10. Performance Auto Supplies (PAS) is a national franchise selling automotive parts and accessories. At corporate headquarters in Chicago, Illinois, top management is developing a model to estimate the annual sales of each regional area. If the regional sales can be predicted, then the total sales for PAS can be predicted. Also, a good sales model can assist regional inventory scheduling and result in more accurate production orders to PAS's contracted manufacturers.

The sales manager at PAS suggested using two predictor variables: (1) the current number of retail outlets in each region and (2) the number of automobiles registered in each region as of April 30 (end of first quarter). Data are as follows:

Region	Annual Sales ($ millions) Y	Number of Retail Outlets X_1	Number of Automobiles Registered (millions) X_2
1	52.5	1,780	21.5
2	24.6	2,470	20.2
3	18.5	450	6.1
4	15.6	440	11.5
5	32.2	1,650	9.2
6	45.0	2,102	10.6
7	33.0	2,305	18.9
8	3.6	121	4.3
9	34.7	1,801	9.1
10	24.6	1,130	5.6
11	40.0	1,650	8.7

a. Estimate the prediction equation. (This requires operation of a multiple-regression computer program.)

b. How much error is involved in the prediction for Regions 1 and 3?

PAS's sales manager is dissatisfied with the regression results because fluctuations in regional economic conditions are not incorporated in the annual sales model. To account for this, a new predictor variable, personal income by region, is added to the regression. Data are as follows:

Region	Personal Income ($ billions)
1	97.2
2	32.5
3	34.6
4	30.2
5	65.3
6	92.7
7	62.1
8	18.6
9	65.2
10	60.5
11	82.0

Questions

a. Does the additional variable, personal income by region, make a significant contribution to the prediction of annual sales?

b. Estimate the annual sales for a new region, Region 12, with the assumption of $37 billion in personal income, 2,000 retail outlets, and 15.5 million registered automobiles.

c. Evaluate the accuracy of the sales estimate for Region 12.

d. If you were a consultant on this case, which variables would you include or exclude in your regression model? Why?

Case Problem: Determinants of Fast-Food Sales

11. The objective of this case is to illustrate how multiple regression can be used to construct a model

of aggregate sales. The subject of this study is a fast-food chain in Hawaii. [23] Because of intense competition, it is important for the chain to be able to determine what factors influence sales and to predict sales given certain scenarios of market and economic development.

Speedy Burger has 13 stores located in various parts of the state. These stores are classified into three groups according to the type of clientele each serves. *Tourist* stores primarily serve tourists, *metropolitan* stores are those frequented by urban customers, and *rural* stores cater to those who live and work in rural areas of the islands. Since each type of store has a different type of customer, it is not unreasonable to expect sales at each type of store to be affected differently by the same set of independent variables.

Data were collected for 28 monthly periods from the 13 stores in the chain. Total monthly sales for each category of store was selected as the dependent variable. The independent variables were:

a. *Consumer variables:*

(1) HOLIDA = Number of school holidays and weekends in the month

(2) VISITO = Visitor (tourist) count for Hawaii in that month (in thousands)

(3) RAIN = Average rainfall in that month (in inches).

b. *Marketing variables:*

(4) NOST = The number of Speedy Burger stores open for business during the month

(5) ADV1 = Speedy Burger advertising, that is, weighted advertising expenditures (see explanation following this list of variables)

(6) ADV2 = Same as ADV1 except different weights

(7) CADV = Weighted advertising expenditures by Speedy's competitors

(8) NEWPRO = Percentage of month during which a new product promotion took place

(9) GAME = Percentage of month during which game promotions occurred

c. *Economic variables:*

(10) PI = Consumer price index for Hawaii.

Special consideration was given to the advertising variables because advertising was expected to have both cumulative and lagged effects on sales. The variable ADV1 represented a 50 percent weight on Speedy's advertising expenditures in the current month, with weights of 100, 80, 70, 60, and 50 percent in those of the preceding five months, respectively. ADV2 had a 33 percent weight on the current month and 100 percent for the previous month. Because of the lagging, the data for the first five months were unusable, leaving 23 monthly observations on which to base the analysis.

Regression results are shown in Table 1. (Numbers in parentheses after the regression coefficients are the standard errors of the regression coefficients.) The computer output reveals that for each class of store, an equation can be fitted with a high degree of explanatory power (as reflected in R^2).

Note that not all variables are relevant to each type of store. For example, the number of holidays is a significant explanatory variable only for tourist stores. Similarly, the promotions appear effective only at tourist stores. Some variables have different effects on different types of stores. Competitors' advertising (CADV) has a positive correlation with sales of metropolitan and tourist stores but detracts from rural sales. In all cases, the advertising by Speedy Burger (when adjusted for lag) contributes to higher sales.

The estimated equations can be used to forecast aggregate sales by store type. Assumed

---

[23] This is an actual analysis prepared by Dr. Jack Suyderhoud, University of Hawaii, College of Business Administration. The name of the client has been altered to maintain the confidentiality of the data source.

TABLE 1   Estimated Coefficients and Test Statistics

```
                              Class of Store
              ---------------------------------------------------
   Variable    Metropolitan    Tourist         Rural

   HOLIDA          ---          2,812(3.52)*      ---
   VISITO          ---          231.6(1.06)       ---
   RAIN        -2,142(-1.25)       ---            ---
   NOST        70,313(3.42)*       ---         92,163(11.14)*
   ADV1        0.3862(1.07)     0.4100(2.28)*      ---
   ADV2            ---             ---          0.65027(3.49)*
   CADV        0.6519(1.97)*    0.6320(2.39)*  -0.4576(-2.57)*
   NEWPRO          ---         22,462(2.09)*       ---
   GAME            ---         10,499(1.48)        ---
   CPI         1,827(4.68)*     1,164(4.06)*   -1,184(-1.95)*
   CONSTANT    -373,290         -148,990        221,780

   SUMMARY STATISTICS

   n                      23              23              23
   STD ERROR          17,478          11,730          12,702
   R2                   0.85            0.91            0.98
   DURBIN-WATSON        2.05            1.94            2.21
```

values of the independent variables are substituted into the estimated relationship and a prediction is made. For example, suppose we expect the independent-variable values next month for metropolitan stores to be:

RAIN = 1 inch (from the National Weather Service)

NOST = 5 (current level)

ADV1 = $98,716 (advertising budget)

CADV = $127,233 (a "best guess")

CPI = 350 (from the general economic forecast).

The forecast aggregate metropolitan sales are thus

$$\hat{Q} = -373,290 - 2,142(1)$$
$$+ 70,313(5) + 0.3862(98,716)$$
$$+ 0.6519(127,233) + 1,827(350)$$
$$\approx \$736,650.$$

Questions

a. Provide an interpretation for the estimated coefficient of the RAIN and CADV variables in metropolitan stores. Are the signs consistent with theory? Explain.

b. Interpret the coefficient of determination, R^2, for the tourist-stores equation.

c. Based on the calculated Durbin-Watson statistics, should adjustments be made for autocorrelation in any model? Explain.

d. Given the set of independent variables, is there reason to suspect multicollinearity? If so, among what variables?

e. Given the definition of the HOLIDA variable, can you explain why it is significant to the tourist stores but not to the others?

References

Barnes, R.; R. Gillingham; and R. Hagemann. "The Short-Run Residential Demand for Electricity." *Review of Economics and Statistics* (November 1981), pp. 541–42.

Bechdolt, B. "Cross-Sectional Travel Demand Functions: U.S. Visitors to Hawaii, 1961–1970." *Quarterly Review of Economics and Business* (Winter 1973), pp. 37–47.

Carlson, Rodney L. "Seemingly Unrelated Regression and the Demand for Automobiles of Different Sizes, 1965–1975: A Disaggregate Approach." *Journal of Business* (April 1978), pp. 243–62.

Farrar, D., and R. Blauber. "Multicollinearity in Regression Analysis: The Problem Revisited." *Review of Economics and Statistics* (February 1967), pp. 92–107.

Gahvari, Firoz. "Demand and Supply of Housing in the U. S., 1929-1978." *Economic Inquiry* 24 (April 1986), pp. 333–47.

Gujarati, Damodar. *Basic Econometrics*. New York: McGraw-Hill, 1978, pp. 167–251.

Haitovsky, Y. "A Note on the Maximization of $\overline{R}^2$." *American Statistician* (February 1969), pp. 20–21.

Houthhakker, H. S., and Lester D. Taylor. *Consumer Demand in the United States, 1929–1970: Analyses and Projection*, 2nd ed. Cambridge, Mass.: Harvard University Press, 1970.

Johnston, J. *Econometric Methods*, 4th ed. New York: McGraw-Hill, 1984.

Leamer, Edward E. "Is It a Demand Curve, or Is It a Supply Curve? Partial Identification through Inequality Constraints." *Review of Economics and Statistics* (August 1981), pp. 319–25.

_____. "Let's Take the Con out of Econometrics." *American Economic Review* 73 (March 1983), pp. 31–43.

Neter, J.; W. Wasserman; and M. Kutner. *Applied Linear Regression Models*. Homewood, Ill.: Richard D. Irwin, 1983.

Savin, N., and K. White. "Estimation and Testing for Functional Form and Autocorrelation: A Simultaneous Approach." *Journal of Econometrics* (August 1978), pp. 1–12.

Thiel, A.; and A. L. Nagar. "Testing the Independence of Regression Disturbance." *Journal of the American Statistical Association* 56 (1961), pp. 793–806.

C H A P T E R

9

FORECASTING

Since successful operation of the firm's business in the future rests upon effective planning, and since effective planning rests upon good forecasting of the firm's business and economic environment, it is fair to say that the firm's continuing success rests upon its ability to make good forecasts. The purpose of this chapter is to explain several methods of forecasting either micro- or macroenvironments, thereby reducing the degree of uncertainty inherent to all future business endeavors.

There are many different ways to classify forecasting methods, but the four most commonly used methods are:

- Mechanical extrapolations
- Barometric techniques
- Opinion polling and intention surveys
- Econometric methods

Although these methods are different, they should not necessarily be regarded as mutually exclusive. Some methods may be more suitable for preparing short-term forecasts such as monthly or quarterly predictions; others may be better for long-term projections of a year or more. Some may be better for forecasting at the macro level, while others may be preferred for forecasting at the level of the firm. In many organizations, two, three, or even all four approaches may be used with various degrees of emphasis and sophistication.

CHAPTER OUTLINE

The chapter is divided into four sections and an appendix:

1. **Mechanical Extrapolations.** This section covers naive models and the techniques of time-series analysis, including the use of moving averages and linear regression.

2. **Barometric Techniques.** This section covers leading, lagging, and coincident indicators, composite indexes, and diffusion indexes.
3. **Opinion Polling and Intention Surveys.** This section covers surveys of economic intentions and sales forecasting.
4. **Econometric Models.** This section covers both single-equation and simultaneous-equations models, and the techniques employed by macroeconomic forecasters.
5. **Appendix 9A: Evaluation of Forecasting.** This appendix covers the need for evaluation of forecasting and some of the ways in which it can be performed.

Mechanical Extrapolations

Extrapolation procedures of one form or another are used extensively by business executives, economists, market researchers, and others engaged in forecasting activities. As a method of prediction, extrapolation may include procedures ranging from simple coin tossing to the projection of trends and other more complex mathematical techniques. Typically, **extrapolation techniques** are distinguished from other forecasting methods in that they are essentially mechanical and are not closely integrated with relevant economic theory. Nevertheless, they are widely used by professional forecasters, probably because they are convenient and also reasonably able to satisfy the needs of management, a point that will be discussed later.

Naive Models

Naive models are ordinarily thought of as continuity models, for they all state that the future value of the variable in question is in some way a function of its present or recent value. Thus, letting Y denote the observed value of the variable under investigation, letting $\hat{Y}$ denote its forecast value, and using subscripts to designate time periods, the following two naive models are typical examples.

1. *No-change model:* The predicted value of the variable for the next period will be the same as its actual value in the present period:

$$\hat{Y}_{t+1} = Y_t. \tag{1}$$

2. *Proportional-change model:* The change in the value of the variable from the current period to the next period, $\Delta Y_{t+1} = Y_{t+1} - Y_t$, will be proportional to the change in the value of the variable from the previous period to the current period $\Delta Y_t = Y_t - Y_{t-1}$. Thus

$$\hat{Y}_{t+1} = Y_t + k\Delta Y_t. \tag{2}$$

The parameter k may be estimated by observation from historical data, by more refined methods such as averaging or statistical regression, or by sheer hunch if there are inadequate data. If $k = 1$, the equation represents an equal-change model.

The great majority of all economic decisions (and probably political and social decisions as well) are made on the basis of naive models such as these. It is not difficult to see why this is so. Naive models are either straightforward or modified projections of the present or the recent past. Hence for most short-term decisions, they provide the most feasible guides for forecasting, since they are simple to apply and require a minimum amount of data or computation.

Time-Series Analysis

A **time series** is a sequence of values corresponding to particular points, or periods, of time. Data such as sales, production, and prices, when arranged chronologically, are thereby ordered in time and hence are referred to as time series. The simple line chart is the most common graphic device for depicting a time series, with the dependent variable (such as sales, production, or prices) scaled on the vertical axis, and the independent variable (time, expressed in years, months, or any other temporal measure) scaled on the horizontal axis.

Why does a time series typically exhibit a pattern of fluctuations? The answer to this question has usually been that at least four sources of variation are at work in an economic time series:

1. Trend (T)
2. Seasonal variation (S)
3. Cyclical variation (C)
4. Irregular forces (I).

Trend represents the long-run growth or decline of the series. **Seasonal variations** due to weather and customs manifest themselves during the same approximate time periods each year (for example, Christmas, Easter, and other seasons when different types of purchases are made). **Cyclical variations**, covering several years at a time, reflect economic prosperities and recessions. And finally, **irregular forces**, such as strikes, wars, and boycotts, are erratic in their influence on a particular series but nevertheless must be recognized.

Of the four forces affecting economic time series, the seasonal factor is fairly easy to measure and predict. The irregular factor is unpredictable but can be adjusted by a smoothing-out process such as a moving average. Hence the trend (which represents persistent growth or decline) and cyclical variation (which is presumably recurrent) have occupied the chief attention of forecasters using time-series analysis.

Since calculation of the trend may require first removing seasonal influence, we will discuss seasonal variation and its adjustment before discussing trend projections and cyclical analysis.

Seasonal Variation and the Moving-Average Technique.   Seasonal variation can be incorporated routinely into forecasts by means of a *seasonal index*, which can be calculated by a *moving-average* technique. A **moving average** is calculated by adding each period's value over some desired length of time and then dividing by the number of

---

EXHIBIT 9–1 **Unadjusted Quarterly Sales, 1985–1989, in Thousands of Dollars**

Quarter	1985	1986	1987	1988	1989
1	$ 190	$ 280	$ 270	$ 300	$ 320
2	370	420	360	430	440
3	300	310	280	290	320
4	220	180	190	200	220
Totals	$1,080	$1,190	$1,100	$1,220	$1,300

---

periods. Using data from Exhibit 9–1, we can show how to create a moving average and construct a seasonal index.

The data shown in Exhibit 9–1 are first rearranged as shown in Exhibit 9–2, after which four-period moving averages, centered moving averages, and seasonal indexes are calculated. These calculations are also shown in Exhibit 9–2 and have been obtained by using a four-step procedure.

Step 1. The four-period moving averages are calculated from successive sets of four quarters of sales, beginning with the first four quarters of the first year:

$$\frac{190 + 370 + 300 + 220}{4} = 270 \qquad \frac{370 + 300 + 220 + 280}{4} = 292$$

$$\frac{300 + 220 + 280 + 420}{4} = 305 \qquad \frac{220 + 280 + 420 + 310}{4} = 307$$

and so on. (Fractions are dropped.) Note that each successive calculation drops the earliest quarter and adds the next successive quarter.

Step 2. As illustrated by the dotted lines in the exhibit, the four-period moving averages obtained in Step 1 are centered *between* quarters, but this is not what we want. What we want are moving averages centered *on the midpoints* of the quarters. To get them, we calculate **centered moving averages**. As illustrated by the solid line around the first two four-period moving averages, the centered moving average for each quarter is calculated as the average of each successive adjacent pair of the four-period moving averages, i.e.,

$$\frac{270 + 292}{2} = 281, \qquad \frac{292 + 305}{2} = 298, \qquad \frac{305 + 307}{2} = 306,$$

and so on.

Step 3. The seasonal indexes are calculated by dividing the centered moving average for the quarter into the actual sales for the quarter:

$$Q_{3/1985} = \frac{300}{281} = 1.07, \qquad Q_{4/1985} = \frac{220}{298} = 0.74,$$

$$Q_{1/1986} = \frac{280}{306} = 0.91, \text{ and so on.}$$

EXHIBIT 9–2   Moving Averages and Quarterly Seasonal Indexes

Year	Quarter	Sales Units of $10,000	Four-Period Moving Average	Centered Moving Average	Seasonal Index
1985	1	190			
	2	370	270		
	3	300	292	281	1.07
	4	220	305	298	0.74
1986	1	280	307	306	0.91
	2	420	297	302	1.39
	3	310	295	296	1.04
	4	180	280	287	0.63
1987	1	270	273	276	0.98
	2	360	275	274	1.32
	3	280	283	279	1.00
	4	190	300	286	0.66
1988	1	300	303	301	1.00
	2	430	305	304	1.42
	3	290	310	307	0.94
	4	200	312	311	0.64
1989	1	320	320	316	1.01
	2	440	325	322	1.37
	3	320			
	4	220			

Step 4. Arrange the seasonal indexes by quarter and calculate the average seasonal index for each quarter. Exhibit 9–3 (page 248) shows the results of this step.

Step 5. Since the figures in Exhibit 9–3 are merely rough estimates of seasonal-index values, perhaps we can improve them by making some adjustments. The first step is to normalize—that is, to make sure that the average of the four average seasonal indexes is 1. We find that:

$$\frac{0.98 + 1.38 + 1.01 + 0.67}{4} = 1.01.$$

This small error could be eliminated by reducing each quarter's value by 0.0025. However, it is better to examine the seasonal-index values for trends or other patterns of behavior. The data in Exhibit 9–3 indicate that Q_1 is increasing, Q_2 oscillates in a fairly regular pattern bout a mean of 1.375, Q_3 seems to be decreasing, and Q_4 first drops, then follows an up and down pattern with a narrow range of movement. These changes should be recognized and incorporated into an adjusted seasonal index.

While there are more formal methods to make these adjustments, we shall be content to use an "eyeball" approach. This means that we exercise our best judgment to adjust the seasonal indexes upward or downward to recognize the trends, while insuring that the average of the four indexes is equal to 1. The result is as follows:

	Q_1	Q_2	Q_3	Q_4
Adjusted seasonal index	0.99	1.38	0.98	0.65

EXHIBIT 9–3   **Data for Calculating Adjusted Seasonal Indexes**

Year	Q_1	Q_2	Q_3	Q_4
1985			1.07	0.74
1986	0.91	1.39	1.04	0.63
1987	0.98	1.32	1.00	0.66
1988	1.00	1.42	0.94	0.64
1989	1.01	1.37		
Totals	3.90	5.50	4.05	2.67
Average seasonal index	0.98	1.38	1.01	0.67

Step 6.   The last step is to make a forecast for each of the four quarters of the coming year; in this case, for 1990. We do this by multiplying the *most recent* centered moving average for the quarter by its respective adjusted seasonal index. Going back to Exhibit 9–2, we see that the most recent centered moving average (last number in the "Centered Moving Average" column) pertains to the second quarter of 1989, the next most recent to the first quarter of 1989, the third most recent to the fourth quarter of 1988, and the fourth most recent to the third quarter of 1988. The resulting quarterly forecasts for 1990 are:

$$Q_1: \quad 316 \text{ (for 1989)} \times 0.99 = 312.84 \approx \$313,000$$
$$Q_2: \quad 322 \text{ (for 1989)} \times 1.38 = 444.36 \approx \$444,000$$
$$Q_3: \quad 307 \text{ (for 1988)} \times 0.98 = 300.86 \approx \$301,000$$
$$Q_4: \quad 311 \text{ (for 1988)} \times 0.65 = 202.15 \approx \$202,000.$$

By flattening the peaks and valleys of the seasonal data, the moving average has deseasonalized the data, thereby revealing the underlying trend. The moving-average technique has both advantages and disadvantages. As a method of determining trend, it is simple and easy to apply, and it tends to present a realistic portrayal of long-run movements. On the other hand, it misses turning points in the trend forecast, it assumes a definite and relatively stable periodicity for the series to which it is applied, and it is unable to calculate moving averages for observations at each end of the series. The difference between the number of observations in the series and the number of moving averages calculated is equal to the number of periods being averaged, with half of the difference at the beginning and half at the end of the series. For example, the moving averages for four quarters as shown in Exhibit 9–2 have no values for the first two quarters and the last two quarters of the series.

Forecasting with a moving average thus becomes a problem of predicting the future course of the moving average based on its most recent level, which of necessity always trails behind the most recent observations in the original series. The use of a moving average for forecasting thus can pose some difficulties unless the average is reasonably stable and easy to predict. Since this is not usually the case with economic data, moving averages have perhaps been more frequently employed as devices for studying the deviations from the trend of a series rather than the trend itself.

Trend Projections.   As a forecasting procedure, the methods of trend projection usually assume that the recent rate of change of the variable will continue in the future. On this basis, expectations are established by projecting past trends into the future, using techniques such as regression analysis. Thus, companies often project sales, GNP, and so forth several years into the future by this procedure.

When predictions are based on trends of past relationships, the trend may be a simple unweighted line, or it may be weighted by attaching the greatest importance to the most recent period and successively lesser degrees of importance to periods in the more distant past.

Unquestionably the most widely used approach for finding the trend in a time series is regression analysis by the method of least squares that was explained in Chapter 7. As its name implies, this method involves fitting a regression line through a series of observed data points in such a way that the squared deviations from this line are minimized. Letting Y = the observed values and $\hat{Y}$ = the forecasted values of a time series, then the sum of the squared deviations between Y and $\hat{Y}$ is:

$$D = \Sigma(Y - \hat{Y})^2. \tag{3}$$

The regression line is represented by the equation $\hat{Y} = a + bt$ where a and b are the estimated parameters and t is the number of a time period. Therefore,

$$D = \Sigma(Y - a - bt)^2. \tag{4}$$

Taking the partial derivatives of D with respect to a and b and setting them equal to zero leads to the following equations:

$$\Sigma Y = na + b\Sigma t \tag{5}$$

$$\Sigma tY = a\Sigma t + b\Sigma t^2 \tag{6}$$

where n = number of observations. These equations are then solved simultaneously to find the values for the parameters a and b. The resulting regression line indicates the trend of the data over time.

Trend estimates are more reliable if they are based on "deseasonalized" data. Seasonal influences should be removed from the data by the moving-average technique illustrated previously before trend is calculated. The trend line for our illustrative problem thus should be calculated from the centered moving averages of Exhibit 9–2. To fit a trend line, we need to find values for ΣY, Σt, ΣtY, and Σt^2, where Y = the centered moving averages and t = time sequence of quarters. These sums are shown in Exhibit 9–4 (page 250).

Then

$$(1) \quad \Sigma Y = na + b\Sigma t \qquad (2) \quad \Sigma tY = a\Sigma t + b\Sigma t^2$$
$$4{,}746 = 16a + 120b \qquad\qquad 36{,}150 = 120a + 1{,}240b.$$

Multiplying the first equation by 7.5, then subtracting it from the second equation, we can solve for b:

$$36{,}150 = 120a + 1240b$$
$$\underline{35{,}595 = 120a + 900b}$$
$$555 = 340b$$

$$b = 1.632352941$$
$$\approx 1.6324.$$

EXHIBIT 9–4   Calculation of Sums for Least Squares Method

Year	Centered Moving Average Y	Time Period t	tY	t^2
1985	281	0	0	0
	298	1	298	1
1986	306	2	612	4
	302	3	906	9
	296	4	1,184	16
	287	5	1,435	25
1987	276	6	1,656	36
	274	7	1,918	49
	279	8	2,232	64
	286	9	2,574	81
1988	301	10	3,010	100
	304	11	3,344	121
	307	12	3,684	144
	311	13	4,043	169
1989	316	14	4,424	196
	322	15	4,830	225
Sums	4,746	120	36,150	1,240

Substituting for b in the first equation, we can solve for a:

$$4,746 = 16a + 120(1.632352941)$$
$$4,746 = 16a + 195.8823529$$
$$16a = 4,550.117647$$
$$a = 284.3823529 \approx 284.3824.$$

Hence the estimated trend line of the deseasonalized data is

$$\hat{Y} = \$284.3824 + \$1.6324t.$$

Our deseasonalized forecast for the second quarter of 1989 would be

$$\hat{Y}_{1989/2} = \$284.3824 + \$1.6324(15) = \$308.8684.$$

When this figure is multiplied by the seasonal index of 1.38, as previously calculated, the resulting forecast is $4,262,384 (since the data were given in units of $10,000).

This illustration shows that the least squares method is a relatively quick way to calculate the trend line even when calculations must be done manually rather than with a computer. If a computer program for linear regression is available, however, it is better to let the computer do the work, not only to avoid arithmetic errors during the process of calculations, but also for the statistics used to evaluate the reliability of the estimated trend line, as explained in Chapter 7. A computer solution to this illustrative problem is shown in Exhibit 9–5.

Trend models have been used both successfully and unsuccessfully in the past. Forecasts based for the years 1929, 1933, 1937, 1973, and 1980 were disastrous for companies that relied upon the trend of preceding years. Yet the method continues in wide use because many economic time series do, for the most part, show a persistent tendency

EXHIBIT 9–5   Computer Solution to Illustrative Problem

```
----------------------REGRESSION ANALYSIS------------------------


HEADER DATA FOR: A:SEO5      LABEL:
NUMBER OF CASES: 16    NUMBER OF VARIABLES: 2

----------------------------------------------------------------


INDEX       NAME            MEAN            STD.DEV.
  1          X             7.5000           4.7610
DEP. VAR.:   Y            296.6250          14.6600

----------------------------------------------------------------

DEPENDENT VARIABLE: Y

VAR.   REGRESSION COEFFICIENT   STD. ERROR   T(DF=  14)   PROB.
X                1.6324            .6978        2.339     .03466
CONSTANT       284.3824

STD. ERROR OF EST. = 12.8669

        r SQUARED = .2810
             r = .5301

            ANALYSIS OF VARIANCE TABLE

   SOURCE       SUM OF SQUARES   D.F.   MEAN SQUARE   F RATIO   PROB
 REGRESSION        905.9559       1       905.9559     5.472    .0347
 RESIDUAL         2317.7941       14      165.5567
 TOTAL            3223.7500       15
```

to move in the same direction for a period of time because of their inherent cumulative characteristics. Therefore, forecasts using the method of trend projection will be right as to the direction of change more times than they will be wrong.

Unfortunately, trend projections fail to detect changes in direction until after they have occurred, although it is the prediction of turning points that is most important to management. If turning points can be detected in advance, management can alter its plans with respect to sales effort, production scheduling, credit requirements, and the like. Otherwise, the mere projection of trends implies a forecast of continuance and no essential change in policy.

Cyclic Models.   When the trend and seasonal variation are removed from an annual series of economic data, the residual structure exhibits certain fluctuating characteristics that have been described by some economists as *business cycles*. World War II produced important changes in the structural variables of the economy and apparently has thereby altered the business cycle. Nevertheless, the use of cyclic models as a prediction method continues among forecasters in many business firms.

The most common practice in constructing forecasting models is to assume a multiplicative structure for the elements so that the relationship is expressed by the formula $O = TSCI$, where O = total behavior, T = trend, S = seasonal variations, C = cyclical variations, and I = irregular variations. The problem in forecasting is to isolate and measure each of these four factors by separating out of the total behavior O the gradual long-term change T, the regular oscillations S occurring within a year, and the regular oscillations C occurring over several years, each measured independently of the others. This problem of assumed relationships among the variables, however, is minor when compared with the following types of measurement problems that arise:

1. In explaining the cyclical mechanism, whether for the total economy or for a particular firm, there is controversy over whether the methods of analysis are really valid. Analysts have shown that apparent cycles can result in a series, not because a cycle actually exists, but simply because of the way in which the data are processed. For example, the use of a moving average may induce an oscillation in a resulting series even if no real cycle exists. In general, summing or averaging successive values of a random series can result in cyclical behavior by the very act itself (known as the *Slutsky-Yule effect*). For these reasons, the conventional method of residual analysis used by most business firms in separating cyclical and random components of time series is by no means a universally accepted procedure. On the contrary, it has been strongly questioned by analysts for many years.

2. The separation of trend and random forces in a time series has also been questioned. Various studies of economic series reveal that perhaps the trend in a series cannot be separated from the short-term movements, and that perhaps both may be generated by a common set of forces. If series of data are observed at fairly close intervals, the random changes from one term to the next may be large enough to outweigh substantially any systematic (causal) effect that may be present, so that the data appear to behave almost like a "wandering series." If the series really is wandering, any movements that appear to be systematic, such as trends or cycles, would be illusory, and their separation and measurement may be highly hazardous. Unfortunately, it is difficult to distinguish by statistical methods a genuine wandering series from one in which the systematic element is weak.

It is apparent that the mechanistic methods of processing time-series data—methods that are in extensive use by many business firms—have a number of shortcomings. Nevertheless, this does not mean that such methods need be discarded. They definitely have certain specific uses and are often well employed as a part of the forecaster's total kit of analytical tools. Their limitations as discussed here are based on their shortcomings when used as the *only* forecasting technique in complex forecasting problems. When traditional methods of time-series analysis are properly utilized, a number of advantages can be derived:

1. The necessary data are usually minimal and often easily obtained either from within the company itself or from outside sources.
2. The analytical calculations, such as the moving average, are usually simple and repetitive, and therefore suitable for computer processing. Hence, these techniques may be particularly well suited for problems in which a large number of variables must be forecast.
3. Only moderate analytical skills are required of the forecasters themselves. The methods are fairly easy to understand and the data processing is straightforward.
4. The method is largely objective, although judgment is involved in choosing fixed or changing seasonal factors, type of trend, and extrapolation of the cyclical component.
5. The resultant forecasts are usually reasonably accurate for the short run, say, a 12-month period.
6. Time-series analysis usually permits the calculation of the degree of error in the forecast. An interval of confidence for the predicted value strengthens the quality of the forecast itself. Forecast errors may be further reduced if identification of dependable trend and seasonal patterns can be made.
7. Once decomposition of the time series has been accomplished, the way is open for a causal analysis of the separate components.

Despite these advantages, time-series analysis, like every other tool, must be used with full awareness of its limitations:

1. Time-series analysis cannot be used when time-series data have not been accumulated; for example, projections are not possible for a new product or a new environment for which no historical records have been kept.
2. Forecasts based on extrapolation of trend, cyclical, and seasonal components of a series assume a strong persistence of time patterns from the past into the future. This may not always be a valid assumption.
3. Strict adherence to the time-series–analysis technique fails to take advantage of the forecaster's knowledge of prospective developments. For example, the forecaster might know that advertising effort will be greater than in the past, and such knowledge should be used to modify the extrapolation.
4. Time-series analysis gives no information about the causal factors influencing the time-series components. It merely provides a basis for causal analysis.

Barometric Techniques

Whereas mechanical methods of forecasting, particularly time-series analyses, are used under the assumption that the future is an extension of the past, the use of barometric techniques is based on the idea that the future can be predicted from certain happenings in the present.

Specifically, barometric methods usually involve the use of **statistical indicators**— selected time series that, when used in conjunction with one another or when combined in certain ways, provide an indication of the direction in which the economy, a particular industry, or a product is heading. The series chosen thus serve as barometers of economic change.

Types of Indicators

The basic concept underlying the statistical-indicator approach to business cycle analysis and forecasting is that various economic activities tend to move through the course of the business cycle in consistent but different time sequences. The most extensive periodic reports on business-cycle indicators have appeared, since October 1961, in a monthly magazine entitled *Business Conditions Digest*, published by the U.S. Dept. of Commerce. This widely quoted source consists for the most part of tables and charts showing the movements of several hundred economic indicators over the business cycle.

Coincident indicators are those that move approximately in phase with the aggregate economy and hence are measures of current economic activity. Some of the coincident indicators regularly reported by the U. S. Dept.of Commerce are:

- Employees on nonagricultural payrolls
- Personal income less transfer payments
- Index of total industrial production
- Manufacturing and trade sales.

Leading indicators tend to reflect future changes in the trend of the aggregate economy. Some of the leading indicators regularly published by the U. S. Dept. of Commerce are:[1]

- Average workweek for production and manufacturing workers
- Average weekly initial claims for state unemployment insurance
- New orders for consumer goods and materials
- Vendor performance: companies receiving slower deliveries
- Index of net business formations
- Contracts and orders for plant and equipment
- Index of new building permits for private housing units
- Changes in inventories on hand and on order
- Change in sensitive materials prices
- Index of stock prices for 500 common stocks
- Money supply
- Change in credit: business and consumer borrowing.

Lagging indicators are those that trail behind aggregate economic activities. Some of the lagging indicators that are regularly reported by the U.S. Dept. of Commerce are:

- Average duration of unemployment
- Ratio of constant-dollar inventories to sales for manufacturing and trade
- Labor cost per unit of manufacturing output: actual data as a percentage of trend

---

[1] Today many business executives use their own leading indicators based on personal experiences and observations.

- Average prime rate charged by banks
- Commercial and industrial loans outstanding
- Ratio of consumer installment credit to personal income.

The turning points of leading, coincident, and lagging indicators relative to the business cycle are illustrated in Exhibit 9–6 (page 256). The exhibit shows that leading indicators begin a downward trend before the peak of the business cycle and begin an upward trend before its trough. The turning points of coincident indicators coincide with the peaks and troughs of the business cycle. The lagging indicators start downward some time after the business cycle has peaked and don't start upward again until some time after the business cycle has reached its trough and has started back up. The relationships between leading, coincident, and lagging indicators usually have an economic basis. In many instances of leading indicators, for example, there are planning, contracting, or purchasing commitments that systematically lead to further economic activities or that are symptomatic of such activities.

Coincident indicators reflect concurrent economic activities and are therefore the most direct of the three relationships. Current sales and production levels, for example, contribute toward establishing a more general level of economic activity.

Finally, lagging indicators may sometimes be viewed as the residual in economic activities, as in the case of post-Christmas business inventories, or as a reflection of business or government commitments already under way. But even though experience is gained through historical evaluation, business executives are not nearly as interested in hindsight as they are in foresight. Consequently, of the three series discussed so far, lagging indicators are the least useful as an aid in formulating future business policy.

As previously mentioned, a number of indicator series are available monthly from the U. S. Dept. of Commerce, and it would seem that they should provide a useful guide for predicting the future course of the economy. Unfortunately, however, they are not as useful for this purpose as they might at first seem because of four limitations.

1. Leading indicators are not always consistent in their tendency to lead. Frequently, some of the series will signal what turns out to be a true change, while the remaining series either fail to signal at all or else signal too late to be of much value for prediction.
2. It is not always possible to tell whether the series is signaling an actual future turning point of the economy or whether it is merely exhibiting a wiggle that is of no real significance.
3. Even if the leading indicators could consistently signal the true turning points of the economy, they would still indicate only the direction of future change, while disclosing little or nothing about the magnitude of the change.
4. Indicator forecasting is not applicable to new-product situations. The development of indicators requires historical records that do not exist for new products.

In the light of these criticisms, the use of leading series as a forecasting device would seem to be a very limited approach at best.

There are also two refinements of statistical indicators that are often used in forecasting. One is the *composite index*, which highlights the timing and pattern of business-

EXHIBIT 9–6   **Movement of Economic Indicators Relative to the Business Cycle**

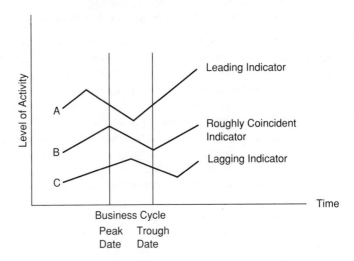

cycle expansion and contraction. The other is the *diffusion index*, which shows the direction and intensity of selected economic time series in a particular category, such as production or consumption. These indexes will be discussed next.

Composite Indexes

A **composite index** is a weighted average of several individual leading indicators. The weight of each indicator is based upon its ability to perform well in six areas related to forecasting:

1. Economic significance
2. Statistical adequacy
3. Consistency of timing at business-cycle peaks and troughs
4. Conformity to business expansions and contractions
5. Smoothness
6. Prompt availability.

Since a composite index is a weighted average of several leading indicators, the result is a smoother index with less random fluctuations than its components. Thus the composite index has a smaller tendency than its component indexes to give false signals.

Diffusion Indexes

The **diffusion index** was developed to answer the question of whether a change in any particular indicator series is really forecasting a reversal in the general trend or whether it is just an isolated development. Diffusion indexes are similar to composite indexes in that they are compiled from a number of leading indicators. But instead of combining a number of leading indicators into a single standardized composite index, the diffusion index reflects the percentage of leading indicators that are rising at some given time. For example, if there are 10 leading indicators that have proven to be relatively reliable predictors of economic movement in a certain area and seven of them are rising at the present time, the diffusion index would be 7/10 or 70 percent. The diffusion index is interpreted to mean that if it is higher than 50 (meaning that more than 50 percent of the indicators are rising), an increase in the economy is predicted, while if it is less than 50, the economy is expected to decline.

Diffusion indexes thus measure rates of change of the aggregate to which the indexes apply; hence diffusion indexes tend to change direction before the aggregates do. This is a useful characteristic for forecasting purposes. Unfortunately, however, the lead of a diffusion index is erratic. Many indexes tend to peak in the early stages of a business expansion and then settle down at a moderate level until the onset of recession. At that point they may fall spectacularly but much too late to be of any value in forecasting.

The prime difficulty with diffusion indexes is that efforts to increase their lead make them harder to interpret, while efforts to simplify their interpretation reduce their lead. Efforts to improve their lead usually require the inclusion of more and more leading series, but this results in increasing instability of the index. Despite the fact that diffusion indexes appear to derive reliability from the aggregation of more than one series, they must be used with caution.

In spite of their shortcomings as reliable indicators of a coming trend, diffusion indexes provide a useful way of examining the breadth and vigor of movement in the business cycle. The student, however, is well advised to regard the diffusion indexes as *aids* to careful study and analysis of underlying economic phenomena rather than substitutes. They cannot substitute completely for the judgment and experience of the forecaster, but they do provide a means of cross-checking judgment against the raw data of business statistics.

Opinion Polling and Intention Surveys

The **opinion-polling** or **sample-survey technique** of forecasting is a subjective method of prediction, amounting largely to a weighted or unweighted average of attitudes and expectations. The underlying assumption is that certain attitudes affecting economic decisions can be defined and measured far enough in advance so that changes in business trends can be predicted. The results are arrived at by asking people about their expectations or intentions as to future economic happenings. Various forms or types of surveys are used in both economic and sales forecasting and are discussed next.

Surveys of Economic Intentions

Among the best-known studies made for forecasting economic activity or some particular phase of it are the following:

1. Surveys of business executives' intentions concerning what to spend on plant and equipment, made independently by the McGraw-Hill Book Company, the U.S. Department of Commerce, the Securities Exchange Commission, and the National Industrial Conference Board.
2. Surveys of consumers' finances and buying plans, made primarily by the Survey Research Center of the University of Michigan under the sponsorship of both industry and government.
3. Surveys of business executives' plans regarding inventory changes, made by the National Association of Purchasing Agents.

All of these surveys are made periodically. On the whole, the more successful ones have been the McGraw-Hill survey of the expenditure plans for plant and equipment (capital-consuming plans) and the Survey Research Center's surveys of consumers' intentions. These account for most of the investment undertaken by the important capital-consuming industries. The record of these surveys has agreed rather well with actual expenditures, except for a few scattered years when the errors could be accounted for by unexpected international political events, such as war or the threat of war. Capital-expenditure plans, since they are so dependent on changes in the structural environment of the economy, could not be expected to remain the same under such unusual circumstances. Other than in these situations, however, the McGraw-Hill surveys have provided a basically sound analysis of capital-expenditure plans. The surveys cover much the same ground as the government survey mentioned before but are available earlier (in *Business Week*) and are widely used for forecasting.

The Survey Research Center of the University of Michigan prepares surveys of consumer finances and buying plans. The surveys, based on samples of several thousand respondents, are designed to

- Evaluate recent developments among consumers
- Provide data for testing hypotheses about economic behavior, that is, functional relationships among variables
- Determine intentions for consumer purchases of automobiles, houses, and major appliances. A single survey provides a cross section of data, while consecutive surveys yield time series of such data.

The results of these surveys have been both good and bad. On the one hand, the surveys seem to do well in foretelling some of the more important turning points of business. On the other hand, the surveys are less useful for predicting the magnitude of change. They have been best suited to predictions covering important decisions only a few months into the future. This is because the average consumer's decisions are affected by a wide array of economic and emotional complexities that are subject to frequent change. The farther we go into the future, the higher the probability that the consumers' finances and intentions will change.

Sales Forecasting

Opinion-polling methods are not confined to forecasting changes in economic conditions; many business firms use variations of the method in forecasting sales.

Executive polling, whereby the views of top management are combined and (subjectively) averaged, is frequently used. The assumption in the use of this approach is that there is safety in numbers since the combined judgment of the group is better than that of any single member. Hence the executives sit as a jury and pass judgment on the sales outlook for the coming year. Generally represented on the jury are people with a diversity of opinions—the sales, production, finance, purchasing, and administrative divisions.

In those companies where forecasts of probable events are derived after a sifting and analysis of market reports, sales data, and formal economic forecasts, the executive-polling approach may be quite successful. Without such careful evaluation, however, the method can easily degenerate into a guessing game yielding sloppy and unfounded predictions. Companies using the executive-polling approach may also combine it with statistical measures of trends and cycles or other analytical tools by raising or lowering the statistical forecast according to their subjective judgments.

Sales-force polling is another variation whereby a composite outlook is constructed on the basis of information derived from those closest to the market. The sales forecast may be built up from the estimates of salespeople made in cooperation with branch or regional managers, or by going directly to jobbers, distributors, and major customers in order to discover their needs.

One advantage is that this method utilizes the first-hand, specialized knowledge of those nearest to the market. It also gives salespeople greater confidence in their quotas developed from forecasts. Obviously, however, salespeople may be unaware of structural changes taking place in their markets and hence incapable of shaping their forecasts to account for those future changes. Also, sound forecasting requires more time and effort than most salespeople can ordinarily devote, and the result is more likely to be an off-the-cuff guess than a prediction. Furthermore, even their guesses may be biased by their quotas and the sales-quota system. Accordingly, firms using this method may need to set up a system of checks and balances whereby the estimates of salespeople are compiled, checked, adjusted, and revised periodically in the light of past experience and future expectations.

Consumer-intentions surveys are still another version of the opinion-polling method applied to sales forecasting. Some automobile companies, for instance, make sample surveys of automobile-buying intentions, which they then project to a national level by weighting the estimate with the average purchase rate and an index of predicted incomes. Similar techniques are used by other firms in forecasting the sales of appliances, furniture, and other durable goods.

Econometric Models

Based on the idea that changes in economic activity can be explained by a set of relationships among economic variables, there has arisen a branch of applied science known as **econometrics**. Breaking the word into its two parts, *econo* and *metrics,* it is evident that its subject matter must deal with the science of *economic measurement*. And this is precisely what econometrics does: it explains past economic activity and predicts future activity by deriving mathematical equations that will express the most probable inter-relationships among a set of economic variables. The economic variables may include disposable income, money flows, inventories, government revenues and expenditures, foreign trade, and so on.

Forecasting by econometric models offers at least two distinct advantages over other methods:

1. The most important advantage of econometric models is their ability to explain quantifiable economic relationships among the many variables that influence economic phenomena. The better management understands the interrelationships among all of these variables, the more accurate its forecasts can be.
2. Econometric models that deal with causal relationships by making explicit assumptions about variables demonstrate a consistency that other methods lack and exhibit flexibility in adjusting to a changing environment. Error data can be used to improve accuracy of the model's parameters, thus improving future forecasts.

Single-Equation Models

Economic theory deals with the science of choices among alternatives, and its method is to construct simplified models of economic reality from which certain laws describing regularities in economic behavior are derived. When these models are quantitatively formulated, they may take the form of econometric models. Such models may be constructed for the total economy for predicting future levels of income, employment, and other aggregate economic variables, or they may be constructed for a particular firm or industry in order to predict sales, production, costs, and related economic variables. Both types of models can be useful, of course, in facilitating decision making and planning by government agencies, business executives, labor unions, political organizations, and similar groups with a direct interest in economic and business conditions. Hence, both types of models are often discussed and illustrated in the literature of economics.

One of the first steps in the construction of an econometric model is to specify the hypotheses that purport to explain the economic phenomenon under investigation. Then these hypotheses are translated into a form suitable for testing, usually one or more mathematical equations.

For example, consider an elementary demand problem in which the industry sales, S, of a certain product during any given time period, t, is a function of the number of households, H, during the period and of consumers' disposable household income, Y, during the previous period. This model is expressed by the unspecified equation

$$S_t = f(H_t, Y_{t-1}). \tag{7}$$

If it is further hypothesized that the relationship among the variables is linear and not exact, the model becomes the specified equation

$$S_t = a + bH_t + cY_{t-1} + \mu_t \tag{8}$$

where a, b, and c are parameters to be estimated from the available data by certain statistical techniques, and μ is a "disturbance" term.

If μ had been excluded from the equation, the relationship would mean that sales are completely determined by the household and income variables. However, by including μ, the equation recognizes that sales will be affected by additional factors besides households and incomes, and hence the forecasted estimates of sales that are derived from the equation will deviate from the actual or realized sales. These other factors represented by μ should be random in nature and, in a statistical sense, normally distributed so that μ will average out to zero. Then, once the parameters are estimated, certain statistical tests may be applied to evaluate the adequacy of the equation as a forecasting device. These were discussed with specific reference to demand forecasting in Chapter 8.

Simultaneous-Equations Models

There are many relatively uncomplicated problems in business and economics that can be solved by expressing the underlying structure in the form of a single mathematical equation. However, when a theoretical structure is complex, as is usually the case, there are simultaneous interrelations among the variables in the system. In that event, a system of equations can be developed to express the complex interactions among the variables. Such a system ordinarily requires a computer solution. The construction of such a model can be illustrated by the following simplified version of an actual model.

Let

$$
\begin{aligned}
C &= \text{Consumption} \\
G &= \text{Government expenditures on goods and services} \\
I &= \text{Investment (net)} \\
K &= \text{Net capital stock at end of period} \\
P &= \text{Nonwage income} \\
W &= \text{Wage income} \\
Y &= \text{National income (or net product)} \\
t &= \text{A given time period; } t-1 \text{ denotes the previous time period} \\
a, \ b, \ c &= \text{Parameters} \\
\mu_1, \ \mu_2, \ \mu_3 &= \text{Disturbance terms or random influences that affect the depen-} \\
& \quad \ \text{dent variable but are assumed to average out to zero.}
\end{aligned}
$$

In order to construct an econometric model, we must now specify various hypotheses that purport to explain the phenomena under investigation. These hypotheses are based on previous studies, empirical findings, or a priori reasoning. Then the hypotheses are translated into a form that is suitable for empirical verification and testing, usually into mathematical equations.

1. Consumption in the current period depends on the current period's income and on consumption in the previous period:

$$C_t = a_0 + a_1 Y_t + a_2 C_{t-1} + \mu_{1t}. \tag{9}$$

2. Investment in the current period is determined by nonwage income earned in the current period and by the net capital stock available at the end of the previous period:

$$I_t = b_0 + b_1 P_t + b_2 K_{t-1} + \mu_{2t}. \tag{10}$$

3. Wages in the current period depend on income in the current period and on time. ("Time" is used as a substitute variable for all other variables that are unspecified but nevertheless exert an influence on wages.)

$$W_t = c_0 + c_1 Y_t + c_{2t} + \mu_{3t}. \tag{11}$$

4. National income or net product in the current period is the sum of consumption, investment, and government expenditures in the current period. (In the real world there are some accounting differences between national income and net product, but these differences are assumed to be sufficiently unimportant to be neglected in this model.)

$$Y_t = C_t + I_t + G_t. \tag{12}$$

5. Nonwage income in the current period is the difference between national income in the current period and wage income in the current period:

$$P_t = Y_t - W_t. \tag{13}$$

6. Net capital stock at the end of the current period is equal to the last period's net capital stock plus current net investment:

$$K_t = K_{t-1} + I_t. \tag{14}$$

This completes the set of hypotheses that we have expressed both in words and in equations for explaining the phenomena being investigated. Note that the last three statements are actually nothing more than definitions or mathematical identities that are needed to complete the model. For convenience, the six equations that comprise the model may now be grouped together as a system of equations:

Equation 9: $\quad C_t = a_0 + a_1 Y_t + a_2 C_{t-1} + \mu_{1t}$

Equation 10: $\quad I_t = b_0 + b_1 P_t + b_2 K_{t-1} + \mu_{2t}$

Equation 11: $\quad W_t = c_0 + c_1 Y_t + c_{2t} + \mu_{3t}$

Equation 12: $\quad Y_t = C_t + I_t + G_t$

Equation 13: $\quad P_t = Y_t - W_t$

Equation 14: $\quad K_t = K_{t-1} + I_t.$

It may be worth noting again that there is a reason for the use of the variables, μ_{1t}, μ_{2t}, and μ_{3t} on the right side of the first three equations. These variables, called **disturbance terms**, allow for the fact that the explicit independent variables in the equations do not account completely for the variations in the dependent variables.

For example, in Equation 9 consumption in the current period is determined by other factors in addition to income in the current period and consumption in the previous period. Some of these other factors may be economic or psychological. Further, there may be errors in the data used to represent the relevant variables. All of these disturbances are represented in Equation 9 by the variable μ_{1t}. If we assume that no known important independent variables have been omitted, then the disturbance terms reflect all of the unknown and unpredictable factors.

Ideally, the variations in these "all other" factors will be small and random in nature, and will tend to cancel each other out so that their overall net effect on the dependent variable is zero. To the extent that this assumption is realized in practice, the remaining explicit variables in the equation will account for the systematic or causal movements in the dependent variable.

The reader should be aware that there is considerably more involved in econometric model building than the brief sketch presented here. Many theoretical and statistical problems exist that must be handled in actual model construction. These paragraphs have merely conveyed a bit of the flavor of the subject for those who are unfamiliar with it.[2]

Techniques of Macroeconomic Forecasters

A study of 13 prominent macroeconomic forecasting organizations was conducted in 1981 by McNees.[3] As shown in Exhibit 9–7 (page 264), five of the forecasters are commercial consulting firms (BMARK, CHASE, DRI, TG, and WEFA); four are university facilities (GSU, KEDI, RSQE, and UCLA); two are corporate activities (MHT is financial and GE is nonfinancial); and one is an activity of the federal government (BEA). The 13th "forecaster" (ASA) is simply the median forecaster of a survey.

The McNees study chose to compare forecast results on 15 of the most common macroeconomic variables as follows:

1. Change in business inventories (billions of current dollars)
2. Civilian employment (millions)
3. Consumer price index (1967 = 100)
4. Federal-government purchases of goods and services (billions of current dollars)
5. Gross national product (billions of current dollars)
6. Housing starts (millions of units)
7. Implicit GNP price deflator (1972 = 100)
8. Investment in residential structures (billions of current dollars)
9. Net exports of goods and services (billions of current dollars)
10. 90-day Treasury-bill rate (percentage)
11. Nonresidential fixed investment (billions of current dollars)
12. Personal consumption expenditures, consumer durables (billions of current dollars)
13. Personal consumption expenditures, nondurable goods and services (billions of current dollars)
14. Real gross national product (billions of 1972 dollars)
15. Unemployment rate (percentage).

There are, of course, many other variables. As shown in column 2 of Exhibit 9–7, the number of variables forecasted ranged from as few as 3 to as many as 1,000.[4]

---

[2] For a more detailed description, see Lawrence R. Klein and Richard M. Young, *An Introduction to Econometric Forecasting and Forecasting Models* (Lexington, Mass.: D.C. Heath, 1980).

[3] Stephen K. McNees, "The Recent Record of Thirteen Forecasters" (reprint), *New England Economic Review,* September-October 1981, pp. 5–21. The reprint corrects several errors in the original article. See also McNees, "The Forecasting Record for the 1970s," *New England Economic Review,* September-October 1979, pp. 33–53.

[4] BMARK used only three variables: gross national product, implicit GNP price deflator, and real gross national product.

EXHIBIT 9–7   Summary Information on 13 Macroeconomic Forecasting Organizations

(1) Forecasting Organization	(2) Number of Macroeconomic Variables Forecasted	(3) Typical Forecast Horizon, Quarters	(4) Frequency of Release, Per Year	(5) Date Forecast First Issued Regularly	(6) Forecasting Technique(s) (Approximate Weights)
ASA (American Statistical Association and National Bureau of Economic Research Survey of regular forecasts, median)	8	45	4	1968	Most participants rely primarily on an "informal" GNP model; the majority also consider econometric model results.
BEA (Bureau of Economic Analysis, U.S. Commerce Department)	about 800	7	8	1967	Econometric model (65%), judgment (25%), current data analysis (5%), interaction with others (5%)
BMARK (Charles R. Nelson Associates, Inc., Benchmark forecast)	3	4	4	1976	Time-series methods (100%)
CHASE (Chase Econometric Associates, Inc.)	about 700	10 to 12	12	1970	Econometric model (70%), judgment (20%), time-series methods (5%), current data analysis (5%)
DRI (Data Resources, Inc.)	about 1,000	8 to 12	12	1969	Econometric model (55%), judgment (30%), time-series methods (10%), current data analysis (5%)
GE (Economic Research and Forecasting Operation, General Electric Co.)	360	8	4	1962	Econometric model (50%), judgment (50%)
GSU (Economic Forecasting Project, Georgia State University)	215	8	12	1973	Econometric model (60%), judgment (30%), current data analysis (10%)
KEDI (Kent Economic and Development Institute)	1,699	10	12	1974	Econometric model (60%), judgment (20%), time-series methods (10%), interaction with others (10%)
MHT (Manufacturers Hanover Trust)	37	4 to 5	4	1970	Econometric model (50%), judgment (50%)
RSQE (Research Seminar on Quantitative Economics, University of Michigan)	about 100	8	3	1969	Econometric model (80%), judgment (20%)
TG (Townsend-Greenspan & Co., Inc.)	about 800	6 to 10	4	1965	Econometric model (45%), judgment (45%), current data analysis (10%)
UCLA (UCLA Business Forecasting Project, Graduate School of Management, University of California, Los Angeles)	about 1,000	8 to 12	4	1968	Econometric model (70%), judgment (20%), interaction with others (10%)
WEFA (Wharton Econometric Forecasting Associates, Inc.)	about 1,000	12	12	1963	Econometric model (60%), judgment (30%), current data analysis (10%)

Source: Stephen K. McNees, "The Recent Record of Thirteen Forecasters," *New England Review*, September-October 1981 (reprint), pp. 5–21.

Exhibit 9–7 also shows that 12 of the 13 forecasts are generated with the help of a large macroeconomic model of the U.S. economy. All of the models require input of the forecaster's assumptions about the future values of several exogenous variables, such as changes in economic policy of the federal government.

The models provide the basis for application of judgment, and according to column 6 of the exhibit, their outputs are weighted from 45 to 80 percent in development of the forecast. All forecasters in the exhibit adjust the mechanical output of the econometric model in the light of newer data, revisions to data, past errors, feedback from users of their forecasts, and expected events of a nature not covered by the model. Sometimes judgmental adjustment includes the predictions of other forecasters. As shown in column 6, judgmental adjustments carry weights of 20 to 50 percent.

Several forecasters emphasized that the interaction between the model and the forecaster's judgment is a two-way street. The forecaster may elect to override the model's preliminary results, but those results may also modify the forecaster's judgment. Further, the relative weights given to the forecasting techniques employed will vary, not only from forecaster to forecaster, but also from prediction to prediction.

One forecasting organization, BMARK, uses an entirely different technique. Its forecasts are generated by autoregressive integrated moving average (ARIMA) time-series equations. Thus its forecasts are based solely on the historical record of the predicted variable, and they are not judgmentally revised even if there is reason to suspect error. Consequently, they serve as benchmarks, or standards for comparison with the results of other techniques.

Summary

In this chapter we have reviewed some of the tools and techniques available to the art and science of economic forecasting, and we have looked at some of the ways in which they are used. We have seen that mechanical extrapolations, barometric techniques, opinion polling, and econometric models all have uses in both long-term and short-term forecasting at all levels of economic activity.

The econometric method is the approach that is best suited for incorporating or utilizing the best features of all methods. Thus to an increasing extent, econometric models are making greater use of other forecasting methods such as leading indicators and up-to-date survey data. These statistics can be incorporated as variables in the model, and the latter can be revised as new information becomes available and new weights become necessary.

Sometimes econometric models have failed to provide better predictions for the following year than less costly models such as simple trend projections. Does this mean that econometric methods should be abandoned? Not at all; if our theoretical understanding and statistical data are good, econometrics can illuminate the darker areas and enhance our ability to predict. For econometrics, to a greater degree than other forecasting methods, is analytical in nature and process-oriented in approach. That is, econometric models almost always describe an ongoing process that yields a value for the dependent variable.

In any forecast, strong forces may come into play and modify existing relationships. The econometrician is aware of this and constantly watches for the emergence of new forces or changes in existing ones so that allowances can be made in the operating model. In this manner, a good econometric model automatically incorporates the necessary degree of built-in flexibility, thereby facilitating the model's use for forecasting purposes. Perhaps the most important use of naive models, therefore, is that they provide a benchmark— a null hypothesis—against which the more sophisticated forecasting methods can be compared.

Whatever method is used, it seems likely that the forecaster's role in the decision-making activities of the firm is apt to grow rather than diminish. The forecaster's contribution to the welfare of the firm is to make management aware, on a timely and continuing basis, of the economic forces at work; and this requires that forecasters subject their own work to constant critical review. However, despite the improved techniques offered by the use of computers, forecasting remains in large part an effort to predict human behavior. Forecasting, therefore, is at least as much art as science and seems likely to remain so in the foreseeable future.

Problems

1. Trend models or projections will usually yield correct forecasts, at least as to the direction of change. If the distinction between a forecasting artist and a forecasting scientist is that the latter is correct more than half the time, the use of trend models would seem warranted. Yet we have been critical of their use. Why? Discuss.

2. "After all, in the final analysis, the best forecasting method is obviously the one that yields the highest percentage of correct predictions." Comment in the light of this chapter.

3. Briefly discuss the nature and pros and cons of the following methods of forecasting business cycles:

   a. Trend projections

   b. Leading indicators

   c. Survey methods

   d. Econometric model building

   e. Any other method or technique.

4. An economist in the Reading Company conjectured the model that sales in any given month are directly proportional to the square of the buyers' incomes in the preceding month, plus a random disturbance.

   a. Write an equation for this month's sales and another equation for next month's sales, using the symbols Y = sales, X = income, t = time, and μ = disturbance term.

   b. If sales this month are 36 and income last month was 3, what sales should be expected next month if income this month is 5?

5. In the most current month, the composite index of 12 leading indicators has just turned down after rising for each of the six previous months. How would you interpret this information?

6. A naive model of the demand for television sets asserts that annual sales of televisions sets vary with the number of families during the year, income per family during the previous year, and all other factors.

   a. Letting Z = sales, Y = income per family, t = time in years, and μ = all other factors, write the equation of the model.

   b. Assume that you are presented with the data in the following table:

Year	Sales	Total Family Income	Number of Families
1	5	18.0	3
2	8	20.0	4
3	10	21.6	6
4	6	21.0	5

Assuming that the "all other factors" have always averaged out to zero, does the model seem to forecast accurately? If the number of families for Year 5 is predicted to be 7, what will your sales forecast be?

7. It has been observed that people's buying plans for the future are highly influenced by their most recent incomes. If this is true, what implication would this have with respect to the use of opinion-polling techniques in forecasting future consumption expenditure?

8. Consider the forecasting model

$$Y_t = AK^t$$

where A and K are known constants. It is interesting to gain an appreciation of the time path of the dependent variable Y_t for different values of A and K, and integer values of t representing discrete time periods.

a. Let $K = 1$ and $A =$ any positive constant. Graph the time path of Y_t from $t = 0$ to $t = 5$, i.e., $0 \leq t \leq 5$.

b. Let $K = 2$ and $A = 0.25$. Graph the time path of Y_t for $0 \leq t \leq 5$. If your graph is correct, you will see why the time path of Y_t is said to explode. The direction of the explosion (i.e., positive or negative) depends upon the algebraic sign of A. What happens when $A > 0$? When $A < 0$? What does the magnitude of K determine?

9. What are the four major sources of variation in a time series? Explain.

10. The Bruxton Leather Goods Company introduced a new product in the first quarter of 1983. Its sales figures for the following eight years appear in the accompanying table.

| | | Quarter | | | |
Year	1	2	3	4	Total
1983	150	120	100	200	570
1984	280	240	190	410	1,120
1985	240	220	180	280	920
1986	270	230	160	390	1,050
1987	290	250	180	440	1,160
1988	340	280	220	490	1,330
1989	300	220	190	420	1,130
1990	300	210	210	460	1,180

a. Using the least squares method, determine the trend line and forecast sales for each quarter in 1991.

b. Use a moving-average approach to forecast sales for the first two quarters of 1991. Compare these forecasts with your forecasts calculated in part (a).

Case Problem: General Steel Corporation

11. For the past 10 years, General Steel Corporation (GSC) has been working actively with several foreign governments in planning heavy industrialization programs. As a result, GSC now has subsidiary iron-and-steel–manufacturing corporations in three foreign countries.

Two years ago, the top managers of GSC began exploring the possibility of opening a subsidiary corporation in Arcadia, a major industrial nation. Since the economic future of Arcadia is of obvious interest to GSC, the firm's economists have been actively engaged in collecting data for the purpose of constructing an econometric model of that country.

According to recent studies by GSC's economic-research department, last year's corporate profits in Arcadia were about $84 billion. Although there is no way of being certain of how much Arcadia's national, provincial, and local governments will spend next year, GSC's economists estimate from present budget information that the amount should be around $150 billion. Also, an analysis of the most recent business cycle in Arcadia, covering several years, indicates that annual consumption expenditures have averaged $80 billion plus 70 percent of national income; investment expenditures have averaged about $40 billion plus 90 percent of preceding year's profits; and tax receipts have averaged about 40 percent of gross national product (GNP). GNP, of course, is composed of consumption, investment, and government expenditures, while national income represents the difference between GNP and tax receipts.

Assume that all disturbance terms average out to zero and use the following symbols to construct an econometric model:

C = Next year's consumption
Y = Next year's national income
I = Next year's investment
P = Preceding year's profits
T = Next year's tax receipts by all levels of government
G = Next year's gross national product
E = Next year's government expenditures by all levels of government.

Questions

a. Construct a five-equation econometric model of Arcadia. The first equation should be for consumption, the second for investment, the third for tax receipts, the fourth for gross national product, and the fifth for national income.[5]

b. Solve the system of equations to find the values of C, I, T, G, and Y.[6]

c. Prepare a diagram of your model. Plot G on the horizontal axis and C, E, and Y on the vertical axis as functions of G. Also plot G as a function of G (a 45° line). Show that $C + I + E = G = 595.9$.

d. Do some contingency forecasting.

(1) Find the value for G if E happens to be $174 billion rather than $150 billion, with everything else as stated previously.

(2) Find the value for G if Arcadia's average tax receipts should be 32 percent of GNP rather than the expected 40 percent, with everything else as stated before (including E at $150 billion).

e. Calculate the government deficit or surplus in the original forecast. Then calculate it for part (d). Finally, briefly discuss the relative effects of the two fiscal stabilizing tools: changes in government spending and changes in tax rates.

f. Discuss briefly some problems you might encounter in actually using this model to make economic forecasts.

g. In the preceding model, investment expenditures in one period depend upon the profits of the preceding period. Suppose, however, that the argument is made that investment expenditures in one period are more closely correlated to both expected profits P^* and the prevailing interest rate i in *that* period; i.e., $I_t = f(P_t^*, i_t)$. Do you think this is a more realistic investment formulation? Explain. Discuss a major problem involved with actually using this formulation in a forecasting model.

References

Armstrong, J. Scott. "Forecasting with Econometric Methods: Folklore versus Fact." *Journal of Business* 51 (October 1978), pp. 549–64.

————. "Research on Forecasting: A Quarter Century Review, 1960–1984." *Interfaces* 16 (January-February 1986), pp. 89–109.

Baltagi, Badi H., and James M. Griffin. "A General Index of Technical Change." *Journal of Political Economy* 96, no. 1 (February 1988), p. 20.

Bohara, A.; R. McNown; and J. T. Batts. "A Re-evaluation of the Combination and Adjustment of Forecasts." *Applied Economics* 19, no. 4 (April 1987), p. 437.

Bureau of Economic Analysis, U. S. Dept. of Commerce. *Business Conditions Digest* (June 1989). Washington, D.C. : U. S. Government Printing Office.

---

[5] You may find it helpful to construct the model by first using lower-case letters such as a, b, c, d, and e to represent the constants, and then substituting the correct numbers for the constants.

[6] HINT: Solve for I first. Then, in solving for C and the other variables, look for substitutions that can be made. Check your answers against the correct answers, which are: C = $330.3 billion; I = $115.6 billion; T = $238.4 billion; G = $595.9 billion; Y = $357.5 billion.

Chambers, John C.; Santinder K. Mullick; and Donald D. Smith. "How to Choose the Right Forecasting Technique." *Harvard Business Review* 49 (July-August 1971), pp. 45–74.

Chow, Gregory C. "Are Econometric Models Useful for Forecasting?" *Journal of Business* 51 (October 1978), pp. 565–71.

Gardner, Everett S., Jr. "Exponential Smoothing: The State of the Art." *Journal of Forecasting* 4 (January-March 1985), pp. 1–28.

Kling, John L. "Predicting the Turning Points of Business and Economic Time Series." *Journal of Business* 60, no. 2 (April 1987), p. 201.

McNees, Stephen K. "The Recent Record of Thirteen Forecasters" (reprint). *New England Economic Review* (September-October 1981), pp. 5–21.

Stock, James H. "Measuring Business Cycle Time." *Journal of Political Economy* 95, no. 6 (December 1987), p. 1240.

Willis, Raymond E. *A Guide to Forecasting for Planners and Managers.* Englewood Cliffs, N. J.: Prentice-Hall, 1987.

Witt, Stephen F., and F. Raymond Johnson. "An Econometric Model of New-Car Demand in the U. K.," *Managerial and Decision Economics* 7, no. 1 (March 1986), pp. 19–23.

APPENDIX 9A   Evaluation of Forecasting

If forecasting is to be improved, there must be some way of measuring its performance. Having one's forecast checked against actual results and against the forecasts and opinions of others can be a disenchanting experience. For their own protection, as well as to encourage intelligent use of their products, economic forecasters should insist upon objective and systematic procedures for review and rigorous evaluation of their work.

Those procedures must recognize that forecasting with complete accuracy is impossible and, fortunately, unnecessary, provided the forecasts are evaluated and used in the proper manner.

Auditing Past Performance

Checking a short-range forecast against the record, when all the data are at hand, is a fairly simple process. Evaluating long-range forecasts may be somewhat more complicated. Sometimes the statistical series has been altered; sometimes the forecast was hedged by unrealized assumptions or other restrictions. In either case, comparison with actual results may be difficult.

Forecast versus Actual Results

The simplest way to evaluate an unconditional forecast is to compare numbers with actual results and state the difference either in dollars or as a percentage of error. We can define forecasting error, ϵ, with respect to any one variable as the difference between a predicted value, P, and an actual value, A, over the forecast horizon, n, expressed in quarters. When the forecast is generated, it is based upon the then current *estimate* of the predicted variable in the previous time period. When the actual value of the forecast base becomes known, the error in the base must be adjusted before the error in the forecast can be measured. The definition of forecast error thus becomes

$$\epsilon_{t+n} = P_{t+n}(A_t - A_t^*) - A_{t+n} \tag{1}$$

where

$$n = \text{The horizon of the forecast, in quarters}$$
$$t = \text{The base time}$$
$$\epsilon_{t+n} = \text{Error in the forecast}$$
$$P_{t+n} = \text{Predicted value of the variable at the forecast horizon}$$
$$A_t = \text{Actual value of the variable in the base period}$$
$$A_t^* = \text{Estimated value of the variable in the base period}$$
$$A_{t+n} = \text{Actual value of the variable at the forecast horizon}$$

Equation (13) actually measures forecasting error as the difference between the predicted cumulative change in the variable $(P_{t+n} - A_t^*)$ and the actual cumulative change, $(A_{t+n} - A_t)$. This is quite desirable because we are usually more interested in the changes in a variable than we are in its future level.

Many economic variables, especially those that exhibit trends, are commonly expressed as annual percent changes. If we assume compound annual rates of growth, the percentage error can be defined as

$$\epsilon\% = \left[\left(\frac{P_{t+n}}{A_t^*} \right)^{4/n} - \left(\frac{A_{t+1}}{A_t} \right)^{4/n} \right] \cdot 100 \tag{2}$$

where n is the forecast horizon.

Summary Measures.   There are a number of summary measures that can be used to summarize individual errors, but most forecast users prefer the average absolute error, *AAE*, as an index of forecasting accuracy.[1]

$$AAE_n = \frac{1}{m} \sum_{t=1}^{m} |\epsilon_{t+n}| \tag{3}$$

where

$$m = \text{Number of errors}$$
$$n = \text{Horizon of the forecast}$$
$$|\epsilon_{t+n}| = \text{Absolute value of the individual error.}$$

Some forecast users prefer a summary measure that penalizes large errors, such as the square root of the mean squared error, *RMSE*:

$$RMSE_n = \sqrt{\frac{1}{m} \sum_{t=1}^{m} \epsilon_{t+n}^2}. \tag{4}$$

---

[1] Equations 1, 2, 3, and 4 have been provided by McNees, "The Recent Record of Thirteen Forecasters," p. 9.

EXHIBIT 9A–1   **Evaluative Criteria and Their Relative Importance as Determined by Forecasting Practitioners and Academicians**

Criteria	Academicians[a]	Practitioners
Accuracy		
R^2		2
Mean square error (*MSE*)	30	20
Geometric *MSE*	1	
Minimum variance	2	4
Theil's U test	3	1
Mean percentage error (*MPE*)	5	5
Mean absolute error (*MAE*)	12	14
Mean absolute percentage error (*MAPE*)	15	7
Minimax absolute error (*MMAE*)	2	
Random forecast errors	1	2
No specific measure	8	14
Ease of interpretation	26	29
Cost time	24	25
Ease of use implementation	26	18
Adaptive to new conditions	10	13
Universality	3	10
Capture turning points	5	6
Robustness	10	3
Incorporates judgmental input	4	2

Source: Robert Carbone and J. Scott Armstrong, "Evaluation of Extrapolative Forecasting Methods: Results of a Survey of Acadamicians and Practitioners," *Journal of Forecasting,* April–June 1982, p. 216.

[a] Out of the 206 persons surveyed, 70 academicians and 75 practitioners responded.

As for academicians and practitioners, Carbone and Armstrong found the evaluation criteria shown in Exhibit 9A–1.

Evaluation.   No matter how good the measurement of forecasting error might be, it is meaningless in isolation. Evaluation requires comparison with other forecasts made for the same period under similar conditions, but this is easier said than done. If all forecast users had exactly the same interests in terms of forecasted variables and horizons, it would be possible to rank the forecasters' past performances from best to worst, using the summary measures noted previously. But this would be no guarantee that such performance will continue into the future.

Furthermore, forecast users do not have identical interests. Those who make economic policy are most concerned with macroeconomic aggregates such as inflation and real growth. Most users, however, are mainly concerned about the products they buy and sell. The horizons of interest may vary from a few hours or days in financial markets to several years for those making capital-budgeting decisions.

The solution to the problem is to treat each variable and horizon separately and let individual forecast users consider what interests them. This means that no expert can say which forecaster is best. Each user must comb through an array of summary measures for each variable and horizon, as illustrated by Exhibit 9A–2.

EXHIBIT 9A–2   **Average Absolute Errors in Forecasted Gross National Product, 1976–1980 (in billions of current dollars)**

	Forecast Horizon (Quarters)							
Forecaster	*1*	*2*	*3*	*4*	*5*	*6*	*7*	*8*
Early quarter								
ASA	17.2	24.7	30.9	35.4	36.6	—	—	—
BEA	20.5	24.3	29.3	32.6	33.3	39.2	—	—
BMARK	21.3	31.5	41.1	52.4	—	—	—	—
Chase	21.4	29.8	46.8	56.9	65.8	76.0	91.8	109.2
DRI	19.2	23.2	31.4	36.8	40.1	43.4	48.7	63.5
GSU	15.3	25.8	29.4	38.5	39.1	40.0	48.3	55.1
RSQE	15.6	25.0	35.6	30.3	39.1	53.3	—	—
WEFA	18.8	22.3	27.5	26.2	31.6	34.0	42.7	48.5
Middle quarter								
KEDI	17.3	28.8	29.4	28.5	24.7	29.7	45.5	51.2
MHT	18.2	24.9	30.5	34.9	47.4	—	—	—
TG	14.6	24.1	24.0	34.9	36.4	34.6	37.4	—
UCLA	14.7	28.4	30.8	35.1	33.2	31.2	—	—
WEFA	13.0	23.7	25.3	27.5	32.8	32.8	37.6	44.4
Late quarter								
Chase	12.7	29.4	44.3	56.8	67.4	78.8	94.9	111.0
DRI	8.4	25.4	25.4	33.9	40.0	41.6	47.0	56.6
GE	16.6	26.6	34.2	34.8	25.2	27.3	33.3	43.5

Source: Stephen K. McNees, "The Recent Record of Thirteen Forecasters" (reprint), *New England Economic Review,* September-October 1981, pp. 13–14.

The exhibit shows the average absolute errors in billions of current dollars for quarterly forecasts of gross national product by the 13 forecasters of the previously referenced McNees study. The McNees study contains similar tables for the other 14 variables listed in the final section of Chapter 9.

The errors are averaged from the second quarter of 1976 through the third quarter of 1980. The forecasters have been grouped according to the release dates of their forecasts. Early-quarter forecasts are based on the preliminary estimates of the preceding quarter's GNP. Middle-quarter forecasts are made near the end of the quarter when many of the previous quarter's actual data are known. Note that two of the forecasters (Chase and DRI) made both early- and late-quarter forecasts, and one (WEFA) made both early- and middle-quarter forecasts.

Exhibit 9A–2 demonstrates that even when relative magnitudes of error are tabulated for a single variable, it is difficult to rank the 13 forecasters. Partly this is because there are gaps in the forecast sets where some forecasters did not cover all quarters or all horizons in each forecast. A second difficulty is the disparity in timing of forecast release dates, as noted before.

As we have seen, evaluation of accuracy is not always fair or relevant and some additional considerations are appropriate. Whatever tests are made, they should be realistic and practical, keeping in mind that even the most elaborate statistical techniques leave wide margins for error. Bald comparisons with perfection prove nothing. Some of the questions that should be asked include:

1. Did the forecast do what it was supposed to do?
2. Were the important changes forecast with respect to magnitude, timing, and direction?
3. Should the errors have been anticipated by the forecaster?
4. Above all, *did the forecast enable better decisions to be made than would have been possible without it?*

Interim Review

The important timing for interim review of forecasts depends upon so many factors that it is difficult to generalize. The best guide is to keep in mind what the interim review is for—to enable management to change an operating policy based on an erroneous forecast before it is too late. The interim review also enables the forecaster to update the forecast to reflect new developments and perform a running check on sources and methodology.

Sometimes the requirement for interim review is inherent in the forecasting schedule. This is common in short-range forecasting, where quarterly forecasts running four or five quarters ahead are made. These can be updated as new data are obtained, which could be monthly or quarterly, or whenever an exceptional event occurs. For longer-term forecasts, reviews might be instituted:

1. When the basic data from which the forecast was developed are changed, as when a published statistical series is revised.
2. When a key assumption undergoes an important change, such as a technological breakthrough.
3. When anticipated bounds on the forecast variable have been breached.

When there is a substantial deviation in the behavior of the forecast data, it is important to determine whether or not the validity of the forecast has actually been impaired. If the forecast represents an anticipated trend, then seasonal, cyclical, or random aberrations do not necessarily invalidate the trend. In the case of long-range forecasts, such as for 10 years, if the trend is off the forecast in the first two or three years, even by a wide margin, the interim review provides the opportunity to look again.

Forecasts should be accompanied by some measure of confidence. Any revisions brought about by the interim review should be announced promptly to all concerned. Reasons for the revisions should be explained concisely and frankly but without apology. Perfect forecasting does not exist and is not to be expected; therefore no apology is in order when perfection has not been achieved.

Selecting a Forecasting Method

There is no single forecasting method that is always more appropriate than other methods. In a sense forecasting is as much art as it is science. In many respects, it is similar to the practice of general medicine, in which the practitioner must consider a wide variety of factors in diagnosing an illness and then prescribing for its cure. Among the factors a forecaster must consider are:

1. Availability and accuracy of historical data
2. Time available to make the analysis

EXHIBIT 9A-3   Cost versus Accuracy in Forecasting

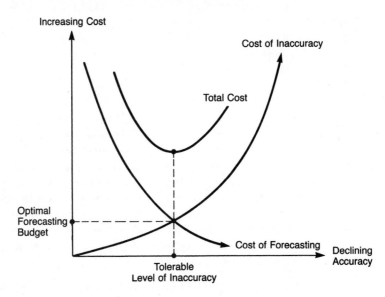

3. Degree of accuracy expected
4. Length of the forecast period
5. Cost of making the analysis and preparing periodic forecasts.

The choice of a particular forecasting method should be decided by comparing the relative costs and benefits of each method. Of course, there is the inevitable trade-off: In order to improve accuracy and thereby lower the costs associated with an inaccurate forecast (excessive inventories, for example), we must use more resources—including time—in preparing the forecast. For example, at one extreme we have very elaborate and expensive econometric models that we hope will reduce forecast errors. At the other extreme we might use expert opinion.

Exhibit 9A–3 illustrates these points and indicates an answer to the question of how much the firm should invest in forecasting. The answer is: Expand the forecasting function to the point at which the marginal cost of inaccuracy from a poor forecast is equal to the marginal cost of preparing a more accurate forecast. Unquestionably, there are difficulties in actually using the rule; nevertheless, it is a correct way of thinking about the problem.

C H A P T E R

10

PRODUCTION ANALYSIS

Once demand for a given product or service has been determined, management decides the most profitable way to employ the firm's resources to produce that good or service. Such decisions involve an understanding of **production functions**.

A production function is simply an input–output relationship between one or more factors of production (input) and the good or service produced (output). This relationship is analyzed and quantified during a production study to determine the most economical combination of input resources to obtain a given level of output. Or conversely, it may involve the determination of the maximum output obtainable from a given level and mix of inputs. A production study may pertain not only to the production of goods (such as automobiles, calculators, or pet foods), but also to the production of services (such as TV repair, hair styling, government assistance, or health care).

A study of production functions is also fundamental to cost analysis. Once a firm's production function has been identified, its cost function can be derived from the production function, provided the market prices of the input factors are known. Hence the production function strongly affects the firm's status in its industry, and the study of production functions is even more basic than the study of cost functions.

CHAPTER OUTLINE

This chapter is divided into two main sections and an appendix:

1. **Production Functions.** Here production is studied in terms of a relationship between output and the input factors of production (resources). Emphasis is on the substitutability of inputs in the attempt to find the combination of inputs that will optimize production in the short run.

2. **Expansion of Production and Returns to Scale.** Here production is studied in terms of the relative increase in output that takes place when *all* factors of production are increased simultaneously by the *same* proportion. Knowledge of possible returns to scale is crucial for determining whether or not the firm should change the size of its plants. It is, therefore, a concept for long-range production planning and investment decisions.

3. **Appendix 10A: Effect of Wage Increases on Jobs.** This appendix shows why unearned wage increases always result in fewer jobs because the profit-maximizing firm will substitute capital for labor.

Production Functions

Production means the transformation of *input factors* of production, such as labor, materials, machinery, and other capital assets, into an *output* over a span of time. The output may be a consumer good ready for purchase by the ultimate consumer, or it may be a producer good intended for input into another product.

Like a demand function, a production function can be expressed as a schedule, a graph, or an equation such as

$$Q = f(X_1, X_2, \ldots, X_n) \tag{1}$$

where Q, a specific output, is a function of the input factors, $X_1, X_2, \ldots, X_n$. For example, X_1 could be direct labor, X_2 could be indirect labor, X_3 could be capital goods such as machinery and equipment, X_4 could be raw materials, X_5 could be management, and so forth. All of these factors of production are commonly aggregated into two basic factors: capital, C, and labor, L, so that in general

$$Q = f(C, L). \tag{2}$$

It is important to remember that a production function relates to some given level of technology. If the technology changes through the upgrading of labor, materials, machinery, equipment, processes, or management, the production function changes accordingly.

At any given time, the input factors of production can be divided into two categories: *fixed inputs* and *variable inputs*.

Fixed inputs are mostly capital inputs (such as land, buildings, and machinery) whose input quantities cannot be changed during the period of time under consideration. Since all factors of production can be varied in the long run, fixed input is a short-run concept—in fact, *the definition of the* **short run** *is that period of time during which some factors of production are fixed.*

Variable inputs are those inputs whose quantities are directly related to the level of production. That is to say, the level of production will change when any of the variable inputs are changed. Hours of labor, bags of fertilizer, and kilowatt-hours of energy are all examples of variable inputs that can be increased or decreased according to the level of output desired.

Production efficiency depends upon the balance that is achieved between fixed and variable inputs. For example, a firm working three shifts would need one operator per machine on each shift. Suppose the firm has two machines, but only four operators to cover all three shifts. The lack of sufficient labor (variable input) would lead to inefficient use of the machinery (fixed input). On the other hand, if the firm has eight operators for only two machines, lack of sufficient machinery would make inefficient use of the labor input. Only when the fixed and variable inputs are balanced with six operators (two per shift) for the two machines does the firm attain maximum production efficiency.

Production-Function Relationships When There Is a Single Variable Input with All Other Inputs Held Constant

In a previous chapter about demand, we found it useful to determine the effect on demand when a single determinant of demand was allowed to vary while all other determinants were held constant. Now, in an analogous situation, we want to find out what happens to output when a single variable input is allowed to vary while all other inputs are held constant. This is expressed by the equation

$$Q = f(X_1 | X_2, X_3, \ldots, X_n). \tag{3}$$

The vertical bar in this equation indicates that the input factors to its right are regarded as fixed in the production process under analysis, while the factor to its left is variable. The quantity of the output product, Q, is the result of combining a variable quantity of input factor, X_1 (e.g., skilled labor or raw materials) with fixed quantities of other input factors $X_2, X_3, \ldots, X_n$ (e.g., land, buildings, equipment, and management).

The fundamental problem in the study of the production function is to discover the probable nature of the input–output relationship. This is discussed in the literature of economic theory under several synonymous headings, such as the "Law of Variable Proportions" or the "Law of Diminishing Returns." The nature and ramifications of this law are explained in the following example.

Suppose an agricultural experiment station in Chile wants to examine the effect of fertilizer on the production of table grapes, which are harvested in March when fresh fruit is out of season in the Northern Hemisphere. The output of grapes depends upon a number of inputs besides fertilizer, such as soil (land), water (rain or irrigation), sunshine, temperature, and labor. By staking out and preparing test plots on a suitable piece of land, all of these inputs can be held constant, with fertilizer alone being allowed to vary.

Suppose the Chilean researchers set up nine test plots, and in each plot they plant cuttings from a single vine. When the new vines are ready to bear fruit, the researchers use the first plot for control by giving it no fertilizer. On the other eight plots, they add increasing amounts of fertilizer. When the grapes are harvested, the harvest from each plot is weighed. The results are then tabulated by plot for comparative purposes. Hypothetical results are shown in Exhibit 10–1 (page 278).

Besides the total product (output of table grapes) in column 2, Exhibit 10–1 shows two other relationships that are of critical interest: average product (column 3) and marginal product (column 4). The average product is simply the total output divided by the total input, $AP_X = Q/X$. The marginal product is the change in output divided by the change in input, $MP_X = \Delta Q/\Delta X$. Although the MP_X is measured between discrete values of X, the units of input (sacks of fertilizer) are infinitely divisible; therefore the underly-

EXHIBIT 10–1   **Production of Chilean Table Grapes on Nine Test Plots**

(1) Amount of Fertilizer (sacks) X	(2) Total Product (pounds) Q	(3) Average Product (pounds/sack) $AP_x = Q/X$	(4) Marginal Product (pounds) $MP_x = \Delta Q/\Delta X$
0	850	—	
			850
10	1,700	170	
			1,800
20	3,500	175	
			3,400
30	6,900	230	
			3,100
40	10,000	250	
			1,500
50	11,500	230	
			1,100
60	12,600	210	
			−1,050
70	11,550	165	
			−1,150
80	10,400	130	

ing function is continuous. This means that the relationships tabulated in Exhibit 10–1 can be used as plot points to obtain the graphs shown in Exhibit 10–2. It also means that calculus can be used in analysis of the production function and its relationships with average product, marginal product, and elasticity.

Exhibit 10–2 shows the relationships between total product, *TP*, marginal product, *MP*, average product, *AP*, and the elasticity of production, ϵ_P, when a single input factor of production is allowed to vary while all other factors are held constant. The horizontal axis of Exhibit 10–2 represents the input quantity of fertilizer, X, in sacks. The vertical axis represents the output of table grapes, Q, in pounds. The upper curve, TP_X, is a graph of the production function, $Q = f(X|X_2, X_3, \ldots, X_n)$. The lines below it represent the average-product function, $AP_X = Q/X$ and the marginal-product function, $MP_X = dQ/dX$.[1] What does the chart reveal? Specifically, what are some of the fundamental properties of the production function?

The Law of Diminishing Returns.   Exhibit 10–2 shows that in a given state of technology and keeping other productive factors constant, additional units of a particular variable input will yield increasing output per unit of input up to a point. But eventually a point is reached beyond which further additions of the variable-input factor yield diminishing returns per unit of input. That is to say, marginal product increases over a

---

[1] Because Exhibit 10–1 contains only discrete values of X and Q, MP_X is calculated as $\Delta Q/\Delta X$. For the continuous function represented by the total product curve, $TP_X = Q = f(X)$, in Exhibit 10–2 the marginal product is its derivative, dQ/dX.

EXHIBIT 10–2   Production Function Relationships

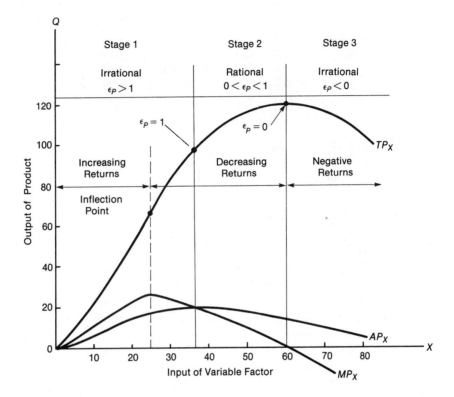

certain range of input up to a point, after which it decreases and eventually becomes negative.

In this illustration, the point of diminishing returns is reached at an input of about 25 units of X. This is the input at which the marginal product, MP_X, is at a maximum. It is indicated on the TP_X curve by the inflection point, that is, the point at which the curve changes from concave upward to concave downward.

The law of diminishing returns applies to virtually all types of production functions, ranging from those that characterize agriculture and automobile production to those that are found in retailing, textile-mill operations, mining, and the service sectors of the economy. It is thus a phenomenon of great significance and generality. Both the total-marginal relationships and the average-marginal relationship are affected by the law of diminishing returns.

The Total-Marginal Relationship.   Exhibit 10–2 reveals the relationship between marginal product and total product, which exhibits the following characteristics:

1. As long as the MP_X curve is rising, the total product curve increases at an increasing rate and is convex to the X-axis.

2. The quantity of input X at which the TP_X curve changes its curvature corresponds precisely to the point at which the MP_X curve peaks. In Exhibit 10–2, this occurs at approximately 25 units of input, as shown by the broken line in the diagram. In accordance with the law of diminishing returns, the output corresponding to the peak of the marginal-product curve is referred to as the point of diminishing (marginal) returns—the point prior to which there are increasing returns to the variable factor and beyond which there are decreasing returns.

3. When the total-product curve reaches its maximum (at 60 units of input in the diagram), MP_X is zero. Beyond this point, the marginal product is negative and the total product declines.

4. In summary, increasing returns to the variable-input factor exist when MP_X is positive and rising; decreasing returns occur when MP_X is positive and falling; negative returns are realized when MP_X is negative and falling.

The Average-Marginal Relationship.   Exhibit 10–2 also reveals what may be called the average-marginal relationship.

1. The average product increases as variable input increases as long as the marginal product exceeds the average product. In Exhibit 10–2 this is the case when the variable input is between 0 and about 38 units.

2. When the marginal product is less than the average product, the average product decreases as variable input increases. In Exhibit 10–2, this is the case when input exceeds 38 units.

3. When the average product is at a maximum, the average product and marginal product are equal. In Exhibit 10–2, this occurs at 38 units of input. It should be noted from the exhibit that even when the marginal product of the variable input turns down from its maximum point, the average product is still rising. It will continue to rise as long as the marginal product is greater than the average product. It will reach its maximum when the marginal product and the average product are equal ($MP_X = AP_X$). This is the point of maximum production efficiency for the variable input. That is to say, this is the quantity of the variable input X that can be used most efficiently in combination with the other factors of production that are being held constant. Business managers need to know this input level in order to make strategic decisions about production in the short run.

The Three Stages of Production.   Exhibit 10–2 also illustrates the three stages of a typical production function.

Stage 1.   This stage extends from zero input of the variable factor to the level of input where the average product is maximum. In this stage, the fixed factors are excessive relative to the variable input. Consequently, output can be increased by increasing the variable input relative to the fixed input. For example, if a large department store were understaffed with sales clerks, sales could be increased by hiring more clerks (the variable factor) relative to floor space and fixtures (the fixed factors). Throughout Stage 1, the marginal product is greater than the average product. The average product is a measure of efficiency; hence efficiency can be improved by increasing the variable input.

Stage 2. This stage extends from the end of Stage 1 (the point where the marginal product and the average product are equal) to the point where the marginal product is zero and the total product is at a maximum. Exhibit 10–2 shows that as the variable input increases from 38 to about 60 units, both marginal product and average product decrease, but are positive. Total output, however, continues to increase until it reaches a maximum when about 60 units of X are input. At this point, $MP_X = 0$ and Stage 2 ends. Stage 2 is a rational stage in which relatively good balance has been achieved between the variable and fixed inputs.

Stage 3. In this stage, in which input is greater than 60 units, the variable-input factor is excessive relative to the fixed factors, the marginal product is negative, and the total product is falling. It is completely irrational to produce in this stage.

The Elasticity of Production.   Exhibit 10–2 also shows the **elasticity of production**, symbolized ϵ_P, which is defined as the fractional change in total output, $\Delta Q/Q$, relative to a slight fractional change in variable input, $\Delta X/X$. Thus

$$\epsilon_P = \frac{\Delta Q/Q}{\Delta X/X} = \frac{\Delta Q}{\Delta X} \cdot \frac{X}{Q} = \frac{\Delta Q/\Delta X}{Q/X}. \tag{4}$$

Since $\Delta Q/\Delta X = MP$ and $Q/X = AP$, we can rewrite production elasticity as

$$\epsilon_P = \frac{\Delta Q/\Delta X}{Q/X} = \frac{MP}{AP}. \tag{5}$$

Thus the elasticity of production is the ratio of the marginal product to the average product, and it is different at every point on the total-product curve. This relationship between marginal product and average product accounts for the various values of ϵ_P shown in Exhibit 10–2 and helps to explain the three stages of production.

In Stage 1, the elasticity coefficient is greater than unity ($\epsilon_P > 1$) because $MP > AP$. This means that a 1 percent change in the X-variable input causes more than a 1 percent change in the output.

At the beginning of Stage 2, $MP = AP$, hence $\epsilon_P = 1$, which means that a 1 percent change in the X-variable input causes a 1 percent change in output. At the end of Stage 2, $MP = 0$, hence $\epsilon_P = 0$, meaning that a slight change in X-variable input will produce no change in output. Between the boundaries of Stage 2, the marginal product is less than the average product, so the elasticity decreases from 1 to 0 as the variable input increases.

The Optimal Hiring Rule for a Single-Variable Input.   In the previous discussion of the average-marginal relationship, it was noted that although peak efficiency occurs at the beginning of Stage 2, where $MP = AP$, this is not necessarily the point of maximum profit. To determine the optimum input–output relationship for maximum profit, we must shift the analysis from *physical* input–output relationships to *economic* relationships. The precise amount of the input variable needed to produce maximum profit will depend upon the price of the input variable, the marginal product of the input variable, and the selling price of the output. To analyze the most profitable level of production, we need to understand the meaning and relationship of *marginal revenue*, *marginal cost*, *marginal product*, and *marginal revenue product*.

Marginal revenue (MR_Q) is the additional revenue obtained when one more unit of output is sold.

$$MR_Q = \frac{\Delta TR}{\Delta Q}. \tag{6}$$

If the price of the product is constant, then the marginal revenue is just the price of the product.

Marginal cost (MC_Q) is the additional cost incurred when one more unit of output is produced. It measures the rate of change in total cost as output changes; i.e.,

$$MC_Q = \frac{\Delta TC}{\Delta Q}. \tag{7}$$

Marginal product (MP_X) is the additional output from employing one more unit of the variable input.

$$MP_x = \frac{\Delta TP}{\Delta X} \tag{8}$$

The **marginal revenue product** of the X input is defined as the additional revenue that results from employing one more unit of the variable input X. It is the economic value of one unit of the variable input. It is calculated as the marginal revenue multiplied by the marginal product of the input. In symbols,

$$MRP_X = MR_Q \cdot MP_X. \tag{9}$$

For example, suppose that the additional output per hour of labor input (MP_L) is 50 units, and the output product sells for \$0.50 per unit (MR_Q). Then

$$MRP_L = \$0.50 \times 50 = \$25.$$

That is, each hour of labor generates \$25 of revenue. If the cost of labor is less than \$25 per hour, the firm can gain additional revenue and additional profit by hiring more labor up to the point where the marginal revenue product of labor is equal to the price or cost of labor. That is, profit will be maximized when

$$MRP_L = MR_Q \cdot MP_L = P_L. \tag{10}$$

Equation 10 can be adapted to any variable input. Hence, in general,[2]

$$MRP_X = MR_Q \cdot MP_X = P_X. \tag{11}$$

The profit-maximizing firm will attempt to employ additional input of each variable production factor up to the point at which the additional revenue generated by one more unit of the variable input is just equal to the unit cost of the input.

Each of the two factors in the marginal revenue product (MR_Q and MP_X) may be either variable or constant. If the firm faces a downward-sloping demand curve, marginal

---

[2] Equation 11 is derived as follows: We know that profit is maximum when marginal cost equals marginal revenue; i.e.,

$$MC_Q = \frac{\Delta TC}{\Delta Q} = \frac{P_X \cdot \Delta X}{\Delta Q} = P_X \left(\frac{\Delta X}{\Delta Q} \right) = \frac{P_X}{\Delta Q/\Delta X} = \frac{P_X}{MP_X} = MR_Q.$$

Hence, from the equality of the last two terms we get

$$MR_Q \cdot MP_X = P_X.$$

revenue will be variable, decreasing as production and sales increase. But if the firm is selling its product in a market where the market sets the price and the firm must take it or leave it, marginal revenue will be a constant.

Marginal product may be variable because of the law of diminishing returns, or it may be constant because there are some inputs to which the law of diminishing returns does not apply. For example, in the manufacture of lawn mowers, the input of a set of wheels generates a marginal product of one lawn mower. This marginal product will never change, no matter what the level of production may be.

The unit price, P_X, of the input factor of production may also be a variable in the sense that it can and will change from time to time. At any given time, however, it will take on some specific value, and it is this value that will determine the optimal level of production.

As previously noted, when the production function is known, the marginal revenue product can be calculated as the marginal product of the input multiplied by the marginal revenue from the output. If the production function is not known, the marginal revenue product of a particular input factor can still be calculated by observing the change in total revenue when one more unit of that input factor enters the production process. This is so because

$$MRP_X = MR_Q \cdot MP_X. \tag{12}$$

But

$$MR_Q = \frac{\Delta TR}{\Delta Q} \text{ and } MP_X = \frac{\Delta Q}{\Delta X}. \tag{13}$$

Hence

$$MRP_X = \frac{\Delta TR}{\Delta Q} \cdot \frac{\Delta Q}{\Delta X} = \frac{\Delta TR}{\Delta X} \tag{14}$$

which is to say that the marginal revenue product is the change in total revenue per unit change in the input factor.

MRP as a Demand Function for Variable Input. The marginal revenue product of a particular input factor constitutes the firm's demand function for that factor. For example, consider Exhibit 10–3 (page 284), which represents a firm's demand for labor as expressed by the marginal revenue product of labor.

The vertical axis in Exhibit 10–3 represents the price of labor in dollars per hour, and the horizontal axis represents the number of people employed by the firm. The downward-sloping curve labeled MRP_L represents the marginal revenue product, in dollars, at levels of employment from 80 to 200.

The exhibit shows that at an average wage of $5.00 per hour, the firm's optimal position is to hire 150 employees, for at that level of employment the MRP_L per hour is equal to the wage of $5.00 per hour. If the firm hires more than 150, MRP_L will decrease. Revenue will increase from increased output and sales, but the total cost of labor will also increase. Because of the lower MRP_L, the increase in the cost of labor will be greater than the increase in revenue.

If the firm hires fewer than 150, the MRP_L will be greater than the wage of $5.00, meaning that by hiring more workers up to the optimum 150, the firm can gain an

EXHIBIT 10–3   **Firm's Demand for Labor Expressed as the Marginal Revenue Product of Labor**

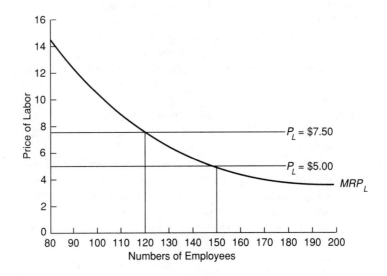

increase in total revenue greater than the increase in total labor cost. Similarly, at an average wage of $7.50 per hour, the firm's optimal position is to use 120 workers. Since the MRP_L shows the optimal quantity of labor demanded for each specific price of labor, it constitutes a demand schedule for labor.

Illustrative Problem

Westland Electronics has been producing automated business-telephone systems for the past 12 years. The company has just completed a two-year renovation of its production facilities, during which investments were made on robotic assembly systems. Westland believes the new systems will be very cost-efficient because they will lower labor costs and increase production capacity. If this proves to be true, Westland plans to intensify its move toward automation. The production-research team at Westland estimates the company's capital production function to be

$$Q = 72C + 15C^2 - C^3 \qquad (15)$$

where

Q = Output of business-telephone systems, in units
C = Units of capital employed, in dollars.

Westland sells all the business-telephone systems it produces at a price of $1,800 each and is currently employing nine units of capital.

Questions

a. What is Westland's current marginal revenue product for capital?

b. If additional capital can be raised at a cost of $100,000 per unit, what is the firm's optimal capitalization?

c. What is Westland's current elasticity of production?

d. Why couldn't the decision on further automation have been made simply on the basis of elasticity?

e. What are some possible real-world effects of decreases in capital costs due to technological advances in such areas as computers and robotics?

Solutions

a.
$$MRP_C = MR_Q \cdot MP_C = \$1,800(72 + 30C - 3C^2)$$
$$= \$1,800(72 + 30(9) - 3(9)^2) = \$178,200$$

b. Since the firm's current MRP_C of $178,200 is greater than the current cost of capital, it would be profitable to continue automation of production facilities until $MRP_C = P_C$.

$$MRP_C = 1,800(72 + 30C - 3C^2) = 100,000$$
$$129,600 + 54,000C - 5,400C^2 = 100,000$$
$$29,600 + 54,000C - 5,400C^2 = 0$$

By the quadratic equation,

$$C = \frac{-54,000 \pm \sqrt{(-54,000)^2 - (4)(-5,400)(29,600)}}{(2)(-5,400)}$$

$$= \frac{-54,000 \pm 59,626.83959}{-10,800} = -0.52100366, +10.52100367.$$

We eliminate the negative answer, leaving

$$C \approx 10.521 \text{ units } \times \$100,000/\text{unit} = \$1,052,100.$$

c. Since Westland is currently employing nine units of capital,

$$\epsilon_P = \frac{MP}{AP} = \frac{72 + 30C - 3C^2}{72 + 15C - C^2} = \frac{72 + 30(9) - 3(9)^2}{72 + 15(9) - (9)^2} = 0.7857.$$

d. Elasticity merely tells us the proportional increase in production that can result from additional capital investment. The marginal revenue product of labor, MRP_L, also must be considered along with the cost of capital in order to determine the effect on profit.

e. As capital costs decrease for investments in such assets as computers and robots, it becomes profitable to incorporate them into production systems. This can lead to greater production efficiency, but an unfortunate side effect is that some categories of labor become less efficient relative to capital. For example, we see robots replacing assembly-line workers and computers replacing middle managers. As technology advances, our labor force must seek to maintain its relative efficiency by upgrading skills and pursuing advanced education.

EXHIBIT 10–4   Units of Output as a Function of Varying Input Combinations of Capital and Labor

Units of Capital	Units of Labor							
	1	*2*	*3*	*4*	*5*	*6*	*7*	*8*
1	3	6	8	9	10	10	9	7
2	6	12	17	21	24	26	25.5	24.5
3	10	24	39	52	61	66	66	64
4	13	30	54	72	85	93	95	95
5	15	37	60	80	100	113	120	121
6	16	42	66	88	106	120	128	132
7	13	46	69	91	108	123	134	140
8	9	46	69	92	109	124	136	144

The Production Function of Multiple-Variable Inputs

In the preceding section, we looked at production as a function of one variable input to obtain an output, Q, with all other inputs held constant. Our purpose was to gain a better understanding of factor productivity and its effect on the production function, which is often called return to factor. Now let's examine a production system with two variable inputs. The basic two-variable production is

$$Q = f(C, L) \qquad (16)$$

where C = capital and L = labor. Equation 16 represents a multivariate function in which two independent variable inputs go into a production process to obtain one kind of output (the dependent variable Q).

To illustrate, we show a hypothetical tabulation of output from varying combinations of capital and labor inputs, i.e., $Q = f(C, L)$. Exhibit 10–4 above shows the outputs obtained from the 64 possible combinations of eight different input quantities of capital and eight different input quantities of labor. Each combination of inputs produces its own level of output, although some output levels are the same.

Since the input values are discrete, these production data can be visually represented by a three-dimensional histogram, as partially illustrated by Exhibit 10–5 (page 287). Each combination of input quantities forms the rectangular base of a block. The height of the discrete block represents output. Taken together, the tops of the blocks form a *production surface*, whose shape can be seen by following the rows of blocks, first in the *X*-direction and then in the *Y*-direction.

The rough stair-step nature of the production surface in Exhibit 10–5 results from the discrete values of the input variables. To get a smooth surface, we must assume a continuous underlying production function for each of the input variables. This means that the input units must be infinitely divisible. The concept is illustrated by Exhibit 10–6.

Continuous Input–Output Curves and Relationships.   The diagrams in Exhibit 10–6 (page 288) have two horizontal axes in the base plane (*X–Y* plane), along which units of input *X* and input *Y* are scaled in a positive direction only. Output is measured vertically. There is one output (*Z*) for each combination of inputs *X* and *Y*. Since an infinite number

EXHIBIT 10–5   Production Surface Resulting from Discrete Production Function

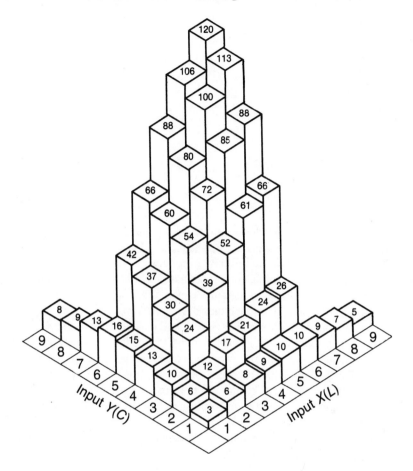

of combinations is possible, there is also an infinite number of outputs, each represented by a point in space. Taken together, these points form a smooth *production surface*.

A production surface may be viewed as a hill, with greater output represented by greater height of the surface. Output is increased as we move up the hill. This is done by increasing one or the other of the inputs, or both at the same time. Thus in Panel A of the exhibit, if the quantity of Y is held constant at Y_1, while X is allowed to vary, a vertical slice at Y_1 that is parallel to the X-axis produces the trace Y_1A on the production surface. Similarly, if the quantity of X is held constant at X_1, a vertical slice at X_1 and parallel to the Y-axis will produce the trace X_1B.

These traces, or surface lines, are simply input–output curves. Each expresses a relationship between output and one variable input while the other variable input is held constant at some specified level. Obviously, since infinitely many vertical slices can be made, there are infinitely many input–output curves that can be drawn. The *slopes* of the input–output curves indicate the *marginal products* of the variable inputs.

EXHIBIT 10–6   **Production Surfaces from Continuous Production Functions**

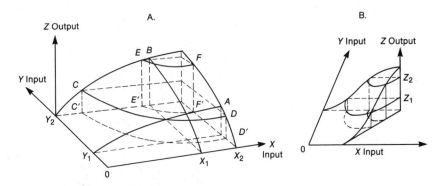

Panel A illustrates a production surface in which both input–output relationships are quadratic. Therefore, the slopes (marginal products) of the individual input–output curves are continuously diminishing. In contrast, Panel B illustrates a production surface in which the underlying production functions are cubic. As previously shown in Exhibit 10–2, in a cubic production function the slope (marginal product) of the individual input–output curves first increases and then decreases. Thus, with increasing inputs of both factors, the production surface is first convex and then concave to the *X–Y* base plane.

The figures in the exhibit illustrate production surfaces that result when the input–output curves for the two factors are similar in shape. That is, both are quadratic in Panel A and both are cubic in Panel B. This need not be the case; the individual factor-output curves may be any shape. Consequently, any number of production surface shapes is possible, depending upon the nature of the underlying univariate production functions.

Factor-Factor Relationships: Isoquants.   A second type of relationship is revealed when the production surfaces of Exhibit 10–6 are sliced horizontally instead of vertically. The height of each horizontal slice represents a special output level, as indicated by Z_1 and Z_2 in Panel B. Associated with each horizontal slice is a contour line around the surface, representing a constant level of output. Such contour lines are called isoquants. In Panel A, line *CD* is one such isoquant, while line *EF* is another isoquant representing a greater level of total output than *CD*. Obviously, the higher we go up the hill, the greater the level of total output represented by a particular isoquant. Since each isoquant is the result of various combinations of inputs, analyses of this type may be said to involve the study of factor–factor relations.

When the isoquants are projected downward onto the base, as shown by the dashed lines *C′D′* and *E′F′*, we get a two-dimensional graph that is much easier to work with. It is customary in economic theory to work with the two-dimensional version of the isoquants rather than with their more cumbersome three-dimensional counterparts. Accordingly, it is in the two-dimensional framework that analyses of the isoquants and other concepts of production are developed in the field of production economics. A typical isoquant map is shown as Exhibit 10–7.

EXHIBIT 10–7   Isoquants from Inputs of Capital and Labor

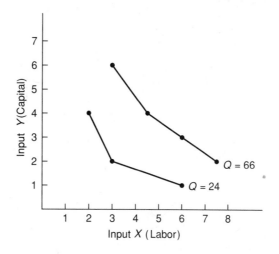

The basic characteristics of isoquants are the same as the characteristics of the in-difference curves that were discussed in Chapter 5, that is, they are infinite in number, continuous, downward-sloping, and convex to the origin, and the farther they are from the origin, the greater the output they represent. An indifference curve was defined as the loci of all combinations of commodities X and Y that yield the same level of satisfaction or utility. Similarly, an isoquant is defined as the loci of all combinations of two input factors that yield the same level of output.

Marginal Rate of Technical Substitution.   In Chapter 5, we showed that the slope of an indifference curve measured the marginal rate of substitution of commodity X for commodity Y. The same concept of substitutability is pertinent to production functions using two variable inputs. The slope of the isoquant measures *the marginal rate of technical substitution* of input X for input Y while maintaining the same level of output. It is calculated as the negative change in Y divided by the change in X:

$$MRTS_{XY} = -\frac{\Delta Y}{\Delta X}. \tag{17}$$

Although a constant $MRTS_{XY}$ is theoretically possible if the two inputs are perfect substitutes for each other, the $MRTS_{XY}$ normally grows smaller as the substitution of X for Y increases. The reason why this is so is that inputs normally tend to complement one another. Two inputs are necessary because each input does something the other cannot do, or cannot do as efficiently. In most activities, capital and labor are not perfect substitutes. Therefore, it takes more and more of one to substitute for less and less of the other. Thus, as we move down the isoquant, ΔY in Equation 17 above grows smaller and ΔX grows larger, making the *MRTS* smaller.

EXHIBIT 10–8   **Isoquants of Inputs That Are Perfect Substitutes or Perfect Complements**

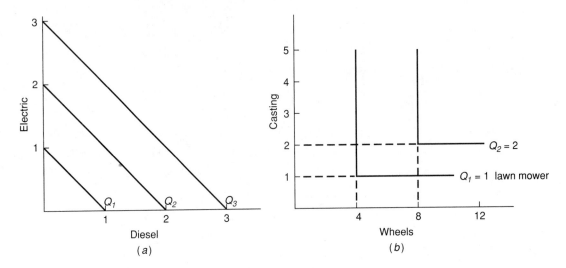

(a)

(b)

Shapes of Isoquants.   The possibility of substitution of input X for input Y and the degree of substitution possible determine the shape and slope of the isoquant. In addition to the normal shape of isoquants illustrated by Exhibit 10–7, there are peculiar shapes associated with perfect substitutes and perfect complements, as shown in Exhibit 10–8. Panel A shows the isoquants resulting from two inputs that are perfect substitutes for one another. For example, an electrified railroad may be able to use either electric or diesel locomotives to pull a train of the same size at the same speed. Thus if for any reason an electric locomotive is not available, a diesel locomotive can be substituted with no change in the output. The $MRTS_{XY}$ is a constant in this case.

Panel B shows the right-angled isoquants resulting from two inputs that are perfectly complementary; i.e., input of a single variable by itself will not produce any output. To obtain output, both X and Y must be input in a fixed ratio. For example, the manufacture of a lawn mower requires an input of one body casting and four wheels, a ratio that never changes. Therefore, if two castings are input, eight wheels must also be input to obtain two units of output, because the two inputs are complementary. Even if 20 wheels are available for input, the output will still be only two units as long as only two body castings are available.

The Economic Region of an Isoquant.   In earlier discussion, we noted that an isoquant is obtained by passing a horizontal plane through a production surface described as a "hill." The resulting trace would, of course, be roughly circular in shape as it goes all around the hill. Technically, the entire circular trace is an isoquant, since every point along it represents the same level of production. But in normal usage, when we refer to an isoquant, we are talking about the part of the trace that slopes downward and to the right, i.e., the heavy line on *EADF* in Exhibit 10–9. The reason why can be explained with the aid of this exhibit.

EXHIBIT 10–9   Economic Regions of Isoquants

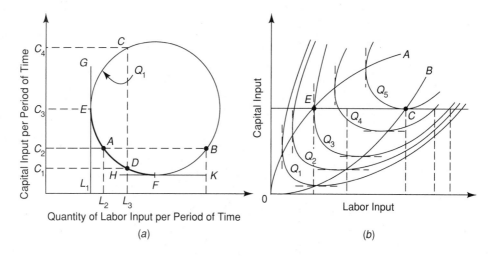

(a)   (b)

To understand this exhibit, let's assume that we have a production surface that represents the outputs resulting from all possible combinations of capital and labor inputs. Then the trace *CADB* in Panel A of the exhibit results from passage of a horizontal plane through this production surface at an output level of, let us say, $Q_1 = 100$ units. The vertical line L_1G is tangent to this trace at point E. Since the point E is on the trace, the output level at E is 100 units.

If we move clockwise from this point along the trace to point C, the output level remains at 100 units despite the fact that *both* capital and labor inputs increase. This is the result of negative marginal products of both capital and labor, manifested in the positively sloped isoquant between points E and C.

In a similar manner, we note the line *HK*, which is tangent to the trace at point F. If we move counterclockwise along the trace to point B, the output level remains at 100 units, but both labor and capital inputs increase. This, too, is the result of negative marginal products of both capital and labor, manifested in the positively sloped isoquant between points F and B.

Clearly, it would be irrational to input the combinations of capital and labor that would lead to the positively sloped isoquant above point E or to the right of point F. Consequently, rational combinations of inputs yielding output of 100 units are restricted to the isoquant between points E and F, where the isoquant curves downward and to the right.

Extending this concept to any number of isoquants, we can define the economic region of any number of isoquants by drawing vertical and horizontal lines tangent to the front side of each equal-output trace, as shown in Panel B of the exhibit. When these points of tangency are joined by smooth curves (lines *OA* and *OB* in Panel B), the area between *OA* and *OB* constitutes the rational economic region, and input combinations outside these lines are irrational.

EXHIBIT 10–10   Isoquant-Isocost Diagram

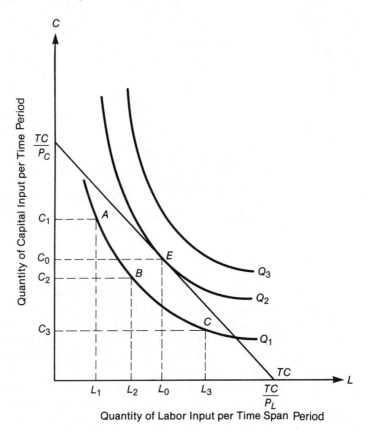

Quantity of Labor Input per Time Span Period

Production Equilibrium: Optimum Multiple-Variable Inputs.   If the marginal products of the respective variable-input factors can be determined and the costs of all input combinations are known, the optimum input combination yields either minimum total costs for a given level of output or maximum output for a given level of total costs.

Many different combinations of inputs will yield a given level of output, but obviously only the least-cost combination will result in optimum production management. Clearly, the least-cost combination depends on the relative prices of the inputs as well as the amount of input factors used. This leads to the following principle or decision rule:

> **Principle:** *The least-cost combination of variable inputs is achieved when a dollar's worth of any variable input adds as much to total output as a dollar's worth of any other variable input.*

Accordingly, if we let MP_A denote the marginal product of A, and PA the price of A, and similarly for other inputs $B, C, \ldots, N$, the equation of minimum cost is

$$\frac{MP_A}{P_A} = \frac{MP_B}{P_B} = \dots = \frac{MP_N}{P_N}. \tag{18}$$

Equation 18 is the *rule of minimum cost* or *least-cost hiring rule*. Its derivation can be demonstrated by an isoquant-isocost approach that is analogous to the indifference-curve/budget-line approach to demand analysis that was discussed in Chapter 5. Suppose we let the two inputs be labor, L (instead of X) and capital, C (instead of Y), as shown in Exhibit 10–10.

If we move along an isoquant from one point to another (as from point A to B to C on the isoquant Q_1), the change in C is $OC_3 - OC_1 = C_3 - C_1 = -\Delta C$, and this causes a loss in production equal to the change in capital multiplied by the marginal product of capital. The change in L is $OL_3 - OL_1 = L_3 - L_1 = \Delta L$, and this causes a gain in production equal to the change in labor multiplied by the marginal product of labor. Since the level of production remains the same everywhere along the isoquant, the loss in production from using less of C is exactly compensated by the gain from substituting more of L. In symbols,

$$-\Delta C \cdot MP_C = \Delta L \cdot MP_L.$$

Dividing both sides of the equation by $-\Delta L \cdot MP_C$, we get

$$\frac{\Delta C}{\Delta L} = -\frac{MP_L}{MP_C}. \tag{19}$$

Thus the slope of the isoquant, $\Delta C/\Delta L$, not only indicates the rate at which one input may be substituted for the other at a given level of output, but also the ratio of the marginal product of labor to the marginal product of capital, $\frac{MP_L}{MP_C}$. This ratio is the marginal rate of technical substitution, labor for capital ($MRTS_{LC}$). Its equation is

$$MRTS_{LC} = -\frac{MP_L}{MP_C}. \tag{20}$$

The other half of the isoquant-isocost approach is the isocost line. "Isocost" means "equal cost," and an **isocost line** is a budget line that defines the quantities of inputs that a given amount of money will buy in various combinations.

In Exhibit 10–10, the isocost line TC represents the sum of money available for purchases of capital and labor, all of which must be spent. If we spend the entire budget on labor, we can buy TC/P_L units and this is the L-intercept. If we spend the entire budget on capital, we can buy TC/P_C units, and this is the C-intercept. If the prices of L and C are constant at all levels of consumption, a straight line between the intercepts, as illustrated in Exhibit 10–10, will trace out all possible combinations of L and C that can be purchased with exactly TC dollars. That is,

$$TC = L \cdot P_L + C \cdot P_C. \tag{21}$$

As shown in Exhibit 10–10, the isocost line is the hypotenuse of a right triangle. Its slope, therefore, is

$$\frac{\Delta C}{\Delta L} = -\frac{TC}{P_C} \div \frac{TC}{P_L} = -\frac{TC}{P_C}\frac{P_L}{TC} = -\frac{P_L}{P_C}. \tag{22}$$

Like the isoquant, the slope of the isocost or budget line is always negative. Since there is an infinite number of isoquants, an isocost line will always be just tangent to some isoquant. This is the point of equilibrium, and it indicates the specific combination of capital and labor that will give the lowest unit cost and lowest total cost of the output level represented by the isoquant. Conversely, the point of equilibrium indicates the highest level of production that can be attained with the indicated budget for capital and labor.

At the point of equilibrium, the slopes of the isoquant and isocost lines are equal, i.e.,

$$-\frac{MP_L}{MP_C} = -\frac{P_L}{P_C}.$$ (23)

Therefore, by cross-multiplying,

$$\frac{MP_L}{P_L} = \frac{MP_C}{P_C}.$$ (24)

Equation 24 can easily be extended to cover any number of input factors, thus becoming the equation of minimum cost previously stated as Equation 18.

The **rule of minimum cost**, or **least-cost hiring rule**, states that if the price of an input rises, the producer should use less of it (thereby increasing its marginal product) and use more of other inputs (thereby decreasing their marginal products) until the ratios *MP/P* are all equal.

As an example, suppose a producer employs two inputs, X and Y, which have the same unit price. Suppose further that at some given level of output, MP_X is 10 units per dollar and MP_Y is eight units per dollar. To minimize costs at that output level, the producer should proceed as follows:

1. Reduce the input of Y by one dollar's worth, thereby reducing output by eight units.
2. Increase the input of X by 80 cents' worth, thereby increasing output by eight units (that is, 4/5 of the marginal product of one dollar's worth of X).

This trade-off between inputs reduces costs by 20 cents while maintaining a constant output volume. It is the best result obtainable at the given volume.

Illustrative Problem

To illustrate the procedure for determining the optimal combination of inputs, let us take the original Cobb-Douglas production function

$$P' = 1.01L^{0.75}C^{0.25}.$$ (25)

Questions

Suppose that the price of labor is $12 per unit and the price of capital is $2 per unit.

a. What is the optimal relationship between input of labor and input of capital?
b. How many units of labor and capital should an employer purchase?

Solutions

a. First we take the partial derivatives to find the marginal products of labor and capital in order to apply the least-cost hiring rule:

$$MP_L = \frac{\partial P'}{\partial L} = (0.75)(1.01)L^{-0.25}C^{0.25} \tag{26}$$

$$MP_C = \frac{\partial P'}{\partial C} = (0.25)(1.01)L^{0.75}C^{-0.75}. \tag{27}$$

The ratio of the marginal products is

$$\frac{MP_L}{MP_C} = \frac{(0.75)(1.01)L^{-0.25}C^{0.25}}{(0.25)(1.01)L^{0.75}C^{-0.75}} = \frac{3C}{L}. \tag{28}$$

The least-cost hiring rule $\frac{MP_L}{P_L} = \frac{MP_C}{P_C}$ can also be written as

$$\frac{MP_L}{MP_C} = \frac{P_L}{P_C}. \tag{29}$$

Hence,

$$\frac{3C}{L} = \frac{12}{2}.$$

Cross-multiplying, we get

$$6C = 12L$$
$$C = 2L$$

which means that regardless of the number of units to be produced, the employer should always use two units of capital for each unit of labor.

The foregoing procedure for finding the optimal ratio of inputs (using partial derivatives to find the marginal products) can be applied to any type of production function, including the power function. The power function (or Cobb-Douglas type), however, has special properties (which are discussed in the next chapter) that make possible a much easier short-cut formula. The short-cut general formula is

$$\frac{X_1}{X_2} = \frac{\text{Exponent of } X_1}{\text{Exponent of } X_2} \cdot \frac{\text{Price of } X_2}{\text{Price of } X_1} \tag{30}$$

where X_1 and X_2 are quantities of two different input factors. Applying the general equation to our specific problem, we let $X_1 = C$ and $X_2 = L$ and get the same answer with a lot less work:[3]

$$\frac{C}{L} = \frac{0.25}{0.75} \cdot \frac{12}{2} = 2$$

so that

$$C = 2L$$
$$L = 0.5C.$$

b. Once the optimal ratio of inputs has been found, the maximum number of units that can be produced depends upon how much money is available to hire or purchase the

---

[3] If a power function has more than two variables, Equation 30 can be used to find the optimal ratio of input for any two variables at a time.

input factors. In this example, since labor costs $12 per unit and capital costs $2 per unit, the total cost is

$$TC = L \cdot P_L + C \cdot P_C = 12L + 2C.$$

Suppose that we have a maximum of $1,000 to spend on labor and capital. Then

$$12L + 2C = 1,000.$$

But since $C = 2L$, we can substitute $2L$ for C, so that

$$12L + 2(2L) = 16L = 1,000$$
$$L = 1,000/16 = 62.5$$
$$C = 2L = 125.$$

We could, of course, get the same answer by substituting $0.5C$ for L, since $L = 0.5C$:

$$12L + 2C = 1,000$$
$$(12)(0.5C) + 2C = 1,000$$
$$8C = 1,000$$
$$C = 1,000/8 = 125$$
$$L = 0.5C = 62.5.$$

When we put these values into the original equation, we get

$$P' = 1.01L^{0.75}C^{0.25} = (1.01)(62.5)^{0.75}(125)^{0.25} = 75.069.$$

Thus approximately 75 units of output is the maximum that can be produced with a production budget of $1,000.

Optimum Multiple-Variable Inputs and Profit Maximization

Now let us consider a productive operation in which there are two input factors of production, capital (C) and labor (L), and one output product (Q). From Equation 18, we know that the cost of production at any level will be minimal when $MP_C/P_C = MP_L/P_L$. Minimum cost certainly is a *necessary* condition for maximization of profit, but is not *sufficient* by itself. Maximization of profit also requires that marginal revenue, MR_Q, equal marginal cost, MC_Q.

By definition,

$$MC_Q = \frac{\Delta TC}{\Delta Q} = \frac{P_X}{MP_X}. \qquad (31)$$

At optimum, therefore,

$$MC_Q = \frac{P_C}{MP_C} = MR_Q \qquad (32)$$

and

$$MC_Q = \frac{P_L}{MP_L} = MR_Q. \qquad (33)$$

Therefore, from Equations 32 and 33,

EXHIBIT 10–11   Expansion Path for Increase of the Firm's Production Capacity

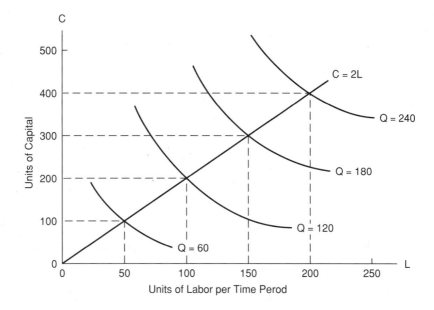

$$MR_Q \cdot MP_L = P_L = MRP_L \tag{34}$$

$$MR_Q \cdot MP_C = P_C = MRP_C. \tag{35}$$

Equations 34 and 35 consider not only the factors related to supply (i.e., marginal product and input prices) but also the factor related to demand (i.e., marginal revenue). Thus the firm's profits are optimal when the marginal revenue product of each input is equal to its price.

Expansion of Production and Returns to Scale

A firm desiring to expand production will do so by increasing expenditures on capital and labor. If the prices of labor and capital remain constant, this will cause the budget line to shift outward in a parallel fashion. Each time the budget line shifts, a new equilibrium point will occur where the budget line is just tangent to an isoquant. A line connecting these equilibrium points constitutes the firm's expansion path, as illustrated by Exhibit 10–11. Since expansion of production requires changes in all inputs, it clearly is a long-run concept.

Exhibit 10–11 depicts the optimal relationship between capital and labor for the Cobb-Douglas production function $P' = 1.01L^{0.75}C^{0.25}$, which was discussed in the previous section. From that discussion we learned that $C = 2L$ is the optimal ratio of capital and labor. In other words, the equation $C = 2L$ is the equation of the expansion path. When this equation is substituted into the production function, the optimal requirements for capital and labor can be calculated for any level of output.

For example, suppose we want to expand production to 10,000 units, using the Cobb-Douglas production function. The optimal requirement for labor will be

$$1.01L^{0.75}C^{0.25} = 1.01L^{0.75}(2L)^{0.25} = (1.01)(2)^{0.25}(L)$$
$$= (1.01)(1.1892071)L = 1.2010992L = 10,000$$
$$L = 8,325.7071 \approx 8,326 \text{ units.}$$

The optimal requirement for capital will be

$$1.01L^{0.75}C^{0.25} = 1.01(0.5C)^{0.75}C^{0.25} = (1.01)(0.5)^{0.75}(C)$$
$$= (1.01)(0.5946036)C = 0.6005496C = 10,000$$
$$C = 16,651.414 \approx 16,651 \text{ units}$$

which is just twice as much as the requirement for labor units. The total budget required to produce 10,000 units of output would be $(8,326 \times \$12) + (16,651 \times \$2) = \$133,214$.

Returns to Scale

In order to develop the expansion path of Exhibit 10–11, we make three basic assumptions: (1) input factor prices remain constant even though we may be using more of them; (2) the production function will not change when production is increased; and (3) the optimal mix of inputs will be maintained. This last assumption leads us to the notion of "scaling up" production. Scaling up requires that all production factors vary simultaneously in the same proportion, as they will if optimal relationships are maintained.

At first glance, it seems reasonable to expect that if we double all inputs at the same time, we will also double the output. In some industries this may be so. In other industries with different production functions, the yield from doubled inputs may be more than or less than doubled. When all factors of production are increased simultaneously by some proportion, one of three results is possible:

1. *Increasing returns to scale*: Output increases by a greater proportion than the increase in inputs.
2. *Constant returns to scale*: Output increases in the same proportion as the increase in inputs.
3. *Decreasing returns to scale*: Output increases by a smaller proportion than the increase in inputs.

The concept of returns to scale is illustrated by Exhibit 10–12. The exhibit represents the base of a production surface upon which are projected three possible traces from the production surface above. They indicate the proportional changes in output when inputs of C and L are increased in the same proportion. The three curves are actually three possible expansion paths, and their slopes indicate returns to scale.

Curve (1) has an increasing slope, reflecting increasing returns to scale. Curve (2) has a constant slope, indicating constant returns to scale. Curve (3) has a decreasing slope, indicating decreasing returns to scale. The positioning of the curves in this exhibit has no significance, as each type of curve will be positioned according to the equation of the expansion path.

EXHIBIT 10–12   Possible Returns to Scale

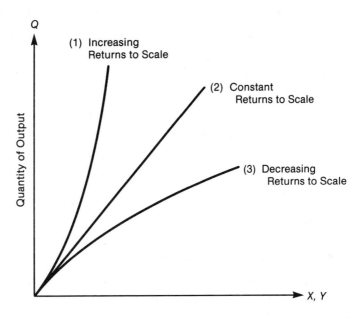

Testing Production Functions for Returns to Scale

In the preceding discussions, we examined optimal relationships between two input variables. If the production function is known, however, it can be analyzed algebraically for returns to scale even if it has more than two input variables. Suppose we have the production function

$$Q = 5X_1 + 3X_2 + 0.5X_3 \qquad (36)$$

where Q = output and X_1, X_2, and X_3 are three different input factors. Assume initial inputs of one unit each of X_1, X_2, and X_3. Total output, therefore, is

$$Q = 5(1) + 3(1) + 0.5(1) = 8.5.$$

Now suppose we increase each input factor by the proportion k. Output will then increase by some proportion, h. The value of h is determined by dividing hQ by Q. If $h > k$, the function yields increasing returns to scale. If $h = k$, the function yields constant returns to scale. If $h < k$, the function yields decreasing returns to scale.

To illustrate, suppose we let $k = 2$, thus doubling the inputs so that $X_1 = 2$, $X_2 = 2$, and $X_3 = 2$. Output is then

$$hQ = 5(2) + 3(2) + 0.5(2) = 17.$$

We calculate $h = hQ/Q = 17/8.5 = 2 = k$. Doubling the inputs ($k = 2$) has doubled the output ($h = 2$). Therefore there are constant returns to scale, since $h = k$.

Homogeneous Functions. Scaling up a production function means multiplying each term of the function by a constant term, k, as we just illustrated. If the constant, k, can then be factored out of the equation, the function is said to be homogeneous of degree n, where n is the exponent of k after it is factored out. The exponent, n, will indicate increasing, constant, or decreasing returns to scale according to whether it is greater than, equal to, or less than 1.0.

For example, when the function

$$Q = 5X_1 + 6X_2 + X_3 \tag{37}$$

is scaled up by k, we get

$$hQ = 5(kX_1) + 6(kX_2) + (kX_3) \tag{38}$$

from which k can be factored out to get

$$hQ = k(5X_1 + 6X_2 + X_3) \tag{39}$$
$$hQ = k(Q)$$
$$h = k \text{ or } h = k^1.$$

The exponent of k is 1. Therefore, we say that the function $Q = 5X_1 + 6X_2 + X_3$ is homogeneous of degree 1. Since $h = k$, the function will yield constant returns to scale. But if we scale up the function

$$Q = X_1^{0.4}X_2^{0.3}X_3^{0.1} \tag{40}$$

by k, we get

$$hQ = (kX_1)^{0.4}(kX_2)^{0.3}(kX_3)^{0.1} = k^{0.8}(X_1^{0.4}X_2^{0.3}X_3^{0.1}) \tag{41}$$
$$hQ = k^{0.8}(Q)$$
$$h = k^{0.8}.$$

Therefore $h < k$.

This function is homogeneous of degree 0.8. Since $h < k$, the function exhibits decreasing returns to scale. In general, the rule is:

- If $n > 1$, then $h > k$, which means increasing returns to scale.
- If $n = 1$, then $h = k$, which means constant returns to scale.
- If $n < 1$, then $h < k$, which means decreasing returns to scale.

Nonhomogeneous Functions. When the production function is nonhomogeneous because the scaling constant k cannot be factored out, the function can still be tested by assigning numerical values to the variables. For example, suppose we have the production function

$$Q = 10L + 0.6LCM + 2.1L^{0.4}C^{0.3}M^{0.2}. \tag{42}$$

Examining this equation term by term, we see that each term has different returns to scale. The first term, $10L$, would yield constant returns to scale. The second term, $0.6LCM$, would yield increasing returns to scale. The third term, $2.1L^{0.4}C^{0.3}M^{0.2}$, would yield decreasing returns to scale. The overall return to scale will thus depend upon which term will exert the strongest influence when scaled up.

To test this function for returns to scale, we need to select some set of reasonable values for the variables, then scale up, and see what happens. Any set of numbers will do, but the easiest is to let all variables equal 1.0 and let $k = 2$. Then

$$Q = 10L + 0.6LCM + 2.1L^{0.4}C^{0.3}M^{0.2}$$
$$= 10(1) + 0.6(1)(1)(1) + 2.1(1)^{0.4}(1)^{0.3}(1)^{0.2} = 12.7.$$

Now suppose we double the inputs, i.e., let $k = 2$. Then

$$hQ = 10(2) + 0.6(2)(2)(2) + 2.1(2)^{0.4}(2)^{0.3}(2)^{0.2} \approx 28.7$$

$$h = \frac{hQ}{Q} = \frac{28.7}{12.7} \approx 2.26.$$

Since $h > k$, we conclude that the function exhibits increasing returns to scale.

Elasticity and Returns to Scale. Since return to scale is defined as the ratio of percent change in output to percent change in input, it clearly is the elasticity of production. Thus for increasing returns to scale, $\epsilon_P > 1$; for constant returns to scale, $\epsilon_P = 1$; and for decreasing returns to scale, $\epsilon_P < 1$.

Variable Returns to Scale

In the preceding discussion of returns to scale, we made the implicit assumption that the change in output proceeds along one of the smooth curves depicted in Exhibit 10–12 to yield increasing, decreasing, or constant returns to scale. In reality, however, the change in output may be more erratic, for at least five reasons:

1. *Indivisibility of some product services.* Rarely is it possible to increase all of the productive factors in exactly the same proportion. As a consequence, some of the factors are always being underworked or overworked relative to others at most levels of output, and this results in alternations of increasing and decreasing returns to scale. For example, doubling the rate of output of an assembly line may still require only one final inspector instead of two; one locomotive may have sufficient horsepower to pull 40 freight cars as adequately as 30; a salesperson may be able to take on a full line of goods instead of a single item at no significant increase in costs; and to a bank, the expense of investigating and managing a loan does not increase in proportion to the size of the loan. These examples from the fields of production, marketing, and finance illustrate that economies may result from stretching each input unit to its full capacity.

2. *Specialization.* Increased scale of operation provides the opportunity for specialization of both human and machine tasks, leading to gains in efficiency. Specialization of management is included in this category. Only large firms can afford resident accountants, lawyers, and economists. However, differences in the degree of specialization possible and the relative effects of labor and machine specialization can lead to varying effects on output.

3. *Machine capacity.* Equipment of larger capacity may be more efficient than smaller machinery. However, the scaling up of machine capacity is necessarily a step function, as compared to the scaling up of labor, which is more nearly a continuous process.

4. *Dimensional factors.* Doubling the diameter of a pipe quadruples its cross section and therefore its carrying capacity. Likewise, halving a pipe's diameter quarters its cross section and carrying capacity. An increase (or decrease) along one dimension of an input factor, accordingly, often yields disproportionate effects on output.

5. *Different rates of production in different machines.* Suppose Machine A fills 15,000 packages per day. Machine B wraps 20,000 packages per day. Both types of machines will be fully utilized only when the output is a multiple of 60,000 packages. Each increment of 60,000 would then fully utilize four production runs of Machine A and three of Machine B. If output is *not* a multiple of 60,000 packages, however, one or both machines will be underutilized periodically, thereby causing fluctuations in output.

Management and Returns to Scale

If management does not fully understand the nature of the contribution that each input variable makes to the total production, attempts to improve profitability by increasing the scale of operations may yield some unpleasant surprises. This is beautifully illustrated in the following passage from a classic work:

> There is a story of a man who thought of getting the economy of large scale production in plowing, and built a plow three times as long, three times as wide, and three times as deep as the ordinary plow and harnessed six horses to pull it, instead of two. To his surprise, the plow refused to budge, and to his greater surprise it finally took fifty horses to move the refractory machine. In this case, the resistance, which is the thing he did not want, increased faster than the surface area of the earth plowed, which was the thing he did want. Furthermore, when he increased his power to overcome this resistance, he multiplied the number of his power units instead of their size, which eliminated all chance of saving there, and since his units were horses, the fifty could not pull together as well as two.[4]

Given a particular technology, an expanding firm can expect to pass through a short phase of increasing returns to scale, then a long phase of constant returns to scale, and finally a phase of decreasing returns to scale. The last stage (decreasing returns) may be avoided through the implementation of an improved technology, which is often made possible by larger output. For example, as a firm grows, so do its data-processing requirements. It may decide to install a computer rather than hire more clerks. This effectively alters the production function, of course, but it may or may not relieve the burden imposed on management by the growth of the firm.

In order to perform its function as coordinator, top management of a growing firm may be able to delegate authority, but ultimately decisions must emanate from a final authority if there is to be uniformity in performance and policy. As the firm grows, increasingly heavy burdens are placed on management so that eventually this factor of production is overworked relative to others and diminishing returns to management set in. Thus it is the growing difficulty of coordination that eventually stops the growth of any firm. To some extent, the development of new scientific methods and techniques of decision making may (1) reduce the time necessary to make a given number of correct

---

[4] J. M. Clark, *Studies in the Economics of Overhead Costs* (Chicago: University of Chicago Press, 1923), p. 116.

decisions or (2) increase the number of correct decisions that can be made within a given time period. However, this would only tend to postpone the realization of decreasing returns to scale rather than avoid them altogether.

Increasing, decreasing, or constant returns to scale reflect changes in production efficiency that result from scaling up productive inputs. But it must be remembered that returns to scale is strictly a production concept. Management's decisions on what to produce and how much to produce must be based first of all upon demand for the product. Even if increasing returns to scale are available, there is no profit in producing what cannot be sold, no matter how efficiently it is produced. On the other hand, if there is a large demand for the product, scaling up may produce greater total profit even if there are decreasing returns to scale. Although the increase in unit cost will reduce the unit profit margin, the total profit may increase because of the increase in sales volume.

In other words, returns to scale is not the only consideration for management when making long-run decisions about production levels. Demand and other factors must also be included in the decision maker's deliberations.

Summary

Production analysis may be undertaken to determine (1) the most economical input of resources to obtain a given level of output or (2) the maximum output that can be obtained from a given level and mix of inputs. Production of any good or service always requires input of two basic factors: capital and labor. In the short run, the study of production thus begins with the study of factor–product relationships, in which one factor is allowed to vary while all others are held constant.

Study of factor–product relationships has led to the *law of variable proportions*, also called the *law of diminishing returns*. This law says that as the input of a factor of production increases, the marginal product varies, first increasing, then decreasing until it becomes negative. Total production will be maximum at the point where the marginal product is zero.

Returns to scale is a long-range planning concept that enables management to estimate the effect of increasing all inputs by the same proportion. If all inputs are increased by some proportion, k, output will be increased by some proportion, h. If $h > k$, the production function exhibits increasing returns to scale. If $h = k$, the function exhibits constant returns to scale. And if $h < k$, the function exhibits decreasing returns to scale.

A production function is said to be homogeneous if the scaling proportion, k, can be factored out of the equation. If so, the exponent of the factored-out k indicates the returns to scale. If the exponent is greater than 1, then $h > k$; if it is equal to 1, then $h = k$; and if it is less than 1, then $h < k$.

If a function is nonhomogeneous, returns to scale can be estimated by giving some numeric value to each variable, and then scaling up. After scaling up, h is calculated as hQ/Q and compared to k to determine the returns to scale.

The analyst must remember that returns to scale and economies of scale are strictly production and cost concepts and have no links to demand. The ultimate decision regarding the size of the production facility must be based on the level of sales that is most profitable for the firm.

Problems

1. What are the basic short-run and long-run production decisions in the following activities?

   a. Airline industry
   b. Automobile industry
   c. Academic activities of a university
   d. Medical doctor's office
   e. Government agencies
   f. Research institutes or "think tanks."

2. Use a graph to explain how the law of variable proportions or law of diminishing returns is reflected in the shape of the marginal-product and total-product curves based on one input variable. Explain the relationship between diminishing returns and the three stages of production.

3. Explain the underlying differences between the law of diminishing returns and decreasing returns to scale. How can these two concepts be utilized in decision making?

4. The soil in Iowa is some of the world's most fertile for the growing of corn. At an Iowa agricultural-experiment station, tests were run to determine the effect of nitrogen on corn production. The tests showed that beginning with one unit of fertilizer, increasing applications of nitrogen yielded increasing harvests of corn, but at a decreasing rate from the beginning. If you were to draw graphs of the production function, marginal product, and average product, what would their shapes be?

5. Refer to Exhibit 10–4.

   a. Assume input of one unit of capital and construct a table showing the total product, average product, marginal product, and production elasticity for input of from one to eight units of labor.

   b. Use these data to construct a graph showing total-product, average-product, and marginal-product curves. Indicate on the graph:

      (1) The level of labor input that maximizes marginal product
      (2) The level of labor input that maximizes average product
      (3) The level of labor input that maximizes total product.

   c. Explain how the law of diminishing returns is reflected in the total-product curve.

6. We have made the point that isoquants are analogous to indifference curves. List the similarities and differences between the ordinal approach to the analysis of utility functions and the isoquant approach to analysis of production functions. Show the similarities and differences in the basic assumptions.

7. Draw an isoquant diagram, plotting the variables capital and labor. Then illustrate situations in which technological improvements result in:

   a. Increased capital productivity
   b. Substitution of capital for labor
   c. Increased use of both capital and labor.

8. Division and specialization of labor are often cited as a partial explanation of the enormous increases in labor productivity that took place during the 19th century. In terms of isoquant curves, how would you fit division and specialization of labor into the concept of the production function? Explain.

9. Giaia, a shoe manufacturer located in Milan, Italy, doubled the size of its factory, the number of machines in it, the number of employees, and the quantity of materials used. As a result, the manufacturer's output increased from 200 to 420 pairs of shoes per day.

   a. Is this an example of increasing returns to scale (often called the economies of large-scale production)?

   b. Giaia then doubled the quantity of managers and found the output fell to 370 pairs of shoes per day. What do you suppose might have happened?

10. Explain or prove the following relationships:

    a. $MRTS_{LC} = \dfrac{P_L}{P_C}$

    b. $MRTS_{LC} = \dfrac{MP_L}{MP_C}$

    c. $\dfrac{MP_L}{MP_C} = \dfrac{P_L}{P_C}.$

11. Sports International of Brisbane, Australia, has developed a new tennis racket that is designed to improve the game of beginners. The key to the new racket's efficiency is a ceramic frame

that is fairly expensive to produce, costing $20 each. However, demand for the new product is estimated to be such that the company can sell the rackets at a price of $50 each. Their production engineers have estimated the production function for output of the new racket to be

$$Q = 350X - 0.5X^2$$

where

Q = Number of finished rackets produced
X = Number of ceramic frames input.

a. What is the marginal product if $X = 50$?

b. Find the level of input that will maximize profit.

c. Find the output at the profit-maximizing level of input.

12. The revenue department of a certain state government employs certified public accountants (CPAs) to audit corporate tax returns and specially trained bookkeepers to audit personal returns. CPAs are paid $62,400 per year, while the annual salary of a bookkeeper is $36,400. An economist studying the department's additional tax collections resulting from auditing tax returns found that the CPAs auditing corporate returns produced an average additional tax collection of $52,000 per auditor-year. In contrast, the bookkeepers produced only $41,600 per auditor-year.

a. If the department's objective is to maximize tax revenue collected, is the present mix of CPAs and bookkeepers optimal? If it is not optimal, explain what reallocation should be made.

b. What assumptions were necessary to find a solution to part (a)? Are these assumptions realistic? If not, explain how realistic conclusions might be reached.

13. Tiger Parts, Inc., is a small Korean manufacturer of automobile shock absorbers, with an estimated weekly production function of

$$Q = 100C^{0.5}L^{0.5}$$

where

Q = Number of shock absorbers produced per week
C = Units of capital employed
L = Number of workers employed, working a 40-hour week.

During the past year, the firm operated efficiently, using 100 units of capital and 25 workers.

a. What was its weekly output last year?

b. What was the marginal product of capital? Of labor?

c. If the price of capital was 66,500 *won* per unit per week, what was the average labor cost per worker per week?

d. The firm's new labor contract with the Brotherhood of Rubber Workers, which goes into effect at the beginning of the coming fiscal year, calls for a wage increase of 10 percent. The cost of capital is also expected to rise to 79,800 *won* per unit. If the firm maintains efficient production, how many units of capital and how many workers will be employed in order to maintain current output?

14. An economics professor developed the following production function for a privately operated business school:

$$Q = 15X^{0.7}Y^{0.2}Z^{0.3}$$

where

Q = Student enrollment
X = Number of teachers
Y = Number of administrative personnel
Z = Number of support personnel.

There are 53 support personnel and four administrative personnel, but one of the administrative staff works only half-time. The tuition fee is $2,500. The average salary of the school's teachers is $45,000. What is the optimum number of teachers?

15. Weld-On, Inc., produces three different types of glue. Each glue requires a separate manufacturing process. Thus each has a unique production function, as follows:

Watertight: $Q = 0.65C^{0.25}L^{0.75}$
Woodbond: $Q = C^2 + 3L$
Plastigrip: $Q = 2C + 5L$

where

Q = Units of glue produced
C = Units of capital used
L = Units of labor used.

a. What are the returns to scale for each product?

b. Where should management concentrate its resources?

c. What other factors and qualifications must be considered in following the strategy chosen in part (b)?

16. Determine whether the following production functions indicate constant, increasing, or decreasing returns to scale. Which of the functions is homogeneous?

a. $Q = 10C^{0.5}L^{0.5}$

b. $Q = 13C + 12L + 0.5M$

c. $Q = C + 2L + 0.7M^{0.3}$

d. $Q = 3C^2 + 8LM$

e. $Q = 1.09C^{0.3}L^{0.3}M^{0.3}$

f. $Q = \sqrt{3L^2 + 0.9C^2 + 4T^2}$.

Case Problem: South Fort Electric

17. South Fort Electric operates a generating plant that converts natural gas to electric power. After detailed analysis of the plant, management estimates its production function to be

$$Q = 5L^{0.2}C^{0.8}G^{0.9}$$

where

Q = Hundreds of kilowatt-hours produced

L = Thousands of labor hours

C = Capital investment (rate base) in millions of dollars

G = Natural gas in hundred thousands of cubic feet.

South Fort Electric currently purchases natural gas for $22 per thousand cubic feet and pays an average wage of $25 per hour, including payroll taxes, pension plan, and other fringe benefits. Its capital investment is $50 million. The public-utilities commission has fixed electric power rates at $18 per hundred-kilowatt hours.

Questions

a. What is the power plant's optimal level of natural-gas consumption?

b. The public-utilities commission permits a 10 percent return on the firm's rate base (capital investment). At the optimal level of gas consumption, is it profitable for South Fort Electric to make additional capital investments?

References

Douglas, Paul H. "Are There Laws of Production?" *American Economic Review* (March 1948), pp. 1–41.

Gold, Bela. "Changing Perspectives on Size, Scale, and Returns: An Interpretive Survey." *Journal of Economic Literature* (March 1981), pp. 5–33.

Gould, J. P., and C. E. Ferguson. *Microeconomic Theory*. 5th ed. Homewood, Ill.: Richard D. Irwin, 1980, chaps. 5 and 6.

Johnston, J. "An Economic Study of the Production Decision." *Quarterly Journal of Economics* (May 1961), pp. 234–61.

Moroney, John R. "Cobb-Douglas Production Functions and Returns to Scale in U.S. Manufacturing Industry." *Western Economic Journal* (December 1967), pp. 39–51.

Mulligan, J. E. "Basic Optimization Techniques: A Brief Survey." *Journal of Industrial Engineering* (May-June 1965), pp. 192–97.

Stokes, H. S., Jr. "An Examination of the Productivity Decline in the Construction Industry." *Review of Economics and Statistics* (August 1981), pp. 496–505.

APPENDIX 10A   Effect of Wage Increases on Jobs

In general, any change in the unit cost of capital or labor will cause a shift in the position and slope of the isocost line. If the unit cost falls, the axis-intercept will move away from the origin. Conversely, if the unit cost rises, the axis-intercept will move toward the origin. Whether costs rise or fall, equilibrium will shift to another isoquant. If the unit cost increases, equilibrium will shift to an isoquant that represents a lower level of production. If the unit cost decreases, equilibrium will shift to an isoquant that represents a higher level of production. In either case, the ratio of capital to labor will change. The theory is illustrated by Exhibit 10A–1 (page 308), which shows the effects of changes in the unit cost of labor while the unit cost of capital remains constant. To understand the diagram, begin with the middle budget line (isocost line), which has an X-intercept at TC/P_{L_1} and equilibrium at point A on the isoquant Q_1. At this level of production, the firm is using C_1 units of capital and L_1 units of labor.

If the unit cost of labor increases from P_{L1} to P_{L2}, the X-intercept of the budget line will move toward the origin to TC/P_{L2}. The equilibrium will shift to point B on the isoquant $Q2$. At this lower level of production, the firm would use C_2 units of capital (more capital) and L_2 units of labor (less labor); that is to say, the firm would have to substitute capital for labor in order to maintain an optimal position.

If the unit cost of labor decreases from P_{L1} to P_{L3}, the X-intercept of the budget line will move away from the origin to TC/P_{L3}. The equilibrium will shift to point C on the isoquant Q_3. At this higher level of production, the firm would use C_3 units of capital (less capital) and L_3 units of labor (more labor); that is to say, the firm would have to substitute labor for capital in order to maintain an optimal position.

The theoretical response of the firm in the preceding discussion is to increase or decrease the level of production. In actual practice, however, the firm is more likely to be committed to a certain level of production by the demand for its product. We shall analyze the effect of an increase in the unit cost of labor under those conditions, but first we make the following observations:

1. Valid analysis requires the use of constant dollars, i.e., dollars that have been adjusted for inflation. An increase in nominal wages that merely offsets inflation does not increase the real cost of labor. Likewise, an increase in the interest rate that merely compensates for an increase in the rate of inflation does not increase the real cost of capital.

2. The news media often make the fundamental error of using wage rates to measure differences in labor costs in different countries. The cost of labor is a unit cost calculated by dividing wages paid by units of output produced. Hence an increase in real wages that is accompanied by a commensurate increase in productivity does not increase the unit cost of labor. But an increase in real wages that is not accompanied by a corresponding increase in productivity is an unearned increase, and unearned increases in real wages threaten jobs. Exhibit 10A–2 (page 309) depicts the process.

Exhibit 10A–2 begins with the firm at equilibrium at point A on the isoquant Q_1, at which the firm offers L_1 jobs. Then the union demands and gets an unearned wage

EXHIBIT 10A–1   Effect of Change of Input Unit Cost on Equilibrium

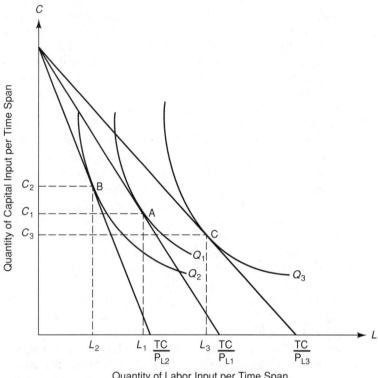

Quantity of Labor Input per Time Span

increase from P_{L1} to P_{L2}. The budget line swings toward the origin and new equilibrium is attained at point B on isoquant Q_2. The number of jobs is reduced to L_2.

This equilibrium, however, requires a lower level of production. The firm does not want to reduce its level of production, so it increases its total cost enough to pay the new wage rate. This causes the new budget line to shift outward in a parallel fashion to a new X-intercept at TC_2/P_{L2} and Y-intercept at TC_2/P_{C1}. But now the budget line is no longer optimal, because it cuts through the isoquant Q_1 at two places.

The firm, however, can reach an optimal point on Q_1 if it substitutes capital for labor. This causes the budget line to move back toward the origin in a parallel fashion until it is just tangent to Q_1 at point C. At this point of equilibrium, the number of jobs has been reduced from L_1 to L_3.

At this point the student may be wondering why, historically, the number of jobs has increased at the same time that wages have increased. Surely some of the wage increases were unearned—so why did the number of jobs increase instead of decrease?

The answer is that many industries have been expanding. The loss of jobs at a given level of production was more than offset by the additional labor required to expand production to a higher level. The process is illustrated by Exhibit 10A–3 (page 310). The exhibit begins with equilibrium at point A on isoquant Q_1, after which an unearned wage increase shifts the equilibrium to point C in the manner explained by the previous discus-

EXHIBIT 10A–2   Effect of an Unearned Wage Increase on Employment

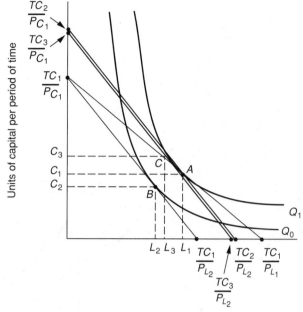

Source: Arthur A. Thompson, Jr., *Economics of the Firm: Theory and Practice,* 3rd ed. (Englewood Cliffs, N.J.: Prentice-Hall, 1981). p. 214.

sion of Exhibit 10A–2. This causes a reduction in jobs from L_1 to L_2. Then the firm initiates an expansion of production that causes the budget line to move outward in a parallel fashion until equilibrium is achieved at point D on the isoquant Q_2. The number of jobs increases to L_3, which is more than the original number at L_1. Note, however, that if the unearned wage increase had not been obtained, the *original* budget line would have shifted outward in a parallel fashion, and equilibrium would have been achieved at point E on Q_2. The number of jobs would have been L_4, which is greater than L_3. So jobs have been lost even as the total number of jobs was rising.

Illustrative Problem

Imagine a hypothetical company in which a small number of workers produce a particular product. Management estimates their production function to be $Q = 500L - L^2$, where Q = number of units output per year, and L is the number of workers. Demand for the product appears to be $Q = 10,000 - 100P$.

Questions

a. What is the optimal number of workers if the average wage in this group of workers is $20,000 per year?

EXHIBIT 10A–3 **The Effect on Employment When Production Is Increased in the Face of Unearned Wage Increases**

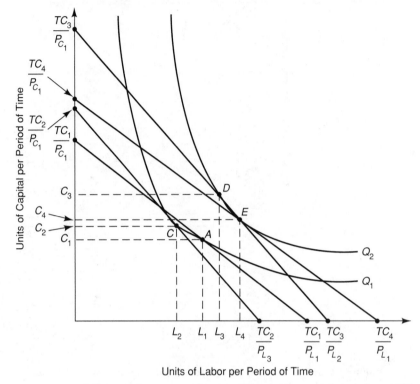

Source: Arthur A. Thompson, Jr., *Economics of the Firm: Theory and Practice*, 3rd ed. (Englewood Cliffs, N. J.: Prentice-Hall, 1971), p.216.

b. Suppose a new union contract increases the average wage to $25,000 per year. What are the company's options, assuming it wants to maximize profit?

Solution

The demand function

$$Q = 10,000 - 100P$$

is the same as

$$P = 100 - 0.01Q$$

from which we get the total-revenue and marginal-revenue functions

$$TR = 100Q - 0.01Q^2$$

$$MR = \frac{dTR}{dQ} = 100 - 0.02Q.$$

Also

$$Q = 500L - L^2$$

EXHIBIT 10A–4   **Marginal Revenue Product of Labor for the Production Function $Q = 500L - L^2$ and the Revenue Function $TR = 100Q - 0.01Q^2$**

Input Units of Labor L	Units of Output Q	Marginal Product MP_L	Total Revenue TR	Marginal Revenue MR_Q	Marginal Revenue Product MRP_L
0	0	—	0	—	—
1	499	498	47,409.99	90.02	44,829.96
2	996	496	89,679.84	80.08	39,719.68
3	1,491	494	126,869.19	70.18	34,668.92
4	1,984	492	159,037.44	60.32	29,677.44
5	2,475	490	186,243.75	50.50	24,745.00
6	2,964	488	208,547.04	40.72	19,871.36
7	3,451	486	226,005.99	30.98	15,056.28
8	3,936	484	238,679.04	21.28	10,299.52
9	4,419	482	246,624.39	11.62	5,600.84
10	4,900	480	249,900.00	2.00	960.00

---

from which we get the marginal product of labor:

$$MP_L = \frac{dQ}{dL} = 500 - 2L.$$

We know that profit is maximized when $MRP_L = MP_L \cdot MR_Q = P_L$. Since we are given a value for only one of the three variables in this equation, we must explore the possible values for MRP_L that may lie within the range of interest in this problem. We do this by tabulating output, marginal product, total revenue, marginal revenue, and the marginal revenue product for 0–10 workers, as shown in Exhibit 10A–4. From the exhibit, we see that if the average wage is now $20,000, the company cannot maximize profit precisely. It will come very close, however, by employing six workers. If the average wage increases to $25,000 per year, the company has only two options: either increase productivity (i.e., marginal product of labor) or reduce the labor force from six workers to five.

We can calculate the increase in productivity that would be necessary to retain six workers on the payroll as follows:

$$MR_Q \cdot MP_L = P_L$$
$$40.72 MP_L = 25,000$$
$$MP_L = 613.94.$$

This is an increase in productivity of approximately 25-26 percent, which is not likely to be attained. Therefore, the company will probably reduce the work force to five workers.

C H A P T E R

11

ESTIMATION OF PRODUCTION FUNCTIONS

In an empirical investigation of production, the goal is to develop a statistical model of the production function that will enable management to understand the behavior of input–output relationships. Such a model can be used to find the optimal input–output relationship in the short run, which is important to the management of current operations. The model can also be used to determine returns to scale in the long run, which is crucial for planning and expansion of the firm.

CHAPTER OUTLINE

In this chapter we look at the methodology for estimating production functions, measurement and its problems, and the analysis of meaningful facts about the production process. This chapter consists of three main sections and an appendix:

1. **Production Measurement.** This section describes three different methods of measuring production functions and the limitations of each method.
2. **Selection of the Production Function.** Guidelines for selecting and fitting a production function to empirical data are discussed in this section, along with the characteristics and properties of various production functions.
3. **Some Empirical Studies of Returns to Scale.** This section presents some empirical production studies of returns to scale for several industries.
4. **Appendix 11A: Quadratic- and Cubic-Curve Fitting.** This appendix shows how observed data points may be fitted to quadratic or cubic curves by simultaneous solution of a system of equations derived by the least squares method.

EXHIBIT 11–1   **Typical Format for the Collection of Time-Series Data**

Year	Output	Capital Input	Labor Input	Materials Input
1969	xxx	xxx	xxx	xxx
1970	xxx	xxx	xxx	xxx
.	.	.	.	.
.	.	.	.	.
.	.	.	.	.
1988	xxx	xxx	xxx	xxx

Production Measurement

The production process being studied may be that of an individual economic entity such as a factory or service organization, or it may be that of an aggregation of economic units within specified economic, geographic, or political boundaries, such as an industry, a trading area, a state, or a nation. The methods used for estimating any production function, however, are the same regardless of whether the entity is an individual operating unit or an aggregate of units. What may differ between cases is the constitution of the data and/or the interpretation of the fitted function.

Methods of Measurement

Empirical estimates of a production function typically use one of the following statistical approaches:

- Time-series analysis
- Cross-sectional analysis
- Engineering analysis.

Time-Series Analysis.   This approach uses historical observations as a data base. The data for a time-series production study may pertain either to a given firm or to a given industry. The data consist of the amount and kind of input resources actually used and the corresponding amount and kind of output actually produced over an extended period of time, as illustrated by Exhibit 11–1.

For example, suppose we want to study production of rubber tires, either by a specific firm or by the industry. In either case, we might gather data on how many tires were produced and how much capital, how much labor, and how much raw materials were used during each year during the 20-year period from 1969 through 1988. We would then attempt to fit these data to one or more of the four most common production functions.

Cross-Sectional Analysis.   Analysis of time-series data is most appropriate for studies of production in a single firm that has not undergone significant changes in technology during the time span analyzed. To develop a production function for an industry is a different problem. Even if all firms in an industry have operated over the same time span, changes in capacity, inputs, and outputs may have proceeded at a different pace for each firm. Thus a cross-sectional analysis may be more appropriate for an industry.

EXHIBIT 11–2   **Format for the Collection of Cross-Sectional Data**

Firm	Output	Capital Input	Labor Input	Materials Input
ABC	xxx	xxx	xxx	xxx
DEF	xxx	xxx	xxx	xxx
.	.	.	.	.
.	.	.	.	.
.	.	.	.	.
XYZ	xxx	xxx	xxx	xxx

Cross-sectional analysis deals with data collected at one particular time or during one particular time period for a number of firms. For example, instead of making observations of the variables for each year over a number of years, the variables are observed for each firm in an industry during one particular year.[1] To illustrate, suppose there are five firms in the tire-manufacturing industry. We might gather data on how many tires were produced and how much capital, labor, and raw materials were used by each of the five firms in 1988. Then we would attempt to fit the data to one of the production curves. This data-gathering format is illustrated by Exhibit 11–2.

Cross-sectional analysis is most effective when different firms have substantially different levels of input and output.

Engineering Analysis.   When good historical data are difficult to obtain or not available, it may be possible for engineers or agricultural scientists to develop data from controlled experiments or from day-to-day working experience. In manufacturing, controlled engineering experiments often consist of small-scale pilot plants. In agriculture, controlled experiments often consist of test plots in which plants may be grown under controlled conditions. Generally speaking, the goal of these experiments is to determine what the inputs (raw materials, capital equipment, and labor) and the resulting output *ought* to be.

Limitations of the Methodology.   Each of the methods we have just outlined suffers from certain limitations, as follows.

Restricted Operating Level.   Time-series and cross-sectional studies are restricted to a relatively narrow range of output levels. For example, suppose that a plant consistently operates at 85–90 percent of capacity. Within that range, variation of inputs and output is often insufficient for good statistical analysis. Extrapolation of the production function to values outside that range may be seriously misleading. For example, marginal product might decrease rapidly above 90 percent of capacity. If the production function derived for values in the 85–90 percent range were to be extrapolated to predict output at capacity, the predicted output might be substantially overstated.

---

[1] In some cases, an appropriate time period might be a particular month or even a particular week. The point is that all observations are taken within one particular time period, whatever that period might be.

Assumed Constant Technology.   Another weakness of time-series analysis is the basic assumption of a relatively constant technology. Some firms or industries may be stagnant enough to warrant such an assumption. Most firms and industries, however, find better, faster, or cheaper ways of producing their output as time goes by. As their technology changes, they are actually creating new production functions. One way of coping with the problem of technological change is to make it one of the independent variables.

The problem of changing technology does not apply to cross-sectional analysis, which accepts each firm's technology as it exists at one particular time. However, there may be widely differing technologies used by different firms within the industry. This means that a production function derived from cross-sectional data is valid for the industry, but is not valid for individual firms.

Assumed Maximum Efficiency.   Data for both time-series and cross-sectional analysis are gathered under the assumption that the combination of inputs chosen by the firm and the resultant output are technically efficient. That is to say, the observed output is assumed to be the most that could be obtained from the observed inputs, regardless of the level of plant utilization. This may or may not be true. For example, if a plant is operating at less than normal or standard capacity, the capital resources in place may be underutilized.

Theoretically, the production function includes only efficient combinations of input factors. If measurements are to conform to this concept, data for any year in a time series or any firm in a cross section in which production was less than normal would have to be excluded from the analysis unless a way could be found to measure the capital input actually used rather than a stock of capital assets available. This is very difficult to do.

Returns to Scale.   The engineering method overcomes the weakness of a restricted range of observations that is characteristic of time-series and cross-sectional data. Since engineering data are acquired by means of experience with production of similar products or by experimentation (such as using pilot plants), the range of applicability is known and the full range, including zero input, can be used to develop the production function. Unfortunately, however, the full-scale plant may not behave exactly like the pilot plant and the returns to scale may not conform to the engineer's expectations.

Another problem with the engineering method is that engineering data usually pertain to only part of the firm's production environment. Engineering data are generally confined to manufacturing activities, or in some cases, to only part of the firm's manufacturing activities. Engineering data do not tell us anything about the firm's marketing or financial activities, even though these activities may directly affect production. For example, lack of demand or the firm's inability to obtain sufficient working capital will change the optimum level of output. The effect of limitations is automatically incorporated into time-series or cross-sectional data, which reflect production as it actually existed. The engineering study, however, is concerned with a production function that does not actually exist. It is difficult to incorporate marketing or financing limitations into an engineering study that is concerned with what the production function ought to be rather than what it is.

Problems in the Measurement of Input and Output Variables

In its most elementary form, production consists of a flow of input resources into a production process from which there emerges an output flow of a single product. Ideally, the flow of output can be measured by the physical quantities produced per period of time and the flow of input can be measured by the physical quantities used or consumed per period of time. Many situations arise, however, in which such simple measurement is not possible, so some other measurement must be developed. For example:

- When the output consists of more than one product or service
- When the inputs cannot be directly associated with the output
- When we desire a production function for an aggregation of economic entities.

Since measurement of output poses somewhat different problems from those associated with the measurement of input, we shall discuss them separately.

Measurement of Input Factors at the Plant or Firm Level.   Input factors for a production process are customarily divided into three categories: direct inputs, indirect inputs, and capital inputs.

Direct Inputs.   **Direct inputs** are input variables, such as direct labor and materials, that go directly into the product. The quantity of direct inputs is constant with respect to *unit* output, but varies with *total* output. For example, each unit of output might require a constant input of two component parts and 20 minutes of labor. If 100 units of output are produced, the total input would be 200 component parts and 2,000 minutes of labor. But if 500 units are produced, total input would be 1,000 parts and 10,000 minutes of labor. That is, the total number of component parts and hours of labor vary directly with the total number of units produced; hence, they are called direct inputs.

Indirect Inputs.   Certain resources that are necessary for production but do not go directly into the product are called **indirect inputs** or **factory overhead**. This category includes labor for set-up or maintenance of plant and equipment, manufacturing supplies, utilities, and supervision of production. These inputs vary with *total* output, but are not always constant with respect to each *unit* of output.

Capital Inputs.   Land, buildings, machinery, equipment, tools, vehicles, and other capital assets utilized by the production process are called **capital inputs** or **fixed inputs** because they are fixed with respect to the total output. That is to say, they do not change when total output changes. Fixed inputs are often lumped together as "overhead."

In estimating a production function we try to measure the flow of inputs into the production process and the flow of outputs from it. In most cases, flow measurements of direct inputs, such as hours of direct labor and units of direct material, are easily obtained from cost-accounting records. Such reports may also include flow measurements of indirect inputs, such as hours of indirect labor, units of factory supplies, and units of utilities consumed. However, if the output consists of more than one product, it may be necessary to allocate portions of the indirect inputs to each product.

A more serious problem arises when we attempt to measure the flow of fixed inputs such as land, buildings, equipment, machinery, vehicles, and other capital assets. Full-cost accounting procedures call for allocation of the cost of such assets to the firm's various products. Although it is not difficult to translate allocation of cost into allocation of physical quantities, such allocations are arbitrary and often highly subjective. Consequently, rather than attempting to measure the quantity of fixed assets that are actually used, many analysts prefer to measure the total quantity or *stock* of fixed assets that are in existence and *available* for use at a given point or over a given span of time, without regard to how they are actually used. In essence, the analyst recognizes that production is a function of the firm's total assets as well as of direct and indirect inputs. Consequently, *flow* measurement may be used for variable and semivariable inputs, and *stock* measurement for fixed assets.

Measurement of Output at the Plant or Firm Level.   If the production model $Q = f(X_1, X_2, \ldots, X_n)$ provides for multiple inputs but only a single output, there is no problem. Output can be measured as the flow of physical units out of the production process. If the output consists of joint products in fixed proportions, there is still no great problem, since measurement of one actually measures both. For example, when a steer is slaughtered for beef, the packing house gets one hide whether it is wanted or not. Measuring the number of carcasses automatically measures the number of hides. But if the output consists of joint products of variable proportions or multiple products, then there is a problem of measurement.

If the products are relatively homogeneous, output might be measured as the sum of common physical units. For example, output of gasoline, kerosene, diesel oil, fuel oil, and other products of an oil refinery might be lumped together and measured as barrels or gallons of refined petroleum products. But if the output consists of many dissimilar products, the sum of their physical units might be meaningless. For example, suppose that an electronics firm is producing integrated circuits that sell for a few dollars each, along with personal computers that sell for hundreds of dollars each. Output could be measured more meaningfully by the dollar value of the products made or shipped during the period of interest.

In some cases it may be necessary to use dollar-value data to measure input variables as well as output. In such cases, the value data of time series must be adjusted for inflation by means of an appropriate price index, such as the consumer price index or the wholesale price index. For cross-sectional analysis, value data collected in different geographic areas should be adjusted to compensate for differences in prevailing wage rates and prices of raw materials.

Some production studies have been conducted using *value added* as the measurement of output. This greatly simplifies the production function, since value added is simply the gross value of the output minus the value of all goods and services used in its production.

Measurement of Aggregate Production

As previously noted, a production function may be developed for certain aggregates of economic entities, such as for an industry, a geographic region, or an entire national economy.

Aggregate Models.   Aggregate models depict the aggregate output Q as a function of aggregate capital C and aggregate labor L:

$$Q = f(C, L). \tag{1}$$

However, the aggregate output Q is a composite of all the individual outputs, that is,

$$Q = (q_1, q_2, \ldots, q_n). \tag{2}$$

Similarly, the aggregate capital input C is the resultant of the amounts and types of capital inputs used at the firm's level,

$$C = (c_1, c_2, \ldots, c_n) \tag{3}$$

while the labor input L is a composite of all labor inputs, such as labor hours:

$$L = (l_1, l_2, \ldots, l_n). \tag{4}$$

In the economy as a whole, or in a large segment of it, the components of Q, C, and L could number in the hundreds. For example, if we were studying shoe manufacturing, the aggregate output of shoes would include hundreds of styles of shoes. In cases like this, some common unit of measurement must be used to express the value of the aggregate output. Usually this takes the form of an *index*, and the model is greatly simplified if an index can be used to represent each variable, both input and output.

Production Indexes.   A number of production indexes are readily available, such as the index of the gross national product (GNP) compiled by the U.S. Dept. of Commerce and the index of industrial production published by the Federal Reserve Board. Data on employment and hours worked are provided by the U.S. Dept. of Labor's Bureau of Labor Statistics, and various other data are compiled by other federal and state agencies. However, reliable estimates of capital inputs are hard to obtain. It may be possible to construct a measure of the stock of capital available from gross investment and depreciation data published by the Dept. of Commerce. Other sources of data include corporations' annual reports, trade-association publications, and the Dept. of Commerce's periodic census of manufacturers and businesses. Whatever the source, the analyst must use extreme caution in dealing with the data.

Problems of Interpretation.   Once appropriate indexes have been established, the development of an aggregate production function proceeds in the same way as the development of a firm's production function, but interpretation of the physical relationships is more difficult. For an individual firm, the production function relates to a specific technological process. For the economy, however, the production function relates to many technological processes employed by individual firms. The resulting model does not represent any particular firm, nor does it represent an average or typical firm, for there is no such thing.

For a particular industry, however, we might expect production processes, the mix of inputs, and the mathematical relationship between inputs and output to be similar for all firms. Even so, it would be risky to make inferences about the production function of a specific firm from the aggregate production function of the whole industry. One source of error could be the misinterpretation of certain inputs, such as specialized skilled labor, which might be fixed for the industry but variable for individual firms. Also, it is quite possible that individual firms might realize increasing returns to scale from expansion when returns to scale for the industry as a whole are limited.

Selection of the Production Function

In the estimation of a production function, our task is to choose an approximating function whose form reflects most accurately the input–output relationship of the production process being investigated. This is easier said than done, because the underlying scheme of a production function may be founded on biological, psychological, physical, or other environmental factors as well as economic considerations. Fortunately, a considerable number of criteria, both economic and statistical, can be used to evaluate the individual properties of the various production functions. Included are such factors as the shape of each of the different curves, measures of marginal product and elasticity associated with each curve, and the relative ease or difficulty with which each production function lends itself to computational procedures.

Linear, quadratic, cubic, or power equations can be fitted to input–output data to derive production functions. In addressing the choice of algebraic production functions, perhaps the most important thing to be said about them is that they are mathematical models that can at best only approximate the true input–output relationship. Intangible factors, catalytic agents, and uncertainties attributable to breakage, spoilage, mistakes, poor communication, errors in judgment, and so forth are not accounted for in the algebraic formulation. Therefore, the model must necessarily be accepted as only an incomplete approximation of the system rather than as a precise formula. Nevertheless, it serves a vital analytical purpose as an abstraction of the real production process under the manager's supervision.

In selecting a production function, the limitations of linear regression must also be kept in mind. If we want to express output as a function of a single input variable while all others are held constant, the mathematical form of the function may be linear, quadratic, cubic, or exponential. But if we want to express output as a function of more than one input, only a linear or power (exponential) function may be used, because these are the only types that can be fitted by multiple regression.

Properties of Production Functions

When analyzing production functions in which total output, Q, is a function of a single input variable, X, while all other variables are held constant, we are most concerned with the measurement of the *average product, marginal product,* and *elasticity of production.* These basic properties of the production function can be expressed in simple algebraic terms or graphically.

Average Product.   Given a production function $Q = f(X)$, in which output, Q, is expressed as a function of input, X, the average product is the ratio of output to input:

$$AP = \frac{Q}{X} = \frac{f(X)}{X}. \qquad (5)$$

Marginal Product. The marginal product is the rate of change in output that results from a one-unit change in input. If inputs are discrete units, the marginal product is

$$MP = \frac{\Delta Q}{\Delta X}. \tag{6}$$

For a continuous production function, the marginal product is the first derivative of the function, which measures the slope of the total-product curve:

$$MP = \lim_{\Delta X \to 0} \frac{\Delta Q}{\Delta X} = \frac{dQ}{dX}. \tag{7}$$

Elasticity of Production. In production economics, elasticity measures return to scale. Consequently, as we shall see later, much empirical research has been directed toward determining the elasticities of production in various industries. The elasticity of production, ϵ_P, is defined as

$$\epsilon_P = \frac{\text{Percentage change in output}}{\text{Percentage change in input}}. \tag{8}$$

As explained in the preceding chapter, at any given point (Q, X) on the production curve, the *point* elasticity of production is

$$\epsilon_P = \frac{\Delta Q/Q}{\Delta X/X} = \frac{\Delta Q}{\Delta X} \cdot \frac{X}{Q} = \frac{\Delta Q/\Delta X}{Q/X} = \frac{MP}{AP}. \tag{9}$$

The formula for *arc* elasticity, E_P, is

$$E = \frac{\left[\dfrac{Q_2 - Q_1}{(Q_2 + Q_1)/2} \right]}{\left[\dfrac{X_2 - X_1}{(X_2 + X_1)/2} \right]} = \frac{Q_2 - Q_1}{Q_2 + Q_1} \cdot \frac{X_2 + X_1}{X_2 - X_1}. \tag{10}$$

In applying this formula, it is assumed that the segment of the curve in question can be adequately approximated by a straight line. This is because the arc formula actually measures elasticity at a point halfway along a straight line between the endpoints of the arc.

Equations for Production Functions with a Single Input

There are five equations that may possibly describe an input–output relationship for empirical measurement when one input factor is allowed to vary while all others are held constant. The five equations are listed in Exhibit 11–3 (page 322) along with equations for their respective average product, marginal product, and elasticity. In each equation,

Q = Total output quantity, in units
X = Input quantity of the single variable of interest, in units
a, b, c, d = Parameters to be estimated.

EXHIBIT 11–3 **Five Equations for Empirical Measurement of a Production Function with One Input Variable**

Type of Equation	General Form	Average Product	Marginal Product	Production Elasticity
Linear	$Q = a + bX$	$\frac{a}{X} + b$	b	$\frac{b}{\frac{a}{X}+b}$
Quadratic I	$Q = a + bX + cX^2$	$\frac{a}{X} + b + cX$	$b + 2cX$	$\frac{b+2cX}{\frac{a}{X}+b+cX}$
Quadratic II	$Q = a + bX - cX^2$	$\frac{a}{X} + b - cX$	$b - 2cX$	$\frac{b-2cX}{\frac{a}{X}+b-cX}$
Cubic	$Q = a + bX + cX^2 + dX^3$	$\frac{a}{X} + b + cX + dX^2$	$b + 2cX + 3dX^2$	$\frac{b+2cX+3dX^2}{\frac{a}{X}+b+cX+dX^2}$
Power	$Q = aX^b$	aX^{b-1}	baX^{b-1}	$\frac{baX^{b-1}}{aX^{b-1}} = b$

The Parameter *a*. It should be noted that the general equation for a linear, quadratic, or cubic function contains a constant parameter, *a*, which is graphed as the *Y*-intercept of the curve. This parameter may or may not have economic significance, depending upon the nature of the production function and the range of observations of the input variable. There may be cases where an input of zero can still produce an output. For example, if we were to study the effect of fertilizer on the production of vegetables, there would be some production even if no fertilizer were applied. In such cases, if the empirical investigation includes input values of zero and near zero in the range of actual observations, the parameter *a* would represent the output when the input is zero.

In cases where the product cannot be produced without the input variable, output will be zero when input is zero. If the empirical investigation includes input values of zero and near zero in the range of actual observations, the graph of the estimated function should pass through the origin. It is often the case, however, that empirical data do not include low levels of input in the range of actual observations. In that case, least-squares–curve fitting may generate a nonzero value for *a*, which may even be negative.

A negative value for *a* clearly has no economic significance, since a negative output is physically impossible. Even a positive constant in the production equation is a mathematical appendage that has no economic significance unless zero and other low levels of input were included in the range of observations. Even then, before accepting that a positive value of *a* has some economic significance, the analyst must determine that some output is possible even when there is no input of the variable under study.

Some other general observations may be made from the equations in Exhibit 11–3.

1. If $X = 0$, the power function and its average product and marginal product also equal zero. Hence the graph of the power function always passes through the origin.
2. For the linear, quadratic, and cubic functions, if $X = 0$, the average product is undefined. For $X = 1$, the average product = 1.

The Linear Production Function

Some properties of the linear production function are illustrated by Exhibit 11–4.

EXHIBIT 11–4   **A Linear Production Function of the Form** $Q = a + bX$

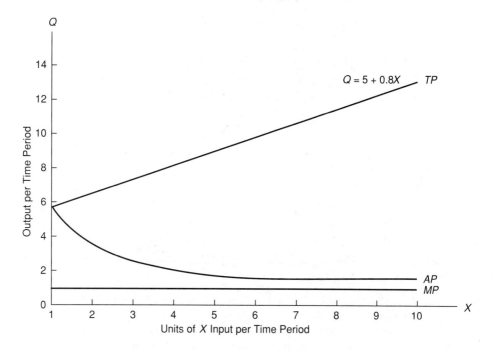

The Average Product.   The graph of this function $\frac{a}{x} + b$ is a hyperbola that is asymptotic to the marginal-product line. As X grows larger, the average product approaches the marginal product but never quite reaches it. Thus the marginal-product and average-product curves never intersect.

The Marginal Product.   The marginal product of the linear production function $Q = a + bX$ is constant at all levels of production, so its graph is just a horizontal line with a Y-intercept at b units of output. Since this is not consistent with the law of diminishing returns, linear functions are rarely assumed in empirical research if output is expected to vary widely as a result of a wide range of input. But for small variations in output within a narrow range of input, the linear assumption may be suitable as a reasonable approximation of the underlying production curve.

Elasticity.   The elasticity of a linear production function is different for each value of X unless the graph of the production function passes through the origin so that $a = 0$. In that special case, the average product coincides with the marginal product and $\epsilon_P = 1.0$ everywhere along the line.

Quadratic I: The Quadratic Function When c Is Positive

As illustrated by Exhibit 11–5 (page 324), the positive sign of parameter c in the production function $Q = a + bX + cX^2$ causes the parabolic production curve to open upward.

EXHIBIT 11–5   Quadratic Production Function When the Parameter c Is Positive

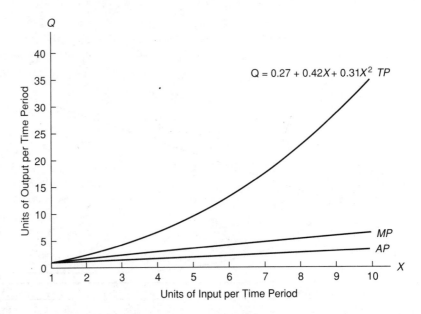

The upward concavity of the curve causes the peculiar property that neither *TP* nor *MP* will have a maximum value; thus the curve clearly violates the law of diminishing returns. However, it can be an accurate representation of a segment of the production function at low levels of input.

Average Product.   The *AP* curve $\frac{a}{X} + b + cX$ is a hyperbolic line segment rising beneath the *MP* curve, but with a shallower slope. If $a = 0$, the *AP* curve becomes an upward-sloping straight line with a *Q*-intercept at $Q = b$. In either case, the *MP* and *AP* curves diverge as input increases.

Marginal Product.   The marginal product $b + 2cX$ is an upward-sloping straight line that intersects the *Q*-axis at $Q = b$, and has the peculiar property of being greater than total product at $X = 1$. This is a mathematical anomaly without any economic significance.

Elasticity.   Even if $a = 0$, elasticity is different at every point along the production curve. Since *MP* and *AP* diverge, with *MP* always greater than *AP*, the production function grows more elastic as input increases.

Quadratic II: The Quadratic Function When c Is Negative

When the parameter c is negative, the quadratic production function exhibits the properties illustrated by Exhibit 11–6.

Average Product.   The *AP* graph $\frac{a}{X} + b - cX$ is a hyperbola that approaches but does not reach the *MP* curve, after which it diverges from the *MP* curve because of a shallower

EXHIBIT 11–6   Quadratic Production Function When the Parameter *c* Is Negative

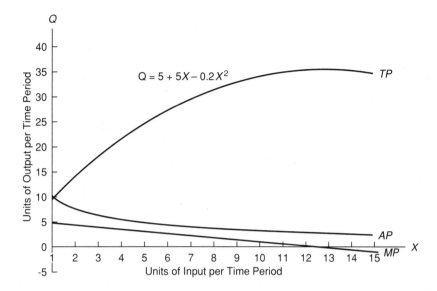

slope. If $a = 0$, the *AP* curve becomes a downward-sloping straight line with a *Q*-intercept at $Q = b$.

Marginal Product.   The marginal product $b - 2cX$ is a downward-sloping straight line that intercepts the *Q*-axis at $Q = b$ and intercepts the *X*-axis at the value of *X* at which total product is maximum. The *MP* line is everywhere less than the *AP* line, except when $a = 0$. In that case, the two lines intersect at $Q = b$ on the *Q*-axis.

Elasticity.   As noted previously, the *MP* function is a straight line, but the *AP* function is not linear; therefore, the ratio *MP/AP* is not constant and elasticity is different at every point along the production curve.

The Cubic Function

Exhibit 11–7 (page 326) illustrates the traditional or classical production function with one input variable, as discussed in the preceding chapter. The data points in the exhibit represent observed values of input and output. The vertical pattern of the dots indicates that the inputs were available only in discrete units. Note that almost all of the dots are concentrated in Stage 2 of the production function. This indicates that management was usually able to keep production within the rational range.

The cubic production function allows for both increasing and decreasing marginal productivity from the input of a single variable resource. If there can be no production without that particular input resource (as shown in Exhibit 11–7), the constant parameter, *a*, will be zero. In that case, the cubic production function exhibits the following properties:

EXHIBIT 11-7   A Cubic Production Function Fitted to Observed Data

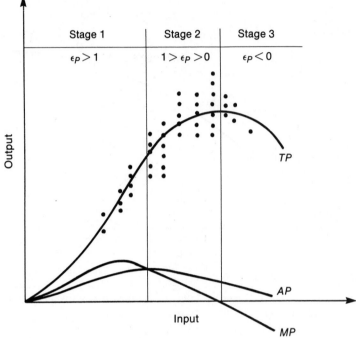

Average Product.   In the absence of the parameter a, the average product of the cubic production function shown in Exhibit 11-7 becomes

$$AP = \frac{Q}{X} = \frac{bX + cX^2 + dX^3}{X} = b + cX + dX^2 \tag{11}$$

which is a quadratic function. Stage 2 begins at the point where the average product is at a maximum and equal to the marginal product.

Marginal Product.   As shown in Exhibit 11-7, the marginal product is also a quadratic function:

$$MP = \frac{dQ}{dX} = b + 2cX + 3dX^2. \tag{12}$$

Since d is always negative in a cubic production function, the marginal product first increases and then decreases. The input value at which MP is maximum marks the inflection point on the TP curve, at which the concavity changes from upward to downward.

Elasticity.   In the absence of the parameter a, the elasticity of production is

$$\epsilon_P = \frac{MP}{AP} = \frac{b + 2cX + 3dX^2}{b + cX + dX^2}. \tag{13}$$

Since this ratio changes whenever X changes, elasticity is different at every point along the curve.

Maximum Efficiency of a Cubic Function. As shown in Exhibit 11–7, maximum production efficiency occurs when AP is maximum. This is the point at which $MP = AP$; that is, when

$$b + 2cX + 3dX^2 = b + cX + dX^2.$$

Collecting terms, we get

$$cX + 2dX^2 = 0.$$

Factoring, we get

$$X(c + 2dX) = 0.$$

Hence we get two solutions for X:

$$X = 0 \quad \text{and} \quad X = -\frac{c}{2d}. \tag{14}$$

The second solution indicates the amount of input factor X that is required when input resources are used most efficiently.

Illustrative Problem

Steven K. is a Peace Corps volunteer who has elected to use his business education to help the people of Sri Lanka in the development of basic industries. He was assigned to the city of Colombo to assist a Sri Lankan entrepreneur in the establishment of a garment factory to produce men's shirts for export. In the course of his work, he observed that the first sewing-machine operators hired by this enterprise were more skilled and therefore more productive than those hired later as the firm grew. Recalling his study of managerial economics, he postulated that the firm's production function might be cubic. After studying the firm's production data for the first year of operation, he used the least squares method of curve fitting to obtain the production function

$$Q = 65X + 8X^2 - 0.0625X^3 \tag{15}$$

where
  Q = Output of finished shirts per month
  X = Number of sewing-machine operators.
  To determine the number of sewing-machine operators needed to maximize production efficiency, he used Equation 14 to get

$$X = -\frac{c}{2d} = -\frac{8}{2(-0.0625)} = \frac{8}{0.125} = 64 \text{ sewing-machine operators.}$$

At this level of input, output would be

$$Q = 65(64) + 8(64)^2 - 0.0625(64)^3 = 20,544 \text{ shirts per month.}$$

The average product (which is at a maximum) is

$$AP = \frac{Q}{X} = \frac{20,544}{64} = 321 \text{ shirts per operator per month}$$

or

$$AP = b + cX + dX^2 = 65 + 8(64) + (-0.0625)(64)^2 = 321.$$

The marginal product, calculated as

$$MP = b + 2cX + 3dX^2 = 65 + 2(8)(64) + (3)(-0.0625)(64)^2 = 321$$

equals the average product at this level of input.

The entrepreneur was also interested in learning the number of operators that would maximize his output. In order to find this level of input, Steven put the marginal function into standard form, set it equal to zero, and solved for X by using the *quadratic equation*

$$X = \frac{-B \pm \sqrt{B^2 - 4AC}}{2A}. \tag{16}$$

Rewriting the MP function in the standard form, he got

$$3dX^2 + 2cX + b = 0$$

that is, $A = 3d$, $B = 2c$, and $C = b$. When $MP = 0$ (that is, at the input that maximizes output),

$$X = \frac{-2C \pm \sqrt{(2c)^2 - 4(3d)(b)}}{2(3d)}$$

$$= \frac{-16 \pm \sqrt{(16)^2 - (4)(3)(-0.0625)(65)}}{2(3)(-0.0625)}$$

$$= \frac{-16 \pm 17.45709025}{-0.375} = -3.885574 \text{ or } 89.21890733.$$

Since a negative input is physically impossible, the input level of X to gain maximum output would be approximately 89 sewing-machine operators. At this level of input, total output would be

$$Q = 65(89) + 8(89)^2 - 0.06258(89)^3 \approx 25,092 \text{ shirts per month.}$$

The Power Function with a Single Input

A power production function that expresses total product as a function of a single input has the form

$$Q = aX^b. \tag{17}$$

If we set the constant, a, equal to 1, the curvature of the function depends on the exponent, b, which in all practical problems is assumed to be positive. (A negative

EXHIBIT 11–8   **Examples of the Power Function $Q = aX^b$ for $a = 1$ and $b > 0$**

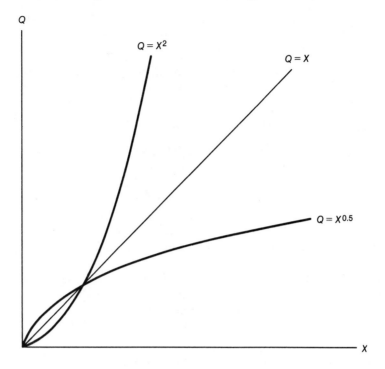

exponent would not make economic sense.) Thus if $b = 1$, the curve is a straight line. For $b > 1$, the curve is convex to the base, while for $b < 1$, it is concave to the base, as shown in Exhibit 11–8.

The marginal-product function, $MP = baX^{b-1}$, allows for increasing, constant, or decreasing marginal activity, but not all three in any one function, as illustrated by the slopes of the curves in Exhibit 11–8. Thus if $b = 1$, both average and marginal product will be constant at the level a. This is the case for the linear function $Q = X$ in Exhibit 11–8.

If $b > 1$, the marginal product will increase as X increases, but in a proportion dependent on the magnitude of b. For the curve $Q = X^2$ in Exhibit 11–8, $MP = 2X$. On the other hand, if $b < 1$, the marginal product will decrease as X increases, again in a proportion indicated by the magnitude of b. For the curve $Q = X^{1/2}$, $MP = (1/2)X^{-1/2} = 1/(2X^{1/2}) = 1/(2\sqrt{X})$.

The elasticity of production for a power function is

$$\epsilon_P = \frac{MP}{AP} = \frac{baX^{b-1}}{aX^{b-1}} = b. \tag{18}$$

Thus we see that the elasticity of production is constant for all values of X and is equal to the exponent of the input variable, which is an interesting and very convenient mathematical property.

Another convenient property is that the function is linear in its logarithms; that is, it can be written

$$\log Q = \log a + b \log X. \tag{19}$$

Graphically, this means the equation plots as a straight line when expressed in its logarithmic form or in its original form on double logarithmic scales. Hence, for simplicity and convenience the equation is estimated statistically in logarithmic form.

Power Functions with Multiple Inputs

Production functions with multiple input variables are more realistic than those with only one. The general form for this type of power production function is

$$Q = aX_1^b X_2^c \ldots X_n^m \tag{20}$$

where Q represents output from the variable inputs, X_i. The coefficient a and the exponents $b, c, \ldots, m$ are constants called parameters, because their values are established at the time of their use. In production measurement, values of the parameters are estimated by linear regression.

In 1928, Professors C. W. Cobb and Paul H. Douglas of the University of Chicago published a seminal study of manufacturing production in the United States. They postulated a production function of the form

$$P' = bL^k C^{1-k} \tag{21}$$

where

P' = Calculated or expected index of manufacturing output over a particular span of time

L = Index of employment in manufacturing industries

C = Index of fixed capital in manufacturing industries

k = A fractional exponent between 0 and 1.

Using annual data for the United States based on the period 1899 to 1922, the function that Cobb and Douglas derived for U.S. manufacturing as a whole was

$$P' = 1.01 L^{0.75} C^{0.25} \qquad (R^2 = .9409) \tag{22}$$

where the variables have the same meaning as described previously, and the three indexes use 1899 as the base year, i.e., 1899 = 100.

R^2 is the coefficient of multiple determination. It represents the proportion of variation in the dependent variable that is accounted for by the independent variables (as explained in Chapter 8). Thus, about 94 percent of the variation in P' is accounted for by L and C in this equation.

Let us examine some of the interesting implications of this analysis:

1. Note that this equation, a power function, is linear in the logarithms but not in the original data. Thus the equation expressed in its equivalent logarithmic form is

$$\log P' = \log 1.01 + 0.75 \log L + 0.25 \log C. \tag{23}$$

2. The marginal products of labor and capital are the respective partial derivatives:

$$MP_L = (0.75)(1.01)L^{-0.25}C^{0.25} = 0.7575L^{-0.25}C^{0.25} \tag{24}$$

$$MP_C = (0.25)(1.01)L^{0.75}C^{-0.75} = 0.2525L^{0.75}C^{-0.75}. \tag{25}$$

3. The average products of labor and capital are

$$AP_L = \frac{P'}{L} = \frac{1.01L^{0.75}C^{0.25}}{L} = 1.01L^{-0.25}C^{0.25} \tag{26}$$

$$AP_C = \frac{P'}{C} = \frac{1.01L^{0.75}C^{0.25}}{C} = 1.01L^{0.75}C^{-0.75}. \tag{27}$$

4. The elasticities of the individual inputs are

$$\epsilon_{PL} = \frac{MP_L}{AP_L} = \frac{(0.75)(1.01)L^{-0.25}C^{0.25}}{1.01L^{-0.25}C^{0.25}} = 0.75 \tag{28}$$

$$\epsilon_{PC} = \frac{MP_C}{AP_C} = \frac{(0.25)(1.01)L^{0.75}C^{-0.75}}{1.01L^{0.75}C^{-0.75}} = 0.25. \tag{29}$$

Because the function is linear in its logarithms, the elasticity of each individual input is simply its exponent. Thus a 1 percent increase in labor results in a 0.75 percent increase in production, and a 1 percent increase in capital results in 0.25 percent increase in production. Since the exponents of these two independent variables are each less than 1, production is relatively inelastic with respect to any one input.

5. The Cobb-Douglas power function is also characterized by the convenient mathematical property of homogeneity that was discussed in the preceding chapter. This is readily illustrated if we multiply each of the input factors in Equation 22 by some constant k:

$$hP' = 1.01(kL)^{0.75}(kC)^{0.25} = 1.01k^{0.75}L^{0.75}k^{0.25}C^{0.25}$$

$$= 1.01k^{(0.75+0.25)}L^{0.75}C^{0.25} = k(1.01L^{0.75}C^{0.25}).$$

Therefore

$$hP' = kP'$$

and

$$h = k, \text{ indicating constant returns to scale.}$$

Every Cobb-Douglas production function is always homogeneous of degree n, where n equals the sum of the exponents. This is true regardless of the number of productive input factors (independent variables) in the equation.

In the original Cobb-Douglas model, input factors were restricted to capital and labor, and their exponents were chosen to add up to one. This restricted the model to production functions yielding constant returns to scale. Later models have relaxed these restrictions so that more than just two input factors may be considered, and the sum of the exponents may be more or less than one.

Returns to scale may be quickly determined by simply adding up the exponents as a whole. It should be emphasized, of course, that where the Cobb-Douglas type of production function has been used, especially at the intrafirm level, it has typically been in the later, rather than in its original form.

Some Empirical Studies of Returns to Scale

Returns to scale and attendant economies or diseconomies are among management's most important considerations in planning for growth. Consequently, many empirical studies of the production function have been performed to estimate elasticity of production, which measures returns to scale. Most of these studies have used a power function because of its convenient properties with respect to elasticity, which were noted in the preceding section.

Studies Using Time-Series Data

For their original study, Cobb and Douglas gathered time-series data on the U.S. manufacturing sector from 1899 to 1922 and converted the data into indexes (as explained in the preceding section).

One of the main problems that Cobb and Douglas sought to solve concerned the economic theory of *imputation:* How is the value of the final product to be allocated to the various factors of production (namely, capital, land, and labor) that collaborated to produce it? In other words, how can we measure the contribution of each input factor to the value of the final product? To answer this question, they computed (by partial differential calculus) the marginal productivities of labor and capital, obtaining $0.75PL^{-1}$ and $0.25PC^{-1}$, respectively. On the basis of these quantities, they imputed the proportion of total product coming from labor as $0.75P$ and the proportion of total product coming from capital as $0.25P$, where P represents the actual index of production in any one year as compared to P', which is the calculated index obtained from the derived production function.

At a later date, Cobb and Douglas revised the output and labor indexes to remove the secular trend from each index.[2] They did this by calculating each annual index as a percentage of its overall trend value and by dropping the condition that the sum of the exponents equal 1. The result of these changes was the function

$$P' = 0.84L^{.65} C^{.30} . \tag{30}$$

This equation indicates an elasticity of about 2/3 for labor and 1/3 for capital. Although the sum of the exponents is slightly less than 1, the difference is not statistically significant. Thus the Cobb-Douglas findings support their original hypothesis of constant returns to scale.

---

[2] "Secular" trend is the long-term or persistent trend of a series. Techniques for its removal are discussed in Chapter 9.

Since the seminal work of Cobb and Douglas, many other production studies using time-series data have been performed. Production functions have been estimated for major sectors of the economy, such as agriculture, mining, and manufacturing. Economists have also developed production functions for geographic regions, such as the Commonwealth of Massachusetts and the Australian states of Victoria and New South Wales. Production functions have even been determined for entire political economies, such as those of New Zealand, Norway, Finland, and the United States.

A particularly interesting application of the Cobb-Douglas function was made in 1975 by a trio of investigators who applied it to time-series data to estimate and evaluate a police production function in the city of Los Angeles.[3]

One of the researchers' problems was to identify meaningful variables in the absence of a physical product. However, they could and did quantify output as the felony arrest rate, *FAR*, calculated as the number of arrests divided by the number of crimes committed. They also identified five independent variables that might be expected to influence the felony arrest rate:

MT = Number of motorcycle teams
FO = Number of field officers
NFO = Number of nonfield officers
CE = Number of civilian employees
XC = Number of newly released criminals in the community.

For the first four of these variables, the number of employees in each class represents joint labor and capital input (for example, a motorcycle officer and the officer's motorcycle). The last variable, *XC*, is an indicator of police knowledge of a potential criminal population. All data were adjusted to eliminate the effect of population changes. The data were then converted to logarithms and multiple-regression analysis was used to obtain the production function

$$FAR = 17.2MT^{0.01}FO^{0.718}NFO^{1.02}CE^{0.74}XC^{0.078}. \tag{31}$$

The coefficient of determination was $R^2 = 0.9013$. The t-ratios for *FO*, *NFO*, and *CE* were 1.66, 2.29, and 2.16, respectively. The t-ratios for *MT* and *XC* indicated that these variables were statistically insignificant. The authors concluded that "the production function analysis indicated that increasing police resources significantly affects police output." The researchers also indicated that "there appears to be some indication of increasing returns (to scale) to the police agency as a whole."

This study suggests that analysis of production functions might be extended to many activities that produce professional services rather than just to those that produce a physical product. Merchandising activities would also seem amenable to a production-function analysis.

---

[3] Jeffery I. Chapman, Werner Z. Hirsch, and Sydney Sonenblum, "Crime Prevention, the Police Production Function, and Budgeting," *Public Finance* 30, no. 2 (1975), pp. 197–215.

Studies Using Cross-Sectional Data

Cobb-Douglas functions have been derived from cross-sectional data for various sectors of the economy in Australia, Canada, and the United States, and for a number of different industries in these as well as other countries. In industry studies, cross-sectional data on firms within the industry are used. Industries studied so far include those that produce chemicals, clothing, coal, electricity, milk, railroad transportation, and rice.

One of the most noteworthy industry studies is Moroney's work on 18 manufacturing industries in the United States.[4] The industries studied were broad groups, such as petroleum, coal, textiles, and primary metals. Moroney's objective was to determine returns to scale in each of these industries. He used cross-sectional analysis rather than time-series data to avoid the problem of having to allocate changes of output observed in a time series between quantity of input and changes in technology. The approach he chose was to estimate the parameters of the logarithmic form of a Cobb-Douglas production function by means of multiple-regression analysis. Specifically, the model was

$$\log \gamma = \log \beta_0 + \beta_1 \log X_1 + \beta_2 \log X_2 + \beta_3 \log X_3 + e \qquad (32)$$

where

γ = Value added
X_1 = Gross capital stock
X_2 = Production labor-hours
X_3 = Nonproduction labor-years
β_i = Elasticity of factor X_i
e = Error term.

Results of the regression analysis are shown in Exhibit 11–9. The following highlights are of particular interest:

1. The coefficients of multiple determination indicate that the power function was a very good fit in all cases.
2. In every industry except rubber and plastics, all of the factor elasticities (β_i) are positive, as expected. Furthermore, when standard statistical tests for significance are applied, 39 out of 54 elasticities are significantly different from zero at the .05 level of significance, indicating a good selection of variables.
3. The most important finding is the output elasticity recorded in column (6) as the sum of the factor elasticities. These indicators of returns to scale range from a minimum of .94713 for petroleum and coal to a maximum of 1.10875 for furniture. Only the elasticity of food and beverages, furniture, printing, chemicals and fabricated metals proved to be significantly different from 1 at the .05 level of statistical significance. Each of these five industries exhibits slightly increasing returns to scale. All of the other industries exhibited constant returns to scale.

---

[4] John R. Moroney, "Cobb-Douglas Production Functions and Returns to Scale in U.S. Manufacturing Industry," *Western Economic Journal*, December 1967, pp. 39–51.

EXHIBIT 11–9   Output Elasticity in Several Manufacturing Industries

(1)	(2)	(3)	(4)	(5)	(6)	(7)
				Elasticity[a]		
			Production	Nonproduction		Coefficient of
	Number of	Capital	Labor	Labor	Total	Determination
Industry	Observations	β_1	β_2	β_3	$\beta_1 + \beta_2 + \beta_3$	R^2
Food and	41	.55529*	.43882*	.07610*	1.07021**	.9865
beverages		(.12101)	(.12793)	(.03746)	(.02128)	
Textiles	21	.12065	.54881*	.33462*	1.00408	.9913
		(.17334)	(.21573)	(.08580)	(.02365)	
Apparel	24	.12762	.43705*	.47654*	1.04121	.9823
		(.08926)	(.08612)	(.09297)	(.03741)	
Lumber	23	.39170*	.50391*	.14533	1.04094	.9509
		(.09316)	(.12467)	(.10157)	(.06014)	
Furniture	22	.20458	.80154*	.10263	1.10875**	.9659
		(.15344)	(.18552)	(.07893)	(.05082)	
Paper and	30	.42054*	.36666*	.19723*	.98443	.9902
pulp		(.04460)	(.09430)	(.07035)	(.01890)	
Printing,	17	.45900*	.04543	.57413*	1.07856**	.9888
etc.		(.05562)	(.17089)	(.19199)	(.03168)	
Chemicals	32	.20025*	.55345*	.33626*	1.08996**	.9701
		(.09879)	(.20996)	(.14650)	(.03693)	
Petroleum	17	.30783*	.54621*	.09309	.94713	.9826
and coal		(.11162)	(.22207)	(.16847)	(.04489)	
Rubber and	16	.48071*	1.03317*	-.45754*	1.05634	.9912
plastics		(.10535)	(.20567)	(.14574)	(.04139)	
Leather	11	.07597	.44124*	.52273	1.03994	.9897
		(.14921)	(.20105)	(.31491)	(.03916)	
Stone,	26	.63167*	.03165	.36592*	1.02924	.9614
clay, etc.		(.10538)	(.22449)	(.20104)	(.04543)	
Primary	29	.37146*	.07734	.50881*	.95761	.9693
metals		(.10260)	(.18842)	(.16433)	(.03454)	
Fabricated	33	.15110*	.51172*	.36457*	1.02739**	.9947
metals		(.07426)	(.09379)	(.09204)	(.01589)	
Nonelectrical	30	.40382*	.22784	.38870*	1.02036	.9804
machinery		(.12827)	(.18375)	(.20542)	(.03122)	
Electrical	25	.36796*	.42908*	.22905*	1.02609	.9832
machinery		(.11869)	(.19225)	(.12937)	(.03640)	
Transportation	29	.23353*	.74885*	.04103	1.02341	.9719
equipment		(.06969)	(.12572)	(.08809)	(.03915)	
Instruments	11	.20557	.81865*	.01978	1.04420	.9969
		(.15204)	(.20592)	(.16806)	(.02437)	

[a] Numbers in parentheses are standard errors of the regression coefficient.

* Significantly different from zero at $P \leq 0.05$ (one-tail test).

** Significantly greater than one at $P \leq 0.05$ (one-tail test).

Moroney concluded that the results of his studies supported the hypothesis that there is a broad range of "optimal" plant sizes in U.S. manufacturing, and that there are constant technological returns to scale in most industries. Similar studies by other investigators in the United States and other countries have yielded slightly different results. Some of these results are shown in Exhibit 11–10 (page 336).

In Exhibit 11–10, the sum of the elasticities in column (7) is the measure of returns to scale. Of the 15 industries studied, 9 have elasticities greater than 1. However, of the 15,

EXHIBIT 11–10   **Estimates of Returns to Scale for Selected Industries**

(1)	(2)	(3)	(4)	(5)	(6)	(7)
					Elasticity	
			Labor	*Capital*	*Raw Materials*	*Total*
Industry	*Country*	*Year*	β_1	β_2	β_3	$\beta_1 + \beta_2 + \beta_3$
Food	United States	1967	.63[a]	.44	—	1.07[b]
Paper	United States	1967	.62[a]	.37	—	0.99[b]
Telephone	Canada	1972	.70	.41	—	1.11
Railroads	United States	1936	.89	.12	.28	1.29
Coal	United Kingdom	1950	.79	.29	—	1.08[b]
Food	United States	1909	.72	.35	—	1.07[b]
Metals and machinery	United States	1909	.71	.26	—	0.97[b]
Gas	France	1945	.83	.10	—	0.93[b]
Cotton	India	1951	.92	.12	—	1.04[b]
Jute	India	1951	.84	.14	—	0.98[b]
Sugar	India	1951	.59	.33	—	0.92[b]
Coal	India	1951	.71	.44	—	1.15
Paper	India	1951	.64	.45	—	1.09[b]
Chemicals	India	1951	.80	.37	—	1.17
Electricity	India	1951	.20	.67	—	0.87

Source: Edwin Mansfield, *Microeconomics*, 3rd ed. (New York: W. W. Norton, 1979), p. 164.

[a] These values for β_1 are the sums of those originally found for production workers and nonproduction workers.

[b] These sums are so close to 1 that the industries may be considered to show constant returns to scale.

10 (marked with a superscripted *b*) have elasticities so close to 1 that we might consider them to exhibit constant returns to scale. This leaves four—railroads in the United States, coal in India, chemicals in India, and telephones in Canada—that showed increasing returns to scale in the years indicated.

Summary

The measurement of production functions is particularly important for long-range planning. In an empirical investigation of production, the goal is to develop a mathematical model that can be used to predict the output that can be obtained from any mix of inputs. Empirical studies can use any of three approaches to measurement: (1) time-series analysis, (2) cross-sectional analysis, or (3) engineering analysis.

Input variables customarily are divided into three classes: (1) direct inputs of labor and materials, (2) indirect inputs that are necessary for production, and (3) capital inputs, often called "overhead." The first two classes are usually measured as a flow of physical resources into the production process. The capital inputs are more difficult to measure because they must be arbitrarily allocated to particular products. Therefore, capital inputs are often measured in terms of the *stock* of capital resources available.

The measurement of output presents problems somewhat different from those encountered in the measurement of input. When more than one product is produced, output may have to be measured by dollar values rather than by quantities of product. Some studies have used *value added* as the output variable.

In the measurement of production in economic entities, both inputs and outputs are aggregates of the corresponding activities in component firms. These production models are greatly simplified by the use of an index to represent each of the variables.

A number of problems must be overcome in the measurement of production. Time-series and cross-sectional data are restricted to the relatively narrow range of observed values. This weakness may be overcome by the engineering method. Unfortunately, engineering data do not cover all of a firm's activities. Time-series and cross-sectional methods also assume that (1) the various observations represent the same production function and (2) the observed production process is technically efficient.

In analyzing production functions, we are most concerned with the measurement of the average product, marginal product, and elasticity. All types of production functions—linear, quadratic, cubic, and power functions—can be estimated from observed data, as follows:

- Linear functions may be fitted to observed data by means of simple linear regression.
- Quadratic and cubic functions may be fitted to observed data by the least squares method described in Appendix 11A to this chapter.
- Power functions may be fitted to observed data by simple or multiple regression after they are changed into their logarithmic form:

$$\log Q = \log a + b \log X$$

for a univariate power function, and

$$\log Q = \log b_0 + b_1 \log X_1 + \ldots + b_n \log X_n$$

for a multivariate power function.

Power-production functions—including functions of the Cobb-Douglas type—have the valuable property that the elasticity with respect to any input variable is equal to its exponent. Furthermore, the sum of the exponents is the function's output elasticity, which is a measure of returns to scale. For this reason, the Cobb-Douglas form has been used in many studies of returns to scale, especially in manufacturing industries. Many of these studies support the conclusion that there is a very wide range of plant sizes that exhibit constant returns to scale.

Problems

1. Explain the criteria to be considered when deciding whether to use time-series, cross-sectional, or engineering data to estimate a long-run production function.

2. Considering the environmental and technological changes in U.S. industries, what method would you suggest for estimating the production functions of

the following industries? Discuss the advantages and limitations of your suggested approach.

   a. Automobile tires
   b. Personal computers
   c. Washing machines
   d. Paper and pulp
   e. Processed foods

3. Explain at least five major problems you might face in constructing a production function for the following:

   a. Operation of your university

   b. U.S. government entity or activity

   c. Sears, Roebuck & Co.

   d. Midas Muffler Shops

   e. Operation of a hospital

   f. Southern Pacific Railroad.

4. Moroney's study concluded that the production functions of most U.S. firms exhibit approximately constant returns to scale. Do you think this may be true for government or university operations as well? Explain.

5. Develop equations for the average product, marginal product, and elasticity of the following production functions:

   a. $Q = 15.7X + 20X^2 - 6.5X^3$

   b. $Q = 15 - 7X - X^2$.

6. A certain production function is given by the equation $Q = 20X - X^2$, where X denotes input and Q is output.

   a. Sketch the total, average, and marginal product curves from $X = 0$ to $X = 10$.

   b. Write the equations for average and marginal output.

   c. If each unit of X costs $5 while each unit of Q can be sold for $2, how many units of X should be utilized?

   d. Regardless of the method you used to work part (c), prove the following proposition: A factor of production is employed up to a point where the marginal revenue product (MRP) is equal to its price.

   e. Discuss the following comment: "Every factor of production is paid what it is worth."

7. Given the production function $Q = 0.84L^{0.70}C^{0.30}$, where Q = units of output, L = units of input labor, and C = units of capital:

   a. What are the marginal and average products of labor and capital?

   b. Show that the production elasticities of labor and capital are equal to their respective exponents.

   c. Restate the production function as a linear function, and show that the production elasticities of labor and capital are the coefficients of their logarithms.

8. For the benefit of its members, the American Corn Growers Association sponsored an analysis of the effects of phosphate fertilizer on corn production. They derived the following production function:

   $$\hat{Q} = 43.2X + 7.5X^2 - 1.1X^3$$

   where

   $\hat{Q}$ = estimated output, in bushels of corn per acre

   X = quantity of phosphate fertilizer, in pounds per acre.

   a. If a farmer were to use 10 pounds of phosphates per acre, what would be the expected production?

   b. What is the elasticity of production at 10 pounds of phosphates per acre?

   c. Should the farmer increase or decrease the amount of phosphates used? Explain.

   d. What is the maximum output possible and how many pounds of phosphates will be required?

9. Refer to the study "Crime Prevention, the Police Production Function, and Budgeting," by Jeffery I. Chapman, Werner Z. Hirsch, and Sydney Sonenblum that was discussed in this chapter.

   a. Assume that you are a professional consultant to your local police department. You have studied the same sort of data as Chapman, Hirsch, and Sonenblum and have arrived at the same production function. Present the case for an increased budget for the police department to the city council.

   b. Now switch hats and assume that you are a professor of business economics engaged by the council to examine the consultant's report and refute it if possible. Prepare your analysis to include both the explicit and implicit implications of the factual information embraced by the consultant's estimated production function. Be specific and itemize your answer.

Case Problem: Reaction Electronics, Inc.

10. In the past, Reaction Electronics has played it by ear when estimating production levels for its Fuzz-

Buster Radar Detection Units. However, in the past few years the company has grown so quickly that rough estimates of needed output have resulted in both demand shortfalls and costly overproduction. Now, however, the company is about to establish a European subsidiary and needs a better understanding of the relationship between inputs and outputs before designing the European plant. The president of Reaction Electronics has hired a managerial economist to tackle this problem and the economist has tabulated the following data for the past 12 months of operations:

Month	Output (units)	Labor (hours)	Capital (units)
1	26,000	90,000	108,000
2	29,000	101,000	114,000
3	31,500	118,000	116,000
4	34,000	132,500	114,500
5	37,000	147,500	111,000
6	40,000	161,000	107,500
7	44,000	174,500	106,000
8	47,000	188,500	107,500
9	51,500	202,500	110,000
10	58,000	215,000	112,500
11	62,000	229,500	114,500
12	67,000	245,000	117,000

Questions

a. What is the estimated linear production function in the form $Q = a + bX_1 + cX_2$?

b. Explain the significance of the linear production function's parameters b and c.

c. Does the function exhibit increasing, decreasing, or constant returns to scale?

d. Transform the data to logarithms either by hand or through a computer. Using your adjusted data, what is the estimated production function in the power form, $Q = aX_1^b X_2^c$?

e. Does the power form exhibit increasing, decreasing, or constant returns to scale?

f. If labor costs $9 per hour and capital costs $11 per unit, what are the most efficient (least-cost) proportions of labor and capital under the power form?

g. Discuss possible benefits from a production analysis such as that performed on Reaction Electronics, Inc.

References

Bernhardt, Irwin. "Sources of Productivity Differences among Canadian Manufacturing Industries." *Review of Economics and Statistics* (November 1981), pp. 504–12.

Caves, Douglas W.; Laurits R. Christensen; and Joseph A. Swanson. "Productivity Growth, Scale Economies, and Capacity Utilization in U.S. Railroads, 1955–75." *American Economic Review* (December 1981), pp. 994–1002.

Cobb, C. W., and P. H. Douglas. "A Theory of Production." *American Economic Review* (March 1928) (Suppl.), pp. 139–65.

Huettner, D. A., and J. H. Landon. "Electric Utilities: Scale Economies and Diseconomies." *Southern Economic Journal* (April 1978), pp. 883–912.

Kopp, Raymond. "The Measurement of Productive Efficiency: A Reconsideration." *Quarterly Journal of Economics* (August 1981), pp. 477–504.

Mansfield, Edwin. *Microeconomics*. 3rd ed. New York: W. W. Norton, 1979, chap. 6.

Schlutter, G., and P. Beeson. "Components of Labor Productivity Growth in the Food System, 1958–67." *Review of Economics and Statistics* (August 1981), pp. 378–87.

Walters, A. A. "Production and Cost Functions: An Econometric Survey." *Econometrics* (January–April 1963), pp. 1–66.

APPENDIX 11A   Quadratic- and Cubic-Curve Fitting

Quadratic functions can be fitted by solving for the parameters a, b, and c in the following system of equations, which has been derived by the least squares method.[1]

$$\Sigma Y = na + b\Sigma X + c\Sigma X^2$$

$$\Sigma XY = a\Sigma X + b\Sigma X^2 + c\Sigma X^3$$

$$\Sigma X^2 Y = a\Sigma X^2 + b\Sigma X^3 + c\Sigma X^4.$$

Cubic functions can be fitted by solving for the parameters a, b, c, and d in the following system of four equations:

$$\Sigma Y = na + b\Sigma X + c\Sigma X^2 + d\Sigma X^3$$

$$\Sigma XY = a\Sigma X + b\Sigma X^2 + c\Sigma X^3 + d\Sigma X^4$$

$$\Sigma X^2 Y = a\Sigma X^2 + b\Sigma X^3 + c\Sigma X^4 + d\Sigma X^5$$

$$\Sigma X^3 Y = a\Sigma X^3 + b\Sigma X^4 + c\Sigma X^5 + d\Sigma X^6.$$

It has been suggested that the quadratic or cubic function may be fitted by first performing a transformation of the general equation by treating each power of X as an independent variable. Thus the general quadratic equation

$$Q = a + bX + cX^2$$

is transformed into the linear equation

$$Q = a + bX + cW$$

where $W = X^2$. In a similar manner, the general cubic equation

$$Q = a + bX + cX^2 + dX^3$$

is transformed into the linear equation

$$Q = a + bX + cW + dZ$$

where $W = X^2$ and $Z = X^3$. Multiple linear regression can then be used to determine the parameters a, b, c, and d, as explained in Chapter 8. Unfortunately, however, the variables W and Z are dependent upon the value of X so the problem of multicollinearity, which is also explained in Chapter 8, will be introduced. Therefore this method should not be used.

---

[1] Standard college-algebra textbooks explain several ways of solving simultaneous equations.

C H A P T E R

12

COST ANALYSIS

"A graduate class in economic theory would be a success if the students gained from it an understanding of the meaning of cost in all its many aspects."

These words—written in 1923 by the noted economist J. M. Clark in his classic work, *Studies in the Economics of Overhead Costs*—are still true today.

What prompted Clark to make this statement is the fact that the study of cost is extraordinarily complex, with all kinds of accounting, financial, economic, engineering, and even legal implications. As we might expect, there frequently is controversy over the nature of costs, how they should be defined, and what costs are relevant for decision making. Actually, most of the controversy evaporates once it is realized that there are different kinds of problems for which cost information is needed, and that the particular information required varies from one problem to another. This means that a thorough understanding of the concept of cost is necessary for a number of basic decisions that management must make for such things as pricing output, controlling costs, planning future production, and planning for profit.

CHAPTER OUTLINE

This chapter is divided into five sections:

1. **The Nature of Costs**. This section discusses the nature of cost and shows that costs may be classified in many different ways. The discussion emphasizes the concept of *relevant costs*—those particular costs that should be considered when making a particular decision.
2. **Theory of Cost**. This section examines the cost–output relationship of economic theory and different cost behaviors.

3. **Cost Behavior in the Long Run**. This section focuses on cost considerations that affect strategic planning for the long run.
4. **Economies and Diseconomies of Scale**. This section discusses the effects on costs of returns to scale, both in the plant and in the firm.
5. **Cost Behavior and Managerial Strategy**. This last section discusses useful applications of cost and production analysis, such as determining the right plant size or making effective use of the learning curve.

The Nature of Costs

All firms maintain books of account that record *explicit* costs incurred in the course of business, such as cash payments for wages, raw materials, taxes, and so forth. While it is *necessary* to consider these explicit costs, it is not *sufficient* to consider these costs alone. Economists and skillful managers recognize that there are *implicit* costs that are never recorded in the books, but nevertheless must be considered in managerial decision making.

To understand this statement, you must understand that whatever their nature, all costs involve a *sacrifice* of some kind. That is to say, if you must give up something in order to get something else, you incur a cost. What you give up may not necessarily be measurable in money. It may not even be tangible. For example, in a modern industrial society, there are certain social costs associated with production, such as noise, congestion, and pollution. There are also psychic costs, such as stress and job dissatisfaction. Inasmuch as these kinds of costs affect worker performance, they should concern management as much as monetary costs.

The point to be stressed here is that in business there are many kinds of costs. In a given situation, moreover, what is identified as a cost is often a matter of the manager's point of view.

The Concept of Relevant Costs

In decision making, managers must identify and use only those costs that are relevant to the decision at hand. By **relevant cost**, we mean a cost that will make a difference in the decision situation. In many business situations, the historical costs provided by accounting records are often the only costs that need to be reckoned with. For example, the recorded explicit costs suffice to fulfill certain legal and financial requirements, such as tax returns, reports to the Securities Exchange Commission, and annual reports to stockholders. But for decision making where the concern is with predicting costs under alternative courses of action, the costs provided by conventional accounting often are not enough.

The most useful estimates of future costs frequently are derived by combining, adjusting, interpreting, modifying, or otherwise manipulating accounting data. In the well-managed firm, therefore, books of account are a basic source of information to be weighed and analyzed in the decision-making process. Books of account, however, record only historical or original cost. In decision making, the relevant cost may be the **replacement cost** rather than the original cost.

Replacement Cost versus Original Cost

Economists differ from accountants in their valuation of assets. Under generally accepted accounting principles, an asset is valued on the books at its original or historical cost. While this approach to asset valuation may seem reasonable, it often is a problem. For example, when there are substantial increases in general price levels, as there were from 1970 to 1982, distortions in the true value of assets occur. Depending upon the method of valuation used, either the value of the inventory is understated on the balance sheet or else the firm's income is overstated on the income statement.

Many economists and cost accountants advocate valuation of assets at replacement cost, at least for management purposes. The rationale is that, broadly speaking, the firm has two business alternatives: (1) use its assets to produce and sell a finished product or (2) dispose of its assets at current market prices. The sacrifice (cost) imposed by choosing to produce and sell therefore should be measured by the market (replacement) value of the assets and not by their original cost.

Manufacturing output and goods purchased for resale are held in inventories pending sale. If prices change while the goods are being held in inventory, the difference between the original cost and the current market value of the goods is a profit or loss. But this profit or loss arises solely through holding goods during a period of rising or falling prices. It should not be attributed to the company's primary business operation, which is selling goods at a price that reflects the value that has been added to them by combining capital and labor in a production process.

As for assets other than inventories of goods being held for sale, such as land, buildings, machinery, equipment, vehicles, and other capital goods, their original costs need to be restated in current inflated dollars so that the true costs of their use can be charged against the company's operations. These problems are discussed in more detail in Chapter 14.

Accounting Cost versus Opportunity Cost

As indicated before, there is a fundamental difference between accounting (absolute) cost and opportunity (alternative) cost.

Accounting cost is the historical outlay of funds for wages and salaries, raw materials, rent, utilities, interest, and so forth. Accounting costs also include estimated periodic reductions in asset valuations, such as depreciation, amortization, and depletion expense.

Opportunity cost is the cost of forgoing certain opportunities or alternatives in favor of pursuing others. Opportunity cost exists because all resources are scarce. A resource that is used for one purpose cannot be used for something else at the same time. For example, consider a firm that chooses to invest $100,000 in a building instead of buying a $100,000 U.S. Treasury bond. The interest that could have been earned on the bond is a forgone opportunity and therefore an opportunity cost. In the firm's cost analysis, this opportunity cost should be added to the building's explicit cost of $100,000.

Decision making when opportunity costs exist involves more than merely comparing explicit costs. It also involves comparison of forgone opportunities. One kind of opportunity or alternative cost is **implicit or imputed cost**. This is a cost that never shows up in the accounting records, but it is nevertheless important for certain types of decisions. For example, when management decides to use a piece of company equipment or a company building in day-to-day operations, it sacrifices the income that could be obtained by renting the equipment or building to someone else. That is an implicit cost. Other examples of implicit cost are the use of fully depreciated property (it could be sold, rented, or salvaged) and the implicit interest on equity capital (which is equal to the explicit cost of borrowing an equal amount).

Incremental Costs and Decision Making

The concept of **incremental cost** is an integral part of the concept of relevant cost. When a decision has to be made in which cost is a factor, only those costs that will change as a result of the decision are relevant. Those are the incremental costs. Costs that do *not* change as a result of the decision are called **sunk costs**. Since they are not affected by the decision, sunk costs are irrelevant. For example, a decision to add a second shift of workers would increase relevant variable costs, such as costs of wages, materials, and supplies, but it would not change the cost already sunk into land, buildings, machinery, and other fixed assets used in production.

It must be emphasized that incremental cost is a *short-run* decision-making concept, based on the existence of sunk costs that can be ignored as irrelevant. In the long run, all costs must be recovered or the business will fail.

Illustrative Problem

Jill, an accounting major at a midwestern college, is on a tight budget, so she has kept careful records on the cost of driving her second-hand automobile. Her records show that when depreciation, interest on her investment (opportunity cost), license fees, parking fees, and insurance are added to her direct operating costs for gas, oil, tires, and maintenance, the total cost comes to $0.36 per mile if she drives 10,000 miles per year.

Jill wants to drive home for Christmas, which is a 500-mile round trip. She can't afford the trip unless she takes other students along to share the cost. She notes that the total cost of the trip at $0.36 per mile would be 500 × $.36 = $180. This would mean that the pro rata cost for herself and four riders would be $36 each, a sum that neither she nor her equally impecunious classmates can afford.

Fortunately, Jill learned about incremental costs during a course in cost accounting and recognizes that her problem is one of short-run decision making. Her objective is merely to cover the added operating cost of making a 500-mile round trip for which only the direct operating costs for gas, oil, tires, and maintenance are relevant. According to Jill's records, these costs amount to 7.3 cents per mile. Thus 500 miles of driving will increase Jill's total cost by 500 × $0.073 = $36.50, not $180. If Jill can find four riders willing to pay $10 each, she will not only get her own transportation at no additional cost, but will even make a small profit on the deal.

Although the concept of incremental cost is simple enough—it involves only those costs that are affected by a decision—it is not an easy concept to apply. A single decision may have indirect as well as direct effects upon costs. Care must be taken, therefore, to properly identify all future changes in costs that will result from a particular decision.

Illustrative Examples

Concept. If a decision requires additional capital investment, the decision maker must consider not only incremental interest, but also any change in the firm's financial risk.

Example. A firm determines that it needs $500,000 in additional capital to carry out a planned expansion of its manufacturing operations. It now must decide whether to raise that sum through the sale of common stock or by issuing corporate bonds. In comparing relevant costs, the decision maker notes that an increase in debt means an increase in the firm's financial risk. This, in turn, may affect the required rate of return on the stockholders' investments (required dividends).

Concept. Incremental costs need not be explicit costs. In some situations they are opportunity costs. That is, the incremental cost is the opportunity forgone by using limited resources in one activity instead of another.

Example. Suppose Product A provides a profit of $50 per unit. If floor space is used to make Product B instead of Product A, then the $50 forgone profit from Product A becomes part of the cost of Product B. (Note also that the allocated rental cost of the floor space is irrelevant because the same rent will have to be paid in either case.)

Concept. Expenses vary differently along different dimensions of a business.

Example. Suppose that a trucking company is operating 10 tractor-trailer rigs, each with a 36-foot trailer. In considering the incremental costs of taking on new business, the company has the alternatives of (1) using more trucks per day or (2) getting more payload per truck. The most economical policy would be to balance the two alternatives such that their incremental costs are equal.

This hypothetical company could get an 11 percent increase in capacity by trading all 10 of its 36-foot trailers for 40-foot trailers, and would not have to buy any more tractors. It could also get an 11 percent increase in capacity by adding one 40-foot trailer to its fleet, but then it would also have to buy an additional tractor. The less expensive of the two alternatives would be the way to go.

Concept. Sunk costs are not relevant costs.

Example 1. A firm orders a special machine, A, at a price of $50,000, putting down a nonrefundable deposit of $2,500, leaving a balance due of $47,500. Before accepting delivery of machine A, the firm finds out that a newly developed machine, B, costing only

$45,000, will be adequate for the purpose it has in mind. In choosing between the two machines, the deposit of $2,500 is *not* a relevant cost to be added to the cost of machine B. The $2,500 deposit is a sunk cost that has already been incurred regardless of which machine is chosen.

Example 2.   A plumbing contractor is offered a contract for $50,000 to install all the plumbing in a new building. His estimated costs for labor and overhead amount to $35,000. All of the materials needed for this job (mostly copper pipe) are in his inventory at an original cost of $20,000. However, since these materials were purchased, the cost of copper pipe has been drastically reduced so that the market value of these materials is now only $12,000, and this market value seems unlikely to change in the near future. If the plumber calculates his costs on the basis of the book value (original cost) of his inventory, he will reject the contract because his total cost would be $55,000. But this would be a mistake. The $8,000 loss from the original cost of the inventory is a sunk cost that will not change whether or not he accepts the contract. The relevant cost for materials is the current replacement cost of $12,000. The total relevant cost is $47,000, meaning there is a profit of $3,000 in the contract.

Concept.   Future relevant costs must also be identified.

Example.   Suppose that a firm's business has slacked off temporarily so that it is operating at substantially less than capacity. The firm is faced with either idling some of its highly trained staff, thereby possibly losing them, or accepting substandard contracts that will cover operating costs, but only part of the overhead.

At first glance, it would seem that the only relevant costs are the operating expenses associated with the substandard contracts. But what will happen in the future when business picks up again? Whether the firm has laid off some of its staff or whether it has tied up its staff with substandard contracts, it will have reduced its capacity to accept standard contracts from which normal profits are possible. If such contracts are refused, that entails an opportunity cost equal to the forgone profits. If the additional contracts are accepted, the firm must incur additional operating cost necessary to expand capacity. Either way, the costs of refusing or accepting future standard contracts are relevant in the original decision to accept or reject substandard contracts.

Incremental Analysis.   Incremental analysis was introduced in Chapter 3 under the heading of "Incremental Profit Analysis." The purpose of incremental analysis is to identify incremental revenue and incremental cost in order to determine incremental profit. Incremental analysis is an analytical tool that can be applied to many practical decision-making problems. In all such problems, it is the difference between alternatives that provides the basis for making the correct decisions. The decision maker must be sure, however, to consider *all* of the effects of each alternative, be they qualitative or quantitative. In Chapter 3, for example, we used the case of a tire manufacturer to illustrate the quantitative aspects of incremental analysis. However, we also pointed out that qualitative considerations, such as the possible effect on the firm's current customers, might affect the decision.

The need for this kind of broad incremental analysis is particularly apparent in the case of a firm that is considering the introduction of a new product. At the very least, decision makers must ask:

1. How will sales of the new product affect sales of existing products? Specifically, is the new product a substitute competing for sales? Or is it a complement, enhancing sales? Will it round out the firm's product line? Or is it unrelated to existing products?

2. How will production of the new product affect production of existing products? Can the new product be manufactured with existing production facilities? Will the new product create a production bottleneck? How will production of the new product affect supplies of labor and materials? How will it affect maintenance and repair of machinery and equipment?

3. How will distribution of the new product affect the firm's distribution system? Will it require new channels?

4. What will be the long-run effects of the production and sale of the new product? What future investments might be required to replace worn-out facilities? Will future expansion or development of other products be affected?

Incremental Cost versus Marginal Cost.   The distinction between incremental cost and marginal cost may seem somewhat fuzzy, and this is not helped by the fact that sometimes the two terms are used as if they were synonymous. There is, however, a fundamental conceptual difference between the two terms. *Marginal cost* refers to the change in the total cost of output when one more unit is produced. One might also refer to the marginal cost of other business functions, such as sales, finance, and administration, as well as to the marginal cost of production in manufacturing, but the concept is restricted to *unitary change of output*.

Incremental cost is a broader concept. It embraces *any* change in the total cost of doing business. For example, a decision to introduce new machinery, develop a new product, or expand into different markets might involve marginal costs of production, but it would involve other costs as well. A decision to float a new security issue, install a data-processing system, or launch a new advertising campaign may not directly entail a change in production costs. It would, however, be likely to change the total cost of doing business.

Conclusions.   Costs can be classified in a number of ways, from both economic and accounting viewpoints. There is no single definition of cost that is applicable to all situations. Because of this fact, the analyst must be sure to use the appropriate measure of cost in a given situation. The decision maker should not try to make one concept of cost do the work of several.

Theory of Cost: Cost–Output Functions

The basic principle of cost theory is that a unique functional relationship exists between cost and the rate of output for a firm; i.e., $TC = f(Q)$. Admittedly, there may be independent variables other than output that will affect cost, such as production lot size and rate of plant utilization, but the costs of these other variables are assumed to remain constant. Accordingly, they are held constant when cost curves are constructed.

The exact nature (i.e., shape) of a given cost curve—fixed, variable, total, average, or marginal—depends on the nature of the underlying production function at given input factor prices. Curves thus derived are static in nature, meaning that they show only how costs differ under alternative output levels when input factor prices are constant.

Fixed Cost versus Variable Cost

Economists generally divide costs into two major categories, *fixed* and *variable*. These terms can be a source of much confusion unless it is clearly understood that they refer to the *total costs* in each category related to the *total output* of the production function. **Fixed costs** are those costs that do not vary directly with (i.e., are not a function of) output. They are costs that require a fixed outlay of funds for each time period, without any relation to output. Examples are such expenditures as rent, property taxes and similar "franchise" payments, interest on bonds, and depreciation of assets.

Total fixed costs are not fixed in the sense that they never change. They may change and frequently do, but they do so in response to developments that are independent of volume, such as change in plant size, insurance rates, or financial arrangements. It follows, therefore, that since total fixed costs in the short run are constant with respect to total output, fixed cost *per unit* will vary with the rate of output, continuously decreasing as output increases over the production range.

A term synonymous with fixed cost, at least to the economist, is *overhead cost*. To the cost accountant, this term is virtually the same as indirect cost. Overhead, in accounting literature, usually is composed of some fixed costs and some costs that are variable in nature. The distinction is unfortunate and can lead to misinterpretations in technical discussions if care is not taken in defining terms.

Variable costs are those costs that are a function of output. Examples of variable costs include materials utilized, power, direct labor, and factory supplies. Total variable cost varies directly, sometimes proportionately, with output. Over certain ranges of production it may vary more or less than proportionately with output depending on the utilization of fixed facilities and resources.

In both economic and accounting theory it is often assumed that variable costs are continuous functions of output. In reality, however, some variable costs remain fixed over considerable ranges of production, and then increase by jumps (i.e., discontinuously) at various levels of output. Costs that exhibit this tendency have been classified as **semivariable (or semifixed) costs**. They consist of a fixed and a variable portion. Examples of such costs are telephone expenses and foremen's wages.

Short-Run and Long-Run Costs

In production analysis, the **short run** is defined as that period of time during which some of the firm's input factors are fixed. For example, the costs of a firm's plant, machinery, and equipment are fixed for some extended period of time. Inherent in the notion of short run, therefore, is the idea of temporarily fixed resource commitments whose expense the firm incurs regardless of the level of output. Because of differences in the nature of their products (consumer goods versus capital goods), production processes (labor-intensive versus capital-intensive), plant size, and level of technology, different firms may have very different time frames constituting their short-run situations. This makes it virtually impossible to say, a priori, what the short-run period is for a given firm in a given industry.

The **long run** refers to a period of time in which no input factors can be assumed to be fixed. All input factors can be changed in the long run, and therefore all long-run costs are variable. The actual period of time that can be regarded as long-run depends upon the relationship of the firm's inputs to its production process. In general, the more capital-intensive a production process is, the longer will be the time period required to change *all* of the factors of production. For example, a new oil refinery might take three years or more to build and place into operation. A nuclear power plant or a dam might take even longer. In contrast, a service industry (e.g., a bank, an employment agency, or an insurance company) that employs relatively small amounts of capital may expand its entire operation in the few months required to hire and train more personnel.

For managerial decision making, the short run is an *operating* concept, since at any given time the firm is operating in the short run. The long run, which embraces many short runs, is a *planning* concept. Whereas decisions concerning day-to-day operations are based upon the firm's short-run cost functions, the firm's plans to expand are greatly affected by its long-run cost function.

Total Cost and Marginal Cost

At any given level of output, total cost is the sum of total fixed cost and total variable cost. In symbols,

$$TC = TFC + TVC. \tag{1}$$

When derived for successive levels of output, the resulting *TC* series thus represents a functional relationship between total cost and output.

Since in the short run, total variable cost comprises the only changing portion of total cost, any change in the aggregate will be the result of and equal to the change in total variable cost. This change, due to a change in output, is called *marginal cost*. That is, marginal cost is the change in total cost resulting from a unit change in output, and it equals the change in total variable cost.

In economic theory, marginal cost is significant for decisions involving the company's allocation of resources and in product pricing, but it has other practical applications as well. At present it is sufficient to note that the concept of marginal cost should not be confused with the notion of differential or incremental cost discussed already.

Cost Behavior in the Short Run

As noted already, the short run is defined as that period of time during which some inputs and their costs are fixed. That is to say, plant size is fixed in the short run. Therefore, short-run total-cost curves are constructed to reflect the combinations of input resources that will produce various levels of output at least cost in a given plant. Since the firm always operates in the short run, short-run cost curves can be used to guide the firm's operating decisions.

Two factors determine the behavior of short-run costs: (1) the character of the un-derlying production function and (2) the prices of the variable inputs to production. If technology remains constant as production increases (i.e., the production functions do not change), the resulting cost curves are mirror images, or *inverses*, of the underlying production functions. Hence, when one is convex, the other is concave. Thus the *shape* of a cost curve depends upon the shape of its underlying production curve; but the *position* of the cost curve on the graphing plane depends upon the price of the input factor, X. If the price of X rises, the cost curve shifts upward, and vice versa.

Average-Cost and Marginal-Cost Curves.   To understand a firm's cost structure and to have a theoretical basis for resolving various kinds of decision problems, it is important to examine several cost curves, all of which can be derived from total-cost data. If we let

$$
\begin{aligned}
Q &= \text{Quantity of output} \\
TC &= \text{Total cost} \\
TFC &= \text{Total fixed cost} \\
TVC &= \text{Total variable cost} \\
ATC &= \text{Average total cost (unit cost)} \\
AFC &= \text{Average fixed cost (unit fixed cost)} \\
AVC &= \text{Average variable cost (unit variable cost)} \\
MC &= \text{Marginal cost,}
\end{aligned}
$$

then

$$ TC = f(Q) = TFC + TVC \tag{1a} $$

from which we can derive

$$ AFC = \frac{TFC}{Q} \tag{2} $$

$$ AVC = \frac{TVC}{Q} \tag{3} $$

$$ ATC = \frac{TC}{Q} = AFC + AVC \tag{4} $$

$$ MC = \frac{\Delta TC}{\Delta Q} \text{ for discrete functions} \tag{5} $$

$$ MC = \frac{dTC}{dQ} \text{ for continuous functions.} \tag{6} $$

We emphasize that *TFC* affects *TC* and *ATC*, but has no effect on *MC*. Exhibit 12–1 illustrates the tabular method of cost analysis, using discrete data to set forth a cost schedule for the production of tennis rackets. Although the data in this exhibit are not complete, there is sufficient information to fill in the blanks. (The student may find it worthwhile to do so.) When the discrete data points are connected, the average fixed cost, average variable cost, average total cost, and marginal cost all show themselves to be continuous curvilinear functions, as illustrated by Exhibit 12–2 (page 352).

Mathematically, average fixed cost, *AFC*, is a rectangular hyperbola that is asymptotic to the horizontal axis, and this will always be true no matter what the shape of the associated total-cost function. This means that *AFC* is constantly decreasing, as shown in Exhibit 12–2. The exhibit also shows that marginal cost (*MC*) first decreases and then increases. Average variable cost (*AVC*) and average total cost (*ATC*) also first decrease and

EXHIBIT 12–1   Cost Schedule for the Production of Tennis Rackets

Quantity of Production (000) Q	Total Fixed Cost ($000) TFC	Total Variable Cost ($000) TVC	Total Cost ($000) TC = TFC + TVC	Average Fixed Cost ($000) TFC/Q	Average Variable Cost ($000) TVC/Q	Average Total Cost ($000) TC/Q	Marginal Cost ($000) ΔTC/ΔQ
1	$50		$ 55.00				
							$ 3.00
2	50	$ 8.00	58.00	$25.00	$ 4.00	$29.00	
3	50		60.50				
							2.50
4	50	13.00	63.00	12.50	3.25	15.75	
5	50		65.00				
							3.00
6	50	18.00	68.00	8.33	3.00	11.34	
7	50		72.75				
							5.25
8	50	28.00	78.00	6.25	3.50	9.75	
9	50		86.00				
							9.00
10	50	45.00	95.00	5.00	4.50	9.50	9.50
11	50	54.50	104.50	4.55	4.95	9.50	
							10.70
12	50	65.20	115.20	4.17	5.44	9.60	
13	50		130.00				
							19.10
14	50	99.10	149.10	3.57	7.08	10.65	
15	50		174.75				
							37.25
16	50	162.00	212.00	3.13	10.13	13.25	
17	50		259.25				
							60.25
18	50	269.50	319.50	2.78	14.97	17.75	
19	50		399.00				
							101.00
20	50	450.00	500.00	2.50	22.50	25.00	

then increase. As the production level increases, *ATC* approaches *AVC*. This is because the gap between them is the unit fixed cost, which grows smaller and smaller as the level of production increases.

Note particularly that the marginal-cost curve intersects both the average-variable-cost curve and the average-total-cost curve at their lowest points. That is to say, marginal cost is equal to average variable cost when average variable cost is at a minimum. Marginal cost is also equal to average total cost when average total cost is at a minimum.

This is easily verified by referring to the cost schedule in Exhibit 12–1. When the sixth unit is produced, the average variable cost of $3 is at a minimum and is equal to the marginal cost of $3. When the eleventh unit is produced, the average total cost of $9.50 is at a minimum, and is equal to the marginal cost of $9.50.

Cost and Production Relationships. As with the total-cost and total-variable-cost curves, the shapes or curvatures of the average-cost and marginal-cost curves are conditioned by the technical nature of the underlying production curves, and not by factor prices. A change in factor prices will shift the curves up or down on the graph, but will not change their shape because their slopes are not affected.

The natural consequence of a constant factor price for varying levels of output is an inverse relationship between (1) average variable cost and average product and (2) marginal cost and marginal product. These relationships may be derived as follows:

EXHIBIT 12–2   Cost Curves for Production of Tennis Rackets

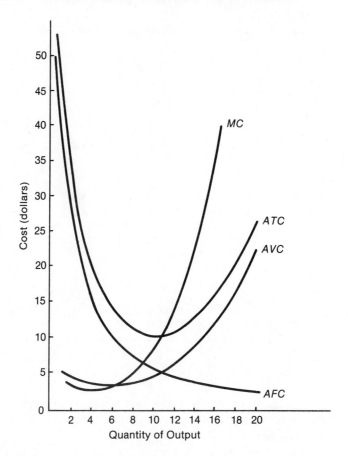

Step 1.   The average variable cost of the output can be expressed as

$$AVC_Q = \frac{TVC_Q}{Q_x} = \frac{P_X \cdot X}{Q_x} = P_X\left(\frac{X}{Q_X}\right) \tag{7}$$

where

AVC_Q = Average variable cost of the output
TVC_Q = Total variable cost of the output
Q_X = Units of output resulting from input of factor X
P_X = Unit price of input factor X
X = Units of input of factor X.

The average product, AP_X, is defined as Q_X/X, which is the reciprocal of X/Q_X in Equation 7. Therefore, the average variable cost can be defined as

$$AVC_Q = P_X\left(\frac{1}{Q_X/X}\right) = P_X\left(\frac{1}{AP_X}\right) = \frac{P_X}{AP_X}. \tag{8}$$

EXHIBIT 12–3   **Relationship between Marginal Product and Marginal Cost, and between Average Product and Average Variable Cost**

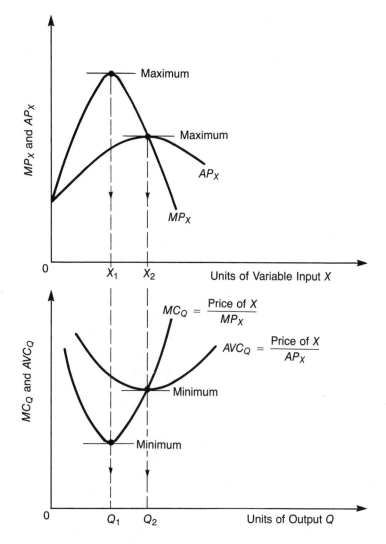

Given that the price of the input factor is constant, we see from Equation 8 that when AP_X increases, AVC_Q decreases, and vice versa. Logically, then, AVC_Q must be at a minimum when AP_X is at a maximum. This inverse relationship is illustrated by Exhibit 12–3.

Step 2. Exhibit 12–3 also shows the inverse relationship between marginal product and marginal cost, which is not affected by fixed input. Therefore, marginal cost of output, MC_Q, can be defined as

$$MC_Q = \frac{\Delta TVC_Q}{\Delta Q_X} = \frac{\Delta X \cdot P_X}{\Delta Q_X} = P_X\left(\frac{\Delta X}{\Delta Q_X}\right) = P_X\left(\frac{1}{\Delta Q_X/\Delta X}\right) = \frac{P_X}{MP_X}. \qquad \textbf{(9)}$$

Given that the price of the input factor is constant, we see from Equation 9 that when MP_X increases, MC_Q decreases, and vice versa. Logically, then, MC_Q must be at a minimum when MP_X is at a maximum.

Step 3. Average total cost, ATC_Q, is the sum of the average fixed cost, AFC_Q, and average variable cost, AVC_Q; i.e.,

$$ATC_Q = AFC_Q + AVC_Q. \qquad \textbf{(10)}$$

Step 4. Going back to Exhibit 12–2, we see that AFC grows smaller as output increases. Thus the ATC curve is asymptotic to the AVC curve. We also note that its lowest point is at a higher level of production than the minimum AVC. This is because when we first increase production beyond the level of minimum AVC, the decline in AFC more than offsets the increase in AVC. As production continues to increase, however, we reach the point where increases in AVC begin to exceed decreases in AFC. This is where the ATC curve turns upward.

Step 5. The most *production-efficient* level of production occurs where $MP_X = AP_X$ and AP_X is at a maximum. This marks the end of Stage 1 and the beginning of Stage 2 of the classic production function that was illustrated by Exhibit 10–2 in Chapter 10, and coincides with the level where $MC_Q = AVC_Q$. This is *not* the most economical or *cost-efficient* level, however, because it does not consider average fixed cost. The most economical, cost-efficient level of production occurs somewhere in Stage 2, at the point of minimum average total cost, ATC.

Illustrative Problem

A certain manufacturing process uses five hours of labor and $100 worth of raw materials for each unit of output. The firm's current level of output is 400 units per week for a working year of 50 weeks. Fixed costs amount to $100,000 per year. Production workers' wages average $12.50 per hour, including payroll taxes, pension plan, and other fringe benefits. In addition, each employee gets two weeks paid vacation per year.

Questions

a. What is the average (unit) variable cost of manufacturing?
b. What is the total unit cost?

Solutions

a. The first step is to determine the full hourly wage including paid vacation. For each worker, the annual wage is 52 weeks × 40 hours × $12.50 = $26,000. The hourly wage then is $26,000 ÷ 50 working weeks ÷ 40 hours = $13 per hour. Then, by Equation (8),

$$AVC_Q = \frac{P_X}{AP_X} = \frac{(5)(13) + 100}{1} = \$165.00 \text{ per unit.}$$

b. Annual production = 400 units per week × 50 weeks = 20,000 units. The unit fixed cost then is 100,000 ÷ 20,000 = $5 per unit. Hence, by Equation 10,

$$ATC_Q = AFC_Q + AVC_Q = \$5 + \$165 = \$170 \text{ per unit.}$$

Elasticity of Total Cost. Since the economic theory of cost deals with relationships between cost and output, can we measure the responsiveness or sensitivity between these variables? The answer to this question, of course, involves the familiar concept of elasticity.

The elasticity of total cost measures the percent change in total cost, *TC*, resulting from a 1 percent change in output, *Q*. Thus, at any point along the total-cost curve,

$$\epsilon_C = \frac{\Delta TC/TC}{\Delta Q/Q} = \frac{\Delta TC}{\Delta Q} \cdot \frac{Q}{TC} = \frac{\Delta TC/\Delta Q}{TC/Q} = \frac{MC}{ATC}. \tag{11}$$

From this equation, it is apparent that the elasticity of total cost is the ratio of marginal cost to average total cost.

Suppose cost elasticity is 1.2. What does it mean?

It means that if output is increased by 1 percent, total cost will increase by 1.2 percent. It means that at the given level of production, marginal cost is 20 percent greater than average cost, as indicated by Equation 11.

If the total-cost function is linear, or if it is nearly linear within the range desired, the elasticity of total cost, E_C, can be estimated with the arc formula,

$$E_C = \frac{\dfrac{TC_2 - TC_1}{(TC_2 + TC_1)/2}}{\dfrac{Q_2 - Q_1}{(Q_2 + Q_1)/2}} = \frac{TC_2 - TC_1}{TC_2 + TC_1} \cdot \frac{Q_2 + Q_1}{Q_2 - Q_1}. \tag{12}$$

This formula gives the average cost elasticity over the range of output between Q_1 and Q_2.

Properties of Short-Run Cost Functions

The generalized or typical cost function is the cubic function

$$TC = a + bQ - cQ^2 + dQ^3. \tag{13}$$

It is the inverse of the generalized (cubic) production function, which first exhibits increasing, and then decreasing marginal product or returns to input. Consequently, as illustrated by Exhibit 12–4 (page 356), the cost function exhibits first decreasing, and then increasing marginal cost. Marginal cost can be measured by the slope of either curve since the shapes of the *TC* and *TVC* curves are identical. The vertical distance between them is the constant total fixed cost, *TFC*.

The classical cost function, as illustrated by Exhibit 12–4, extends over the entire capacity of the production plant, from zero output with $TVC = 0$ to maximum-capacity

EXHIBIT 12–4   Generalized Short-Run Total-Cost Function

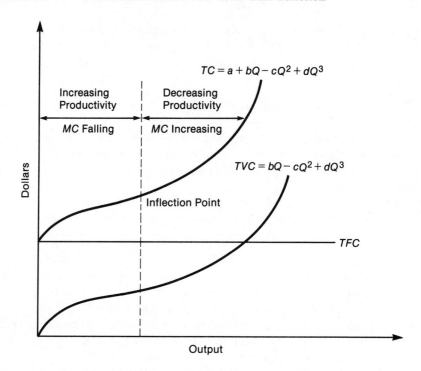

output with maximum total cost. Within that range, there may be segments of the curve that exhibit linear or quadratic properties. If so, they will have the characteristics depicted in Exhibit 12–5, which shows the mathematical properties of linear, quadratic, and cubic cost functions.

In general, we note the following:

1. The constant parameter, a, may be taken to represent total fixed costs unless the cost function has been obtained by regression analysis of production data that do not cover low levels of production. In that case, the constant term of the regression equation does not represent fixed cost, but merely indicates a Y-intercept that serves to properly locate the regression line in the production range of interest. In either case, when it is removed from the total-cost equation, the remainder represents total variable cost.
2. Marginal costs are derivatives of the equations for total costs.
3. The quantity a/Q represents average fixed cost. When it is removed from the equation for average total cost, the remainder represents average variable cost.
4. Cost elasticity is the ratio of marginal cost to average total cost.

Economic interpretations of some of these mathematical properties are discussed next.

Linear Cost Functions.   Exhibit 12–6 (page 358) illustrates the cost curves associated with a linear cost function, $TC = a + bQ$. As we shall explain in the next chapter, the re-

---

EXHIBIT 12–5   Cost Curves Associated with Various Cost Functions

Function	Linear	Quadratic I	Quadratic II	Cubic
TC	$a + bQ$	$a + bQ - cQ^2$	$a + bQ + cQ^2$	$a + bQ - cQ^2 + dQ^3$
TFC	a	a	a	a
TVC	bQ	$bQ - cQ^2$	$bQ + cQ^2$	$bQ - cQ^2 + dQ^3$
ATC	$\frac{a}{Q} + b$	$\frac{a}{Q} + b - cQ$	$\frac{a}{Q} + b + cQ$	$\frac{a}{Q} + b - cQ + dQ^2$
AFC	$\frac{a}{Q}$	$\frac{a}{Q}$	$\frac{a}{Q}$	$\frac{a}{Q}$
AVC	b	$b - cQ$	$b + cQ$	$b - cQ + dQ^2$
MC	b	$b - 2cQ$	$b + 2cQ$	$b - 2cQ + 3dQ^2$
ϵ_C	$\frac{b}{\frac{a}{Q}+b}$	$\frac{b-2cQ}{\frac{a}{Q}+b-cQ}$	$\frac{b+2cQ}{\frac{a}{Q}+b+cQ}$	$\frac{b-2cQ+3dQ^2}{\frac{a}{Q}+b-cQ+dQ^2}$

---

sults of empirical research suggest that firms in widely differing industries enjoy linear cost functions over a fairly broad range of what might be called normal production. One explanation for this phenomenon is that within the normal range of production, the fixed and variable inputs can be combined in minimum cost proportions at each level of output. If the cost function were to be extended to include higher levels of output, however, the linear function would no longer be valid. This is because it does not recognize the law of diminishing returns. That is, the equation does not allow for total cost to turn upward, even as output levels approaching the physical capacity of the plant are reached.

Note that average variable cost (*AVC*) and marginal cost (*MC*) are constant and equal. The average-total-cost (*ATC*) curve is asymptotic to that of average variable cost. Within the normal range of production, the *ATC* curve flattens out and remains nearly constant.

Quadratic Cost Functions.   As shown in Exhibit 12–5, two types of quadratic functions are possible. The first type is described by the general equation $TC = a + bQ - cQ^2$. The associated cost curves are shown in Exhibit 12–7 (page 358). As always, the *ATC* curve is asymptotic to the *AVC* curve. Average variable cost falls at a constant rate as output increases, and marginal cost decreases even faster. Unfortunately for the firm, this happy situation is unlikely to occur in a normal range of output. It may occur at the start-up of production, where fixed factors are excessive in relation to variable inputs. Decreasing marginal costs thus are attributable to more efficient use of fixed factors, which also causes the average variable cost to decrease.

The second type of quadratic cost function is described by the equation $TC = a + bQ + cQ^2$. The associated cost curves are illustrated in Exhibit 12–8 (page 359). As shown in panel B, the *AVC* curve constantly increases, with *MC* rising even faster. Since the *ATC* curve is asymptotic to the *AVC* curve, it must cut through the *MC* curve. The intersection, where $MC = ATC$ and cost elasticity is therefore 1, marks the most cost-effective level of production.

Cubic Cost Functions.   The typical total-cost function of economics textbooks is not usually of a linear or quadratic form, but rather of the cubic type, $TC = a + bQ - cQ^2 + dQ^3$, which exhibits the law of variable proportions. The curves associated with

EXHIBIT 12–6   **Linear Cost Function:** $TC = a + bQ$

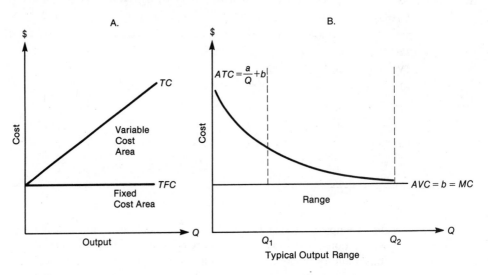

EXHIBIT 12–7   **Quadratic Cost Function:** $TC = a + bQ - cQ^2$

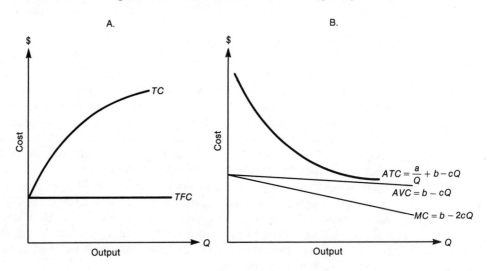

EXHIBIT 12–8   **Quadratic Cost Function:** $TC = a + bQ + cQ^2$

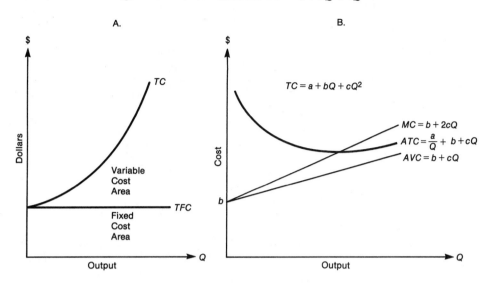

A.

B.

$TC = a + bQ + cQ^2$

$MC = b + 2cQ$

$ATC = \dfrac{a}{Q} + b + cQ$

$AVC = b + cQ$

this cost function are illustrated by Exhibit 12–9 (page 360). Since the *TC* function is cubic, the *ATC* and *MC* curves are quadratic, first falling, and then rising. The switch from decreasing to increasing marginal cost (when *MC* is at a minimum) corresponds to the inflection point of the curvature of the cubic function. The intersection of the *MC* and *ATC* curves, where $MC = ATC$ and $\epsilon_C = 1$, marks the most cost-effective level of output. If the firm increases output to a higher level, it encounters increasing costs for such things as maintenance of machinery and overtime pay for labor. Total costs thus rise at an ever-increasing rate.

Cubic functions such as these represent, for the most part, strictly theoretical generalizations. Attempts to fit cubic curves to empirical data have met with varying and, at best, only moderate degrees of success (to be discussed in the next chapter). One reason that a cubic function does not readily fit empirical data is that the data usually are confined to the range of normal operations. As was shown earlier, the cost function in the normal operating range tends to be linear, and marginal costs are likely to be constant.

Illustrative Problem

The total cost function for Randolph Enterprises is
$$TC = 100Q - 3Q^2 + 0.1Q^3.$$

Questions

a. Determine the level of output that will minimize unit cost.
b. Determine the level of output that will minimize marginal cost.
c. Find the cost elasticity when $Q = 12$.

EXHIBIT 12–9 **Cubic Cost Curves and the Elasticity of Total Cost**

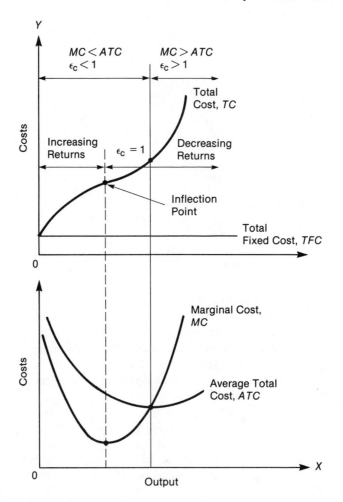

Solutions

a. Unit cost is average total cost, which is

$$ATC = \frac{TC}{Q} = \frac{100Q - 3Q^2 + 0.1Q^3}{Q} = 100 - 3Q + 0.1Q^2$$

The level of output at which unit cost is minimal is found by taking the first derivative of the ATC function, setting it equal to zero, and solving for Q:

$$\frac{d\,ATC}{dQ} = -3 + 0.2Q = 0$$

$$Q = 15.$$

This solution can be tested to determine whether it represents a minimum or a maximum by taking the second derivative of the ATC function:

$$\frac{d^2 ATC}{dQ^2} = 0.2.$$

Since the second derivative is positive, it indicates a minimum.
b. Marginal cost is the first derivative of the total-cost function:

$$MC = \frac{dTC}{dQ} = 100 - 6Q + 0.3Q^2.$$

To find the level of output that minimizes marginal cost, we take the first derivative of the MC function, set it equal to zero, and solve for Q:

$$\frac{dMC}{Q} = -6 + 0.6Q = 0$$
$$Q = 10.$$

Again we use the second derivative to test this solution,

$$\frac{d^2 MC}{dQ^2} = 0.6$$

which is positive, indicating a minimum.
c. Cost elasticity when $Q = 12$ is

$$\epsilon_C = \frac{MC}{ATC} = \frac{100 - 6Q + 0.3Q^2}{100 - 3Q + 0.1Q^2}$$

$$= \frac{100 - 6(12) + 0.3(12)^2}{100 - 3(12) + 0.1(12)^2} = \frac{71.2}{78.4} = 0.908.$$

Cost Behavior in the Long Run

As we noted earlier, cost behavior in the short run is an *operating* concept. At any given time, now or in the future, the firm will operate an existing plant that incurs a set of fixed costs. Operational decision making thus is concerned with minimizing variable costs.

In contrast, cost behavior in the long run is a *planning* concept. It is based on the premise that all input factors can be varied and that for each possible output level, there is a least-cost combination of input factors. Therefore, it is possible to construct a plant of optimum size for any desired level of production.

Because of the flexibility afforded in the long run, the firm must begin the planning process by first establishing the technology and production methods that are or will be available for the firm's expansion. The firm is then free to choose the size of the plant and the kinds of equipment that are most suitable to its desired level of production. When the firm actually increases its plant size, some of the production factors will become fixed. The firm will again be operating in the short run, and a short-run average-cost function will be established.

This is illustrated by Exhibit 12–10 (page 362), which shows the short-run average cost (*SRAC*) curves for four successively more efficient plant sizes. Each plant operates most efficiently at a level of output corresponding to the lowest point on its *SRAC* curve. We call this level of output the **design capacity** of the plant.

If the plant size can be varied, the production manager will try to find the lowest

EXHIBIT 12–10   Average Short-Run Costs for Four Different Plant Sizes

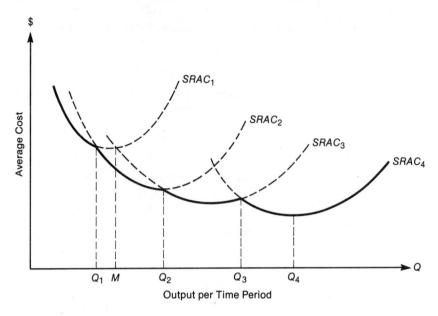

average cost for each of several levels of production. Taking the smallest plant, it can be seen that the lowest short-run average cost occurs when *M* units are produced. The diagram shows, however, that *M* units can be produced at lower cost in the second plant, which has a larger capacity. Pursuing this line of reasoning further, we conclude that it is most efficient to produce up to Q_1 units in Plant 1, from Q_1 to Q_2 units in Plant 2, from Q_2 to Q_3 units in Plant 3, and from Q_3 to Q_4 units in Plant 4. This choice is indicated on the diagram by the solid line connecting these points. This solid line is the long-run average cost curve, *LRAC*.

Of course, a firm actually has many more than four plant sizes to choose from. Indeed, depending on the divisibility of productive units and their technical nature, there may be an infinite number of plant sizes available, each with its own short-run average-cost curve and design capacity. When the points of intersection of all these *SRAC* curves are joined together, the result is the smooth *LRAC* curve illustrated by Exhibit 12–11.

In Exhibit 12–11, only five of the infinite number of possible *SRAC* curves have been drawn. Or, to put it another way, all but five of the intersecting *SRAC* curves have been erased. This leaves each of the remaining *SRAC* curves just tangent to the *LRAC* curve at the point of intersection with the (erased) *SRAC* curve for the next larger plant.

Exhibit 12–11 further illustrates the relationship between the long-run and short-run average-cost functions. Suppose that the firm is producing Q_1 units of output in Plant 1, which has the short-run average cost curve $SRAC_1$. If the firm wants to expand output to Q_2 units, production would take place at point *A* on $SRAC_1$, at a cost of C_1 dollars. But the cost would be substantially less in a larger plant with $SRAC_2$ at a cost of C_2 dollars. The reduction in cost would be $C_1 - C_2$.

EXHIBIT 12–11   **Short-Run Average-Cost Curves for Various Sizes of Plants and Resulting Long-Run Average Cost Curve**

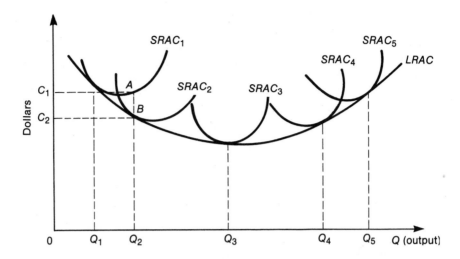

The *LRAC* curve envelops the entire family of *SRAC* curves. The U shape of the *LRAC* curve implies that expansion of plant size results in lower and lower units costs until the optimum size is reached. This occurs at Q_3 units of output, where the *LRAC* curve is at its lowest point. Thereafter, further increase in production will require successively larger plants and successively higher unit costs.

The *LRAC* curve is tangent to only one point on each *SRAC* curve. At the optimal plant size, the tangency occurs at the lowest point on both the short-run and long-run average-cost curves, as shown by $SRAC_3$. For all other plant sizes, the tangency point occurs: (1) to the left of the minimum-cost point (design capacity) on all short-run curves that are to the left of the optimum curve $SRAC_3$ and (2) to the right of the minimum-cost point (design capacity) on all short-run curves that are to the right of the optimum curve. Therefore, for outputs less than Q_3, it is more economical to operate at less than design capacity, underutilizing a plant that is slightly larger than necessary. Thus it would be cheaper to produce output Q_2 with a plant designated by $SRAC_2$ than with one represented by $SRAC_1$. Conversely, at outputs beyond the optimum level Q_3, it is more economical to operate at a somewhat higher level than design capacity, overutilizing a plant with a design capacity that is slightly smaller than the required production. Thus it is cheaper to produce Q_4 units with plant $SRAC_4$ than with $SRAC_5$.

The *LRAC* curve of Exhibit 12–11 is U-shaped; however, empirical research has indicated that the *LRAC* curve may be L-shaped, as shown by Exhibit 12–12 (page 364). Here, once the minimum *LRAC* is reached at a plant with the capacity to produce $Q*$ units, successively larger plants can maintain that same minimum *LRAC*. This means that there is a wide range of plant sizes in which there is no particular cost advantage to any one size.

EXHIBIT 12–12   L-Shaped Long-Run Average-Cost Curve of a Single Plant

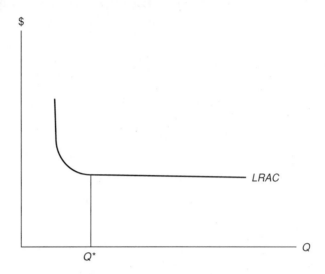

Economies and Diseconomies of Scale

In the preceding chapters on production, we defined returns to scale as the proportionate increase or decrease in output that results from an increase in all input factors of production, and noted that it is a long-run concept. If there are increasing returns to scale while the prices of input factors remain the same, then there are corresponding decreases in long-run unit cost. We call this **economies of scale**. On the other hand, decreasing returns to scale result in increasing long-run unit cost, and we call this **diseconomies of scale**. Economies or diseconomies of scale may be obtained either within single plants or for the firm as a whole. The output–cost relationships and the input–output relationships continue to be mirror images of each other.

Economies of Scale at the Plant Level

There are at least eight different reasons why economies may be achieved when the plant size is enlarged more or less to scale:

1. *More efficient use of labor from subdivision and specialization.* For example, in a small manufacturing plant using, say, two machinists, the machinists might be required to sweep up around their machines. Thus they would spend part of their time doing janitorial work at machinist's wages. As the plant expands, janitors could be hired for clean-up work at janitor's wages, leaving machinists free to spend all of their time doing what they do best.
2. *Machine execution of simplified work elements.* For example, computers are capable of performing repetitive tasks involving manipulation of data, and they can do it better, faster, and cheaper than human beings.

3. *In-house performance of specialized tasks.* For example, a small firm may use an outside duplicating service for occasional copying of documents. As the plant size grows, the increased need for copying may justify the purchase of a duplicating machine.

4. *Specialization and higher capacity of machines.* A machine that is designed to perform a specialized operation is usually more cost-efficient than a general-purpose machine. Higher-capacity machines also offer savings. For example, a machine with twice as much capacity does not cost twice as much to buy or operate.

5. *Centralization and integration of manufacturing stages into a single continuous process.* An example is provided by steel mills in which raw steel goes into the rolling mills while it is still hot.

6. *Use or sale of by-products.* For example, when coke is made from anthracite coal, naphtha is obtained as a by-product. When gasoline is made from crude oil, other products such as kerosene, diesel oil, and fuel oil are also produced in the refining process. By-products are also common in the meat-packing, chemical, and paper-products industries.

7. *Quantity discounts on purchases.* A firm that buys in large quantities can demand and get volume discounts from suppliers.

8. *Savings on transportation costs by owning and operating the firm's own vehicles.* Many large companies, while not in the trucking business, own and operate more trucks than some of the smaller trucking companies.

Diseconomies of Scale at the Plant Level

When a plant becomes too large, certain diseconomies may set in:

1. The sheer size of a plant may cause bottlenecks in the production process.
2. Traffic jams and other difficulties in moving materials into, within, and out of the plant may increase transportation costs.
3. Distribution of a very large volume of finished goods may become more costly.
4. Finally, ineffectual coordination and supervision sets in as plant size increases.

Economies of Scale for Multiplant Firms

In multiplant firms, distinctive production and cost functions exist for the firm as a whole as well as for each of its component plants. Ideally, each plant would be of optimal size, meaning that no further economies are possible by changing plant sizes.[1] If the firm expands by adding more plants, each of which is of optimal size for its location, then the shape of the resulting *LRAC* for the firm determines the degree to which economies of scale can be realized by expansion of the firm.

---

[1] This does not mean that all plants are of the same size, even if they are producing the same product. It simply means that in each plant's geographic location, the cost environment is such that the minimum short-run average cost coincides with the minimum long-run average cost, as illustrated in Exhibit 12–11.

EXHIBIT 12–13   Some Possible Long-Run Average-Cost Curves for a Multiplant Firm

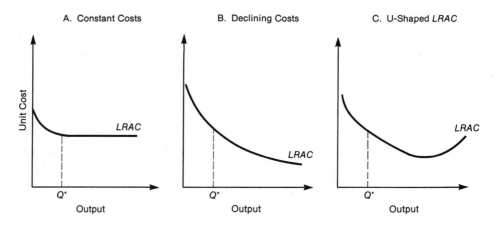

Even under ideal circumstances, there are at least three different shapes that could be assumed by the firm's long-run cost curve, as illustrated by Exhibit 12–13. In each panel of the exhibit, Q^* indicates the level of output of the first optimally sized plant. In Panel A, the *LRAC* curve for the firm levels off when the first optimally sized plant is established. No matter how many optimally sized plants are added to increase the size of the firm, no further economies of scale can be achieved.

In Panel B, long-run average cost for the firm continues to decline as additional (optimally sized) plants are added. The tendency for long-run average costs to fall as the firm expands its scale of operations is a reflection of cost economies that are frequently encountered with increasing size of the firm. Some of the reasons for economies of scale as the firm grows may be:

1. Putting several plants under one management economizes on top-echelon management. Also, a large firm can afford specialized staff, such as lawyers, tax accountants, and economists.
2. A larger firm may be able to serve the full range of its customers' needs, or use a common distribution system for many products, or use a common technology to manufacture a variety of products.
3. Large firms can realize the economies of mass marketing, with nationwide distribution and promotion.
4. The large firm has a definite advantage in the financial markets. In general, large firms can negotiate lower interest rates on loans and lower costs of floating stock or bond issues to obtain capital.

In Panel C of Exhibit 12–13, economies of scale beyond Q^* are realized up to a certain size of the firm. After that, diseconomies of scale may set in, although there is some disagreement among economists about what happens to long-run average costs once economies of scale have been fully realized by the firm. Some economists think that long-run average costs then remain constant. Others think that the *LRAC* will ultimately rise because of problems of coordination and control by management. As the firm becomes larger, decision making and coordination become more complex and difficult. Therefore, the burden of administration becomes disproportionately greater and diminishing returns to management set in.

The minimum efficient size of the firm is affected by the available economies of scale both within the plant and within the firm. Thus, all three shapes of *LRAC* curves, as depicted in Exhibit 12–13, have been detected in U.S. firms, with different shapes holding in different industries.

Cost Behavior and Managerial Strategy

There are many useful applications of cost and production analysis in decision making. Two of the more important applications are the choice of plant size and the effective use of the learning curve.

Minimum Efficient Scale (MES)

The shape of the long-run average-cost curves of production plants is important not only because it governs cost-efficient plant size, but also because it indicates the number of firms that will emerge in an industry. Returning to Exhibit 12–13, we see that Q^* is the level of output that first minimizes the long-run average cost of the plant. This is the minimum size or scale of the plant that is cost-efficient, when "cost-efficient" means lowest *LRAC*. Hence we can refer to this plant size as the **minimum efficient scale** or *MES*. The *MES* is an important consideration in a firm's decision as to whether to operate more than one plant, as shown by the following illustrative problem.

Illustrative Problem

International Therapeutics, Inc., is a manufacturer of a piece of equipment used by physical therapists at hospitals and clinics throughout the United States and Canada. At the present time, all of the firm's production takes place at a single plant located in the midwestern United States. Because of the growth of demand for its product as well as the high costs of transportation of its goods, the firm is considering a multiplant strategy to replace its centralized production. The estimated demand for the firm's product is

$$P = 1,880 - 0.02Q.$$

The total-cost function, including both production and transportation, is

$$TC = 500,000 + 80Q + 0.01Q^2$$

and the firm believes that this cost function would remain the same in a multiplant operation.

The profit-maximizing level of production at the single plant is the level at which marginal revenue equals marginal cost:

EXHIBIT 12–14   Marginal Cost, Average Total Cost, and Marginal Revenue in a Single Plant Producing 30,000 Units and Six Plants with Capacity of 7,100 Units Each

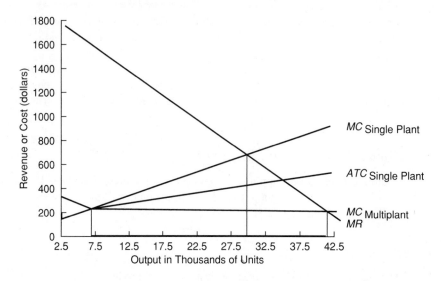

$$MR = 1,880 - 0.04Q = 80 + 0.02Q = MC$$
$$-0.06Q = -1,800$$
$$Q = 30,000 \text{ units}$$

for which the optimal price is

$$P = 1,880 - 0.02(30,000) = \$1,280 \text{ per unit.}$$

Maximum profit is

$$\pi = TR - TC = PQ - TC$$
$$= 1,280(30,000) - 500,000 - 80(30,000) - 0.01(30,000)^2$$
$$= \$26,500,000.$$

If the company embarks upon a multiple-plant strategy, it would want each plant to operate at its *MES*, which is the lowest possible unit cost.

$$ATC = \frac{TC}{Q} = \frac{500,000 + 80Q + 0.01Q^2}{Q} = 500,000Q^{-1} + 80 + 0.01Q$$

$$\frac{dATC}{dQ} = -500,000Q^{-2} + 0.01 = 0$$
$$0.01Q^2 = 500,000$$
$$Q^2 = 50,000,000$$
$$Q = 7,071.067812 \approx 7,100.$$

Hence the minimum efficient scale for the firm's plants would be a standard operating capacity of approximately 7,100 units. At this level, MC and ATC are approximately equal, and both are lower than in the single plant producing 30,000 units. Furthermore, the marginal cost will remain constant throughout total production by the firm, as shown by Exhibit 12–14.

At an output of 30,000 units,

$$MC = 80 + 0.02Q = 80 + 0.02(30,000) = \$680.$$

At an output of 7,100 units,

$$MC = 80 + 0.02Q = 80 + 0.02(7,100) = \$222.$$

As shown on the exhibit, spreading the total production over a number of small plants instead of one large plant enables the firm to achieve a constant marginal cost that is equal to the average total cost at minimum efficient scale. In this example, the profit maximizing level of production and sales for the firm will be the level at which marginal revenue equals a marginal cost of $222.

$$MR = 1,880 - 0.04Q = 222$$
$$-0.04Q = -1,658$$
$$Q = 41,450 \text{ units}$$

Output at this level would require $41,450/7,100 \approx 6$ plants with a capacity of 7,100 units each. If production of the 41,450 units is divided as evenly as possible among the six plants, four plants would produce 6,908 units each and two plants would produce 6,909 units each. Total cost for producing 6,908 units would be

$$TC = 500,000 + 80Q + 0.01Q^2$$
$$= 500,000 + 80(6,908) + 0.01(6,908)^2 = \$1,529,844.64$$

and total cost for producing 6,909 units would be

$$TC = 500,000 + 80Q + 0.01Q^2$$
$$= 500,000 + 80(6,909) + 0.01(6,909)^2 = \$1,530,062.81$$

The total cost for producing 41,450 units thus would be:

$$TC_{total} = \$1,529,844.64(4) + \$1,530,062.81(2) = \$9,179,504.18.$$

In order to sell 41,450 units, the price would be reduced to

$$P = 1,880 - 0.02Q = 1,880 - 0.02(41,450) = \$1,051$$

which is $229 less than the $1,280 that is optimal under a single-plant operation. The firm's profit would be

$$\pi = TR - TC = PQ - TC = \$1,051(41,450) - \$9,179,504$$
$$= \$43,563,950 - \$9,179,504 = \$34,384,446.$$

This is $7,884,446 more than the $26,500,000 earned from production of 30,000 units in a single plant. It should be further noted that these calculations assume that each of the six small plants incurs the same fixed cost as the single large plant. If fixed costs could be reduced in each of the smaller plants, the increase in profits would be even greater.

The MES as a Barrier to Entry. The *MES* may be viewed as the smallest plant with which a new firm can enter a particular industry. Since all firms within an industry can be expected to have similar long-run average costs, the relationship of the size of the *MES* plant to total industry output reflects the difficulty of entry into a particular industry. To illustrate, suppose two industries have a different *MES*. Industry A produces 10 billion units of output annually and has an *MES* of 1 million units. Industry B produces 10 million units annually and has an *MES* of 100,000 units.

An *MES*-sized plant in Industry A would produce 0.01 percent of the industry output. A much smaller *MES*-sized plant in Industry B would produce 1.0 percent (100 times as much) of the industry output. Although the *MES* of Industry B is only one tenth as large as the *MES* of Industry A, it would be much more difficult to raise enough capital and find enough skilled labor to start up in Industry B because its *MES* represents a far greater proportion of the total industry output.

MES and Competitiveness. In the preceding example, we could expect more vigorous competition in Industry A than in Industry B simply because of the relatively greater start-up costs in Industry B. Competition will tend to be most vigorous in industries where the *MES* is small compared to industry demand. When the *MES* is large compared to industry demand, its greater relative cost constitutes a barrier that limits the number of competitors.

The effect of the *MES* on the competitiveness of an industry is also determined by the slope of the firm's *LRAC* at outputs less than the *MES*. Looking again at Exhibits 12–11 and 12–12, we see that the effect of operating somewhat to the left of Q_3 in Exhibit 12–11 would be much less severe than operating somewhat to the left of Q^* in Exhibit 12–12. Thus we conclude that the level of competition in an industry is influenced both by the shape of the *LRAC* curve and by the size of the *MES* plant relative to total industry output.

The Effect of Transportation Costs on Minimum Efficient Scale. Some of the most important determinants of optimal plant size and location are the costs of moving raw materials to the plant and moving finished goods from the plant to customers. Long-run transportation costs can be expected to rise when plant size is increased. This will affect optimal plant size as illustrated by Exhibit 12–15. The exhibit shows that when only production costs are considered, the minimum efficient scale is at Q_1^*. When transportation costs are added to production costs, however, the *MES* is reduced to Q_2^*. The implication is that as the ratio of transportation costs to production costs rises, the minimum efficient scale will fall. This is why small, relatively inefficient plants producing such things as sand and gravel, cement, coal, or milk can be profitable when located near important markets. Conversely, when transportation costs are relatively insignificant (as for products such as breakfast cereal, computer chips, cigarette lighters, and ball-point pens), the tendency is for worldwide markets to be served from a few large-scale plants.

The Effect of Demand Expectations on Choice of Plant Size

So far, we have said that the optimally sized plant is the one with the lowest unit cost for a given level of output. This is something that can be estimated quite accurately. Unfortunately, however, it is not so easy to determine the most cost-effective way of producing the level of output that will satisfy the *expected demand* in the long run.

To illustrate the importance of expected demand upon plant selection, consider the probability distributions of demand illustrated in Exhibit 12–16. The exhibit shows two possible probability distributions of demand for the same product. In the two cases, the expected demand is the same—about 2,000 units. However, Distribution N shows a narrower range of deviation from the expected value than Distribution W.

EXHIBIT 12–15   **Effect of Transportation Costs on Minimum Efficient Scale**

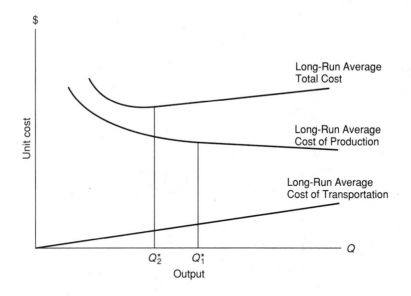

EXHIBIT 12–16   **Probability Distributions of Two Demand Functions with the Same Expected Value**

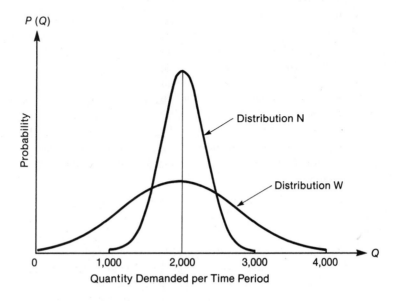

EXHIBIT 12–17   Average-Total-Cost Functions of Alternative Plants

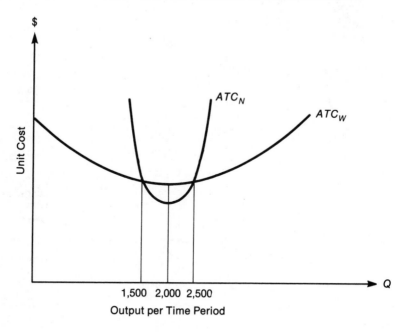

Now suppose that we have a choice of two different plants to produce 2,000 units, with average-total-cost curves as illustrated by Exhibit 12–17. As we see in the figure, Plant N, with ATC_N, is a highly mechanized (capital-intensive) plant designed to produce 2,000 units at its lowest unit cost. However, any deviation from this target output drives up costs very rapidly.

Plant W, with ATC_W, also achieves minimum average cost at a production level of 2,000 units. However, it is a more general design, so that deviations from the target level of production escalate costs more slowly. From the diagram, it is clear that production between 1,500 and 2,500 units is less costly in Plant N. Outside that narrow range, production is much less costly in Plant W.

Which plant should we choose? The answer depends upon the probability distribution of demand combined with the cost at various levels of output. An appropriate yardstick might be the expected average total cost. It can be calculated for each plant by multiplying the unit cost (ATC) at each level of production (within the contemplated range of production) by the probability of demand for that quantity, and then summing the results. In symbols,

$$E(ATC_i) = \sum_{j=1}^{n} P_{ij}ATC_{ij} \qquad (14)$$

where

$\quad E(ATC_i)$ = Expected average total cost of the ith plant design

$\qquad P_{ij}$ = Probability of demand for the jth level of production in the ith plant

$\quad ATC_{ij}$ = Average total cost (unit cost) at the jth level of production in the ith plant

$\qquad n$ = Number of output levels being considered.

This formula considers probable demand as well as cost behavior at various levels of production. With this information on hand for each plant design being considered, the most advantageous design soon becomes evident.

Learning Curves and Economies of Scale

For many (but not all) manufacturing and service-oriented activities, both managers and workers become more proficient as they gain experience with the production process. Managers find more efficient production procedures and better ways to use equipment. Workers gain in skill so that they work better and faster, reducing waste from defects, improving the quality of their output, and increasing the marginal product of labor. Empirical analysis has found that when periodic output, production technology, and input factor prices are held constant, the cost per unit tends to decline by a stable percentage, often around 20 percent, each time the cumulative output is doubled.

As the cumulative total output from a given level of input increases, the decline in unit costs is the effect of the firm's **experience factor**. The experience factor is defined as the ratio of unit cost (*ATC*) in the second time increment to the unit cost in the initial time increment; that is,

$$\text{Experience factor} = \frac{ATC_1}{ATC_0} \qquad (15)$$

where

ATC_0 = Unit cost during the initial time increment
ATC_1 = Unit cost during the next time increment.

Equation 15 assumes a constant level of periodic production during both time increments. Thus the cumulative production at the end of Increment 1 is double the cumulative production at the end of Increment 0. Increment 2, however, would be four times the length of the initial time increment, Increment 3 would be eight times as long, and so forth.

The firm's experience factor is reflected in the firm's **learning curve**. The learning curve can be expressed as a decaying exponential curve with the equation:

$$ATC_t = e^{kt}ATC_0 \qquad (16)$$

where

ATC_t = Unit cost during the *t*th time increment, where t = number of times cumulative output has doubled since production began
ATC_0 = Initial unit cost (average total cost during the initial time period, such as the first month)
e = Base of natural logarithms ($= 2.71828\ldots$)
k = The natural logarithm of the experience factor calculated by Equation 15.

Exhibit 12–18 (page 374) shows a learning curve in which unit cost is reduced by 20 percent each time the cumulative output is doubled. The learning curve reflects the fact that many improvements in production methods become obvious as soon as production begins and these improvements generally are readily implemented. As time goes by, additional improvements are harder to come by. Thus the learning curve shows a substantial

EXHIBIT 12–18   **A Typical Learning Curve in Which Unit Cost is Reduced by 20 Percent Each Time the Cumulative Output Is Doubled**

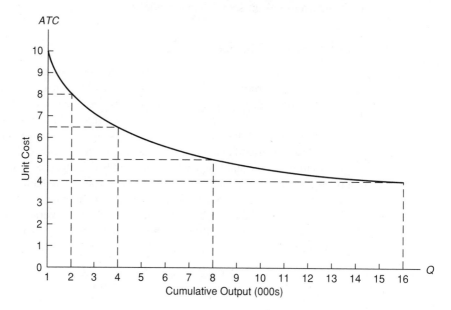

reduction in unit cost at the outset, with smaller and smaller cost reduction as the cumulative production grows larger.

Unfortunately, tracing the cost savings resulting from the learning curve is anything but an easy matter because there are so many other factors besides the experience factor that can affect unit costs. For example, technological improvements to increase productivity, such as the redesign of a component so that it takes less time to assemble, will tend to shift cost curves downward. Changes in input factor prices will tend to shift cost curves upward if prices increase or downward if prices decrease. Economies of scale also may be available if the level of periodic output increases.

In order to identify the learning curve, it must be possible to isolate its effects from the effects of these other factors by holding the other factors constant. For example, if the same number of units is output each month with plant and equipment that does not change and if input factor prices remain constant, then we can reasonably ascribe reductions in unit cost to the experience factor and the learning curve.

Illustrative Problem

During the initial month of production, the unit cost of a new product was $50. During the second month, the same level of monthly production has been maintained (which means that *cumulative* production has doubled), input-factor prices have remained constant, and there have been no technological improvements of the production process. By the end of the second month, unit cost has dropped to $40 as management and workers have gained experience in production of the product.

Question

Other things remaining constant, what unit cost can be expected by the end of the third month?

Solution

At the end of the second month, cumulative production has doubled over the initial month. Therefore, from Equation 15,

$$\text{Experience factor} = \frac{\$40}{\$50} = 0.8$$

meaning that for each time increment in which cumulative output is doubled, average unit costs will be 80 percent of average unit costs in the previous time increment.

At the end of the second month, cumulative output of the previous month has been doubled once. The second month's cumulative output will be doubled at the end of the fourth month. Therefore, at the end of the third month, the cumulative output will be doubled 1.5 times. By Equation 16,

$$ATC_{1.5} = e^{(1.5)(ln0.8)}(\$50) = e^{-0.3347}(\$50) = (0.7155)(\$50) = \$35.78.$$

Equation 16 makes use of the experience factor of Equation 15. The learning curve can also be expressed by an equation that uses the **learning rate**, which is the reciprocal of the experience factor, i.e., 1 minus the experience factor:

$$ATC = aQ^b \qquad (17)$$

where

Q = Cumulative volume of output

a = The initial unit cost; i.e., the average total cost of the first unit produced

b = The learning rate; i.e., the rate by which cost is changed each time cumulative production has doubled.[2]

Since Equation 17 is linear in its logarithms, linear regression of empirical data can be used to find the parameters a and b.

Illustrative Problem

The Jonesville Manufacturing Corporation began production of a new product 10 weeks ago, and has been producing 100 units per week. The company's cost-accounting records show the following unit costs of production:

---

[2] If cost is reduced when cumulative production has doubled, the exponent b will be a negative number.

Week	Cumulative Volume Q	Unit Cost ATC
1	100	$12.51
2	200	10.01
5	500	7.46
8	800	6.41
10	1,000	5.97

Question

What will the unit cost be when the cumulative production reaches 2,000?

Solution

$ATC = aQ^b$, hence $\log ATC = \log a + b \log Q$. Then by the least squares method of simple linear regression that was described in Chapter 7:

Logarithm of Cumulative Production log Q	Logarithm of Unit Cost log ATC	log Q × log ATC	(log Q)²
2.000000000	1.097257310	2.194514619	4.00000000
2.301029996	1.000434077	2.302028821	5.294739041
2.698970004	0.872738827	2.355495917	7.284439084
2.903089987	0.806858029	2.342381466	8.427931473
3.000000000	0.775974331	2.327922993	9.000000000
$\sum \log Q$ 12.90308999	$\sum \log ATC$ 4.553262575	$\sum \log Q \log ATC$ 11.52234382	$\sum (\log Q)^2$ 34.0071096

$$b = \frac{n \sum \log Q \log ATC - (\sum \log Q)(\sum \log ATC)}{n \sum (\log Q)^2 - (\sum \log Q)^2}$$

$$= \frac{5(11.52234382) - (12.90308999)(4.553262575)}{5(34.0071096) - (12.90308999)^2}$$

$$= \frac{-1.139437653}{3.54581671} = -0.321347025 \approx -0.3213$$

$$\log a = \frac{\sum \log ATC - b \sum \log Q}{n}$$

$$= \frac{4.553262575 - (-0.321347025)(12.90308999)}{5}$$

$$= \frac{8.699632157}{5} = 1.739926431 \approx 1.7399.$$

Since $\log ATC = \log a + b \log Q$,

$$ATC = 10^{1.739926431} Q^{-0.321347025}$$
$$= 54.94477905 \, Q^{-0.321347025}.$$

When $Q = 2,000$,

$$ATC = 54.94477905(2,000)^{-0.321347025}$$
$$= \$4.776945239 \approx \$4.78.$$

Learning by experience improves efficiency at all levels of production. Therefore, the effect of the learning curve on long-run average cost is similar to any other technological advance; that is, it shifts the *LRAC* curve downward. Since the effect of the learning curve is the same at all levels of production, the *LRAC* curve shifts downward in a parallel fashion.

Economic literature often describes the learning-curve concept as a cause of economies of scale, but this is a mistake. Although both economies of scale and the learning curve affect costs of production, they are two different concepts. Economies of scale are measured as movement along the *LRAC* as a change in the level of production per time period takes place. The effect of the experience factor is measured as the shift in the vertical position of the *LRAC* as the cumulative output increases over time while the level of production per time period remains constant.

The Learning Curve and Corporate Strategy

The learning curve is not applicable to all industries, but there can be important strategic implications in those specific industries where it does apply. In general, the firm has three avenues of competition open to it: price, product, and promotion. The learning process often leads to improvement of the product at no additional cost. The improvement may be one that makes the product more useful or more attractive to all potential buyers, or it may be a customized version that will sell for a higher price. Thus the learning curve can affect the firm's ability to compete on the basis of product quality. In today's markets, however (particularly in international markets), it will be of the most strategic importance if it enables the firm to compete primarily on the basis of price.[3]

To compete primarily on the basis of price, the firm must achieve costs that are lower than those of its competitors. This will not happen unless the cost reductions offered by the experience factor are substantial, i.e., 20 to 30 percent. This is much more apt to be the case in industries that are characterized by the development of many new products, the frequent modification of old products, or the frequent development of new production techniques, rather than in mature industries with stable and well-known production methods. Many such industries exist or are in the process of development in Japan, Korea, and Taiwan. The strategic importance of the learning curve will be even greater if the new products are standardized (as are semiconductors or generic drugs).

It is important to note that skillful management is necessary to obtain the benefits of the learning curve. Managers must monitor potential sources of increased productivity and

---

[3] The learning curve has nothing to do with promotional competition.

facilitate continuous feedback from workers who have been motivated to reduce costs. These are oft-noted attributes of the Japanese style of management, and the Japanese have used the experience factor with great skill in establishing prices for their products.

In the United States, some companies have established incentive-pay programs for increased productivity. The learning curve thus enables employees and employers to benefit together, as employees receive greater compensation and the firms that employ them realize greater profits.

Skillful management of the experience factor can enable a firm to achieve and maintain a position of dominant leadership in a given market. A firm that knows its costs will be reduced by 20 to 30 percent each time its cumulative production doubles can enter the market with a penetration price below its initial cost and below its competitors' costs. The lower price can increase the firm's market share and the larger volume gives the firm greater opportunity for learning. Thus the strategy contributes to its own success.

Summary

A thorough understanding of cost concepts is necessary for optimal allocation of resources to production, for product pricing, and for cost control. Costs can be classified in many different ways, and cost concepts differ considerably, depending upon who uses them.

The theory of cost is concerned with both short-run and long-run costs. Business firms always operate in the short run, and operational decision making is concerned with minimizing costs of variable inputs. Planning, however, is based on the concept that all inputs are variable in the long run.

Two factors determine the behavior of short-run costs: (1) the character of the underlying production function and (2) prices of the variable inputs. In analyzing the total-cost function, we develop and graph functions representing marginal cost, average fixed cost, average variable cost, and average total cost (which may also be called unit cost). The elasticity of cost measures the percent change in total cost that results from a 1 percent change in the quantity produced, which is also the ratio of marginal cost to average total cost, MC/ATC.

Economies of scale may be realized at either the plant level or the firm level. Within the constraints of existing technology, it is possible to construct an optimally sized plant for whatever level of production is desired. In choosing a plant size, the probability distribution of expected demand must be considered. If the probability distribution is confined to a narrow range, a specialized plant designed to produce the expected demand at lowest cost might be appropriate. But if the spread is wide, it might be better to design a more generalized plant to give reasonable, but not necessarily the lowest, cost over a wider range of output. An important determinant of plant location is the cost of transportation.

Long-run average cost ($LRAC$) may be used to determine the minimum efficient scale (MES) of a firm's plants. The MES is the size of the plant that incurs the lowest possible $LRAC$. Management must determine whether it will be more profitable to produce the firm's product in a single plant or in a number of plants, each of minimum efficient scale. In multiplant firms, economies of scale in areas of management, marketing, and finance may accrue to the firm in addition to those realized from plants of optimal size.

For many manufacturing activities, both managers and workers become more proficient as they gain experience with the production process. The learning curve is measured as the percentage by which costs are reduced each time cumulative production is doubled. Since it applies to all levels of production, the effect of the learning curve is a downward shift in the long-run average-cost curve.

Problems

1. Differentiate between incremental costs and sunk costs. Are all sunk costs fixed costs? Are all fixed costs sunk costs? Discuss.

2. In estimating the annual cost of owning a fully paid-for $15,000 automobile, you might show the following cost entry: "Interest on investment at 10 percent: $1,500." What would this mean? Explain.

3. Road-Ready Tire Company manufactures and sells about 1,000 tires a day at a unit cost of $16 and wholesale price of $25. The company has an unexpected opportunity to sell additional tires under private labels to three different retail outlets.

   1. Able's Auto Accessories offers to buy 1,000 tires for $23 each.

   2. Baker's Auto Accessories offers to buy 1,000 tires at $20 each.

   3. Charlie's Auto Accessories offers to buy 1,000 tires for $18 each.

   Road-Ready figures its unit costs on these additional tires to be $17 for the first 1,000 tires, $18 for the second 1,000 tires, and $19 for the third 1,000 tires.

   a. If there are no other considerations, which of these orders should Road-Ready agree to fill?

   b. What fundamental principles are involved here?

4. Until a year ago, Amy B. and Cora C. were employed by a photocopying and printing firm. Each of them received a salary of $20,000 per year. One year ago, they quit the firm to go into the photocopying business for themselves. Each of them put up $3,000 for working capital, which they agreed would be recovered from their first year's profits. They found a suitable location at a lease rent of $1,500 per month, and leased the necessary duplicating machines at an annual cost of $30,000. Business was very good during their first year, during which they spent $10,000 on supplies and other operating costs and took in $125,000 from sales.

   a. What were their explicit and implicit costs during their first year of operation?

   b. Assuming that neither woman has a strong preference for self-employment, should they remain in this business? Analyze and discuss their situation.

5. Six months ago, William N. opened a shop to manufacture advertising novelties. It took a month to locate and remodel a suitable building and install machinery and equipment, so actual manufacturing operations did not begin until the second month. William's records for the first six months showed the following output and total cost:

Month	Output Q	Total Cost TC
1	0	$3,000
2	1,000	9,000
3	1,100	9,600
4	1,050	9,300
5	1,075	9,450
6	1,080	9,480

   Use the data in the table to develop equations for *TC*, *TFC*, *TVC*, *AVC*, and *MC*.

6. Accuro Division of Metropolitan Instruments Company manufactures devices to measure blood pressure. Accuro's normal production rate is 260 units per week at a total cost of $3,200. At full capacity it can produce 340 units per week at a total cost of $3,800.

a. What is the average unit cost under normal operating conditions?

b. What is the average variable cost per unit?

c. What is the total fixed cost?

d. What is the average fixed cost per unit under normal operating conditions?

e. A British distributor offers to buy 50 units per week from Accuro over a one-month period, to be test-marketed in Europe under a different brand name. The distributor offers a price of $10 per unit. Should Accuro accept the offer? What is the least price Accuro should accept for this kind of arrangement?

7. The total-cost function of a neckwear-manufacturing company is $TC = 8 + 12Q - 6Q^2 + Q^3$, where TC = total cost in hundreds of dollars per month and Q = output in hundreds of ties produced per month.

a. What is the equation for average total cost?

b. What is the equation for average variable cost?

c. What is the equation for marginal cost?

d. Plot the total and fixed cost curves for $Q = 1$ through 5. Plot the ATC, AVC, and MC curves for these values of Q. Back up your graph with a complete cost schedule.

8. Dream Furniture Company has been experiencing operating losses in its plant for a number of months and the company's management is debating whether or not to shut down operations.

a. What cost factors should management consider for this decision?

b. Is there a difference between abandonment and shutdown?

c. Is it possible for the company to recover part of its plant cost while operating at a loss? (HINT: What is the role of depreciation and its influence on cash flow?)

9. The managers of a sheet-metal works that manufactures and installs ducting for air-conditioning systems has developed the following cost function:

$$TC = 24 + 4.5Q - 3Q^2 + 0.05Q^3$$

where Q = linear feet of standard ducting installed.

a. Determine the level of output at which ATC is minimized.

b. Determine the level of output at which AVC is minimized.

c. Prove that $MC = AVC$ at the level of output where AVC is minimum.

d. Calculate the cost elasticity of the production function.

10. Consider the classic cubic total-cost function. Assume that labor is the only variable input and the wage rate is constant. Then explain why both the average-variable-cost and marginal-cost curves are U-shaped.

11. Motivated by rapidly increasing costs of diesel fuel and by rather strong evidence that fuel economy depends upon vehicle speed, the Highway International Trucking Company has undertaken a study to determine the relationship between vehicle speed and fuel efficiency for its truck fleet. The bottom line of the study is an equation that relates miles per gallon, MPG, to the average speed in miles per hour, MPH:

$$MPG = 0.11MPH - 0.001MPH^2.$$

a. Find the optimal average speed to minimize fuel consumption.

b. The company estimates that diesel fuel will cost an average of $1 a gallon during the upcoming year. Calculate the fuel cost per mile if the fleet is driven at (1) the optimal average speed, (2) an average speed of 50 mph, and (3) an average speed of 60 mph.

c. The company's drivers are currently paid by the route, rather than by mileage or hours (within limitations, of course). However, a suggestion has been made to utilize a new compensation scheme in which drivers would be paid $15 per hour. Explain how each of these possible compensation arrangements (pay by the route, pay by the mile, and pay by the hour) is related to the previously determined optimal speed. (It is not necessary to find the precisely correct answer to the question, although a graph or an appropriately constructed table will help.)

Case Problem: L & S Freighters, Inc.

12. L & S Freighters, Inc., is a trucking company currently operating at full capacity. Its current equipment consists of 10 semitrailer rigs, each with a tractor and an almost-new 36-foot trailer. The company has an opportunity to increase its business by 10 percent, but will have to increase its capacity in order to accept the additional business. Capacity can be increased either by making more trips per day or by getting more payload per trip.

   The company finds that new 40-foot trailers sell for $20,000, but because of the size of the order and the good condition of its old trailers, the dealer will give a trade-in allowance of $10,000 per trailer. A new tractor of the size they need costs $80,000 when fully equipped.

Questions

   a. What are the company's alternatives?
   b. Discuss the pros and cons of each alternative.

Case Problem: Sealift Shipping Lines

13. Sealift is a container shipping company based in Singapore. Business is expanding, so management is investigating the purchase of new containers from a manufacturer in Japan. The present containers are cubic with a reinforced base and corrugated metal sides and top. They have 1,000 cubic feet of cargo space. The Japanese manufacturer reports that the reinforced base costs $7.00 per square foot and the corrugated metal costs $3.20 per square foot. The containers can be built in any size.

Questions

   a. What is the present cost of metal per cubic foot of cargo space?
   b. Management is considering building larger containers in hopes of reducing costs. Sketch a graph of metal cost as it relates to cargo space (assume a cubic container). What is the optimal size of a container?
   c. Discuss the problem of size. For example, how big do you build a warehouse, football stadium, or oil tanker?

Case Problem: Fertile Farm, Inc.

14. Fertile Farm, Inc., has fertilizer plants located throughout the United States. Its phosphate division in Oakland, California, is presently under review by top management. Last year's prices for raw phosphates climbed by over 60 percent to $0.75 per pound, and each bag of fertilizer contains four pounds of raw phosphates. The price rise is a result of environmental regulation levied on South Pacific island suppliers because of their strip-mining practices. However, since new deposits of phosphates have been recently discovered in Florida, it is unknown whether prices will continue to rise.

   Top management is attempting to find out how high phosphate prices can go before the Oakland fertilizer plant should shut down. To assist in this task, the accounting department has forecast the following costs for next year. Included is some important supplementary information.

	Annual Production (thousands of bags)		
Cost Forecast (× $1,000)	70	100	120[a]
Raw materials other than phosphates	$210	$300	$360
Variable manufacturing costs[b]	145	195	280
Fixed costs:			
Insurance	20	20	20
Property taxes	12	12	12
Depreciation (building, equipment, and other)[c]	50	50	50
Maintenance[d]	70	70	70
Cost of capital[e]	86	86	86
Totals	$593	$733	$878

[a] Maximum production capacity is 120,000 bags per year.

[b] A charge of $0.30 per bag is included for depreciation of processing machinery. The machinery originally cost $360,000 and had an estimated life of 12 years if production averaged 100,000 bags per year. With four years of useful life remaining, the market value of the machinery is only $25,000, but to replace it would cost $600,000.

[c] This is a 10 percent annual write-off. The actual deterioration of these assets is not related to production, but is based on time and obsolescence factors. Present market value is $150,000, with four years of useful life remaining. Replacement cost is expected to be $600,000.

[d] One-third of this amount is required whether or not the plant is operating.

[e] Fertile Farm requires a 10 percent return on investment.

Because of low farm prices and a very competitive fertilizer market, the price of Fertile Farm's phosphate fertilizer is expected to remain at $11.25 per bag for the foreseeable future. If management should decide to shut down, plant engineers estimate $10,000 in additional costs. Another factor in management's decision is a land-use hearing presently in the courts. If Fertile Farms wins the case, the plant's waterfront property can be rezoned from industrial to commercial, increasing its value from $500,000 to $2,400,000.

Questions

a. Using the available cost figures, prepare a report for next year that analyzes the cost of shutting down for one year. Use this cost to show the break-even price that could be paid for phosphates at each level of production. Be explicit with regard to all costs.

b. What conclusions can be drawn from your cost analysis? Discuss other factors involved in the shutdown decision.

c. Because of the questionable returns of its phosphate division, management is considering termination of the Oakland facility. Assess the plant's profitability, assuming that phosphate prices remain stable. Should the facility be terminated?

d. What effect would the land-use ruling have on your decision?

Case Problem: Performance Motors Inc. (PMI)

15. PMI specializes in automobile modification. Recently it received a contract from a large Detroit auto manufacturer to modify 1,500 stock cars with a high-performance package that will increase the cars' horsepower and handling capabilities. For meeting the terms of the contract PMI will receive $2,150 per car.

The chief accountant for PMI has spent a week going over the contract and estimates the following costs:

1. Direct labor: 33,000 hours at $18 per hour.
2. Parts needed from existing inventories originally cost $325,000. However, current replacement costs are $410,000.

3. Additional necessary parts will be purchased at a cost of $750,000.
4. A calibrated cylinder resurfacer will be required to increase engine compression. The machine rents for $65,000 for the life of the contract.
5. To finance the six-month project, PMI will need a loan of $600,000. PMI's current credit rating results in an interest rate of 12 percent.
6. To consult on the project, a renowned Italian race-car designer will be brought in at a cost of $39,000.
7. Variable overhead costs are allocated to projects by a $5 charge per direct labor hour.
8. To obtain the required return on capital, standard procedure at PMI is to charge enough for a 75 percent profit margin on both direct labor costs and the purchase price of all materials used.

Slumping U.S. auto sales over the past few years have resulted in excessive capacity at PMI. Thus acceptance of this contract will not interrupt present or future production schedules.

Questions

a. Which costs are relevant to PMI's decision? Is each cost explicit or implicit?

b. Should PMI accept or reject the auto-modification contract?

c. Assume that the oil glut, through its effect in reducing gas prices, has spurred the demand for powerful, high-performance cars. PMI now has contracts to maintain production capacity for over two years. Under these conditions, have the relevant costs changed? Should PMI accept or reject the contract?

Case Problem: Shadow Screen Inc.

16. Shadow Screen Inc., located in Los Angeles, manufactures shadow screens for color-television sets made in the United States, the United Kingdom, West Germany, and the Far East. Output of its Los Angeles plant is exported to many Asian locales, such as Singapore, Hong Kong, and Korea, but not to Japan. Because of its rising labor costs in the United States and increasing de-

mand for its products in Asia, the management of Shadow Screen has decided to establish a manufacturing unit in Singapore, to be operational by the end of this year. Shadow Screen's industrial engineers estimate the cost function of the new plant to be

$$TC = 800,000 + 40Q + 0.0025Q^2$$

in U.S. dollars, where

TC = Total cost
Q = Units of production.

Although Shadow Screen is a leader in the worldwide market, it is facing increasing competition in the Asian market from several French, German, and Japanese newcomers. Market demand in Asia is expected to be 200,000 units next year, and is expected to grow 20 percent annually for the next five years. Shadow Screen expects to sell 15,000 units next year, and to maintain its share of the market as it grows thereafter.

Questions

a. What is the expected total cost and average cost for sales of 15,000 units?

b. Calculate the output level that will yield the lowest average total cost, or maximum efficient production scale (MEPS).

c. In order to maintain a profit margin of 25 percent at a production level of 15,000 units, what price should be charged? What is the expected profit?

d. With a 20 percent annual increase in sales, when will the firm reach maximum efficient production scale (MEPS); that is, the minimum average total cost?

e. Estimate Shadow Screen's market share and the most efficient market share for next year. (HINT: Most efficient market share = MEPS/industry sales.) Determine the potential for future competition in the industry.

f. Assume that the estimated cost function is subject to a standard error of ±$85,000. What is the probability of holding cost below $2 million next year?

References

Abernathy, W. J., and K. Wayne. "Limits of the Learning Curve." *Harvard Business Review*, 52 (September-October 1974), pp. 109–19.

Anthony, Robert N. "What Should 'Cost' Mean?" *Harvard Business Review* (May-June 1970), pp. 121–31.

Bassett, Lowell. "Returns to Scale and Cost Curves." *Southern Economic Journal* (October 1969), pp. 189–90.

Berndt, Ernst R., and Catherine J. Morrison. "Capacity Utilization Measures: Underlying Economic Theory and an Alternative Approach." *American Economic Review* (May 1981), pp. 48–52.

Ghemawat, Pankaj. "Building Strategy on the Experience Curve." *Harvard Business Review*, 63 (March-April 1985), pp. 143–49.

Hubbard, L. J, and P. J. Dawson. "Ex Ante and Ex Post Long-Run Average Cost Functions," *Applied Economics*, 19, no. 10 (October 1987), p. 1411.

Koot, Ronald S., and David A. Walker. "Short-Run Cost Functions of a Multiproduct Firm." *Journal of Industrial Economics* (April 1970), pp. 118–28.

McElroy, F. W. "Return to Scale of Cost Curves: Comment." *Southern Economic Journal* (October 1970), pp. 227–28.

Miller, Edward, M. "The Extent of Economies of Scale: The Effect of Firm Size on Labor Productivity and Wage Rates." *Southern Economic Journal* (January 1978), pp. 470–87.

Revier, Charles F. "The Elasticity of Scale, the Shape of Average Costs, and the Envelope Theorem." *American Economic Review*, 77, no. 3 (June 1987), p. 486.

Shephard, A. Ross. "A Note on the Firm's Long-Run Average Cost Curve." *Quarterly Review of Economics and Business* (Spring 1971), pp. 77–79.

Walters, A. A. "Production and Cost Functions: An Econometric Survey." *Econometrics* (January-April 1963), pp. 1–66.

C H A P T E R

13

EMPIRICAL ESTIMATION OF COST FUNCTIONS

Empirical studies of cost functions are undertaken in order to project current and past costs into future operations. Empirical studies may be used to project either short-run or long-run cost functions. Knowledge of the firm's *short-run* cost function is essential for current operational decisions, such as finding the most efficient level of production or pricing output. Knowledge of the firm's *long-run* cost function is essential for proper planning of the firm's future operations. It provides a guide to economies of scale and the optimum size for both the plant and the firm.

CHAPTER OUTLINE

In this chapter, we shall discuss the techniques and problems associated with empirical cost measurement for a firm or group of firms, in both the short run and the long run. The chapter is divided into two sections:

1. **Estimation of Short-Run Cost Functions.** This section discusses methods and some of the problems of estimating short-run cost functions and some results of short-run cost studies.
2. **Estimation of Long-Run Costs.** This section discusses the purposes of long-run cost studies, the methods and problems of empirical estimation of long-run costs, and some results of actual long-run cost studies.

Estimation of Short-Run Cost Functions

The analysis of short-run costs reveals how a firm's costs vary in response to changes in output within a time span short enough that the size of the plant may be regarded as fixed.

Methods of Estimation

The two basic methods by which an analysis of short-run costs can be undertaken are the econometric or statistical approach and the engineering approach.[1]

Econometric or Statistical Approach.   The statistical approach combines regression analysis with economic theory to measure the net effect of output variations on cost. The basic assumption is that the firm has been operating efficiently, or at least that inefficiencies can be isolated. Frequently the goal is to construct a cost function from time-series or cross-sectional data that will reflect as closely as possible the static cost curve of economic theory. However, since the empirical curve is at best only an average of past relationships, it is not an exact replica of the theoretical cost curves.

Engineering Method.   In the engineering approach, emphasis is placed primarily on the nature of physical relationships such as pounds of supplies and materials used, or rated capacity. These relationships are then converted into dollars to arrive at an estimate of costs. This method uses data about the firm's production facilities and technology to determine the most efficient combination of raw materials, capital equipment, and labor for various levels of production. "Most efficient" means "at the lowest unit cost." In determining a firm's most efficient cost structure, the engineering method charges each unit of output with costs that *ought* to be incurred rather than with costs that have actually occurred in the past. Hence this is the method used to establish standard costs for cost-accounting purposes. This method may also be particularly useful when good historical data are difficult or impossible to obtain.

These approaches to cost measurement should not be regarded as mutually exclusive or even competitive, but rather as supplementary or complementary to one another. As always, the emphasis placed on any method depends on the purpose of the investigation (i.e., what it is that management really wants?), time and expense considerations, and the availability of data.

Understanding the Essentials of Cost Measurement

Our aim in developing a cost function is to quantify the relationship between a firm's costs and its rate of output. The cost function may be expressed mathematically as an equation or graphically as a cost curve.

---

[1] Cost accountants may recognize five ways of approximating cost functions: (1) industrial engineering, (2) account analysis, (3) visual fit, (4) regression analysis, and (5) high–low method. Closer examination reveals, however, that account analysis is a method of preparing data for regression analysis, and the visual fit and high–low methods are simply crude shortcuts for fitting a regression line to cost data.

If the shape of the cost curve depended solely on the rate of output, solving the problem would be fairly simple. In reality, however, costs depend on a number of factors in addition to output. Therefore it is necessary to understand what costs are to be included and how they are measured in order to arrive at a cost function that reasonably expresses the cost–output relation.

Measurement Procedures.   Generally speaking, three preliminary activities must take place before a cost function can be derived empirically from available data: (1) an appropriate time period for study must be chosen; (2) technical homogeneity must be assured; and (3) the cost data must be adjusted if necessary. [2]

Time Period of Measurement.   The choice of an appropriate time period on which to base the analysis involves three important considerations: *normality, variation of output,* and the *observational time unit* chosen.

Normality. The time period chosen for analysis should be a **normal** or typical one for the firm, so far as this is possible. This means that the period covered should be one that was reasonably static; i.e., one in which changes in technology, plant size, efficiency, and other dynamic occurrences that may have a significant bearing on costs were either nonexistent or at least at a minimum. Admittedly, a completely static period is probably impossible to find. Still, a period in which changes were relatively minor is acceptable if the data can be adjusted in a compensatory manner. If compensatory data adjustment is not possible, the cost function will not reflect the typical type of cost behavior desired.

Variation of Output. The time period chosen for observation should be one in which there were sufficiently wide variations in output to obtain enough observations for a regression analysis. Furthermore, if the results are to be used as a guide for future planning, the selected period should be as recent as possible. Generally speaking, the more recent the data, the more relevant they are for future planning. On the other hand, if the normality conditions stated in the preceding paragraph are satisfied, a longer period may be statistically preferable.

The Observational Time Unit. Within the time period chosen for analysis, observations will be made in **observational time units**, such as a day, week, month, quarter, or year. The observational time unit should be the shortest unit of time (within the time period chosen for analysis) in which complete data can be collected. An observational time unit of a week or a month will allow measurement of slight variations of output more readily than will a quarter or a year. Further, the cause-and-effect relationship between output and cost is easier to see in the shorter observational time units. A month is often the time unit chosen in cost studies, although analyses have also been conducted using quarterly or annual data.

Technical Homogeneity. If production conditions change, significant cost variations may result. Changes in production conditions may involve raw materials, equipment, the

---

[2] These procedures pertain to the investigation of long-run as well as short-run costs.

frequency of production lags, and so forth. Since changes of this kind can contaminate the study data, the plant chosen for a statistical cost analysis should be characterized by input and output structures that are as **technically homogeneous** as possible.

On the *input* side, "technically homogeneous" means that input factors can be measured by identical or very similar units within factor classes. For example, if a small machine is replaced by one of larger capacity when output rises above a certain level, this change will introduce a variation in average fixed cost.

On the *output* side, technical homogeneity has two requirements. First, the number of different products produced should be small enough to facilitate measurement. Second, these products should not undergo significant cost changes (due, for example, to changes in composition or style) during the period of analysis. If these conditions of output homogeneity are not met, it may be necessary to construct a weighted index of output for products or classes of products according to some logical criterion. For example, in a cost study performed for a manufacturer, the weights used for the output index were the direct labor costs of specific products.

Various techniques are available for measuring output. For example, in a study of production costs for steel, it was found that inventory fluctuations (the difference between production and shipments) were relatively small. Consequently, tons shipped rather than tons produced was found to be a more useful measurement of output.

In a cost analysis of a men's-clothing factory, square feet of woolen cloth of a specific grade used in production was chosen as the measure of output as well as input. Conversion coefficients for other types of materials used by the company were derived from the woolen-cloth measurement.

Cost-Data Adjustment.   Decisions about the proper choice of data and the types of adjustments needed to correct the data must be made if they are to be recast into a meaningful cost function. The problem as a whole breaks down into three parts: *cost inclusion, deflation*, and *cost–output timing*.

Cost Inclusion. Since the object of cost analysis is to arrive at a cost–output relation, only those elements of cost that vary with (are functionally related to) output should be included. Thus, factory overhead, which has a functional relationship to production, might be included. Company overhead, which has no direct connection to production of the product, would not be included in the cost of production.[3]

Sometimes a series of preliminary correlations must be made to determine which costs should and should not be included in the final analysis. Simple linear regression can be used to determine strength of correlation between input and output, from which inferences can be drawn about the correlation between input costs and total cost.

For example, suppose we want to study the cost of manufacturing television sets. A regression analysis of $Y = f(X)$, where X = the input of picture tubes and Y =

---

[3] After the unit cost of production has been determined, company overhead may be arbitrarily allocated to the various products to determine a fully allocated unit cost for the purpose of pricing the products.

the output of television sets would undoubtedly reveal a 1:1 correlation between X and Y.[4] This would indicate that the cost of picture tubes should be included. In contrast, if X = the company president's salary and Y = the output of television sets, a regression analysis would show little or no correlation, indicating that the company president's salary should not be included.

It should be mentioned that results are likely to be more reliable in most statistical cost analyses when total costs rather than average costs are used. Marginal-cost and average-cost functions can be readily derived mathematically from the total-cost function if desired, or the marginal- and average-cost figures can be derived by simple arithmetic if a cost table or schedule is constructed from the total-cost equation.

Deflation. In the construction of empirical cost functions, the data must often be "reduced" or "deflated" to a particular base period if the results are to be meaningful. Wages and equipment price indexes are readily available and are frequently used for such purposes, or analysts may construct their own indexes if it seems desirable. In any event, the purpose of deflating the data is to adjust for significant inflationary changes in input prices during the period of analysis.

Cost–Output Timing. A third area of cost-data adjustment addresses the problem of obtaining the correct correspondence of cost and output. Costs are not normally recorded in the books of account in such a manner that they can be readily associated with output variations. Technical engineering estimates usually are necessary if the correct timing associations are to be established between cost and output.[5] Of particular importance in this respect are certain costs that are usually charged as a function of time, such as depreciation (which is often calculated on a straight-line basis). These costs, or portions thereof, should first be adjusted or recalculated as a function of the output rate before being incorporated in the overall cost function.

Decision Making and Relevant Costs. Some of the difficulties encountered during statistical cost analysis stem from an inaccurate identification of relevant costs. Since managerial decision making is future-oriented, the only relevant costs are future costs. Historical costs available in a firm's records may point to the future, but they may have to be modified before they can be used for decision making.

It is also important to recognize that opportunity costs—not recorded on company accounts—have an important bearing on the future. Indeed, opportunity costs may be the largest and most important consideration in a short-run decision problem. That is to say, what the firm won't do but could do might be the key issue.

---

[4] The correlation of 1:1 is based upon the fact that one picture tube is required for the manufacture of one TV set. If, however, there is some breakage of picture tubes involved, total production may require more than one picture tube per TV set.

[5] Some costs lead or lag the corresponding output. Consider, for example, the maintenance of machinery, buildings, and equipment. When production peaks at or near full capacity, routine maintenance may be deferred until a slack period occurs. When this maintenance finally is performed (during the first slack period), its cost properly belongs to the earlier period of high output. Charging maintenance costs elsewhere would result in a distortion of the cost function.

Statistical Method of Cost Estimation

The statistical method of cost estimation can be explained by the following illustrative problem.

Illustrative Problem

The HyTech Toy Company, located in Hong Kong, is a manufacturer of innovative electronic recreational products for both children and adults. The company produces a variety of video games and battery-operated remote-controlled toy automobiles, boats, and airplanes in a number of price ranges. The company's records show the following sales and cost data for the past five years.

Sales ($1,000)	Total Fixed Cost ($1,000)	Total Variable Cost ($1,000)	Total Cost ($1,000)
250	50	100	150
275	55	118	173
300	60	150	210
280	60	112	172
315	65	142	207

Questions

a. How is output being measured?
b. What assumptions must the company make if it wants to use the data to estimate its cost function?
c. Estimate the firm's cost function by linear regression.
d. Interpret the regression equation. How much is the firm's profit?

Solutions

a. Because of the variety of products and the range of prices for individual products, output is being measured by the dollar value of sales.
b. The company must assume that the costs were incurred with a constant technology and within such a narrow range of output that a linear cost function will provide a reasonable estimate of costs.
c. Only the data on sales (the independent variable) and total cost (the dependent variable) are required for the linear regression. When these data are input to a linear-regression program on a computer, the results are as shown in the table on the following page. The computer printout provides the regression equation:

$$TC = 0.985(S) - 97.231$$

with $r^2 = .9163$, meaning that 91.6 percent of total cost is accounted for by production and sales.

```
----------------------REGRESSION ANALYSIS------------------------

HEADER DATA FOR: A: HYTECH TOY              LABEL:
NUMBER OF CASES: 5    NUMBER OF VARIABLES: 2

-----------------------------------------------------------------

INDEX       NAME              MEAN          STD.DEV.
  1         sales           284.0000        24.8495
DEP. VAR.:  cost            182.4000        25.5597

-----------------------------------------------------------------

DEPENDENT VARIABLE: cost

VAR.   REGRESSION COEFFICIENT   STD. ERROR   T(DF=  3)    PROB.
sales             .9846            .1718       5.732     .01054
CONSTANT        -97.2308

STD. ERROR OF EST. = 8.5365

          r SQUARED = .9163
                  r = .9573

            ANALYSIS OF VARIANCE TABLE

SOURCE          SUM OF SQUARES   D.F.    MEAN SQUARE   F RATIO  PROB.
REGRESSION         2394.5846       1     2394.5846     32.860   .0105
RESIDUAL            218.6154       3       72.8718
TOTAL              2613.2000       4
```

d. Since the sales and cost data are both in thousands of dollars, the regression equation may be interpreted as saying that the firm's total cost will be 98.5 percent of sales minus $97,231. Since profit equals total revenue minus total cost,

$$\pi = S - TC = S - [0.985(S) - 97.231] = 0.015(S) + 97.231$$

thousands of dollars which may be interpreted as saying that profit will be $97,231 plus 1.5 percent of sales.

The preceding problem illustrates that statistical analysis of cost data proceeds in two major steps.

Step 1.   Gather, Classify, and Tabulate Data.   As we have just seen, the selection and adjustment of relevant data, the choice of appropriate time periods, and the problem of technical homogeneity are very real and necessary concerns. Once these considerations

EXHIBIT 13–1   Development of Cost Schedules

(1) Output (units) Q	(2) Total Cost TC	(3) Total Fixed Cost TFC	(4) Total Variable Cost TVC	(5) Average Total Cost $ATC = TC/Q$	(6) Average Variable Cost $AVC = TVC/Q$	(7) Marginal Cost $MC = \Delta TVC/\Delta Q$
0	$100	$100	$0	—	—	—
50	230	100	130	$4.60	$2.60	$2.60
100	285	100	185	2.85	1.85	1.10
150	360	100	260	2.40	1.73	1.50
·	·	·	·	·	·	·
·	·	·	·	·	·	·
·	·	·	·	·	·	·
500	890	100	790	1.78	1.58	1.51

have been addressed and adequate data have been gathered on output and associated costs, the analyst's next task is to develop cost schedules like the one illustrated in Exhibit 13–1.

The first three columns in Exhibit 13–1 contain the empirical data gathered by the analyst. Column 1 contains the level of output, arranged in ascending order. Column 2 contains the total cost associated with each level of output. Column 3 contains the fixed cost, which by definition does not change with the level of output. Column 4 contains the total variable cost, which equals $TC - TFC$. The remaining columns are easily calculated from these data by the formulas shown in the exhibit.

Step 2.   Derive an Appropriate Cost Function.   The complete table in Exhibit 13–1 is, of course, a presentation in tabular form of a set of *discrete* cost functions. What we want, however, is a set of *continuous* cost functions in the form of equations and graphs from which future costs at any level of production may be estimated. Once the preliminary considerations are out of the way, there remains the problem of choosing the type of equation or curve that seems to fit the data best, justified as much as possible by economic theory.

With a table of data as illustrated by Exhibit 13–1, equations can be developed for total cost, average variable cost, or marginal cost as a function of total output, i.e., $TC = f(Q)$, $AVC = TC/Q$, or $MC = \Delta TVC/\Delta Q$. Since there is only one independent variable, the analyst may choose to fit the data to a linear, quadratic, cubic, or power function by the least squares techniques described in Chapter 11. The choice of one curve or the other depends upon how well the mathematical properties of the function represent the economics of the particular case. If there is no particular reason for choosing one over the others, the data might be fitted to all four curves to see which one gives the best fit.

In some cases, the objective of cost analysis might be to develop an equation for total cost as a function of the output quantities of several products, i.e., $TC = f(Q_1, Q_2, \ldots, Q_n)$. Multiple regression can be used to fit a straight line or a power curve to the data, but not a quadratic or cubic curve.

Illustrative Problem

The Plimpton Manufacturing Plant No. 1 has a capacity of 1,000 units per month. During the past nine months, output has varied between 80 and 95 percent of capacity. At the lower levels of production, the productivity of its skilled work force has held variable costs to a minimum, but at higher production levels variable costs have risen as a result of the hiring of less skilled workers and payment for some overtime work.

Variable costs include direct costs of material and labor plus indirect costs or factory overhead. Fixed costs exclusive of factory overhead have remained at a constant $10,000 per month. Fifty percent of the factory overhead and 80 percent of direct costs are for wages. The company's records show the following production-cost data:

Month	Output (units)	Direct Cost	Factory Overhead
1	800	$ 8,000	$1,600
2	825	8,500	1,600
3	850	9,000	1,700
4	850	8,800	1,660
5	850	8,800	1,680
6	900	9,500	1,800
7	950	10,000	2,000
8	900	10,350	2,240
9	850	9,000	2,000

The company has just signed a new contract with the union that grants a 10 percent increase in wages. The company plans to maintain production at 85 percent of capacity throughout the coming year and it expects fixed costs to remain the same.

Question

What can the company expect the new unit cost to be?

Solution

The first step is to adjust the recorded variable data to reflect the anticipated increase in labor costs. Let

$$DC_1 = \text{Direct cost previously recorded}$$
$$DC_2 = \text{Direct cost after the wage increase.}$$

Then, since 80 percent of direct cost is for wages and wages will be increased by 10 percent, wages will be $1.1(0.8)DC_1$, while the remainder of the direct cost is unchanged, at $0.2DC_1$:

$$DC_2 = (1.1)(0.8)DC_1 + (0.2)DC_1 = 0.88DC_1 + 0.2DC_1 = 1.08DC_1.$$

By similar reasoning, the factory overhead (semivariable costs), FO_2, can be calculated as

$$FO_2 = (1.1)(0.5)FO_1 + (0.5)FO_1 = 0.55FO_1 + 0.5FO_1 = 1.05FO_1$$

and

$$TVC = DC_2 + FO_2.$$

When these factors are applied to the data previously given, we get the following table:

Output (units) Q	Direct Cost DC	Factory Overhead FO	Total Variable Cost TVC
800	$ 8,640	$1,680	$10,320
825	9,180	1,680	10,860
850	9,720	1,785	11,505
850	9,504	1,743	11,247
850	9,504	1,764	11,268
900	10,260	1,890	12,150
950	10,800	2,100	12,900
900	11,178	2,352	13,530
850	9,720	2,100	11,820

When the output and total-variable-cost data are input to a linear-regression program on a computer, the output is as follows:

```
---------------------------REGRESSION ANALYSIS---------------------------

HEADER DATA FOR: A: PLIMPTON MFG. PLANT NO. 1    LABEL:
NUMBER OF CASES: 9    NUMBER OF VARIABLES: 2

-------------------------------------------------------------------

INDEX      NAME          MEAN            STD.DEV
  1         Q          863.8889          45.2616
DEP. VAR.:  TVC       11733.3333       1002.2261

-------------------------------------------------------------------
DEPENDENT VARIABLE: TVC

VAR.   REGRESSION COEFFICIENT   STD. ERROR   T(DF=  7)    PROB.
Q              19.5153             3.9545       4.935     .00168
CONSTANT      -5125.6780

STD. ERROR OF EST. = 506.2508

        r SQUARED = .7767
          r = .8813

          ANALYSIS OF VARIANCE TABLE

SOURCE          SUM OF SQUARES   D.F.      MEAN SQUARE    F RATIO  PROB.
REGRESSION       6241628.8136     1       6241628.8136   24.354 1.685E-03
RESIDUAL         1794029.1864     7        256289.8838
TOTAL            8035658.0000     8
```

The computer printout shows a total-variable-cost function of

$$TVC = 19.5153Q - 5125.678.$$

Production at 85 percent of capacity will be 850 units per month, for which the total variable cost will be approximately

$$TVC = 19.5153(850) - 5125.678 = \$11,462.33.$$

Total cost will be

$$TC = TVC + TFC = \$11,462.33 + \$10,000 = \$21,462.33$$

and the unit cost will be

$$ATC = TC/Q = 21,462.33/850 = \$25.25.$$

Empirical Short-Run Cost Studies

Since the 1930s, economists have conducted many studies of short-run cost functions in widely differing industries. Most studies used time-series data. Some used engineering data. Regardless of the method used or the kind of industry that was investigated, the same conclusions were reached:

1. Most short-run cost functions are linear over the normal range of output. That is to say, short-run marginal costs are constant while short-run average total costs decline slightly in the normal range of output.
2. While some U-shaped marginal- and average-cost curves exist, they seem to be the exception rather than the rule. This is illustrated by Exhibit 13–2 (page 396), which shows the results of some studies that employed statistical analysis of time-series data.

Reasons for Apparent Linear Cost Functions.   Eight of the 15 studies listed in Exhibit 13–2 found clear evidence of a linear cost function. Do studies such as these invalidate the theoretical curvilinear cost functions that were discussed in Chapter 12? Not at all. There are several reasons why the true underlying curvilinear cost function may not be apparent in an empirical investigation.

Slight Curvature of the True Function.   If the true function is curvilinear but the curvature is slight, the fact that the line actually bends may not be detected because of random scatter or an insufficient number of observation points. This is no cause for concern. As Joel Dean reported in his study of a department store:

> The unexplained scatter of observations is great enough to permit a cubic of the traditional form to be fitted in each case. However, the curvature would be so slight as to be insignificant from a managerial viewpoint, so that it could scarcely affect any economic conclusions which might be derived from the linear functions. [6]

---

[6] Joel Dean, *Managerial Economics* (Englewood Cliffs, N.J.: Prentice-Hall, 1951), p. 254.

EXHIBIT 13–2   Some Empirical Investigations of Short-Run Costs

Investigator(s)	Date	Type of Industry	Findings
Broster	1938	Railways in United Kingdom	Operating cost per unit of output falls
Dean	1936	Furniture	Constant MC, $SRAC$ "failed to rise"
Dean	1941	Leather belts	No significant increase in MC
Dean	1941	Hosiery	Constant MC, $SRAC$ "failed to rise"
Dean	1942	Department store	MC declining in one department, constant in two
Ehrke	1933	Cement	Ehrke interprets as constant MC, but Apel (1948) argues that MC is increasing
Eiteman and Guthrie	1952	Manufacturing	MC below AC at all outputs below capacity
Ezekiel and Wylie	1941	Steel	Declining MC, but large standard errors
Hall and Hitch	1939	Manufacturing	Majority have decreasing MC
Johnston	1960	Electricity in United Kingdom	ATC falls, then flattens, tending toward constant MC up to capacity
Johnston	1960	Multiple food-products processing	Direct cost is linear; MC is constant
Lester	1946	Manufacturing	AVC decreases up to capacity levels of output
Mansfield and Wein[a]	1958	Railways in United Kingdom	Constant MC
Nordin	1947	Light plant	Increasing MC
Yntema	1940	Steel	Constant MC

Source: A.A. Walters, "Production and Cost Functions: An Econometric Survey" *Econometrica,* January 1963, pp. 1–66.

[a] Used engineering method rather than time-series analysis.

Plant Design.   In actual production systems, plants are designed to operate within a narrow range of normal output. Within this range, the use of capital inputs may be matched with variable inputs in such a way that a fairly constant ratio is maintained. For example, a manufacturing firm can increase production by setting up an additional assembly line in which the ratio of capital (fixed factor) to labor (variable factor) remains constant. In other words, there is a variable employment of the fixed factor; hence the rate of usage of each unit of capital is almost constant regardless of the level of production. Under such circumstances, the law of diminishing returns does not hold. The marginal cost of output remains constant, and a linear cost function is the result.[7]

---

[7] Researchers advancing this explanation make a distinction between variable employment of the fixed factor (a short-run concept) and variable magnitude of the fixed factor (a long-run concept). For example, a large enough floor area can be used for either one or two assembly lines in the short run.

Normal Range of Operation.   Finally, we have to consider that these studies covered only those periods in which the firm was operating in its normal range of output. No observations were included at very low or very high levels. If the firm were operating at or near capacity, a very rapid increase in marginal costs could be expected. As the firm attempts to get more production out of its fixed facilities:

1. It is likely that wage premiums will have to be paid either for overtime or for additional shifts. A third shift, especially, not only draws higher wages but also is less productive than a day shift.
2. As the equipment is used more intensively, it breaks down more often, running up maintenance costs and creating hangups in production.
3. Marginal or obsolete equipment may have to be used.
4. Hiring standards may have to be lowered to get enough labor.

In other words, everything the firm does to squeeze out the last ounce of capacity has to be done less efficiently and at greater cost. This conclusion has been supported by surveys of manufacturing firms concerning the rate at which they would prefer to operate. Most firms respond that they prefer to operate in the neighborhood of 90 percent of capacity. Apparently, these firms expect to achieve optimum efficiency—and therefore minimum average total cost—at about 90 percent of capacity. The clear implication is that getting the last 10 percent would cause marginal and average costs to rise.

Estimation of Long-Run Costs

Planning for the future requires a study of long-run costs to determine whether or not management has achieved an optimal scale of plant for the technology to be used. Long-run cost studies are particularly important for three purposes:

1. Expansion Decision.   Appropriate expansion enables the firm to obtain a more efficient base of operation with lower unit costs. (Refer to Exhibit 12–11 in the preceding chapter.) Lower unit costs enable a reduced output price that will make the firm more competitive.

2. Merger Decision.   Long-run cost behavior can help management to decide on the advisability of a merger. As already noted, a firm that expects economies of scale as a result of expanding its base of operations has a positive incentive to do so as long as the costs of such expansion do not exceed the benefits obtained. The long-run cost curve can at least serve as a guide in arriving at an answer.

3. Evaluation of Economic Efficiency.   Another reason for studying the individual firm's long-run cost behavior is that economies of scale are apt to become the crucial issue leading to federal-government approval or disapproval of mergers of large firms. In the general climate of deregulation, the current practice of the Antitrust Division of the U.S. Dept. of Justice with respect to mergers is much more relaxed than it has been in the past. Nevertheless, if a potential merger can be shown to result in an unfair competitive advantage owing to anticipated cost savings, the Antitrust Division may step in to bar the arrangement.

Conversely, the federal government will be likely to approve the merger or expansion of large companies when it feels the public interest will be served. For example, joint research by IBM and Motorola to produce high-definition television (on which the Japanese are also working) has been partially funded by the U.S. government, presumably in the belief that the joint effort for more economic efficiency will make the firms more competitive in the international marketplace.

Another example is the recent formation of a consortium by three of the nation's top research institutions: International Business Machines Corporation (IBM), American Telephone & Telegraph Company (AT&T), and the Massachusetts Institute of Technology (MIT). These three have invited other companies to join them in research leading to commercial applications of high-temperature superconductors, apparently with the approval of the U.S. government.

The economies of scale wrought by an integrated telephone system, the formation of the quasi-public Amtrak passenger rail system, and the "rescue" from bankruptcy of several aerospace and air carrier concerns through mergers provide examples of government-approved expansion of already large enterprises. Furthermore, the breaking up of General Motors into smaller units has been thwarted to date, perhaps in part because it has been successfully argued that the American consumer would ultimately suffer by paying higher prices for motor vehicles produced by smaller, less efficient firms.

Methods of Long-Run Cost Estimation

The empirical analysis of long-run costs is similar to the analysis of short-run costs, but considerably more complex. The complexity arises because the analyst

1. Must first determine the relative efficiency of plants of various sizes.
2. Must then project this information into the future in the shape of a long-run average cost curve (*LRAC*).
3. Must find the shape of the least-cost production curve for plants of different sizes in order to determine relative efficiency.
4. Must select an appropriate method for estimating long-run costs. The methods available are statistical analysis of cross-sectional or time-series data, the engineering method, and the survivor method, all of which are discussed next.

Statistical Methods

Statistical analysis in general includes both time-series analysis and cross-sectional analysis.

Time-Series Analysis.   Although regression analysis of time-series data is the most common method of short-run statistical analysis, it is rarely used for the estimation of long-run costs. In theory, it might be possible to extend the method to long-run cost analysis by examining the growth (increase in output level) of a single firm over a long span of time. More often than not, however, significant expansion of the firm is accompanied by changes in technology and other kinds of changes that result in new and different production and cost functions. Because of this, extrapolating the time-series data into a single long-run cost curve would not be valid.

Cross-Sectional Analysis.   Statistical analysts avoid the difficulty just described by using cross-sectional data to compare at some specific time the cost–output relationships of firms and plants whose sizes are different. In this way, the output level of each firm or plant becomes a primary independent variable.

Cross-sectional analysis eliminates many of the problems associated with time-series data. For example, since all cross-sectional data pertain to the same time, there is no need to adjust for price changes. But a number of other problems arise from differences among firms (or among plants in the same firm). These problems include:

1. *Differences in technology.* If a study involves a number of different-sized plants, the differing sizes may indicate differences in technology, particularly if the different-sized plants are owned by the same firm.

2. *Differences in factor prices.* Regional differences may be expected in input-factor prices, such as wage rates and transportation costs.

3. *Differences in cost-accounting practices.* The depreciation of assets and the amortization of major expenses such as research and development are generally guided by tax laws rather than economic considerations. Even within the tax laws, different methods of depreciation and amortization are allowed, and these make a substantial difference in recorded costs. Generally accepted accounting principles permit different methods of valuing assets for costing purposes, such as FIFO (first-in, first-out) and LIFO (last-in, first-out).[8] Moreover, many assets are valued at historical cost rather than at replacement cost, and opportunity costs are entirely overlooked. On top of everything else, cost accountants must make arbitrary allocations of overhead costs and joint costs of production. The basis for such allocations may differ considerably from firm to firm and even from plant to plant within the same firm. All of these considerations add up to a substantial distortion of true cost–output relationships.

4. *Differences in methods of payment for input factors.* Total compensation for labor typically includes more than wage payments. Additional compensation may include such things as vacation with pay, sick pay, health insurance, life insurance, retirement plans, profit sharing, and many other employee benefits. These "sweeteners" vary widely from firm to firm, and their actual cost is extremely difficult to estimate.

5. *Differences in operating efficiency.* Even if the data problems listed previously are resolved satisfactorily, there is still one more problem with cross-sectional analysis, namely, the assumption that each firm is operating efficiently in the most efficient plant available for production at the level it has chosen. In other words, each firm is assumed to be operating at the point on its long-run average-cost curve (*LRAC*) at which costs are minimal. If this assumption is not valid, then the derived-cost curve will lie above the true *LRAC*, and costs will be overstated. Perhaps more of a problem than cost overstatement would be the distortion of the true curvature of the *LRAC*, so that available economies (or diseconomies) of scale would be mis-stated.

---

[8] See an intermediate accounting text for a detailed explanation of FIFO, LIFO, and other methods of valuing inventory and calculating cost of goods sold.

The Engineering Method

The **engineering method** of cost analysis rests upon a thorough understanding of the underlying physical-production function and the analyst's ability to hold constant such factors as production technology and efficiency, product mix, and input-factor prices. By developing standard costs based upon currently available production technology, the engineering method avoids many of the cost-accounting problems of resource valuation and cost allocation. The cost analyst first determines the best (least-cost) combination of inputs to achieve a given level of output. Each input quantity is then multiplied by the projected input price. The output level and the sum of input costs then become coordinates of a point on the long-run cost curve. Since the sum of the input costs can be changed only by changing the mix of inputs, the effect is to isolate the effect of changes in input from all other factors.

Thus we see that the engineering method avoids the contamination of data by extraneous factors that is so troublesome in statistical methods. In particular, it avoids the mixture of old and new technology that is inherent in historical data. But the engineering method is not without its own problems. Indeed, it suffers from at least three important limitations:

1. *Omission of certain costs.* The engineering method deals only with production costs. But total costs associated with a product or line of products necessarily include the marketing costs of distributing and selling the product(s) plus some share of administrative and financing costs. The engineering method ignores these other costs except to the degree that they are arbitrarily allocated as overhead.

2. *Subjective estimation of costs.* The engineering method deals not with costs that have actually been incurred, but with costs as they ought to be under ideal conditions. This necessarily involves subjective opinion rather than facts, not only as to what the costs should be, but also as to what the ideal conditions are and the degree to which they can be achieved. Thus, given the same basic problem, it would not be unusual for two analysts to reach two different conclusions.

3. *Lack of orientation to the future.* The essence of long-run analysis is prediction of the future, but the engineering method deals with currently available technology and current factor prices that may soon become obsolete. The engineering method often proves inadequate when production functions are extended beyond the range of existing systems, or when they are extrapolated from pilot-plant operations to full-scale facilities.

Despite its limitations, the engineering method does avoid the most serious problems of statistical methods, and it is the only method available for estimating the long-run costs of producing a new product when no historical data are available.

The Survivor Method

The survivor method was first developed in 1958 by George Stigler[9] of the University of Chicago, who was awarded the Nobel Prize in economics in 1982. The basic idea of the

---

[9] George J. Stigler, "The Economies of Scale," *Journal of Law and Economics*, October 1958, pp. 54–71.

survivor method is that the more efficient firms will survive over the long run, while less efficient firms will be driven out of the industry by competition. (More efficient firms are those with lower long-run average costs.)

The technique of the survivor method is to classify the firms in an industry by size, and then to determine the share of industry output or capacity that is provided by each class over a number of years. If the market share of a particular class grows larger over time, that size of firm or plant is deemed to be more efficient, i.e., to have lower average costs. These empirical findings can then be used to develop a long-run cost curve.

For example, suppose that in a given industry both the smallest and the largest firms suffered declining market shares, while midsized firms enjoyed increasing market shares. This would indicate a U-shaped long-run cost curve, with economies of scale first increasing, then remaining relatively constant, and then decreasing.

The survivor method is more direct and easier to apply than other techniques for looking at economies of scale. It avoids the statistical method's problems of resource valuation and allocation of overhead cost and the problems associated with the hypothetical aspects of the engineering method. However, it obviously cannot be used unless the industry under study has been established long enough for trends to become apparent. This method has other limitations as well:

1. *The basic premise may not be true.* The basic premise of the survivor method is that all firms operate in a highly competitive environment, in which survival depends upon the ability to minimize long-run average costs, which implies maximum efficiency. However, many firms—particularly large firms—manage to survive without attaining maximum efficiency. As long as a firm's selling prices are above the unit costs of its products, the firm will survive.

2. *Relative efficiency is not measured.* The survivor method will show that increasing or decreasing returns to scale may exist, thereby indicating an optimal size, but the method does not show the relative inefficiency of operating at a scale larger or smaller than optimum. That is to say, it does not show whether operating at a different scale is *somewhat* inefficient or *very* inefficient.

3. *The method does not deal with changing technology.* The survivor method is concerned with analysis over a long span of time. This makes it especially vulnerable to data contamination caused by changing technology.

Some Results of Long-Run Cost Studies

Exhibit 13–3 (page 402) summarizes the results of 10 empirical studies of long-run costs reported by Professor A. A. Walters and one conducted and reported by V. Gupta.

It is interesting to note that 7 of the 11 studies listed in Exhibit 13–3 used the statistical method of cross-sectional analysis. Three researchers chose the engineering method, and one researcher used a questionnaire to obtain data. None of the studies reported by Walters used the survivor method. It has been used, however, first by Stigler and later by Allen. In 1930, 1938, and 1951, Stigler studied steel production by different-sized companies.[10] He found that returns to scale increased at low levels, decreased at high

---

[10] Ibid.

EXHIBIT 13–3   Results of Empirical Studies of Long-Run Costs

Investigator(s)	Type of Industry	Method[a]	Findings
Bain	Manufacturing (U. S.)	Q	Small economies of scale in multiplant firms
Gupta	Manufacturing (India)	CS	*LRAC* L-shaped in 18 industries, U-shaped in 5, linear in 6
Moore	Manufacturing (U. S.)	E	Economies of scale generally
Alpert	Metals (U. S.)	E	Economies of scale to 80,000 lbs./month, then constant returns
Johnston	Coal mining (U. K.)	CS	Wide dispersion of costs per ton
Holton	Retailing (Puerto Rico)	E	*LRAC* is L-shaped, but Holton argues that inputs of management may be undervalued at high outputs
Barts	Railways (U. S.)	CS	*LRAC* increasing in East, decreasing in South and West
Johnston	Road passenger transport (U. K.)	CS	*LRAC* either falling or constant
Dhrymes and Kurz	Electricity (U. S.)	CS,TS	Substantial economies of scale
Johnston	Electricity (U. K.)	CS	*LRAC* of production declines (no analysis of distribution)
Nerlove	Electricity (U. S.)	CS	*LRAC*, excluding transmission costs, declines then shows signs of increase

Sources: A. A. Walter, "Production and Cost Functions," *Econometrica,* January 1963, pp. 1–66; V. Gupta, "Cost Functions, Concentration and Barriers to Entry in 29 Manufacturing Industries in India," *Journal of Industrial Economics,* November 1968, pp. 57–72.

[a] CS = cross section, E = engineering, Q = questionnaire, TS = time series, LRAC = long-run average cost

---

levels, and were nearly constant in the broad middle range. These results are depicted in Exhibit 13–4.

Stigler also used the survivor method to examine the automobile industry, for which he discovered an L-shaped curve. That is, economies of scale were achievable at relatively low levels of production and were followed by constant returns to scale, but there were never any diseconomies at relatively high levels of production. In a later study of the Portland cement industry, using the survivor method, Allen also found an L-shaped long-run cost curve.[11] Many other researchers, using different methods, have obtained similar results. This has led researchers to advance the hypothesis that typical long-run average cost curves are L-shaped, as depicted in Exhibit 13–5, rather than U-shaped.

Conclusions.   In the long run, when a firm can change its use of any and all inputs, it will strive for just the right size to produce its output at the lowest possible cost. The right size depends upon the behavior of long-run costs as applied to a plant or to the firm as a

---

[11] Bruce T. Allen, "Economies of Scale in the Portland Cement Industry, 1965–1971," working paper, Michigan State University; and "Vertical Integration and Market Foreclosure: The Case of Cement and Concrete," *Journal of Law and Economics*, April 1971, pp. 251–74.

EXHIBIT 13–4   Long-Run Average Cost in the Steel Industry as Determined by the Survivor Method

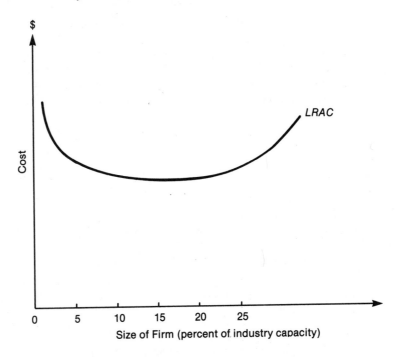

EXHIBIT 13–5   Apparent Shape of Long-Run Average-Cost Curve in Many Industries

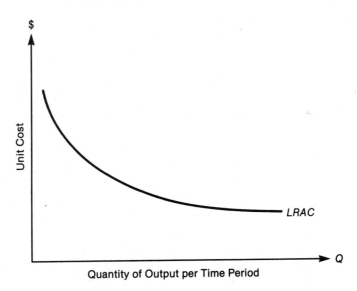

whole. The long-run average cost (*LRAC*) curve for a plant will indicate its optimal size. When the firm has time to adjust each of its plants to optimal size for its location, the *LRAC* for the firm will indicate the optimal size for the firm. Thus the number and size of the plants in a particular industry are largely determined by the behavior of long-run costs.

In theory, *LRAC* curves are U-shaped for both plant and firm. A number of empirical studies have found, however, that the right side of the *LRAC* curve did not turn up within the normal range of production. Consequently, the *LRAC* curve is L-shaped, indicating that there is room in those industries for firms or plants, as the case may be, to grow larger without increasing long-run average costs.

Summary

Management needs to know the firm's short-run cost function to make operational decisions and it needs to understand the firm's long-run cost function to make planning decisions. Both short-run and long-run cost functions can be estimated by analysis of empirical data.

For estimating the short-run cost function, the most common method is statistical analysis of time-series data. When such data are not available, the engineering method may be used. In preparing for empirical analysis, the analyst must deal with at least four major problems:

1. Selecting and adjusting cost data to account for inflation, to obtain the proper correspondence between cost and output, and to eliminate irrelevant costs.
2. Selecting appropriate observation periods.
3. Assuring the technical homogeneity of both input and output.
4. Projecting historical costs into the future and including opportunity costs in the analysis.

The procedure for statistical analysis is to gather the pertinent data and then fit a theoretical cost curve by means of linear regression or other least squares techniques. In a number of empirical studies, analysts have found clear evidence of a linear cost function. This does not invalidate the law of diminishing returns. It merely indicates that the short-run cost function is approximately linear within the observed range of output.

The most common methods of estimating the firm's long-run cost function are statistical analysis of cross-sectional data, analysis of engineering data, and the survivor method. Each method has certain advantages and limitations.

Cross-sectional analysis eliminates many problems associated with time-series data. However, it must contend with a number of difficulties, including the following:

1. Differences in technology among plants within a firm or among firms within an industry.
2. Regional differences in input-factor prices.
3. The nature of accounting data, which are usually the only cost data available.
4. Valuation of assets at historical cost rather than replacement or opportunity cost.
5. Arbitrary allocations of overhead costs and joint costs of production.

6. Different methods of payment for input factors, especially fringe benefits to labor.
7. The assumption that each plant and firm is operating efficiently, which may not be true.

The engineering method has certain distinct advantages, such as a constant, current technology as a basis for cost functions. By developing standard costs, the engineering method avoids many of the problems of resource valuation and cost allocation. However, the method suffers from certain limitations, as follows:

1. It is restricted to production costs and ignores selling, distribution, and administrative costs.
2. It deals with costs as they ought to be, rather than as they are.
3. It deals with current technology and current factor prices rather than the technology and costs of the future.

The survivor method classifies firms according to size, then examines each class over the long run. If a certain-sized class obtains a larger share of the market over time, that size is deemed to be more efficient than other sizes.

A number of empirical studies have discovered long-run average cost curves that either are U-shaped with a very broad flat bottom, or else are L-shaped, with no cost upturn at the higher levels of output.

Problems

1. In recent years large corporations have been actively pursuing acquisition or merger possibilities.

   a. Why might mergers or acquisitions be beneficial?

   b. Do results of actual long-run cost studies support or reject the theory behind antitrust legislation against large corporate mergers?

2. Business, especially American business, is often accused of short-sightedness. Critics claim that many companies lack long-range planning and instead seem to focus on short-run profits.

   a. Given the availability of various methods of cost analysis, why don't more companies conduct long-run studies?

   b. We often read about "Japan Incorporated." How could this concept be more useful in long-range industrial planning?

3. The most efficient plant size in an engineering sense is one for which the *ATC* is as low as possible. Explain whether or not this is also the most efficient plant size in an economic sense, assuming your perspective is that of the individual firm.

4. An accountant in your company plotted a scatter diagram of production and cost data taken from the past six months of operations. Sketching in an approximate total-cost curve *TC*, the accountant presents this work for your evaluation.

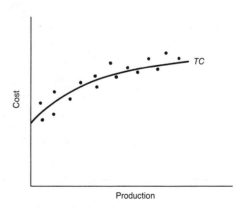

   a. What type of cost analysis has the accountant made?

b. What form of cost equation best fits the given *TC* curve?

c. Is this *TC* curve a reasonable assumption for the company to follow?

5. Flex-Rack Inc. has been experimenting with new tennis racket designs. Using a new fiber material, it plans to produce a small number of rackets for market testing. After analyzing available technology and production facilities, Flex-Rack estimated its total cost function for the new racket to be

$$TC = 975 + 18Q - 0.1Q^2.$$

a. What type of cost analysis is Flex-Rack using?

b. Develop the cost schedule for an output range of 0 to 100, using increments of 20 (but include the level of production at which *MC* = 0).

c. Using the cost schedule, graph the total cost function. Include curves for *TVC* and *TFC*.

d. On a second graph show the *ATC*, *AVC*, and *MC* curves.

e. What assumption is being made when Flex-Rack estimates cost according to the approximated cost function?

6. The manufacture of television sets for the U.S. market is an international endeavor in which the United States, Japan, South Korea, and Singapore are the principal producers. Surveys of the television production facilities in these countries were conducted in 1979 and again in 1989. The following results were obtained:

Plant Capacity ($\times$ 10,000)	Percentage of Industry Capacity 1979	1989
0.0–1.5	9.8	6.6
1.5–2.3	5.2	4.7
2.3–3.4	4.3	4.8
3.4–5.0	5.6	5.1
5.0–7.3	6.2	5.9
7.3–8.9	8.3	14.6
8.9–13.1	9.8	18.4
13.1–15.7	9.3	14.8
15.7–18.4	11.2	8.3
18.4–20.0	16.4	9.6
More than 20.0	13.9	7.2

a. We have postulated short-run cost functions to be either linear, quadratic, or cubic. Which of these best fits these data? Explain the reasons for your choice.

b. What type of long-run cost analysis is appropriate for these data? What assumptions are necessary when using this technique of cost analysis?

c. What conclusions might be drawn from these data about long-run average costs for television manufacturers?

Case Problem: Steel Producers of America

7. Because of the intense competition from both Europe and Japan, Steel Producers of America organized a group of experts to investigate cost–structures in various ailing steel markets. Assume that the following cost-output data for the month of August represent activities of steel producers manufacturing coil tension springs such as those used in automobile suspensions.

Company	Production	Cost/Unit
1	7,500	$53.00
2	11,000	54.00
3	14,500	52.50
4	15,000	51.00
5	18,500	49.50
6	19,500	50.00
7	28,000	47.00
8	67,000	43.00
9	118,000	43.50
10	150,000	43.50

Questions

a. Plot the data on an output–cost graph sketching a smooth curve of best fit.

b. If all cost and output calculations were made at one point in time, what type of cost analysis does this represent? Is it a long-run or short-run analysis?

c. Determine the relationship between output and cost. Does it exhibit increasing, decreasing, or constant returns to scale?

d. Do the data perfectly fit your approximated cost curve? What might have caused deviations to occur?

e. What advice for the future might the cost experts give to tension-spring manufacturers?

f. Discuss the pros and cons of applying this type of cost analysis to the U.S. computer industry.

References

Bain, Joe S. "Survival-Ability as a Test of Efficiency." *American Economic Review* (May 1969), pp. 99–104.

Benston, George J. "Multiple Regression Analysis of Cost Behavior." *Accounting Review* (October 1966), pp. 657–72.

————. "Economies of Scale in Financial Institutions." *Journal of Money, Credit and Banking* (May 1972), pp. 312–41.

Christensen, L. R., and W. H. Greene. "Economies of Scale in U.S. Power Generation." *Journal of Political Economy* (August 1976), pp. 655–76.

Douglas, Paul H. "The Cobb-Douglas Production Function Once Again: Its History, Its Testing, and Some New Empirical Values." *Journal of Political Economy* (October 1976), pp. 903–15.

Frech, Ted H. E., and Paul B. Ginsburg. "Optimal Scale in Medical Practice: A Survivor Analysis." *Journal of Business* (January 1974), pp. 23–36.

Gold, B. "Changing Perspective on Size, Scale, and Returns: An Interpretive Survey." *Journal of Economic Literature*, 19 (March 1981), pp. 5–33.

Henderson, James M., and Richard E. Quandt. *Microeconomic Theory: A Mathematical Approach.* 3rd ed. New York: McGraw-Hill, 1980.

Johannes, James M., Paul D. Koch, and Robert H. Rasche. "Estimating Regional Construction Cost Differences." *Managerial and Decision Economics*, 6 (June 1985), pp. 70–79.

Johnston, J. *Statistical Cost Analysis.* New York: McGraw-Hill, 1960, pp. 136–88. These pages summarize, in a few paragraphs each, the main features and conclusions of more than two dozen well-known statistical cost studies. Chapter 6, pp. 169–94, presents criticisms and evaluations of statistical cost analyses.

Longbrake, William A. "Statistical Cost Analysis." *Financial Management* (Spring 1973), pp. 48–55.

Mansfield, E. "Industrial R&D in Japan and the United States: A Comparative Study." *American Economic Review* (May 1988) pp. 223–28.

————. "The Speed and Cost of Industrial Innovation in Japan and the United States: External vs. Internal Technology." *Management Science* (October 1988) pp. 1157–168.

McDougall, Gerald S., and Dong W. Cho. "Demand Estimates for New General Aviation Aircraft: A User-Cost Approach." *Applied Economics* 20, no. 3 (March 1988), p. 315.

Shepherd, William G. "What Does the Survivor Technique Show About Economies of Scale?" *Southern Economic Journal* (July 1967), pp. 113–22.

Walters, A. A. "Production and Cost Functions: An Econometric Survey." *Econometrics* (January-April 1963), pp. 1–66.

Wheelwright, Steven C., and W. E. Sasser, Jr. "The New Product Development MAP." *Harvard Business Review* (May-June 1989), pp. 112–27.

Williams, Martin. "Firm Size and Operating Costs in Urban Bus Transportation." *Journal of Industrial Economics* (December 1979), pp. 209–18.

C H A P T E R

14

PROFIT: CONCEPTS, MEASUREMENT, PLANNING, AND CONTROL

Profitability is the ultimate test of management's ability to fulfill its coordinative functions of decision making and planning. In the final analysis, profits, not losses, provide the basis for a firm's well-being and growth in the marketplace. In this chapter we examine the forces that contribute to or reduce profits and the ways by which managers may plan for and control profitability.

CHAPTER OUTLINE

This chapter is divided into four sections:

1. **Measurement of Profit: Accounting versus Economic Concepts**. This section examines accounting and economic concepts of profit and associated measurement problems. The concept of replacement-cost accounting is also discussed.
2. **Profit Theories**. This section examines some of the theories of profit that have been developed by economists.
3. **Profit Planning and Control**. Two profit-planning concepts (the *profit budget* and *break-even analysis*) are explained. Also explained are the concepts of the *margin of safety* and *operating leverage*.
4. **Profit-Centers Concept**. This section discusses the establishment, evaluation, and control of decentralized profit centers in large organizations.

Measurement of Profit: Accounting versus Economic Concepts

Before discussing the problems of measuring profits, the difference between accounting profit and economic profit must be understood. Accountants and economists both define profit as revenues minus costs. The difference lies in the definition of costs.

The accountant defines **costs** as those *explicit* charges entered on the company's books. All revenue above these costs is called "accounting profit" or "business profit." The economist also accepts those explicit charges as costs, but adds to them the following *implicit* economic costs:

1. The entrepreneur's wages; that is, the compensation the entrepreneur could earn by working for someone else.
2. Forgone rental income on real property and fully depreciated assets owned and used by the business, which could be received by leasing or selling the property to another firm.
3. The minimum return that would be just enough to compensate the owners for their capital investment and that presumably could be earned by putting the money to work in somebody else's business at equivalent risk.

These items are all deemed to be costs for the simple reason that entrepreneurs who fail to secure in the long run a net revenue at least equal to the sum of these costs would withdraw from the business. Why? Because it would improve their economic position to lease or sell the business property, invest the proceeds elsewhere, and hire out to another firm. This is the basis for the technical, economic meaning of cost. *Cost is the minimum compensation necessary to keep a given resource or factor of production in its stated employment in the long run.*

Cost, in the economic sense, is thus viewed as a payment necessary to keep resources out of the next most attractive alternative employment. A payment that is below economic cost will result in an eventual shift of the resource to the alternative opportunity—hence the term **opportunity cost**.

Illustrative Problem

Question

Under the accounting and economic definitions of cost, how would the following items be treated?

1. Salaries of professional managers in large corporations
2. Corporate headquarters:
   a. Owned by the company
   b. Rented, not owned by the company
3. Long-term capital from
   a. Bonds
   b. Preferred stock
   c. Common stock
   d. Retained earnings

EXHIBIT 14–1   Accounting versus Economic Concepts of Cost

Item	Accountants	Economists
Executive salaries	Recognized as explicit overhead expense	Recognized as explicit cost
Owned headquarters	Partially recognized by depreciation costs; however, land cannot be depreciated.	Cost measured by what the building would bring in if rented to someone else.
Rented headquarters	Recognized as explicit overhead expense	Recognized as explicit cost
Interest on bonds	Recognized as explicit financing cost	Recognized as explicit cost
Dividends on preferred stock	Classified as distribution of earnings; not recognized as a cost	Recognized as explicit cost similar to interest on bonds
Dividends on common stock	Classified as distribution of earnings; not recognized as a cost	Recognized as implicit opportunity cost
Capital from retained earnings	Not recognized as cost	Recognized as implicit opportunity cost equal to what the retained earnings could earn if invested elsewhere
Home storage	Might be recognized as cost under current income-tax law	Might be recognized as cost under current income-tax law
Time spent in preparation of unsuccessful proposal	Not recognized unless the consultant is incorporated and paying himself an hourly wage	Recognized as the imputed value of the consultant's time

4. Closet in proprietor's home used as a storage facility for the business
5. Time spent on proposal for consulting contract that the consultant fails to obtain.

Solution

The accounting and economic concepts of what constitutes a cost are the same for some items but differ for others, as shown in Exhibit 14–1.

To the accountant, all revenue in excess of explicit costs recorded on the books of account is profit. To the economist, revenue in excess of explicit costs plus opportunity cost is **economic profit**. It may also be called "excess profit" or "surplus profit" since it is an amount in excess of (or surplus to) recovery of opportunity cost. This concept of economic profit is the key to managerial decision making in business enterprises.

This does not mean that the accounting concept is useless. Various factors compel the periodic determination and reporting of accounting profits. Periodic financial reports are required by:

1. Stockholders (owners), who want to know how their investments are faring
2. Tax collectors, both state and federal, who want their share of the profits, if any

3. The Securities Exchange Commission, which requires certain financial reports from publicly held corporations
4. Bankers and other financiers, who want to monitor the progress of firms in which they have investments
5. Management, which needs financial data for decision making and control, and as a measure of success (or failure) of past decisions.

Problems in Measuring Accounting Profit

Given the discrepancy between the accountant's and the economist's concepts of profit, certain problems emerge in the periodic calculation of profit for reporting purposes. Accountants, for legal and other reasons, are concerned only with historical facts. Further, generally accepted accounting principles decree that the books must carry only those entries that can be substantiated by reasonably objective evidence in the form of *source documents*, such as invoices, receiving reports, canceled checks, and bank statements. Thus, **accounting profit** is an *ex post facto* concept based on past transactions as recorded on the company's books. Unfortunately, this leads to incomplete cost analyses. The failure to give consideration to certain economic costs has already been discussed. In addition to these oversights, even more serious errors arise from the generally accepted accounting techniques themselves.

The difficulties that exist in accounting methodology are not due to the failure of the accounting profession to produce the right techniques. Rather, they arise simply because the true profitability of an investment cannot be precisely determined until the process has been terminated. For any period other than the full life of the investment, profits can only be estimated. This, in turn, means that revenues and costs must, to some extent, be arbitrarily allocated to the period in question. The problem is that generally accepted and perfectly legal cost-accounting methods can vary these allocated costs by as much as 40 percent. These wide variations are particularly apparent in the procedures for calculating depreciation expense and for valuation of assets.[1]

The Economic Concept of Replacement-Cost Accounting

The accountant has the necessary role of recording and reporting what has been done in the past. While there are cogent reasons why accountants insist upon using historical costs to value assets and also refuse to recognize any profits held in the inventory, there are equally persuasive arguments in favor of relaxing such practices for the purposes of managerial decision making. From an internal, managerial perspective, the economist's concept of *replacement-cost accounting* can give management a much more accurate picture of how well or how poorly the firm is doing.

Since the economist views economic profit as a surplus in excess of all explicit and opportunity costs, past outlays have only partial significance. Cost allocations arising

---

[1] Extended discussion of the depreciation and valuation of assets is beyond the scope of this book. The best source of information on depreciation is IRS Publication 534, *Depreciation*. Complete discussions of techniques for valuation of assets can be found in standard cost-accounting texts.

from these past transactions must be modified by current facts and expectations for the future. Thus, the profit earned in some period is equal to the growth in the value of the enterprise from the beginning of the period to the end of the period (after adjusting for any distributions by the firm or contributions to the firm during the period). This increase in value is a reflection not only of what we ordinarily understand to be the results of operations during the period, but also of changes in values of assets (plant, equipment, inventories). Thus, in an economic sense, *profit is the difference between the cash value of the enterprise at the beginning and end of the period.*

By using replacement cost to calculate the cost of goods sold and the value of goods remaining in inventory, a manager can calculate the firm's true profit as the difference between the cash value of the enterprise at the beginning and end of the period. Further, the manager can separate profit or loss into two components: *trading profit or loss* and *holding profit or loss.* Trading profit or loss is realized from the company's primary business, which is producing (or buying) and selling goods. Holding profit or loss is realized from having goods stored in inventory while prices rise or fall, a matter over which the firm has no control.

Trading profit may be defined as net sales minus operating expenses and the replacement cost of goods that were sold. (Traders are well aware that goods that are sold must be replaced if the business is to continue.) It is important to understand that replacement cost is the price that is expected to prevail at the time of the next purchase. If the supplier has issued a new price list since the last purchase was made, the new price should be used. Otherwise, in the absence of any knowledge of further price changes, the last price paid may be assumed to be the replacement cost.

Holding profit or loss has nothing to do with the trading skills of the persons managing the enterprise. It is defined as the difference between replacement cost and the actual prices paid for all items that were available for sale. Thus it is more a capital gain or loss that results from a general increase or decrease in prices. In calculating holding profit or loss, all quantities of goods that were available for sale must be accounted for. This includes the beginning inventory and all goods purchased during the period. If prices rose during the period, there was a gain simply from holding the goods in inventory. If prices fell, there was a loss.

Illustrative Problem

Suppose that a hypothetical company deals in a completely homogeneous product and makes all transactions in cash. Suppose further that it has the following balance sheet as of December 31, 1990:

Cash	$30,000
Inventory: 3,000 units @ $10	30,000
Total assets	$60,000
Owner's equity	$60,000

Now suppose the following activities take place in 1991:

Sales	20,000 units @ $15	$300,000
Purchases	3,000 units @ $10	30,000
	15,000 units @ $11	165,000
	5,000 units @ $12	60,000
Operating expenses		20,000

Cash on hand at the end of the accounting period is:

Cash on hand, January 1		$ 30,000
Plus sales		300,000
		$330,000
Subtract:		
Purchases	$255,000	
Operating expenses	20,000	$275,000
Cash on hand, December 31		$ 55,000

Also on hand are 6,000 units of merchandise. Since we have no knowledge of any further price change, we assume the replacement cost to be the last price paid, i.e., $12 per unit, for a total of $72,000. Thus the cash value of the enterprise at the end of the period would be:

Cash	$ 55,000
Inventory: 6,000 units @ $12	72,000
Cash value of the firm, December 31	$127,000

The increase in cash value of the firm (economic profit[2])is:

Cash value of the firm, December 31	$127,000
Cash value of the firm, January 1	60,000
Economic profit	$ 67,000

Trading profit is:

Sales		$300,000
Operating expenses	$ 20,000	
Replacement cost of goods sold:		
20,000 units @ $12	240,000	260,000
Trading profit		$ 40,000

----

[2] Under generally accepted accounting methods, the firm's income statement as of December 31, 1991, would show operating income of $55,000 if the LIFO (last-in, first-out) method is used to calculate the cost of goods sold. But if the FIFO (first-in, first-out) method is used, the operating income would amount to $66,000. The difference of $11,000 in operating income is due solely to the difference in the method of inventory valuation, and these results reveal ample grounds for the continuing controversy in the accounting profession. See an intermediate accounting text for an explanation of FIFO and LIFO methods.

Holding profit is:

3,000 ($12 − $10) =	$ 6,000	Beginning inventory @ $10
3,000 ($12 − $10) =	6,000	First purchase @ $10
15,000 ($12 − $11) =	15,000	Second purchase @ $11
5,000 ($12 − $12) =	-0-	Third purchase @ $12
Holding profit	$27,000	

The trading profit of $40,000 plus the holding profit of $27,000 add up to the economic profit of $67,000.

The preceding illustration shows how the economist's definition of profit can lead to better profit analysis. A decision maker should be in a better position to understand and evaluate profit performance when profit is viewed in the comprehensive manner just shown, rather than as a single figure without any breakdown and separation of its basic sources. Further, the economist's concept of economic profit avoids the necessity of stating the inventory value at a historical cost that may be substantially different from its current replacement cost.

Profit Theories

The history of economic thought abounds in profit theories. Each of the many theories that have been offered, however, tends to focus upon just a few of the various aspects of profit (e.g., its source, components, or function). Nevertheless, most profit theories can be classified as one of three major types:

1. Compensatory or functional theories
2. Friction and monopoly theories
3. Technology and innovation theories.

This classification is not exhaustive. Furthermore, it should not be taken to mean that one type of theory may not contain elements of other types. It merely points out the main differences in orientation that have emerged historically in the course of thinking about profit. For this reason, this classification represents a fair arrangement of the major issues involved in profit analysis and a convenient starting point for approaching them in managerial decision making.

Compensatory or Functional Theories

This group of theories holds that economic profits are the necessary payments to the entrepreneur in return for coordinating and controlling production. It is the entrepreneur who organizes the factors of production into a logical sequence, plans their efficient combination, and establishes policies to see that production is carried out. Profits, therefore, are compensation for fulfilling these functions successfully.

Functional theories were proposed in the early 19th century, before the advent of large corporations. At that time, the entrepreneur was regarded as a higher type of laborer, similar in certain ways to an individual proprietor. When attempts were made later, however, to apply functional theories to modern publicly owned corporations with their separation of ownership and control, the results appeared confusing and contradictory.

In the corporate form of business organization, the coordinative function is usually delegated by the owners (stockholders) to professional salaried executives. If executive remuneration is taken to be profits despite its contractual form, the theory still leaves unexplained the residual income of the enterprise that goes to the stockholders who exercise no active control over the business.

The only alternative, if functional theories are to be consistent with their original definition, is to allocate a share of the entrepreneurial function to stockholders. But attempts to do this are not in accord with the reality that the corporation is an organization of active leadership by managers and passive ownership by stockholders. With the growing importance of the large corporation as a dominant type of business organization in the U.S. economy, functional-profit theories have lost much of their usefulness. Around the turn of the century, a group of friction and monopoly theories emerged to take their place.

Friction and Monopoly Theories

In contrast to functional theories, **friction theories of profit** hold that profits are not attributable to any particular function. Rather they are the result of unanticipated changes in cost conditions or demand for a product that provide a temporary windfall to the recipient of the surplus. For example, the 1988 Olympic games in Seoul, Korea, brought profit bonanzas to hotels, restaurants, and even homeowners with spare rooms to rent. When the games were over, of course, profits went back to normal.

Another example is the recent Japanese spending of about $2 billion for purchases of real estate in Hawaii at inflated prices by Hawaiian standards, though they seemed like bargains to Japanese accustomed to Tokyo prices. The owners of private homes, hotels, and commercial properties bought by the Japanese have reaped windfall capital gains.

Monopoly theories of profit are extensions of friction theories. They hold that some firms are able to obtain monopoly positions that enable them to reap above-normal profits for an extended period of time. A patent, a copyright on computer software, a franchise, or the ownership of a particularly favorable business location may give a firm an effective monopoly for a long time. Other factors that may introduce monopoly are economies of scale, high capital requirements that prevent the entry of competitors, technical advances, market dominance or control, protection from imports, and control of any resource whose supply is scarcer than the demand for it.

Technology and Innovation Theories

Like the monopoly theories just discussed, this group of theories is an extension of the friction theories. Technology and innovation theories hold that new technology gives rise to **inventions**, and inventions adapted to business use become **innovations**. Many inventions, of course, do not become innovations. But those that do, being dynamic phenomena, upset the equilibrium of an otherwise static system.

A successful innovation can give the innovating firm above-normal profits until competition develops. For some innovations, this can take quite a long time, but for others the honeymoon is soon over. For instance, McDonalds, Kentucky Fried Chicken, and Xerox each enjoyed a long period of virtual monopoly in their respective fields before serious competition arose. But in the field of personal computers, for example, each innovation seems to be matched by the competition almost as soon as it is announced.

From a business standpoint, an innovation may embrace any one of a wide variety of activities, such as the discovery of new markets, the differentiation of products (thereby gaining wider consumer acceptance), and the development of a new product.

The development of new technology with commercial uses is the result of industrial research and development (R&D) that may or may not have been conducted by the innovating firm. Industrial research can be classified as either **basic research**, which seeks to expand technical knowledge in a particular industry without having any particular application in mind, or **applied research**, which sets out to develop new products or new processes with commercial value. That is to say, basic research lays the foundation for new technology and applied research develops it. Technology that has been developed as a result of a firm's own R&D may be referred to as internal technology, while technology developed by organizations outside of a particular firm may be referred to as external technology.

The innovation process progresses through two stages: (1) invention, which begins at the start of R&D and ends when the product or process is developed, and (2) commercialization, which begins when the product or process is developed and ends when it is first introduced to the marketplace. Research and development is a costly activity, of course. If a firm can develop innovative new products or processes by using external technology, it often gains a competitive advantage. The advantage lies not only in the avoidance of the cost of R&D, but also in the speed with which the innovation can be developed and commercialized. The speed with which a firm is able to translate an invention into a commercial product or process often makes the difference between success or failure in the international marketplace.

The Rewards and Costs of Innovation: Japan and the United States

A number of accounts of Japanese superiority in the commercialization of innovations has been published. A recent two-year study by Mansfield has concluded, however, that the Japanese advantage exists only in certain industries and even there is not as great as some had thought.[3] The Mansfield study focused on two areas (the speed and cost of innovation, and returns from industrial research), while also addressing the role of government.

The Speed and Cost of Innovation.   Data were obtained by a random sampling of 50 Japanese and 75 U.S. firms in the following industries: chemicals (including pharmaceuticals), rubber, machinery (including computers), instruments, metals, and electrical equipment. These data showed that Japanese firms tended to develop and commercially

---

[3] Edwin Mansfield, "Industrial Innovation in Japan and the United States," *Science*, 241 (September 30, 1988), pp. 1771–1772.

introduce new products and processes faster than the U.S. (about 18 percent faster according to the Japanese data or 6 percent faster according to the U.S. data), but the picture varied from industry to industry. In machinery, both Japanese and U.S. data showed a substantial differential. In the instruments industry, Japanese data showed a substantial differential, but the U.S. data did not. In chemicals, both Japanese and U.S. data showed that no large differential existed.

The data showed that the Japanese introduce new products and processes faster than the Americans, besides doing it at lower cost. The overall average differential was 23 percent according to the Japanese data or 10 percent according to the U.S. data. The cost differential also varied from industry to industry. In machinery and instruments, for example, the cost differential was substantial, but little difference existed in chemicals.

To learn whether these time and cost differentials depended upon the use of internal or external technology, 30 matched pairs of Japanese and U.S. firms of approximately the same size in the same industry were selected at random. These firms were drawn from the chemical industry (defined to include pharmaceuticals and petroleum), machinery industry (to include computers), the electrical-equipment industry, and the instrument industry. Each firm said how much time and money it devoted to the development and commercialization of each new product that it introduced during the period 1975–1985 and whether the product was based on internal or external technology. The following results were indicated:

1. The Japanese firms tended to have cost and time advantages over U.S. firms if the innovations were based on external technology. If innovations were based upon internal technology, there seemed to be no significant difference.
2. Overall, U.S. firms spent almost as much time and money on innovations based on external technology as on those based on internal technology. In the invention stage, they spent somewhat less time and money on an innovation based on external technology, but in the commercialization stage, they spent at least as much on the one based on external technology as on the one based on internal technology.
3. In Japan, firms spent about 25 percent less time and 50 percent less money on an innovation based on external technology as on one based on internal technology. This was true of every industry included in the study.
4. The largest contrast between the Japanese and U.S. firms occurred in the commercialization phase of the innovation process. In the United States, the commercialization of an innovation based on external technology took more time and approximately the same amount of money as the commercialization of one based on internal technology. In Japan, however, it took about 10 percent less time and about 50 percent less money. The difference lay in the strategy employed. The Japanese tended to emphasize reduction of production costs. The Americans tended to spend heavily on positioning their innovations optimally in the marketplace. The differences are portrayed in Exhibit 14–2.

Returns from Industrial Research.   The study suggests that U.S. firms have profited more than the Japanese from basic research, while the Japanese have profited more from applied research. There are several factors that may explain the higher estimated rate of return from applied R&D in Japan:

EXHIBIT 14-2 Percentage Distribution of Innovation Costs of 100 Japanese and U.S. Firms, 1985

Percentage of Innovation Cost Going for:

Industry and Nationality	Applied Research	Preparation of Product Specifications	Tooling and Prototype or Pilot Plant	Mfg. Equip. and Facilities	Manu- facturing Start-up	Marketing Start-up
All industries combined[a]						
Japan	14	7	16	44	10	8
United States	18	8	17	23	17	17
Chemicals						
Japan	18	9	13	42	6	11
United States	29	7	13	22	13	17
Electrical and instruments						
Japan	21	7	18	26	18	10
United States	16	8	11	26	18	21
Machinery						
Japan	6	5	20	58	5	6
United States	6	11	23	20	21	18
Rubber and Metals						
Japan	9	8	6	66	6	5
United States	15	4	15	45	15	6

Source: E. Mansfield, "Technological Creativity: Japan and the United States," *Business Horizons,* March–April 1989, p.49.

[a] The sample sizes are: all industries combined, 100; chemicals, 36; electrical and instruments, 20; machinery, 30; and rubber and metals, 14.

1. A rich stockpile exists of external technology more advanced than Japan's from which the Japanese may draw at relatively low cost.
2. A relatively small percentage of industrial R&D for noncommercial purposes is financed by the Japanese government.
3. The Japanese firms focus on process technology rather than product technology. This has enabled the Japanese firms to pick up a new product of external technology and greatly reduce its cost of production.

The lower Japanese rate of return from basic research may be attributable to differences between the two countries in the basic research provided by universities. In the United States, there often is a close working relationship between basic researchers in industry and in the universities. In Japan, university research is less highly regarded and plays a lesser role.

Given the higher returns to Japanese firms from applied research, it is not surprising that expenditures on R&D have increased more rapidly in Japan than in the United States. By 1986, Japanese manufacturers were increasing their spending on R&D from about 2.0 percent of their net sales to about 2.7 percent. This may be compared to the 2.8 percent of net sales expended on R&D by U.S. manufacturers in 1985. A detailed breakdown by industry is shown in Exhibit 14–3.

Because data on total R&D expenditures are difficult to interpret, the Mansfield study included data concerning composition of R&D expenditures from 50 matched pairs of Japanese and U.S. firms in the chemical, electrical equipment, instruments, machinery, rubber, and metals industries. The firms included in this sample perform about 25 percent of the R&D conducted in each country. Exhibit 14–4 (page 422) contains a tabulation of these data.

From the detailed information obtained from the 100 firms, Mansfield notes that the Japanese seem to devote about the same percentage of their R&D expenditures to relatively risky and long-term projects as do the Americans. Nevertheless, the pattern of industrial R&D is quite different in the two countries. Almost half of the American expenditures were devoted to development of entirely new products and processes, whereas only one third of the Japanese expenditures went for this purpose. An even more striking difference lay in the allocation of R&D resources between projects devoted to improvement of *product* technology and projects devoted to improvement of *process* technology. The U.S. firms spent two thirds of their resources on new products and product improvement and one third on new processes and process improvements. The Japanese proportions were just the reverse, with one third going to products and two thirds to processes. This emphasis on process improvement has enabled the Japanese to take state-of-the-art products developed elsewhere and produce them more cheaply than the originators.

The Role of Government.   The Mansfield study concludes that although the U.S. response to technological challenge from the Japanese and others must come in large part from American firms and research organizations, the U.S. government does have an important role to play. That role is not to make detailed decisions about which specific designs and types of commercial products should be developed and at what price; rather, it is to emphasize broad policies that will stimulate civilian technology. Three points are suggested:

EXHIBIT 14–3   **Company R&D Funds as a Percentage of Net Sales, Japan and the United States**

Industry	Japan (1986)	United States (1985)
Food	0.8	0.4
Textiles	1.2	0.5
Paper	0.7	1.3
Chemicals	3.8	4.7
Petroleum	0.4	0.7
Rubber	2.9	2.2
Ferrous metals	1.9	0.5
Nonferrous metals	1.9	1.4
Fabricated metal products	1.6	1.3
Machinery	2.7	5.8
Electrical equipment	5.1	4.8
Motor vehicles	3.0	3.2
Other transportation equipment	2.6	1.2
Instruments	4.5	9.0
Total manufacturing	2.7	2.8

Source: E. Mansfield, "Technological Creativity: Japan and the United States," *Business Horizons,* March-April 1989, p. 50.

1. Even though the United States cannot expect to appropriate all or most of the benefits from basic research, available evidence suggests that enhanced public investment in basic research will have a high economic payoff with a high rate of social return.
2. Government agencies might be able to help U.S. firms become more adept at imitation of foreign developments by supporting the gathering of information about foreign technologies.
3. Agencies such as the National Science Foundation might consider additional support for university research related to process technologies. Also the U.S. Dept. of Defense and NASA (which have helped to develop advanced manufacturing technology for certain industries) might consider doing more to transfer what they have learned to civilian industry in general.

Profit Planning and Control

Profit planning refers to operating decisions in the area of product line, volume of production, and pricing. Whatever the firm's profit goals may be, profit planning must take into account the expected demand for the firm's products, its capacity to meet the demand, and all of its costs. A good profit plan will establish objectives and prescribe the means for achieving them. It will also establish a timetable for actions necessary to carry out the plan. Profit management is not only a vital function for directing short-run operations but also is essential for optimizing investment and financing decisions in the long run. This will help to allocate scarce resources to the firm's activities in the most efficient manner.

A number of approaches to profit planning are commonly used by accountants and economists. We shall discuss two of them:

EXHIBIT 14–4 Composition of R&D Expenditures, 100 Firms (50 Matched Pairs), Japan and the United States, 1985

Industry and Nationality	Basic Research	Applied Research	Percentage of R&D Expenditures Devoted to:			
			Products (Rather than Processes)	New Products and Processes	Projects with Less than 0.5 Probability of Success	Projects that Will Last Longer than 5 Years
All industries combined[a]						
Japan	10	27	36	32	26	38
United States	8	23	68	47	28	38
Chemicals (including drugs)						
Japan	11	42	48	42	24	39
United States	11	39	74	43	39	41
Machinery (including electrical equipment and computers, instruments, metals, and rubber)						
Japan	9	23	32	28	26	37
United States	4	9	62	51	16	36

Source: E. Mansfield. "Technological Creativity: Japan and the United States," *Business Horizons*, March-April 1989, p. 51.

[a] The sample sizes are: all industries combined, 100; chemicals, 36; electrical and instruments, 20; machinery, 30; and rubber and metals, 14.

- The profit budget
- Break-even analysis.

Each of these may be used separately or in combination with the other, depending upon the information available and the purpose of the analysis.

The Profit Budget

A **profit budget** is derived from a projected or *pro forma* income statement based upon the most recent income statement of the firm, with appropriate adjustments for expected changes in costs, prices, and anticipated demand over the period covered by the profit budget. From these figures, of course, either a profit or a loss can be forecast.

Usually, the manager of each department, activity, or profit center submits a proposed budget that goes to the firm's controller for evaluation, adjustment, consolidation, and location of funding sources. Thus, the *planning* aspect of profit budgeting enables managers at all levels to anticipate their needs for work force, materials, equipment, and financial resources, and to plan accordingly.

The profit budget is used for *coordination* and *control* of the firm's activities as well as for *planning*. Therefore, good practice requires that it be flexible, with periodic review and revision.

The *coordinating* aspect of profit budgeting is a side effect of the preparation and periodic revision of the budget. The executive who is responsible for drawing up the budget for one activity cannot perform the necessary duties without extensive consultation with, and input from, managers of all other interacting activities. The very process of drawing up a budget forces a coordination of the firm's activities that otherwise might not take place.

The *control* aspect of the profit budget, unlike coordination, is not automatic. Nevertheless, when the budget is used properly, it enables management to maintain a systematic check on the results of current operations and their relation to previous forecasts. When wide variations between predictions and results are observed, the causes can be analyzed to discover ways to improve profitability.

Break-Even Analysis

Break-even analysis is a technique of profit planning that assumes that both revenue and cost are functions of output, hence profit is a function of output. The technique contains many variations and applications, and only a few of its essential characteristics are highlighted here in order to provide a basic understanding of its nature and relation to managerial decision making.

The economic basis of break-even analysis stems from the cost–output and revenue–output functions of the firm, as illustrated by Exhibit 14–5 (page 424). The exhibit shows the total-revenue curve, *TR*, the total-cost curve, *TC*, and the net-profit curve, *NP*, as functions of output when all output is sold.[4] It represents the short-run cost and revenue

---

[4] This graph was previously shown as Exhibit 3–1 in Chapter 3.

EXHIBIT 14–5   Cost–Volume–Profit Relationships

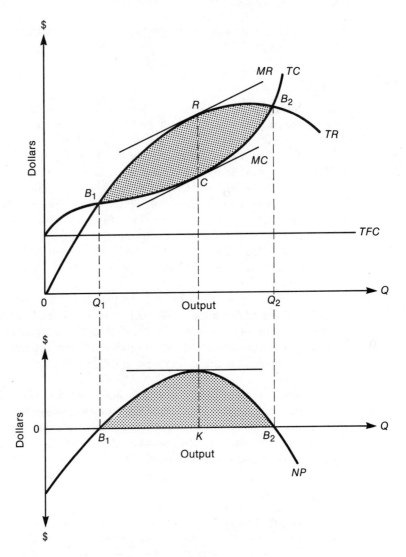

data for a single firm under static conditions, that is, with a given fixed plant and no changes in technology. The total-revenue curve, determined by the price per unit times the number of units sold, is concave downward, indicating that the firm can sell additional units only by charging a lower price per unit.

The total-cost curve represents the sum of total fixed costs and total variable costs ($TC = TFC + TVC$). As outlined in a previous chapter, total fixed costs are those that do not vary with (are not a function of) output. Total variable costs are those that do vary with (are a function of) output. In Exhibit 14–5, the variable-cost area lies between the TC and TFC curves.

The difference between total revenue and total cost is net profit, *NP*, as shown by the shaded area on the upper panel of the exhibit and on the lower panel, where net profit is plotted as a separate function. Net profit is maximum at output level *K* (on the lower panel), at which level $TR - TC$ is maximum on the upper panel. At this level of output, the slope of the total-revenue curve (which is marginal revenue, *MR*) is equal to the slope of the total-cost curve (which is marginal cost, *MC*), indicating that $MR = MC$; and the slope of the *NP* curve is zero. The graph reveals two break-even points at B_1 and B_2, corresponding to the output levels Q_1 and Q_2, where the firm's total revenues just cover its total costs and where net profit is zero.

The curvilinear functions depicted in Exhibit 14–5 may pertain to a wide range of output. At the first break-even point, Q_1, the firm first recovers its costs, and output beyond this point produces profits. The second break-even point at Q_2, however, may actually be far beyond the firm's capacity to produce. Consequently, within the relatively narrow range of production around the first break-even point, linear representations of the *TR* and *TC* functions provide adequate approximations of the underlying curves and are much easier to develop and interpret. Consequently, break-even analysis normally uses linear functions and linear break-even charts.

Linear Break-Even Analysis

The following symbols will be used in our discussion of linear break-even analysis:

$$
\begin{aligned}
TR &= \text{Total revenue} \\
TC &= \text{Total cost} \\
TFC &= \text{Total fixed cost} \\
AFC &= \text{Average (unit) fixed cost} \\
TVC &= \text{Total variable cost} \\
AVC &= \text{Average (unit) variable cost} \\
TCM &= \text{Total contribution margin} \\
ACM &= \text{Average (unit) contribution margin} \\
P &= \text{Price} \\
\pi &= \text{Profit} \\
Q &= \text{Level of production, in units} \\
Q_B &= \text{Break-even level of production, in units} \\
S_B &= \text{Break-even sales volume, in dollars} \\
\%_B &= \text{Break-even production as a percentage of capacity.}
\end{aligned}
$$

Linear break-even analysis assumes that (1) total cost and total revenue are linear functions and (2) total fixed cost (which reflects scale of plant) is constant, with no changes in technology. In other words, linear break-even analysis assumes static conditions, and therefore is a short-run concept. The basic concept is illustrated by Exhibit 14-6 (page 426). In the upper panel, the *TR* line is determined by price per unit times the number of units sold. The *TC* line represents total fixed cost plus total variable cost, $TFC + TVC$, where total variable cost is equal to average, or unit, varible cost, *AVC*, times the number of units produced, *Q*. The variable-cost area lies between the *TC* and *TFC* lines. The difference between total revenue and total cost is profit, as shown by the shaded area.

EXHIBIT 14–6   **Break-Even Chart and Net Profit Curve**

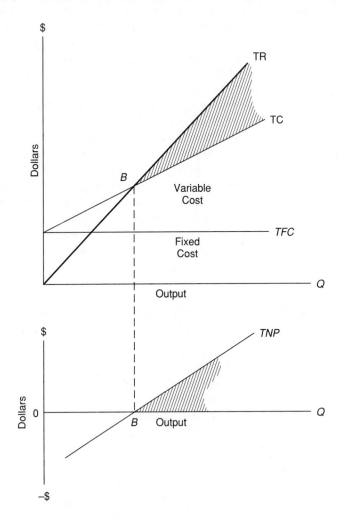

The lower panel shows total net profit, *TNP*, as a function of output. To the left of the break-even point, *B*, there is a loss. As output passes the break-even point, profits rise, as indicated by the shaded area, indefinite boundaries on the right sides of the shaded areas in both panels indicate that profit will further increase as output increases.

Contribution Margin

Business executives do not usually think of profit in the economic sense as total revenue less total cost. Instead, for short-run decisions where a portion of the firm's capital is already a sunk investment and hence immobile, they use a more appropriate profit concept known as **contribution margin** or **contribution profit**—the difference between revenue

EXHIBIT 14–7   Contribution Margin

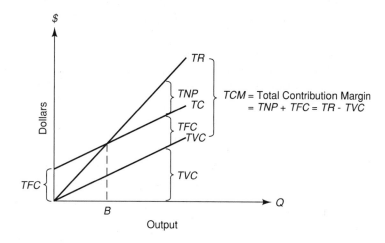

and variable cost. Thus, if a product sells at $1 per unit and the average variable cost per unit equals 30 cents, then each unit sold recovers the 30-cents cost and fetches an additional 70 cents. The 70 cents is the average, or unit, contribution to the payment of fixed costs and profit. Hence it is called the average contribution profit (*ACP*) or, more properly, the average contribution margin (*ACM*). The sum of the contribution margins on all units sold is the total contribution profit (*TCP*) or total contribution margin (*TCM*). In symbols,

$$ACM = P - AVC \tag{1}$$

that is, the average contribution margin is equal to the selling price of the product minus its unit variable cost. It follows that

$$TCM = Q(ACM) = TR - TVC = TFC + \pi \tag{2}$$

that is, the total contribution margin is equal to the average or unit contribution margin multiplied by the number of units sold, which is equal to the total revenue minus the total variable cost, which is equal to the total fixed cost plus profit.

Exhibit 14–7 illustrates the concept of contribution margin and its relationship to total revenue and elements of cost. At the break-even point (*B*), $TR = TC$ and profit (*TNP*) = 0. Therefore $TCM = TFC$ at the break-even point. We also see that

$$TR = TCM + TVC = TFC + TVC + TNP. \tag{3}$$

Illustrative Problem

Martin L. has a glass-blowing concession at a marketplace frequented by tourists. He turns out little figurines in glass that sell for $12 each. Martin's fixed costs consist of the rent on his concession booth and the depreciation on his tools and equipment, which amounts to a total of $500 per week. Martin pays himself an hourly wage. Materials and his labor cost an average of $7 per figurine. In order to make the concession worthwhile, Martin figures he must earn an average of $200 per week more than his wages and other expenses.

Question

Assuming that Martin can sell all the figurines he can produce as fast as he can produce them, how many per week must he produce to achieve his profit goal?

Solution

The average contribution margin is

$$ACM = P - AVC = \$12 - \$7 = \$5.$$

Martin must earn his fixed cost of $500 plus his desired profit of $200 out of the contribution margin of his sales. Since each unit contributes $5 toward this goal, the number of units he must produce is

$$Q_B = \frac{TFC + TNP}{ACM} = \frac{500 + 200}{5} = \frac{700}{5} = 140 \text{ units.}$$

We also note that the total contribution margin is the total revenue minus the total variable cost, i.e., $TCM = TR - TVC$. In this illustration,

$$\begin{aligned} TR &= 140 \text{x} \$12 = \$1,680 \\ TVC &= 140 \text{x} \$7 = \$980 \\ TCM &= TR - TVC = \$700 \end{aligned}$$

which is just enough to pay the fixed cost of $500 plus the desired profit of $200.

Algebraic Techniques

The assumption of linear revenue and cost functions permits the development of simple algebraic procedures for handling break-even problems. There are three ways of expressing the break-even point:

1. As an output quantity, in units
2. As a percentage of plant capacity
3. As a volume of sales, in dollars.

Each of these calculations requires a different expression of the contribution margin.

Break-Even Quantity.   To derive a formula for the break-even point in terms of quantity sold, we first observe that, by definition, break-even means the point at which $TR = TC$ and $\pi = 0$. Substituting, we get

$$P \cdot Q_B = TFC + TVC = TFC + AVC \cdot Q_B$$

$$P \cdot Q_B - AVC \cdot Q_B = TFC$$

$$Q_B(P - AVC) = TFC.$$

Hence the break-even quantity is

$$Q_B = \frac{TFC}{P - AVC} = \frac{TFC}{ACM}. \tag{4}$$

That is to say, the break-even quantity is calculated as the total fixed cost divided by the average (unit) contribution margin, which is the difference between price and average variable cost. Since $\pi = 0$ at this level of production and sales, the ACM also equals average fixed cost, AFC.

Break-Even Percentage of Capacity.   If the break-even point is desired in terms of a percentage of plant capacity, the break-even quantity, Q_B, is divided by the plant capacity, Q_{max}. This decimal fraction may be multiplied by 100 to obtain a percentage figure:

$$\%_B = \frac{Q_B}{Q_{max}}(100) = \frac{TFC}{(P - AVC)} \times \frac{100}{Q_{max}}. \tag{5}$$

Break-Even Sales Volume.   If the break-even point in terms of sales dollars is desired, the contribution margin is expressed as the fraction of price or revenue that contributes to payments of fixed costs:

$$S_B = \frac{TFC}{1 - (AVC/P)} \tag{6}$$

or

$$S_B = \frac{TFC}{1 - (TVC/TR)}. \tag{7}$$

   In Equation 6, dividing the average (unit) variable cost by the sales price gives the proportion of the sales price that is required to pay variable cost. When this figure is subtracted from 1, the remainder represents the proportion of the sales price that is available to pay fixed cost. When this decimal fraction is divided into the total fixed cost, the result is the number of sales dollars necessary to break even.

   Equation 7 yields the same result because $1 - (AVC/P) = 1 - (TVC/TR)$. Either Equation 6 or Equation 7, whichever is more convenient, may be used to find the break-even sales volume.

Illustrative Problem

Suppose an airline can carry a maximum of 10,000 passengers per month on one of its routes at a fare of $85. Variable costs are $10 per passenger, and fixed costs are $300,000 per month.

Questions

a. How many passengers must be carried in order to break even?
b. What is the break-even load factor (percentage of capacity)?
c. What is the break-even point in sales dollars?

Solutions

a. If we want to find the number of passengers necessary to break even, we calculate by Equation 4:

$$Q_B = \frac{TFC}{P - AVC} = \frac{(\$300,000)}{\$85 - \$10} = 4,000 \text{ passengers.}$$

Note that Equation 4 establishes TFC/ACM as the break-even quantity. Hence, at the break-even point,

$$TR = P \cdot Q_B = P \cdot \frac{TFC}{ACM} = (\$85) \frac{(\$300,000)}{\$75} = \$340,000$$

and

$$TC = TFC + TVC = TFC + Q_B(AVC) = TFC + \frac{TFC}{ACM}(AVC)$$

$$= \$300,000 + \frac{(\$300,000)}{\$75}(\$10) = \$340,000.$$

Thus $TR = TC$, which is the definition of "break even."

b. To find the break-even load factor, we use Equation 5:

$$\%_B = \frac{TFC}{(P - AVC)} \times \frac{100}{Q_{max}} = \frac{(\$300,000)}{\$75} \times \frac{100}{(10,000)}$$

$$= 4,000 \times 0.01 = 40\%.$$

c. To find the break-even dollar volume of sales, we use Equation 6:

$$S_B = \frac{TFC}{1 - (AVC/P)} = \frac{(\$300,000)}{1 - (\$10/\$85)} = \frac{(\$300,000)}{0.882352941} = \$340,000.$$

This answer agrees with our previous calculation that the break-even quantity is 4,000 passengers, because $4,000 \times \$85 = \$340,000$.

Planning for Profit

In order to project the production and sales necessary to meet a planned-profit goal, the planned profit is treated as an additional increment of fixed cost. Letting π stand for the planned profit, the basic equations then become

$$Q_B = \frac{TFC + \pi}{P - AVC} = \frac{TFC + \pi}{ACM}. \tag{8}$$

If the break-even percentage of capacity is desired, then

$$\%_B = \frac{TFC + \pi}{(P - AVC)Q_{max}} = \frac{TFC + \pi}{(ACM)Q_{max}}. \tag{9}$$

If the break-even sales in dollars is desired, then

$$S_B = \frac{TFC + \pi}{1 - (AVC/P)} = \frac{TFC + \pi}{1 - (TVC/TR)}. \tag{10}$$

Reusing our preceding example of the airline, suppose that management sets a profit target of $200,000. Then the break-even points would be

$$Q_B = \frac{(\$300,000 + \$200,000)}{\$75} = 6,667 \text{ passengers}$$

$$\%_B = \frac{(\$300,000 + \$200,000)}{\$75(10,000)} = 0.6667 = 66.67\%$$

$$S_B = \frac{(\$300,000 + \$200,000)}{1 - (\$10/\$85)} = \frac{(\$500,000)}{0.882352941} = \$566,667.$$

In this example, no provision was made for payment of income taxes. In general, if r denotes the tax rate expressed in decimal form, then profit after taxes, *PAT*, is related to profit before taxes, *PBT*, in the following way:

$$PAT = PBT - (r)(PBT)$$

that is

$$PAT = (1 - r)PBT$$

hence

$$PBT = \frac{PAT}{(1 - r)}.$$

Thus, in the preceding example, at the corporate tax rate of 34 percent, a profit after taxes of $200,000 would require a profit before taxes of

$$PBT = \frac{(\$200,000)}{1 - 0.34} = \frac{(\$200,000)}{0.66} = \$303,030.30.$$

That is, a 34 percent tax on $303,030.30 is $103,030.30, leaving $200,000 profit after taxes. This calculation can be incorporated directly into the break-even–sales planning formula if desired:

$$S_B = \frac{TFC + (PAT/0.66)}{1 - (AVC/P)} = \frac{300,000 + \left(\frac{200,000}{0.66}\right)}{0.8824} = \$683,398.$$

Similarly, if management is contemplating an action that will involve additional fixed commitments (e.g., floating a new bond issue that will require the firm to make periodic interest payments in the future), these increments in fixed cost can be added to the numerator of the preceding formula, and the additional sales revenue needed to cover these extra costs can thus be calculated.

Break-Even–Point Alternatives

As was previously shown, profit is represented on a break-even chart by the area between the total-revenue and total-cost curves beyond the first break-even point. Obviously, this area can be enlarged by increasing the volume of sales. However, the increase in units sold is eventually limited by plant capacity. The profit area can also be enlarged by shifting the break-even point to a lower level of production and sales. This can be achieved by manipulating any or all of the equation's three variables in the following manner: (1) reduce the fixed cost, (2) reduce the variable cost, and/or (3) raise the price.

To illustrate these concepts, we have depicted linear cost relationships in Panel A of Exhibit 14–8, based on the following data:

$$
\begin{aligned}
\text{Plant capacity} &= 100 \text{ units per day} \\
AVC &= \$7 \text{ per unit} \\
P &= \$12 \text{ per unit} \\
TFC &= \$400 \text{ per day} \\
Q_B &= 80 \text{ units per day} \\
TR(\text{at capacity}) &= \$1{,}200 \text{ per day} \\
TC(\text{at capacity}) &= \$1{,}100 \text{ per day}.
\end{aligned}
$$

The shaded area in Panel A represents profit at levels of production beyond the break-even point of 80 units per day. If we want to reduce the break-even point to 40 units, (Q_B), we might do it in one of three ways previously mentioned.

Reduce Fixed Cost.   We use Equation (4) to find the fixed cost for which the break-even output will be 40 units.

$$
\frac{TFC}{P - AVC} = \frac{TFC}{\$12 - \$7} = 40
$$
$$
TFC = \$5(40) = \$200.
$$

Equation (4) indicates that the break-even point will be reduced in direct proportion to a decrease in total fixed cost. The darker shaded area in Panel B represents the gain in profit caused by reduction of total fixed cost.

Reduce Average Variable Cost.   The break-even point can also be achieved by reducing average variable cost. The reduction necessary to achieve a break-even point of 40 units is calculated as follows:

$$
Q_B = \frac{TFC}{P - AVC}
$$
$$
Q_B(P - AVC) = TFC
$$
$$
AVC = P - \frac{TFC}{Q_B} = \$12 - \frac{\$400}{40} = \$12 - \$10 = \$2 \text{ per unit.}
$$

The darker shaded area in Panel C indicates the increase in profit caused by reducing the unit variable cost. However, it should be noted that a 50 percent reduction in the break-even point requires a 71.4 percent reduction in variable cost from $7 to $2; i.e., each 1 percent reduction in the break-even point requires a 1.43 percent reduction in unit variable costs.

Increase Price.   The increase in price necessary to achieve a break-even sales volume of 40 units may also be determined by manipulating Equation (4):

$$
Q_B = \frac{TFC}{P - AVC}
$$

EXHIBIT 14–8   Break-Even–Point Alternatives

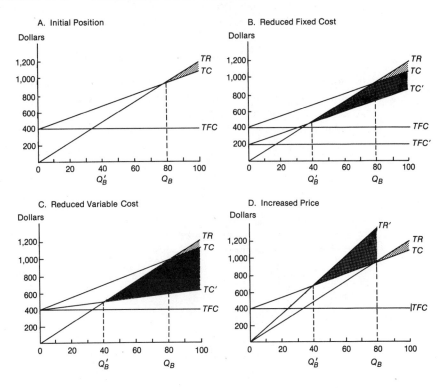

$$Q_B(P - AVC) = TFC$$

$$P = \frac{TFC}{Q_B} + AVC = \frac{\$400}{40} + \$7 = \$17.$$

With an increase in price from \$12 to \$17, a decrease in the quantity sold might be expected. The decrease may be calculated using Equation 5 as

$$\%_B = \frac{TFC}{(P - AVC)} \times \frac{100}{Q_{max}} = \frac{(40,000)}{(17 - 12)100} = 80\%.$$

When compared with Panel A, Panel D shows that even with sales reduced to 80 percent of capacity, a sizable increase in profits could result from reducing the break-even point by raising the price.

Margin of Safety

In the preceding illustrations, only one of the elements (fixed cost, variable cost, or price) was changed at a time, but in reality more than one may be changed simultaneously. One way of measuring the overall effect of multiple changes is to look at the ratio of profit to total fixed cost. This margin of profit stands between the profit the firm is making or expects to make and the loss it would take if sales were to drop below the break-even point. Hence this ratio is called the **margin of safety** and the larger it is, the better.

The margin of safety may be calculated in two ways. First,

$$MS = \frac{\pi}{TFC} \tag{11}$$

with profit, π, and total fixed cost, TFC, expressed in dollars. We may also recognize that profit is the revenue derived from sales above the break-even point and that total fixed cost is equal to revenue from the break-even quantity. Therefore, the margin of safety may also be expressed as a ratio of quantities:

$$MS = \frac{\pi}{TFC} = \frac{P(Q_S - Q_B)}{PQ_B} = \frac{Q_S - Q_B}{Q_B} \tag{12}$$

where

P = Selling price
Q_S = Total number of units sold
Q_B = Break-even quantity.

Use of the margin-of-safety concept may be illustrated by the following problem.

Illustrative Problem

The Superior Waste Management Company produces solid-waste–disposal units that are sold to stores, factories, and other commercial users for $35,000 each. The plant is currently producing 48 units per year, which represents 60 percent of its 80-unit capacity. Total fixed cost is $600,000 and the average variable cost per unit is $20,000.

The firm is contemplating a change in design that will increase the average variable cost by $1,000 per unit. Also an advertising campaign could be launched, at a cost of $120,000, to announce that the new improved model will sell for $2,000 less than the old one. The marketing manager estimates that these measures will increase sales to 90 percent of plant capacity. The firm's top management is faced with four alternatives:

• *Alternative A:* Maintain current conditions; that is, make no changes.
• *Alternative B:* Carry out all of the contemplated changes; that is, change the design, reduce the price, and conduct the advertising campaign.
• *Alternative C:* Change the design and reduce the price, but do not conduct the advertising campaign.
• *Alternative D:* Change the design and conduct the advertising campaign, but do not reduce the price.

Question

Assuming the marketing manager is right about the increase of sales to 90 percent of capacity, which alternative should be chosen?

Solution

To evaluate the four alternatives, we examine the break-even quantity, sales quantity, profit, and margin of safety.

Alternative A:

$$Q_B = \frac{TFC}{P - AVC} = \frac{\$600,000}{(\$35,000 - \$20,000)} = 40 \text{ units}$$

$$Q_S = 48$$

$$\pi = Q_S(P - AVC) - TFC = 48(\$15,000) - \$600,000 = \$120,000$$

$$MS = \frac{\pi}{TFC} = \frac{\$120,000}{\$600,000} = 0.20 = 20\%$$

Alternative B:

$$Q_B = \frac{(\$600,000 + \$120,000)}{(\$33,000 - \$21,000)} = \frac{\$720,000}{\$12,000} = 60 \text{ units}$$

$$Q_S = (0.9)(80) = 72 \text{ units}$$

$$\pi = (0.9)(80)(\$12,000) - \$720,000 = \$144,000$$

$$M_S = \frac{\$144,000}{\$720,000} = 0.20 = 20\%$$

Alternative C (for $\pi = \$144,000$, same as Alternative B):

$$Q_B = \frac{\$600,000}{\$12,000} = 50 \text{ units}$$

$$Q_S = \frac{\pi + TFC}{P - AVC} = \frac{(\$144,000 + \$600,000)}{\$12,000} = 62 \text{ units}$$

$$M_S = \frac{\$144,000}{\$600,000} = 0.24 = 24\%$$

Alternative D (for $\pi = \$144,000$, same as Alternative B):

$$Q_B = \frac{\$720,000}{\$14,000} = 52 \text{ units}$$

$$Q_S = \frac{(\$144,000 + \$720,000)}{\$14,000} = 62 \text{ units}$$

$$M_S = \frac{\$144,000}{\$720,000} = 0.20 = 20\%$$

These computations may be summarized as follows:

Alternative	Sales Quantity	Break-Even Quantity	Profit	Margin of Safety
A	48	40	$120,000	0.20
B	72	60	144,000	0.20
C	62	50	144,000	0.24
D	62	52	144,000	0.20

From the preceding table, Alternative C emerges as a clear winner. It generates the same increased profit as Alternative B, but with fewer sales, a lower break-even point, and a greater margin of safety. Alternative D can generate the same level of profit, but with a higher break-even point and a much lower margin of safety.

Operating Leverage: Sales Elasticity of Profit

If sales increase or decrease, what is the effect on profits? To measure the sensitivity of profits to sales, we can use a formula for the sales elasticity of profits:

$$s\epsilon_\pi = \frac{\Delta\pi/\pi}{\Delta Q/Q} = \frac{\Delta\pi}{\Delta Q} \cdot \frac{Q}{\pi}. \tag{13}$$

If we assume that the sales price of the output will remain constant without regard to the level of output, then operating profit and operating leverage depend upon three variables: (1) the level of output and sales, Q; (2) the level of fixed costs, TFC; and (3) the unit variable cost, AVC.

Even among plants with the same output capacity, the cost structure may vary from a labor-intensive plant with relatively lower fixed costs and relatively higher variable costs to a capital-intensive plant with relatively higher fixed costs and relatively lower variable costs. If both plants charge the same price for their outputs, the capital-intensive plant with higher fixed costs and lower unit variable costs will experience greater variation in profit as sales increase or decrease. That is to say, the capital-intensive firm will have more *operating leverage*.

Operating leverage is a measure of the extent to which fixed production facilities, as distinguished from variable inputs, enter the firm's operations. Operating leverage actually is the sales elasticity of profit, so it can be computed from Equation 13. For break-even analysis assuming linear relationships, Equation 13 can be manipulated to show that the degree of operating leverage at any level of production can be calculated as the ratio of the total contribution margin, TCM, to operating profit, π. In symbols,

$$OL_Q = \frac{TCM_Q}{\pi}. \tag{14}$$

Equation 14 may be derived from Equation 13 as follows:

$$\pi = PQ - (AVC)(Q) - TFC$$

and

$$\Delta\pi = P(\Delta Q) - (AVC)(\Delta Q).$$

Therefore, by substitution,

$$OL_Q = \epsilon_Q = \frac{\frac{\Delta\pi}{\pi}}{\frac{\Delta Q}{Q}} = \frac{\frac{P(\Delta Q)-(AVC)(\Delta Q)}{PQ-(AVC)(Q)-TFC}}{\frac{\Delta Q}{Q}}$$

$$= \frac{(Q)(\Delta Q)(P - AVC)}{(\Delta Q)[Q(P - AVC) - TFC]} = \frac{Q(P - AVC)}{Q(P - AVC) - TFC}$$

$$= \frac{Q(ACM)}{Q(ACM) - TFC} = \frac{TCM}{\pi} \tag{14a}$$

where

π = Profit
Q = Level of output, in units
OL_Q = Operating leverage at output level Q
P = Selling price of output
AVC = Average or unit variable cost
ACM = Average or unit contribution margin
TCM = Total contribution margin.

Note that total fixed cost in this formulation bears a minus sign. This means that the larger the fixed cost, the greater will be the operating leverage. Hence, for any given level of sales, operating leverage is greater for the more capital-intensive firm. However, the break-even equations [Equations 4, 5, 6, and 7] make it clear that the more capital-intensive firm will have a higher break-even point than the labor-intensive firm. Therefore, whether or not the capital-intensive firm enjoys a cost advantage depends upon its level of output. At lower levels of production, the labor-intensive plant has an advantage. At higher levels, the capital-intensive firm has an advantage. And there is a level of output at which they are equally efficient.

Application of Break-Even Analysis and Operating Leverage

To illustrate the points made in the preceding paragraph, let us return to the Superior Waste Management Company.

Illustrative Problem

The Superior Waste Management Company now has obtained distributors for its solid-waste–disposal units in the Far East. At a price of US $33,000, the sales potential is so great that the firm will have to build an additional plant to provide the increased output. Two designs have been submitted by the firm's engineering department and management must choose one of them.

Design A consists of merely duplicating the existing facility, in which case the total-cost equation is expected to remain

$$TC_A = \$600,000 + \$21,000(Q).$$

Design B is a new design that utilizes more capital equipment. Its estimated total cost function is

$$TC_B = \$780,000 + \$18,000(Q).$$

Questions

a. At what level of production does neither plant have an advantage? How do you interpret this information?

b. How much profit would be earned at that level of production?

c. What is the break-even point for each plant design?

d. Compare the profit and operating leverage at several possible quantities of output. Which design is more sensitive to changes in output and sales?

e. Since they are entering new markets, the company's managers are not sure how many units will be sold. The vice president for marketing believes that the most likely number is 70 units annually, give or take 15 units. What is the probability that sales will be sufficient to favor choice of Plant B? What is the probability that sales will be 70 units or more?

Solutions

a. The production level at which neither design has an advantage is found by simply setting their cost equations equal to each other and solving for Q:

$$TC_A = TC_B$$
$$\$600,000 + \$21,000Q = \$780,000 + \$18,000Q$$
$$\$3,000Q = \$180,000$$
$$Q = 60.$$

As already noted, a capital-intensive plant generally involves larger fixed costs but smaller variable costs than a plant that is labor-intensive. At small output rates a capital-intensive plant is more costly, but as output increases, so does its cost advantage. We interpret the answer to mean that for output of less than 60 units, Plant A is more efficient. For output of more than 60 units, Plant B is more efficient. For output of 60 units, they are equally efficient.

b. Both plants earn $120,000 at an output of 60 units, computed as follows:

$$\pi = TR - TC = PQ - TC$$
Plant $A : \pi = 33,000(60) - 600,000 - 21,000(60) = \$120,000$
Plant $B : \pi = 33,000(60) - 780,000 - 18,000(60) = \$120,000.$

c. Break-even points are

$$Q_B = \frac{TFC}{P - AVC}$$

Plant A : $Q_B = \dfrac{600}{33 - 21} = 50$ units

Plant B : $Q_B = \dfrac{780}{33 - 18} = 52$ units.

The break-even point of 50 units for Plant A versus 52 units for Plant B demonstrates that the more capital-intensive a plant is, the higher its break-even point.

d. Exhibit 14–9 shows a comparison of profit and operating leverage for the two plants at various levels of output. Clearly, profit at Plant B is more sensitive to change in output than it is in Plant A. This is because operating leverage is higher for Plant B at all levels of production above its break-even point. Therefore, earnings at Plant B drop much faster when production and sales fall, and they rise much faster when production and sales rise, than at Plant A.

EXHIBIT 14–9   **Comparison of Break-Even Output and Operating Leverage of Two Plants**

Level of Output	Plant A P= $33,000 TFC=600,000 AVC= 21,000		Plant B P= $33,000 TFC=780,000 AVC= 18,000	
	Profit	Operating Leverage	Profit	Operating Leverage
0	−$600,000	0.0	−$780,000	0.0
40	−120,000	−4.0	−180,000	−3.3
50	0	∞	−30,000	−25.0
52	24,000	26.0	0	∞
55	60,000	11.0	45,000	18.3
60	120,000	6.0	120,000	7.5
65	180,000	4.3	195,000	5.0
70	240,000	3.5	270,000	3.9
75	300,000	3.0	345,000	3.3
80	360,000	2.7	420,000	2.9

e. Assuming that the probability distribution of future sales is normal, we can interpret the marketing VP's remarks to mean that the mean of the probability distribution is 70 units (μ = 70) and the standard deviation is 15 units (σ = 15). This is shown in Exhibit 14–10. At the level of production where neither plant has an advantage, $TC_A = TC_B$, therefore $TC_A - TC_B = 0$; i.e.,

$$\$600,000 + 21,000Q - (\$780,000 + \$18,000Q)$$
$$= -\$180,000 + 3,000Q = 0 \qquad (15)$$
$$Q = 60.$$

A straight line representing Equation 15 is drawn in Exhibit 14–10 to pass through the level of production at which neither plant has an advantage; i.e., at Q = 60. To the right of this point, Plant B has an advantage, and to the left Plant A has an advantage. To answer the question asked previously, we must first determine the probability that sales will equal or exceed 60 units. The shaded area in Exhibit 14–10, measured as a percentage of the total area under the distribution, provides the information we want. It is measured by carrying out the following steps:

1. Translate the mean and standard deviation into the appropriate Z-value.

$$Z = \frac{X - \mu}{\sigma} = \frac{60 - 70}{15} = \frac{-10}{15} = -0.67.$$

2. Refer to Table E in the Appendix at the end of this book and find the probability corresponding to Z = 0.67; it is 0.2486. Since our Z-value is negative, 0.2486 is the value of the shaded area to the left of the mean.

3. Determine the total shaded area; it is 0.2486 + 0.5000 = 0.7486. This means that the probability is about 75 percent that Plant B will be more profitable than Plant A. Of course, management might also use the same technique to determine the probabilities for other sales estimates.

4. The probability that sales will equal or exceed the mean value of 70 units is 50 percent.

EXHIBIT 14–10   **Probability Distribution of Sales and Relative Cost Advantage of Two Plants**

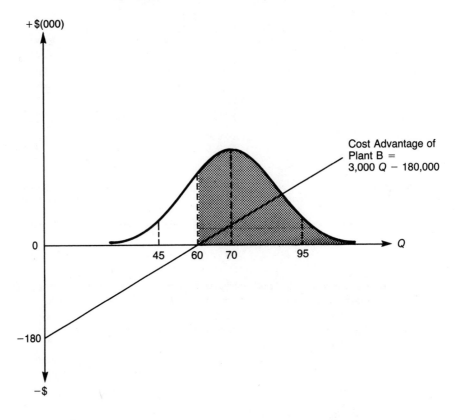

Evaluation of Break-Even Analysis

Break-even analysis is a method of short-run profit planning and control, based on the assumption that there is a unique functional relationship between the profits of a firm and its level of output. Output, as stated earlier, may be measured in terms of physical units, dollar value of sales, percentage of plant capacity, or any other relevant index. Profit, on the other hand, is more explicit and usually represents the difference between total revenue and total cost for the period under study. As an analytical device, break-even methods have as their chief advantages simplicity, ease of comprehension by management, and relative inexpensiveness compared to other more sophisticated techniques. Most, if not all, of the required data can be taken directly from the firm's cost-accounting records and financial statements.

The static profit–output relationship that underlies the notion of break-even analysis assumes a continuation of the same relative sales and expense patterns. It takes no account of uncertainty, that is, the possible changes in revenues, costs, and technology that result from changing business conditions. Thus, the assumption in break-even analysis that there is a simple relationship between profits and output is an oversimplification of the facts. Profit depends upon output, to be sure, but it also is affected by production processes, selling effort, the composition of demand, and a multiplicity of other factors internal and external to the firm.

A characterization of profit more in keeping with the facts would thus take into account its multiple relationships. To the extent that firms experience rapid changes in their main cost components, in their sales mixture, in their advertising and promotional policies, and/or in their technology and product design, the oversimplified traditional break-even techniques must be applied with great caution and due consideration of their weaknesses. However, when properly used, cost–volume–profit analysis provides the necessary background for decisions about such things as pricing strategies, promotion and advertising expenditures, channels of distribution, and output contracting.

Decentralized Profit Centers

At the beginning of this chapter, we noted that profit budgeting is closely connected with management of the company's operations. There are two primary means of control: (1) clear statements of policies and procedures that provide direction for the firm's activities before they occur and (2) timely corrective measures in response to feedback. It is in this second area that the profit budget serves as a yardstick by which managerial or organizational performance can be measured and corrected if necessary.

As an organization grows larger and more complex, effective coordination and control by top management becomes more difficult and complicated. Many companies have resolved this problem through decentralization. A truly decentralized firm is organized as a combination of semiautonomous units, each of which is a profit center. Largely as a result of the continuing success achieved by the decentralized organization of many large U.S. firms, this technique has won increasing favor among large multinational firms for management of their organizations both in the United States and abroad. Managers of subordinate units, which may be divisions of the parent company or separate corporations, are given authority to plan their selling campaigns, establish selling prices, determine their materiel and personnel requirements, select their sources of supply from either inside or outside the company, and determine their marketing and distribution channels. The subordinate unit manager's responsibility and authority tends to be complete with respect to all short-run decision making. In other words, division managers run their divisions as if the divisions were independent corporations, whether or not they are so organized.

The top executive group of the parent firm retains responsibility for all matters of long-run policy, particularly with respect to capital expenditures; the establishment, disestablishment, and merger of decentralized units; and the selection and evaluation of division managers. In fulfilling this last responsibility, there is a tendency for top management to use profit as a yardstick by which to measure a division manager's performance. After all, profit is the ultimate measure of the firm's well-being. However, top management sometimes finds that determining and using profit measures for purposes of internal control are more difficult and controversial matters than establishing profit measures for the company as a whole.

Divisional Profit

In a decentralized firm, where management responsibility has been delegated to the heads of divisions that may or may not be organized as separate corporations, there is a need for appropriate profit measures for evaluating performance of division executives and for guiding their decisions. A profit measure that will function properly must exclude all factors over which the division managers have no control. This means that it must be independent not only of the decisions handed down from the top but also of the superior or inferior performance of other divisions with which the one in question does business.

Such a measure is **controllable divisional profit**, which is essentially the earnings available after deducting from divisional (or subordinate-company) revenues all variable divisional costs such as cost of goods sold and administrative and selling expenses, as well as any overhead costs directly subject to the the control of division managers.

Allocation of Cost.   Many facilities and services may be used jointly by two or more divisions of the company (e.g., general administrative services, research, maintenance personnel, and equipment). Furthermore, one division is likely to use more of these common facilities and services than another, but the amount of such use is not necessarily related to the volume of a division's business. This complicates the problem of allocating such costs among the various operating units.

Interdivisional Transactions.   It is also very likely that one division will have business relationships with another involving transfer of goods, by-products, and/or services. If established market prices exist for such transfers, the problem is relatively simple, but if no market prices exist, a system of (arbitrary) transfer prices must be established. Since the purchasing division has no control over the efficiency with which such products and services have been produced (and for which there are no established market prices to permit objective testing of their supply prices), it should not be placed in a position of having its own performance hindered or helped by the supplying division's performance.[5]

Evaluating Managerial Performance

Even after controllable divisional profit has been determined, there remains the problem of evaluating the divisional management. By what yardstick should it be measured? Comparisons of absolute dollar figures are meaningless when divisions differ in such things as size, products, marketing conditions, and operating equipment.

Perhaps we should use return on investment (*ROI*), but the problems in applying this yardstick are also quite formidable. We have already mentioned the transfer-pricing problem, but there are at least three other major difficulties in using *ROI* as a yardstick.

1. *Differences in depreciation base and methods.* Accelerated depreciation decreases *ROI* in the early part of the asset's life and increases *ROI* in the latter part. Fully depreciated assets no longer create depreciation expense and hence increase *ROI*. Leasing of assets hides them from view and also increases *ROI* on the diminished investment base.

---

[5] See Appendix 16A to Chapter 16 for a broader discussion of transfer pricing.

2. *Relative riskiness of investments.* Return on investment takes no account of the fact that one investment may be riskier than another. Given two investments that are equally successful in achieving their expected return, the one with the higher risk should be expected to yield the higher return—but this does not reflect superior management performance.

3. *Effect of evaluation period.* Evaluation usually takes place once a year, but large investments frequently take considerably more than a year to pay off. For example, the development of a new product and successfully marketing it internationally can be expected to take more than a year. In the meantime, of course, *ROI* might be quite low or nonexistent. Executive evaluation at short intervals may force these managers into undue emphasis on short-run profits at the expense of the long-run welfare of the firm. American management, for example, has often been criticized for its emphasis on short-run profits. In contrast, Japanese management is often praised for its emphasis on long-term objectives, which include lifetime employment of corporate executives and emphasis on productivity.

Another way to evaluate divisional performance is to compare actual results with budgeted results. After all, the budget is a negotiated document with performance goals and objectives that have been agreed to by the managers and their superiors. The difficulty with this approach is that this, too, is a measure of short-run performance when, in fact, an evaluation of long-run performance may be more appropriate.

Evaluating Departmental Performance. In many respects, the task of evaluating departmental performance within a division is just as formidable as the task of evaluating divisions of the firm. One of the stickiest and most persistent problems at both levels is the fair and equitable allocation of fixed overhead costs. What one manager may consider to be fair and equitable might not seem that way to another.

Conclusions about Decentralized Control. If the discussion of decentralized control seems to raise more questions than answers, it is because that is the nature of the problem. It is unlikely that anyone has developed a completely satisfactory, universally applicable method for evaluating managerial performance, and possibly no one ever will. In many situations, it might make more sense to ignore profit figures altogether and evaluate efficiency instead, as measured by minimization of costs. Ultimately, of course, minimization of costs will enhance profits.

Whatever procedure is adopted, the following rule of thumb should apply: If the evaluation or cost-allocation scheme does not lead managers to make decisions that benefit the organization as a whole, then it should be changed or discarded.

Summary

Any discussion of profit requires that the difference between accounting profit and economic profit be understood. Both accountants and economists define profit as revenues minus costs. The difference lies in the definition of costs. The accountant defines costs as those *explicit* charges entered on the company's books. The economist also accepts those explicit charges as costs, but adds to them the *opportunity cost* of the wages of capital.

The economist values both goods sold and goods retained in inventory at replacement cost. Profit or loss can then be calculated as the difference in cash value of the firm at the beginning and end of the accounting period. Using replacement cost also permits separation of economic profit (loss) into two parts:

1. *Trading profit (loss)* is the direct result of the firm's primary business, which is the making (or buying) and selling of goods.
2. *Holding profit (loss)* is a capital gain or loss that results from a general increase or decrease in price while goods are being held for sale.

The history of economic thought abounds in profit theories, but most of them fall into three major categories:

1. *Compensatory or functional theories*, which hold that economic profit is the reward for above-average efficiency in the production and marketing of the firm's product.
2. *Friction and monopoly theories*, which hold that unanticipated changes in cost conditions or demand for the product can lead to surplus profits for some period of time.
3. *Technology and innovation theories*, which hold that profits are the rewards for innovation, that is, the reward for adapting an invention to business use.

A profit budget serves the functions of planning, coordination, and control of the firm's activities. The budgeting process enables managers to anticipate their needs, and forces a coordination of the firm's activities that otherwise might not take place. A profit budget enables management to maintain a systematic check on the company's operations in terms of planned versus actual results.

Break-even analysis is an adjunct to profit planning that graphically or algebraically portrays the probable effects of alternative courses of action. Simple algebraic formulas can be used to determine the output and sales required to break even or to earn a target profit.

Operating leverage is the sales elasticity of profit, which measures the sensitivity of profits to changes in output and sales. It can be calculated as the ratio of total contribution profit to operating profit. Operating leverage can be used to determine the relative advantage or disadvantage of capital-intensive operations versus labor-intensive operations at various levels of output.

Break-even analysis is simple, easy to understand by management, and relatively inexpensive to perform. Its weakness is the assumption that profit is a simple function of output. In reality, profit is also affected by production processes, selling effort, the composition of demand, and a multiplicity of other factors both internal and external to the firm.

On the control side, a formidable task is the evaluation of divisions and divisional managers of a decentralized firm, and departmental performance within divisions. One of the toughest problems at both levels is the fair and equitable allocation of fixed overhead costs. One suggested method of short-run evaluation is to simply compare actual performance with budgeted performance. Whatever procedure is adopted, it must lead managers to make decisions that benefit the whole organization.

Problems

1. In reporting the cost of leases, large business firms are now required to "capitalize" future lease payments and record the capitalized value as a liability and also as an asset. Both of these values are then reduced as lease payments are made. Previously, these lease payments were treated as ordinary expenses in the year in which they were made. From the economist's point of view, explain which method you believe more accurately measures the value of the firm at any given time.

2. What is meant by contribution margin? Can it be positive when total profit is negative? Can it be negative when total profit is positive?

3. Return on investment (*ROI*) is frequently used to evaluate the profit performance of semiautonomous divisions within a corporation. Discuss some limitations of using this method. Can you suggest an alternative approach? Explain.

4. In break-even analysis, if a linear revenue function is used, one is assuming that all units of output are sold at a constant price. What assumption is made when a nonlinear revenue curve is used? Is either of these assumptions very realistic from a practical point of view? Discuss.

5. Vincent quit his $36,000 a year job as a wholesale liquor salesman to work full-time on his growing Polish vodka distributorship. He began the year with $20,000 in cash and 1,400 bottles of Polish vodka. The following is a record of purchases made during the year.

Date	Number of Bottles	Price per Bottle
Jan 1	100	$7.50
Mar 7	500	8.25
May 14	1,000	8.50
Jul 2	800	8.50
Oct 3	500	9.00
Dec 6	600	9.50

At the end of the year, Vincent calculated total sales of $72,000 and operating expenses of $10,000. The ending inventory is 1,300 bottles, and he has just received notice from the importer of a price increase to $10 a bottle.

a. What is the ending cash value of Vincent's distributorship?

b. What is the total economic profit for operations during the year?

c. Separate the total economic profit into trading and holding profit.

d. If you were Vincent, would you stay in business? Analyze the situation and explain your answer.

6. Data for last month's activity at a division of the Albritton Company appear in the accompanying table.

	Product			
	A	B	C	Total
Sales	$100,000	$60,000	$90,000	$250,000
Variable costs	50,000	50,000	60,000	160,000
Allocated fixed costs	24,000	14,400	21,600	60,000
Profit (loss) before taxes	$ 26,000	$ (4,400)	$ 8,400	$ 30,000
Federal income taxes (34%)	8,840	(1,496)	2,856	10,200
Net profit	$ 17,160	$ (2,904)	$ 5,544	$19,800

a. Calculate the break-even sales volume for the division as a whole.

b. Sales in the upcoming month are expected to change as follows: (1) Product A, up 10 percent; (2) Product B, down 20 percent; and (3) Product C, up 5 percent. Based on this new information, calculate the new break-even sales volume. Also, determine the divisional profit or loss for the upcoming period.

c. Albritton's president feels the division should eliminate Product B because of its previous profit performance and the pessimistic forecast for the upcoming month. Do you agree with this decision? Why or why not?

7. Suave Hats, Inc., manufactures men's hats in Hong Kong and sells them in the United States at US$5 each. Its total fixed cost is US$1,000 per week, and its average variable cost is US$3 per unit.

a. How many hats per week must the company sell to break even?

b. What would the company's profit be at its normal production capacity of 1,000 hats per week?

c. The company has been operating at its normal production capacity, but production is going to be disrupted for several days while the company moves its factory to larger quarters. The president of Suave decides to produce an additional 500 hats for inventory at an estimated average variable cost of $3.50 per hat. What will be the expected incremental profit (or loss) on the sale of the 500 additional hats?

d. During the period when the company was moving its factory, it was able to dispose of only 300 of the 500 additional hats at the regular price of $5. However, a department store has now offered to take the remaining 200 hats under a private label at $2 each. If the management of Suave accepts the offer, what will be the incremental effect of the 500 units?

8. South of the Border, Inc., operates a factory in Guadalajara, Mexico, where it makes men's raincoats for sale in the United States, Latin America, and Europe. The raincoats sell for the equivalent in buyers' currency of US$40 each, from which the average contribution profit is US$15 per coat. Last year total fixed costs were US$5.4 million; this year, through a major cost-reduction effort, total fixed costs are expected to be US$3.9 million.

a. How many raincoats did South of the Border, Inc., need to sell last year in order to break even?

b. How many must it sell this year in order to break even?

c. How many raincoats must the company sell this year in order to earn a before-tax profit equal to 20 percent of sales?

9. Long Wei-Lin is preparing to manufacture designer jeans at a new plant in Chiang Mai, Thailand, for export to the United States and Europe. Since "Long" is the Chinese word for "dragon," the firm has been named Dragon Goods, Ltd., and the jeans will be distinguished by a patch on the hip pocket with an embroidered dragon on it.

Costs for the first year of operation are estimated to be, in U.S. dollars,

Rent	$1,500 per month
Direct labor	$3.30 per hour
Raw materials	$3.00 per pair of jeans
Overhead	$975 per week
Interest on capital	$1,350 per month.

It takes 20 minutes of direct labor to make a pair of jeans, which are expected to sell for $9.10 each.

a. How many pairs of jeans must be sold to break even the first year?

b. After a successful first year, Long Wei-Lin foresees a decline in demand for designer jeans as a result of changing tastes and possibly a weakening world economy. If he wants a break-even point of 13,000 units, how much of a reduction in fixed costs would be necessary?

c. What three alternative methods are available for reducing the break-even point? Using each of these methods, what adjustments must be made to meet the break-even point of 13,000 units?

d. Considering the uncertain demand conditions faced by Dragon Goods, what combination of the three methods for reducing break-even points is most appropriate? Why?

10. Monkeypod, Ltd., is a newly formed company in the Hawaiian wood-products industry. It will specialize in monkeypod-wood bowls for sale to both tourists and island residents. Before constructing any production facilities, management conducted market research to see what the monthly demand for this product is on each of the islands most visited by tourists, with the following results.

Island	Demand/Month
Oahu	8,000
Maui	3,000
Kauai	2,300
Hawaii	2,000
Total	15,300

After considering the market survey, the facilities development team suggested two alternatives for plant construction:

1. Build one large plant on Oahu with a capacity of 16,000 units per month, fixed cost of $32,000 per month, and variable cost of $4 per unit.

2. Build four plants, one on each island, with production capacities of 8,000 units on Oahu, 3,000 units on Maui, 2,500 units on Kauai, and 2,000 units on the Big Island (Hawaii). The total fixed cost for the four facilities would be $40,000 per month with variable costs of $3.50 per unit.

   a. What are the total-cost equations for each alternative?

   b. Given the market-survey results, which of the given production alternatives should be chosen?

   c. If the monkeypod bowls sell for $9.50 each, how much profit will be realized from your chosen alternative?

   d. Discuss possible reasons for the differing cost structures between the two production alternatives.

   e. If the demand for bowls is expected to rise significantly next year, would this alter your decision? Explain. Include economies of scale in your discussion.

11. IBN Water Purification, Inc., is evaluating two possible designs for a new production facility to replace its present obsolete facility. The total-cost functions for the two facilities are

$$TC_1 = \$550,000 + \$600Q$$
$$TC_2 = \$300,000 + \$825Q.$$

Both plants would produce an identical desalination device that would sell for $2,600 per unit. IBN foresees no change in demand and intends to estimate sales from an average of the past seven years, as follows:

Year	Sales($000)
1	$1,100
2	1,075
3	1,200
4	1,250
5	1,150
6	1,100
7	1,125

a. Which plant design is labor-intensive and which is capital-intensive? Explain.

b. Calculate the operating leverage for both plant designs.

c. Find the level of production at which neither plant design has an advantage.

d. Considering the sales information given, which plant design has a greater probability of cost savings?

Case Problem: Dutch Line Furniture Company

12. Dutch Line Furniture Company produces natural-oak wood chairs. The chairs sell for $135 each, variable costs are $50 each, and fixed costs total $120,000 per year. Current production is 3,500 chairs per year, which is plant capacity. Because of excess demand, Dutch Line is planning to expand plant capacity by 1,500 chairs. The plant expansion will incorporate some new high-speed equipment that will result in a reduction of variable costs by 40 percent. Because of its reputation for quality, Dutch Line can sell every chair it produces.

Questions

a. What is the break-even output before and after the plant expansion?

b. What is the operating leverage at current capacity?

c. What would be the operating leverage at capacity after plant expansion?

d. Will the plant expansion increase or decrease the margin of safety at capacity?

e. Would you advise Dutch Line to expand? Explain.

Case Problem: U.S. Automobile Industry

13. Since the Japanese auto influx of the late 1970s, the big three U.S. auto manufacturers have tried reducing prices, giving rebates, and offering discount financing in order to increase sales. Com-

mon sense tells us that sales are elastic to price. In other words, by lowering the price we can increase sales. However, with further analysis it becomes apparent that there are actually two forms of elasticity to be considered when adjusting prices:

1. Price elasticity of demand, which measures the effect of price reductions on demand and thus on revenues

2. Cost elasticity, which measures the effect of increased sales volume on production and thus on costs.

Both elasticities should be considered by U.S. auto manufacturers when they attempt to compete by means of price reductions. However, corporations using such price reductions have focused on price elasticity of demand while often neglecting the effects on costs.

Actual demand studies conducted on new automobiles have estimated price elasticities of demand ranging from 0.5 to 1.5. The higher the coefficient of elasticity, the greater the percent increase in quantity demanded that will result from a price decrease. For our analysis assume a liberal elasticity measurement of 1.5, which should maximize any benefits from a price reduction. We will explore the effects of an auto manufacturer's reducing car prices by $400.

The auto industry is considered to be an oligopoly market structure. Thus competition can be expected to meet any price reduction, as indicated by the rebate war of the late 1970s and the interest-rate competition during the 1980s. As a result, price reductions do not result in a relative advantage but instead a general price change by all producers. Assume the following conditions before price reductions:

Average car price	$9,000 per car
Expected sales volume	1,000,000 cars
Average total cost	$8,200 per car
Total variable cost	$6.4 billion.

Questions

a. Calculate the present total fixed cost, average fixed cost, and average variable cost.

b. What is the present break-even point?

c. What is the change in total revenue resulting from the $400 price reduction?

d. Calculate the profit before and after the price reduction.

e. Because of the price reduction, revenues have been reduced by $400 per car. Was there any effect on the cost per car? What is the average total cost after reducing the price?

f. Discuss possible conclusions from your calculations.

g. Would higher or lower variable cost, relative to total cost, help justify price reductions? Explain.

h. Use the following formulas to determine the price elasticity of demand necessary for a given price reduction while keeping profits constant:

$$\%Q = \frac{PR}{\pi - PR + (1 - \frac{TVC}{TC})ATC}$$

where

$\%Q$ = Percentage increase in output quantity required

PR = Price reduction, in dollars

π = Unit profit at the old price

TVC = Total variable cost

TC = Total cost

ATC = Average total cost per unit.

The elasticity coefficient is then

$$\epsilon = \frac{Q(\pi + ATC)}{PR}.$$

At what elasticity would the $400 price reduction be justified?

i. What advice would you give to the auto manufacturers? Why do U.S. manufacturers continue to give price reductions?

j. Discuss possible recessionary effects on auto sales.

References

Dearden, John. "Measuring Profit Center Managers." *Harvard Business Review*, no. 5 (September-October 1987), p. 84–88.

Forbes, Kevin F.; and Dennis C. Mueller. "Profits in the Long Run." *Southern Economic Journal* 54, no. 1 (July 1987), p. 470.

Jacobson, Robert. "The Validity of ROI as a Measure of Business Performance." *American Economic Review* 77, no. 3 (June 1987), p. 470.

Horngren, Charles T. *Cost Accounting, A Managerial Emphasis*. 5th ed. Englewood Cliffs, N.J.: Prentice-Hall, 1982.

Mansfield, Edwin. "Industrial Innovation in Japan and the United States." *Science* 241 (September 30, 1988), 1771–1772.

————. "Technological Creativity: Japan and the United States." *Business Horizons* (March-April 1989), pp. 48–53.

Meimaroglou, M. C. "Break-Even Analysis with Stepwise Varying Marginal Costs and Revenue." *Budgeting* (November 1986), pp. 1–7.

Reinhardt, U. E. "Breakeven Analysis for Lockheed's Tri-Star: An Application of Financial Theory." *Journal of Finance* (September 1973), pp. 821–38.

Riggs, James L. *Engineering Economics*. 2nd ed. New York: McGraw-Hill, 1982. The discussion on multiple products and nonlinear break-even analysis in Chapter 3 is particularly recommended.

15

MARKET STRUCTURE AND PRICING ANALYSIS

In previous chapters we discussed (1) possible objectives of the firm and the profit-maximization model, (2) determinants and measurement of demand, (3) the production function and the concept of optimal employment of resources, (4) the nature and behavior of costs, including economies of scale, and (5) profit planning and control. Having studied these elements, we are now in a position to examine how demand, production, cost, and profit objectives interact to determine price/output decisions in various market structures.

In this chapter, price/output decisions in the four market structures of perfect competition, pure monopoly, monopolistic competition, and oligopoly are discussed. The next chapter addresses special topics in pricing such as pricing objectives and methods, price discrimination, pricing of multiple products, pricing of joint products, and transfer pricing.

CHAPTER OUTLINE

The chapter is divided into six sections and an appendix:

1. **Market Structures**. This section examines five important determinants of market structure: (1) sellers' characteristics, (2) buyers' characteristics, (3) product characteristics, (4) conditions of market entry and exit, and (5) economies of scale. The section ends with a brief introduction to equilibrium analysis.

2. **Perfect Competition**. This section presents the characteristics of a perfectly competitive market structure and analyzes a firm's pricing and output decisions in both the short run and the long run.
3. **Pure Monopoly**. This section examines the theoretical model of pure monopoly and analyzes both short-run and long-run equilibrium in this market structure.
4. **Monopolistic Competition**. This section examines a market structure in which firms compete while still retaining some elements of monopoly. It analyzes a firm's equilibrium situation in both the short-run and the long-run.
5. **Oligopoly**. This section examines four different types of oligopoly models: (1) price-leadership models, (2) the kinked–demand-curve model, (3) cartels and formal collusion, and (4) market-share models.
6. **Nonprice Competition**. The last section of the chapter discusses nonprice competition provided by product differentiation and advertising.
7. **Appendix 15A: Market Power and Profit-Maximizing Advertising.** This appendix discusses the Lerner index of market power and the profit-maximizing advertising/sales ratio.

Market Structures

Market structure refers to the nature and degree of competition in the market for a particular good or service. The general theory of pricing postulates a spectrum of market structures that range from **perfect competition** at one extreme to **pure monopoly** at the other. In between lies **imperfect competition**, in which a number of intermediate market structures are possible. For convenience, market structures in imperfect competition are divided into two classes: **monopolistic competition** and **oligopoly**.

A number of determinants influence the market structure for any particular product or group of products. In general, determinants of market structure fall into five major independent categories:

1. The number and nature of the sellers
2. The number and nature of the buyers
3. The nature of the product
4. The conditions of entry into and exit from the market
5. Possible economies of scale.

Each of these categories is discussed in more detail in the following subsections.

The Effect of Seller Characteristics on Market Structure

The nature and degree of competition are influenced by the number and size of the firms operating in the market in relation to the size of the market. Thus the continuum of market structures ranges from many small sellers in perfect competition (no one of which can produce a significant portion of the total market supply) to only one seller in a pure monopoly. Agricultural commodities provide particularly good examples of purely competitive markets with many relatively small sellers, while utilities offer examples of markets close to pure monopolies.

The Effect of Buyer Characteristics on the Market Structure

The nature and degree of competition are also influenced by the number and size of buyers in the market. If there is only one large buyer (the condition is called **monopsony**) or only a few relatively large buyers (this condition is called **oligopsony**), there cannot be much competition among suppliers. The market price will be established by what the large buyers are willing to pay. Monopsony or oligopsony characterizes government purchases of complex systems, the market for automotive components purchased by the large automobile manufacturers, local labor markets where there is only one large employer, and local agricultural markets where the entire crop is purchased by a few large processors.

The Effect of Product Characteristics on Market Structure

The most important characteristic of a firm's product is the degree to which the product is differentiated from all others in the same market. Product differentiation thus is closely related to elasticities of demand. Products that are close substitutes, as indicated by high positive cross elasticity coefficients, will be marketed in a different structure from products with greater or lesser differentiation. At one extreme, a perfectly elastic standard product (no differentiation) is a necessary condition for perfect competition. At the other extreme, a product with no close substitutes (extreme differentiation) is a necessary condition for pure monopoly.

Conditions of Entry and Exit

Economic theory holds that profitability within a particular market will attract the entry of new firms, and lack of profitability (losses) will drive weaker firms out. In the model of perfect competition, both entry and exit are assumed to be free from any obstruction. At the other extreme, a pure monopoly can exist only if barriers to entry are so high that no other firm can enter the market.

There are many potential barriers to the entry of new firms into a particular market, and the height of these barriers plays a crucial role in determining the structure of the market. Factors that may bar market entry include:

1. Costs of developing a differentiated product plus promotional costs necessary to penetrate the market.
2. Demand conditions, especially price elasticity. For example, if there is limited demand for a price-inelastic product in a market that is already being fully supplied, it will be very difficult for a new firm to carve out a share of the market for itself.
3. Control by existing firms over the supply of factors of production.
4. Control by existing firms over channels of distribution.
5. Legal and institutional factors, such as patents and franchises.

6. Potential economies of scale.
7. Capital requirements.
8. Technological factors.

Economy of Scale

Possible economies of scale in production provide the best explanation of why there are large firms in some industries, but not in others. When large economies of scale are possible, firms that can grow large enough to achieve such economies have a competitive edge. Other things being equal, smaller firms with higher marginal costs are unable to compete and drop out of the market. Consequently, the market comes to be served by a small number of firms, each of which is large enough to attain the available economies of scale. When the economy of scale is such that it can be fully achieved only if one firm provides all that is demanded, then a **natural monopoly** exists.

Equilibrium Analysis

In any market structure, the firm must determine the level of production that will maximize profit or minimize loss. This process is called **equilibrium analysis**. Equilibrium analysis is performed for the short run and for the long run.

Short-run equilibrium is an operating concept based on two fundamental assumptions:

1. The firm is operating plant(s) of fixed capacity with some fixed costs.
2. Because of the relatively short time frame of short-run analysis, market demand is relatively stable.

Long-run equilibrium is a planning concept based upon the following assumptions:

1. In the long run all assets are variable, making the firm free to alter the size of its plant(s) and any other element of production.
2. Except in pure monopoly, market supply will be stabilized by the entry and exit of profit-maximizing firms into or out of the industry. In the case of monopoly, the monopolist will adjust plant size to supply the profit-maximizing quantity.

Having examined the determinants of market structure, we are now ready to discuss the firm's output and pricing decisions in terms of reaching equilibrium in four basic models: perfect competition, pure monopoly, monopolistic competition, and oligopoly.

Perfect Competition

The model of **perfect competition** envisions a market structure with the following characteristics:

1. *Many small sellers of a homogeneous or standard product.* Market supply is the aggregate production of many small sellers and no one seller produces enough to significantly affect market supply. However, if all sellers move in the same direction at the same time, market supply will be affected. For example, a low market price of wheat in one year may cause all wheat farmers to reduce their plantings for the next year.

2. *Many small buyers.* Since the product is homogeneous, buyers are indifferent to the source of the product. Market demand thus is the aggregate demand of all buyers, no one of which is large enough to significantly affect demand. However, if all buyers move in the same direction at the same time, they will shift the demand curve. For example, there is an upsurge in the demand for eggs at Easter time and in the demand for lettuce in hot weather.

3. *Free entry and exit.* In the long run, there is free entry into and exit out of the market. Barriers to entry or exit are either very low or nonexistent.

4. *Free mobility of economic resources.* There are no artificial restraints upon supply, demand, or price of either input factors of production or output of the product, and all resources are freely mobile.

5. *Perfect information.* Each buyer and seller operates under conditions of certainty, being endowed with complete knowledge of prices, quantities, costs, and demand.[1]

6. *The firm is a price taker and quantity adjuster.* Market price is determined by the interaction between market supply and market demand. Consequently, individual firms have nothing to say about price. Individual firms cannot sell their product at more than market price, because no one will buy it, and it would be irrational to sell at less than the market price. Therefore, each individual firm in a purely competitive market is a taker of the market price. Why? Because the output of each individual firm is too small to influence the market price. By the same token, because the individual firm's share of the market is so insignificant, each firm can sell all it can produce at the market price. Thus each firm sees its demand curve as a horizontal line, and the firm's only decision is how much to produce in order to maximize profit or minimize loss.

Although some of the assumptions of the perfectly competitive model may seem unrealistic, use of the model in economic theory has been increasing in recent decades for two quite different reasons. One reason is that the model can be used as an ideal, or yardstick, against which all other models can be compared and evaluated. The other reason is that the model has been quite useful for explaining and predicting behavior of the market and of the firm in circumstances that fit the model.

Short-Run Equilibrium

In a perfectly competitive market, the firm's task is to maximize profit or minimize loss with a given cost function and a price fixed by the market. Analysis begins with market equilibrium between the market supply curve, *S*, and the market demand curve, *D*, as shown in Panel A of Exhibit 15–1 (page 456). The market-clearing price is thus established at *P*.

Panel B shows that the firm can sell all it wishes at the market price. Therefore, the firm sees its demand curve as a horizontal line that is both the average-revenue curve (*AR*) and the marginal-revenue curve (*MR*) since both *AR* and *MR* are equal to the

---

[1] The model of *pure* competition, as opposed to *perfect* competition, does not require perfect information on the part of buyers and sellers. In pure competition, buyers and sellers may be unaware of pertinent market facts to various degrees.

EXHIBIT 15–1   Profit-Maximizing Price and Output for a Firm in Pure Competition

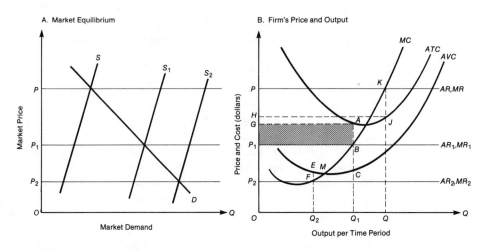

A. Market Equilibrium

Market Demand

B. Firm's Price and Output

Output per Time Period

market price, *P*. Panel B also shows the curves representing the firm's marginal cost, *MC*, average total cost, *ATC*, and average variable cost, *AVC*. These cost curves include a "normal profit," (a return on investment based on the firm's opportunity cost).

As we have noted in previous chapters, the firm's profit will be maximized when *MC* = *MR*. This occurs at point *K* in Panel B, indicating an optimal production of *Q* units and a price of *P* dollars. The unit price, *P*, is greater than unit cost, *ATC*, by *JK* dollars. This represents unit profit. Hence there is a total economic profit represented by the rectangle *JKPH*.

Illustrative Problem

Zebra Coffee Delight, Inc., is one of many small independent processors of Brazilian coffee. The industry's weekly supply and demand functions are estimated to be

$$Q_S = 5,000P \text{ and } Q_D = 90,000 - 4,000P$$

where

Q_S = Quantity supplied per week, in metric tons (2,204.6 pounds)
Q_D = Quantity demanded per week, in metric tons
P = Price per metric ton, in thousands of U.S. dollars.

Zebra's cost function is

$$TC = 4 + 4Q + Q^2.$$

Questions

a. What is the market price?
b. What is the profit-maximizing level of output by Zebra?
c. What are Zebra's total revenue, total cost, unit cost, and profit at the profit-maximizing level of output?

Solutions

a. Market price is established at the point where market supply and market demand are equal:

$$Q_S = 5,000P = 90,000 - 4,000P = Q_D$$
$$9,000P = 90,000$$
$$P = 10, \text{ i.e.,}$$
$$P = \$10,000/\text{metric ton} \approx \$4.54/\text{pound.}$$

b. Profit is maximum when marginal revenue = marginal cost. In a perfectly competitive market, marginal revenue is just the market price, which is 10.

$$MR = 10$$
$$TC = 4 + 4Q + Q^2$$
$$MC = \frac{dTC}{dQ} = 4 + 2Q$$

At optimum,

$$MR = MC$$
$$4 + 2Q = 10$$
$$Q = 3 \text{ metric tons or 6,613.8 pounds.}$$

Alternative solution

$$\pi = TR - TC = PQ - TC = 10Q - (4 + 4Q + Q^2) = -4 + 6Q - Q^2$$
$$\frac{d\pi}{dQ} = 6 - 2Q$$
$$Q = 3$$

To complete the exercise, we take the second derivative and check its sign to see whether Q represents a maximum (negative sign) or a minimum (positive sign):

$$\frac{d^2\pi}{dQ_2} = -2.$$

Hence π is maximum at $Q = 3$. When $Q = 3$, $MC = 4 + 2Q = 10$, which is equal to marginal revenue. At any greater level of production, $MC > MR$, and at any lower level of production, $MC < MR$.

c. (1) $TR = PQ = 10(3) = 30$, i.e., \$30,000 per week.
   (2) $TC = 4 + 4(3) + (3)^2 = 25$, i.e., \$25,000 per week.
   (3) $ATC = TC/Q = 25/3 = 8.33333$,
       i.e., \$8,333.33 per metric ton or \$3.78 per pound.
   (4) $\pi = TR - TC = \$30,000 - \$25,000 = \$5,000$ per week.

Now let us suppose that the market equilibrium is upset by events that cause a shift in either the market-demand or the market-supply curve. A good example is the bumper grain crop of 1982, which shifted the market-supply curve to the right and drove the price down below cost for many farmers. A change in price calls, of course, for a different optimal quantity of production.

To illustrate, suppose the supply curve shifts from S to S_1 in Panel A of Exhibit 15–1, creating a new market price of P_1. Now the firm's $MR = MC$ at point B in Panel B, and $Q = Q_1$. The price is now less than total unit cost, ATC, but greater than unit variable cost, AVC. Consequently, the firm will lose some, but not all of its fixed cost. Its loss is represented by the shaded rectangle ABP_1G.

A firm in this position will continue to produce in the short run. Why? Because if it shuts down, it will have no revenue and lose all of its fixed cost. If the firm continues to produce, it will recover all of its variable cost and some of its fixed cost, thus minimizing its loss.

If the market price drops to P_2, which is below the firm's minimum average variable cost, the firm must shut down, because if it continues to operate, it will lose all of its fixed cost and some of its variable cost as well.

The Firm's Short-Run Supply Curve. We see in Exhibit 15–1 that at each different price, the firm's output level is determined by the intersection of the marginal-revenue and marginal-cost curves, where $MR = MC$. The points of intersection between the MR curve and the MC curve follow the MC curve as the price changes. Hence the firm's short-run supply curve is simply its marginal-cost curve, except that the lower end of the supply curve terminates at point M, where $MC = AVC$. below this point, the firm would be losing all of its fixed cost and some of its variable cost and therefore would shut down in order to limit its loss to its total fixed cost.

Long-Run Equilibrium

To understand the process of reaching long-run equilibrium, remember that the model of perfect competition assumes there are no barriers to impede the entrance of new firms into the industry or to hinder the exit of firms that may want to leave. Those firms that do remain in the industry beyond the short run can adjust plant size in the long run to obtain maximum efficiency. With costs reduced to a minimum, these more efficient firms are in a position to survive whatever the market does.

Exhibit 15–2 shows how the market and the firms within it arrive at long-run equilibrium with market demand held constant. Panel A of this exhibit shows supply and demand in the market. Panel B shows the long-run average total cost, $LRATC$, and long-run marginal cost, $LRMC$, of a typical plant, which we assume has been constructed for maximum cost efficiency.

1. Given the demand curve D and the supply curve S_1 in Panel A, a market-clearing price of P_1 becomes established. Since this price is the firm's marginal revenue, the profit-maximizing firm will produce Q_1 units of output. At this level of production, the price is higher than the $LRATC$, which results in substantial economic profit.

2. The economic profit being earned by firms in the industry at a price of P_1 attracts new firms. Their added production shifts the supply curve rightward to S_2, which lowers the market price to P_2. Each firm reduces its output to the optimal quantity Q_2, with the

EXHIBIT 15–2   **Adjustment to Long-Run Equilibrium in a Purely Competitive Market**

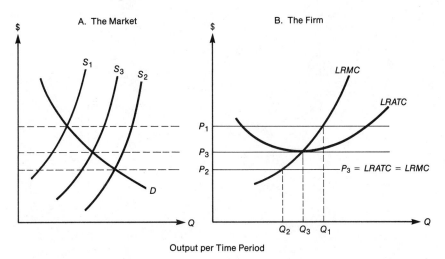

Output per Time Period

result that $P_2 < LRATC$. The less efficient firms will then drop out, shifting the supply curve leftward to S_3 where the price is P_3.

3. At the price P_3, the typical firm's optimum production is Q_3, where $P = LRMC$. At this level of production, the $LRATC$ is at a minimum since $LRATC = LRMC$. Thus the typical firm earns no economic profit while producing and selling the product at the lowest possible long-run average total cost.

The preceding model rests on the assumption of perfect knowledge that was stated earlier. In real life, of course, knowledge is not perfect. There may be lack of information, misinformation, miscalculations by managers as well as circumstances over which managers have no control and little, if any, foreknowledge. For example, the weather determines the size of the wheat, corn, and soybean crops. A farmer must decide how much to plant without knowing how large the harvest will be. Such uncertainties cause frequent adjustments to the number of producers in the industry and to the market supply, but the tendency toward long-run equilibrium where $P = LRATC = LRMC$ *is unmistakable.*

The Impact of New Technology on Long-Run Equilibrium and International Trade. Although international markets for personal computers, VCRs, compact-disc players, stereo TV monitors, and other electronic goods do not precisely fit the assumptions of the perfectly competitive model, there are enough similarities among goods of competing sellers and enough sellers to make the model applicable. For example, IBM personal computers and all of their clones use the same standardized operating system, regardless of which country produces them. Software vendors develop their programs to be compatible with the operating system rather than for any particular make of computer.

EXHIBIT 15–3   The Effect of Cost-Reducing New Technology upon Long-Run Equilibrium

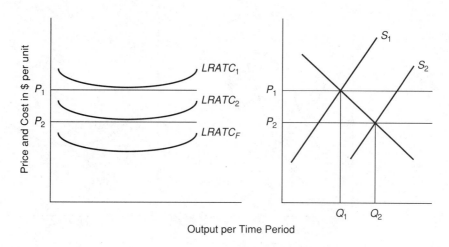

Output per Time Period

Exhibit 15–2 in the preceding section showed how economic profits are squeezed out for firms operating in a perfectly competitive market. In some industries, however, the introduction of new technology further reduces long-run average total cost until new equilibrium is reached at a much lower price and a much higher level of production and sales. The process is illustrated by Exhibit 15–3. The exhibit shows initial long-run equilibrium with the industry supply S_1 and a market-clearing price of P_1, which corresponds to the typical firm's lowest *LRATC*. New technology lowers the typical firm's *LRATC* to the point where the lowest *LRATC* equals P_2. For a short time, maintaining the price P_1 may provide economic profits, but if the market is perfectly competitive, the new technology is freely available to anyone. New firms will enter the market, increasing the supply to S_2 with a market-clearing price of P_2, which is equal to the lowest cost on the typical firm's *LRATC*.

This phenomenon has been particularly evident in the industries producing electronic goods and other high-tech products, where dramatic reductions in price have been accompanied by equally dramatic increases in demand for these products. The phenomenon has also strongly affected international trade in these products.

When all nations have access to the same technology, the nation with the lowest labor costs can produce the product with the lowest *LRATC* and therefore with a lower price than all others. This is illustrated by $LRATC_F$ in Exhibit 15–3. Firms with $LRATC_F$ can charge any price they wish between P_2 and the lowest point of $LRATC_F$ and firms with $LRATC_2$ will be unable to compete. In this way, South Korea has come to dominate the international market for microwave ovens.

The Market's Long-Run Adjustment to Increased Demand.   In the preceding section, we examined the results of a shift in the market-supply curve while the market-demand curve remained constant, i.e., while only price was allowed to vary. Now we want to

EXHIBIT 15–4   **Long-Run Supply Curves for Constant-Cost, Increasing-Cost, and Decreasing-Cost Industries**

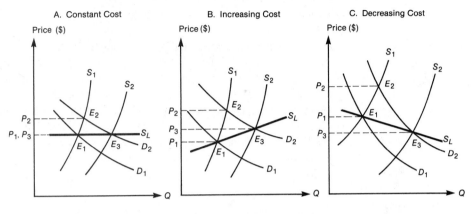

Quantity Produced per Period of Time

determine what happens when the market-demand curve is caused to shift by changes in demand determinants other than price, as depicted in Exhibit 15–4.

Each of the panels in Exhibit 15–4 depicts what happens to market supply and market price when demand is increased. In each panel, we begin with the market-demand curve D_1 and the market-supply curve S_1. Equilibrium is at point E_1 where the market-clearing price is P_1. Then, for any of a number of reasons, the demand curve shifts to D_2. In each panel, market equilibrium immediately and temporarily shifts to E_2, with a higher market price of P_2.

At the higher market price, firms already in the industry then increase production to gain additional profit. The possibility of economic profit may also attract new firms into the market. In either case, output increases, causing the supply curve to shift to the right. In each panel, new market equilibrium is gained at E_3, with a market price of P_3. The value of P_3, however, depends upon what happens to production costs when firms in the industry increase production to satisfy the increased demand.

1. *Constant production cost.* If a particular industry does not require a significant share of the total supply (in the whole economy) of the input resources it uses, prices of the input factors of production are not driven up as production increases. Since the *LRATC* does not increase for firms in the industry, equilibrium is achieved at the original price, i.e., $P_3 = P_1$, as shown in Panel A. When the initial equilibrium point, E_1, is connected with the final equilibrium point, E_3, the resulting long-run supply curve is horizontal.

2. *Increasing production cost.* Panel B depicts an industry that requires a significant share of the total resources available. When production increases to meet the increased demand, firms in this industry must bid up the prices of input factors in order to obtain a sufficient supply. Therefore, their minimum *LRATCs* (which equal price) are greater.

The market goes through the same sort of transition as discussed previously, from initial equilibrium at E_1 with price P_1, through interim equilibrium at E_2 with price P_2, to final equilibrium at E_3 with price P_3. This time, however, the long-run supply curve connecting E_1 and E_3 has an upward slope, while the final price, P_3, is higher than the initial price, P_1.

3. *Decreasing production cost.* Panel C again depicts the transition from E_1 and P_1 through E_2 and P_2 to E_3 and P_3. This time, the long-run supply curve slopes downward and the ultimate price, P_3, is lower than the initial price, P_1. This situation occurs when expanding production enables firms to (1) take advantage of new technology and (2) realize economies of scale. These two factors may work together to decrease the costs of production. This situation may often be observed in the developing countries of Asia. As their industries grow, production costs are reduced by volume purchases of raw materials, reduced shipping charges, and other economies of scale.

Pure Monopoly

The model of pure monopoly lies at the opposite end of the market-structure continuum from perfect competition. In general, monopoly power exists anywhere along the continuum where the seller exercises some degree of control over a product's price and quantity supplied in the market. This broad definition covers any seller outside of perfect or pure competition, and takes in most firms in the U. S. economy. Monopoly power is greatest, of course, in a **pure monopoly**, which has the following characteristics:

1. *One seller.* There is only one seller, which supplies the entire market.
2. *No close substitute.* The seller's product is so differentiated from others that no close substitute exists.
3. *No entry allowed.* Barriers to entry are so high that no other firm can enter the market.

These characteristics place complete control of the market in the hands of the monopoly, which must decide how much to produce and how much to charge for its product. The output level and price will be chosen, of course, to maximize profit.

The assumption of insuperable barriers to entry is crucial to the maintenance of the monopoly in the long run. This means that even when the monopoly is earning economic profits, additional suppliers are unable to enter the market. The most common barriers to entry are:

1. Legal or institutional factors, such as patents or franchises
2. Economies of scale that require very large capital outlays
3. The monopoly's control of input supplies
4. Demand conditions, such as the market's inability to absorb additional production
5. Technology controlled by the monopoly.

Real-world examples that completely fulfill all of the theoretical conditions for pure monopoly are rare, if they exist at all. However, the position of pure monopoly is approached by firms providing electricity, natural gas, local telephone communications, cable-TV service, and some transportation services. These monopolies arise because the

EXHIBIT 15–5   **Unregulated Monopoly's Output, Price, and Profit**

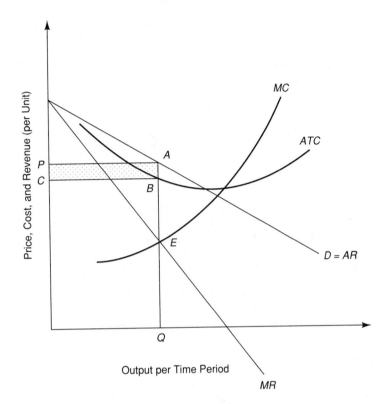

economies of scale are such that it is most efficient to let one firm produce and sell all that is demanded at a market-clearing price. These are called **natural monopolies**. Usually, such firms are granted a government franchise to monopolize a defined area in exchange for submitting to government regulation. A regulated monopoly has its prices set by a public-utilities commission or similar body such that those prices allow the monopoly a specific rate of return on investment.

An unregulated monopoly, however, has complete control of output and price. Therefore, it can set the output and price to maximize profit. It does so by setting $MR = MC$ to find the optimal output.

Short-Run Monopoly Equilibrium

Since a monopoly supplies the entire market, the firm's demand curve is just the downward-sloping market-demand curve, as illustrated by Exhibit 15–5. The exhibit depicts the short-run equilibrium of a monopoly with the market demand curve, D, the marginal-revenue curve, MR, the marginal-cost curve, MC, and the unit-cost curve, ATC. Profit is maximized at the level of output where $MR = MC$. To find the profit-maximizing output and price, we draw a vertical line through the intersection of the MR and MC curves such that it reaches the horizontal axis at Q, intersects the unit cost curve (ATC) at point B, and reaches the demand curve (D) at point A. Then we draw a horizontal line from point A to the vertical axis at P, and another horizontal line from point B to the vertical axis at C. Point C marks the unit cost and point P marks the selling price at which Q units of the product will be demanded. As the graph is drawn, the monopoly enjoys an economic profit represented by the shaded rectangle, $ABCP$.

Illustrative Problem

The Savemore Home Improvement Center has an exclusive franchise for distribution of Lawn King lawn mowers in the Kansas City metropolitan area. Lawn King lawn mowers are generally acknowledged to be the best in the industry and there are no close substitutes. A market-research firm engaged by Savemore has estimated the monthly market demand for Lawn King lawn mowers to be:

$$Q = 2,000 - 5P.$$

Savemore estimates its total monthly cost for purchasing, warehousing, and marketing the Lawn King line to be

$$TC = 100 + 4Q + 0.4Q^2.$$

Questions

a. How many Lawn King lawn mowers should the firm purchase and sell in order to maximize profit? What should the selling price be, and how much profit can be made?
b. If Savemore lowers the price for the Lawn King mower to $300, what is the average price elasticity of demand? Can a profit be made at a price of $300? If so, how much?
c. If Savemore wants to maximize revenue, what should it do about the price? What is the revenue-maximizing price? How many lawn mowers will be sold at this price? Would maximization of revenue still be profitable?
d. Savemore has decided to run a month-long sale of Lawn King lawn mowers as a loss leader to promote sales of other merchandise in its store. It will sell the mowers at cost, but not below cost. What should the sale price be?

Solutions

a. Since the demand function is $Q = 2,000 - 5P$, its inverse is

$$P = 400 - 0.2Q$$

so that

$$TR = PQ = 400Q - 0.2Q^2$$

and

$$MR = \frac{dTR}{dQ} = 400 - 0.4Q.$$

Also total cost is $TC = 100 + 4Q + 0.4Q^2$, therefore marginal cost is

$$MC = 4 + 0.8Q.$$

Profit is maximized when $MR = MC$; therefore

$$400 - 0.4Q = 4 + 0.8Q$$
$$-1.2Q = -396$$
$$Q = 330$$

hence

$$P = 400 - 0.2Q = 400 - 0.2(330) = \$334.00.$$

Alternative solution

$$\text{Profit, } \pi = TR - TC = 400Q - 0.2Q^2 - 100 - 4Q - 0.4Q^2$$
$$= -100 + 396Q - 0.6Q^2$$
$$\frac{d\pi}{dQ} = 396 - 1.2Q = 0$$
$$Q = 330.$$

Maximum profit is

$$\pi = -100 + 396(330) - 0.6(330)^2 = \$65,240.$$

b. At a price of $300, the quantity demanded would be

$$Q = 2,000 - 5P = 2,000 - 5(300) = 500.$$

The average price elasticity of demand is

$$E = \frac{(Q_2 - Q_1)(P_2 + P_1)}{(Q_2 + Q_1)(P_2 - P_1)} = \frac{(500 - 330)(300 + 334)}{(500 + 330)(300 - 334)}$$
$$= \frac{107,780}{-28,220} = -3.82$$

meaning that sales of Lawn King lawn mowers are very sensitive to price. At a price of $300, profit would be

$$\pi = TR - TC = PQ - TC$$
$$= 300(500) - 100 - 4(500) - 0.4(500)^2 = \$47,900.$$

c. At maximum revenue, $MR = 0$:

$$MR = 400 - 0.4Q = 0$$
$$0.4Q = 400$$
$$Q = 1,000 \text{ units}$$
$$P = 400 - 0.2Q = 400 - 0.2(1,000) = \$200$$
$$\pi = TR - TC = PQ - (100 + 4Q + 0.4Q^2)$$
$$= 200(1,000) - 100 - 4(1,000) - 0.4(1,000)^2$$
$$= -\$204,100.$$

Clearly, maximizing revenue is a losing proposition.

d. Selling at cost means that the price should be such that profit equals zero:

$$\pi = -100 + 396Q - 0.6Q^2 = 0.$$

Then by the quadratic formula,

$$Q = \frac{-396 \pm \sqrt{(-396)^2 - (4)(-0.6)(-100)}}{2(-0.6)}$$

$$= \frac{-396 \pm \sqrt{156,576}}{-1.2} = 0.25, 659.7 \approx 0, 660.$$

Eliminating the option to sell nothing, the lowest possible price is

$$P = 400 - 0.2Q = 400 - 0.2(660) = \$268.$$

Long-Run Monopoly Equilibrium

Since a monopoly has no competition because entry of new firms is effectively barred, economic profit is not eliminated in the long run as it is in the case of pure competition. Hence the monopoly's long-run strategy is to adjust plant size as demand conditions warrant to achieve maximum profit. To do this, the monopoly must determine whether a plant of different size and cost, with a different price and output, will yield a greater profit than the current plant does in the short run. In making this determination, the relevant consideration is long-run marginal cost, as illustrated by Exhibit 15–6.

In Exhibit 15–6, the monopoly begins with short-run equilibrium at output Q_1 and price P_1, with Q_1 established by the intersection of the MR curve and the short-run marginal-cost curve, $SRMC_1$. At this level of production and sales, using a single plant, the monopoly is earning the economic profit ABP_1C_1. However, long-run cost equilibrium is achieved at the level where marginal revenue is equal to long-run marginal cost, $LRMC$. This calls for Q_2 units, at a price of P_2, from a plant whose short-run average cost, $SRATC_2$, is just tangent to $LRATC$ at Q_2 units of production and whose short-run marginal cost, $SRMC_2$, is equal to $LRMC$ and MR at Q_2 units of production. Under these conditions profit is enlarged to the area EGP_2C_2. This is the best the monopoly can do, but it *can* do it because the monopoly can adjust its plant size as it pleases and there is no competition in the market.

Monopolistic Competition

The extremes of perfect competition and pure monopoly are theoretical models that are remote from many actual market situations. Thus in the late 1920s and early 1930s, many economists attempted to develop models of imperfect competition that could characterize market structures between those two extremes. One of the most noteworthy of those models is **monopolistic competition**.[2]

The monopolistic-competition model pictures an industry with four distinguishing characteristics:

---

[2] E. H. Chamberlin, *The Theory of Monopolistic Competition* (Cambridge, Mass.: Harvard University Press, 1933).

EXHIBIT 15–6   Monopolist's Long-Run Equilibrium

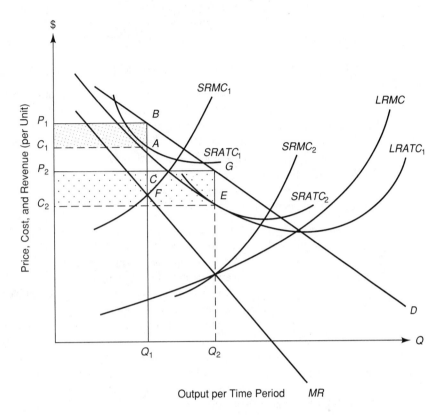

Output per Time Period   *MR*

1. There is a relatively large number of firms offering slightly differentiated products, with each firm satisfying a small portion of the total market demand for the general type of goods produced by these firms.
2. The market consists of firms that produce similar products that are close substitutes for one another. The substitutability of these products provides the element of competition in monopolistic competition.
3. Because of product differentiation, each firm possesses a monopoly over its own version of the general product. Therefore, each firm may set its own price, but within limits imposed by competition. Product differentiation thus provides the element of monopoly in monopolistic competition.
4. Some barriers to entry do possibly exist so that entry is not *completely* free. Nevertheless, entry is relatively easy.

Short-Run Equilibrium in Monopolistic Competition

The firm's demand curve in monopolistic competition is downward-sloping and highly elastic because of the large number of close substitutes for the firm's product. Because its product is differentiated, the firm in monopolistic competition is free to choose its output level and set its price with maximum profit as its objective, but there are limits to this freedom. If the firm can persuade its customers that its product is superior to close substitutes and worth a higher price, it may be able to charge a higher price than its competitors—but not much higher, because the competing products are still close substitutes.

The shape of the firm's demand curve will depend upon three factors:

1. The total demand for the whole product group. **Product group** means a set of several closely related and substitutable but not identical goods that serve the same general purpose for consumers. Hence we may speak of the market for men's shoes, beer, or bedroom furniture although there are many producers offering different brands and different qualities of these goods at different prices.
2. The firm's share of the group market.
3. The firm's use of advertising and other forms of nonprice competition to increase demand for its product.

Under these circumstances, it is not possible to draw a stable, unambiguous demand curve for the firm. However, to the extent that each firm is able to know or estimate its demand curve, it will behave in the same way as a monopolist. There are so many firms in monopolistic competition that the behavior of one firm has little effect upon the others. For example, a furniture manufacturer in North Carolina might reduce its price by 10 percent to try to increase sales. Whatever increase the firm gets is not at the expense of any other one competitor. Rather, it is taken out of the market shares of many competitors. Since the firm's competitors are not greatly affected, they are unlikely to make retaliatory moves against the price cutter. This leaves the firm free to maximize profit by producing at the level where $MR = MC$, as was shown in Exhibit 15–5. In the short run, then, there is little or no difference between the analysis of monopoly and the analysis of monopolistic competition.

Long-Run Equilibrium in Monopolistic Competition

The process by which firms in monopolistic competition reach long-run equilibrium is illustrated by Exhibit 15–7. This exhibit displays the long-run average-total-cost curve, *LRATC*, and the long-run marginal-cost curve, *LRMC*, of a firm in monopolistic competition. These curves intersect at point *A*, where the firm's *LRATC* is minimum.

The equilibrating process begins with the downward-sloping demand curve, D_1, and its associated marginal-revenue curve, MR_1. The firm is producing Q_1 units, at which level $MR_1 = LRMC$ at point *F*. The optimal quantity, Q_1, clears the market at a price of P_1 dollars and a unit cost of *H* dollars. The firm earns an economic profit of $(P_1 - H)$ dollars per unit multiplied by Q_1 units. This profit is represented by the rectangle $HBCP_1$.

The economic profit available in this market attracts new firms and some existing firms may expand to take advantage of the favorable market situation. This has two effects upon individual firms: (1) the firm's market share is reduced because the total market is being divided among more firms and (2) the increased supply of close substitutes puts downward pressure on prices. This causes the typical firm's demand curve to move

EXHIBIT 15-7   Long-Run Equilibrium in Monopolistic Competition

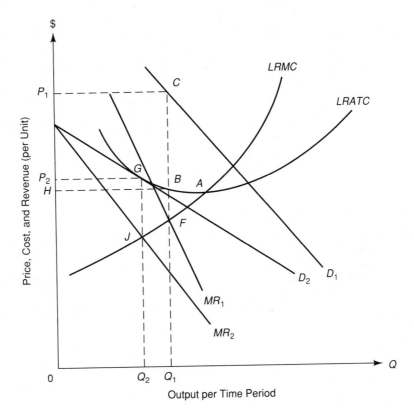

downward and become more elastic, as shown in the exhibit by the demand curve D_2 and its associated marginal-revenue curve MR_2.

If too many new firms enter the market, the demand curves will fall below some firms' *LRATCs*. These firms will be forced out of the market. When they leave, the demand curves of the remaining firms shift upward and grow somewhat less elastic. This juggling will continue until the market finally settles down with each firm at equilibrium with its demand curve just tangent to its *LRATC* at point *G* on the diagram. The long-run marginal cost, *LRMC*, is equal to MR_2 at point *J*. The firm will be producing Q_2 units at a price P_2, which is just equal to the long-run average total cost at point *G*.

From this diagram, we can see that the competition in monopolistic competition tends to squeeze out economic profits in the long run. Unlike perfect competition, however, equilibrium does *not* occur at the point of the lowest long-run average total cost, i.e., at point *A*. Does this mean that monopolistic competition is less efficient than perfect competition? Technically, yes, but only if you place no value on having a variety of products to choose from. A price slightly higher than the minimum possible *LRATC* and a slightly excessive unused capacity in each firm is what consumers gladly pay for the privilege of choice.

Illustrative Problem

April Showers Company is a medium-sized manufacturer of sprinkler heads. The firm has recently developed a square-spraying sprinkler head that greatly improves lawn watering and requires less water than conventional circular-spraying sprinkler heads. The firm's engineers estimate the long-run total-cost function to be

$$LRTC = \$500,000 + \$400Q$$

where Q = output in units of 1,000 sprinkler heads. The cost function includes a return on investment of 15 percent. The firm's marketing department estimates demand will be

$$Q = 2,500 - 0.5P$$

where P is the price per 1,000 sprinkler heads.

Questions

a. Determine the profit-maximizing output and price.
b. Determine the profit at the optimum output.
c. Determine sales-maximizing price and profit.
d. Determine output, price, and profit at long-run equilibrium. (Assume a parallel shift in the demand curve.)
e. What is April Showers' demand function at long-run equilibrium?

Solutions

a. $Q = 2,500 - 0.5P$, which is equivalent to $P = 5,000 - 2Q$. Therefore,

$$TR = PQ = (5,000 - 2Q)Q = 5,000Q - 2Q^2.$$

Hence

$$MR = 5,000 - 4Q.$$

Total cost is given as

$$TC = 500,000 + 400Q.$$

Hence

$$MC = \frac{dTC}{dQ} = 400.$$

Maximum profit occurs when $MR = MC$:

$$
\begin{aligned}
5,000 - 4Q &= 400 \\
4Q &= 4,600 \\
Q &= 1,150 \text{ units} \\
P &= 5,000 - 2(1,150) = \$2,700.
\end{aligned}
$$

b. Profit = Total revenue − Total cost:

$$
\begin{aligned}
\pi &= PQ - TC = (1,150)(\$2,700) - \$500,000 - (\$400)(1,150) \\
&= \$2,145,000.
\end{aligned}
$$

c. Total revenue (sales) is maximized when marginal revenue equals zero:

$$MR = 5,000 - 4Q = 0$$
$$4Q = 5,000$$
$$Q = 1,250$$
$$P = 5,000 - 2(1,250) = \$2,500.$$

d. At long-run equilibrium, the new demand curve is tangent to the *LRATC* curve at the point where their slopes are equal. Now we must find their slopes.

Since the demand curve shifts in parallel fashion, its slope remains the same, i.e., -2.0. Therefore, the new demand function is $P = a - 2Q$.

To find the slope of the *LRATC* curve, we calculate the *LRATC* function and take its derivative:

$$LRATC = \frac{LRTC}{Q} = \frac{500,000 + 400Q}{Q} = \frac{500,000}{Q} + 400$$

$$\frac{dLRATC}{dQ} = -\frac{500,000}{Q^2}.$$

Since the slope of the *LRATC* curve is identical to the slope of the demand curve,

$$-2 = -\frac{500,000}{Q^2}$$
$$2Q^2 = 500,000$$
$$Q^2 = 250,000$$
$$Q = 500$$

$$P = LRATC = \frac{(500,000) + (400)(500)}{500} = \$1,400$$

$$\pi = TR - LRTC = 1,400(500) - 500,000 - 400(500) = 0.$$

That is to say, at long-run equilibrium, all economic profit has been squeezed out.

e. To establish a new demand equation, we substitute $P = 1,400$ and $Q = 500$ into the demand equation $P = a - 2Q$:

$$1,400 = a - 2(500)$$
$$a = 1,400 + 1,000 = 2,400.$$

Hence the new demand function is

$$P = 2,400 - 2.0Q$$

or its inverse

$$Q = 1,200 - 0.5P.$$

Evaluation of Monopolistic Competition

The model of monopolistic competition has been criticized chiefly on the ground that its nature and characteristics cannot be empirically verified or demonstrated.[3] Its critics

[3] Harold Demsetz, "The Welfare and Empirical Implications of Monopolistic Competition," *Economic Journal*, September 1964, pp. 623–41, and "Do Competition and Monopolistic Competition Differ?" *Journal of Political Economy*, January–February 1968, pp. 146–68.

contend that other models are as well or better suited for explanation of the firm's behavior. For example:

1. If products are only slightly differentiated and there are a large number of small sellers, the firm's demand curve is so nearly horizontal that the model of pure competition provides an adequate explanation.
2. In markets where there are strong brand preferences, it usually turns out that a small number of sellers are dominating a limited market; thus the market is actually an oligopoly. (Oligopolies are discussed in the next section of this chapter.)
3. If a firm sells a product for which there are no close substitutes, the firm enjoys a monopoly even if it is a very small firm.
4. One of the key assumptions of the model of monopolistic competition is that firms are relatively small and so numerous that an action by one firm has little or no influence upon other firms. This assumption is clearly unrealistic.[4] An action such as price change by one firm may have no effect at all on firms in distant markets, but it may strongly influence other firms nearby. Again, the oligopoly model is more realistic. For example, the Yellow Pages of the 1989 telephone book for Honolulu list 28 retail hardware stores. But when the city is divided into the neighborhood markets where people actually buy hardware, each market has only two or three stores. The owners of these stores are keenly aware of the competition from the others in their neighborhood. If one store advertises a sale at reduced prices, the others soon counter with sales of their own.

The chief value of the model of monopolistic competition is that it explains how economic profit is squeezed out of the markets served by small businesses at prices somewhat but not much higher than the firm's lowest long-run average total cost.

Oligopoly

As previously noted, many economists argue that the vast majority of business firms, whether large or small, operate under the market structure of **oligopoly**. The term oligopoly is used to describe a market in which the dominant share of the market is supplied by a small number of firms. Oligopolies display the following characteristics:

1. *A small number of firms.* All oligopolistic firms are large relative to the market because they are so few. In absolute terms, they may be large or small, depending upon the size of the market.
2. *Products may be homogeneous or differentiated.* Homogeneous products include steel, cement, and newsprint. Automobiles, cereals, beer, and soap are examples of differentiated products.
3. *Interdependence.* A key feature of an oligopoly is the interdependence and competitive interaction among its members. Whatever one firm does affects all others. The greatest

---

[4] Lester G. Telser, "Monopolistic Competition: Any Impact Yet?" *Journal of Political Economy*, March-April 1968, pp. 312–15.

uncertainty facing management is not *whether* competitors will react to a decision—it is certain that they will—but *how* they will react.

All models of oligopoly recognize the interdependence of firms therein, but unlike the models of perfect competition and pure monopoly, there is *no* generally accepted equilibrium theory to explain the output and pricing behavior of oligopolists. Many models of oligopoly have been proposed, but discussion in this chapter will be limited to four of the most prominent:

1. Price-leadership models
2. Kinked–demand-curve model
3. Cartelization and formal-collusion model
4. Market-share model.

Price-Leadership Models

In many oligopolies, a pattern has been observed in which one firm sets a price and all the others follow. The two distinct patterns of price leadership that have been observed most often are (1) barometric and (2) dominant-firm.

Barometric Price Leadership.   **Barometric price leadership** gets its name from the fact that one firm acts as a "barometer," reflecting changing market conditions or costs of production that require a change in price. First one firm, then another, may fulfill this role by announcing price changes that they hope will be followed by others in the market. If the other competing firms in the oligopoly do not agree with the barometer firm's assessment of the market or cost situation, they might respond to the barometric leader's action with a series of higher or lower price changes. A certain amount of jockeying back and forth may take place until a general consensus on what the price should be is reached, either by trial and error, or by explicit collusion (which is illegal in the United States, but not in some other countries).

The barometric price leader doesn't need great market power, nor does it need to be a dominant firm with a lower cost structure than the others. The barometric price leader will lead only if the changes it makes are agreeable to the rest of the industry. For example, if the barometric leader announces a price increase and the rest of the industry refuses to go along with it, the leader will have to back down by reverting to the old price, no matter why it found the price increase to be warranted.

There is no glory and no particular gain from being the leader. Indeed, sometimes the first firm to announce a price increase must endure a great deal of harsh criticism. Consequently, there is no struggle for power, and the role of the barometric price leader easily passes from one firm to another.

Dominant-Firm Price Leadership.   The model of **dominant-firm price leadership** envisions a market in which one firm has become the leader because it is bigger and has a lower cost structure than other competing firms. Because of its market power, the dominant firm can behave as if it were a monopoly, setting its output level where $MR = MC$ and pricing accordingly to maximize its profit. Each competing firm

EXHIBIT 15–8   Dominant Firm Price Leadership

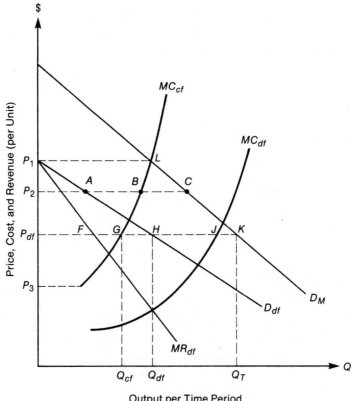

Output per Time Period

may sell all it wishes at the dominant firm's price, setting its output at the level where its marginal cost equals the dominant firm's price. Consequently, the competing firms must behave as if they were price takers in a purely competitive market.

If the competing firms can sell all they wish at the dominant firm's price, does this leave any of the market for the dominant firm? Yes, indeed it does. Keep in mind that the competing firms all have marginal costs higher than the dominant firm's at any given level of production. Therefore the market share of the competing firms is restricted by their higher costs.

The model is illustrated by Exhibit 15–8. In this exhibit:

D_M = The market-demand curve
MC_{cf} = The collective marginal-cost curve of the competing firms[5]

---

[5] MC_{cf} is also the competing firms' collective short-run supply curve. The bottom of this curve is cut off at the level of their collective average variable cost, which is equal to the price P_3. The competing firms will not supply anything at a price lower than P_3.

MC_{df} = The marginal-cost curve for the dominant firm, which is lower than the collective marginal cost of the competing firms.

In order to find the dominant firm's profit-maximizing output and price, we must first find the dominant firm's demand curve, which is, of course, somewhere below the market-demand curve. To do this, we proceed as follows:

1. At a price of P_1, which corresponds to the intersection of MC_{cf} with D_M, the competing firms would be willing to supply the entire market. Hence, the dominant firm's demand would be zero at that price and the P-intercept of the dominant firm's demand curve, D_{df}, is at P_1. At this price, the competing firms' demand curve and MR curve would be the horizontal line P_1L, which intersects their MC_{cf} line at point L.

2. At a price of P_2, the competing firms would be willing to supply P_2B units, since the competing firms' MR is just the price that is equal to MC_{cf} at point B. This leaves BC units for the dominant firm to supply. From this fact, we can plot point A such that $P_2A = BC$. The dominant firm's demand curve is just a straight line from P_1 through point A and continuing downward.[6]

3. To establish the dominant firm's marginal-revenue function, we recall that for the linear demand curve $P = a - bQ$, $TR = PQ = aQ - bQ^2$. Hence, $MR = dTR/dQ = a - 2bQ$, meaning that the slope of the MR curve is just twice that of the demand curve. Therefore, to locate MR_{df}, we need only to measure halfway from any point on the demand curve, D_{df}, to the vertical axis and draw a straight line from P_1 through that point.

When the dominant firm's marginal-revenue curve has been established, the dominant firm finds the output quantity, Q_{df}, and price, P_{df}, such that $MC_{df} = MR_{df}$. The competing firms can sell all they wish at that price. The amount each firm will want to sell is determined, of course, by its marginal cost. Since the competing firms' profits are also maximum when their respective marginal revenues equals their respective marginal costs, they will elect to sell a total of Q_{cf} units at the dominant firm's price, P_{df}. The total supplied to the market is Q_T, which is equal to $Q_{df} + Q_{cf}$.

What keeps the competitors in line? Presumably, it is because the dominant firm is the most efficient firm with the lowest cost structure. The exhibit shows that if the competitors lowered the price, their optimal position (where $MR = MC$) would be at a lower level of production and sales. By lowering the price, they would simply lose a share of the market.

Although dominant firms have been identified in a number of industries in the past, dominance typically does not last very long. The position of the dominant firm is eroded by the growth of markets, the entry of new firms, and technological change, and these processes have been intensified by international competition.

---

[6] Since the dominant firm's demand function is assumed to be linear, two points are all we need to draw the line. If the dominant firm's demand function were assumed to be curvilinear, the process of locating points on the curve would be repeated for successively lower prices until the price P_3 is reached.

The Kinked–Demand-Curve Model

Price rigidity has often been observed in oligopolies. For example, the price of steel rails remained at $28 per ton for 15 years between 1901 and 1916, and stuck at $43 for 11 years between 1922 and 1933. Another example is sulfur, which stood within a few cents of $18 per ton for 12 years between 1926 and 1938. In 1939, the kinked–demand-curve model was proposed by Sweezy[7] and by Hall and Hitch[8] as an explanation of price rigidity in oligopolies. As depicted in Exhibit 15–9, the model assumes that the firm is operating in an oligopoly where there is strong interaction among competing firms and the price of similar products has stabilized in the industry.

Exhibit 15–9 assumes P_1 dollars as the firm's price and Q_1 units as the firm's output at that price. Two demand curves, D_F and D_K, pass through point K, which is located at the coordinates (Q_1, P_1). The curve D_F represents the firm's demand curve if its competitors' prices are fixed. The demand curve D_K represents the firm's demand curve if its competitors match any price changes by the firm.

The demand curve D_F indicates that by reducing its price from P_1 to P_2, the firm could enlarge its share of the market from Q_1 units to Q_2 units. But if the firm does this, the other firms in the industry will defend their market shares by making the same price reduction. Therefore, the highly elastic segment of the demand curve KD_F moves to the less elastic position KD_K. Consequently, the quantity demanded will increase by only a small amount, from Q_1 to Q_A, and the firm's share of the market will remain approximately the same.

On the other hand, if the firm thinks that the other firms will match any price increase, the relevant demand-curve segment would be KW on D_K. An increase in price from P_1 to P_3 would reduce the quantity demanded only to Q_3. But if the other firms do not go along with the price increase, the relatively inelastic segment KW of D_K swings down to coincide with the more elastic segment CK of D_F. The actual change in the quantity demanded is from Q_1 to Q_B units of output and sales. Therefore, a relatively small increase in price would incur a large loss of market share.

Because of the reactions that can be expected from a firm's competitors if the firm changes its price, as explained already, a firm in an oligopoly is unlikely to try to manipulate prices to gain market advantage, and this may be true even when the firm's cost function changes.

Since the kinked demand curve, $C_K D_K$, has two different slopes, as shown by the heavy line in Exhibit 15–9, the model derives two different MR curves with a gap between them at the output level Q_1, which corresponds to the kink at point K. As shown in Exhibit 15–9, the discontinuity in the MR curve allows many different marginal-cost curves to pass through the gap between points A and B, and all of them would equal MR at Q_1 units of output. This means that marginal cost could rise all the way from point B to point A without any incentive to change the level of output or price.

---

[7] Paul M. Sweezy, "Demand under Conditions of Oligopoly," *Journal of Political Economy*, August 1939, pp. 568–73.

[8] R. L. Hall and C. J. Hitch, "Price Theory and Business Behavior," *Oxford Economic Papers*, May 1939, pp. 12–45.

EXHIBIT 15–9   The Kinked–Demand-Curve Model of Oligopoly.

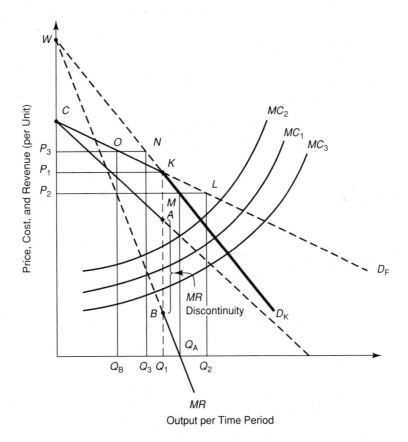

The kink in the demand curve will be more pronounced and the width of the gap therefore greater when the following conditions exist:

1. There are only a small number of firms in the market.
2. The sizes of most firms in the market are about the same.
3. The products are standard or nearly so.
4. There is no collusion.

These factors contribute to the intensity of interaction among competing firms in an oligopoly.

Illustrative Problem

Safe Ride Products markets its products in an oligopoly in which all makers of similar products are keenly aware of what each other is doing. Safe Ride Products perceives the demand function for its new road-emergency kit to be a kinked line with two different slopes.

Above the kink,

$$D_1 : Q_1 = 85 - P_1 \text{ or } P_1 = 85 - Q_1$$

while below the kink,

$$D_2 : Q_2 = 32.5 - 0.25P_2 \text{ or } P_2 = 130 - 4Q_2$$

where

Q = Output in thousands of units
P = Price in dollars.

The firm's total cost, *TC*, is

$$TC = 375 + 25Q + 0.6Q^2$$

Questions

a. Using the kinked–demand-curve model, what is the firm's output, price, and profit at the kink?
b. Are this output, price, and profit optimal?
c. Graph this problem.

Solutions

a. The kink in the firm's demand function occurs at the intersection of the two differently sloped segments:

$$\begin{aligned} D_1 = 85 - Q &= 130 - 4Q = D_2 \\ 3Q &= 45 \\ Q &= 15. \end{aligned}$$

At the kink, $P = P_1 = P_2$:

$$P_1 = 85 - 15 = \$70 \text{ or } P2 = 130 - 4(15) = \$70$$
$$\pi = TR - TC = 70(15) - 375 - 25(15) - 0.6(15)^2 = \$165(000).$$

b. The output, price, and profit are optimal if $MR = MC$:

$$\begin{aligned} TR_1 &= 85Q - Q^2 \\ MR_1 &= 85 - 2Q = 85 - 2(15) = \$55. \end{aligned}$$

This is the upper limit of the *MR* gap. Also

$$\begin{aligned} TR_2 &= 130Q - 4Q^2 \\ MR_2 &= 130 - 8Q = 130 - 8(15) = \$10. \end{aligned}$$

This is the lower limit of the *MR* gap. Marginal cost can range from a low of $10 to a high of $55 at $Q = 15$ without changing the optimal output (15 units) and price ($70). We note that

$$\begin{aligned} TC &= 375 + 25Q + 0.6Q^2 \\ MC &= 25 + 1.2\ Q = 25 + 1.2(15) = \$43. \end{aligned}$$

Since this marginal cost falls within the gap between $10 and $55, we conclude that profit is maximum at an optimal output of 15 units selling for $70 per unit.

c. Exhibit 15–10 shows a graph of the problem.

EXHIBIT 15–10   Graph for Illustrative Problem Using a Kinked–Demand-Curve Model of Oligopoly

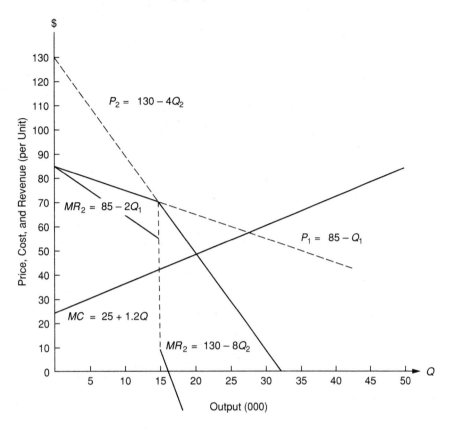

Output (000)

Evaluation of the Kinked–Demand-Curve Model.   The kinked–demand-curve model has been questioned on at least two counts:[9]

1. The assumption that price cuts will be matched by the competition, but that price increases will be ignored, may not be true. For example, if the price is at or very near to the top of the *MR* gap, any increase in cost would call for a raise in price. Hence we could have a barometric-leadership situation in which the competitors will be happy to follow the firm's lead in raising price. Conversely, if the price is very

---

[9] George J. Stigler, "The Kinky Oligopoly Demand Curve and Rigid Prices," *Journal of Political Economy*, October 1947, pp. 432–49. See also Walter J. Primeaux and Mark R. Bomball, "A Reexamination of the Kinky Oligopoly Demand Curve," *Journal of Political Economy*, July–August 1974, pp. 851–62; and Walter J. Primeaux and Mickey S. Smith, "Pricing Patterns and the Kinky Oligopoly Demand Curve," *Journal of Law and Economics*, April 1976, pp. 189–99.

close to the bottom of the gap in the competitors' *MR* curve, the competitors may decline to match a price cut that would drive their marginal revenues down to or below their marginal costs.

2. There are other valid explanations for price rigidity, such as nationally advertised prices, catalogued prices, reluctance to disrupt customer relations, and fears that recurrent price cuts may trigger a price war.

Empirical evidence has given little support to the model as a theory of long-run pricing strategy in oligopolies. It may have some validity as an explanation of short-run pricing behavior in a new industry in the early stages of development when competitors have not yet learned very much about each other's behavior.

Cartels and Collusion

In an oligopoly, where there is a small number of producers, all firms could benefit if they could get together and behave as if they were a monopoly. If they could agree upon prices, output level, market areas, use and construction of productive capacity, advertising expenditures, and the purchase and use of inputs, they could then act as a monopoly to maximize the total profit to be divided up among them. When such an agreement is reached openly and formally, the group is called a **cartel**. If a covert, informal agreement is reached, it is **collusion** or **conspiracy**.

Cartels are legal in Europe and many other parts of the world, and multinational U.S. firms may become involved in them in foreign markets. For example, U.S. airlines can legally be members of the International Air Transport Association (IATA) cartel. But within the United States, all forms of cartelization are illegal under most circumstances. Collusive agreements about prices are always illegal. Most other agreements about other important market variables have almost always been invalidated by the courts, but there are important exceptions. Most notably, certain farm products, such as milk, are marketed under cartel-like arrangements.

Cartelization arises because firms want to eliminate uncertainty and improve profits by stabilizing market shares, stabilizing prices, reducing competition, putting excess capacity to work, or outlining spheres of interest and eliminating unnecessary promotional costs. Cartelization or collusion is most successful when most, if not all, of the following specific structural conditions are present in a market.

1. *Small number of sellers*. This makes it easier to reach and enforce a formal or informal agreement.
2. *Similar cost conditions for all sellers*. This makes for equitable profits.
3. *Minimal or nonexistent product differentiation*. This makes it easier to agree upon a set of rules and eliminates the need for exceptions to the rules.
4. *Inelastic demand*. This enables the cartel to increase the price of the product without incurring a commensurate decrease in sales.
5. *High barriers to entry*. To avoid competition, new firms are kept from entering the market.
6. *Stability of the industry*. This enables the cartel to make and enforce rules.
7. *Depressed economic conditions*. In hard times, firms seek ways to avoid cut-throat competition, thus making cartelization more attractive.

EXHIBIT 15–11   **Allocation of Production of Two Members of a Cartel**

Output Unit	Marginal Cost		
	Firm One	Firm Two	Cartel
1	$5	$7	$5
2	$6	$8	$6
3	$7	$9	$7
4			$7
5			$8
6			$9

8. *Little or no excess capacity.* This makes it easier for the cartel to allocate production quotas without creating a temptation to cheat.

The cartel's problems of determining price and allocating production are exactly the same as for a firm with multiple plants with different cost structures, except that the cartel's plants are not owned by the cartel as a group. To create a simple illustration, suppose a cartel consists of two members. Each member can produce three units with the marginal costs shown in Exhibit 15–11.

This exhibit shows that if the cartel allocates production one unit at a time until it reaches the total capacity of each firm, each successive unit will go the the firm with the lowest marginal cost for that unit. Thus the first and second units go to Firm One at costs of $5 and $6, respectively. The third and fourth units go to either firm, one to each at a marginal cost of $7. This exhausts Firm One's capacity. The fifth and sixth units go to Firm Two at marginal costs of $8 and $9, respectively, and this exhausts Firm Two's capacity. Marginal costs for the cartel are just the unit-by-unit marginal costs of all of its firms, arranged in ascending order.

Actually, however, the cartel will not allocate the entire capacity of its members. Rather, it will allocate production such that the marginal cost *of the cartel* is equal to the marginal revenue *of the cartel*. The cartel's marginal revenue depends, of course, upon the total market demand, as illustrated by Exhibit 15–12 (page 482).

This exhibit shows Firm One with a lower cost structure than Firm Two. Firm One has the marginal-cost curve MC_1, and Firm Two has the marginal-cost curve MC_2. The cartel's marginal-cost curve MC_C, is derived as shown in Exhibit 15–11. In the total market, which has the demand curve D_M and the marginal-revenue curve MR_M, the intersection of MC_C and MR_M determines the cartel's profit-maximizing output of Q_C units at a price of P_C.

Each firm in the cartel is allocated a share of the cartel's total production Q_C such that the firm's marginal cost is equal to the cartel's profit-maximizing marginal revenue. This results in production of Q_1 units by Firm One and Q_2 units by Firm Two. The price to be charged by each firm is just the cartel's profit-maximizing price. Since the cartel's price is always higher than the average total cost of the least efficient member, all firms in the cartel will make a profit; but the lower-cost (more efficient) firms will make more profit than the higher-cost (less efficient) firms. The profits made by Firm One and Firm Two are shown as shaded areas in Exhibit 15–12, where it is clear that the profit going to Firm One is substantially greater than the profit going to Firm Two.

EXHIBIT 15–12   Market Allocation in a Two-Firm Cartel

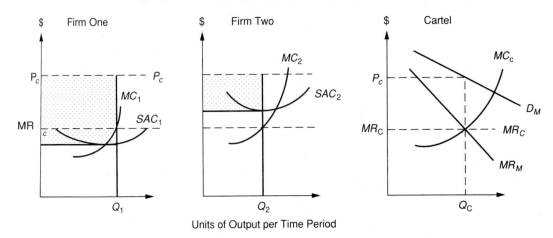

Units of Output per Time Period

The foregoing discussion illustrates the allocation of output according to the firm's individual outputs, but there are other bases as well. Among these are historical market shares, plant capacity (which may be determined in a number of different ways), and a bargained solution based on economic power. The problem is that while firms may all agree that maximizing the cartel's profits is beneficial, they seldom agree that the division of the spoils is equitable. This leads to cheating—subversion of the agreement—by individual members.

Since the cartel's price is always higher than the free-market price without the cartel, most or all of the firms in the cartel will develop some excess capacity, and the most efficient firms will develop the most excess capacity. The temptation to cheat is always very strong among all firms, but for the most efficient firms with excess capacity and relatively constant or decreasing unit cost, the temptation may prove to be irresistible. Exhibit 15–13 shows how a cheating firm (in this case, Firm F) can greatly increase its profits by slightly undercutting the cartel price to the point where $MR_F = MC_F$, and its excess capacity is put to work.

Exhibit 15–13 shows Firm F's marginal-cost curve, MC_F, average-total-cost (unit-cost) curve, ATC, demand curve, D_F, and the associated marginal-revenue curve, MR_F. The cartel price, P_C, and the cartel's marginal revenue, MR_C, are indicated by horizontal dashed lines. The cartel's MR_C line intersects the firm's marginal-cost curve, MC_F, at point A. Projecting downward to the horizontal axis determines Q_C, the cartel's allocation to Firm F. Projecting upward from A, we intersect the ATC_F curve at point B and locate point C on the P_C line. Projecting leftward to the vertical axis from point B determines the firm's unit cost, ATC_C, under the cartel's allocation of production. The firm's profit is represented by the shaded area $P_C C B ATC_C$.

Since all of the members of the cartel are charging the same price, P_C, a small decrease in price by Firm F can be expected to bring a relatively large increase in demand for Firm F's output. That is to say, Firm F has a very elastic demand curve that passes through

**EXHIBIT 15–13   Undercutting the Cartel's Price to Increase a
Member Firm's Profits**

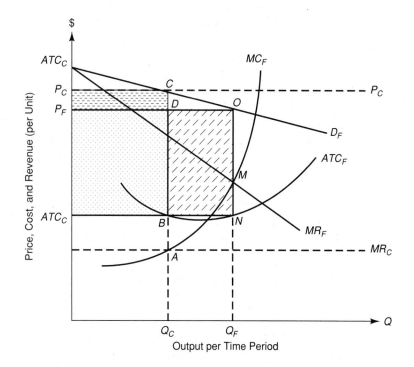

point *C* with a relatively shallow slope. The firm's profit-maximizing output and price are determined by the intersection of the firm's marginal-revenue and marginal-cost curves at point *M*. Projecting downward from *M* to the horizontal axis determines the firm's profit-maximizing production, Q_F. Projecting upward from Q_F, we pass through the ATC_F curve at point *N* and reach the firm's demand curve at point *O*. Projecting leftward from *O* gives us the firm's new price, P_F. Projecting leftward from *N* gives us the firm's new unit cost. Because of the shape of the ATC_F curve in this exhibit, the new unit cost is ATC_C, the same as before, but this may or may not be the case.

The area $P_C C D P_F$ represents the reduction in profit due to the reduction in price. The area *ONBD* represents the increase in profit due to the increased level of production and sales, and the increase in profit is clearly larger than the decrease. The firm's profit is represented by the area $ATC_C P_F ON$.

Cheating on the agreement is one of the major reasons why cartels eventually break up. Other reasons are:

1. The presence of maverick producers in the market that won't go along with the cartel. For example, Mexico, Norway, and the United Kingdom have all refused to join the Organization of Petroleum Exporting Countries (OPEC) after discovering large amounts of oil in their respective territories.

2. Periodic adoption of new corporate strategies to meet changing business conditions, which may cause members to drop out of the cartel.

3. Frequently changing supply and demand conditions that make the cartel price structure obsolete. OPEC's struggle to maintain the cartel price in the face of a worldwide increase in the supply of oil and a decrease in demand (because of conservation) provides a good example.

Market Share Model

Another model that attempts to explain pricing behavior of firms in an oligopoly is the market share model. The market share model shows that prices tend to be similar for products sold by oligopolists even when the competing firms' costs are different. The market share model addresses four cases:

1. The case where the competitors have equal market shares and the same marginal costs.

2. The case where the competitors have equal market shares but different marginal costs.

3. The case where the competitors have different market shares but the same marginal costs.

4. The case where the competitors have different market shares and different marginal costs.

Case 1: Equal Market Shares and the Same Marginal Costs.   Suppose we have an oligopoly with just two firms, Firm A and Firm B. The two firms produce a standard product, have exactly the same production and selling costs, and have divided the market between them with each holding half of the total market. The case is illustrated by Exhibit 15–14.

Exhibit 15–14 shows the market demand curve, D_M, and the demand curves for the two firms. Since each firm has half the total market, their demand curves and associated marginal revenue curves are placed one on top of the other and labeled $D_{A,B}$ and $MR_{A,B}$. They also share the same marginal cost curve, $MC_{A,B}$. Both firms will choose to operate at the production and sales level at which $MR = MC$. Consequently, each will produce Q units of the product, selling it at a price of P dollars, and each will earn an economic profit represented by the shaded area on the diagram.

The important point is that there is no pricing conflict here because both firms maximize profit at the same price. Neither firm has any incentive to try for a larger market share by lowering its price, because this would only provoke a price war with the other firm. Under the circumstances, neither firm could win a price war. Both would end up with a smaller profit.

Case 2: Equal Market Shares but Different Marginal Costs.   Now let us suppose that Firm A and Firm B have equal market shares, but Firm B's marginal costs are higher than Firm A's, as shown on Exhibit 15–15 (page 486).

EXHIBIT 15–14   Two Firms with Equal Market Shares and the Same Production and Selling Costs

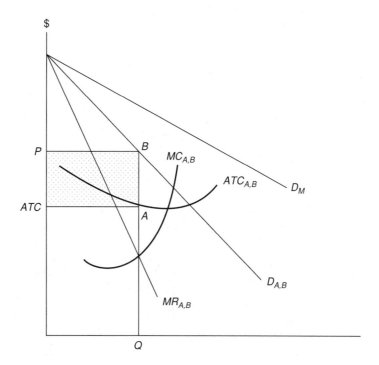

There could be a number of reasons why Firm B has higher marginal costs than Firm A. Perhaps Firm B is producing the product in an obsolete plant requiring a large amount of expensive labor while Firm A has introduced a high level of automation in its production process. Perhaps Firm B is geographically located such that its freight-in costs are substantially higher than Firm A's. Whatever the reason for the difference in marginal costs, it is clear that they lead to a pricing and market share conflict. Firm B's profit-maximizing output is less than Firm A's, and its profit-maximizing price is higher.

If its products are sufficiently differentiated from Firm A's, Firm B may be able to persuade its customers that its product is worth the higher price. Even so, it must give up some of its market share. But if the competing products are very close substitutes, then Firm B must meet Firm A's price or perhaps lose all of its market share.

The higher-cost, higher-price firm has only a few options: (1) attempt collusion to persuade the competitor to charge a higher price (which is illegal and can lead to a prison sentence); (2) initiate a price war with the competitor, which will hurt the higher-cost firm more than the lower-cost firm; or (3) bring costs into line with the competitor's. If the firm is unable to match the competitor's costs, then it must either do the best it can while meeting the competitor's price or else give up the competition and produce something else.

EXHIBIT 15–15   **Output and Pricing by Two Firms with Equal Market Shares but Different Marginal Costs**

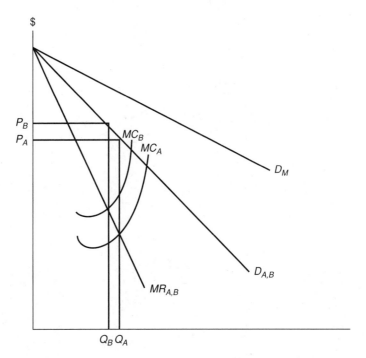

Case 3: Different Market Shares and the Same Marginal-Cost Function.

When firms have the same marginal-cost function but different market shares, pricing conflict may or may not arise, depending upon what happens to marginal costs as production and sales increase. The concept is illustrated by Exhibit 15–16.

Each panel in the exhibit shows two firms. Firm A has 60 percent of the market and Firm B has 40 percent. Panel A shows rising marginal costs as production and sales increase, due to increasing scarcity of input resources. Panel B shows constant marginal costs, reflecting an abundance of input resources and no appreciable economies of scale. Panel C shows decreasing marginal costs due to economies of scale. In each panel, the firm with the higher marginal cost suffers a price disadvantage because it must charge a higher price if it wants to maximize profit.

Panel A.   Both firms face rising marginal cost as production increases. Thus Firm A, with the lion's share of the market, incurs higher marginal cost than Firm B. So Firm A is faced with a dilemma. If it attempts to hold onto its share of the market, it must cut its price to meet that of Firm B. But if it does that, its market share may increase because of the increase in demand at the lower price, and the additional production will cause its marginal cost to rise even higher. If the firm chooses to simply hold onto its market share without satisfying the additional demand, it will have to accept reduced profits.

EXHIBIT 15–16   **Output and Pricing by Two Firms with Equal Marginal Costs but Different Market Shares**

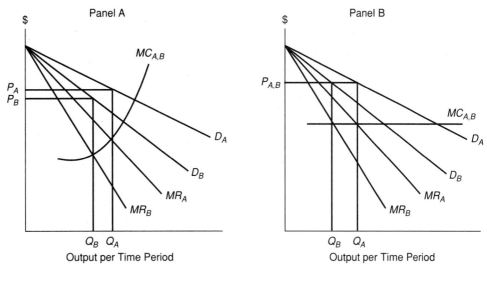

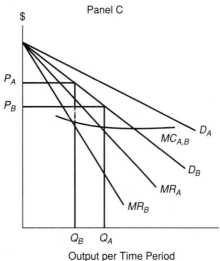

The solution seems to be to scale down its operation and let Firm B have a larger share of the market.

Panel B.   This panel shows the situation if marginal costs remain constant when production rises. The two firms will maximize their profits by charging the same price, and each will maintain its share of the market.

Panel C.   This panel shows what happens if substantial economies of scale are available. Firm A, with the larger share of the market, is able to produce at a lower cost than Firm B and therefore can price the product lower than Firm B would like to see. Firm B, as the underdog in this competition, may attempt to hang onto its share of the market by directing buyer attention away from price. Some of the strategems it might use are:

1. Concentrate on producing a superior product.
2. Engage in unconventional distribution of the product.
3. Appeal to a special class of buyers.
4. Mount a superior promotional campaign.
5. Engage in direct personal selling.

Ploys like these have enabled some smaller companies to compete against the giants despite their higher costs. As a general rule, however, custom will go to the lower-priced product, other things being equal. Substantial returns to scale, then, can enable one firm to dominate the industry and behave in the manner previously described as the model of dominant-firm price leadership.

Case 4: Different Market Shares and Different Marginal Costs.   In the normal course of events, product differentiation and different degrees of product acceptance lead to different market shares. Marginal costs also tend to be somewhat different because of differences in regional wages and transportation costs and differences in production technology. When both market shares and costs differ among competitors in an oligopoly, differences in costs and preferred (profit-maximizing) prices may be wide or narrow, and such a wide range of results is possible that we can't graph all the possibilities. It is certain, however, that the ease with which customers can switch to a lower-priced product will guarantee that some means will be found to bring all the competitors' prices into a very narrow range.

The four cases of the market-share models all lead to the same conclusion. Oligopolists really have no choice about charging the same or nearly the same prices for comparable products, no matter what their market shares or cost structures might be.

Nonprice Competition: Product Differentiation and Advertising

The preceding discussion of market structures focused on price as a means of competition. However, price competition at best merely moves the seller along the firm's demand curve. Moreover, if a firm cuts price to increase sales, it provokes retaliation by competitors. Product differentiation and advertising can provide effective competition in a much more subtle way. Product competition is perceived by competitors as much less aggressive than price competition, and their reaction is much slower. Furthermore, the advertising that is necessary to establish product differentiation in the mind of the consumer can have the salutary effect of shifting the firm's demand curve to a higher level.

Product differentiation may be broadly defined as anything that causes a buyer to prefer one product to another. Therefore, product differentiation, if it exists at all, exists in the mind of the consumer. It isn't necessary for the difference to *be* real—it is only necessary for the consumer to *think* it is real. Such persuasion may be a result of incessant advertising and other forms of promotion that instill brand-name recognition. For example, a store may offer Clorox bleach, Purex bleach, and a store brand in identical bottles and identical quantities at three different prices. The label on each bottle may reveal identical chemical composition of the contents. Yet customers will pay more for the highly advertised brands. Apparently they perceive a difference in the products by virtue of brand-name recognition. This, of course, reveals the intimate connection between product differentiation and promotion.

Of course, there can be and are some real differences among similar products. These may arise from many sources, such as:

1. Patents, trademarks, and copyrights
2. Differences in quality and durability
3. Differences in design, style, fit, color, and packaging
4. Conditions surrounding the sale, such as the courtesy of sales personnel, a good shopping location, a comfortably air-conditioned store, and convenient shopping hours
5. Guarantees and warranties, including policies on the return of merchandise
6. Method, time, and cost of delivery
7. Availability of repair services.

The Role of Advertising

Advertising, which is the principal cost of product differentiation, can provide the consumer with information by describing the goods and services available and by identifying their sellers. The theory of information developed by Stigler more than forty years ago holds that advertising can reduce search costs for both buyers and sellers.[10] From a welfare standpoint, informative advertising is quite desirable. Nevertheless, a considerable amount of product differentiation can result from advertising that is uninformative or even deceptive and untruthful. Advertising thus has the potential to make the marketplace more perfect or to disrupt its functioning, and therein lies the problem in any discussion of the welfare role of advertising. Despite all the claims of proponents and opponents, advertising is neither all good nor all evil. Without *informative* advertising, however, there can be little effective product differentiation in the consumer's mind, which is the only place it matters.

Measurement of Product Differentiation

It is much easier to talk about the degree of product differentiation in qualitative terms than to settle upon a meaningful quantitative measurement. Four quantitative measurements of product differentiation have been proposed at one time or another:

1. *Advertising-to-sales ratio.* This is the measurement most often used. Advertising expenditure as a percentage of sales dollars ranges from less than 1 percent for auto-

---

[10] George J. Stigler, *The Economics of Advertising* (Homewood, Ill.: Richard D. Irwin, 1944).

mobiles and petroleum products to more than 20 percent for drugs and cosmetics. The higher the ratio, the less real differentiation exists in the products. One of the difficulties with this measurement is that products may be visibly differentiated by nonadvertising selling costs, such as distinctive packaging.

2. *The coefficient of cross elasticity of demand.* As explained in Chapter 6, cross elasticity measures the change in demand for one product in response to a change in the price of another product that is either a substitute or complement. Measurement of product differentiation, however, applies only to substitutes for which a high cross elasticity indicates little differentiation. That is to say, if the products are *close* substitutes, demand for one will be very sensitive to the pricing of the other.

This measure suffers from a pair of difficulties. First, the second product must be a carefully selected, close substitute. For example, a low cross elasticity between two makes of refrigerators could indicate a high degree of product differentiation. But if the cross elasticity between corn and pig-iron is near zero, it merely indicates that the products are not substitutes. The second difficulty is that the cross product must undergo significant price changes before cross elasticity can be observed and measured. Hence, cross elasticity does not provide as sharp a measuring tool as we would like to have.

3. *Entropic measurement.* An **entropic measurement** of product differentiation looks at the extent of customer loyalty to a brand or a merchant. *Entropy* is a term drawn from thermodynamics by way of communication theory. It refers to the degree of disorder or randomness in a system.

On a scale of 0 to 1, a homogeneous product would rate a 0, because customers would buy completely at random from any seller in the market, since there is no differentiation of the product. At the other extreme, if a product is so differentiated that customers always buy a particular brand or from a particular merchant, the entropy measurement would be 1.

Entropic measurement is highly subjective in nature. Further, it cannot establish whether the entropic behavior of the consumer is the result of product differentiation or the result of price.

4. *Product-differentiation barriers.* This approach classifies product differentiation as high, medium, or low by the extent to which product differentiation acts as a barrier to market entry by new firms. Such classification is based not only on advertising-to-sales ratios, but also on any other facet of product differentiation the observer is aware of that would require expenditure of capital by a newcomer seeking to enter the market. This approach requires a knowledgeable observer, and the results can be no better than the quality of information possessed by the classifier.

Summary

Market structure refers to the nature and degree of competition within a market. The five major indicators of market structure are (1) the number and nature of sellers, (2) the number and nature of buyers, (3) the nature of the product, (4) the conditions of entry and exit, and (5) possible economies of scale.

The general theory of pricing postulates a continuum of market structures that ranges from perfect competition at one end to pure monopoly at the other. *Perfect competition* is a market structure with many small sellers and buyers of a homogeneous product. Market price is set at the equilibrium between market supply and market demand, and both buyers and sellers must either take it or leave it. All resources are assumed to be completely mobile, and market entry and exit are free from all barriers. Thus when an economic profit is being made, enough new firms will enter the market to drive the price down and squeeze out all economic profit. Long-range equilibrium is obtained when the price is set equal to the lowest possible long-run average total cost.

In *pure monopoly*, there is only one seller of a product that has no close substitute. A natural monopoly exists when economies of scale are so great that it is most efficient for one firm to supply the entire market. Other monopolies may arise from patents or franchises or from control of raw materials. The monopolist faces a downward-sloping demand curve. However, since the barriers to entry are so high that no competitor can enter the market, the monopolist is free to optimize profit at the level of production and sales for which marginal revenue equals marginal cost.

Between the extremes of perfect competition and pure monopoly lies the realm of imperfect competition, in which two market structures have been postulated: monopolistic competition and oligopoly. *Monopolistic competition* is a market structure in which there are many small sellers of weakly differentiated products that are close substitutes. Because of product differentiation, each firm has a limited monopoly over its own version of the product. Therefore, the firm faces a downward-sloping, highly elastic demand curve and sets its output and price where $MR = MC$, the same as in a pure monopoly.

The situation differs from pure monopoly, however, in that the firm faces competition. Firms seeking to enter the market must undergo the cost of developing a differentiated product and the promotional cost of penetrating the market. Thus a cost barrier to entry exists, but entry still is relatively easy. As new firms enter, the demand curves for all firms shift to the left and become more elastic. At long-run equilibrium, the firm's demand curve is just tangent to its long-run average-total-cost (*LRATC*) curve. Since the demand curve slopes downward, the point of equilibrium is somewhat to the left of the lowest possible *LRATC*. Thus equilibrium is obtained at a slightly higher price than would be obtained in perfect competition.

Oligopoly is a condition of imperfect competition in which a few sellers supply most of the market with products that may be either homogeneous or differentiated. An oligopoly is characterized by the interdependence of its members, such that any decision by one firm affects all others. Four models of oligopoly have been discussed:

1. Price-leadership models, in which one firm takes the lead in establishing a price and the others follow.
2. The kinked–demand-curve model, which assumes that the competition will follow a firm's price decreases but not its price increases.
3. The cartelization–and–formal-collusion model, in which sellers act in concert as if they were a monopoly, to maximize profits.
4. The market-share model, which shows the interlocking effects of market share and marginal cost.

All of the foregoing models focus on price competition. At best, however, price competition merely moves the firm along its established demand curve. Nonprice competition in the form of product differentiation and advertising can do even better—it can shift the entire demand curve to a higher level.

"Product differentiation" may be broadly defined as anything that causes the consumer to prefer one product to another. Product differentiation exists in the mind of the consumer. It need not be real as long as the consumer thinks it is real. Thus, anywhere from one fourth to three fourths of all advertising is "fluff" designed to persuade the consumer that the advertiser's product is different from competing goods although it really is not. Good, informative advertising is necessary to bring real differences to the consumer's attention.

Four approaches have been tried to measure product differentiation: advertising-to-sales ratio, coefficient of cross elasticity, entropic measurement, and product-differentiation barriers. None of these approaches has proved to be very accurate or meaningful.

Problems

1. Name a few industries that might provide examples of perfect competition, monopolistic competition, oligopoly, and pure monopoly. Do the characteristics of these industries fit the theoretical market structures exactly? What problems are encountered when theoretical models are applied to real-world markets?

2. Agriculture is often characterized as operating in a perfectly competitive market. Does one farmer compete with another farmer? If so, in what way?

3. The OPEC cartel effectively increased oil prices during the 1970s, resulting in tremendous profits for member countries. What economic factors have led to disunity among OPEC ranks in the 1980s?

4. In 1982, traces of heptachlor were discovered in Hawaii's milk supply. Although the problem was corrected, demand for milk fell by 20 percent. In 1983, both the state dairy-owners' association and individual producers resorted to advertising to increase the fallen demand for dairy products. Was there likely to be a difference in the motives of these two advertisers?

5. Explain how monopolistically competitive firms are similar to purely competitive firms, and how they differ.

6. List the reasons why research, development, and innovation are more likely to occur under oligopoly than under any other market structure.

7. Many firms contribute money and executives' time to so-called "social responsibilities" such as charities and civic projects. Is such behavior consistent with maximizing profit in the long run? Under what market structures would firms be most likely and least likely to engage in such behavior? Explain.

8. It seems clear that the market structure in which a firm must do business has a strong influence on the firm's output and pricing decisions. Moreover, in the world market in which there is free trade (more or less), domestic firms' decisions about output and price are strongly influenced by the production of substitute goods in other countries.

    a. Does this mean that U. S. firms need to study the market structures of other countries in order to understand the world market structure?

    b. What facet of foreign production has the greatest impact on the output and pricing decisions of U. S. firms?

    c. How do government subsidies and other unfair trade practices influence the output and pricing decisions of other countries?

9. Security Lock, Inc., is a major U. S. producer of magnetic door locks. In recent years, Security Lock has suffered substantial short-run losses in the international market because of cut-throat price competition from companies in England, France, and West Germany. However, these companies have also suffered substantial losses, and so have proposed that Security Lock join them in an international cartel that would give the four firms a high degree of monopoly power. Since their biggest market would be the United States, the cartel has asked Security Lock to propose production and pricing policies for their approval. Assuming that Security Lock's participation is legal, how could Security Lock proceed?

10. Fisco Farms is a relatively small producer of wool in New Zealand. Fisco's total-cost function is

$$TC = 6,500 - 600Q + 20Q^2$$

where

Q = Hundred-weight (cwt) of wool (100 pounds)

TC = Total cost, in dollars.

If the market price for wool is $10 per pound,

a. Determine Fisco's profit-maximizing output and price.

b. Determine the maximum total profit.

c. Determine ATC at the maximum-profit output.

d. Suppose wool prices decline to $5 per pound, with no change in cost. Should Fisco continue to operate?

e. Describe the condition of long-run equilibrium in a competitive market. How is such an equilibrium obtained?

f. What are Fisco's ATC and output at long-run equilibrium?

11. The Sharpit Manufacturing Company dominates the manufacture of pencil sharpeners because of its highly cost-efficient operation. Its market-research department estimates demand for the Sharpit brand pencil sharpener as

$$Q = 600 - 0.5P$$

where

Q = Output, in units

P = Price per unit, in dollars.

The production department reports that the total-cost function, TC, is

$$TC = 50,000 + Q^2.$$

a. Calculate the profit-maximizing output and price.

b. Calculate profit at the profit-maximizing output.

c. Calculate revenue-maximizing output and profit at that level.

d. What is the level of output and profit at minimum average total cost?

e. What is the price elasticity of demand at the most profitable price?

12. Ace MiniComp Company developed a compact computer system that can fit in an ordinary briefcase. At first, there was no competition in the marketplace. The estimated demand and total production cost were

$$Q = 3,000 - 2P$$
$$TC = 250,000 + 650Q$$

where

Q = Output of computer systems

P = Price of each computer system, in dollars

TC = Total cost.

a. Determine profit-maximizing output and price under the demand and cost functions just stated. Also find total profit.

b. Determine the revenue-maximizing output, price, and profit under the demand and cost functions just stated.

c. Now it is a few years later and there are many similar products on the market, although some product differentiation is evident. Because of the competition, Ace MiniComp's sales have declined and its demand curve has shifted in a parallel fashion so that all economic profit has been eliminated. Assuming that Ace's cost function remains the same, determine its new demand function, output, and price at equilibrium.

13. The Aloha Greeting Card Company produces greeting cards for all occasions that feature reproductions of photographs of Hawaii's most scenic attractions. Cards are produced in a modern plant using the latest technology in an effort to hold

down costs and deliver a quality product at a reasonable price. The cards are packaged 50 to a box and shipped to buyers all over the world. Weekly demand is currently estimated to be

$$Q = 10,000 - 1,000P$$

where

Q = Output per week, in boxes of 50 cards
P = Price per box.

The firm's total weekly cost of production is estimated to be

$$TC = 5,000 - 4Q + 0.005Q^2$$

a. Calculate the profit-maximizing output and price per box.

b. Calculate maximum profit per week.

c. Calculate revenue-maximizing output and price.

d. Calculate output, price, and profit at minimum unit cost.

e. Calculate the price elasticity of demand at the most profitable price.

NOTE: Round output to whole units, price to dollars and cents, and profit to whole dollars.

Case Problem: Carbine, Inc.

14. Carbine, Inc., is one of four major manufacturers of high-quality specialty steel. Attempting to establish pricing and production policies has been difficult for Carbine because its demand curve has reacted inconsistently. An economist hired by Carbine to analyze the situation found two different demand functions and a cost function, as follows:

$$P_1 = 550 - Q$$
$$P_2 = 750 - 3Q$$
$$TC = 15,000 + 200Q + 0.3Q^2$$

where

P = Price per ton of specialty steel
Q = Output of specialty steel, in thousands of tons
TC = Total cost, in dollars.

Questions

a. Describe the market structure and model that seem to fit the data just given.

b. Graph the curves for demand, marginal revenue, and marginal cost.

c. Determine Carbine's profit-maximizing price and output.

d. Determine the maximum profit.

e. Purchasing newly developed furnaces changes Carbine's total-cost function to

$$TC = 17,500 + 125Q + 0.3Q^2.$$

Determine the new profit-maximizing price and output. What is the maximum profit?

Case Problem: Bethlehem Car Company

15. Suppose the railway-freight-car–manufacturing industry consists of seven firms, which produce four basic types of freight cars:

- *Flat cars*, used for such goods as lumber, pipe, automobiles, and heavy machinery
- *Hopper cars*, used for such goods as grains, fertilizers, dry chemicals, and general merchandise
- *Box Cars*, used for such goods as grains, bagged fertilizers, dry chemicals, bagged cement, and general merchandise
- *Tank cars*, used for transportation of liquids of any type

In addition to price, industry demand is sensitive to factors such as

- Forecast demand for rail transportation
- Prime rate of interest
- Railroad earnings per ton-mile.

Among the seven firms, the Bethlehem Car Company is considered to be dominant because of its lower cost of production. Consequently, when Bethlehem sets the price, the other firms are forced to follow that price in order to compete at all. However, Bethlehem will allow the competing firms to sell all they wish to sell at that price. Bethlehem's market research indicates that industry demand for box cars in the coming year will be

$$Q_B = 40,000 - 0.5P$$

where

Q_B = Forecast industry sales, in number of boxcars
P_B = Price per boxcar, in dollars.

Bethlehem's expected cost function for the manufacture of boxcars is

$$TC_B = 100,000 - 15,000Q_B + 2.5Q_B^2.$$

Further, Bethlehem's management has learned that the marginal cost of boxcar production by the smaller competing firms is

$$MC_C = 50,000 + 2Q_C.$$

Questions

a. Determine Bethlehem's demand curve and marginal-revenue curve.

b. Determine the profit-maximizing output and price for Bethlehem Car Company.

c. Determine the output for the combined competing firms.

d. What conditions are necessary for Bethlehem Car Company to continue in its dominant role?

Discussion Topics

16. It has been said that gigantic firms—such as General Motors, General Electric, and Alcoa—operating in oligopolies are primarily responsible for producing higher-quality consumer goods, and that breaking them up to obtain more active price competition could be counterproductive. Do you agree or disagree? Critically analyze your position both pro and con.

17. Where economies of scale have led to the formation of large firms in an oligopoly, barriers to entry of new firms are extremely high in terms of both the required technical know-how and the required capital investment. For example, the five leading U.S. steel manufacturers average over $8 billion in assets. Can you suggest desirable methods to overcome these barriers in steel as well as in other oligopolistic industries?

18. George Stigler, a Nobel Prize–winning economist, has argued that government is primarily responsible for the existence of monopoly. He cites public utilities, federal and state labor laws, agricultural-support programs, local building codes, and licensing restrictions as examples of government-sponsored monopoly that increase inefficiencies. Do you agree or disagree? Explain. What is the significance of the government's 1983 breakup of AT&T?

19. Your local power company and the U.S. Postal Service are close to being pure monopolies. How can their performances be evaluated to decide whether they are doing an efficient job?

References

Bain, Joe S. *Barriers to New Competition*. Cambridge, Mass.: Harvard University Press, 1965.

Baumol, William J. *Economic Theory and Operations Analysis*. 4th ed. Englewood Cliffs, N.J.: Prentice-Hall, 1977.

Demsetz, Harold. "Do Competition and Monopolistic Competition Differ?" *Journal of Political Economy* (January-February 1968), p. 146–68.

————"Barriers to Entry." *American Economic Review* (March 1982), pp. 47–57.

Fershtman, Chaim; and Kenneth L. Judd. "Equilibrium Incentives in Oligopoly." *American Economic Review* 77, no. 5 (December 1987), p. 927.

Holthausen, D. M. "Kinky Demand, Risk Aversion, and Price Leadership." *International Economic Review* 20 (June 1979), pp.341–48.

Kling, A. "Imperfect Information and Price Rigidity." *Economic Inquiry* 20 (January 1982), pp. 145–54.

Koch, James. *Industrial Organization and Price Level*. 2nd ed. Englewood Cliffs, N.J.: Prentice-Hall, 1980.

Nelson, Phillip. "The Economic Consequences of Advertising." *Journal of Business* (April 1975), pp. 213–41.

Palda, Kristian S. "The Measurement of Cumulative Advertising Effects." *Journal of Business* (April 1965), pp. 162–79.

Panzar, John C., and James N. Rosse. "Testing for 'Monopoly' Equilibrium." *Journal of Industrial Economics* 35, no. 4 (June 1987), p. 443.

Pyatt, F. G. "Profit Maximization and the Threat of New Entry." *Economic Journal*, (June 1971), pp. 242–55.

Rotenberg, Julio J.; and Garth Saloner. "The Relative Rigidity of Monopoly Pricing," *American Economic Review* 77, no. 5 (December 1987), p. 917.

Scherer, F. M. *Industrial Market Structure and Economic Performance*. 2nd ed. Chicago: Rand McNally, 1980, chaps. 5–8.

Silberston, Aubrey. "Survey of Applied Economics: Price Behavior of Firms." *Economic Journal* (September 1970), pp. 511–82.

Stigler, George, J. "Price and Non-Price Competition." *Journal of Political Economy* (February 1968), pp. 149–54.

Telser, Lester. "Monopolistic Competition: Any Impact Yet?" *Journal of Political Economy* (March-April 1968), pp. 312–15.

Wilson, Charles A. "On the Optimal Pricing Policy of a Monopolist." *Journal of Political Economy* 96, no. 1 (February 1988), p. 164.

APPENDIX 15A   Market Power and Profit–Maximizing Advertising

Market power may be defined as the ability to influence noticeably the price or quantity of some commodity in the market. In the models of market structure that were discussed in this chapter, market power ranged from zero for firms in perfect competition to complete control for a pure monopoly.

We have also seen that the element of monopoly in imperfect markets requires product differentiation, and the greater the differentiation, the greater the monopoly power. Further, we have seen that differentiation is promoted by informative or persuasive advertising. Finally, we have seen that in all market structures, profit-maximizing equilibrium exists at the level of production and sales at which marginal revenue equals marginal cost, with a price established by the demand function for that level of sales. Thus the three great action variables are *price*, *product*, and *promotion*, over which most firms have some control. There may be other action variables as well, such as changes in methods of distribution or dealer incentives.

Maximum profit will be realized when the last dollar spent on each action variable results in the same incremental profit. In mathematical notation,

$$\frac{M\pi_P}{C_P} = \frac{M\pi_A}{C_A} = \frac{M\pi_Q}{C_Q} = \cdots = \frac{M\pi_N}{C_N} \tag{1}$$

where

$M\pi_i$ = Marginal profit from the ith action
C_i = Cost of the ith action
P = Subscript indicating price
A = Subscript indicating advertising and other forms of promotion
Q = Subscript indicating changes in product quality, composition, packaging, etc.
N = Subscript indicating the Nth action of N actions.

Measurement of Market Power

The best known measurement of market power is the **Lerner Index**:

$$I = \frac{P - MC}{P} \tag{2}$$

where

P = Price
MC = Marginal cost
I = Index of market power.

The numerator of the Lerner Index represents economic profit. Under conditions of perfect competition, where all economic profit is squeezed out, $MR = P = MC$ and the Lerner Index $= 0$, indicating that the firm has no market power at all. The maximum magnitude of the Lerner Index is 1, which could occur only if $MC = 0$. As long as $P > MC$, the Lerner Index is positive; but if $MC > P$, it is negative.

When the firm is maximizing profits at equilibrium, where $MR = MC$, the Lerner Index is the reciprocal of the absolute value of the price elasticity of demand; i.e.,

$$I = \frac{1}{|\epsilon_D|}. \tag{3}$$

This can be shown with the aid of the formula for marginal revenue that was developed in Appendix 6:

$$MR = P(1 - \frac{1}{|\epsilon_D|}). \tag{4}$$

At equilibrium, $MR = MC$; therefore,

$$MC = P(1 - \frac{1}{|\epsilon_D|}). \tag{5}$$

Expanding the right side,

$$MC = P - \frac{P}{|\epsilon_D|}. \tag{6}$$

Subtracting P from both sides,

$$MC - P = -\frac{P}{|\epsilon_D|}. \tag{7}$$

Reversing the signs,

$$P - MC = \frac{P}{|\epsilon_D|}. \tag{8}$$

Dividing both sides by P,

$$\frac{P - MC}{P} = \frac{1}{|\epsilon_D|} = I. \tag{9}$$

From the explanation of price elasticity in Chapter 6, the student should recognize that Equation 9 is equivalent to saying that the Lerner Index measures market power in terms of the deviation of the slope of the demand function from zero.

Profit-Maximizing Advertising

It has been demonstrated by Dorfman and Steiner[1] that when the product (and other) variables are held constant, the profit-maximizing advertising-to-sales ratio is

$$\frac{A}{S} = \frac{P - MC}{P}(\epsilon_{Q \cdot A}) \tag{10}$$

where

$$A/S = \text{Advertising/sales ratio}$$
$$\frac{P - MC}{P} = \text{Lerner Index of market power}$$
$$\epsilon_{Q \cdot A} = \text{Elasticity of output with respect to advertising expenditures.}$$

Equation (10) may be interpreted as saying that the more market power a firm has, the more of its sales dollar it will spend on advertising. This is because there is a strong correlation between market power and product differentiation; and the fundamental purpose of advertising is to establish product differentiation in the mind of the consumer.

With some algebraic manipulation, Equation 10 also shows how the effects of advertising expenditure upon product price are related to the firm's advertising/sales ratio, in the following five steps.

Step 1.   Begin with Equation 10:

$$\frac{A}{S} = \frac{P - MC}{P}(\epsilon_{Q \cdot A}). \tag{10}$$

---

[1] Robert Dorfman and Peter O. Steiner, 'Optimal Advertising and Optimal Quality," *American Economic Review*, December 1954, pp. 826–36.

Step 2.   Rewrite the Lerner Index as the reciprocal of the price elasticity of demand:

$$\frac{A}{S} = \frac{1}{\epsilon_{Q \cdot P}}(\epsilon_{Q \cdot A}). \tag{11}$$

Step 3.   Replace the elasticity symbols with their definitions:

$$\frac{A}{S} = \frac{1}{\left(\dfrac{\Delta Q/Q}{\Delta P/P}\right)} \cdot \frac{\left(\dfrac{\Delta Q/Q}{\Delta A/A}\right)}{1} = \frac{\left(\dfrac{\Delta Q/Q}{\Delta A/A}\right)}{\left(\dfrac{\Delta Q/Q}{\Delta P/P}\right)}. \tag{12}$$

Step 4.   Carry out the indicated division by inverting the denominator and multiplying:

$$\frac{A}{S} = \frac{\Delta Q/Q}{\Delta A/A} \cdot \frac{\Delta P/P}{\Delta Q/Q}. \tag{13}$$

The left-hand term is the elasticity of quantity sold with respect to advertising; that is, it measures the sensitivity of sales to expenditures on advertising.

Step 5.   Simplify the fraction in Equation 13, getting

$$\frac{A}{S} = \frac{\Delta P/P}{\Delta A/A} = \frac{\%\ \text{change in price}}{\%\ \text{change in advertising expenditures}} = \epsilon_{P \cdot A}. \tag{14}$$

Equation 14 says that the more sensitive price is to expenditure on advertising, the larger the percentage of the sales dollar that will be spent on advertising, which is just a formal acknowledgment of a common-sense notion.

The problem with the preceding theoretical work is that it ignores the passage of time. However, there is ample empirical evidence to support the concept that advertising expenditures more nearly have the properties of an investment than an expense. That is, the returns do not necessarily materialize in the same time period as the expenditure. On the contrary, returns from good advertising campaigns will continue to be received for many years to come.[2] The appropriate measurement of advertising returns, therefore, is the present value of a future stream of profits, as follows:

$$PVA = \sum_{t=1}^{n} \frac{S_t - C_t}{(1 + r)^t} = \sum_{t=1}^{n} \frac{\pi_t}{(1 + r)^t} \tag{15}$$

---

[2] One study found that it took seven years for the company to reap 95 percent of the sales generated by its advertising dollars. (See Kristian S. Palda, "The Measurement of Cumulative Advertising Effects," *Journal of Business*, April 1965, pp. 162–79; also Palda, *The Measurement of Cumulative Advertising Effects* (Englewood Cliffs, N.J.: Prentice Hall, 1964).

where

$$PVA = \text{Present value of advertising in base year, } t = 0$$
$$S_t = \text{Sales in year } t$$
$$C_t = \text{Cost of sales in year } t$$
$$\pi_t = \text{Profit in year } t$$
$$r = \text{The firm's discount rate (cost of capital).}$$

The advertising should be undertaken if $PVA \geq 0$. In spite of the empirical evidence that advertising is an investment, the accounting profession continues to treat it as a periodic expense. No allowance is made for the image, goodwill, and future profits that are being generated. Consequently, the real value of the firm's assets is considerably more than its book value.

C H A P T E R

16

PRICING
PRACTICES
AND DECISIONS

In the theoretical frame of reference established in the preceding chapter, simple models of various market structures were constructed to explain the firm's output and pricing decisions under *static* conditions of cost and demand. In each model, the firm's objective was assumed to be maximization of profit, and the objective was achieved by adjusting output so that marginal revenue was equal to marginal cost.

In the *dynamic* environment of the real world, managements have fairly well defined pricing objectives that are based upon *planned* profits and *long-range* profit horizons, and these objectives may differ somewhat from the profit-maximization principle. In addition, management must deal with production and pricing under a variety of conditions, which may include pricing of a single product in multiple markets, pricing of multiple products in one or more markets, pricing of joint products, and transfer pricing between divisions of a firm. Pricing, therefore, is frequently done for broad product groups within the framework of the company's overall profit position and objectives. Consequently, specific pricing policies may differ among firms, reflecting different orders of priorities among competing objectives.

CHAPTER OUTLINE

In this chapter, we are concerned with the pragmatic side of pricing decisions. The chapter is divided into four sections and an appendix:

1. **Pricing Objectives.** This section discusses three categories of pricing objectives that are commonly pursued.

2. **Pricing Methods and Approaches.** This section focuses on cost-plus pricing and incremental-cost pricing.
3. **Price Discrimination.** This section explains the three degrees of differential pricing and shows how differential pricing can maximize profits.
4. **Optimal Pricing of Multiple Products.** This section deals with several of the more common problems of pricing multiple products.
5. **Appendix 16A: Transfer Pricing.** This appendix shows how to develop profit-maximizing prices for goods or services that are sold by one division of a firm to another division.

Pricing Objectives

Empirical studies have revealed that the typical and collateral pricing goals of U.S. companies tend to fall into three categories, namely:

1. Pricing to achieve a target return on investment
2. Pricing to realize a target market share
3. Pricing to meet or match competition.

Pricing to Achieve a Target Return on Investment

A **target-return price** is a price designed to yield a predetermined average return on capital for specific products and product groups or divisions over the long run. Most corporations tend to use stockholders' equity plus long-term debt in measuring return on capital.[1] In allocating fixed costs among products or divisions, firms usually establish a standard cost for each product based on an assumed rate of production—typically 70 to 80 percent of capacity—and an assumed product mix.

Since target returns are established on the basis of "normal" or average periods, year-to-year profits may at times be higher or lower than the predetermined targets. There is some evidence to support the notion that firms probably do not as a general rule set prices so as to maximize profits, at least in the short run.

A concomitant issue with regard to the target-return criterion is the selection of the profit target itself. Executives who have been asked about this question have responded by saying that their company's margins are based on one or more of the following considerations:

• What is believed to be a "fair" or reasonable return
• Industry custom
• A desire to equal or better the company's recent average return
• Use of a specific profit target as a means of stabilizing the firm's market share and industry prices.

---

[1] Partnerships and proprietorships would use net worth plus long-term debt.

In most cases, the target rate of return is regarded by firms as a long-run objective, and this is true regardless of the specific criteria of choice. The target rate of return tends to range between 10 and 20 percent after taxes, with an average of about 15 percent.

There is a close relationship between target return on investment as a pricing *objective* and cost-plus pricing (discussed in the next section) as a pricing *method*. In most companies, cost-plus pricing, in one form or another, is the chief means of achieving the objective. The "cost" may be based on an estimate of standard cost and standard volume for a specific group of products; the amount of the "plus" may vary with the pricing executive's goal—whether it be a target return on investment or some other objective.

Pricing to Realize a Target Market Share

Pricing to achieve a minimum or maximum *market share* of domestic and/or international markets is often cited as a firm's pricing objective. For example, General Electric claims that its products rarely have more than 25 percent of any given market, and that it is the company's policy not to exceed 50 percent market share because it would then become too vulnerable to competition. Japanese automakers are using voluntary quotas to limit the export of their cars to about 22 percent of the U.S. market, thereby maintaining a higher, more profitable price than it would take to expand their market share.

Pricing to Meet or Match Competition

Pricing to meet or to match competition is sometimes cited as the objective of a pricing policy. To some extent this type of policy, if it can be called such, may be due largely to fear of losing competitive status in the marketplace. Recently, U.S. automakers have attempted to camouflage price cuts by offering them in the form of factory rebates or low-priced financing. When Chrysler started this type of price reduction, GM and Ford quickly countered with price rebates and special financing of their own.

Pricing Methods and Approaches

A firm may pursue its pricing objectives through a variety of methods and approaches. We shall limit our discussion to the two most important methods: cost-plus pricing and incremental-cost pricing.

Cost-Plus Pricing

The most widely used method of pricing is known as **cost-plus pricing**. It is a procedure whereby the price is determined by adding a fixed markup of some kind to the cost of producing or acquiring the product. Thus development of a cost-plus price requires two basic steps: determination of the relevant cost and determination of what the "plus" should be.

Determination of the relevant cost differs somewhat among the three basic types of business: manufacturing, merchandising, and service. In turn, determination of the "plus" will depend, in part, on how the cost was determined.

Cost-Plus Pricing in Manufacturing. Manufacturers most often use a cost-accounting method that develops a standard unit cost of production. The standard cost may be the **standard variable cost** (which consists of standard allowances for direct labor and direct materials) or it may be the **standard absorption cost** (which is the standard variable cost plus factory overhead). Standard unit costs are normally developed as part of the firm's budgeting process, and are based upon forecasted demand for the product (which establishes the standard output) and expected prices of the input factors of production. Thus the standard costs are carefully predetermined target costs that should be attained at the forecast level of production.

Allocation of company overhead costs (selling, administrative, and financial costs) to the product is not standardized under cost-accounting procedures, and different companies may deal with the allocation of overhead costs in different ways. If all costs have been fully allocated to the product, the markup is all profit. If some overhead costs have not been allocated, then the markup should be high enough to cover the unallocated costs as well as profit.

Cost-Plus Pricing in Merchandising. In the case of a merchandising operation, either wholesale or retail, unit variable costs are simply the unit prices that the merchant pays for the merchandise. The markup on these costs should be sufficient to cover store overhead and profit.

Cost-Plus Pricing in Service Industries. Customers of auto-repair shops, TV-repair shops, plumbers, electricians, and other tradespeople expect to be billed on a **time-and-materials basis**. That is, there will be one charge for the hours worked and another charge for the parts used. The price of labor and the price of the materials may each be calculated on a cost-plus basis. In each case, the wholesale cost of the materials and the wages actually paid to the workers must be marked up enough to cover all overhead costs as well as profit.

"Time and materials" does not always mean the actual time required to complete the job. In some cases, the charge for time may be based upon a standard, such as the flat-rate manual used by auto-repair shops. The flat-rate charge for time has permeated the professions as well, particularly the medical profession. In part, this is due to the way in which medical-insurance companies set allowable fees for specific treatments.

The "Plus" in Cost-Plus. The markup added to cost—the "plus" in cost-plus—may be the same for all of the firm's products, or different for each one. It may be expressed as a set number of dollars, but is more likely to be a percentage of cost. The specific formula used by a particular firm may be geared to long-standing industry practice, to competitive conditions, to break-even analysis, or to capital-investment requirements.

The formula for the markup percentage is

$$\text{Markup rate} = \frac{\text{Price} - \text{Cost}}{\text{Cost}}. \tag{1}$$

For example, if a product costing \$8 is priced at \$10, the markup on cost would be

$$\frac{\$10 - \$8}{\$8} = 0.25 = 25\%.$$

The "plus" of cost-plus may also be expressed as a profit margin in the price. In the preceding example, profit is $10 − $8 = $2, which is 20% of the price. Conversion from one expression to the other is quite easy by means of the formulas:

$$\text{Markup rate} = \frac{\text{Profit margin}}{1 - \text{Profit margin}} = \frac{0.20}{1 - 0.2} = 0.25 \tag{2}$$

$$\text{Profit margin} = \frac{\text{Markup rate}}{1 + \text{Markup rate}} = \frac{0.25}{1 + 0.25} = 0.20 \tag{3}$$

where both markup rate and profit margin are expressed as decimal fractions.

Illustrative Problem

The WTT Corporation manufactures integrated circuits (ICs) for electronic devices. The company's budget reflects a standard production level of 1.5 million units with a standard unit absorption cost of $1.50. (**Standard unit absorption cost** is a cost-accounting term that means standard direct labor + standard direct materials + standard factory overhead. Since it includes the fixed cost of factory overhead, it is not the same as average variable cost (*AVC*); rather, it is the total cost of production per unit.) Company overhead is budgeted at $2.25 million for administration, financing, and marketing of the ICs.

Questions

a. What is the ratio of company overhead to the total standard absorption cost of production?
b. What is the fully allocated unit cost?
c. What is the selling price if the company marks up to obtain a 40 percent profit margin?

Solutions

a. The total standard absorption cost is 1.5 million units × $1.50 = $2.25 million. The ratio of company overhead to standard production cost is $2.25/$2.25 = 1.0; that is to say, company overhead is 100 percent of the standard total-production cost.
b. To get the fully allocated unit cost, we must add company overhead to the standard total cost of production and then divide by the standard output of 1.5 million units. The result is the average total cost, *ATC*:

$$ATC = \frac{1.5(\$1.50) + \$2.25}{1.5} = \frac{\$4.50}{1.5} = \$3.00.$$

c. From Equation 1,

$$\text{Markup rate} = \frac{\text{Profit margin}}{1 - \text{Profit margin}} = \frac{0.4}{0.6} = 0.67$$

$$P = ATC + (\text{Markup rate} \times ATC) = \$3.00 + (0.67)(\$3.00)$$
$$= \$3.00 + \$2.00 = \$5.00 \text{ per unit.}$$

Cost-Plus and Profit Maximization.   As previously noted, marginal analysis is specifically designed to maximize profits in the short run by determining the level of output at which marginal revenue equals marginal cost. In contrast, cost-plus pricing is basically a long-run concept, in which a markup on cost is established to achieve a target return that the firm considers to be satisfactory, but not necessarily maximum. That is to say, the cost-plus pricing method does not necessarily attempt to maximize profit, but neither is profit maximization ruled out as an objective of the firm.

Although cost-plus is basically a long-run concept, cost-plus may be preferred to marginal analysis even in the short run, simply because marginal analysis requires information about marginal revenue and marginal cost (both of which may depend upon the level of output required to satisfy demand for the product) with a degree of precision that is difficult and sometimes impossible to obtain.

Besides the statistical problems of demand estimation that were discussed in Chapters 7 and 8, there are the added problems of product interdependence both inside and outside the firm and the uncertainty of competitors' actions in the future. Cost estimation encounters the same statistical problems as demand estimation, with the additional complications of joint costs and the allocation of overhead. Add to all these problems the uncertainties inherent to the future, such as weather, economic conditions, and labor union negotiations, and it is easy to see why managers may turn to something a little less complicated than marginal analysis.

Does this mean that firms using cost-plus pricing have abandoned profit maximization? Not really. In determining the markup to be applied to unit cost, managers must think of many relevant factors, such as the nature of the product, the turnover rate of the product, degree of risk involved in the business, customary markups in the industry, inventory costs, target rate of return, the mode of payment for the product (cash-and-carry versus sales on credit), and perhaps other factors, but the key variable is the price elasticity of demand, i.e., the sensitivity of demand for the product to price.

Competitive pressure in the marketplace forces firms to consider the price elasticity of demand, and this leads to a high level of flexibility in cost-plus pricing. In the grocery business, for example, demand for staple products such as bread, milk, and coffee is highly elastic due to industry-wide competition. Therefore, their prices carry low markups. In contrast, demand for items such as salt, spices, and brand-name ice cream is much less sensitive to price, so their prices carry higher markups.

Can we tell if cost-plus pricing is maximizing profit? Yes, we can, but only if we are able to determine the price elasticity of the product. First, let us recall from Chapter 6 that

$$MR = P\left(1 + \frac{1}{\varepsilon}\right) \tag{4}$$

where

MR = Marginal revenue
P = Price
ε = Price elasticity of demand.

We know that profit is maximized when marginal revenue equals marginal cost, i.e., $MR = MC$. Therefore, when (and only when) profit is at a maximum, we can substitute

MC for *MR* in Equation 4, getting

$$MC = P\left(1 + \frac{1}{\varepsilon}\right). \tag{5}$$

Dividing both sides by $1 + \frac{1}{\varepsilon}$, we get

$$P = \frac{MC}{1 + 1/\varepsilon} = MC\left(\frac{1}{1 + 1/\varepsilon}\right). \tag{6}$$

Price can be expressed as the marginal cost times the sum of 1 plus the markup rate. Let m = markup rate. Then,

$$MC(1 + m) = MC\left(\frac{1}{1 + 1/\varepsilon}\right). \tag{7}$$

Dividing both sides by *MC*, we get

$$1 + m = \frac{1}{1 + 1/\varepsilon} \tag{8}$$

$$m = \frac{1}{1 + 1/\varepsilon} - 1. \tag{9}$$

Equation 9 indicates that the markup rate varies with the price elasticity of demand. Exhibit 16–1 (page 508) shows markup rates for price elasticities from –1.25 to –5.0.

Equation 9 implies that products with different elasticities should have different markup rates even if they have the same marginal cost. Equation 9 also reinforces the common-sense notion that the more price-sensitive the product is (i.e., the higher the price elasticity), the smaller should be the markup rate. It must be clearly understood, however, that *m* is optimal if and only if ϵ is the elasticity at the profit-maximizing price.

If a firm is able to estimate the price elasticity at a particular price, Equation 9 can be used to test that price for optimality. The procedure is as follows:

Step 1. Obtain the actual markup rate by the formula:

$$\text{Markup rate} = \frac{\text{Price} - \text{Cost}}{\text{Cost}}.$$

Step 2. Calculate the test markup rate, *m*–test, from Equation 9:

$$m\text{-test} = \left(\frac{1}{1 + 1/\varepsilon}\right) - 1. \tag{10}$$

Step 3. Compare the actual markup rate with the *m*–test rate. They will be the same if and only if the price is optimal. If the *m*–test rate is less than the actual markup rate, the actual markup rate is too high. If the *m*–test rate is greater than the actual markup rate, the actual markup rate is too low.

The convenience of cost-plus pricing does not mean that marginal analysis should be abandoned by the firm that uses cost-plus pricing. On the contrary, if enough information can be obtained, marginal analysis provides a useful basis for evaluating the firm's

EXHIBIT 16–1   **Profit-Maximizing Markup Rates for Various Price Elasticities**

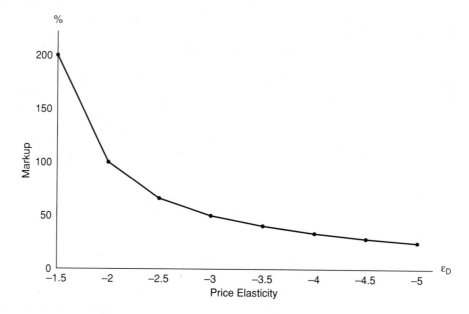

pricing policies. Acquiring information is expensive, of course, and the cost of acquiring information must be added to the other costs before analysis takes place. It should also be noted that neither marginal analysis nor optimum cost-plus pricing guarantees a profit. Under some conditions of cost and demand, the best an optimal price can do is to minimize loss.

Illustrative Example

The Modern Carpet Company purchases a certain grade of carpeting at a wholesale price of $7.50 per square yard. The firm has marked up the wholesale price by 260 percent, resulting in a retail price of $27 per square yard. The firm has reason to believe that the price elasticity of demand at that price is −1.5. Is that price optimal?

Solution

At a price elasticity of –1.5, the *m*–test statistic is

$$m\text{-test} = \frac{1}{1 + 1/\varepsilon} - 1 = \frac{1}{1 + 1/(-1.5)} - 1$$

$$= \frac{1}{1 - 0.66666667} - 1 = 2.0 = 200\%.$$

Since this is less than the actual markup of 260 percent, the actual markup (and the resultant price) is too high.

Evaluation of Cost-Plus Pricing.   Some of the main reasons for using cost-plus pricing are the following:

1. It offers a relatively simple and expedient method of setting price by the mechanical application of a formula.
2. It provides a method for obtaining adequate ("fair") profits.
3. It is desirable for public relations purposes when costs have risen because it provides a rationale for a price increase.

Some of the main criticisms of cost-plus pricing are as follows:

1. It has been said that cost-plus pricing fails to take demand into account, as measured in terms of buyers' desires and purchasing power. This criticism does not stand up under empirical investigation. Firms that market different product lines often have a different markup policy for each line, according to demand elasticities and competitive pressures. Clear evidence that firms using cost-plus pricing do pay attention to demand was provided by the airline industry when deregulation took place. Widespread introduction of discounts and special fares indicated that the airlines were paying close attention to demand conditions and to their competition. The automobile industry provides another example. When demand slackens, manufacturers use devices such as rebates and low-cost financing to lower the marked-up price.

2. It has also been said that cost-plus pricing fails to recognize the roles of such important cost concepts as **avoidable cost**[2] and opportunity cost as guides for pricing decisions. This, of course, is a generality that may be true in some cases, but is certainly not true in all. There is nothing in the cost-plus method to prevent inclusion of opportunity costs. They may be included in the cost, just as is done in marginal analysis, or they may be treated as normal profits to be included in the markup.

3. Another criticism has been that cost-plus pricing fails to reflect competition in terms of rivals' reactions and the possible entry of new firms. For example, in an industry that prices by the cost-plus method, if company margins are above the level necessary to cover operating costs and yield "normal profits" per unit at capacity, new firms will tend to enter the industry as long as no considerable excess capacity is already present. The results will be a smaller market share for each firm, and therefore higher unit overhead

---

[2] Avoidable costs are the firm's expenses of doing a job as compared with its expenses if it does nothing. The difference represents potential savings by doing nothing.

costs and lower profits per firm. The same thing, of course, can be said about the profit-maximization model. Indeed, as was shown in a previous chapter, this is how an industry moves from short-run profit maximization to long-run equilibrium.

Incremental-Cost Pricing

"The economist who understands marginal analysis has a full-time job in undoing the work of the accountant!"

This quotation is indicative of a viewpoint that has long been held by many economists. It simply refers to the fact that accounting practices and most business executives are concerned with allocating average costs rather than incremental costs. As previously noted in Chapter 3, incremental profit analysis is concerned with *any* and *all* changes in revenues, costs, and consequent profits that result from a particular decision. Thus, in any business, there is likely to be a substantial difference between the cost of each company activity as it is carried on the accounting books and the "extra" cost—the so-called incremental cost—which indicates whether or not the activity should be undertaken. For many pricing decisions, the incremental costs are the only "true" and relevant costs to be considered.

Incremental cost provides business executives with an essential guide for *short-run* production and pricing decisions. For if a business executive is considering, say, a reduction in price in order to increase sales, the executive must know whether the incremental revenue gained from the increase in sales will cover the increase in costs. If the incremental revenue exceeds the incremental cost, profits will be expanded accordingly.

Thus, while incremental costs should not *determine* a product's price, they should set a floor while demand conditions set a ceiling on possible prices. Many profitable pricing decisions lie within this range.

"Fully distributed" or "fully allocated" cost, on the other hand, is an economically invalid criterion for certain types of short-run pricing decisions, since it is based on arbitrary apportionments of unallocable costs among various products, departments, and divisions. There is no economic basis for holding a certain product or group of products responsible for any given share of unallocable costs. Whether the particular price of a product is above or below its fully distributed cost is of no economic significance as far as its minimum price is concerned in a particular short-run pricing decision. In the long run, however, all costs must be recovered.

The appropriate use of incremental analysis requires a thorough examination of the *total* effect of the decision in question, both in the short run and in the long run. For example, the decision to introduce a new product should be based on *all* changes in costs and revenues that will result from the decision. This includes the effects on the production, cost, and sales of existing products. Will production of the new product cause any bottlenecks? Will it increase the requirement for maintenance or shorten the useful life of existing machinery and equipment? If the new product is a substitute or complement for one or more of the firm's other products, how will the other products' sales be affected? Thus we see that the relatively simple concept—consider only those factors that are changed by the decision—is not easy to apply.

Price Discrimination

What is meant by the terms **price discrimination** and **differential pricing**? Both terms describe in general a method that can be used by some sellers to tailor their prices to the specific purchasing situations or circumstances of their buyers. Specifically, either term may be defined as the practice by a seller of charging different prices to the same buyer or to different buyers for the same good or service, without corresponding differences in cost.[3]

Price discrimination (differential pricing) has been a subject of controversy for many years. It involves both economic implications and regulatory problems. The economic aspects are our concern in this chapter. The regulatory aspects are discussed in the next chapter.

Degrees of Price Discrimination

For analytical purposes, it is convenient to distinguish among three degrees of differential pricing.

First Degree. In differential pricing of the first degree, the seller charges the same buyer a different price for each unit bought, thereby extracting the maximum total receipts. By shading the price down to the buyer for each additional unit purchased, the seller obtains a larger total revenue than if the same price per unit were charged for all units bought. This is a purely theoretical situation. In real life, of course, in order to sell a given quantity of goods, all units are sold at the same price. As illustrated by Exhibit 16–2 (page 512), Q_4 units would be sold at a price of P_4 dollars. The triangle $P_0M_4P_4$ represents the additional revenue that could be realized under first-degree differential pricing, but never is. This triangle is called the *consumer's surplus*, as explained in Chapter 5.

Second Degree. Differential pricing of the second degree, more commonly known as **volume discounting** or **quantity discounting**, involves the same underlying principle as first-degree differential pricing, except that the seller charges different prices for blocks of units instead of for individual units. By charging a higher price for smaller quantities, the seller receives a higher total revenue than if a single price were charged.

Third Degree. Differential pricing of the third degree occurs when the seller segregates buyers according to income, geographic location, individual tastes, kinds of uses for the product, or other criteria, and charges different prices to each group or market despite equivalent costs in serving them. Thus, as long as the demand elasticities among different buyers are unequal, it will be profitable to the seller to group the buyers into separate classes according to elasticity, and charge each class a separate price. This is

---

[3] From a theoretical standpoint, a better statement would define differential pricing or price discrimination as the sale of technically similar products at prices that are not proportional to marginal costs. However, laws that deal with price discrimination do not distinguish types of cost, thus leaving wide margin for interpretation.

EXHIBIT 16–2   **Differential Pricing of the First and Second Degree**

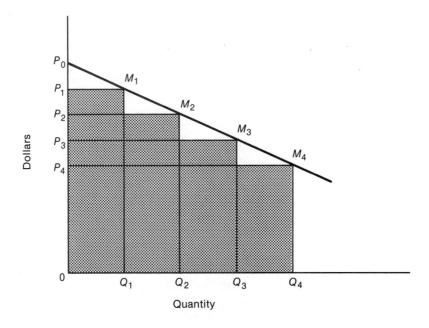

what is referred to more generally as **market segmentation**, that is, the carving up of a total market into homogeneous subgroups according to some economic criterion. From the standpoint of pricing, the criterion usually employed is that of demand elasticity, and it is often applied in a practical manner via certain indirect means, as will be seen shortly.

The Conditions for Differential Pricing

Three practical conditions are necessary if a seller is to practice price discrimination effectively: multiple demand elasticities, market segmentation, and market sealing.

Multiple Demand Elasticities.   There must be differences in demand elasticity among buyers due to differences in income, location, available alternatives, tastes, use of the product, or other factors.

Market Segmentation.   The seller must be able to partition (segment) the total market by segregating buyers into groups or submarkets according to elasticity. Profits can then be enhanced by charging a different price in each submarket.

Market Sealing.   The seller must be able to prevent—or natural circumstances must exist that will prevent—any significant resale of goods from a lower-priced submarket to a higher-priced one. Leakage in the form of resale by buyers between submarkets will tend to neutralize the effect of different prices and narrow the effective price structure toward a single price to all buyers.

Basis for Price-Differential Structures

In view of these conditions, what practical techniques can sellers use to establish a structure of price differentials? In the following discussion, we shall examine differential price structures based on quantity, time, or product use. This classification, it will be seen, cuts across the three degrees (forms) of price discrimination but places major emphasis on the most interesting and important one—price discrimination of the third degree.

Quantity Differentials.   Three types of quantity differentials are particularly worth noting because of their significance in business practice. They are cumulative discounts, quantity discounts, and functional discounts.

Cumulative Discounts.   Cumulative discounts are based upon total quantity bought over a period of time (such as a year). They are granted by sellers as a concession to large buyers, or for the purpose of encouraging greater buyer loyalty, or because they may reduce costs by facilitating forward planning in production, stabilizing seasonal output variations, and reducing investment in inventories.

Quantity Discounts.   Quantity discounts are based upon the quantity purchased at *one* time and its delivery to one location. They are granted in order to encourage larger orders, which reduce the seller's unit costs of selling, accounting, packing, delivery, and other handling and shipping costs.

Functional Discounts.   Functional or distributor discounts are granted to distributors according to their position in the product's channel of distribution. The discounts are from the manufacturer's list price (i.e., the manufacturer's suggested retail price) and they are designed to provide compensation for each distributor's particular marketing function. For example, if the retailer expects a discount from the wholesaler of 30 percent off list price, the manufacturer might give the wholesaler 45 percent off list. Thus the wholesaler's revenue would be 15 percent of list price times the number of units sold to retailers.

Time Differentials.   A second class of differential pricing achieves market segmentation through the medium of *time*. As in other kinds of price differentials, the object from the seller's standpoint is to capitalize on the fact that buyers' demand elasticities vary, but in this case as a function of time. Two classes of time differentials may be distinguished, extending from the narrowest to the broadest "slice of time." These are called *clock-time differentials* and *calendar-time differentials*.

Clock-Time Differentials.   When demand elasticities of buyers vary within a 24-hour period, the seller has the opportunity of exploiting these differences through price differentials. In this approach, the seller charges a higher price for the product in the more inelastic period and a lower price during the more elastic interval. Common examples are day and night rates on long-distance telephone calls and matinee and evening admission charges in movie theaters.

Calendar-Time Differentials.   Price differentials may be based not only on elasticity differences within a day, but on differences between days, weeks, months, or seasons as well. In addition to telephone rates and theater prices, which exhibit weekend variations in addition to intraday (i.e., clock-time) price differences, other examples of calendar-time price differentials are found in the sale of services by recreational facilities such as golf courses, tennis courts, and swimming pools; the sale of food by some restaurants; and seasonal variations in the costs of clothing, resort accommodations, and vacation trips. Calendar-time differentials thus refer to any variable price structure based on time that extends beyond the 24-hour period of clock time.

Seasonal variations, since they occur within a year and are due strictly to weather and custom, are more broadly a function of time in that variations of weather and in custom (e.g., Christmas and Easter buying) are recurrent and fairly periodic. Hence, seasonal variations may justifiably be placed in the category of calendar-time differentials from the standpoint of the seller who is considering this type of pricing structure.

Product-Use Differentials. A third classification of price discrimination is the segregation of buyers according to their use of the product. For example, electric and gas companies establish separate rate structures for residential and commercial users; telephone companies distinguish between residential and business phones; and public carriers set separate charges for senior citizens, other adults, and children despite equal time and space costs of serving all three groups.

Profit Maximization with Price Discrimination

In order to practice third-degree price discrimination, a firm must be able to identify and segregate distinct markets with different elasticities, that is, with different demand functions. Each market is then treated as a separate entity and a price can be set in each market either by marginal analysis or by cost-plus pricing. As previously noted, cost-plus pricing does not necessarily provide maximum profit, although it can. But if the firm can identify the demand function or the price elasticity in each separate market, the marginal-analysis model can be used to determine profit-maximizing prices.

The condition for maximum profit using price discrimination is that the marginal revenue shall be the same in all markets and equal to marginal cost. That is to say, the additional revenue gained from selling one more unit in Market A shall be equal to the additional revenue obtained by selling one more unit in Market B, which shall be equal to the additional revenue gained by selling one more unit in Market C, and so on for any number of markets. If the *MR*s are not equal, the firm can increase its revenue and profit by selling more to the market(s) with the higher *MR*. The concept is illustrated by Exhibit 16–3, which depicts price discrimination in two markets.

Exhibit 16-3 shows that the firm's marginal revenue is the horizontal summation of the marginal revenues of the two markets. The firm's production level is established by the intersection of the firm's marginal revenue, MR_T, with its marginal cost, MC. The sales allocation to each market is established where the market's marginal revenue equals the firm's marginal cost. The procedure for maximizing profit in the two-market situation depicted by Exhibit 16–3 is demonstrated by the following illustrative problem.[4]

---

[4] If a problem involves more than two markets, the solution will require the use of partial derivatives, as shown in Appendix 16B at the end of this chapter.

EXHIBIT 16–3   Price Discrimination in Two Markets

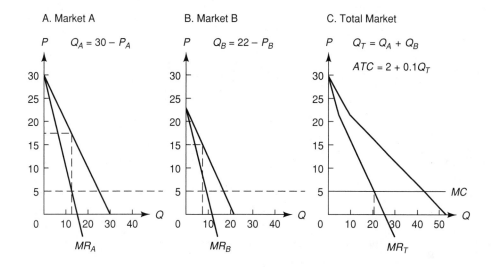

A. Market A   B. Market B   C. Total Market

$$Q_A = 30 - P_A \qquad Q_B = 22 - P_B \qquad Q_T = Q_A + Q_B$$

$$ATC = 2 + 0.1Q_T$$

MR_A MR_B MR_T

Illustrative Problem

The Thaitronics Corporation was established in 1983 in Bangkok, Thailand, as a wholly owned subsidiary of FTT Corporation. Thaitronics manufactures memory boards for computers, which it sells in the United States (Market A) and Europe (Market B). The daily demand in the United States is $Q_A = 30 - P_A$ and in Europe is $Q_B = 22 - P_B$. The average total cost is $2 + 0.1Q_T$, where $Q_T = $ total output, in units.

Questions

a. Find the optimal sales quantity and price in each market under price discrimination.
b. Find the maximum profit using price discrimination.
c. Find the maximum profit without price discrimination.

Solutions

a. Proceed as follows:
Step 1.   At optimum, $MR_A = MR_B$; hence find the equations for MR_A and MR_B, set them equal, and solve for MR_A as a function of Q_B:

Market A	Market B

$$\begin{array}{ll} Q_A = 30 - P_A & Q_B = 22 - P_B \\ P_A = 30 - Q_A & P_B = 22 - Q_B \\ MR_A = 30 - 2Q_A & MR_B = 22 - 2Q_B \end{array}$$

$$MR_A = 30 - 2Q_A = 22 - 2Q_B = MR_B$$
$$-2Q_A = -8 - 2Q_B$$
$$Q_A = Q_B + 4$$

Step 2.   Find the marginal cost in terms of Q_B:

$$ATC = 2 + 0.1Q_T$$
$$TC = (2 + 0.1Q_T)Q_T = 2Q_T + 0.1Q_T^2$$

$$MC = 2 + 0.2Q_T = 2 + 0.2(Q_A + Q_B) = 2 + 0.2Q_A + 0.2Q_B$$
$$= 2 + 0.2(Q_B + 4) + 0.2Q_B = 2 + 0.2Q_B + 0.8 + 0.2Q_B$$
$$= 0.4Q_B + 2.8$$

Step 3.   At maximum profit, $MR_B = MC$:

$$MR_B = 22 - 2Q_B = 0.4Q_B + 2.8 = MC$$
$$-2.4Q_B = -19.2$$
$$Q_B = 8$$
$$Q_A = Q_B + 4 = 8 + 4 = 12$$

Step 4.   Find the optimal price for each market:

$$\text{Market } A : P_A = 30 - Q_A = 30 - 12 = \$18$$
$$\text{Market } B : P_B = 22 - Q_B = 22 - 8 = \$14$$

b. The maximum profit using price discrimination is

$$\pi = TR - TC = \$18(12) + \$14(8) - 2(20) - 0.1(20)^2 = \$248$$

c. Without price discrimination, $P_A = P_B = P$. Hence

$$Q = Q_A + Q_B = 30 - P_A + 22 - P_B = 52 - 2P$$
$$P = 26 - 0.5Q$$
$$MR = 26 - Q.$$

Also, we know that $MC = 2 + 0.2Q$, and at optimum, $MR = MC$:

$$26 - Q = 2 + 0.2Q$$
$$1.2Q = 24$$
$$Q = 20$$
$$P = 26 - 0.5Q = 26 - 10 = \$16$$
$$\pi = TR - TC = \$16(20) - 2(20) - 0.1(20)^2 = \$240.$$

The preceding illustrative problem demonstrates that the profit-maximizing total quantity is the same whether or not there is price discrimination; but profit is greater when price discrimination can be practiced.

Optimal Pricing of Multiple Products

Our discussion so far has been based on the assumption that the firm produces only one product. In modern industry, however, the typical firm produces several products for a number of reasons, not the least of which is the avoidance of the risk inherent to reliance on sales of a single product. Multiple products may also strengthen the firm's competitive position. Whatever the reason for producing more than one product, this multiplicity creates four different kinds of relationships.

1. *Demand relationships* arise when the products are either substitutes or complements for each other.
2. *Cost relationships* arise when multiple products are produced in the same facility. Cost sharing among several products may give the firm a competitive edge in pricing the products.
3. *Production relationships* arise when more than one product results from a single production process. Usually there is a primary product and one or more by-products that may be produced in either fixed or variable proportions. Disposing of the by-products may be profitable or costly, depending upon their nature.
4. *Capacity relationships* arise when the firm is able to use excess or idle capacity to produce one or more additional products. As new products are added, the sharing of fixed costs alters the optimal output and price structure for all products.

Product-Line Pricing

Many firms produce product lines; that is, groups of products that are related either as substitutes or complements. The key economic feature with respect to pricing a company's product line is the cross elasticity of demand, which was discussed in Chapter 6.

Pricing of Substitute Goods.   The production of substitute goods by a firm reflects an effort to segregate market sectors that have different demand elasticities. For example, Procter & Gamble produces Ivory, Zest, Safeguard, Camay, and Lava handsoaps for people with different tastes and preferences. General Motors produces Chevrolet, Pontiac, Buick, Oldsmobile, and Cadillac automobiles for buyers with different income levels as well as different tastes.

Although each of these product lines competes with similar products of other companies, they also compete "in house" with each other. There are numerous examples of firms that produce substitute products for internal as well as external competition. These include meat packers, automobile manufacturers, tire makers, clothing producers, cigarette firms, soap companies, and pharmaceutical houses, to name only a few. Pricing policies that push the sales of one product may consequently hurt the sales of another of the firm's products as well as other firms' competing products. How then should these products be priced?

In practice, two common methods of product-line pricing for substitute goods can be distinguished:

1. *Set prices on the entire line of products by the same method.* Essentially, a markup method of pricing is used on the entire line of products, with the same margin used for all similar products in the line. The specific technique is to price the products in proportion to costs, with the choice of costs being either *full costs* or *transformation costs*. **Transformation costs** are the expenditures for labor and overhead required to transform (convert) raw materials into finished products.

2. *Price the product by varying the size of the markup with the level of costs.* Thus, the more costly the product, the higher the markup, and hence the higher the price. Automobile pricing is a good example of this approach.

Despite their widespread use in industry, both of these methods are defective because they take no account of differences in demand, differences in competitive conditions, and differences in the degree of market maturity of each product in the line. Furthermore, the accounting methods used to divide joint costs among products of the same firm cannot be justified economically. By definition, joint costs are those costs that have no natural connection to any one product but are common to all. Therefore, allocations of joint costs to specific products are necessarily arbitrary. This results in prices that reflect the subjective allocation of common costs.

What, then, should be the appropriate method for setting price? Ideally, the optimum price in a market sector is the one that yields the largest total-contribution margin. Approached in this way, the product-line price structure would aim at the correct objective: that of *exploiting the difference in demand elasticities between market sectors,* as explained in the previous section.

Pricing Complementary Goods

The second type of demand interrelation is complementarity. The degree of complementarity among products can take several forms:

1. Complementarity may take the near-extreme form of fixed proportions (e.g., watch cases and watch mechanisms, automobile radiators and engine blocks, houses and furnaces).
2. Complementarity may lie in different degrees of variable proportions (e.g., turpentine and paint, cameras and film, compact-disc players and CDs).
3. Complementarity may take the most remote form when the various products in the line are not jointly related in use but merely augment the firm's general reputation (e.g., dentrifrices and soap by a firm such as Procter & Gamble, where the ultimate product being sold is personal hygiene).

In a certain sense, all products of a firm can be viewed as complementary if they enhance one another's acceptability. In any event, the fundamental pricing principles are not materially altered. The ultimate objective, as with substitute goods, is to arrive at a price structure that produces the largest total-contribution margin according to the separate demand elasticities of market segments. An essential difference, however, is that the cross elasticity of complementary goods is negative. Therefore, a decrease in the price of one of a set of complementary goods leads to increased demand for the others. The practical consequence is that sellers will frequently find it more profitable to price one item low, or even at a loss, in the hope of selling a complementary item at an above-average profit margin. For example, the purchaser of an inexpensive Polaroid camera is usually a repeat customer for Polaroid film.

Loss Leaders.   **Loss leaders** illustrate one type of product-line pricing of complementary goods. Most commonly encountered in retailing, this practice refers to the selling of a commodity at less than invoice cost or at a price sharply below customary price, and publicizing the fact through advertising. The intention is (1) to draw in customers who will buy other products and/or (2) to arouse enough consumer interest to eventually shift the demand curve to the right.

In the first case, the complementarity is between different products at the same time, and the losses on the loss leader are unimportant if they are more than offset by the gains on the complementary items. In the second case, the complementarity reveals a time dimension between present and future demand, with the hope that present losses will encourage future sales and profits. Magazine trial subscriptions and student rates on theater tickets are two examples.

The name "loss leader" is actually a misnomer, for intelligent management can in reality increase its profits by careful selection and pricing of its loss leaders. Therefore, a good loss leader is actually a profit leader.

Tie-In Sales.   **Tie-in sales** or **tie-in contracts** require buyers to combine other purchases with the featured goods so that in effect the seller is offering the purchaser a joint product. Normally, the featured or "lever" commodity must be difficult to substitute, not easily dispensed with, and relatively more inelastic in demand than the subsidiary item.

An ideal opportunity for tie-in sales exists when the seller possesses an exclusive and essential patent, as in the classic example of the American Shoe Machinery Company, which compelled shoemakers to purchase other materials and intermediate products as a condition of purchasing shoe machinery. (The practice was later ruled to be illegal.)

Packaged deals that offer a customer the chance to "buy one and get one free" are legal and may be considered a type of tie-in practice. For example, the customer who buys a tennis racket may get a package of strings without charge. Packaged sales are often encountered as a method of introducing a new product.

Two-Part Tariff.   Still another illustration of complementarity in practice is the **two-part tariff.** Here the buyer pays two different prices for a joint product consisting of a fixed and a variable component. For the fixed portion, the buyer pays a set price independent of utilization. For the variable flow of services, the buyer makes separate payment according to the amount used. Examples include:

1. Basic installation charge for electric wiring, gas-transmission lines, or telephone lines and the variable payments dependent on use.
2. The minimum charge for public-utility services and the variable payments for units purchased.
3. The entry fee to an amusement park and the variable payments for each individual entertainment.
4. The cover charge in a nightclub and separate charges for food and drink consumed.

Multiple-Product Pricing Strategy: Utilizing Plant Capacity

One reason for pursuing a multiple-product strategy is to make full use of plant capacity. Whenever existing production fails to utilize the firm's productive resources at an optimum level (which is not necessarily 100 percent of capacity), a certain portion of its fixed inputs are being wasted. If another product can be produced and sold at a price greater than its incremental cost, it would pay the firm to do so.

Looking at the situation from another angle, if the fixed costs can be spread over more products, the firm's profitability will be enhanced. This leads to a persuasive argument that business firms are more in the business of selling their unique productive capacities than they are of selling this or that product.

The process of selling plant capacity in the form of a variety of products can be illustrated with the aid of Exhibit 16–4, which depicts a plant that is capable of producing two products, A and B, *with no significant difference in cost factors*. What is the optimal level of output for each product? The exhibit shows the following:

1. There is only one marginal-cost curve, MC, regardless of which product is being produced.

2. The marginal-revenue curve for Product A extends from the Y-intercept at Z to the X-intercept at Q_2. If only Product A is produced, the profit-maximizing output is Q_1 units, which is the production level at which $MR = MC$ (at point R).

3. The productive capacity beyond Q_1 units is available to produce Product B. Therefore, suppose we cut off production of Product A at Q_1 and begin production of Product B. The vertical dashed line at Q_1 then becomes the origin for our diagram of the marginal revenue of Product B (also drawn with a dashed line). This marginal-revenue line MR_B extends between U and Q_5, crossing the marginal-cost curve at V, which corresponds to an aggregate output of Q_3 units of Products A and B. That is, we would produce Q_1 units of Product A and $(Q_3 - Q_1)$ units of Product B.

4. The production of Q_3 units of A and B is not optimal, for MR_B at point V is clearly greater than MR_A at point R. The decision rule for allocating output is that the marginal revenue of A and B must be equal to each other and to marginal cost, as discussed in the previous section. We can increase profits by producing fewer units of A and putting the resources saved into production of B.

5. On our diagram, we shall change the product mix by sliding the triangle UQ_1Q_5 to the left. Now keep in mind that the left side of the moving triangle marks the upper limit on production of Product A and the right side (hypotenuse) represents MR_B. As we move the triangle to the left, the intersection between MR_B and MC, which began at point V, moves down the MC curve. At the same time, the intersection between the left side of the triangle and MR_A, which began at point R, moves up the MR_A curve. We stop moving the triangle when it reaches the position TQ_AQ_4, because at this position, MR_A at point S is equal to MR_B at point W and both are equal to MC. Points S and W lie on a horizontal line of *equal marginal revenue*, EMR, so that $MR_A = MR_B = MC$. This satisfies the conditions for maximum profit.

6. The optimal production quantities are Q_A units of Product A and $(Q_B - Q_A)$ units of Product B.

This process can be extended to any number of products as long as the marginal-cost curve does not change. Exhibit 16–5 depicts the way in which prices may be determined for three products being produced in optimal quantities, that is, when $MR_A = MR_B = MR_C = MC$. The prices P_A, P_B, and P_C are picked off the respective demand curves D_A, D_B, and D_C for the quantities Q_A, Q_B, and Q_C.

The model depicted by Exhibit 16–5 assumes that the firm is able to enter new markets with each additional product, and that in each market the price is greater than the marginal cost. The new markets are entered in the order of their profitability. Thus we see that for each successive product in Exhibit 16–5, the price is somewhat lower and the marginal

EXHIBIT 16–4   **Optimal Output of Two Products from a Single Plant**

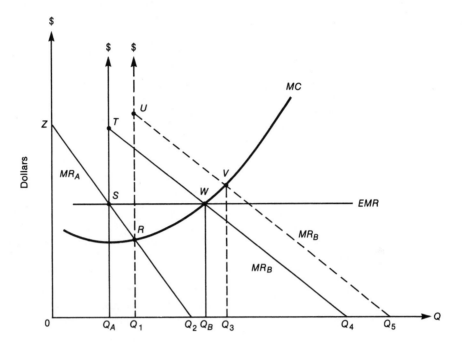

EXHIBIT 16–5   **Pricing of Multiple Products to Utilize Plant Capacity**

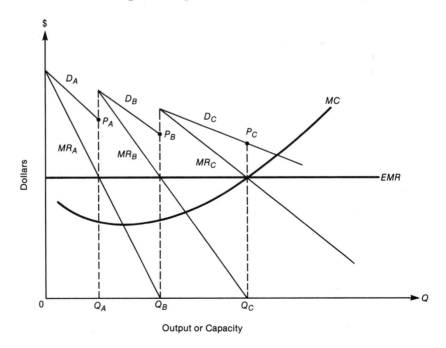

cost somewhat higher. Equilibrium is reached when no more markets can be found in which new products may be sold for a price greater than marginal cost, or when the firm's productive capacity has been reached.

Limitations of the Model.   This model has several weaknesses. First, it ignores demand interdependence, and second, it assumes the firm's capacity can be easily altered to produce a variety of products. Actually, the model can be reshaped to handle either of these cases, although the arithmetic can become somewhat complex.

With respect to plant capacity, the issue may not be so much a matter of whether adjustments can be made in a physical sense as it is a matter of the costs involved in making them. For example, when an airliner is divided into two sections, the physical aspect of creating the new product—seats in a first-class section—is accomplished quite easily by putting a partition in the aircraft and providing first-class passengers with "free" cocktails and other amenities. But the important economic question is whether or not the greater incremental revenues from the new product can offset the added costs.

With respect to demand interdependence, the market conditions for a single product may range from near monopoly to pure competition. In many cases, the firm may arrive at equilibrium in the perfectly elastic market of pure competition in which $P = MR = MC$. This is a common condition that almost all multiproduct firms encounter sooner or later; that is, they produce some products on which they make no economic profit because the price is no greater than the marginal cost. Such products may eventually be discontinued. In many cases, however, products that make no profit, or even suffer slight losses, are continued for strategic reasons other than profit. For example, products may be retained to round out the firm's product line, to retain customer goodwill, or to keep open channels of distribution that might otherwise be closed.

Loss leaders, as previously discussed in this chapter, are examples of products priced at a loss for strategic reasons. Closely akin to this is the supermarket practice of keeping markups very low on staple items such as flour, coffee, and soap. Price elasticity is high on staple items because of industry-wide competition and the consumer's knowledge of what the prices "ought to be." Thus advertising of low prices on staple items has an effect similar to advertising loss leaders.

In some cases, no-profit or money-losing products are necessary to keep the organization intact. Construction companies and consulting firms of all types often will "buy a contract" (offer their services below cost) in order to keep their labor force intact between more profitable projects. In such cases, the incremental short-run loss of buying the contract has to be weighed against the costs of first losing and then replacing professional staff or skilled labor when a more lucrative contract is obtained.

Optimum Pricing of Joint Products

Joint products result from production processes that naturally yield multiple products. A decision to run the production process automatically produces the entire product group. By-products may be used, sold, or otherwise disposed of. For example, the processing of sugar cane results in a by-product called *bagasse*, which is the residue of the cane stalk after the juice has been squeezed out. Bagasse is burned to make steam to generate electricity. By-products that cannot be used or sold create a problem (and a cost) of disposal.

The ratio or proportion of joint products may be either fixed or variable. For example, the slaughter of one steer produces one carcass and one hide, a proportion that never changes. In contrast, a petroleum refinery always produces a spectrum of products ranging from gasoline to fuel oil, but it does control and can vary the proportions of the various outputs.

Joint Products in Fixed Proportions.   Since there is only one production process, there is no economically sound way to allocate costs to the individual products. The demand curves, however, can be and usually are quite different for the main product and the by-products. Determination of the optimal output and prices involves optimization of the total marginal revenue from all products in relation to marginal cost. In making that determination, however, we must remember that total revenue from each individual product is maximum when its marginal revenue equals zero. This means that neither product may be sold beyond the quantity where its individual $MR = 0$. Any further sales would carry negative marginal revenue, and the firm would be losing money on each unit sold. We shall explain the optimizing procedure with the help of Exhibit 16–6 (page 524).

Exhibit 16–6 depicts two cases of the joint products A and B produced in the fixed proportion 1:1. In both cases, the marginal revenues of the by-products are added to obtain the joint marginal revenue, MR_T; i.e., $MR_T = MR_A + MR_B$. In order to maximize profit, we must find the level of production at which $MR_T = MC$. In Panel A, this occurs at the production level Q_C. At Q_C level of output, both MR_A and MR_B are greater than zero and Q_C is less than Q_M, at which $MR_B = 0$. Therefore, Q_C is the optimal level of production and sales of both products.

In Panel B, $MR_T = MC$ at Q_C units of production, but Q_C is greater than Q_M, which is the maximum sales level for the by-product. If Q_C units of the by-product are sold, each unit sold in excess of Q_M bears a negative marginal revenue, which means the firm would be losing money on each such unit. Therefore, $(Q_C - Q_M)$ units of the by-product cannot be sold, and producing Q_C units of both products is not the optimal solution.

The optimal solution is found by concentrating on the main product after Q_M units have been reached. From zero to Q_M units of production, the marginal revenues of both products are positive; therefore the joint marginal-revenue curve MR_T is relevant. After Q_M units, only MR_A is positive; therefore only MR_A is relevant. The shift from MR_T to MR_A occurs at point B on the diagram, and the relevant marginal-revenue curve is indicated by the heavy line ABK. This curve intersects the MC curve at point K, which indicates that the optimal level of production is Q_3. This means that maximum profit occurs when Q_3 units of each product are produced. The entire output of the main product is sold, but only Q_M units of the by-product are sold. The remaining $(Q_3 - Q_M)$ units must be dumped, destroyed, or otherwise disposed of.

In the past, the cheapest method of disposal has too often been indiscriminate dumping on land or in rivers or the ocean. Legally and environmentally sound disposal methods

EXHIBIT 16–6   Output and Price Determination of Two Products, A and B, Produced in Fixed Proportions

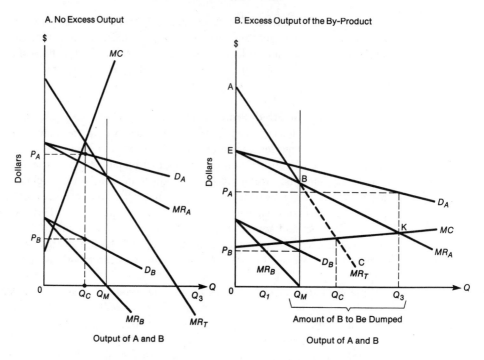

may incur additional costs. These additional costs can be quite substantial, and thus provide a powerful incentive to the company to find new uses and new markets for the unwanted by-product.

A problem of optimizing the production and sales of joint products in fixed proportions is best approached in a step-by-step manner, as follows:

Step 1. Develop or obtain the demand and associated marginal revenue functions for both products in the form $P = f(Q)$.

Step 2. Set the marginal revenue of each product equal to zero and solve for the maximum sales level, Q^*, for each product. Designate the higher value of Q^* as Q_{Amax} and its product as the main product A. Designate the Q^* with the lower value as Q_{Bmax} and its product as the by-product B.

Step 3. Add the marginal-revenue functions MR_A and MR_B to obtain the joint–marginal-revenue function MR_T.

Step 4. Obtain or develop the total-cost function and take its derivative to get marginal cost, MC.

Step 5. Set $MR_T = MC$ and solve for Q^*.

Step 6. Compare Q^* with Q_{Bmax}. If $Q^* \leq Q_{Bmax}$, the problem is solved (i.e., profit is maximized when Q^* units of each product are produced and sold—the situation in Panel A of Exhibit 16–6) and you can go to Step 8.

Step 7. If $Q^* > Q_{Bmax}$, set $MR_A = MC$, and solve for a new Q^*. This will be the optimal level of production. Q^* units of Product A will be sold, but only Q_{Bmax} units of Product B will be sold. The remaining $(Q^* - Q_{Bmax})$ units will be disposed of some other way, but not sold. (This is the situation in Panel B of Exhibit 16–6.)

Step 8. Use the demand functions for Products A and B to find the prices at which the optimal quantities can be sold.

Step 9. Write the profit equation and calculate the profit at optimum output and sales of the two products.

Illustrative Problem

The Excelsior Wood Products Company produces millwork from raw lumber. The production process is such that for every unit of their primary product (Product A) they get one unit of salable scrap (Product B). The firm estimates its demand and cost functions as

$$Q_A = 800 - 2P_A$$
$$Q_B = 150 - P_B$$
$$TC = 600 + 4Q + 3Q^2.$$

Questions

a. Find the profit-maximizing level of output, level of sales, and price for each product.
b. Find the maximum profit from making and selling both products.

Solution

Follow the steps just outlined.

Step 1.

$Q_A = 800 - 2P_A$	$Q_B = 150 - P_B$
$P_A = 400 - 0.5Q_A$	$P_B = 150 - Q_B$
$TR_A = 400Q_A - 0.5Q_A^2$	$TR_B = 150Q_B - Q_B^2$
$MR_A = 400 - Q_A$	$MR_B = 150 - 2Q_B$

Step 2.

$400 - Q_A = 0$	$150 - 2Q_B = 0$
$Q_A = 400$	$Q_B = 75$

Product B is the by-product with maximum sales of 75 units.

Step 3. Since in joint production, output quantity $Q_A = Q_B = Q$,

$$MR_T = 400 - Q_A + 150 - 2Q_B = 550 - 3Q$$

Step 4.

$$TC = 600 + 4Q + 3Q^2$$
$$MC = 4 + 6Q$$

Step 5.

$$MR_T = 550 - 3Q = 4 + 6Q = MC$$
$$9Q = 546$$
$$Q^* = 60.67$$

Step 6.

$$Q^* = 60.67 < Q_B = 75$$

Therefore, optimal production per time period is an average of 60.67 units of each product.

Step 7. Not required, since the sale of 60.67 units of the by-product is allowed.

Step 8.

$$P_A = 400 - 0.5Q_A = 400 - 0.5(60.67) = \$369.67$$
$$P_B = 150 - Q_B = 150 - 60.67 = \$89.33$$

Step 9.

$$\pi = TR_A + TR_B - TC = \$369.67(60.67) + \$89.33(60.67)$$
$$- 600 - 4(60.67) - 3(60.67)^2 = \$15,962.30 \text{ per time period.}$$

Joint Products in Fixed Proportions Other Than a 1:1 Ratio.   If the joint products are produced in fixed proportions other than 1:1, we must first remember that the cost function pertains to output of the main product. Therefore, we want to establish a ratio of 1:x, where x is the number of units of by-product produced per unit of main product.

For example, suppose that the cost function and the demand functions for Product A and Product B of the preceding illustrative problem remain the same, but the production technology changes such that the joint production ratio becomes $Q_A{:}Q_B = 2{:}3$. We note that the ratio 2:3 is the same as 1.0:1.5. Hence $Q_A = Q$ and $Q_B = 1.5Q_A$. By making appropriate substitutions of $1.5Q_A$ for Q_B and vice-versa, the procedure previously described for a 1:1 ratio can be followed.

Joint Products in Variable Proportions and Fixed Product Prices.   When the firm is able to vary the proportions of the joint products, optimal pricing soon becomes quite complex because a large number of combinations must be considered. Conceptually, what is needed is a set of isocost curves that will depict the loci of all combinations of output that can be produced for a given total cost. One such set is depicted on Exhibit 16–7.

1. The curvilinear isocost curves in Exhibit 16–7 are called **product-transformation curves** or **production-possibility curves**. Each curve represents all possible variations in the proportional output of Products A and B for a given constant cost. The curves are concave to the origin to reflect the reasonable assumption that it becomes increasingly difficult to produce more of one product and less of the other as we approach the ends of the curve. As we move outward from the origin, each curve reflects a higher level of total cost. The levels shown are for $TC = 120$, $TC = 200$, and $TC = 320$.

2. Exhibit 16–7 also shows a set of **isorevenue lines**, $TR = 140$, $TR = 240$, and $TR = 340$. They represent all combinations of output of Products A and B that

EXHIBIT 16–7   **Output Determination of Joint Products with Variable Proportions and Fixed Product Prices**

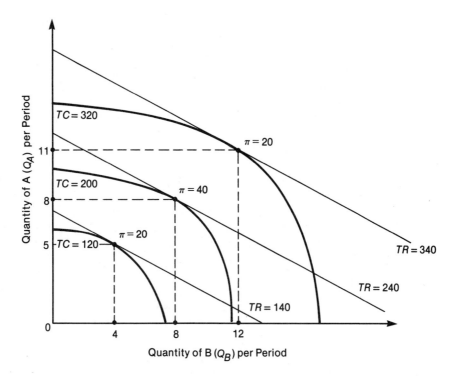

will produce the same revenue. The lines are straight because they are drawn under the assumption of constant product prices—in this illustration P_A = \$20 and P_B = \$10.

3. An optimal combination of A and B can be found for any given isocost by finding its tangency with an isorevenue line. For TC = 120, Q_A = 5 and Q_B = 4; for TC = 200, Q_A = 8 and Q_B = 8; and for TC = 320, Q_A = 11 and Q_B = 12.

4. Finally, the diagram suggests that there is also an optimal total budget for producing the two joint products. As in most other situations, this optimal output combination occurs at the point of profit maximization. In our illustration this occurs with a budget of 200, which yields a total profit of 40. However, there is an infinite number of budgets that would have to be examined to determine whether any of these offers a profit greater than 40. Again, the use of calculus or linear programming can be helpful in searching for the point of maximum profits.

Summary

Simplified models of market structure show how the firm may maximize profit in a static situation by producing at a level where marginal revenue equals marginal cost. In a dynamic situation, however, managements must deal with multiple objectives, multiple products, multiple markets, multiple plants with different marginal costs and revenues, and a considerable degree of uncertainty.

Empirical research indicates that several objectives are pursued in pricing: (1) achieving a target return on investment, (2) realizing target market share, or (3) meeting or matching competition.

The firm may pursue its pricing objectives through a variety of methods, but the two most important methods are *cost-plus pricing* and *incremental-cost pricing*.

The *cost-plus method* of pricing consists of two parts: establishing the cost and establishing the plus (or markup). The determination of relevant cost differs somewhat among manufacturing, merchandising, and service industries, and the way in which the markup is determined will depend upon what is included in cost. In all cases, however, the cost-plus must include a satisfactory profit. This may be less than maximum in the short run in order to improve profits in the long run. Thus cost-plus is a long-run pricing concept closely related to target-return objectives.

Incremental-cost pricing provides business executives with an essential guide for short-run production and pricing decisions. The appropriate use of incremental analysis requires a thorough examination of the total effect of the decision in question, both in the short run and the long run. Then a price can be set that will cause incremental revenue to exceed incremental cost.

Price discrimination is defined as the practice of charging different prices to different buyers of the same product without corresponding differences in cost. It exists in three degrees.

In first-degree price discrimination, the seller charges a different (lower) price for each successive unit bought. Differential pricing of the second degree is more commonly known as volume or quantity discounting. Quantity discounts may be based upon either one-time or cumulative purchases, or may be offered according to the function of the buyer (such as wholesaler, jobber, retailer) in the chain of distribution.

Differential pricing of the third degree occurs when the seller is able to segregate and seal off markets according to the price elasticities of the buyers. Different markets can then be charged different prices, with higher prices in the more inelastic groups. Differentials may be based on time (either clock time or calendar time) or product use. Whatever the basis for discrimination, profit is maximized when the marginal revenue in each market is equal to the marginal cost of the product; i.e., $MR_A = MR_B = \ldots = MR_N = MC$.

When the firm produces multiple products, relationships arise in the areas of demand, cost, production, and capacity. In pricing substitute goods, the firm competes with itself as well as with other firms. Two approaches to the pricing of multiple products are common. One is to price the entire line by the same method, such as a percentage markup on cost. The other method is to vary the profit margin with the level of costs; that is, to place a higher markup on more costly goods. A better way would be to exploit any differences in price elasticities of the various products.

In pricing complementary goods, lowering the price of one good increases demand for both. Hence for many products sold in retail stores, loss leaders (goods sold at or below cost) have proved to be very profitable. Tie-in sales and two-part tariffs are also commonly used in pricing complementary goods.

Joint products present a different problem, since the by-product arises automatically in production of the main product. Optimal pricing requires that the joint marginal revenue equal marginal cost; however, the by-product may not be sold beyond the quantity at which its marginal revenue falls to zero. Joint products may be produced in fixed proportions or in variable proportions, with either fixed or variable prices for both inputs and output. Thus the problem of pricing joint products can become very complicated. The general principle to be followed is that the ratio of marginal revenue to marginal cost should be the same for all products.

Problems

1. If most firms tend to set prices on the basis of costs (for example, cost-plus), why should companies ever show losses on their profit-and-loss statements?

2. Would you expect the markup on staple items (potatoes, flour, and sugar, for example) in a supermarket to be higher or lower than the markup on nonstaples? From the perspective of the *individual* supermarket, which of the two product groups has the more elastic demand? Does the relationship between markup and elasticity, generally recognized as being inverse, seem to hold for staples and non-staples? Finally, which of the two groups would include the more attractive candidates for a loss leader? Explain.

3. In the book-publishing business, it is inherent in the royalty arrangement that the publisher's pricing policy results in an economic conflict between the author and the publisher. In the great majority of cases, the author's royalty is a percentage of the total revenue that the publisher receives on the sale of the book. The publisher, however, determines the price of the book (and also incurs all costs of manufacturing, promotion, and distribution). It follows, therefore, that the price that maximizes profit for the publisher is higher, and the output lower, than the price and output that maximize royalty payments for the author. Why? Demonstrate this proposition graphically, using marginal analysis.

4. The A2Z Company manufactures small electrical appliances that are sold in U.S. markets built up by substantial promotion of the A2Z brand. Among its better known products is a food blender. At a standard production level of 100,000 units, the standard fully allocated cost is $10 per unit, of which

$6 is average variable cost. The normal markup on cost is 50 percent.

The firm receives an offer from a Canadian firm to buy 50,000 units, with the Canadian firm's brand imprinted instead of A2Z, to be sold only in Canada. The Canadian firm offers a price of $12 per unit. Manufacture of the additional 50,000 units will require a second shift and will increase standard variable costs to $8 per unit. Should A2Z Company accept the Canadian firm's offer? Back up your answer with suitable calculations.

5. Identify the pricing principle(s) involved in each of the following pricing practices:

   a. The price of liquid detergent per ounce is found to decrease with larger-sized containers.

   b. A movie theater charges one price for adults, a second for children, and a third for students.

   c. A bakery charges only half as much for day-old bread as it does for fresh bread.

   d. There is a several-hundred–dollar difference between comparably equipped Chevrolets, Pontiacs, and Cadillacs.

   e. A photo-processing concern charges 35 cents each for 1–5 prints from a negative, 30 cents each for 6–10 prints from the same negative, and 25 cents each for more than 10 prints from the negative.

   f. On a certain round-trip flight, an airline charges $30 less for passengers flying weekdays than for those taking the same flight on weekends.

   g. Subscriptions to many periodicals are cheaper if more than a year's subscription is purchased. Also, the publisher often offers a substantial discount to students and educational institutions.

h. Many utilities charge different prices to private versus industrial users.

6. Saturn Publishing Company puts out two monthly magazines called *Action* and *Brisk*. The company charges the same price for both magazines, but the sales of *Brisk* are about twice those of *Action*. Both magazines are among the leaders in their field, with combined sales of 5 to 6 million copies a month. In this sales range, therefore, the marginal cost of producing the two magazines is practically constant. Further, it has been established on the basis of previous pricing experiments in various markets that the elasticity of demand is equal for the two magazines at the present price.

Recently, the president of the company asked whether it is consistent with profit maximization for the two magazines to have the same price. The sales manager replied that in order for Saturn to maximize its profits, it ought to charge a higher price for *Brisk* than for *Action*, since demand is greater for the former.

The president has called you in as a consulting economist to settle the question. Both the president and sales manager studied economics while in college and are fairly familiar with such concepts as average revenue, marginal revenue, marginal cost, and so forth. Can you provide them with an analytical solution to the problem?

7. The World Cup Company manufactures two types of professional-quality tennis rackets. The *Champion* is of regular dimension (90 Series) and the *Winner* has a larger hitting area (110 Series), but the two rackets may be considered as substitutes in the marketplace. The demand functions are

$$Q_C = 800 - 4P_C + 8P_W$$
$$Q_W = 300 + 2P_C - 6P_W$$

where

Q = Quantity demanded
P = Price
C = Subscript denoting the *Champion* racket
W = Subscript denoting the *Winner* racket.

Their unit cost functions are

$$ATC_C = 10 + 0.5Q_C$$
$$ATC_W = 15 + 0.125Q_W$$

where ATC = average total cost (fully allocated unit cost).

a. Determine optimum output and price for each racket.

b. Determine profit for each type of racket at optimum output.

8. The Kentucky Pride Distillers make and distribute a premium-grade whiskey in two distinct markets, one in the Midwest and one in the South. Estimated demand functions in the two markets are

$$Q_1 = 180 - 2P_1$$
$$Q_2 = 70 - 0.5P_2$$

while unit cost is

$$ATC = 10 + 0.1Q$$

where

Q_1 and Q_2 = Quantities demanded, in six-bottle cases
P_1 and P_2 = Price per case
ATC = Average total cost (fully allocated unit cost) per case.

a. Assume that third-degree price discrimination is possible. Then find:

1. The profit-maximizing sales level and price for each market

2. The maximum profit for the firm

3. The price elasticity of demand for each market at optimum sales level.

b. Calculate the profit-maximizing sales level and price if price discrimination is not practiced.

c. Compare the firm's profits with and without price discrimination.

9. The Green Pastures Dairy produces butter and cottage cheese in fixed proportions of one unit of butter to one unit of cottage cheese. The dairy's economic advisor has estimated demand for the two products as

$$P_B = 75 - Q_B$$
$$P_C = 60 - 3Q_C$$

where P = price, Q = quantity demanded, and the subscripts B and C represent butter and cottage cheese, respectively. The cost of the joint production of butter and cheese is

$$TC = 300 + 15Q + Q^2$$

where TC = total cost in dollars.

a. Determine the optimal quantity of each product to be produced and sold in order to maximize profit.

b. Determine the optimal price of each product.

c. Calculate the maximum total profit on both products.

Case Problem: Precision Electronics Company

10. Precision Electronics Company is a rapidly growing manufacturing company in one of Asia's developing nations. The chief executive officer and other top executives of the firm received their business training in U.S. universities and are familiar with the concept of third-degree price discrimination. In 1988, the firm began producing a 19-inch color-TV set with advanced electronic features. After due consideration of demand in the firm's domestic market and in the U.S. market, the sets were priced at $325 in the U.S. market and at the equivalent of US$475 in local currency in the domestic market. Unfortunately, the practice of exporting a product at a lower price than is charged at home is called "dumping" by the United States and is illegal there.

In the summer of 1988, the U.S. Trade Representative's Office found Precision Electronics guilty of dumping its color TVs. Precision Electronics protested the decision, pleading that its costs were higher in its domestic market, but the United States was unmoved. The tariffs on all Precision Electronics products were increased by 15 percent as punishment for dumping the color-TV sets. This effectively destroyed the U.S. market for Precision Electronics TV sets and made it more difficult to market any other products.

In 1989, Precision Electronics persuaded the United States to drop the additional tariff, but the U.S. market for its color-TV sets was gone. Late in 1989, however, the firm developed a new electronic device to improve the performance and usefulness of VCRs. After surveying both markets, the firm estimated demand for this product to be $Q_D = 100 - 2P$ units per day in the domestic market and $Q_F = 80 - 4P$ units per day in the U.S. market. The marginal cost of production is a constant $10; however, a certain piece of equipment limits production to 50 units per day.

Questions

a. Determine the optimal price in each market under price discrimination. Would the U.S. price be legal under U.S. law?

b. If price discrimination is not practiced, what is the optimum price and how many units would be sold in each market?

c. Why would a nation's firms want to "dump" their products in a foreign market?

d. How is an exporting firm's ability to dump its products abroad affected by the import policy of the nation where it is located?

e. What difference does the pricing strategy (i.e., price discrimination or no price discrimination) make in the firm's level of employment (a) if the marginal cost is constant? (b) if the marginal cost curve slopes upward?

References

Cowling, Keith, and A. J. Rayner. "Price, Quality, and Market Share." *Journal of Political Economy* (November-December 1970), pp. 1292–1309.

Hayes, Beth. "Competition and Two-Part Tariffs." *Journal of Business* 60, no. 1 (January 1987), pp. 41–50.

Kardasz, Stanley W., and Kenneth Stollery. "Price Information in Canadian Manufacturing Industries." *Applied Economics* 20, no. 4 (April 1988), pp. 473–83.

Katz, Michael L. "The Welfare Effects of Third-Degree Price Discrimination in Intermediate Goods Markets." *American Economic Review* 77, no. 1 (March 1987), pp.154–67.

Koch, J. V. *Industrial Organization and Prices*. 2nd ed. Englewood Cliffs, N.J.: Prentice-Hall, 1980.

Lanzillotti, Robert F. "Pricing Objectives in Large Companies." *American Economic Review* (December 1958), pp. 921–40.

MacDonald, Glenn, and Alan Slivinski. "The Simple Analytics of Competitive Equilibrium with Multiproduct Firms." *American Economic Review* 77, no. 5 (December 1987), pp. 941–53.

Monroe, Kent B., and Albert J. Della-Bitta. "Models for Pricing Decisions." *Journal of Marketing Research* 15 (August 1978), pp. 413–28.

Png, I. P. L., and D. Hirshleifer. "Price Discrimination through Offers to Match Price." *Journal of Business* 60, no. 3 (July 1987), pp. 365–83.

Silberston, Aubrey. "Surveys of Applied Economics: Price Behavior of Firms." *Economic Journal* (September 1970), pp. 511–82.

Sparkes, J. R.; P. J. Buckley; and H. Mirza. "A Note on Japanese Pricing Policy." *Applied Economics* 19, no. 6 (June 1987), pp. 729–32.

Wolinsky, Asher. "Brand Names and Price Discrimination." *Journal of Industrial Economics* 35, no. 3 (March 1987), pp. 255–68.

APPENDIX 16A   Decentralization and Transfer Pricing

As business firms grow, top management must resolve four central problems dealing with subordinate divisions or units: (1) how to allocate resources, activities, and responsibilities to subordinate units, (2) how to motivate the subordinate units for high performance, (3) how to coordinate and evaluate the performance of the subordinate units, and (4) how to minimize the growing cost of internal communications and the growing difficulties of coordination. As we noted in Chapter 14, the solution to these problems often involves decentralization of the organization into autonomous divisions.

In today's business world one may see divisions getting larger and the firms producing a wider variety of products. One may also see divisions moved overseas to obtain lower production costs or to move production closer to markets. Sometimes these relocated divisions are reorganized as wholly owned subsidiaries.

The autonomous divisions of a decentralized firm are expected to be profit or investment centers, but they are really more than that. In a truly successful decentralization, each division contributes to the success of the company by contributing to the success of other divisions as well as to its own success. One of the ways in which divisions cooperate is in the production of goods or services by one division for use by another division. Since the transfer of such products involves a transaction between autonomous units, it becomes necessary to establish a transfer price at which the product may be sold by one division and purchased by the other.

Transfer pricing is not confined to exchanges between divisions. It applies to pricing any exchange of goods or services between organizational units. Thus the cost accountants' allocation of service-department costs to production departments is actually a form of transfer pricing. However, since we are concerned with economic rather than accounting aspects of transfer pricing, and for the sake of simplicity, we shall confine our discussion to exchanges between divisions or subsidiaries.

The Nature and Objectives of Transfer Pricing[1]

Information about transfer prices affects many crucial decisions about the acquisition and allocation of a firm's resources. Ideally, transfer prices should provide each manager with the information necessary to coordinate inputs and outputs with other units so that profits are maximized for the firm as a whole.

When goods and services are exchanged between divisions, the monetary values to be assigned to these exchanges is often the most troublesome aspect of the firm's control system. In establishing transfer prices, three inherent and sometimes conflicting problems must be solved:

1. **Goal congruence.** This is the problem of insuring that the division management's goals coincide with those of the firm.
2. **Incentive.** This is the problem of providing division managers with the incentive to pursue the firm's goals rather than their own.
3. **Autonomy.** This is the problem of providing guidance without undermining the division managers' authority and freedom to make independent decisions.

There is no all-inclusive rule that will invariably lead to the optimal economic decision. This is because the three problems of goal congruence, incentive, and autonomy must all be dealt with at the same time. In any particular situation, however, the following general rule may provide a useful first step in analysis:

> *The lowest transfer price should be based upon the sum of (1) incremental cash outlay (which sometimes may be approximated by total variable costs) and (2) opportunity costs for the firm as a whole.*

Incremental cash outlay means the cash outflows that are directly associated with the production and transfer of the goods or services in question. **Opportunity costs** means the maximum contribution to profits that is forgone by the firm if the goods are transferred internally rather than sold externally. If an external market exists, the opportunity cost per unit is market price less unit variable cost. If no outside market exists, the opportunity cost might be zero; but it also might be the forgone proceeds from the sale of the productive facilities or forgone profits from their use to produce something else.

We see then that there are two basic circumstances under which transfers and transfer pricing take place: (1) when there is an external market for the goods or services and (2) when there is no external market and the division's only customer is another division. Since the latter circumstance is perhaps the most common and most troublesome, we shall discuss it first.

Transfer Pricing When There Is No External Market

Transfer Pricing at Marginal Cost.   Suppose a firm has two divisions. Division A, located in California's Silicon Valley, manufactures a critical component of the final

---

[1] Extracted from Charles T. Horngren and George Foster, *Cost Accounting: A Managerial Emphasis*, 6th ed. (Englewood Cliffs, N.J.: Prentice-Hall, 1987), chap. 22.

EXHIBIT 16A–1   Transfer Pricing with No External Market

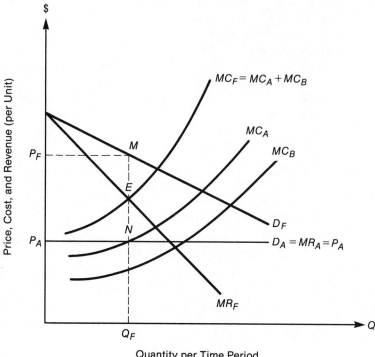

Quantity per Time Period

product, for which there is no external market. Division B, located across San Francisco Bay in Fremont, California, completes assembly and packaging of the final product and markets it throughout the United States and Canada. Since there is no external market for Division A's product, its only customer is Division B. On the other hand, Division B's only source of the product is Division A. Hence, the production by Division A is precisely equal to the demand by Division B. Exhibit 16A–1 illustrates the determination of the transfer price.[2] The exhibit conveys the following information:

MC_A = Division A's marginal cost of producing components for Division B.
MC_B = Division B's marginal cost of completing the firm's product.
MC_F = The firm's marginal cost, which is the vertical summation of $MC_A + MC_B$.
D_F = Demand for the firm's product.
D_A = Demand for Division A's product by Division B.
MR_A = Division A's marginal revenue, which is equal to D_A because the price is constant.

---

[2] Exhibit 16A–1 assumes that Division A's production unit matches Division B's unit requirement on a one-to-one basis. For example, if Division B needs three of the components produced by Division B for each unit of the finished product, then Division A's production unit must contain three components, and Division A's marginal cost must be established accordingly.

MR_F = The firm's marginal revenue, derived from the firm's demand curve, D_F.

E = The intersection of MR_F and MC_F, marking the relationship that will maximize the firm's profits.

Q_F = The profit-maximizing quantity of the firm's finished product, obtained by projecting downward from point E to the horizontal axis.

P_F = Profit-maximizing price of the firm's finished product, obtained by projecting upward from point E to point M on the demand curve, D_F, then horizontally to the vertical axis.

N = The intersection of Division A's marginal cost curve, MC_A, with the line projected downward from point E to Q_F, at which $MR_A = MC_A$. Since the quantity demanded from Division A is precisely equal to Q_F (the firm's output by Division B), Division A's demand curve, D_A, is a horizontal line passing through point N.

P_A = The transfer price, equal to MC_A at the required level of production, Q_F. Division A's marginal revenue will also be the transfer price, hence $P_A = MR_A = MC_A$.

Given the demand function for the firm's product and given the cost functions of the two divisions, the profit-maximizing transfer price can be found as follows:

1. Find the marginal-revenue curve for the firm, MR_F, from the demand curve, D_F.
2. Find the firm's marginal cost, $MC_F = MC_A + MC_B$.
3. Set $MR_F = MC_F$ and solve for the profit-maximizing P_F and Q_F.
4. Substitute the value of Q_F for Q_A in the marginal-cost function MC_A and solve for MC_A. This is the transfer price.

Illustrative Problem

The Lawn-Care Products Company is organized into two divisions. The Heads Division manufactures a patented sprinkler head. The Lawn Systems Division uses these sprinkler heads in the customized lawn-sprinkler systems that it assembles and installs. The Systems Division buys the sprinkler heads from the Heads Division in units of 10 sprinkler heads each. Demand and cost functions have been estimated as follows:

Demand for Lawn Care systems: $P_L = 500 - 0.1Q_L$
Marginal cost in Heads Division: $MC_H = 10 + 0.001Q_H$
Marginal cost in Systems Division: $MC_S = 100 + 0.005Q_S$.

Question

How many units of sprinkler heads will be demanded of the Heads Division and what should the transfer price be?

Solution

Follow the four steps prescribed previously.

Step 1.
$$P_L = 500 - 0.01Q_L$$
$$MR_L = 500 - 0.02Q_L$$

Step 2.
$$MC_L = MC_H + MC_S = 10 + 0.001Q_H + 100 + 0.005Q_S$$
Since $Q_H = Q_S = Q_L$ at the profit-maximizing level of output,
$$MC_L = 110 + 0.006Q_L$$

Step 3.
At optimum, $MR_L = MC_L$

$$500 - 0.02Q_L = 110 + 0.006Q_L$$
$$0.026Q_L = 390$$
$$Q_L = 15,000$$

Step 4.
The transfer price is the Heads Division's marginal cost at a production level of 15,000 units.
$$MC_H = 10 + 0.001Q_H = 10 + 0.001(15,000) = \$25 \text{ per unit of 10 sprinklers heads or}$$
$2.50 each head.

Transfer Pricing When an External Market Exists

When there is an external market for the selling division's product, the selling division may produce more or less than the buying division needs. If the selling division produces more than the buying division needs, the surplus can be sold in the external market. If the selling division produces less than the buying division needs, the buying division can obtain the rest of its needs in the external market. Either way, the selling division is free to pursue maximization of its own profit. The transfer price, however, will depend upon whether the external market is perfectly competitive or imperfectly competitive.

Transfer Pricing with a Perfectly Competitive External Market.   For the case of a perfectly competitive external market, we shall illustrate the derivation of a transfer price with the aid of Exhibit 16A–2. The exhibit conveys the following information:

D_B = Demand curve for the firm's product, which is assembled and sold by Division B.

D_A = Demand curve for Division A's product. Since the product is sold in a perfectly competitive external market, D_A is a horizontal line.

MR_A = The marginal-revenue curve for Division A, which coincides with the demand curve D_A.

P_A = The price of Division A's product. Since the product may be sold in a perfectly competitive external market, the price P_A is the price established by that market and constitutes the marginal revenue, MR_A, for Division A.

MC_A = The marginal cost of selling Division A's product.

EXHIBIT 16A–2   **Determination of Transfer Price When a Perfectly Competitive External Market Exists for the Product**

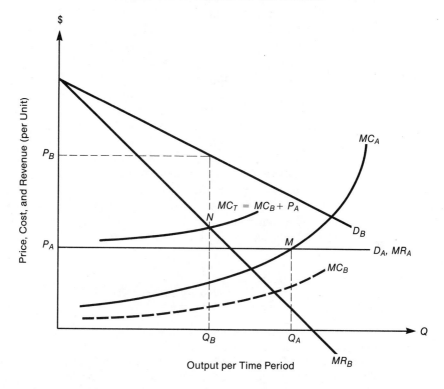

Output per Time Period

MC_B = Marginal cost to Division B of assembling and marketing the firm's product, *excluding* the purchases from Division A or the external market.[3]

MC_T = Marginal cost of producing the firm's product, *including* purchases from Division A or the external market, i.e., $MC_T = MC_B + P_A$. Since Division A will establish production at a level where $MR_A = MC_A$, then $MC_T = MC_B + MC_A$.

M = The intersection of Division A's marginal-cost and marginal-revenue curves.

Q_A = The profit-maximizing output by Division A, obtained by projecting downward from point M.

N = The intersection of Division B's marginal-cost and marginal-revenue curves.

Q_B = The profit-maximizing output of the firm's product by Division B, which is also the quantity of Division A's product purchased by Division B (at a price of P_A). Q_B is obtained by projecting downward from point N.

P_B = Selling price of the firm's completed product by Division B, obtained by projecting upward from point N to the demand curve D_B and then horizontally to the vertical axis.

---

[3] In some firms, the two divisions might be a production division and a marketing division. In that case, the transferred product is the ultimate product and MC_B represents promotional, selling, and perhaps administrative costs.

The exhibit shows that Division A will operate at its profit-maximizing level of production, Q_A units. It will sell Q_B units to Division B at the price P_A and the remainder in the external market at the same price.

Given the demand function for the firm's product (Division B's product), the external market price for Division A's product, MC_A, and MC_B, the profit-maximizing allocation of Division A's output may be calculated as follows:

1. Set $MR_A = MC_A$ to determine Division A's profit-maximizing level of output.
2. Use Division B's demand function to determine MR_B.
3. Find Division B's marginal cost, MC_T, by adding the transfer price to the marginal cost of assembling and marketing the product, MC_B. The transfer price is the external market price, since the external market is perfectly competitive.
4. Find Division B's profit-maximizing output by setting $MC_T = MR_B$. This is the quantity of Division A's product that Division B will buy, provided Division A's output is equal to or greater than Division B's requirement. If not, Division B will buy all of Division A's output and the remainder of its needs in the open market. If Division B's requirement is less than Division A's output, Division A will fill all of Division B's requirement and sell the remainder of its output in the open market.

Illustrative Problem

The AutoSafe Products Company in Cincinnati, Ohio, manufactures a high-quality automobile seat belt that is considered to be very competitive. The company is organized into two autonomous divisions, one for manufacturing and the other for marketing. The marketing division buys the product from the manufacturing division and distributes it to automobile manufacturers and wholesale parts distributors in the United States and Canada. The manufacturing division can also export as much of its output as it wishes to foreign distributors at a price of $25 per unit.

After careful study of the firm's cost accounting and sales records, a recently hired MBA has developed the following cost and demand functions:

For the manufacturing division:

$$TC_{mfg} = 37,500 + 12Q_{mfg} + 0.0005Q_{mfg}^2$$

For the marketing division:

$$Q_{mkt} = 50,000 - 1,000P_{mkt}$$
$$TC_{mkt} = 25,000 + 10Q_{mkt} + 25Q_{mkt} = 25,000 + 35Q_{mkt}.$$

The total-cost equation for marketing reflects $25,000 fixed cost plus a marketing and distribution cost of $10 per unit plus the transfer price of $25 per unit paid to the manufacturing division.

Questions

a. Find the profit-maximizing output for the manufacturing division and its profit (π_{mfg}).
b. How many seat-belt units will be sold to the marketing division and how many to foreign distributors?

c. What will be the marketing division's profit-maximizing price and how much profit (π_{mkt}) will it make?

Solutions

a. Maximum profit occurs when $MR_{mfg} = MC_{mfg}$. Since the manufacturing division can sell as much as it wishes to foreign distributors at a price of $25 per unit, that is both its transfer price and its marginal revenue. Therefore,

$$MR_{mfg} = 25$$
$$TC_{mfg} = 37,500 + 12Q_{mfg} + 0.0005Q_{mfg}^2$$
$$MC_{mfg} = 12 + 0.001Q_{mfg} = 25$$
$$Q_{mfg} = 13,000 \text{ units per time period}$$
$$\pi_{mfg} = TR_{mfg} - TC_{mfg} = PQ_{mfg} - TC_{mfg}$$
$$= 25(13,000) - 37,500 - 12(13,000) - 0.0005(13,000)^2$$
$$= 325,000 - 37,500 - 156,000 - 84,500 = \$47,000.$$

b. The marketing division's profit-maximizing sales occurs when $MR_{mkt} = MC_{mkt}$. Its marginal cost is the $25 per unit transfer price paid to the manufacturing division plus $10 per unit for marketing and distribution. Its marginal-revenue function is

$$Q_{mkt} = 50,000 - 1,000P_{mkt}$$
$$P_{mkt} = 50 - 0.001Q_{mkt}$$
$$MR_{mkt} = 50 - 0.002Q_{mkt}$$

When $MR_{mkt} = MC_{mkt}$,

$$50 - 0.002Q_{mkt} = 35$$
$$Q_{mkt} = 7,500 \text{ units per time period.}$$

Hence, the manufacturing division will sell 7,500 units per time period to the marketing division and (13,000 − 7,500) = 5,500 units per time period to foreign distributors.

c. The marketing division's profit-maximizing price and profit are

$$P_{mkt} = 50 - 0.001Q_{mkt} = 50 - 0.001(7,500) = \$42.50$$
$$\pi_{mkt} = TR - TC = 42.5(7,500) - 25,000 - 35(7,500)$$
$$= \$31,250 \text{ per time period.}$$

Transfer Pricing with an Imperfectly Competitive External Market. Now let us again consider the situation where Division A produces a component used by Division B in the assembly and marketing of the firm's product. Let us say also that the component produced by Division A can be sold in an external market, but this time the market is *imperfectly* competitive. Under these conditions, Division A can maximize its profits by means of price discrimination between Division B and the external market. The procedure can be illustrated with the aid of Exhibit 16A–3 (page 540).

Recall from the discussion of price discrimination in Chapter 16 that the price-discriminating firm sets its prices such that marginal revenue in each market is equal

EXHIBIT 16A–3   **Transfer Pricing with an Imperfectly Competitive External Market**

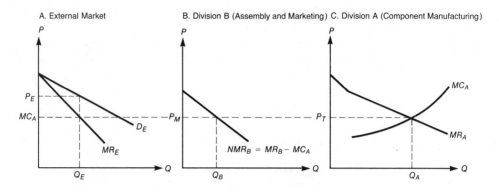

to the firm's marginal cost. Panel A presents the downward-sloping demand curve, D_E, of the imperfect external market for Division A's component with its associated marginal-revenue curve, MR_E.

In the Division B market, the relevant marginal revenue is the net marginal revenue derived by subtracting the cost of the component purchased from Division A from the marginal revenue derived from demand for Division B's product (which is the firm's product as assembled and marketed by Division B). The cost of the component purchased from Division A is just Division A's marginal cost, as shown on Panel B of the exhibit.

As shown in Panel C, Division A's marginal revenue is the horizontal summation of the division's marginal revenue in both markets, i.e., $MR_A = MR_E + MR_B$, where MR_B is the net marginal revenue of Division B, that is, $MR_B - MC_A$. Division A's optimal output level is Q_A units, at which level $MR_A = MC_A$ and the transfer price $P_T = MC_A$.

At the transfer price of P_T dollars, Division B will purchase Q_B units of Division A's product. In the external market, the optimum sales level is Q_E units, which will clear the market at a price of P_E dollars, which is more than the transfer price, P_T. Setting the transfer price equal to Division A's marginal cost insures that Division B will demand from Division A a quantity that will maximize profit for the firm as a whole as well as for both divisions.

International Transfer Pricing

When transactions between divisions or subsidiaries of a multinational company take place across national boundaries, the buying and selling units must meet the differing requirements of their respective jurisdictions with respect to customs duties, tax rates, rules of competition, customary business practices, floating exchange rates, and government regulations. The differences create problems with respect to transfer pricing, but they also create opportunities to increase profits to the firm by manipulation of transfer prices. These opportunities include the following:

1. *Tax savings*. If a company produces a product in a country with low taxes on corporate earnings for transfer to another division in a country with high taxes on corporate

earnings, it can increase taxable earnings in the low-tax country and decrease earnings by an equal amount in the high-tax country by simply charging a high transfer price.

2. *Reduced duties.* If goods are being transferred into a country with high ad valorem import tariffs, low transfer prices keep the dutiable base and duty low. (An ad valorem tariff is a percentage of the value of dutiable goods.)

3. *Repatriation of dividends.* In countries where direct repatriation of dividends is restricted (such as the Peoples' Republic of China), income can be shifted out of the country by charging lower transfer prices for goods shipped out to another division of the company.

4. *Financing of new subsidiaries.* Unusually low transfer prices to a new subsidiary can help it to show a healthy profit and thereby obtain local credit.

5. *Control of public and labor relations.* In situations where high profits might cause customers or local governments to demand lower prices or might encourage labor unions to demand higher wages, the payment of higher transfer prices can lower the visible profits.

Despite all these opportunities for profitable manipulation of transfer prices, most U.S. firms claim that they deal with foreign subsidiaries "at arm's length." In both buying and selling, the foreign subsidiaries are treated as if they were unrelated parties or independent companies. The only exceptions are subsidiaries in developing countries such as India and Pakistan, where tax rates on distributed profits are 70 percent or more.

Several constraints have acted to bring about arm's-length transactions. Among these are the profit-center concept and the expanding role of tax and customs authorities.

The Profit-Center Concept.   Manipulation of transfer prices may destroy the validity of profits as a measure of performance. There are two methods of manipulating transfer prices within the profit-center concept. One is to share the total realized profits between the parent company and subsidiary. The other is to keep two sets of books. One set would be for tax and other local purposes, and the other set would be for management control purposes. In either case, it is debatable whether the gain from manipulating transfer prices is greater than the resulting cost and increased complexity of measuring performance.

Expanding Role of Tax and Customs Authorities.   Governments are aware of the possibilities of transfer-price manipulation to reduce taxes and customs duties. Most nations have stepped up their surveillance of multinational business operations within their borders so as to maximize their tax revenues or assure fair treatment of their subsidiaries. The United States is foremost in the world in this regard. The U.S. Treasury's transfer-price review program covers not only the sale of tangible goods, but also the transfer of intangible property such as patents and trademarks, the use of tangible property, and the pricing of money and services.

The general rule developed by the Treasury is called the **arm's-length formula.** It specifies methods of conforming to the arm's-length formula, but the general principle is that the two parties in the transaction must bargain as if they were independent entities. However, even U.S. regulations appear to leave room for a company to reduce its transfer price in order to meet competition or to penetrate a new market. Consequently, most companies still have the opportunity to increase system-wide profits and to support marketing goals by judicious use of alternative transfer-pricing strategies.

Problems

1. Suppose a vertically integrated firm is organized into two autonomous divisions. Division A manufactures an essential component for the firm's product. The product is assembled, packaged, and marketed by Division B. What should Division A's transfer price be:

   a. If there is no external market for Division A's product?

   b. If there is a perfectly competitive external market for Division A's product?

   c. If there is an imperfectly competitive external market for Division A's product?

2. The Flamingo Corporation is organized into two autonomous divisions for the manufacture and sale of power lawn mowers. The Small Engine Division produces gasoline engines of a type that can be bought or sold in outside competitive markets at a price of $30 each. At that price, the Small Engines Division has a profit margin of 20 percent. Its marginal cost is $MC_E = 0.08Q_E$, where Q_E is the total number of engines produced and sold in any market.

The Lawn Products Division buys the engine and manufactures the remaining components. Marginal cost, MC_M, of the finished lawn mower is $0.1Q_M$ plus the cost of the engine. Demand for the finished product is

$$Q_M = 750 - 5P_M$$

where

Q_M = Quantity demanded
P_M = Price of each lawn mower.

   a. When the Lawn Products Division buys engines from the Small Engines Division, what should the transfer price be?

   b. What are the profit-maximizing output level and price for the Lawn Products Division?

   c. What are the profit-maximizing output level and price for the Small Engines Division?

   d. How many engines should be exchanged between the divisions and how many should be bought or sold in the open market?

References

Benke, Ralph L., Jr., and James D. Edwards. *Transfer Pricing: Techniques and Uses*. National Association of Accountants, 1980.

Burns, Jane O. "Transfer Pricing Decisions in U. S. Multinational Corporations." *Journal of International Business Studies* (Fall 1980), pp. 23–29.

Choi, Frederick, and Gerhard Mueller. *International Accounting*. Englewood Cliffs, N.J.: Prentice Hall, 1984, pp. 432–69.

Horngren, Charles T., and George Foster. *Cost Accounting: A Managerial Emphasis*. 6th ed. Englewood Cliffs, N.J.: Prentice Hall, 1987, chap. 25.

Kant, Chander. "Foreign Subsidiary, Transfer Pricing and Tariffs." *Southern Economic Journal* 55, no. 1 (July 1988), p. 162.

Merville, Larry; and William Petty. "Transfer Pricing for the Multinational Firm." *Accounting Review* (October 1978), pp. 935–51.

Robock, Stefan H.; Kenneth Simmonds; and Jack Zwick. *International Business and Multinational Enterprises*. 3rd ed. Homewood, Ill.: Richard D. Irwin, 1983, pp. 532–36.

Tang, Roger Y. W. *Transfer Pricing Practices in the United States and Japan.* Praeger, 1979.

Yunker, Penelope J. *Transfer Pricing and Performance Evaluation in Multinational Corporations: A Survey Study.* Praeger, 1982.

APPENDIX 16B   Price Discrimination in More than Two Markets

If a price-discrimination problem involves more than two markets, the solution will require the use of partial derivatives. This is a general procedure that can be used to solve price-discrimination problems involving any number of markets (including just two).

Illustrative Problem

The Thaitronics Corporation, a wholly owned subsidiary of FTT Corporation, manufactures memory boards for computers, which the firm has been selling in the United States (Market A) and Europe (Market B). After several months of operation, the top managers of Thaitronics have obtained sufficient experience to revise their estimates of demand in the United States and Europe, and they have also decided to enter a third market in the Far East (Market C). Cost of production remains at

$$TC = 2Q_T + 0.1Q_T^2.$$

Their estimates of demand in the three markets now are:

Market A (United States): $P_A = 30 - Q_A$
Market B (Europe): $P_B = 22 - Q_B$
Market C (Far East): $P_C = 32 - Q_C.$

Questions

a. Find the optimal quantity and price for each market under price discrimination.
b. Find the maximum profit under price discrimination.
c. Find the maximum profit without price discrimination.

Solutions

To find the optimal quantity and price in each market:

Step 1. Find the total cost of production for all three markets.
$$\begin{aligned}
TC &= 2Q_T + 0.1Q_T^2 = 2Q_A + 2Q_B + 2Q_C + 0.1(Q_A + Q_B + Q_C)^2 \\
&= 2Q_A + 2Q_B + 2Q_C + 0.1(Q_A + Q_B + Q_C)(Q_A + Q_B + Q_C) \\
&= 2Q_A + 2Q_B + 2Q_C + 0.1(Q_A^2 + 2Q_AQ_B + 2Q_AQ_C + Q_B^2 + 2Q_BQ_C + Q_C^2) \\
&= 2Q_A + 2Q_B + 2Q_C + 0.1Q_A^2 + 0.2Q_AQ_B + 0.2Q_AQ_C + 0.1Q_B^2 + 0.2Q_BQ_C \\
&\quad + 0.1Q_C^2
\end{aligned}$$

Step 2. Develop the profit function as total revenue from all three markets minus total cost.

$$TR_A = (30 - Q_A)Q_A = 30Q_A - Q_A^2$$
$$TR_B = (22 - Q_B)Q_B = 22Q_B - Q_B^2$$
$$TR_C = (32 - Q_C)Q_C = 32Q_C - Q_C^2$$

$$\pi = TR - TC = TR_A + TR_B + TR_C - TC$$
$$= 30Q_A - Q_A^2 + 22Q_B - Q_B^2 + 32Q_C - Q_C^2 - 2Q_A - 2Q_B - 2Q_C - 0.1Q_A^2$$
$$- 0.2Q_AQ_B - 0.2Q_AQ_C - 0.1Q_B^2 - 0.2Q_BQ_C - 0.1Q_C^2$$
$$= 28Q_A - 1.1Q_A^2 + 20Q_B - 1.1Q_B^2 + 30Q_C - 1.1Q_C^2 - 0.2Q_AQ_B$$
$$- 0.2Q_AQ_C - 0.2Q_BQ_C$$

Step 3. Take the partial derivatives of the profit function, set them equal to zero, and solve the resulting system of equations.

$$\frac{\partial \pi}{\partial Q_A} = 28 - 2.2Q_A - 0.2Q_B - 0.2Q_C = 0$$

$$\frac{\partial \pi}{\partial Q_B} = 20 - 2.2Q_B - 0.2Q_A - 0.2Q_C = 0$$

$$\frac{\partial \pi}{\partial Q_C} = 30 - 2.2Q_C - 0.2Q_A - 0.2Q_B = 0$$

Since the number of equations is equal to the number of variables, we can use the row operations of matrix algebra to solve for Q_A, Q_B, and Q_C. The first step is to rewrite the equations as

$$2.2Q_A + 0.2Q_B + 0.2Q_C = 28$$
$$0.2Q_A + 2.2Q_B + 0.2Q_C = 20$$
$$0.2Q_A + 0.2Q_B + 2.2Q_C = 30.$$

Next, enter the coefficients of the variables and the right-hand sides of these equations into a matrix, as follows:

Q_A	Q_B	Q_C	RHS
2.2	0.2	0.2	28
0.2	2.2	0.2	20
0.2	0.2	2.2	30

Note that the coefficients of the variables form an $n \times n$ matrix (in this case a 3×3 matrix), while the values of the right-hand side (RHS) of the equations form a one-column vector.

Matrix algebra uses an iterative procedure of row operations to convert the $n \times n$ matrix into an identity matrix in which the principal diagonal contains all ones and all other cells contain zeros. It takes one iteration for each row to achieve this result. When it has been done, the RHS vector contains the solution to the problem. The iterations, which are easily programmed on a computer, proceed as follows:

Iteration 1:

(1) Divide row 1 by the contents of cell 1,1. This will place a 1 in row 1, column 1, as follows:

Q_A	Q_B	Q_C	RHS
1.0	0.09090909	0.090909	12.72727
0.2	2.2	0.2	20
0.2	0.2	2.2	18

(2) Multiply row 1 by the contents of cell 2,1 and subtract the result from row 2. This will place a zero in column 1 of row 2.

(3) Multiply row 1 by the contents of cell 3,1 and subtract the result from row 3. This will place a zero in column 1 of row 3. At the end of iteration 1, the matrix is

Q_A	Q_B	Q_C	RHS
1.0	0.09090909	0.09090909	12.7272727
0.0	2.18181818	0.18181818	17.4545455
0.0	0.18181818	2.18181818	27.4545455

Iteration 2:

(1) Divide row 2 by the contents of cell 2,2. This will place a 1 in row 2, column 2.

(2) Multiply row 2 by the contents of cell 1,2 and subtract the result from row 1. This will place a zero in column 2 of row 1.

(3) Multiply row 2 by the contents of cell 3,2 and subtract the result from row 3. This will place a zero in column 2 of row 3. At the end of iteration 2, the matrix is

Q_A	Q_B	Q_C	RHS
1.0	0.0	0.08333334	12
0.0	1.0	0.08333334	8
0.0	0.0	2.16666666	26

Iteration 3:

(1) Divide row 3 by the contents of cell 3,3. This will place a 1 in row 3, column 3.

(2) Multiply row 3 by the contents of cell 1,3 and subtract the result from row 1. This will place a zero in column 3 of row 1.

(3) Multiply row 3 by the contents of cell 2,3 and subtract the result from row 2. This will place a zero in column 3 of row 2. This is the last iteration and the solution is in the RHS column.

Q_A	Q_B	Q_C	RHS
1.0	0.0	0.0	11
0.0	1.0	0.0	7
0.0	0.0	1.0	12

The optimal quantities are 11 units per day in Market A, 7 units per day in Market B, and 12 units per day in Market C.

Step 4. After finding the optimal quantity to be sold in each market, use their respective demand functions to find the profit-maximizing price in each market:

$$\text{Market A} : P_A = 30 - Q_A = 30 - 11 = \$19$$
$$\text{Market B} : P_B = 22 - Q_B = 22 - 7 \ \ = \$15$$
$$\text{Market C} : P_C = 32 - Q_C = 32 - 12 = \$20.$$

Step 5. Verify your solution by proving that $MR_A = MR_B = MR_C = MC_T$.

$$MR_A = 30 - 2Q_A = 30 - 2(11) = 8$$

$$MR_B = 22 - 2Q_B = 22 - 2(7) \ \ = 8$$

$$MR_C = 32 - 2Q_C = 32 - 2(12) = 8$$

$$MC_T = \frac{dTC}{dQT} = \frac{d(2Q_T + 0.1Q_T^2)}{dQ_T} = 2 + 0.2Q_T$$

$$= 2 + 0.2(11 + 7 + 12) = 2 + 0.2(30) = 8$$

The maximum total profit, π, achieved by price discrimination is

$$\pi = TR - TC = TR_A + TR_B + TR_C - TC$$

$$= (\$19)(11) + (\$15)(7) + (\$20)(12) - 2(30) - 0.1(30)^2 = \$404$$

Maximum total profit that can be achieved without price discrimination is

$$Q = Q_A + Q_B + Q_C = 30 - P_A + 22 - P_B + 32 - P_C$$
$$= 84 - 3P$$

since without price discrimination, $P_A = P_B = P_C = P$. Hence

$$P = 28 - 0.333Q$$

$$\pi = TR - TC = PQ - TC = 28Q - 0.333Q^2 - 2Q - 0.1Q^2$$
$$= 26Q - 0.433Q^2$$
$$\frac{d\pi}{dQ} = 26 - 0.866Q = 0$$
$$Q = 30$$
$$P = 28 - 0.333(30) = \$18.$$

Substituting $Q = 30$ into our profit function, we get

$$\pi = 26Q - 0.433Q^2 = 26(30) - 0.433(30)^2 = \$390.$$

C H A P T E R

17

THE ECONOMIC ROLE OF GOVERNMENT

Although the American system is often described as "free enterprise," it is not and never has been a laissez faire system. In Article I, Section 8 of the U.S. Constitution, the first eight of the eighteen clauses that spell out the powers of Congress pertain to economic matters. Thus, besides its traditional functions of maintaining law and order, the government is charged with overseeing the economic system to make sure that it operates in the public interest.

In the real world, market structures are not perfect. They have certain flaws and limitations that require government intervention to promote the general welfare. Flaws and limitations in the American economic system include the following:

1. Although the benefits of competition are recognized, the private-enterprise system does not guarantee that competition will exist. Disproportionate market power can be wielded by some of the participants, such as big business or organized labor.
2. The market economy does not necessarily provide for desirable social and environmental conditions such as clean air and water and safe living and working conditions.
3. The private-enterprise system does not provide products and services that are consumed collectively for the benefit of all, such as parks, highways, traffic signals, weather forecasts, police and fire protection, and national defense. These public goods and services must be provided by government.
4. Inequality of opportunity persists for women, ethnic minorities, and some other groups.

Congress has been granted the power to provide for the general welfare and to regulate commerce. Under these clauses, federal-government intervention in the marketplace has taken four major forms:[1]

1. *Antitrust policy* seeks to control concentration of economic power in the marketplace and keep it within acceptable limits through a market structure that is efficient in performance and fair to all. This is done by prohibiting unnatural monopolies and unfair competition.

2. *Regulation* seeks to (1) preserve freedom of choice and consumer sovereignty in the marketplace and (2) maintain desirable social and environmental conditions such as clean air and water and safe living and working conditions. Regulation controls the activities of business firms, including natural monopolies such as public utilities, for the benefit of the consumer and society as a whole.

3. *Incentives* in the form of tax breaks or subsidies encourage business firms to conduct research and development, to undertake new ventures, and to modify production schedules to increase external social benefits or decrease external social costs (such as pollution).

4. *Public ownership* provides for production by the federal government of public goods and services such as airports, seaports, inland waterways, interstate highways, bridges, dams, national forests, national parks, wilderness areas, and other recreational facilities.

Although these four forms of government intervention are clearly economic in nature, the necessary legislation and subsequent regulatory enforcement often become political issues because of the maneuvering of special-interest groups. The most prominent of these groups are representatives of agriculture, labor, various industries, small business, the professions (medicine, law, education), environmentalists, and consumers. Within each of these broad categories, there are hundreds of smaller, more specialized groups, all clamoring for legislative or executive attention. Competing or cooperating with others, whichever is expedient, each special-interest group seeks legislation or executive orders to advance its particular cause. Consequently, the laws and executive directives that are intended to provide economic support and regulation of private enterprise are actually the result of a political bargaining process in which there is a trade-off between economic efficiency and some other desirable outcome. For example, if a given change in regulatory policy will provide significant benefits to the poor, society may willingly bear the costs of a substantial loss in economic efficiency.

CHAPTER OUTLINE

A full-scale study of government regulation and other intervention in the U.S. economy is far beyond the scope of this book. Rather, in this chapter we shall provide an overview of government activities designed to support and regulate business. We shall attempt

---

[1] In the following discussion of government intervention, the primary reference is to intervention by the federal government. It should be recognized, however, that some forms of intervention, such as regulation of utilities, are more apt to be performed at the state or local level. The word "government" will be used here to encompass whatever level of government is appropriate to the subject being discussed.

to explain the economic underpinnings of regulation and to outline the more important types of regulation that business decision makers may have to deal with. In particular, we shall discuss:

1. **Economic Externalities.** Topics discussed in this section include the reasons why exchange in a perfectly competitive market may fail to achieve economic efficiency, the economic impact of externalities, incentives for beneficial externalities, and dealing with negative externalities.
2. **Regulation of Public Utilities.** This section discusses problems in the regulation of public utilities and other natural monopolies and the effects of inflation on regulated monopolies.
3. **Restraint of Market Power and Unfair Competition.** This section discusses antitrust laws, the measurement of economic concentration, mergers, and the controversy over mergers.
4. **Enforcement of Antitrust Laws.** This section discusses actions taken under the Sherman and Clayton Acts against restrictive agreements and monopoly. Actions by the Federal Trade Commission are also covered, and problems of enforcement are discussed.
5. **Behavior of the Regulatory Agencies.** This section covers two theories that have been proposed to explain the observed behavior of regulatory agencies.
6. **Deregulation and Privatization Trends.** This section discusses reasons for the current deregulation of major sectors of the economy and the growing privatization of public services.

Economic Externalities

An **externality** is a market imperfection that arises when persons not directly involved in an economic transaction nevertheless receive benefits or bear costs as a result of that transaction. Since externalities are not reflected in the pricing of goods or services in the marketplace, the result is a misallocation of resources. Without some sort of intervention in the marketplace, there will be too little production of goods with beneficial (positive) externalities, and too much production of goods with harmful (negative) externalities.

Positive Externalities

A **positive externality** is a benefit not reflected in prices. It may come about by direct benefit or service to others or it may be by indirect cost reduction to other firms. It may arise in the course of either production or consumption.

Example 1. If a firm expands production by building a new plant in a small town, merchants in the town will profit when the new plant's employees spend their wages.

Example 2. When Henry Ford introduced the automobile assembly line, the increased production of automobiles greatly increased the demand for steel. Since large economies of scale were possible in the steel industry, the cost of steel was reduced. All users of steel benefited from Ford's innovation, but Ford received no compensation from them.

Example 3. The owner of an old house in run-down condition pays a contractor for a thorough remodeling and renovation. The house increases in value, and that is what the owner paid for. But if (as often happens) the improvement in that house causes the whole neighborhood to look better, then values of all homes will rise. The neighbors get a "free ride" or positive externality.

Negative Externalities

A **negative externality** is a cost of resource use that is not reflected in the price of a product. It also can arise as a result of either production or consumption. An external *diseconomy* of production arises when expansion of the firm's production results in adverse effects (social costs) that are not paid for by the firm and are therefore not reflected in the prices of its products. An external diseconomy of consumption arises when the purchase and consumption of a good or service results in disutility for people not involved in the transaction.

Example 1. Increased output of a manufacturing plant may put strains on the local transportation system that increase costs for all users.

Example 2. If a firm dumps noxious or toxic wastes into a river, municipalities downstream must spend large sums on purification, and the river provides fewer benefits to those who would like to use it for swimming, boating, or fishing.

Example 3. If a firm spews wastes into the air, the health and property of downwind residents may be adversely affected.

Example 4. All but one of the home owners in a run-down neighborhood renovate and remodel their homes. As a result, the lone exception looks even worse than before and suffers a loss in value.

The Economic Impact of Externalities

Some externalities, such as the pleasure gained from viewing a well-tended garden or the discomfort of standing on a crowded bus, may seem to have no great social significance, and certainly cannot be given a dollar value. Yet when they are taken all together, externalities have a profound economic impact.[2]

> *Example.* It is no accident that industries tend to cluster in particular locations. We associate steel with Pittsburgh, automobiles with Detroit, rubber with Akron, and financial institutions

---

[2] Externalities must not be confused with secondary price effects. Secondary price effects take place within a market system. For example, sale of wheat to the Soviet Union in 1972–1973 caused a rise in the price of wheat products in the United States. Externalities are conveyed outside of the price system directly to the persons affected.

with New York. This clustering has taken place because new firms were attracted to locations where established firms provided positive externalities such as pools of skilled labor, specialized financial institutions, suppliers of raw materials, and transportation systems—all developed at the expense of firms already in place. Locations that lack these necessities, such as inner-city ghettos and less developed countries, are much less attractive to industry.

Managers of both private and public enterprises need to be aware of the economic, social, and environmental effects of externalities that stem from their operations. A private firm's management should analyze the firm's operations to determine what positive or negative externalities may be generated in the normal course of business. If positive benefits are identified, they should be emphasized in the firm's public-relations activities. If negative externalities are recognized, the firm should seek to remedy them through internal action, if possible. If not, the firm should prepare for and attempt to influence the remedies that may be imposed by government.

The management of a public enterprise also must identify the positive and negative externalities its activities generate. The negative externalities call for a remedy, of course; but it is the positive externalities that must be most clearly understood, because they may be the only justification for expanding or even continuing the public enterprise.

Misallocation of Resources.   The most serious consequence of either positive or negative externalities, regardless of whether the enterprise is private or public, is the misallocation of resources. In the case of positive externalities, the result is underutilization; that is, society is not using enough resources in the production of a particular good or service. Negative externalities also result in misallocation of resources. Misallocations of resources from positive and negative externalities are illustrated by the following cases.

Illustrative Case 1: Sunshine Solar Systems, Inc.

Sunshine Solar Systems, Inc., manufactures solar-energy systems for heating water. The solar systems are sold in an imperfectly competitive market, so the firm faces a downward-sloping demand curve and the associated marginal-revenue curve as depicted in Exhibit 17–1 (page 550). Within the firm's normal range of output, its average variable cost is constant and thus equal to its marginal cost. At equilibrium, E_1, where $MR = MC$, the firm maximizes profits by producing Q_1 units.

The firm's solar-energy systems reduce the demand for other fuels, especially imported oil, with the result that oil prices go down. This means that costs go down for all products that use oil in their production, and the reduction in oil prices is especially beneficial to transportation systems, both private and public.

Clearly, there is an external social benefit from the production of solar-energy systems. If we add the value of the positive externality to the price of the product, the result is the marginal-social-benefit curve, MSB. Thus if the firm could be paid for the social benefit it generates, equilibrium would be at E_2. Optimal output would be Q_2, which would require a greater allocation of resources to production of solar-energy systems. The difference between Q_2 and Q_1 represents underproduction and therefore underutilization and misallocation of resources.

EXHIBIT 17–1   Misallocation of Resources When Positive Externalities Exist

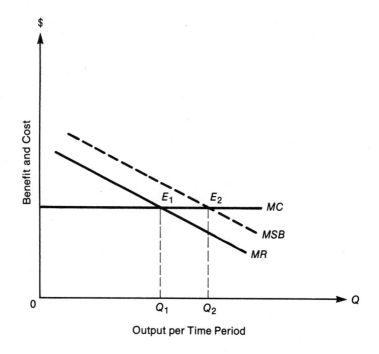

Output per Time Period

Illustrative Case 2: Regional Light & Power Co.

The Regional Light & Power Company burns coal in order to generate electricity. The company has installed scrubbers and other antipollution devices, but its stacks still emit a considerable amount of air pollutants. As the firm increases production to meet the growing demand for electrical power, the intensity of air pollution also grows. This condition is depicted in Exhibit 17–2 by the marginal-social-cost curve, MSC.

Again for simplicity's sake, Exhibit 17–2 depicts a firm with constant marginal cost. As long as the firm does not pay for the pollution it causes, equilibrium occurs at E_1, where $MR = MC$. The cost of pollution is represented by the rectangle $C_0C_1FE_1$, all of which is borne by society at large. But if the firm must pay for pollution, its equilibrium would be at E_2, and production would be cut back to Q_2 units. The cost of pollution would be reduced to the rectangle $C_0C_2E_2G$, all of which would be borne by the firm and its customers. The difference between Q_1 and Q_2 represents overutilization and misallocation of resources.

EXHIBIT 17–2   Misallocation of Resources When Negative Externalities Exist

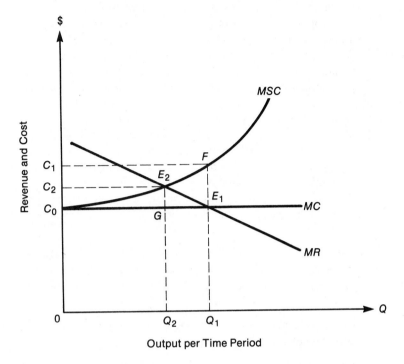

Output per Time Period

Whether externalities are positive or negative, the problem is that a private firm, which controls the level of production, has no incentive to produce either more or less than the profit-maximizing output at which the firm's marginal revenue equals the firm's marginal cost. Consequently, there may be substantial government intervention in the marketplace either to supply the missing incentives to produce more when the externality is beneficial or to produce less when the externality is harmful.

Encouragement of Beneficial Externalities

When beneficial externalities exist, some people pay while others get a "free ride." There are two basic ways of solving the free-ride problem: (1) prevent those who do not pay from receiving any benefits or (2) insure that everyone who receives benefits pays.

The first technique is often employed by private enterprise. For example, suppose that a developer plans to renovate all of the houses in a blighted city neighborhood. If the developer buys and remodels them one at a time, the surrounding property owners get a free ride as the values of their properties increase too. The solution is for the builder to buy all of the old houses at the same time. Then the increase in value of surrounding properties as each one is renovated will be internalized to the benefit of the developer.

The second technique (insuring that everyone who receives benefits pays) is more suitable to government action, and may result in the provision of public goods paid for by taxation.

Public Goods.   If a beneficial externality is nonexclusive, meaning that people cannot be excluded from its benefits no matter who pays for it, the good is classed as a **public good**. Examples of public goods are national defense, police and fire protection, immunization, and education.

If the good is not only nonexclusive, but also of a nature such that its consumption by one person does not reduce the amount available for others, then it is said to be a **pure public good**. If a pure public good is available to anyone, it is available to all at no extra cost.

Government intervention is appropriate when beneficial externalities exist and it is not feasible to exclude free riders from those benefits. Thus there is general agreement that the government should provide pure public goods, such as flood-control dams, police and fire protection, and national defense. Unfortunately, there is no way to measure the economic benefits of public goods. Consequently, there is no agreement on how much of these goods should be provided. The decisions on what to provide and how much to provide thus become political rather than economic decisions.

Subsidies.   Many different goods are partly private and partly public. In such cases, the government may provide incentives for the expansion of private production with a subsidy rather than (or in addition to) the direct provision of the public good.

Direct Subsidies.   Subsidies may be direct or indirect. Direct subsidies generally have taken one of two forms:

1. *Low-cost financing*. For example, Federal Housing Administration and Veterans Administration financing has broadened home ownership by subsidizing the construction industry.
2. *Special tax treatment*. Examples include:
   a. *Depletion allowances*, which encourage the development and exploitation of natural resources.
   b. *Investment tax credits* for certain types of business investments that result in social benefits such as job creation or energy independence.

At the municipal level, some communities have lured industry with a combination of low-cost financing and tax moratoriums.

Indirect subsidies.   Indirect subsidies by the federal and state governments include the entire transportation infrastructure—a network of highways, waterways, seaports, and airports that make interstate and foreign commerce possible. Government construction of dams has also indirectly subsidized a number of industries. Besides the benefits of flood control, water may be provided for irrigation of farmlands. The creation of artificial lakes has also created a demand for marinas, campgrounds, motels, recreational vehicles, boats, camping equipment, and all of the other paraphernalia associated with water sports and recreation.

Subsidies for the installation of solar-heating devices provide a more recent example. Solar-heating devices clearly provide benefits for which a householder is willing to pay, at least up to a point. But society at large also benefits by a reduction in the demand for energy derived from imported oil. Therefore, in the past both federal and state governments have encouraged solar installations by means of tax credits.

Grants of Operating Rights.   Production of goods or services with positive externalities may also be promoted by grants of operating rights in selected areas of the public domain. A classic example is control of the airwaves by the Federal Communications Commission (FCC). The spectrum of radio frequencies is a natural resource that exists in a limited quantity but is not depleted by use. It belongs to nobody in particular, but to everybody in general. Therefore, if it were not regulated, the price for its private use would be zero. At that price, it might well be overused or used inefficiently. Consequently, the government regulates the use of radio frequencies and limits usage to selected licensees.

The number of licenses that can be granted is necessarily limited by the physical restrictions of the radio-frequency spectrum. Each license gives its holder the right to use only a particular frequency or set of frequencies. Once granted, the license is almost always renewed routinely unless it is shown that renewal of the license would be harmful. In effect, an FCC license is a semipermanent grant of a monopoly. Consequently, some economists have suggested that FCC licenses be periodically auctioned off to the highest bidders, thus capturing some of the monopolists' economic profits for the public treasury.

Federal, state, and sometimes municipal regulatory agencies also grant public franchises in the form of charters or licenses. Industries controlled in this way include banks and other savings institutions, insurance companies, and securities dealers.

Public franchises are granted only to those firms that can demonstrate financial soundness, fiscal responsibility, and the ability to serve the needs of the public in their area. Any time that a firm fails to meet these criteria, its right to operate may be withdrawn. Since the mere threat of withdrawing operating rights is usually sufficient to insure compliance, grants of operating rights can be an effective form of regulation. Many critics point out, however, that it can be rendered ineffective if there are no clear, consistent, and workable standards of performance. Television programming is most often cited as a case in point.

Grants of Patents.   A U.S. **patent** is an exclusive right conferred by the federal government to an inventor for a limited period (currently 17 years). It authorizes the inventor to make, use, transfer, or withhold an invention, which the inventor might do even without a patent; but it also gives the inventor the right to exclude others or to admit them on particular terms, a power that the inventor enjoys only with a patent.

Patents thus are a means of promoting invention by granting temporary monopolies to inventors. But the patent system, it is held, has also been used as a means of controlling output, dividing markets, and fixing prices of entire industries. Since these are perversions of the patent law that have a direct effect on competition, they have been subject to criticism by antitrusters, and the courts have increasingly come to limit the scope and abuses of patent monopoly. Among the chief issues have been the standard of patentability, the right of nonuse by the patentee, the use of tying contracts, the employment of restrictive licenses, and the practices of cross licensing and patent pooling.

Dealing With Negative Externalities

One way of reducing the production of a negative externality is to direct its cost back upon the firm that is generating the externality. This can be done on a regular basis by taxation and on an irregular or ad hoc basis by fines and penalties for prohibited behavior.

For example, a truck's license tag will cost many times more than an automobile tag, on the grounds that its heavier weight will do more damage to the roads. However, a limitation also is imposed as to how much the loaded truck can weigh, even when properly licensed. If the truck exceeds this weight, additional taxes in the form of fines and penalties will be imposed on its operator.

Undesirable behavior can also be checked by subsidies. For example, the Internal Revenue Code offers special tax breaks to firms that install pollution-control devices. Alternatively, it would be possible to tax or fine the firm for emitting pollution.

The choice of control method—subsidy or taxation—raises an important political issue. A subsidy implies that the firm has the right to pollute, and that society is willing to pay it to forgo that right. Taxation implies that society owns the environment and has a right to clean air and water. Therefore, the polluter must pay damages for the harm being caused. When the potential for harm is great, taxation can be raised to a prohibitive level, causing the undesirable activity to cease altogether.

Illustrative Problem

The Salt Lake Chemical Company is engaged primarily in the production and sale of Product A. The production process is such that for each unit of A that is output, the company also gets one unit of Product B, which is a liquid. Demand for Product B is such that most of it, but not all of it, can be sold at a profit. At present, it costs nothing to get rid of the unwanted by-product. The company simply opens a valve and dumps it into the lake, where it creates pollution that is definitely harmful to the environment. The county health authorities are insisting that this pollution must be stopped and they propose to install meters on the discharge pipes and charge the company $1,000 per unit of discharge into the lake.

The firm's cost accountants have estimated demand and cost functions as follows:

$$P_A = 8,000 - 6Q_A$$
$$P_B = 600 - Q_B$$
$$TC = 45,000 + 10Q + 6Q^2.$$

Questions

a. What is the firm's profit-maximizing output and price for each product if there is no charge for pollution? How much is profit?

b. What is the firm's profit-maximizing output and price after the pollution charge is imposed?

c. What is the cost of cleaning up the pollution?

Solutions

a. This is a problem in optimizing joint production, as discussed in Chapter 16.

Step 1. Set MR_A and $MR_B = 0$ in order to determine limit on sales of by-product.

$$P_A = 8,000 - 6Q_A \qquad\qquad P_B = 600 - Q_B$$
$$MR_A = 8,000 - 12Q_A = 0 \qquad\qquad MR_B = 600 - 2Q_B = 0$$
$$Q_A = 666.67 \qquad\qquad Q_B = 300$$

This means that maximum sales of Product A is 667 units and of Product B is 300 units. Any production of the by-product B in excess of 300 units will be dumped.

Step 2. Find the marginal cost of manufacturing the two products.

$$TC = 45,000 + 10Q + 6Q^2$$
$$MC = 10 + 12Q$$

Step 3. Set the joint marginal revenue $(MR_A + MR_B)$ equal to marginal cost and solve for the optimal output, Q.

$$MR_A + MR_B = MC$$
$$8,000 - 12Q_A + 600 - 2Q_B = 10 + 12Q$$

Dropping the subscripts, because $Q_A = Q_B$,

$$8,600 - 14Q = 10 + 12Q$$
$$26Q = 8,590$$
$$Q \approx 330 \text{ units of each product.}$$

This is more of Product B than can be sold. Therefore this solution is not optimal.

Step 4. Set marginal revenue of Product A equal to marginal cost and solve for Q:

$$8,000 - 12Q_A = 10 + 12Q$$
$$24Q = 7,990$$
$$Q \approx 333 \text{ units of each product.}$$

Step 5. Find the optimal price for each product, keeping in mind that only 300 units of Product B will be sold and the rest dumped:

$$P_A = 8,000 - 6Q_A = 8,000 - 6(333) = \$6,002 \text{ per unit}$$
$$P_B = 600 - Q_B = 600 - 300 = \$300 \text{ per unit.}$$

Step 6.

$$\pi = TR - TC = \$6,002(333) + \$300(300)$$

$$-\$45,000 - \$10(333) - \$6(333)^2 = \$1,375,002$$

b. The firm is faced with a choice of selling the excess production of the by-product at a loss (i.e., with negative marginal revenue) or of paying the county's pollution tax for dumping the excess. It will pay the company to sell at a loss up to the point where the negative MR equals the pollution charge (which is also a negative number since it represents a reduction in the firm's marginal revenue on the units that are dumped).

$$MR_B = 600 - 2Q_B = -1,000$$
$$-2Q_B = -1,600$$
$$Q_B = 800$$

That is, it would pay the company to sell up to 800 units of the by-product before paying any pollution tax. This is more than the company will produce. Therefore the optimal level of production is where the joint marginal revenue equals marginal cost. This level is 330 units of each product to be produced and sold, as calculated in Step 3. The optimal prices would be

$$P_A = 8,000 - 6Q_A = 8,000 - 6(330) = \$6,020 \text{ per unit}$$
$$P_B = 600 - Q_B = 600 - 330 = \$270 \text{ per unit.}$$

c. The cost to the company of eliminating pollution is the difference between maximum profit before the pollution charge and maximum profit afterward:

$$\pi_1 = TR_1 - TC_1$$
$$= 333(6,002) + 300(300) - 45,000 - 10(333) - 6(333)^2 = \$1,375,002$$
$$\pi_2 = TR_2 - TC_2$$
$$= 330(6,020) + 330(270) - 45,000 - 10(330) - 6(330)^2 = \$1,374,000$$
$$\pi_1 - \pi_2 = \$1,375,002 - \$1,374,000 = \$1,002.$$

Government Control of Operations.   Like subsidies and tax policies, government operating controls are intended to reduce undesirable externalities by mandating some actions and prohibiting others. Unlike subsidies and tax policies, however, operating controls rely upon nonmonetary incentives, although fines and even imprisonment can be used to punish violators.

While control of pollution immediately comes to mind, the fact is that almost every facet of business activity is subject to some government regulation.

Regulation of Public Utilities

A natural monopoly occurs when economies of scale are such that the long-run average cost declines throughout the entire range of production that can be absorbed by a particular market. This means that maximum efficiency (lowest-cost production) can be achieved only when one firm produces all that the market demands.

The situation of continuously falling long-run average costs is characteristic of capital-intensive industries with relatively large fixed costs. As the fixed costs are spread over more and more units, the average or unit cost declines. As long as average cost is declining, marginal cost is less than average cost. Thus almost all utilities—gas, electric, water, sewers—and many transportation facilities are natural monopolies.

The existence of a natural monopoly poses a dilemma because, as we saw in Chapter 15, a monopoly seeks to maximize profits by restricting output, as illustrated by Exhibit

EXHIBIT 17–3   Profit-Maximizing Output under Monopoly

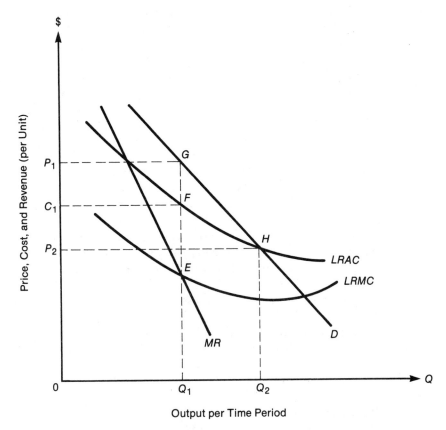

17–3. The exhibit shows the market demand curve, *D*, its associated marginal-revenue curve, *MR*, the monopolist's long-run marginal-cost curve, *LRMC*, and the long-run average-cost curve, *LRAC*. (The *LRAC* curve includes normal profit.)

Without government interference, the monopoly will reach equilibrium at a production level of Q_1 units, at which $MR = LRMC$. By producing Q_1 units at a long-run average cost of C_1 dollars and a price of P_1 dollars, the monopoly will earn an economic profit of $(P_1 - C_1)$ dollars per unit. Total economic profit is represented by the rectangle $P_1 C_1 F G$. Clearly, however, the monopoly could increase production all the way to Q_2 units by giving up its economic profit. At a price of P_2 dollars, the monopoly would recover all of its long-run average cost, which includes normal profit or required return on investment.

Obviously, the general public would be better off with the monopoly producing more output at a lower price. The question is: How can it be induced to do so? The most common answer is: By regulation of prices and profits. That simple answer, however, hides a number of sticky problems.

Problems in Regulation of Public Utilities

Although Exhibit 17–3 presented the theoretical foundation for the regulation of natural monopolies, in reality it is not possible to determine precisely the amount of fixed assets necessary to support a given level of production nor the precise *LRAC* schedule. Further, in the case of utilities, the utility serves several classes of customers (such as residential, commercial, and industrial), each of which has its own demand schedule and price elasticity, but the utility has only one *LRAC* schedule. This means that there are many different combinations of rate schedules that can be used to produce the required level of profit, but there is no rational way in which costs can be divided up and used as a basis for the user-class rates.

From these difficulties come the problems of pricing the output and determining the appropriate level of investment, as well as the encouragement of inefficient production. In addition, there are problems with regulatory delays and costs. These problems are all related, but they are separated for the sake of discussion in the paragraphs that follow.

Pricing the Output.   Theoretically, the regulated price is such that the monopoly recovers its fixed and variable costs plus an allowed return on investment (*ROI*). The actual output, however, will be determined by the actual demand at the price set by the regulatory commission.

If the regulating agency has guessed wrong about demand, and has set the price too high (such as at P_1 in Exhibit 17–3), the regulated monopoly will enjoy some degree of economic profit. However, since the *ROI* is limited, the excess profits will be allocated to system expansion, thus becoming part of the investment base on which allowed *ROI* is calculated. The firm will grow at a faster-than-optimal rate. If the price is set too low, the required *ROI* will not be attainable, and the firm will not expand.

Appropriate Level of Investment.   The utility's allowable return on investment is calculated as a percentage of the *rate base,* which is roughly equal to fixed assets. If the allowed *ROI* is more than the cost of capital, it will pay the utility to shift to more capital-intensive methods of production by expanding fixed assets. On the other hand, if the allowed *ROI* is too low, the utility may not expand its capacity rapidly enough to satisfy future demand, and might be forced to continue less capital-intensive but relatively inefficient methods of production. Either way, regulation can lead to something less than an optimal combination of the input factors of production.

Encouragement of Inefficiency.   Since a regulated monopoly is guaranteed a certain return on investment, there is little incentive to be careful about costs. Inefficiency thus tends to be protected, as illustrated by Exhibit 17–4.

Exhibit 17–4 depicts two regulated utilities, Firm A and Firm B, operating under identical circumstances at different locations. The two firms have been granted the same allowed return on investment (*AROI*) by their regulatory agencies, so that $AROI_A = AROI_B$. (The *AROI* may include normal profit, or required *ROI*, plus some extra allowance to provide funds for expansion.) The curves labeled AC_A and AC_B represent their respective cost functions, not including any return on investment. The curves

EXHIBIT 17–4   Promotion of Inefficiency by Regulation

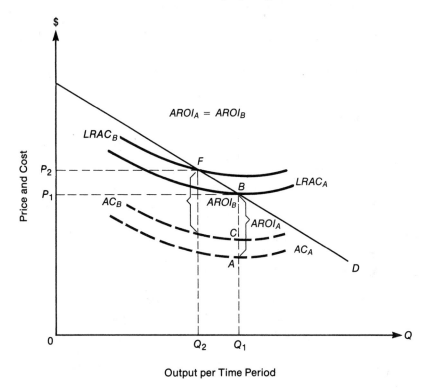

Output per Time Period

labeled $LRAC_A$ and $LRAC_B$ represent their respective long-run average costs, including *AROI*.

At the regulated price of P_1 dollars, both firms produce Q_1 units of output. Firm A, being more efficient, earns the full allowed return on investment, *AROI*, measured by the distance *AB* on the exhibit. But Firm B, being less efficient, can earn only the amount represented by the distance *CB*, which is less than the full *AROI*. Firm B therefore asks for a rate increase from its regulatory agency on the grounds that its earnings are less than its long-run average cost, $LRAC_B$ (which includes the allowed *ROI*). When the regulatory agency grants the rate increase, the price goes to P_2 and Firm B's output falls to Q_2 units. Firm B earns the full allowed return on investment, *AROI*, measured by the distance *EF* (which is equal to *AB*), while continuing its inefficient operation at a lower level of output.

Regulatory Costs and Delays.   Regulatory costs stem from two major sources. First, there are the routine administrative costs of maintaining a regulatory commission and of maintaining necessary records within the regulated monopoly. Second, there are the careful and expensive economic analyses that are made by both proponents and opponents of a proposed rate increase. Ultimately, all of these costs are borne by consumers.

In addition to cost, the regulatory process imposes a substantial delay between the time a necessary rate increase is proposed and the time it is approved. This is because regulation of natural monopolies is a political process. The regulatory-commission members are either elected directly or else are appointed by elected officials who must answer to the electorate, who are the monopoly's customers. When a rate increase is proposed, it cannot be approved until public hearings have been held, at which time all who wish to be heard may testify. The monopoly's customers are naturally opposed to any rate increase, and they are able to put a great deal of political pressure upon the regulatory commission. Often they succeed in denying or at least delaying reasonable and necessary rate increases.

The Effects of Inflation

Regulatory lag can work either for or against the regulated monopoly. For example, during the 1950s and 1960s, economies of scale and technological improvements resulted in lowered costs, while reduction in rates lagged behind. In the 1970s and early 1980s, however, the tide turned. Inflation and high interest rates drove up costs while rate increases lagged behind. Utilities, lacking sufficient funds, began to delay repairs and postpone investments in new equipment. Consequently, the quality of service suffered.

Inflation also magnifies the distortion caused by the use of average cost in setting rates. As we saw in Exhibit 17–3, it is assumed that economies of scale keep the marginal cost below average cost. However, regulatory commissions are prone to calculate average costs from historical (book) costs, rather than current replacement costs. Consequently, marginal cost is actually greater than the average cost on which the regulated price is based. Setting prices below the marginal cost of production encourages wasteful use by the consumer.

Restraint of Market Power and Unfair Competition

Throughout U.S. history, there has been a libertarian distrust of power, whether it be political or economic. The elaborate system of checks and balances established by the Constitution serves to prevent concentration of political power. On the economic side, incorporation laws passed in the 1850s enabled stockholders to pool their economic resources without having to pool their political resources as well. The effect has been to permit the coexistence of big business with democracy.

The growth of big business in this country has been watched by the people with mixed feelings of pride and suspicion, with clear recognition that economic power and political power go hand in hand. Consequently, antitrust policy sometimes has been used to prevent undue concentration of corporate power.

Antitrust Laws

Conventional wisdom says that in order to preserve a market economy, natural monopolies must be strictly regulated and unnatural monopolies must be prohibited altogether.[3]

---

[3] Exceptions to the rule are monopolies created by franchises, patents, and copyrights. However, the government does place certain limits on the rights bestowed by such grants.

In its efforts to maintain competition, the federal government's chief weapon against monopolies has been a set of acts passed by Congress, commonly called the antitrust laws. The substantive provisions of the most important antitrust laws are as follows.

The Sherman Act (1890). This was the first attempt by the federal government to regulate the growth of monopoly in the United States. The provisions of the law were concise (probably too concise). It declared the following to be illegal:

1. Every contract, combination, or conspiracy in restraint of trade that occurs in interstate or foreign commerce.
2. Any monopolization or attempt to monopolize, or conspiracy with others in an attempt to monopolize, any portion of trade in interstate or foreign commerce.

Violations of the act were made punishable by fines and/or imprisonment, and persons injured by violators could sue for triple damages.

The act was surrounded by uncertainty due to its failure to state precisely what kinds of actions are prohibited. Also, no special agency was created to enforce the law until 1903, when the Antitrust Division of the U.S. Dept. of Justice was established under an assistant attorney general. In order to put some teeth into the Sherman Act, therefore, Congress passed the Clayton Act and the Federal Trade Commission Act.

The Clayton Act (1914). Aimed at practices of unfair competition, the Clayton Act was concerned with four specific areas: price discrimination, exclusive or tying contracts, intercorporate stockholdings, and interlocking directorates. About these it said:

1. For sellers to discriminate in prices between purchasers of commodities is illegal where the effect is to substantially lessen competition or tends to create a monopoly. However, such discrimination is permissible where there are differences in the grade, quality, or quantity of the commodity sold.
2. For sellers to lease, sell, or contract for the sale of commodities on condition that the lessee or purchaser not use or deal in the commodity of a competitor is illegal if such exclusive or tying contracts substantially lessen competition or tend to create a monopoly.
3. For corporations engaged in commerce to acquire the shares of a competing corporation, or the stocks of two or more corporations competing with each other, is illegal if such intercorporate stockholdings substantially lessen competition or tend to create a monopoly.
4. For corporations engaged in commerce to have the same individual on two or more boards of directors is an interlocking directorate, and such directorships are illegal if the corporations are competitive and if any one has capital, surplus, and undivided profits in excess of $1 million.

Thus price discrimination, exclusive and tying contracts, and intercorporate stockholdings were not declared by the Clayton Act to be absolutely illegal but rather, in the words of the law, to be illegal only when their effects "may be substantially to lessen competition or tend to create a monopoly." On interlocking directorates, however, the law made no such qualification; the fact of the interlock itself is illegal, and the government need not find that the arrangement results in a reduction in competition.

The Federal Trade Commission Act (1914).   The Federal Trade Commission Act served primarily as a general supplement to the Clayton Act by stating broadly and simply that "unfair methods of competition in commerce are hereby declared unlawful." Essentially, both the Clayton Act and the Federal Trade Commission Act were directed toward the prevention of abuses, whereas the Sherman Act emphasized the punishment of abusers. Moreover, under the Federal Trade Commission Act, the Federal Trade Commission (FTC) was established as a government antitrust agency with federal funds appropriated to it for the purpose of attacking unfair competitive practices and safeguarding the public by preventing the dissemination of false and misleading advertisements. It was no longer necessary to await private suits brought by private parties on their own initiative and at their own expense in order to curb unfair practices in commerce.

The Wheeler-Lea Act (1938).   An amendment to part of the Federal Trade Commission Act, the Wheeler-Lea Act was passed to protect consumers against unfair practices. The act makes illegal "unfair or deceptive acts or practices" in interstate commerce. Thus a consumer who may be injured by an unfair trade practice is, before the law, of equal concern as the merchant who may be injured by an unfair competitive practice. The act also defines "false advertising" as "an advertisement other than labeling which is misleading in a material respect" and makes the definition applicable to advertisements of foods, drugs, curative devices, and cosmetics.

The Celler-Kefauver Antimerger Act (1950).   The Celler-Kefauver Antimerger Act is an extension of Section 7 of the Clayton Act, which made it illegal for corporations to acquire the stock of competing corporations. But that law, the FTC argued, left a loophole through which monopolistic mergers could be effected by a corporation acquiring the *assets* of a competing corporation. The Antimerger Act plugged the loophole in the Clayton Act by making it illegal for a corporation to acquire the stock or assets of a competing corporation if the effect may be "substantially to lessen competition, or tend to create a monopoly." The act thus bans all types of mergers—*horizontal* (similar plants under one ownership, such as steel mills), *vertical* (dissimilar plants in various stages of production, integrated under one ownership), and *conglomerate* or *circular* (dissimilar plants and unrelated product lines)—provided the commission can show that the effects *may* substantially lessen competition or tend toward monopoly.

The intent of Congress in passing the act was that there be a maintenance of competition. Accordingly, the act was intended to apply to mergers of large firms or of large firms with small firms, but not to mergers among small firms that may be undertaken to strengthen their competitive position.

Mergers

A **merger** is an integration of two or more firms under a single ownership. Mergers play an important role in a free-enterprise economy, in that less efficient firms are swallowed by the more efficient. Thus mergers often result in redeployment of productive assets and facilitate the efficient flow of investment capital. But it is also possible for mergers to have an adverse effect on competition by:

1. Reducing the number of firms capable of entering concentrated markets
2. Reducing the number of firms with the capability and incentive for competitive innovation
3. Increasing the barriers to entry in concentrated markets
4. Diminishing the vigor of competition by increasing actual and potential customer–supplier relationships among leading firms in concentrated markets.

Mergers may be classified as horizontal, vertical, or conglomerate.

Horizontal Mergers.   A **horizontal merger** is one in which different plants producing similar products are brought under a single ownership. Three reasons are often advanced for such expansion:

1. To meet the demands of a growing market
2. To take advantage of economies of scale in production and distribution
3. To increase market share and market power.

With respect to economies of scale, few mergers result in actual savings in production costs. The merger is more likely to result in the closing of redundant, inefficient plants and the elimination of excess capacity in the industry (a desirable result). Substantial savings can be realized in the costs of selling and distributing the product, but the most compelling reason is the desire for increased market power.

Vertical Mergers.   A **vertical merger** is one in which firms engaged in different stages of the chain of production and distribution are united under one ownership. For example, a manufacturing firm might integrate backward to obtain control of a source of raw material or forward to obtain control of sales outlets for its products. Two major reasons for vertical mergers exist:

1. *To reduce costs.* For example, substantial cost reductions were obtained in the steel industry when the furnaces were integrated with the rolling mills, thus eliminating costly reheating steps in the production process.
2. *To gain control over the economic environment.* For example, Firestone has complete vertical integration from rubber plantations through manufacturing facilities to retail outlets. Its supply of raw materials is secure, as is its access to the ultimate consumers of its tires and other rubber products.

Vertical mergers may also enhance the firm's market power. However, they are not controlled unless they result in a monopoly, or have undesirable horizontal effects at one level or another of the chain of production and distribution.

Conglomerate Mergers.   A **conglomerate merger** is one in which different companies producing different products are brought under a single ownership. Such diversification enables the acquiring company to spread risk, find good use for idle capital, add a line of products to its marketing capacity, or simply gain in economic power.

Recent Developments Concerning Mergers

The role of big business and the degree of government intervention needed to guard against the real or imagined evils of big business are long-standing subjects of debate. Since the late 1960s, this debate has taken on new dimensions as the economy has contended with inflation, recession, monetary devaluation, trade imbalances, and a continuing energy crisis.

Waves of merger acquisitions tend to rise and fall as conditions change in the economy. When return on investment is low and costs of production are rising, corporations may seek higher returns by investing in other companies. In 1981, 2,395 mergers and acquisitions were recorded, which was the largest number since 1974. In dollar value, the mergers in 1981 broke all records for the third year in a row, with acquiring companies paying $82.9 billion for their acquisitions. In some cases, takeover offers to common stockholders were 50 percent or more above market value. The year also saw 12 transactions that each exceeded $1 billion in value.

Mergers slacked off during the recession years of 1982 and 1983, before beginning a steep growth. The number of completed mergers and acquisitions reached a new peak in 1986 with well over 4,000 deals completed. In 1988, mergers set new records for total dollars (well over $200 billion), size of the average deal (more than $120 million), and the number of billion-dollar deals (more than 40).

Technically, every merger is subject to scrutiny by the Antitrust Division of the U.S. Dept. of Justice. On June 14, 1982, the Antitrust Division issued new guidelines that enabled companies seeking mergers to determine whether or not their proposal would likely be challenged. The guidelines included the following policy statement:

> While challenging competitively harmful mergers the Department seeks to avoid unnecessary interference with that larger universe of mergers that are either competitively beneficial or neutral. In attempting to mediate between these dual concerns, however, the Guidelines reflect the congressional intent that merger enforcement should interdict competitive problems in their incipiency.[4]

This phraseology is taken to mean that the Dept. of Justice recognizes that once a merger takes place, it can't be unscrambled. Therefore, policy is to prevent harmful mergers from taking place.

In order to determine whether or not a proposed horizontal merger is harmful, the Dept. of Justice will examine: (1) concentration and market shares, (2) ease of entry of new firms into the industry, and (3) other factors that "affect the likelihood that a merger will create, enhance or facilitate the exercise of market power."[5] In particular, the department will consider factors that relate to the ease and profitability of collusion.

In evaluating a vertical or conglomerate merger, the department examines its horizontal effect in three major areas of concern: (1) elimination of specific potential entrants into the market; (2) barriers to entry in primary or secondary markets, or both; and (3) facilitating collusion. In the third category the department is particularly concerned about vertical

---

[4] U.S. Dept. of Justice, Antitrust Division, *Merger Guidelines* (Washington D.C.: U.S. Government Printing Office, 1982), p. 3.

[5] Ibid, p. 22.

integration to the retail level, about the elimination of a disruptive buyer in a downstream market, and the possible evasion of rate regulation by a public utility.

In general, the Dept. of Justice will not oppose mergers in industries where the market share of the industry's largest firms is relatively low, or in markets where entry is relatively easy. Apparently, the Dept. of Justice has come to believe that such mergers can result in reduced costs and lower prices that will make the merged concern more competitive in world markets. The presumption seems to be that some reduction in domestic competition is a small price to pay for increased competitiveness against foreign producers.

Enforcement of Antitrust Laws

Although Congress succeeded in passing the antitrust laws, it failed to define, and left up to the courts to interpret in their own way, the meaning of such terms as "monopoly," "restraint of trade," "substantial lessening of competition," and "unfair competition." For business executives, therefore, these are areas of uncertainty that need to be clarified if decisions are to be made and plans formulated to guide a firm's future course of action.

Enforcement of antitrust laws is very similar to enforcement of traffic laws. The law against speeding is self-enforcing to the extent that every driver knows about it and takes precautions against violating the law, or at least against getting caught. Most people support laws against speeding, but not so many get upset when someone does it. At the same time, the amount of speeding that takes place depends to a large extent upon how vigorously the law is enforced.

In the same fashion, business executives are aware of the antitrust laws and desire to avoid actions that will attract the attention of the Antitrust Division of the Dept. of Justice or the Federal Trade Commission. Consequently, antitrust compliance plays a large role in business planning for expansion. The more vigorous the antitrust enforcement, the more wary become the business planners.

When enforcement of antitrust laws becomes necessary, it is effected on a case-by-case basis. That is, an order or decision resulting from an action is applicable not to an entire industry, but to only the defendants in a particular case. Cases tried under the Sherman Act may originate in the complaints of injured business executives, suggestions made by other government agencies, or the research of the Antitrust Division of the Dept. of Justice. About 90 percent of the cases, it has been estimated, arise from complaints issued by injured parties.

The Federal Trade Commission Act, on the other hand, is enforced by the FTC. When its orders become final, however, they are enforced through suits brought by the Dept. of Justice.

Finally, with respect to the Clayton Act, the FTC and the Dept. of Justice have concurrent jurisdiction in its enforcement. In practice it is usually a matter of which agency gets there first.

Illustrative Cases

Following are some key historical cases that illustrate the legal doctrines embodied in antitrust laws:

Price Fixing in the Tobacco Industry.   Conspiracy to fix prices is illegal and subject to both civil and criminal penalties. Moreover, firms may be found guilty of price fixing without any evidence of communications among the firms, as the American Tobacco Company, R. J. Reynolds, and Liggett & Myers found out in 1946. The prosecution proved that (1) their retail prices were identical and (2) all three had pressured retailers against lowering prices. This involved raising prices in the heart of the 1930s depression when both tobacco-leaf prices and labor costs were falling. In refusing to review the case, the Supreme Court ruled that conspiracy may be inferred from the acts of the accused.

The IBM Case.   The government filed suit against IBM in 1969, charging that at one time IBM monopolized the computer market by selling its products only in packages and by pricing its new equipment below cost. The remedy sought was divestiture, requiring that IBM be broken up into several smaller companies.

The government's suit inspired the filing of 16 private suits as well, all of which IBM won in federal courts. IBM management promised the government a stiff fight and gave it to them, spending $300 million in the process, and causing government expenditures of $26 million in what Robert H. Bork, then a Yale law professor, characterized as "the Antitrust Division's Vietnam." In the meantime, rapid technological change in the computer industry, including changes in marketing methods pursued by all competitors, so weakened the government's case that the Antitrust Division decided to drop it.

The AT&T Case.   The government's suit against American Telephone and Telegraph Company (AT&T) was the biggest antitrust action since the Rockefellers' Standard Oil Trust was broken up in 1911. The Antitrust Division of the Dept. of Justice filed suit in November 1974, charging that AT&T had abused its telephone monopoly by freezing out competitors on equipment and long-distance service. While the case dragged on, telephone-equipment manufacturers, data-processing companies, and cable-television systems had to try to plan in a state of uncertainty. At the same time, the Dept. of Commerce worried about the possibility that the Japanese would gain an advantage in telecommunications.

Finally, after the government had spent about $25 million to prosecute the case, and AT&T had spent about $360 million defending itself, the adversaries reached an out-of-court settlement that William Baxter, assistant attorney general, said "completely fulfills the objectives of the Antitrust Division and is also very much in the interests of AT&T and its shareholders."

The nature of the settlement was a sort of "good news, bad news" announcement for AT&T and the other interested parties. From AT&T's point of view, the bad news was that it had to spin off the 22 Bell-system telephone companies in which it had controlling interest. These companies' $80 billion assets represented about two thirds of AT&T's total assets. This was bad news for local Bell-system customers, too, because the newly independent companies would no longer have local telephone service subsidized by AT&T's long-distance earnings.

More bad news for AT&T was the loss of monopoly on long-distance telephone service. But that was good news for long-distance callers, who now enjoy the benefits of price competition in long-distance service. The good news for AT&T was that it could keep its minority interest in two Bell-system local telephone companies and continue to operate Bell Laboratories and its manufacturing arm, Western Electric. The best news of all was that AT&T became free to enter into competition on cable, videotext communications, and digital data transmission, where the greatest growth in communications promises to be.

The NCAA Case.   Prior to June 27, 1984, the National Collegiate Athletic Association's (NCAA's) contracts with major television networks required the networks to schedule appearances by at least 82 college teams in football games played within a two-year period, but limited the telecasts of football games by any one college team to six times in the two-year period. Individual colleges were forbidden to negotiate television contracts on their own.

In 1981, the Board of Regents of the University of Oklahoma and the University of Georgia Athletic Association filed suit charging the NCAA with illegal monopoly control of football telecasts. On June 27, 1984, the Supreme Court ended the NCAA's 33-year monopoly, ruling that the NCAA's exclusive power to regulate the number of television appearances by a college team constituted an "unreasonable restraint of trade," in violation of the Sherman Antitrust Act. The Court said that the NCAA practice of limiting the number of games that could be televised and setting artificially high prices for television rights "restricted rather than enhanced the place of intercollegiate athletics in the nation's life."

Enforcement Trends

Initiation of antitrust prosecution is, of course, a political as well as a legal action. That is, the kind of cases that will be prosecuted depends upon the political philosophy of the executive branch of government. Members of the FTC and the key personnel of the Dept. of Justice and its Antitrust Division are political appointees. We can expect them to be attuned to the views of the president. Therefore, the tenor of antitrust prosecution may change with a change of presidents.

Monopoly.   Concerning monopoly, the state of the law is less certain and the position of the courts less consistent than in cases involving restrictive agreements.

Prior to 1945.   It was the position of the court that the mere size of a corporation, no matter how impressive, is no offense, and that it requires the actual exertion of monopoly power, as shown by unfair practices, in order to be held in violation of the law. This has been called the "good trust versus bad trust" criterion.

1945 to 1980.   The decision against the Aluminum Company of America (ALCOA) in 1945 and decisions handed down in various antitrust cases since 1945 reversed this outlook. In the case against ALCOA, Judge Learned Hand turned the trend in judicial thinking on monopoly. It was the court's opinion that the mere size of a firm *is* an offense, no matter how monopolistic power may have been gained. The company's good behavior is irrelevant, for "Congress did not condone 'good' trusts and condemn 'bad' ones; it forbade all." The company was a monopoly because its market share was 90 percent and that "is enough to constitute a monopoly; it is doubtful whether 60 or 64 percent would be enough; and certainly 33 percent is not."

Since 1980.   At the present time, judgments regarding monopoly are based on consideration of such factors as the number and strength of the firms in the market; their effective size with respect to their production technology; the availability of competitive substitutes; foreign competition; national security interests; and the public's interest in lower costs and uninterrupted production.

Judging from recent cases, it would seem that monopoly per se may be deemed illegal even when there is no proof of intent to monopolize and even if the monopolistic power was lawfully acquired. Monopoly power may be condemned even if it is never abused. However, the recent settlements of the AT&T and IBM cases would seem to indicate that the Antitrust Division may be returning to the notion that bigness per se is no offense.

Unfair Trade Practices.   In enforcing the laws relating to monopoly, unfair trade, and deception, the FTC uses three methods:

1. The *cooperative* method, which involves conferences on an individual and industry-wide basis in order to secure voluntary compliance
2. The *consent* method, whereby the commission may issue a stipulation to the violator stating that the company agrees to discontinue illegal practices
3. The *compulsory* method, which involves legal action based upon the issuance of formal complaints.

In general, the commission obtains its evidence for making complaints from its own investigations, from injured competitors, from consumers, and from other government agencies. About 10 percent of the cases actually selected arise from the commission's own investigations; the remaining 90 percent are derived from the other sources, particularly from the complaints of injured parties.

Behavior of the Regulatory Agencies

We have seen that the chief instrument of government intervention is the regulatory agency, which is supposed to work for the public good. But there are many different opinions as to what the public good may be, and regulatory agencies often are accused of engaging in strange economic behavior.

A regulatory agency is established by an act of a legislative body, which also outlines the composition, functions, and operating criteria of the agency. But the legislative mandate is usually broad enough and vague enough to allow a regulating agency a great deal of latitude in working out the details of its operations. The attitude of the agency may sometimes be established by its director. The longer the agency operates, the more deeply entrenched become the collective practices of its bureaucracy. These questions then arise: What determines the philosophy of the regulatory agency? What governs the behavior of the regulators?

The Capture Theory

Regulatory agencies are supposed to operate in the public interest by molding firms' behavior toward socially desirable ends. But the **capture hypothesis** advanced by George Stigler in 1971 holds that no matter why regulatory agencies are established, they end up promoting the interests of the firms they are supposed to be regulating.[6]

The capture theory notes that the state's power to prohibit or compel and to give or take money in the form of subsidies or taxes is the power to help or hurt any particular industry. Since regulatory agencies have the power to control prices and the entry of new firms, they are the ideal means of running a de facto cartel, if only they can be captured by the industry. Consequently, regulation may be actively sought by an industry despite some of the petty annoyances of the regulations.

Capture of a regulatory agency by the industry it regulates is not too difficult for two reasons:

1. A regulatory agency must have a good working knowledge of the industry it regulates. Consequently, its key personnel are apt to be hired from the industry. Furthermore, there is a natural tendency for friendly personal relationships to develop from frequent contact between regulators and industry executives.
2. The industry's product is just one of many that are bought by consumers, who are also apt to be completely unorganized as a lobbying group. Regulated firms, in contrast, have the resources and incentives to carefully present their positions to their regulators. Consequently, at any regulatory hearing, regulated firms will be well prepared and well represented at whatever cost is necessary, while consumers or the general public often will not be.

Stigler contends that pro-industry policies of regulatory agencies are to be expected under the current system of selecting and rewarding regulators, and that they will continue unless the system is changed.

The Share-the-Gains, Share-the-Pains Theory

Prudent regulators, whether elected or appointed, can retain their jobs by maximizing the approval of their constituency. The regulator's constituency consists of three disparate groups:

1. The legislative body that established the agency and monitors its behavior
2. The industry that is being regulated
3. Customers of the industry that is being regulated.

Each of these groups will have something to say about the agency's performance, and the

---

[6] George J. Stigler, "The Theory of Economic Regulation," *Bell Journal of Economics and Management Science* (Spring 1971), pp. 3–21; see also George J. Stigler, *The Citizen and the State: Essays on Regulation* (Chicago: University of Chicago Press, 1975).

opinion of each group must be given some weight. The Peltzman model[7] suggests that the regulators perform a balancing act, leaning first one way, then another, but always ending up in a neutral position.

In Peltzman's view, regulatory agencies do not allow themselves to be captured by one side or another—that would be far too risky for the regulators. They can be moved by pressure if there is no counterpressure, but they will seek the middle ground. For example, if a product proves to be unsafe, an agency may tighten its standards, but not until the manufacturer has had an opportunity to redesign the product. When it comes to safety, an agency will usually err on the side of excessive prudence. The regulator's motto is "Better safe than sorry." Thus children's toys are barred from the market on the basis of what a child *might* do, rather than on what children ordinarily do.

While there is no doubt that government regulations impose substantial costs on producers, there is no single answer to the question of who pays the bill. If we assume that regulation is imposed even-handedly upon all firms within a particular industry, the answer will depend on two circumstances: (1) the market structure in which the firm sells its products and (2) whether or not close substitutes exist.

If demand is inelastic or if no close substitutes exist, increases in marginal costs can be passed on to customers. But in markets where demand is highly elastic and close substitutes do exist, some and perhaps most regulatory cost increases must be absorbed by the firm's owners, employees, and suppliers.

Deregulation and Privatization Trends

Although government regulation of the U. S. economy began more than 100 years ago, it was greatly expanded and became increasingly burdensome during the 1950s and 1960s. Consequently, there was and still is a widespread feeling in the business community that regulation has gone too far and needs to be reevaluated. In response, Congress has substantially deregulated banking, transportation, communications, and other industries since 1970. Some of the major deregulatory activities since 1970 are shown in Exhibit 17–5.

Reasons for Deregulation

Economists and business executives who press for deregulation do not quarrel with the philosophical reasons for government intervention that have been discussed in this chapter. Rather, they criticize market distortions and inefficiencies, excessive and inefficient regulation, the sheer mass of regulations, and the excessive cost of regulation.

Market Distortions and Inefficiencies.   Market distortions and inefficiencies caused by regulation are manifested in three different ways. First, when goods not produced

---

[7] Sam Peltzman, "Toward a More General Theory of Regulation," *Journal of Law and Economics* (August 1976), pp. 211–40.

EXHIBIT 17–5   Deregulatory Activities since 1970

Year	Industry	Deregulatory Activity
1970	Banking	Federal Reserve Board frees interest rates on bank deposits of $100,000 or with maturities of six months or less.
1975	Stock brokers	Securities Exchange Commission prohibits fixed commissions on stock sales.
1978	Air transportation	Congress deregulates the airlines.
1979	Communications	Federal Communications Commission allows AT&T to sell unregulated services such as data processing.
1980	Banking	Congress allows banks to pay interest on checking accounts and increases competition for business loans.
	Ground transportation	Congress deregulates trucking and railroads.
1982	Savings & loan (S & L)	Congress allows S&L institutions to make commercial loans and related investments.
	Ground transportation	Congress deregulates intercity bus services.
	All industries	Dept. of Justice and Federal Trade Commission relax merger guidelines.
1986	Banking and S&L	Interest rates for passbook and statement savings accounts are deregulated.

in a natural monopoly are price-controlled, the inevitable result is poor distribution, shortages, and inefficient consumption. Second, regulation that controls or denies entry into the market stifles the vigorous competition that leads to better products and better service at lower cost to the consumer. Third, regulation of natural monopolies too often protects inefficient production at excess cost.

Excessive and Inefficient Regulation.   According to a study by the U.S. Dept. of Commerce, the percentage of GNP under regulation increased from 8.2 percent in 1965 to 23.7 percent by 1975. Another study determined that fully 77 percent of the increase was caused by the growth in health and safety regulations.[8] These are the regulations most often complained about. In too many cases, government regulators have not only specified the standards that must be met, but also have specified the means of compliance, whether or not the specified means are cost-effective. It would be more efficient to simply specify the desired results, and then leave it up to the firms to find the best way to comply.

The Sheer Mass of Regulations.   By 1980, the *Code of Federal Regulations* totaled 800,000 pages and occupied 52 large bookshelves. Furthermore, regulations emanating from different agencies are frequently contradictory to the point where compliance is

---

[8] Paul W. MacAvoy, "Overview of Regulatory Effects and Reform Prospects," in *Reforming Regulation*, eds. T. B. Clark, M. H. Kosters, and J. C. Miller, III (Washington, D.C.: American Enterprise Institute, 1980).

impossible. For example, the U.S. Dept. of Agriculture requires that a sausage maker's kitchen floor be washed frequently for sanitary reasons, but the Occupational Safety and Health Administration (OSHA) demands that it be kept dry for safety reasons.

Excessive Cost of Regulation. In a study of the annual cost of federal regulation in 1976, Murray Weidenbaum, later to become chairman of President Reagan's Council of Economic Advisors, estimated the administrative costs of regulation to be $3.2 billion annually and the compliance costs to be $62.9 billion annually, for a total of $66.1 billion per year.[9] In a later study made for the Joint Economic Committee, Weidenbaum estimated the 1979 costs of regulation to be more than $100 billion. As Milton Friedman (among others) has observed, "There is no such thing as a free lunch."

It is fair to argue that the costs of regulation would not be excessive if commensurate benefits could be shown on the other side of the ledger. Unfortunately, this cannot be done. Measuring benefits is even more difficult than measuring costs, especially where the benefit is an improvement in safety. Nevertheless, the discipline of attempting a cost–benefit analysis of proposed regulations might bring out many facts that are now overlooked.

Another problem is that costs tend to rise exponentially as we approach perfection. For example, the cost of reducing air pollution by, say, 85 percent might be within reason. But the cost of getting rid of that last 15 percent might be astronomical and far more than what it's worth. At some point there is an equilibrium between costs and benefits. The regulators and the regulated need to work together to find that point. But it is unlikely that an industrial society can ever be totally safe and totally unpolluted.

The Effects of Deregulation

There is no doubt that deregulation will remain one of the main economic issues of the 1990s, so it will be quite some time before all the evidence of its effects is available. Still, we are able to see some of the effects of deregulation that has already taken place.

Deregulation of the Airline Industry. Prior to 1978, the Civil Aeronautics Board (CAB) determined who could enter the airline business, what routes each airline could fly, and what fares they could charge. Under this system of regulation, airline fares per passenger-mile were below cost on some routes and well above cost on others. The CAB forced the airlines to continue service on unprofitable routes but did not permit them to enter into price competition on profitable routes. Consequently, the airlines entered into nonprice competition with such frills as in-flight movies, gourmet food, and better service. These frills increased their costs and the airlines were not as profitable as other industries.

Under the Airline Deregulation Act of 1978, the CAB lost its authority over domestic routes after 1981, lost its authority over pricing, mergers, and acquisitions on January 1,

---

[9] Murray Weidenbaum, *Business, Government and the Public*, 2nd ed. (Englewood Cliffs, N.J.: Prentice Hall, 1981).

1983, and went out of business altogether at the end of 1984. Thus the airline industry has been completely deregulated since the beginning of 1985, and the result has been a complete restructuring of the industry.

Between 1976 and 1983, the number of certified air carriers for freight and passengers almost tripled, and some more new carriers entered the market after deregulation was completed. Most carriers restructured their route system into a "hub–spoke" arrangement in which certain key airports served as the hubs from which the airline routes radiated. This arrangement permits an airline to carry its passengers over relatively long distances with only one stop (at a hub) during which the passengers might change planes, but would not have to change terminals. This is a convenience for passengers, but is also a source of congestion at hub terminals.

Before deregulation, the airlines served primarily business and middle-income travelers. After deregulation, price competition has drawn moderate-income and vacation travelers away from other forms of transportation, and these people now constitute the bulk of airline passengers.

The rising number of air travelers coupled with the growth of hub–spoke systems has resulted in great congestion at key airports, and the infrastructure for air travel has not kept up with the growth of air traffic. New airports are necessary and the air-traffic–control system is badly in need of expansion.

Consumers, of course, are delighted with the lower air fares, but from the consumer's point of view, deregulation is not an unqualified success. Unregulated price competition has produced such a myriad of discount fares, hedged about with restrictions, that travel agents have to maintain complex computer programs that must be revised frequently just to know what is being offered at any given time. The airlines have eliminated the costly frills that were offered in nonprice competition before deregulation. They have increased the loading density by about 25 percent on the long-haul routes, so flying is not as comfortable as it used to be. Passengers often complain of deteriorating service, with overbooking, dirty cabins, and poor treatment by airline personnel. Recent incidents of structural failure of aircraft in flight have also raised questions about the adequacy of the airlines' maintenance programs. These are faults over which the airlines can exert control.

Passengers also complain of inadequate ground facilities and long runway delays. These are the results of overloading an inadequate infrastructure, which is the responsibility of government.

Restructuring of the airline industry has also resulted in the elimination of weaker carriers through bankruptcy or merger. By the end of 1987, eight carriers controlled 94 percent of all domestic air travel in the United States. The vigor of price competition is waning and the industry seems to be evolving into an oligopoly.

Deregulation of Financial Services.   The deregulation of financial-service institutions has been a particularly difficult problem because of their peculiar nature. In other industries, when a company goes on the skids, only the stockholders are at risk. Financial institutions, however, operate with depositors' money. When a financial institution goes on the skids, depositors as well as shareholders are at risk. For this reason, depositors' money must be at least partially protected by insurance and government regulation. The dilemma is how to give consumers the free-market benefits of efficiency and innovation without losing that critical element of safety for the depositors' money.

The three major sectors of financial services are brokerage, thrift institutions, and commercial banking. The effects of deregulation have been quite different in each of these three sectors.

Deregulation of Securities Brokerage.   The largest regulatory change for the securities industry was the SEC's prohibition of fixed brokerage commission rates in 1975. This was followed in 1982 with the adoption of Rule 415, which permitted companies to register huge blocks of securities one time and then store these securities "on the shelf" until an opportune time for issue. The effect of this rule was to reduce the cost of issuing the securities by opening the process to competitive bidding. Of course, the gain to the issuing companies is a loss to the underwriting profits of investment bankers.

The elimination of fixed commission rates brought the discount brokers into being. Although the discount houses have only about 20 percent of the retail business, their very existence puts a check on what bigger firms can charge their retail customers. Consequently, commissions paid to full-service brokers have risen less than half as much as inflation overall. The number of security analysts has decreased by about 20 percent and many of the smaller brokerage firms either have failed or have been swallowed up by mergers with larger houses.

The increased competition has resulted in lower prices for both corporate and retail customers. At the same time, the squeeze on profits has caused brokerage firms to move into higher-risk ventures where they have to put their own capital on the line.

Deregulation of Thrift Institutions.   All depository institutions were deregulated by the Depository Institutions Deregulation and Monetary Control Act of 1980, which was the widest reform of the banking system since the 1930s. Depository institutions include commercial banks, thrift institutions, savings and loan associations (S&Ls), mutual savings banks, and credit unions. The main purpose of the act was to remove or diminish differences among depository institutions with regard to the types of deposits they can offer, the rates of interest they can pay, the reserves they must hold, and their access to Federal Reserve services. Two of the most noticeable results for consumers are the availability of higher interest rates on various types of deposits and the ability to write checks on accounts in the thrift institutions. All "Regulation Q" restrictions on interest rates payable on savings were phased out by 1986.[10]

In hindsight, the deregulation of the savings and loan associations and other thrift institutions proceeded through a series of blunders. When interest rates were deregulated in 1980, the thrifts' portfolios contained long-term, low-interest, fixed-rate mortgages. The thrifts should have been given at least three years to convert their portfolios to adjustable-rate mortgages before interest rates were deregulated. Instead, the interest rates were cut loose first and it wasn't until a year later that the thrifts were allowed to

---

[10] Regulation Q of the Federal Reserve System put a ceiling on the rate of interest that could be paid by commercial banks on demand and saving accounts.

make loans with adjustable-rate mortgages. As the gap between earnings on the fixed-rate mortgages and the payout on higher rate deposits widened, Congress in 1982 allowed the thrifts to get into commercial lending and other higher-risk investments.

The second mistake was the failure to increase supervision of the thrifts. Thrift managers took advantage of the situation by attempting to increase their earnings with little or no risk to themselves. After all, the depositors are covered by insurance, aren't they?

The third mistake was the lowering of the thrifts' capital requirements. Equity capital is the cushion that allows the institution to absorb temporary losses without endangering the depositors and taxpayers. The net result of these three mistakes has been the failure of hundreds of thrift institutions and a taxpayer bailout of the depositors that may prove to be in excess of $250 billion.

Deregulation of Commercial Banks.   Mechanisms of the market have worked better for commercial banks, first because they were never required to make a certain percentage of fixed-rate mortgages, as the thrifts were, and second, because their commercial lending was performed by experienced commercial-loan officers, something the thrifts did not have. The commercial banks, however, are not uninhibited players in a free market, and never will be as long as they carry federal deposit insurance.

It has been argued recently that commercial banks in the United States need more room to maneuver so they can hold their own in international competition. Foreign banks operating without the restrictions placed on U. S. banks are beginning to dominate world financial markets. By the end of 1987, 8 of the 10 largest banks in the world were Japanese.

In the 1950s, loans to U.S. corporations provided about 90 percent of a typical bank's income. Today, such loans account for less than 4 percent as more and more corporations turn to the securities market for financing. This is why commercial banks are appealing for breaking down the wall between commercial and investment banking.

Is Antitrust Policy Necessary?

No less than five different evaluations of antitrust policy can be seen in the literature:

1. *First opinion*. The very existence of free enterprise depends upon antitrust legislation, which is both actually and potentially beneficial.

2. *Second opinion*. Antitrust laws would be good if they were enforced, but underfunding and understaffing of enforcement agencies have hampered enforcement. Some observers have even suggested that such underfunding and understaffing of enforcement agencies has occurred because there are elements within the government that are not opposed to monopolies and large oligopolies.

3. *Third opinion*. Substantial changes in the antitrust laws are needed to increase their effectiveness. Antitrust laws should be enforceable and the punishment for their violation should be compelling enough to insure that they will be obeyed. Extensive enforcement, therefore, would not be necessary. Most observers belong to this group.

4. *Fourth opinion*. Antitrust laws should be applicable only to the United States because they can have monopolistic, perhaps imperialist, results overseas. For example, it really doesn't matter to Central American banana growers whether the price of bananas is set in a free market in the United States or by a cartel.

5. *Fifth opinion.* It is questionable whether there is any connection between antitrust policy and economic growth, employment, and wage and price levels. The holders of this opinion point out the difficulty of measuring the results of antitrust policy. They suggest it would be useful to compare the performance of an economy before and after antitrust, and note that the U.S. growth rate in the last quarter of the 19th century was greater than after World War II. They also suggest that it might be instructive to compare the economies of countries where monopolies flourish, such as Japan, with countries where few monopolies exist, such as Brazil.

Privatization of Public Services

While deregulation has been taking place, there has also been a movement to turn over to private enterprise—to **privatize**—certain services that have traditionally been performed by federal, state, or local governments. The advocates of privatization argue that there are many activities where private firms can do the job more efficiently and at lower cost than the government can. The drive for privatization is taking place in other countries as well as in the United States, and is perhaps most noteworthy in Great Britain, where the previous nationalization of several key industries has been reversed by privatization. It is particularly interesting to note that the Eastern European countries now breaking away from the Soviet Union, and even the Soviet Union itself, are turning to privatization as a way out of their economic difficulties with state-owned and state-operated industries.

Privatization can take a number of forms, of which the following are the most significant:

1. *Management contracts.* The public agency contracts with a private firm for operation of a publicly owned facility.
2. *Service contracts.* The government contracts with private enterprise for provision of public services.
3. *Private provision of services.* The government permits private enterprise to provide public services, either in place of a public enterprise or in competition with it.
4. *User fees.* The government attempts to finance public services in whole or in part by charging higher fees to those who use them.
5. *Divestiture.* Government-owned enterprises are sold or closed down.

Government operations and services that have been privatized in one place or another include mail delivery, correctional facilities, trash collections, public transportation, fire protection, public-park and road maintenance, private-property assessment, and airport facilities.

Private Postal Services. In the United States, private firms are forbidden by law from providing first-class postal services, but are allowed to compete with the U. S. Postal Service in the other classes. Firms such as United Parcel Service (UPS), Federal Express, and Emery Worldwide have been particularly successful in providing fourth-class service (parcel post). UPS, for example, handles twice as many parcels as the U.S. Postal

Service, with lower rates, faster deliveries, and 80 percent less damage to parcels, and UPS makes a profit doing it.[11]

Private Operation of Correctional Facilities.   All over the United States, states and counties are faced with the problem of overcrowded prisons and jails. Public officials—caught between the need for expansion of jails, prisons, and other correctional facilities on the one hand, and local or state governments' reluctance to raise taxes for new construction on the other—are increasingly turning to private enterprise for more efficient and less costly operation of correctional facilities. The federal government also is turning to private enterprise. Some examples of such privatization are:

1. The Federal Bureau of Prisons has contracted out all of its halfway-house operations.
2. A private firm built and now operates a holding facility for the Immigration and Naturalization Service (INS) in Houston, Texas, at a cost to the INS of $24 per day per prisoner. This is about 35 percent lower than the cost of a comparable publicly operated facility.
3. Private firms own and operate about 1,500 facilities in various locations for the detention of some 30,000 juvenile offenders.
4. Florida contracts with a private company for food service to inmates in correctional institutions in Dade, Broward, and Polk counties. The cost is about as much as the state paid to provide the same service.
5. The states of Georgia, Texas, and California are conducting studies about the possibility of establishing private prisons.

Private Garbage Collection.   Garbage collection is a public service that is particularly well suited to privatization in whole or in part. This is because the whole job can be easily segmented into routes that can be served by small business entrepreneurs. Studies of private garbage collection have revealed improved service at lower cost.

Urban Public Transportation.   There are about 330,000 school buses operating in the nation, and about 90,000 of them are operated by private contractors. A single private firm also provides the top four or five managers of more than 50 municipal bus and rail systems in 28 states. These locations include Kansas City, Missouri, and Dallas and Corpus Christi, Texas.

Private Fire Protection.   One of the oldest privately provided public services is fire protection, and it is a growing industry today, with 17 private companies now operating in 14 states. Benefits of privatization of fire-fighting, ambulance, and paramedical services are reported to include faster response to emergencies and cost reductions averaging 25 percent.

Private Operation and Maintenance of Public Parks.   Almost all of the major cities in the United States have turned over all or part of the maintenance and operation of their parks to private firms. Private maintenance has reduced costs by about 20 percent in some places and private operation often has improved service.

---

[11] Jonathan N. Goodrich, "Privatization in America," *Business Horizons* (January-February 1988), p. 13.

Private Maintenance of Streets, Highways, and Bridges.   Contracting with private firms for routine maintenance work such as graveling of roads, surface dressing, sealing of paved roads, patching potholes, and control of vegetation is a common practice throughout the United States.

Private-Property Assessment.   Some states forbid property assessment by private firms, but Ohio requires it. The quality of assessment in Ohio, when measured by the relationship between assessment and actual selling price, is said to be the best in the nation. At the present time, about 10 percent of all assessment work is conducted by private firms.

Private Improvement and Operation of Airports.   Amid much controversy, proposals for private renovation and operation of airports at Los Angeles, California, Albany County, New York, and Peoria, Illinois, are being considered as of this writing. Proponents of private operation of airports point out that privatization will relieve local government from the necessity to raise large sums of money for airport modernization and that private investors can also raise funds more quickly than local government. Private operators expect to make a profit from landing fees and terminal rents. Opponents of airport privatization argue that a sell-off of airports would simply create private monopolies that would charge all the traffic would bear at great cost to consumers. They point to the private operation of Heathrow and Gatwick airports at London, England, where there is a cap on landing fees but extremely high charges for parking facilities and passenger lounges. A reasonable compromise between the two points of view might be the private operation of the airport as a regulated public utility.

The Future of Privatization: Pros and Cons

From a government perspective, privatization of a particular service may accomplish the following goals:

1. Reduce costs
2. Increase efficiency
3. Improve the delivery and quality of services
4. Reduce government bureaucracy
5. Shake up an ineffective government unit or break the power of an obstructive union
6. Overcome the government's limited capacity to provide a particular service
7. Provide entrepreneurial and business-expansion opportunities for many private citizens.

Not surprisingly, government employees (particularly government-employee unions) are opposed to privatization. Their arguments may be summarized as follows:

1. Government workers become unemployed when a private firm takes over.
2. Privatization means a lower quality of service.
3. The government loses control and accountability.
4. The government pays too much for the private service.
5. There is a possibility of corruption and scandal.

Unfortunately, these arguments have proven to be true in some cases, but the problems have been avoided in well-managed contracts where:

1. A contractor was selected who had the know-how and equipment to do the job, had adequate financial resources and stability, and had a reputation for excellent work.
2. The contractor was paid on time.
3. The contract was carefully drawn to specify the exact performance required, with penalties for sloppy or incomplete work.
4. A government agent was appointed to oversee the work and the government required regular reports about job performance, costs, and complaints.
5. The general public was encouraged to provide feedback about the services or products of the contractor.
6. Contracts were canceled for nonperformance or serious violations and the contractor promptly replaced.

Privatization can be expected to grow as more and more companies enter this specialized market, for a number of reasons:

1. Privatization affords money-making opportunities for individuals and firms.
2. In keeping with a worldwide trend, public services will become increasingly based upon technology developed by private firms. Government will have to rely upon privatization to obtain the necessary technology.
3. As the nation becomes more service-oriented, the need for public services will outstrip local government's ability to provide them. Privatization will fill the gap.
4. Privatization offers opportunities for reducing cost while improving service quality.
5. The movement toward privatization has been fostered at the highest levels of the federal government.
6. Privatization is a normal outgrowth of the nation's market-enterprise economic system.

Summary

Government intervention in the U.S. economy is necessary to compensate for market failure. Market failure arises from two main sources:

1. *Externalities*. These arise when persons not involved in a market transaction nevertheless receive benefits or bear costs as a result of the transaction. The most serious externality is pollution of the environment.
2. *Structural failure*. This occurs as the market structure departs from perfect competition and becomes an oligopoly or monopoly. A special class of structural failure is the natural monopoly, which is regulated.

Government intervention to deal with externalities is designed to provide incentives to increase the output of beneficial externalities or decrease the output of harmful externalities. Incentives to increase output may include grants of operating rights, patents, subsidies, and tax relief. The government may also provide public goods, such as roads and dams, and public services, such as police and fire protection and national defense.

Incentives to decrease harmful output include tax penalties and government control of operations.

A natural monopoly occurs when economies of scale are such that the long-run average cost declines throughout the range of production that can be absorbed by a market. Natural monopolies are regulated by public-utility commissions, which set the price high enough to provide an adequate return on investment.

Market power and concentration are controlled by antitrust laws. The chief prohibitions contained in the antitrust laws may be summarized as follows:

1. It is flatly illegal, without any qualification, to:
   a. Enter a contract, combination, or conspiracy in restraint of trade (Sherman Act, Section 1).
   b. Monopolize, attempt to monopolize, or combine or conspire to monopolize trade (Sherman Act, Section 3).
2. When and if the effect may be substantially to lessen competition or tend to create a monopoly, it is illegal to:
   a. Acquire the stock of competing corporations (Clayton Act, Section 7).
   b. Acquire the assets of competing corporations (Clayton Act, Section 7, as amended by the Antimerger Act in 1950).
   c. Enter exclusive or tying contracts (Clayton Act, Section 3).
   d. Discriminate unjustifiably among purchasers (Clayton Act, Section 2).

Thus the laws taken as a whole are designed not only to prevent the growth of monopoly but to maintain competition as well. Because the effects of regulation have often been much different from what was intended, and because of excessive zeal on the part of some regulatory agencies, a reaction has resulted in demands for deregulation of private industry. There are also growing efforts to privatize many government activities in order to improve service and lower costs.

Problems

1. Critically evaluate government policies with respect to the following:
   a. Tax credits for the installation of solar-energy devices in private homes
   b. Investment tax credits for businesses
   c. Medicare
   d. Import taxes (tariffs)
   e. Excise taxes
   f. Sales taxes.

2. Discuss three different ways of dealing with pollution. Who bears the cost? In your opinion, which way is preferable?

3. Critically evaluate the economic impact of government policy toward:

   a. Transportation subsidies (maritime, highway, rail, and air)
   b. Agricultural subsidies (dairy products, grains, tobacco, and sugar).

4. Suppose that two unregulated firms are allowed to compete in the production and sale of electrical power in the same city.
   a. What would the economic impact be?
   b. How could the economic results be improved?

5. The Friendly Electric Company has petitioned the public-utility commission in its state for permission to practice "time-of-day" pricing. This means that electricity consumed during certain hours of the day—late at night, for example—would be priced lower than electricity consumed during periods of

peak demand. The company argues that this pricing scheme will enable it to lower overall rates. Evaluate this proposal.

6. Paradise Valley Electric Power Company is regulated by a public-utilities commission (PUC) of which you are a member. The PUC has established an allowable rate of return for the utility of 16 percent before taxes. The utility's costs have risen substantially due to inflation, and it has requested a rate increase to yield a 20 percent return before taxes. The following pertinent information has been verified:

   1. The rate base (assets) is $3 billion.
   2. The average operation of machinery and equipment is 50 percent of capacity, and generates 12 billion kilowatt-hours (kwh) of electricity per annum.
   3. Operating costs average 6.5 cents per kwh, not including return on investment (*ROI*).

      a. Calculate the price per kwh if the before-tax rate of return is held to 16 percent.

      b. Calculate the price per kwh if the before-tax rate of return is increased to 20 percent.

7. a. Suppose that tomorrow morning, all grocers in Chicago, without previous public notice, raise their prices for milk by 3 cents per quart. Does this action prove the existence of an agreement or constitute an offense on the part of the grocers?

   b. What would your answer be if all automobile manufacturers announced at the same time a 5 percent price increase next year on all new model cars? Explain.

8. In an industry characterized by price leadership without prior arrangement, is there likely to be a charge of combination or conspiracy leveled against that industry if (a) prevailing prices are announced by the industry's trade association rather than by a leading firm, (b) all firms in the industry report their prices to their industry trade association, (c) all firms in the industry quote prices on a basing point system, that is, the delivered price is the leader's price plus rail freight from the leader's plant, and (d) all firms follow the leader not only in price but in product and sales policies as well? (These four questions should be answered as a group rather than individually.)

9. "To say that the degree of competition depends on the number of sellers in the marketplace is like saying that football is more competitive than tennis." Do you agree? Explain. (Hint: Can you describe different forms of competition, in addition to price competition, that exist in U. S. industry?)

10. It is generally stated that growth, stability, flexibility, economy of scale, and vertical integration are some primary objectives of mergers.

    a. With respect to growth, it has been said that "a firm, like a tree, must either grow or die." Evaluate this statement.

    b. Why may instability be a motive for merger? Instability of what?

    c. What is meant by flexibility as a motive for merger? (Hint: Compare flexibility with vulnerability.)

    d. How could a merger achieve economy of scale?

    e. How could a merger achieve vertical integration?

11. (Library research) Examine the IBM case in detail. What antitrust provisions were alleged to have been violated? How extensive were the alleged damages? Was corporate morality ever an issue? Did government prosecution have any effect on IBM's corporate policies or on the general public?

12. The Hygrade Cement Company is located in a small midwestern city with a population of 80,000. The company's manufacture of Portland cement employs about 10 percent of the town's work force and provides 100 percent of its air pollution. Because of complaints about the plant's discharge of particulate matter into the air, the city council is considering actions to induce or force the firm to reduce its air pollution. Three alternatives are being considered:

    1. Require the firm to reduce its discharge of particulates by 85 percent.
    2. Impose a tax of $7 per ton of particulates discharged.
    3. Leave the situation unchanged.

Each alternative has consequences for the town's employment as well as for the firm's profits, as follows:

Action	Impact on Profits	Impact on Employment
Reduce discharge 85%	−40%	−18%
Tax discharge	−20	−8
Forget it	0	0

a. What do you think the council should do? Why?

b. Are there other factors that should be considered?

c. Why does the 85 percent reduction in particulates have such a drastic effect on employment?

13. In considering regulation to improve automobile safety, there is considerable controversy over the requirement to install air bags that automatically inflate to cushion the impact of a head-on crash. Opponents of the air bags advocate seat belts instead. They argue that seat belts not only are much cheaper than air bags, but also are effective in rollovers and other crashes where air bags are useless. Proponents of air bags counter with the argument that seat belts don't work when people don't use them, but air bags require no action on the part of occupants of the car. What are the economic arguments for and against the following proposals?

a. Compulsory installation of air bags.

b. Compulsory installation of seat belts and stiff fines for people who do not use them. (Some countries already have this law.)

c. A car buyer should have the right to choose whether to buy seat belts, air bags, both, or neither.

14. The Intellectual Club is a group of economists, environmentalists, and exofficials of the government of a certain developing country in Southeast Asia. In 1973, a local firm entered a joint venture with one of Japan's largest steel companies to produce locally a fine specialty steel. However, the production process was such that sulfur products were discharged into the air. The Intellectual Club complained bitterly about the air pollution, but the government refused to shut down the plant because it was providing employment, paying taxes, and otherwise providing the economic

benefits that flow from a primary industry. However, the government indicated it would entertain the idea of a pollution tax if the Intellectual Club could justify such a tax and determine how much it should be. The club learned that the steel plant had installed certain equipment that partially recovered sulfur from the plant's smokestacks. The recovered sulfur was used in the production process or sold. When steel and sulfur are jointly produced in a constant ratio of one unit of steel, Q_A, to one unit of sulfur, Q_B, their respective demand functions are estimated as

$$P_A = 5,000 - 2Q_A$$
$$P_B = 400 - Q_B$$

The total cost of joint production of steel and sulfur is

$$TC = 20,000 + 5.6Q + 2.8Q^2.$$

a. Determine the optimal output, prices, and profit without a pollution tax.

b. Estimate the minimum tax that must be charged to induce the firm to eliminate the sulfur pollution.

c. Critically evaluate the economics of externalities as it pertains to the emigration of a polluting industry to other nations.

15. Provide the economic rationale for deregulation of the following industries:

a. Trucking

b. Airlines

c. Oil

d. Natural gas

e. Communications.

Case Problem: The Nader Recommendations

16. Several years ago a Nader task force investigating antitrust activity came up with the following recommendations:

1. Limit the size of any one firm to $2 billion in assets.

2. Break up any industry with a four-firm concentration ratio of 50 percent or more, or with an eight-firm concentration ratio of 70 percent or more.

3. Require any firm in the top 500 corporations to divest an amount of assets equal to the assets of any firm that it acquires.

4. Levy a 100 percent tax on all advertising expenditures of any firm that possesses incipient market power in excess of a certain percentage of the total sales revenue of the industry.

5. To preserve the public interest, convert any private defense contractor into a public corporation if its business with the government exceeds 75 percent of its sales revenue over a five-year period.

Questions

a. Critically evaluate each of the five recommendations.

b. Do you agree that highly concentrated industries have greater economic power and tend to have larger profits? Why? Justify your answer with some concrete evidence.

c. The crucial issue involved here is whether or not monopoly power can benefit the American public. In your outside readings have you noted situations where this type of power does work to the benefit of the American people?

Case Problem: The AT&T Case

17. Refer to the AT&T antitrust case in the text of this chapter.

Questions

a. Leonard Hyman (analyst at Merrill Lynch, Pierce, Fenner & Smith) described the AT&T divestiture as a wrenching experience for AT&T. "It's going to split apart the family," he said, "But the business that will remain is still an enormous entity, with annual profits of $2 billion to $3 billion." In the light of this statement, critically evaluate the statement by William Baxter, the assistant attorney general, that the agreement "completely fulfills the objectives of the Antitrust Division and is also very much in the interests of AT&T and its shareholders."

b. In your opinion, what political issues were involved in the settlement of the case? Can you provide any evidence to support your opinion?

c. The AT&T case took six years and the expenditure of at least $385 million, all of which will eventually be paid for by taxpayers and users of telephone services. Can you think of ways the system might be reformed so that such enormous costs of litigation can be avoided?

d. In your opinion, has the AT&T settlement served the public interest? Establish and categorize criteria upon which to base your opinion.

e. Testimony by former Secretary of Defense Harold Brown established a security link between national defense and the communications industry. Should there be a national policy of protecting certain monopolies in the interest of national security? How could such a criterion be applied to antitrust cases?

Case Problem: Consortiums for International Competition

18. The U.S. trade deficit has averaged more than $120 billion annually since 1982 and the imbalance of trade with Japan has been particularly acute, being more than $50 billion in 1988 alone. The need to be competitive against Japan and other nations has given rise to a new form of organization: the consortium. A consortium in this case is an alliance of corporate competitors who pool their resources for research and development in order to compete effectively in the international marketplace.

During the years 1983–1988, more than 100 consortiums registered with the U.S. Dept. of Justice. Their R&D activities range from development of artificial intelligence to the more efficient manufacture of semiconductors. Over the same period, the U.S. government's attitude toward consortiums evolved from passive permissiveness to open support.

Questions

a. Read the article entitled "Can Consortiums Defeat Japan?" in the June 5, 1989 issue of *Fortune* magazine.

b. Discuss the pros and cons of the double standard in antitrust policy: domestic cartels are prohibited in order to preserve domestic competition but consortiums are permitted in order to improve U.S. competitiveness in the international marketplace.

c. Should the U.S. government protect the development of a high-definition–television (HDTV) industry from foreign competition?

d. Should the relationship between the U.S. government and U.S. industries become more like "Japan, Inc."?

e. Consider factors that impact the U.S. balance of trade, such as U.S. and foreign business organization, enforcement of property rights, unfair restrictions against the entry of U.S. goods into foreign markets, the burden of defense, and cultural differences. How can the U.S. balance of trade be improved?

Case Problem: Value Hardware

19. Value Hardware operates 23 stores in southern California. Total sales climbed to a record $18 million in 1988 with an average contribution margin of 30 percent. Value Hardware's management attributed much of its 1988 success to an exclusive six-year contract with LS Corporation for a dealership in Olympia paints, which LS Corporation manufactured. The contract began in January 1986.

Olympia paints were heavily promoted in Value Hardware advertising and accounted for about 20 percent of total sales. An additional 20 percent of sales were attributable to purchases of complementary goods such as paint brushes, rollers, and step ladders.

In 1989, the LS Corporation merged with a national chain of hardware stores. As a result of the merger, LS Corporation pulled Olympia paints out of the Value Hardware Stores. Although Value Hardware replaced Olympia with another brand, paint sales dropped 25 percent and total sales were down 10 percent in 1989.

Previous projections by Value Hardware's management forecast that Olympia paint sales could be expected to increase 5 percent per year for the duration of the six-year contract. However, future sales of the replacement line of paints were not expected to increase above the 1989 level. On January 3, 1990, Value Hardware filed an antitrust suit for triple damages against LS Corporation.

Questions

a. What antitrust laws might Value Hardware allege were violated?

b. Analyze the total economic loss sustained by Value Hardware as a result of cancellation of the Olympia paint dealership.

References

Auerback, Alan J. *Corporate Takeovers: Causes and Consequences*. Chicago: University of Chicago Press, 1988.

Blair, Roger, and David L. Kaserman. *Antitrust Economics*. Homewood, Ill.: Richard D. Irwin, 1985.

Christiansen, Gregory B. and Robert H. Havenman. "Public Regulations and the Slowdown in Productivity Growth." *American Economic Review* (May 1981), pp. 320–25.

Curran, John J. "Does Deregulation Make Sense?" *Fortune* (June 5, 1989), pp. 181–96.

Dorfman, Robert. "Incidence of the Benefits and Costs of Environmental Programs." *American Economic Review* (February 1977), pp. 333–40.

Gatti, James F. *The Limits of Government Regulation*. New York: Academic Press, 1981.

Goodrich, Jonathan N. "Privatization in America." *Business Horizons* (January-February 1988), pp. 11–17.

Gordon, Daniel V. "The Effect of Price Deregulation on the Competitive Behavior of Retail Drug Firms." *Applied Economics* 20, no. 5 (May 1988), p. 641.

Moore, Thomas Gale. "U.S. Airline Deregulation: Its Effects on Passengers, Capital, and Labor." *Journal of Law & Economics* 29 (April 1986), pp. 1–28.

Peltzman, Sam. "Toward a More General Theory of Regulation." *Journal of Law and Economics* (August 1976), pp. 211–40.

———— "The Gains and Losses from Industrial Concentration." *Journal of Law and Economics* (October 1977), pp. 229–63.

Scherer, Frederic M. *Industrial Market Structure and Economic Performance*. 2nd ed. Skokie, Ill.: Rand McNally, 1980.

Smith, W. James; Michael B. Vaughan; and John F. Formby. "Cartels and Antitrust: The Role of Fines in Deterring Violations at the Margin." *Southern Economic Journal* 53, no. 4 (April 1987), p. 985.

Stigler, George J. "The Theory of Economic Regulation." *Bell Journal of Economics and Management Science* (Spring 1971), pp. 3–21.

———— "The Economists and the Problem of Monopoly." *American Economic Review* 72 (May 1982), pp. 1–11.

"The Odds in a Bell–IBM Bout." *Business Week* (January 25, 1982), pp. 22–26.

Turner, Donald F. "The Definition of Agreement Under the Sherman Act: Conscious Parallelism and Refusals to Deal." *Harvard Law Review* (February 1962), pp. 655–706.

U.S. Dept. of Justice. *Merger Guidelines* (June 14, 1982).

Uttal, Bro. "How to Deregulate AT&T." *Fortune* (November 1981), pp. 70–75.

Waters, L. L. "Deregulation—For Better, or for Worse?" *Business Horizons* (January-February 1981), pp. 88–91.

Weidenbaum, Murray L. *Business, Government and the Public*. Englewood Cliffs, N.J.: Prentice-Hall, 1979.

———— "The High Cost of Government Regulation." *Challenge* (November-December 1979), pp. 32–39.

C H A P T E R

18

CAPITAL
BUDGETING

Capital budgeting involves the planning of expenditures for assets from which returns will be realized in future time periods. The firm's growth and development, and perhaps even its ability to survive in a competitive environment, depend upon a continuous flow of new investment ideas. Consequently, a well-managed company will place great emphasis on the development of good capital-budgeting proposals. Ideas are sought not only from the company's executives, but also from rank-and-file workers who are given bonuses for suggestions that lead to profitable investments.

Capital budgeting is an integral part of managerial and financial decision making about a firm's long-run strategy, and whole textbooks have been written about it. Therefore, a complete discussion of capital budgeting is beyond the scope of this book. Rather, this chapter presents an overview of the capital-budgeting process and a limited discussion of some of its technical aspects.

CHAPTER OUTLINE

This chapter is divided into four sections:

1. **Overview of Capital Budgeting**. This section discusses the fundamental types of decisions that must be made in the course of capital budgeting and explains the optimal approach to capital budgeting.
2. **Estimating the Cost of Capital**. This section discusses basic principles for estimating a firm's cost of capital.
3. **Estimating Cash Flows**. This section discusses procedures for estimating cash flows.

589

4. Evaluating Investment Proposals. This section discusses five commonly used methods for the evaluation and ranking of capital-budgeting proposals. It then presents some survey data on the capital-budgeting methods actually used by some large U.S. corporations.

Overview of Capital Budgeting

Two fundamental types of decisions must be made in the capital-budgeting process: financing decisions and investment-selection decisions. Exhibit 18–1 shows how these parts fit together within the firm's environment. It pictures the capital-budgeting process as a continuous self-perpetuating system in which the firm draws upon external capital markets and its own internal accumulated earnings for the capital needed for profitable investments. In turn, the earnings of the firm flow partly to the external capital markets in the form of interest on debt and dividends to stockholders and partly back into the firm's pool of retained earnings.

Financing Decisions

Financing decisions involve the amount and kind (debt or equity) of financial capital to be raised, the amount of dividends to be paid to the owners, and the amount of earnings to be retained in the corporation. Ideally, decisions about financing investments are made in conjunction with the selection of investments.

Investment-Selection Decisions

Investment-selection decisions will determine both the total amount of capital expenditures to be undertaken in the planning period and the specific projects selected. Typical decisions in this area include the following:

1. *Expansion decisions*, such as building or acquiring additional plant facilities.
2. *Replacement decisions*, such as the replacement of existing equipment.
3. *Modernization decisions*, such as the remodeling of a plant or the installation of automated machinery to effect more efficient operation.
4. *Pollution-control decisions*, such as the installation of scrubbers on smokestacks or the acquisition of land for disposal of waste materials.
5. *"Seed" investment decisions*, such as research and development, advertising, market research, training, and professional consulting services.
6. *Operating investment decisions*, such as increasing inventories or accounts receivable, or development of a new product line.

All of these decisions require an estimate of future demand as a crucial first step. If demand is weaker than forecast, the firm may be unable to recover the costs of capital-budgeting decisions such as decisions to incur debt. Even if demand is strong, the firm must also consider forecasts of technological change, competition, the possibility of improving the productivity of its workers, opportunities for cost reduction, and the prospects for improving the quality of its output.

EXHIBIT 18–1   The Capital-Budgeting Process

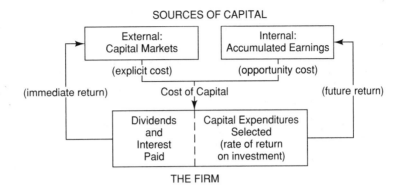

Once a project that requires capital budgeting has been identified, the project must be evaluated before an investment decision can be made. At a minimum, the analysis will include:

1. Estimating the cost of capital
2. Estimating cash flows
3. Evaluation of the investment proposal
4. Ranking capital-investment projects.

Each of these basic steps will be discussed in the sections that follow.

Estimating the Cost of Capital

As we have seen, a firm's cost of capital is an essential factor in investment decision making. At the outset, we shall define cost of capital or, more specifically, **marginal cost of capital** as the cost of acquiring the next increment of capital to be utilized by the firm.

As shown in Exhibit 18–1, sources of capital to the firm are presumed to be: (1) the capital markets, which include many different types of financial intermediaries, and (2) earnings of the firm accumulated from previous time periods. Each specific source of capital has its own cost, which becomes a component part of the overall cost of capital to the firm.

How do we measure a firm's cost of capital? The most widely recommended method is to calculate the weighted average of the current cost of funds to the firm from all sources. This amounts to calculating the cost of debt and the cost of equity, as will be explained shortly.

Before discussing methods of calculating the cost of capital, let us note a fallacy in reasoning that often arises. Suppose that the cost of debt funding is 10 percent before taxes (or 6.6 percent after taxes) and the cost of equity funding is 15 percent. Then suppose that an investment project under consideration is to be financed by debt. It is tempting to think that the cost of capital for the project is the cost of debt, because

EXHIBIT 18–2   Calculating a Firm's Cost of Capital

Method of Financing	*(1)* Current Market Value	*(2)* Percentage of Total Capital	*(3)* Current Market Cost Before Taxes	*(4)* Current Market Cost After Taxes *(34%)*	*(5)* Weighted Cost *(2)×(4)*
Long-term debt	$35,000	35%	10.0%	6.6%	2.3%
Preferred stock	10,000	10	8.0	8.0	0.8
Common stock	30,000	30	20.0	20.0	6.0
Retained earnings	25,000	25	18.0	18.0	4.5
	$100,000	100%			13.6%

the new project is being financed by debt. This thinking is fallacious, however, because in order for a firm to be able to engage in debt financing, it must have an adequate equity base. This is necessary because when a firm incurs a debt, it also incurs the legal obligation to make periodic interest payments before its earnings can be distributed to owners or stockholders. Hence the existence of an equity base provides a safety cushion for creditors.

Because the interest paid on debt is a deductible expense for the purpose of calculating income tax whereas the dividends paid to stockholders are not deductible, the cost of debt is less than the cost of equity. Therefore, as long as the firm can earn more on its total assets than the interest rate it pays on its debt, the owners will benefit from debt financing by receiving higher earnings. This is known in business finance as **trading on the equity** or by the preferred term **leverage**.

On the other hand, interest on the debt is a legal obligation that must be paid whether or not the firm has any earnings; therefore debt increases the financial risk undertaken by the firm. Obviously, the greater the proportion of total assets that are financed by debt instead of equity, the greater the potential economic loss to the owners in case of a decline in earnings. Thus leverage is a two-edged sword that can increase either the firm's earnings or its losses in the same proportion.

This leads to the notion that an "optimal" or "best" financial structure exists for each firm, or at least there is a range within which the debt/equity ratio is approximately ideal. Accordingly, when a firm incurs additional debt financing, it thereby uses up some of its existing equity base. If it continues, the firm's financial structure will become unbalanced in favor of debt.

Logically, therefore, it is often recommended that a calculation of the cost of capital be based on a weighted average of *all forms of financing* that the firm currently uses, including all forms of debt and equity. Furthermore, the estimates should be based on current market costs of debt and equity rather than on historical costs or book values. This is because investment decisions are made in the present on the basis of current and future costs. Exhibit 18–2 illustrates the weighting procedure used to calculate the cost of capital this way.

Note from this example that the cost of debt is an expense or deductible item for income-tax purposes, whereas the cost of equity is not.[1] The cost of capital, in this case 13.6 percent, is the minimum that must be earned on the total assets of any project. Of course, management may also wish to add a safety margin to this estimate, but the current cost of capital at least indicates the minimum prospective profitability necessary to undertake a particular investment.

Explicit Costs of Different Methods of Financing

Each method of financing brings some net amount of funds into the firm (after payment of costs such as underwriting) and requires some future cash outflows, such as interest payments, repayment of principal, or payment of dividends. The discount rate that equates the present value of the net inflows with the present value of the expected outflows is the explicit cost of the particular source of financing. The general equation, then, for the explicit cost of any method of financing is

$$I_0 = \frac{C_1}{1 + r} + \frac{C_2}{(1 + r)^2} + \ldots + \frac{C_n}{(1 + r)^n} \tag{1}$$

where

I_0 = The net income, or yield, from the method of financing, i.e., the net cash inflow after paying the costs of acquiring capital, such as underwriting charges and commissions.

C_t = The cash outflow in the period t where $t = 1, 2, \ldots, n$.

  (1) In the case of bonds or mortgages, C_t is the interest paid in time period t, plus any payment on principal.

  (2) In the case of preferred stock, C_t is the dividend on the preferred stock, which is calculated at the interest rate specified on the preferred-stock certificate.

  (3) In the case of equity financing, C_t is the dividend that is expected to be paid to the owners of the common stock in time period t.

r = The discount rate that expresses the before-tax cost of the method of financing.

  (1) In the case of debt financing, r is the interest rate specified on the debt instrument (bond or mortgage).

  (2) In the case of preferred stock, r is the specified dividend (expressed as an interest rate).

  (3) In the case of equity financing, r is the cost of equity capital.

This approach is used in making the cost estimates for each specific source of capital, as explained next.

Cost of Debt. The explicit cost of debt is determined not only by the rate of interest specified in the debt instruments but also by the method of repayment, the yield of the

---

[1] Of course, if the firm does not earn a profit, there are no income taxes and the cost of debt is the full interest rate. Likewise, if the firm earns $75,000 or less, the tax rate is lower and the cost of debt is higher.

debt issue, and the assumptions that are made about the tax rates expected over the life of the debt.[2]

In debt financing, three outcomes are possible: (1) the yield is equal to the face value of the debt instruments; (2) the yield is less than the face value of the debt instruments; and (3) the yield is greater than the face value of the debt instruments.

For example, suppose a firm issues one hundred 8-percent bonds with a face value of $1,000 each. The firm must make interest payments of $8,000 per year for eight years plus a single payment of $100,000 to retire the bonds at the end of eight years. The present value of the cash outflow is:

$$\$8,000\left[\frac{1 - (1.08)^{-8}}{0.08}\right] + \frac{\$100,000}{(1.08)^8} = \$100,000$$

which is just the face value of the bonds. If the yield (cash inflow) from sale of the bonds is equal to their face value, the before-tax cost of debt is equal to the interest rate specified in the debt instruments, which in this case is 8 percent. To get the after-tax cost, we calculate $r(1 - t_c)$, where t_c is the corporate income-tax rate. If the firm in this example has an income-tax rate of 34 percent,[3] the after-tax cost of this issue is $(0.08)(1 - 0.34) = 0.0528$ or 5.28 percent.

If the yield is more or less than the face value of the debt instruments, the first step in calculating the cost of debt is to determine the periodic cash outflows, which are the C_t in Equation 1. The next step is to determine the discount rate r in Equation 1, which represents the before-tax cost of debt. Solving for r requires a trial-and-error method that requires repeated calculations of the present value of the payments on the debt. The procedure is best performed by a computer, but can be performed with the aid of a hand-held calculator. The procedure is demonstrated in the following illustrative problems.

Illustrative Problems

First Problem

The Dixie Doodle Corporation makes an ice-cream bar, called the Dixie Doodle, which is popular in the Southeastern United States. The firm's profits are such that it is in the 34 percent income-tax bracket. The company needed approximately $500,000 in additional capital in order to expand its distribution to the Southwest, which it attempted to borrow by issuing 500 five-year 8-percent bonds. After paying the costs of floating the bond issue, the yield was $475,000. What is the before-tax and after-tax cost of this debt?

---

[2] There are also implicit costs of debt such as working-capital requirements, issuing of additional debt, and others. Obviously, these must also be considered in the decision to raise capital through debt or by other means.

[3] In 1989, the corporate income tax was graduated up to taxable incomes of $335,000. Corporations with taxable incomes in excess of $335,000, in effect, pay a flat tax at a 34 percent rate.

Solution

The firm will pay annual interest of $1,000 × 0.08 = $80 per bond × 500 bonds = $40,000. Also, at the end of the fifth year, the firm will redeem the bonds at their face value of $1,000 each × 500 = $500,000.

The interest rate on the bonds offers a starting point for our calculations of the present value of the discounted cash outflow. If the cash outflow is discounted by the stated interest rate on the bonds, its present value will always be equal to the face value of the bonds; i.e.,

$$PV = \$40,000 \left[\frac{1 - (1.08)^{-5}}{0.08} \right] + \frac{\$500,000}{(1.08)^5} = \$500,000.$$

In this case, the present value, $500,000, of the discounted cash outflow when discounted at the stated interest rate of 8 percent is greater than the yield of $45,000. This means that the cost of the debt is greater than the stated interest rate. Therefore, we shall repeatedly calculate the present value (*PV*) of the cash outflow, using successively higher discount rates, until *PV* is less than yield, as follows:

Discount Rate	Present Value	Yield
.080	$500,000	$475,000
.085	490,148	$475,000
.090	480,552	$475,000
.095	471,202	$475,000

Now we know that the cost of debt is somewhere between 9.0 and 9.5 percent. We can diagram the situation as

$$0.005 \begin{cases} u\{ & 0.090 & 480,552 \,\}\, 5,552 \\ & 0.090 +u & 475,000 \\ & 0.095 & 471,202 \end{cases} \Bigg\} 9,350.$$

Setting up the ratio and proportion,

$$\frac{u}{0.005} = \frac{5,552}{9,350}.$$

Cross-multiplying,

$$9,350u = 0.005(5,552) = 27.76$$
$$u = 0.002968983$$

Before-tax cost = 0.090 + 0.002968983 = 0.092968983 ≈ 9.3%
After-tax cost = (1 − 0.34)(.093) = 0.06138 ≈ 6.1%.

Note: The interpolation performed above is a linear interpolation of a nonlinear function. Therefore it has a built-in error. The error can be minimized by keeping the spread between the too-small and too-large discount values as small as possible.

Second Problem

The Hytech Pharmaceuticals Company floated a bond issue to raise capital for expansion just after receiving very favorable publicity about the company's future. The issue consisted of 250 9-percent 10-year $1,000 bonds, which were snapped up at a premium price. After paying all expenses of floating the issue, the company netted a yield of $275,000. The company is in the 34 percent income tax bracket. What is the firm's before-tax and after-tax cost of this debt?

Solution

The company will pay annual interest of $0.09 \times \$1,000$ per bond = $\$90 \times 250$ bonds = $22,500 for 10 years. At the end of 10 years, it will redeem the bonds at their face value of $250,000.

Again in this problem, the interest rate on the bonds offers a starting point for our calculations of the present value of the discounted cash outflow. If the cash outflow is discounted by the stated interest rate on the bonds, its present value is equal to the face value of the bonds; e.g.,

$$PV = \$22,500 \left[\frac{1 - (1.09)^{-10}}{0.09} \right] + \frac{\$250,000}{(1.09)^{10}} = \$250,000.$$

In this case, the yield is more than the face value of the bonds, so the present value of the discounted cash outflow when discounted at the stated interest rate is less than the yield. This means that the cost of the debt is less than the stated interest rate. Therefore, we shall repeatedly calculate the present value of the cash outflow, using successively lower discount rates, until PV is greater than yield, as follows:

Discount Rate	Present Value	Yield
.090	250,000	$275,000
.085	258,202	$275,000
.080	266,775	$275,000
.075	275,740	$275,000

Now we know that the cost of debt is somewhere between 7.5 and 8.0 percent. We can diagram the situation as

$$0.005 \begin{cases} u\{ \begin{matrix} 0.075 \\ 0.075 + u \\ 0.080 \end{matrix} & \begin{matrix} 275,740 \\ 275,000 \\ 258,202 \end{matrix} \} 740 \end{cases} 17,538.$$

Setting up the ratio and proportion,

$$\frac{u}{0.005} = \frac{740}{17,538}.$$

Cross-multiplying,

$$17,538u = 0.005(740) = 3.7$$
$$u = 0.00021097$$
$$\text{Before-tax cost of debt} = 0.075 + 0.00021097 = 0.07521097 \approx 7.5\%$$
$$\text{After-tax cost of debt} = 0.075(0.66) = 0.0495 \approx 5.0\%.$$

Third Problem

In the case of mortgages and serial bonds, periodic payments are made on the principal as well as on the interest. For example, suppose that the Dixie Doodle Corporation's bonds (from the first problem in this example) were serial bonds to be retired at the rate of 100 bonds per year. The cash outflow would be:

Cash Outflow	Year				
	1	2	3	4	5
Principal	$100,000	$100,000	$100,000	$100,000	$100,000
Interest	40,000	32,000	24,000	16,000	8,000
Total outflow	$140,000	$132,000	$124,000	$116,000	$108,000

The present value of the cash outflow at 8 percent discount is

$$\frac{\$140,000}{1.08} + \frac{\$132,000}{(1.08)^2} + \frac{\$124,000}{(1.08)^3} + \frac{\$116,000}{(1.08)^4} + \frac{\$108,000}{(1.08)^5} = \$500,000$$

which is greater than the yield of $475,000. Using the trial-and-error procedure previously described on a computer, we find that the before-tax cost of capital is 10.08 percent and the after-tax cost is 6.65 percent.

Cost of Preferred Stock.   Preferred stock has features of both debt and equity. Like bonds or mortgage loans, preferred stock specifies a rate of return to the investor that is fixed as a percentage of the face (par) value of the instrument. Unlike debt, however, the payment of these dividends is not a legal requirement. If the company falls upon hard times, the directors can omit the preferred dividend without danger of being forced into bankruptcy. No dividends can be paid on common stock, however, until the dividends on the preferred stock have been paid.

For tax purposes, payment of dividends on preferred stock is classed as a distribution of earnings rather than a tax-deductible expense. Thus while preferred stock provides financial leverage, its cost is much higher than the cost for debt as long as the firm is profitable. On the other hand, the financial risk of debt is largely avoided when preferred stock is used instead.

In determining the cost of preferred-stock financing, we assume that the directors intend to pay the preferred dividends on time, and we therefore treat preferred stock as a perpetual debt. The cost, then, is simply the annual dividend divided by the yield. For example, if a firm obtains a yield of $98 per share on an issue of par $100, 7 percent preferred stock, the cost is $7/$98 = 7.14 percent. If the preferred stock has a call option and the company intends to call it in after some specific time, Equation 1 may be used to calculate the cost.

Cost of Equity Capital.   Equity capital consists of funds obtained from the sale of common stock plus the retained earnings of the firm. The market price of a common stock is based upon investors' expectations and attitude toward risk. Each investor has in mind some minimum rate of return (from dividends and capital gains) that constitutes a threshold of investment. The individual or institution will invest when the expected rate of return is at or above this threshold, and will divest when it falls below the threshold. Thus the cost of equity capital may be defined as the minimum rate of return that will leave the market price of the common stock unchanged.

The investor makes a decision to invest, hold, or divest on the basis of the market price of the common stock. In return for the price of a share, the investor expects to receive a future stream of income composed of periodic dividends and, finally, the market price of the stock when it is sold. Since these increments of income are to be received in the future, they must be discounted to reflect the time value of money. The market price of common stock, then, is simply the present value of the expected value of a future stream of income, which can be expressed by the equation

$$V = \frac{D_1}{1 + k} + \frac{D_2}{(1 + k)^2} + \ldots + \frac{D_n}{(1 + k)^n} + \frac{S}{(1 + k)^n} \tag{2}$$

where $D_1, D_2, \ldots, D_n$ represents a series of cash dividends received at the end of each of the respective periods over the life of the investment; S is the market value at the end of n periods; k is the investor's discount rate (required rate of return); and V is the present value of a share of stock.

To show why this is so, suppose that an investor buys a share of common stock at a price of $100, expecting to receive a dividend of $5 at the end of one year and then to be able to sell the stock for $110. The return will be the gain over the original investment, $15, divided by the original investment of $100, which gives a return of 15 percent. If we substitute these data into Equation 2 and solve for k, we get the same answer, 15 percent.

Now let us suppose that the investor, after receiving the first-year dividend of $5, decides to keep the stock for two years before selling, basing this decision on information or belief that the second-year dividend will be $6.50, and that the price of the stock at the end of two years will be $120. When we substitute into Equation 2 and solve for k, we again get $k = 15$ percent. This illustrates that the price of the stock is the present value of a discounted stream of dividends plus a discounted terminal value. But the terminal value is just the price that another investor is willing to pay, which is a discounted stream of dividends plus a discounted terminal value, and so on. Thus we see that the price of a stock is based on a stream of earnings in perpetuity.

If a company's dividends are expected to grow at some constant rate, then the dividend in any period is equal to the most recent dividend multiplied by the compound growth factor. By manipulating Equation 2, it can be shown that the cost of equity capital, k_e, is the ratio of the next expected dividend, D_1, to the current price, P_0, plus the rate of growth, g:

$$k_e = \frac{D_1}{P_0} + g. \tag{3}$$

This assumes, however, that dividends will grow at a constant rate forever. There may be firms for which this is a reasonable expectation, but in most cases the rate of growth can be expected to taper off from time to time. If both the timing and the magnitude of changes in the growth pattern can be estimated, then Equation 2 can be used to derive the cost of equity capital.

But what about companies that pay no dividends? Not only do their stocks often sell well, but they sometimes sell for very high prices. How does this happen? The answer, of course, is that investors expect a terminal value high enough that they are willing to forgo dividends. In the meantime the company is reinvesting its earnings, which it hopes will mean greater earnings in the future.

How can the cost of capital be estimated for a company that pays no dividends? One way is by examining the growth in the market price of the stock. For example, if a firm's stock price has increased over several years at a compound rate of 10 percent and this growth is expected to continue, one might accept 10 percent as the cost of equity capital for that firm.

Earnings–Price Ratio. The earnings–price ratio is just one of many pieces of information that investment analysts use to evaluate a stock. In two special situations, the earnings–price ratio may reflect the firm's cost of equity capital. The first case is that of the firm whose earnings per share are expected to remain constant and that pays out all earnings as dividends. The other case is a firm that does not have investment opportunities yielding more than the cost of equity capital but can invest a constant proportion of its earnings in projects that provide a perpetual return just equal to the cost of equity capital. In situations where investors expect growth in the corporation's earnings, the earnings–price ratio is a very uncertain measure of the firm's cost of equity capital, since earnings–price ratios of less than the yield on government bonds are quite common.

Cost of New Stock Issues. When a new issue of stock is sold, the net yield to the firm will be somewhat less than the market price of the stock because of flotation costs. Consequently, the cost of equity capital on new financing will be somewhat higher than the market would indicate. Flotation costs include the difference between the sale price and the proceeds received by the company (called the *underwriting spread*), registration expenses, and other out-of-pocket costs such as printing and postage.

Cost of Retained Earnings. Although today it is recognized that the use of retained earnings is not cost-free, as some writers have contended in the past, there still is much controversy over the measurement of the cost. Some authorities feel that the cost of equity capital should be adjusted downward to reflect the tax effect, but a strong case can be made for simply using the cost of equity capital as the cost of retained earnings.

There is general agreement that the cost of retained earnings is an opportunity cost equal to the value of the dividend forgone by the stockholders. This cost may be defined as the rate of return that permits the shareholder to be indifferent between (1) a cash-dividend payment and (2) the investment project financed by retained earnings.

In a world free of taxes, we might reason that if the firm paid out all of its earnings as dividends, then the only way it could attract these earnings back into its capital structure would be to sell stock. The price of the stock would be determined by the cost of equity capital as previously defined; hence the cost of retained earnings is just the cost of equity capital. On the other hand, there are those who point out that even in a world without taxes, there still are brokerage fees. Therefore the stockholder could not be indifferent unless the cost of equity capital were somewhat higher than the cost of retained earnings. More precisely, the cost of retained earnings would be the cost of equity capital multiplied by 1 minus the brokerage rate. For example, if the brokerage rate were 1 percent, the cost of retained earnings would be 99 percent of the cost of equity capital.

In the real world, of course, there are taxes as well as brokerage fees and they are levied at different rates. Therefore, the cost of retained earnings is the cost of equity capital times $(1 - t_p)$, where t_p is the personal-income tax on ordinary income. For example, if the investor were paying 28 percent personal-income tax and 1 percent brokerage fees, the cost of retained earnings would be $(1 - 0.28)(1 - 0.01) = 71.3$ percent of the cost of equity capital.

This is a very neat solution except for the problem of determining the composite personal-tax rate for all stockholders. Rough estimates suggest that for the average investor, personal-tax rates are about 24 percent, but there can be very large institutional stockholders that are tax-exempt. In very small firms or closely held corporations, it might be possible to ascertain the tax rate by questioning all stockholders. In large publicly held firms, this would be impossible and estimates would have to be used.

Another approach to evaluating the cost of retained earnings is the **external-yield criterion**. In this approach, the cost of retained earnings is defined as the forgone opportunity to invest in other firms of similar risk. This criterion is not affected by, and need not be concerned with, personal tax rates, as it simply measures what the firm could get by direct investment. The external-yield criterion is economically justifiable and can be applied consistently. As a general rule, however, since we assume equilibrium in the marketplace between risk and return, we would expect the external yield to be the same as the cost of equity capital to the firm.

Leverage and the Cost of Capital

Going back to Exhibit 18–2, it is reasonable to ask: How were the amounts in column 2, Percentage of Total Capital, arrived at in the first place? Since long-term debt has the lowest cost, would it not be logical to raise as much capital as possible from this source and thereby lower the weighted average cost? For example, if additional bonds were sold for $15,000 and the proceeds used to buy back and retire common stock, the weighted average cost of capital would decline to 11.6 percent.

But why stop there? Why not continue until there is nothing but debt in the capital structure? What factors usually impede such an excessive use of debt? Finally, is there an optimal debt/equity ratio?

Optimal Debt/Equity Ratio.   It is generally well understood that when a firm engages in debt financing to the extent that debt constitutes a rather large part of its capital structure, the firm exposes itself to risks that increase in rapid geometric fashion compared with the increase in the debt itself. This is reflected, of course, in the leveraged effect on corporate earnings, but it also results in a reduction of the earnings yield (earnings–price ratio) of the stock, since the debt service (payment of interest) must be paid out of earnings.

Let us look in more detail at the relationships between the cost of capital and the debt/equity (D/E) ratio by examining Exhibit 18–3, which illustrates this relationship for one set of hypothetical conditions.

To keep things simple, preferred stock and retained earnings are ignored, leaving only the cost of debt, k_d, and the cost of equity, k_e, to consider. When the debt/equity ratio equals zero, meaning that the firm has no debt, the weighted average cost of capital,

EXHIBIT 18–3 **Leverage and the Cost of Capital**

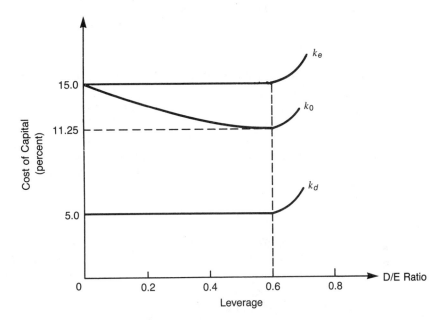

k_0, equals the cost of equity, k_e. Then, as debt is brought into the capital structure, and assuming its cost is less than the cost of equity, k_0 declines. Specifically, we know that

$$k_0 = \alpha k_d + (1 - \alpha)k_e \tag{4}$$

where α is the proportion (percentage) of total capital in the form of debt.

The diagram in Exhibit 18–3 shows $k_e = 15$ percent and $k_d = 5$ percent until the debt/equity ratio of 0.6, at which point $\alpha = 0.375$, is reached.[4] The weighted average cost of capital, k_0, declines throughout this range as α grows larger and $(1 - \alpha)$ grows smaller. When the debt/equity ratio reaches 0.6, k_0 (the weighted cost of capital) begins to rise, since both k_d (the cost of debt) and k_e (the cost of equity capital) increase in response to a growing apprehension on the part of both creditors and owners about the future solvency of the firm. In short, each group now demands a higher return because of the added risk exposure placed upon them.

Of course, optimal debt/equity ratios can be expected to vary among industries and even among firms within a given industry, depending upon the unique circumstances in each. For example, firms with rather stable sales and earnings, such as public utilities, tend to have high debt/equity ratios. Still, there are wide variations among individual utilities that are usually a reflection of the sales and earnings stability of each firm's principal customers. Also, it is not necessary that k_d and k_e turn up at the same point, as indicated in the diagram. This is done for ease of the presentation and does not reflect a theoretical or pragmatic argument.

---

[4] The *D/E* ratio $= \alpha/(1 - \alpha)$.

There is considerable controversy, of both theoretical and practical natures, as to the real-world existence of optimal debt/equity ratios. While we cannot explore the vast literature in this area—indeed, during the early 1960s it dominated the field of finance—the consensus now seems to favor the approach we have presented.

The Cost of Capital Reformulated.   To close our discussion of leverage, let us reformulate the costs of equity and debt capital. As we have seen, these reflect investors' valuations of a company's stock and debt instruments, respectively. Investors, of course, in determining these values, consider a variety of factors, and certainly one that is most important is the rate of return available on a **risk-free** investment such as a Treasury security.[5] In a sense, this risk-free rate establishes a rate "base" upon which all other rates depend. When viewed in this manner, a firm's cost of capital can be formulated as:

$$k_0 = R_f + \rho_1 + \rho_2 \tag{5}$$

where

R_f = Rate of return on the risk-free investment
ρ_1 = A risk premium on the firm's securities, reflecting business risk
ρ_2 = A risk premium for the degree of leverage in the firm's capital structure, reflecting financial risk
k_0 = The firm's cost of capital.

An illustration of this formulation appears in Exhibit 18–4.

Values for ρ_1 will depend upon the business activity of the firm. For example, banks typically have very low risk premiums because of the relative stability of their earnings over time, while automobile manufacturers have much higher premiums that reflect the inherent instability of their activities.

Estimating Cash Flows

One of the most important steps in the analysis of a proposal for capital expenditure is the estimation of cash flows. Many variables are involved in a forecast of the cash flowing out of the firm's treasury and the cash flowing back in as a result of the investment. Obtaining a reasonably accurate estimate may involve the time and attention of many of the firm's departments and many individual employees. The three major elements of estimating cash flows are:

1. Estimating the magnitude and the timing of cash receipts and cash outlays
2. Estimating the magnitude and timing of costs

---

[5] *Risk-free* means the investor expects to receive both the promised interest and face value of the security at its maturity date. In fact, many government securities are purchased at a discount from their face value, and the investor actually achieves the expected yield by receiving the face value at maturity. Notice that risk-free does not mean the investor can always recover the amount initially invested in the government security before its maturity date. If interest rates happen to increase after the purchase of the security, its market rate declines, and sale at that time results in a loss. To this extent, the security is not risk-free.

EXHIBIT 18–4   **Effect of Leverage (D/E Ratio) on the Firm's Cost of Capital**

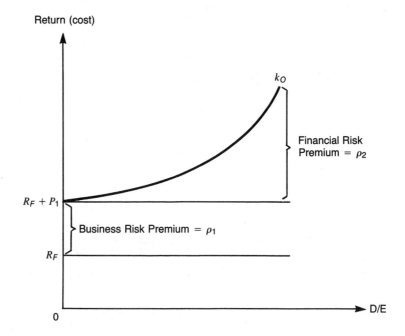

3. Estimating salvage values and working capital to be recovered upon conclusion of the project.

These elements are particularly difficult to forecast for investment proposals that involve something new to the firm, such as the introduction of a new product or entry into a different type of business. These difficulties can be made more manageable by following three simple, common-sense rules:

1. Cash flows must be estimated on an incremental basis. All cash flows that will change if the project is implemented, whether or not they are directly related to the project, must be included. For example, cash sales of an existing product may be affected by the introduction of a new product, particularly if the new product is a substitute for the existing product. On the other hand, cash flows that will remain the same whether or not the project is implemented are not relevant.
2. Cash flows should be constructed on an after-tax basis. That is to say, taxes must be included as a cash outflow.
3. The effect of depreciation expense upon taxes must be calculated, but depreciation is a noncash expense that should not be deducted from the cash inflow.

A spreadsheet is the most common and most efficient way to analyze cash flows, especially if a computer with a spreadsheet program is available. Such programs enable the analyst to vary the estimates of cash-flow items and quickly observe the results on the net cash flow. Exhibit 18–5 (page 604) shows a typical spreadsheet.

EXHIBIT 18–5   Spreadsheet Analysis of Estimated Cash Flows from a Proposed Project

	A	B	C	D	E	F	G	H	I	J
1	JUPITER BOTTLING WORKS									
2	FIVE-YEAR PROJECTION OF ESTIMATED CASH FLOWS FOR PROJECT "A"									
3							Cost of		NPV	Payback
4	Item	1990	1991	1992	1993	1994	Capital	IRR	($million)	(Months)
5										
6	Investment ($million)	1.500					12.0%	15.2%	0.128	38
7										
8	Sales, in $million	1.500	1.750	1.850	2.000	2.100				
9	Costs, in $million									
10	Production	0.750	0.875	0.925	1.000	1.050				
11	Sales	0.300	0.350	0.370	0.400	0.420				
12	Administration	0.075	0.088	0.093	0.100	0.105				
13										
14	Net cash flow	0.375	0.437	0.462	0.500	0.525				

Evaluating Investment Proposals

Management rarely is able to predict the precise liquidation or resale value of an investment at the time it is made. It follows, then, that in the typical case the *true rate of return on an investment cannot be known until the ownership of the investment has terminated*. Hence, prior to actual termination of ownership, it is necessary to accept the best *estimated* return as a reasonable measure of the investment's profitability. Several methods are available for measuring the estimated return from an investment. Three methods can be categorized as discounted cash flow (*DCF*) methods, and there are two other methods in common use, as we shall discuss shortly.

Discounted-Cash-Flow (DCF) Methods

Three methods of investment evaluation are based upon the present value of discounted cash flows: (1) the internal rate of return (*IRR*), (2) the net present value (*NPV*), and (3) the benefit/cost ratio, which may be expressed as a profitability index (*PI*).

Internal Rate of Return (*IRR*).   Most people think of the rate of return on investment as simply the ratio of annual receipts to original cost. Actually, this definition is correct for one special kind of investment, but for no other. The rate of return from a permanent, nondepreciating, nonappreciating asset producing a periodically uniform stream of income can be measured by the ratio of annual receipts to original cost. Even so, to the extent that the liquidating value or resale value of the asset at the time of liquidation or sale is greater or less than the original outlay, the true rate of return will be greater or less than the rate defined by this ratio.

What, then, is the technically correct meaning of **internal rate of return**? A precise definition is as follows:

> **Definition:**   The *internal rate of return* on an investment is the interest rate that equates the present value of the net cash flows from the investment with the present value of the cash expenditures relating to the investment. **Net cash flow** means cash receipts minus cash expenditures in any given period. That is to say, the internal rate of return on an investment is the discount rate at which an investment is exactly repaid by its discounted net receipts.[6]

---

[6] The rate of return on investment is a well-conceived theoretical concept that goes by various aliases in the economic literature. Among the more important of these are *marginal efficiency of capital*, a phrase made famous by John Maynard Keynes, and the closely related concept of *internal rate of return* used here. But while it is a concept well founded in theory, it presents many practical problems to anyone desiring to apply it to actual cases. This is because the solution for the internal rate of return, r, depends on both the amounts and the timing of the cash flows, both of which are estimates. Hence, insistence on a precise solution for r would be unrealistic, since the value of r can never be more than an estimate. It is worth repeating at this point that *the rate of return on an investment can never be stated with precision until the ownership of the investment has been terminated.*

The basic equation for calculation of the internal rate of return is

$$C_0 = \frac{R_1 - C_1}{1 + r} + \frac{R_2 - C_2}{(1 + r)^2} + \ldots + \frac{R_n - C_n}{(1 + r)^n} + \frac{S}{(1 + r)^n} \qquad \text{(6)}$$

where

C_0 = The initial cost of the investment
R_t = Cash receipts during time period t ($t = 0, 1, 2, \ldots, n$)
C_t = Cash expenditures during time period t
S = The liquidation value of the investment in the form of salvage value and/or recovery of working capital
r = The internal rate of return, which is the discount rate at which the discounted stream of future net receipts equals the initial cost of the investment.

If the *IRR* is greater than the firm's cost of capital, the proposed investment is acceptable. If the *IRR* is less than the cost of capital, the proposed investment is a loser that should not be undertaken. If the *IRR* is equal to the cost of capital, the investment is technically acceptable, but the firm has nothing to gain by making it.

The internal rate of return, r, is the unknown value in Equation 6. Solving for r requires a trial-and-error procedure similar to the one described previously under the heading "Cost of Debt." It is best performed by a computer, but there is a procedure that can be performed with a hand calculator, as shown in the following illustrative problem.

Illustrative Problem

The Acme Machine Works is contemplating the purchase of a new machine at a cost of $44,000. The new machine will produce an item that rounds out the firm's line of goods and is expected to increase sales by $12,000 per year. An additional $6,000 in working capital will be required to finance the added inventory and accounts receivable that will result from the estimated increase in sales. The economic life of the machine is expected to be seven years, at which time the scrap or resale value is predicted to be about $9,000. The firm pays 34 percent income tax, and has a cost of capital of 12 percent.

Question

Assuming straight-line depreciation and a forecasted cash inflow of $12,000 a year, calculate the internal rate of return on this investment. Should the investment be undertaken?

Solution

We begin by listing the essential factors to be considered:

1. Cost of asset	$44,000
2. Working capital needed	$6,000
3. Total investment: (1) + (2)	$50,000
4. Economic life	7 years
5. Scrap or resale value at the end of 7 years	$9,000

6. Allowed depreciation: (1) − (5) $35,000
7. Annual depreciation: (6) ÷ (4) $5,000
8. Capital recovery at the end of 7 years: (2) + (5) $15,000
9. Net annual cash inflow, before income tax $12,000
10. Annual taxable income: (9) − (7) $7,000
11. Annual income tax: (10) × 0.34 $2,380
12. Net annual cash inflow after tax: (9) − (11) $9,620

Notice that depreciation is not a cash-flow item. It is used only to calculate the income tax, which is a cash outflow. The preceding list shows that we have a uniform series of cash inflows of $9,620 per year for seven years. At the end of the seventh year, we recover $6,000 in working capital plus salvage of $9,000, for a total capital recovery of $15,000.

The first step is to calculate the discounted cash flow with r set at the firm's cost of capital, 12 percent:

$$DCF = \$9,620 \left[\frac{1 - (1.12)^{-7}}{0.12} \right] + \frac{\$15,000}{(1.12)^7} = \$50,688.58.$$

This *DCF* is slightly larger than the initial investment of $50,000. Therefore the discount rate is too low. This means that the *IRR* is more than the cost of capital, making the project acceptable. This judgment may be confirmed by calculating the *IRR*. First, we repeatedly calculate the *DCF* with successively higher discount rates, until the *DCF* is smaller than the initial investment.

Discount Rate	DCF	Initial Investment
0.120	$50,688	$50,000
0.121	$50,507	$50,000
0.122	$50,327	$50,000
0.123	$50,148	$50,000
0.124	$49,970	$50,000

Now we know that the *IRR* lies between 12.3 and 12.4 percent, which is slightly more than the firm's required return on investment.

Net Present Value (*NPV*). If we let k equal the firm's cost of capital and use it to discount the cash flows, we then have

$$NPV = -C_0 + \frac{R_1 - C_1}{1 + k} + \frac{R_2 - C_2}{(1 + k)^2} + \cdots + \frac{R_n - C_n}{(1 + k)^n} + \frac{S}{(1 + k)^n} \tag{7}$$

where

> NPV = The net present value of all cash flows (in or out) resulting from an investment
> R_t = Cash returns (inflow) in time period t ($t = 0, 1, 2, \ldots, n$)
> C_t = Cash expenditures (outflow) in time period t (C_0 = initial investment)
> k = Cost of capital.

Note that Equation 7 is the same as Equation 6 except that the discount rate is the cost of capital and the initial investment is subtracted from the present value of the discounted cash flow to get the net present value.

The decision criterion for the *NPV* approach is to accept proposals with a positive *NPV* and reject proposals with a negative *NPV*. If the *NPV* = 0, the proposal is technically acceptable, but the firm has nothing to gain by investing.

Illustrative Problem

A firm with a cost of capital of 12 percent is contemplating the purchase of a new machine for $44,000. An additional $6,000 in working capital will be required to finance the added accounts receivable and inventory that will result from the estimated increase in sales generated by use of the new machine.

The economic life of the machine is expected to be seven years, during which it is expected to produce a net cash inflow of $12,000 per year. At the end of seven years its scrap or resale value is predicted to be about $9,000.

Depreciation will be taken under the Modified Accelerated Cost Recovery System (MACRS) prescribed by the Internal Revenue Service (IRS).[7] The new machine will be classed as five-year property, for which the prescribed rates of depreciation are 15 percent of original cost for the first year, 22 percent for the second year, and 21 percent per year for the next three years, at which time the original cost will be fully recovered.

Question

Evaluate this investment, using both rate of return and net present value.

Solution

We begin by setting up a table to determine the net after-tax cash flow from the seven-year life of the machine, as shown in Exhibit 18–6. This exhibit shows that the firm will recover $9,000 in salvage at the end of seven years. This is taxable income, since the machine will be fully depreciated at the end of the fifth year. The firm also recovers the working capital of $6,000, which was part of the original investment of $50,000 ($44,000 for the machine and $6,000 for working capital). Recovery of capital is not taxable.

NPV. The net present value of this investment is computed as follows:

$$NPV = -50,000 + \frac{10,164}{1.12} + \frac{11,211}{(1.12)^2} + \frac{11,062}{(1.12)^3} + \frac{11,062}{(1.12)^4} + \frac{11,062}{(1.12)^5}$$

$$+ \frac{7,920}{(1.12)^6} + \frac{7,920}{(1.12)^7} + \frac{5,940}{(1.12)^7} + \frac{6,000}{(1.12)^7} = \$2,189.$$

The net present value is positive. Therefore the investment is acceptable.

---

[7] See IRS Publication 534 for approved methods of depreciation.

EXHIBIT 18–6 **Calculation of Net Cash Flow**

(1) Year	(2) Operating Profit and Capital Recovery	(3) Depreciation 5-Year ACRS	(4) Taxable Income (2)−(3)	(5) Taxes: 34% of (4)	(6) Net Cash Flow (2)−(5)
1	12,000	6,600	5,400	1,836	10,164
2	12,000	9,680	2,320	789	11,211
3	12,000	9,240	2,760	938	11,062
4	12,000	9,240	2,760	938	11,062
5	12,000	9,240	2,760	938	11,062
6	12,000	0	12,000	4,080	7,920
7	12,000	0	12,000	4,080	7,920
7	9,000	0	9,000	3,060	5,940
7	6,000	0	0	0	6,000

IRR. A computer program calculates the internal rate of return to be 13.3 percent. Since this is more than the firm's cost of capital, the investment is acceptable.

Benefit/Cost Ratio or Profitability Index. Another approach to evaluating projects is to calculate their **benefit/cost ratios**. A project's benefit/cost ratio (*B/C*) is just the present value of the net cash flows per dollar of investment, expressed as a decimal number. When this ratio is expressed as a percentage, it is called the **profitability index** (*PI*).

Ranking of Capital-Investment Projects

Capital-budgeting theory holds that the firm should raise the necessary capital for all nonconflicting proposals that promise to increase the value of the stockholders' shares. In the real world, however, there are many reasons why the firm cannot or should not raise enough capital for all of the investment opportunities that it faces. Hence the decision maker may be confronted not only with conflicting or mutually exclusive proposals (e.g., either buy new machines or renovate the machine shop) but also with the necessity for capital rationing. In either case, the decision maker's problem is to rank investment proposals in such a way that the available capital may be fully invested in the most profitable combination.

The critical factor in ranking investments is the measurement of the expected return. We have defined three methods of measuring the return: the internal rate of return, the net present value, and the benefit/cost ratio or profitability index. Although all three methods rest upon the discounted cash flow for each proposal, the ranking of multiple investment proposals by each of the three methods may be quite different, as explained next.

EXHIBIT 18–7   **Cash Flows for Two Mutually Exclusive Proposals**

	Cash Flow	
Year	*Project A*	*Project B*
0	$(22,856)	$(22,856)
1	8,500	0
2	8,500	5,000
3	8,500	10,000
4	8,500	15,000
5	8,500	19,516
Total cash inflow	$42,500	$49,516
Less initial investment	22,856	22,856
Net cash inflow	$19,644	$26,660
Net present value @ 15% discount rate	$5,637	$5,779
Internal rate of return	25.0%	22.0%

Ranking by *NPV* and by *IRR*: Inherent Conflict.   The preceding illustrative problem demonstrated that in the evaluation of a single project, the *IRR* and the *NPV* indicate the same evaluation—the proposal is either acceptable or unacceptable. Without further analysis, one might think that if alternative investment proposals are ranked in order of their *IRR*s and in order of their *NPV*s, the ranking would be the same. This is *not* the case, however, because the implicit assumption about the reinvestment of cash flows is different between the two methods.

The net-present-value method assumes that cash inflows are reinvested at a rate equal to the cost of capital (or whatever discount rate is chosen as the cutoff criterion), and *all* projects are evaluated against this *same* assumed rate of reinvestment.

In contrast, the internal-rate-of-return method assumes that the cash inflows from each separate project are reinvested at the internal rate of return for that separate project. This means that *different* projects with *different* IRRs have *different* assumed rates of reinvestment. This can lead to conflicting conclusions, as illustrated by Exhibit 18–7.

In Exhibit 18–7, we have two mutually exclusive proposals to be ranked in order of desirability. Both proposals have the same initial cost, but the magnitude and timing of the cash flows are quite different. Since they are mutually exclusive, only one can be selected.

If we evaluate by the net-present-value method, all cash flows in both projects are discounted by the same 15 percent cost of capital, and the implicit assumption is that all cash flows can be reinvested to yield 15 percent. This seems to be an even-handed basis for judgment; if so, Project B clearly is superior since it has a larger net present value.

If we evaluate by the internal-rate-of-return method, we see that Project A has an internal rate of return of 25 percent, compared with only 22 percent for Project B. This is because we have made the implicit assumption that the cash flows from Project A will be reinvested at 25 percent, while the cash flows from Project B can be reinvested at only 22 percent. There seems to be no logical reason why the $8,500 received from Project A in year 2 would bring 25 percent in another investment while the $5,000 received

EXHIBIT 18–8   Profitability Index versus Net Present Value: Ranking by Profitability Index

Project	Funds Required	Present Value of Discounted Returns	Benefit/Cost Ratio and Profitability Index
A. Buy new machine	$100,000	$127,000	1.27 = 127%
B. Expand advertising	100,000	122,000	1.22 = 122%
C. Expand plant	1,500,000	1,785,000	1.19 = 119%
D. Renovate existing plant	800,000	920,000	1.15 = 115%
E. Replace truck fleet	900,000	918,000	1.02 = 102%

from Project B in the same year would yield only 22 percent when reinvested. We must conclude, then, that ranking by rate of return is erroneous in this case.

Ranking by Benefit/Cost Ratio or Profitability Index.   When a project's benefit/cost ratio is expressed as a percentage, it is called the *profitability index*. Either the benefit/cost ratio or the profitability index provides a convenient method for screening proposals and for ranking investments that require identical cash outlays. For investments of differing magnitude, however, ranking by a profitability index should be used with caution, as illustrated by Exhibit 18–8. In the exhibit, these projects clearly are ranked correctly if the investor's primary criterion is to receive the maximum return from each dollar invested. If the investor's goal, however, is to maximize the total return from the available capital, the ranking would be as shown in Exhibit 18–9 (page 612). These exhibits show that Project C will yield more than 10 times as much as Project A, even though its profitability is 8 percent less.

Which ranking method should we choose? If the firm has substantial resources and is intent upon maximizing its owners' wealth, ranking by the *NPV* appraisal will indicate the projects with the highest profit-maximizing potential. If the firm's resources are more constrained, it might be a better policy to invest each available dollar where it will get the highest return, as indicated by the *PI* ranking.

Other Methods of Investment Evaluation

In addition to the three methods just discussed, there are at least two short-cut devices or rule-of-thumb techniques that can be used to evaluate and rank capital-investment proposals: the **average rate of return** and the **payback period**. Neither of these, it should be emphasized, yields the correct answer that is obtained by the discounted-cash-flow procedures, but they do provide rough approximations.

Average Rate of Return.   The average rate of return from an investment may be calculated in two different ways. One way is to add up the expected profits per time period and then divide the total by the number of periods to get an average profit per time period. This figure is then divided by the initial investment to get the average rate of return. In symbols,

EXHIBIT 18–9   Profitability Index versus Net Present Value: Ranking by Net Present Value

Project	Funds Required	Present Value of Discounted Returns	Benefit/Cost Ratio and Profitability Index
C. Expand plant	$1,500,000	$1,785,000	1.19 = 119%
D. Renovate existing plant	800,000	920,000	1.15 = 115%
E. Replace truck fleet	900,000	918,000	1.02 = 102%
A. Buy new machine	100,000	127,000	1.27 = 127%
B. Expand advertising	100,000	122,000	1.22 = 122%

$$r_{avg} = \frac{\pi/n}{C_0}. \qquad (8)$$

Some analysts prefer to use the net cash flow for each period rather than profits. (The difference between profit and net cash flow is depreciation, which is charged as an expense in profit calculations, but is not a cash outflow item.) This is a better approach because it considers the amount of cash actually available for the firm's use. Even so, it is inferior to *DCF* methods because it ignores the time value of money.

Payback Period.   The **payback period**, also called the **payout or payoff period**, is the length of time required for the net cash inflows from a given investment to equal its original cost (cash outflow). It may be calculated either before tax or after tax, the latter being more important.

To simplify the use of this tool, it is typical to estimate a uniform annual cash inflow over the life of the project. Hence, if the original investment is represented by C_0 and the uniform (average) annual cash flow is represented by R, the payback period, P, is expressed as

$$P = \frac{C_0}{R}. \qquad (9)$$

Equation 9 represents the before-tax payback. The relationship between the before-tax and after-tax payback depends on both the tax rate and the productive life of the product.[8] Representing depreciation by D and assuming a 34 percent tax rate, the payback after tax (*PAT*) becomes[9]

$$PAT = \frac{C_0}{0.66(R + D)} = \frac{1.5C_0}{R + D}. \qquad (10)$$

---

[8] Discussion of an after-tax payback seems meaningful only for projects that are actually profitable, that is, their productive life is greater than the before-tax payback period.

[9] For extremely long lived projects such as hydroelectric plants and dams, the depreciation charge approaches zero and the after-tax payback approaches 1.5 times the value of the before-tax payback. Hence, with a 34 percent tax rate, the after-tax payback will, for all depreciable investments, lie somewhere between the before-tax payback at the lower limit and 1.5 times that value at the upper limit.

Under the conditions previously stated, it is clear that: (1) given the life of the project, profitability will vary inversely with the payback period and (2) given the payback period, profitability will vary directly with the life of the project. It is easy enough, therefore, to understand the insistence of management on short-payback investments. However, the tool is often too blunt to be used in selecting among alternative projects that differ in terms of cost, payback, and productive life. In such cases, a more precise analysis is needed.

It is worth pointing out, at the risk of being obvious, that a short payback is not necessarily coincident with high profitability. For example, if the productive life of the project is even shorter than the payback period, the return on the investment will be negative. If the project life and payback period are equal, the investment return is zero. In either case, an economic loss is incurred.

Another weakness of the payback method is that it ignores all cash returns after recovery of the initial investment, although these after-payback returns could differ greatly between two projects with the same payback period.

An argument is sometimes offered that the payback method deals with project risk, albeit in an indirect manner. This argument is based on the notion that for most projects, risk is perceived as increasing over time, which means that cash flows received in more distant years are thought to be riskier than those received in current years. Thus, ranking projects on the basis of their payback periods also ranks them according to their relative riskiness. However, this is not a direct measurement of risk since it fails to consider the dispersion or variation of cash flows for any given year. In other words, a project may pay for itself in a few years if the estimated cash flows for those years are actually received; but if there is a high probability that the cash flows will not be received, then the project must still be considered risky despite its short payback period.

Current Practice by Major U.S. Firms.   In a study of capital-budgeting practices, Gitman and Forrester[10] selected 268 firms for investigation. They used two criteria as a basis for selection: (1) the selected companies were among the 600 firms that experienced the greatest growth in stock price in the period 1971–1976 and (2) the firms also made the largest capital expenditures in the year 1969. Questionnaires were sent to these 268 firms and 112 responded by indicating which of the five capital-budgeting methods discussed previously were used as primary and secondary techniques. Although the study was undertaken more than a decade ago, there is no reason to believe that the companies' choices of techniques have changed greatly since then. The results of the study are tabulated in Exhibit 18–10 (page 614).

This exhibit brings out several interesting points:

1. Although the *NPV* is both technically superior and easier to calculate than the *IRR*, only 9.8 percent of the firms said they used *NPV* as their primary method, while 53.6 percent used *IRR*.

---

[10] Gitman, J. L., and J. R. Forrester, "A Survey of Capital Budgeting Techniques Used by Major U.S. Firms," *Financial Management* (Fall 1977), pp. 66–71.

EXHIBIT 18–10 **Capital-Budgeting Techniques Used by 112 U.S. Corporations, by Percentage of Respondents**

Technique	Primary	Secondary
Net present value	9.8%	25.8%
Internal rate of return	53.6	14.0
Profitability index	2.7	2.2
Average rate of return	25.0	14.0
Payback period	8.9	44.0

2. Approximately two thirds of the respondents used one of the *DCF* methods as their primary method, while one third used the less accurate average rate of return or payback period.

3. All of the firms used both a primary and secondary method of evaluation, and 44 percent used the payback period as their secondary evaluation method. This seems to indicate that the payback method was being used as a constraint to be satisfied rather than as a benefit criterion to be maximized.

Summary

Capital budgeting is concerned with the evaluation of investment proposals to determine whether or not they should be undertaken. After identifying possible investment proposals, the firm must perform four basic tasks: (1) estimate cash flows, (2) estimate the cost of capital, (3) evaluate each investment proposal, and (4) rank the investment proposals from the most profitable to the least profitable.

Cash flows should be estimated on an incremental after-tax basis. A spreadsheet is the most efficient way to estimate the after-tax cash flows, particularly if calculation is done on a computer.

A firm's cost of capital is an essential criterion for investment decision making. The cost of capital must be known before investment selection can be undertaken, since otherwise it would be impossible to determine a cut-off point with respect to all the investment alternatives available to the firm. The cost of capital tells us which investments should be undertaken and which should be rejected.

The firm's sources of capital are presumed to be: (1) the capital markets, which include many different types of financial intermediaries, and (2) earnings of the firm accumulated from previous time periods. Each specific source of capital has its own cost, which becomes a component of the overall cost of capital to the firm. The overall cost of capital should be the weighted average of all forms of financing that the firm currently uses, based on current or projected market costs of debt and equity.

Obviously, the greater the proportion of total assets that are financed by debt instead of equity, the greater the potential economic loss to the owners in case of a decline in earnings. On the other hand, if the firm can earn more on its total assets than the interest rate it pays on its debt, the owners will benefit by receiving higher earnings. This is known in business finance as "trading on the equity" or by the preferred term *leverage*.

This leads to the notion that an "optimal" or "best" financial structure exists for each firm, or at least there is a range within which the debt/equity ratio is approximately ideal.

Five methods for evaluating and ranking investment proposals are commonly used by U.S. corporations: (1) internal rate of return, (2) net present value, (3) benefit/cost ratio and/or profitability index, (4) average rate of return, and (5) payback period. The first three of these methods are based upon discounted cash flows. The last two do not consider the time value of money.

The five methods do not necessarily reach the same conclusions about the evaluation and ranking of investment proposals. The internal-rate-of-return approach assumes that cash flows from each individual project are reinvested at the internal rate of return for that project. Thus the returns from different projects are reinvested at different rates of return. The net-present-value approach discounts all cash flows by the firm's cost of capital and assumes reinvestment at the firm's cost of capital. Thus the returns from all projects are reinvested at the same rate of return. This difference in assumptions about reinvestment may cause projects to be ranked differently under *IRR* than under *NPV*. The conclusion is that net present value provides a more theoretically sound ranking than internal rate of return.

The benefit/cost ratio or profitability index ranks investment proposals according to the ratio of the present value of discounted returns to the initial investment. When the investment proposals involve widely differing initial investments, the profitability index may rank small investments ahead of much more profitable proposals.

The average rate of return from an investment may be calculated from estimates of either profits or net cash flows. (The difference between profit and net cash flow is depreciation, which is charged as an expense in profit calculations, but is not a cash outflow item.) Expected profits or net cash flows per time period are added up. Next the total is divided by the number of periods to get an average profit per time period. This figure is then divided by the initial investment to get the average rate of return. Using the net cash flow for each period rather than profit is the better approach because it considers the amount of cash actually available for the firm's use. Even so, it is inferior to *DCF* methods because it ignores the time value of money.

The payback period, also called the payout or payoff period, is the length of time required for the net cash inflows from a given investment to equal its original cost (cash outflow). It may be calculated either before tax or after tax, the latter being more important.

The relationship between the before-tax and after-tax payback depends on both the tax rate and the productive life of the product. A short payback is not necessarily coincident with high profitability. Another weakness of the payback method is that it ignores all cash returns after the payback period.

A study of the capital-budgeting practices of 112 U.S. firms brought out several interesting points:

1. Although the *NPV* is both technically superior and easier to calculate than the *IRR*, only 9.8 percent of the respondent companies said they used *NPV* as their primary method, while 53.6 percent used *IRR*.
2. Approximately two thirds of the respondents used one of the discounted-cash-flow methods as their primary method, while one third used the less accurate average-rate-of-return or payback-period method.

3. All of the firms used both a primary and secondary method of evaluation, and 44 percent used the payback period as their secondary evaluation method. This seems to indicate that the payback method was being used as a constraint to be satisfied rather than as a benefit criterion to be maximized.

Problems

1. A firm estimates that it can raise $5 million of capital at a cost of 10 percent, $4 million more at a cost of 12 percent, $3 million more at a cost of 14 percent, $2 million more at a cost of 16 percent, and $1 million more at a cost of 18 percent. The total amount raised would be sufficient for five investment proposals, as shown in the accompanying table.

Capital Projects	Required Investment ($ millions)	Rate of Return
A	3.0	20%
B	4.0	18%
C	5.0	14%
D	2.0	11%
E	1.0	10%

a. Draw a diagram of the information just given with respect to the firm's marginal cost of capital and the return on investment proposals. Which proposals are acceptable? (*Hint:* Let the horizontal axis represent the required investment and the vertical axis represent the cost of capital and rate of return.)

b. Redraw the diagram, adding smooth curves representing the demand for capital and the marginal cost of capital (*MCC*). What assumptions are reflected in the smooth curves?

c. If the firm is faced with these smooth curves, how much will it invest and what will be the cost of and return on the last dollar invested?

2. Under what conditions might a firm be better off to select a project with a rapid payback than one with the highest rate of return?

3. Explain the fundamental difference between the net-present-value and internal-rate-of-return methods of investment analysis.

4. Three investments—A, B, and C—are compared in the accompanying diagram. Answer the following questions related to the diagram.

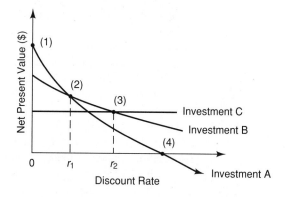

a. Is one investment preferable to the other two at all discount rates? Explain.

b. Provide a brief interpretation of points (1), (2), (3), and (4).

c. Describe the cash-flow pattern for Investment C.

5. a. In the capital structure of most firms, debt financing costs less than equity financing. Explain why this is so.

b. If debt financing costs less than equity financing in a firm's capital structure, why doesn't the firm use debt financing alone?

6. a. Carefully explain the concept of cash flow, contrasting it with net income.

b. Determine the annual cash flows for the following investment, which is expected to have a four-year life:

1. Initial cost: $400,000, fully depreciable for tax purposes (straight-line method, no salvage value, and a tax rate of 34 percent)

2. Annual net income after depreciation but before taxes: $150,000.

c. If the required rate of return on an investment of this type is 20 percent, should the investment be made? Support your answer with suitable computations.

7. A wealthy uncle intends to give you a gift upon graduation. You have a choice of a new car for $15,000 or an investment trust of the same amount invested in securities that will earn 8 percent interest compounded annually for the next 40 years. Since you are now 22 years old and plan to retire at age 62, the trust would fit rather nicely into your plans. On the other hand, you are going to need transportation, and it would be nice to own a new car.

a. How much will you have in the trust in 40 years?

b. If you expect inflation to average 5 percent a year over the next 40 years, what will be the purchasing power of the fund's terminal value in today's dollars?

c. Which will you choose: the trust or a new car? Why?

8. The XYZ Company is considering two mutually exclusive projects, each requiring an initial investment of $15,000 and each lasting for five years. The estimated cash inflows are given in the accompanying table.

Project	Year 1	2	3	4	5
A	5,000	5,000	5,000	5,000	5,000
B	—	5,000	12,000	8,000	5,000

The firm's cost of capital is 20 percent. For each proposal, find

a. The net present value

b. The internal rate of return

c. The profitability index.

9. The London Shipping Company is considering investing $28,000 in new conveying equipment. It is estimated that the new equipment will result in direct labor savings of $11,000 annually over the 10-year life of the equipment. An additional $10,000 in working capital will be required, which will be entirely recovered at the end of the 10-year period. If the company requires a 20 percent minimum return on investment, should it go ahead with this project? (Disregard tax and depreciation considerations and assume a zero salvage value.)

Case Problem: The Jason Company

10. The Jason Company is considering replacing one of its old machines with a new and more efficient one. The old machine is still in good working condition and will last for at least 20 more years. The new machine, delivered and installed, costs $10,000 and is expected to save $1,900 annually in direct costs as compared with the old machine. The new machine has a 10-year economic life, with zero salvage value.

The Jason Company can borrow money at 10 percent, but it does not expect to negotiate a loan for this particular purpose. The management of the company requires a return of at least 20 percent before taxes on this type of investment. Disregard all taxes for the time being.

Questions

a. Assuming that the old machine has a zero book value and a zero salvage value, should the company buy the new machine?

b. Suppose the present machine, now four years old, originally cost $8,000 and has been depreciating at a straight-line rate of 10 percent annually. Its present book value, therefore, is equal to original cost less accumulated depreciation, or $8,000 − $3,200 = $4,800. Its salvage value, however, is zero. Should the Jason Company buy the new machine?

c. Suppose, in part (b), that the salvage value is currently $3,000 but will decline to zero if the machine is held for another 10 years. Should the company purchase the new machine?

d. What if the annual savings were cut in half and the economic life were doubled? In other words, if the annual savings were $950 for 20 years, should the company purchase the new machine? (Assume everything else is the same as in part (a).)

Year	Main-tenance	Harvest-ing	Depre-ciation	Over-head	Total Cost/Acre	Sales	Profit or (Loss)/Acre
1	$269	$ 0	$ 80	$146	$ 495	$ 0	$(495)
2	195	0	80	146	421	0	(421)
3	266	0	80	146	492	0	(492)
4	244	0	80	146	470	0	(470)
5	412	0	80	146	638	0	(638)
6	338	419	110	159	1,026	669	(357)
7	368	673	110	159	1,310	1,560	250
8	389	900	110	159	1,558	2,234	676
9	409	1,019	110	159	1,697	2,674	977
10	429	1,127	110	159	1,825	3,120	1,295
11	429	1,151	110	159	1,849	3,343	1,494

e. Assume now that the Jason Company must pay a 34 percent tax, that it uses straight-line depreciation, and that the company's cost of capital is 10 percent after taxes. If the facts are the same as for part (a), should the company buy the new machine?

Case Problem: Hamakua Plantation

11. Hamakua Plantation is an agricultural corporation formed to pursue diversified agriculture on former sugar-cane lands on the Big Island of Hawaii. One of its holdings is a 10-acre plot planted in papayas. Because of numerous problems with plant disease, the high cost of labor required for harvesting and packing the fruit, and difficulties with transportation of the fruit to market, the firm has been clearing no more than $100 per acre per year on papayas. This has caused management to seek an alternate use for the land. One suggestion has been made to plant the 10 acres in macadamia nuts, for which there is a growing market, with supply unable to keep up with demand. However, it takes 6 years from planting to the first crop, and 11 years to reach full production.

Working with experts from the College of Tropical Agriculture at the University of Hawaii, Hamakua's controller has assembled the following estimate of costs and revenues over the first 11 years after planting:[11]

Initial investment:

Equipment and buildings	$7,000
Establishing the planting (10 acres)	1,250
	$8,250

Annual costs may be classified as:

1. Orchard maintenance, which includes weed control, fertilizing, pruning, inarching, rat control, and raking and burning leaves

2. Harvesting, which includes gathering, husking, drying, and sorting the nuts

3. Depreciation of buildings and equipment

4. Overhead, which includes land rent, taxes, indirect labor, and interest on investment.

Annual costs per acre are projected in the table above.

The company's cost of capital is 15 percent, and income taxes are 34 percent.

Problem

Prepare a suitable analysis to determine whether the company should continue growing papayas on the 10 acres in question, or whether the firm would be better off in the long run to switch to macadamia nuts.

---

[11] Based on J. T. Keeler and E. T. Fukunaga, *The Economic and Horticultural Aspects of Growing Macadamia Nuts Commercially in Hawaii* (Agricultural Bulletin No. 27, Hawaii Agricultural Experiment Station, University of Hawaii, June 1968).

References

Bierman, Harold, Jr., and Seymour Smidt. *The Capital Budgeting Decision.* 4th ed. New York: Macmillan, 1984.

Durand, David. "Comprehensiveness in Capital Budgeting." *Financial Management* (Winter 1981), pp. 7–13.

Gitman, L. J., and J. R. Forrester. "A Survey of Capital Budgeting Techniques Used by Major U.S. Firms." *Financial Management* (Fall 1977), pp. 66–71.

Kim, S. H., and E. J. Farragher. "Current Capital Budgeting Practices." *Management Accounting* (June 1981), pp. 26–30.

Landskroner, Y. "Optimal Production and Portfolio Investment Decision." *Managerial and Decision Economics* 9, no. 3 (September 1988), p. 221.

Marsh, P. "The Choice between Equity and Debt: An Empirical Study." *Journal of Finance* (March 1982), pp. 121–42.

Schall, Lawrence D.; Gary L. Sundem; and William R. Geijsbeek, Jr. "Survey and Analysis of Capital Budgeting Methods." *Journal of Finance* (March 1978), pp. 281–87.

A P P E N D I X

DISCOUNT
TABLES AND
CHARTS;
COMMON
LOGARITHMS;
STATISTICAL
TABLES;
DERIVATIVE
FORMULAS

TABLE A   Present Value of a Uniform Series: PVUS

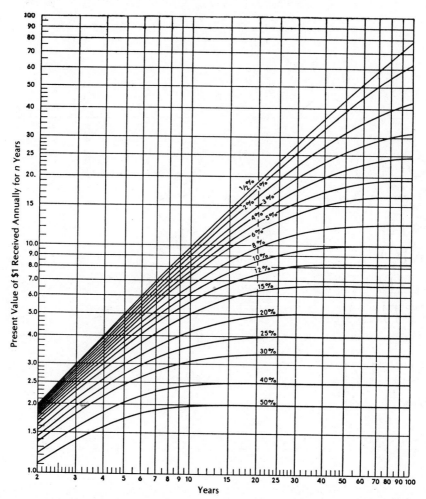

Source: Adapted from Norman Barish, *Economic Analysis for Engineering and Management Decision Making* (New York: McGraw-Hill, 1962).

TABLE A (concluded)   Present Value of $1 Received Annually for N Years

$$PV = \left[\frac{1 - (1 + k)^{-N}}{k}\right]$$

Years (N)	1%	2%	4%	6%	8%	10%	12%	14%	15%	16%	18%	20%	22%	24%	25%	26%	28%	30%	35%	40%	45%	50%
1	0.990	0.980	0.962	0.943	0.926	0.909	0.893	0.877	0.870	0.862	0.847	0.833	0.820	0.806	0.800	0.794	0.781	0.769	0.741	0.714	0.690	0.667
2	1.970	1.942	1.886	1.833	1.783	1.736	1.690	1.647	1.626	1.605	1.566	1.528	1.492	1.457	1.440	1.424	1.392	1.361	1.289	1.224	1.165	1.111
3	2.941	2.884	2.775	2.673	2.577	2.487	2.402	2.322	2.283	2.246	2.174	2.106	2.042	1.981	1.952	1.923	1.868	1.816	1.696	1.589	1.493	1.407
4	3.902	3.808	3.630	3.465	3.312	3.170	3.037	2.914	2.855	2.798	2.690	2.589	2.494	2.404	2.362	2.320	2.241	2.166	1.997	1.849	1.720	1.605
5	4.853	4.713	4.452	4.212	3.993	3.791	3.605	3.433	3.352	3.274	3.127	2.991	2.864	2.745	2.689	2.635	2.532	2.436	2.220	2.035	1.876	1.737
6	5.795	5.601	5.242	4.917	4.623	4.355	4.111	3.889	3.784	3.685	3.498	3.326	3.167	3.020	2.951	2.885	2.759	2.643	2.385	2.168	1.983	1.824
7	6.728	6.472	6.002	5.582	5.206	4.868	4.564	4.288	4.160	4.039	3.812	3.605	3.416	3.242	3.161	3.083	2.937	2.802	2.508	2.263	2.057	1.883
8	7.652	7.325	6.733	6.210	5.747	5.335	4.968	4.639	4.487	4.344	4.078	3.837	3.619	3.421	3.329	3.241	3.076	2.925	2.598	2.331	2.108	1.922
9	8.566	8.162	7.435	6.802	6.247	5.759	5.328	4.946	4.772	4.607	4.303	4.031	3.786	3.566	3.463	3.366	3.184	3.019	2.665	2.379	2.144	1.948
10	9.471	8.983	8.111	7.360	6.710	6.145	5.650	5.216	5.019	4.833	4.494	4.192	3.923	3.682	3.571	3.465	3.269	3.092	2.715	2.414	2.168	1.965
11	10.368	9.787	8.760	7.887	7.139	6.495	5.988	5.453	5.234	5.029	4.656	4.327	4.035	3.776	3.656	3.544	3.335	3.147	2.752	2.438	2.185	1.977
12	11.255	10.575	9.385	8.384	7.536	6.814	6.194	5.660	5.421	5.197	4.793	4.439	4.127	3.851	3.725	3.606	3.387	3.190	2.779	2.456	2.196	1.985
13	12.134	11.343	9.986	8.853	7.904	7.103	6.424	5.842	5.583	5.342	4.910	4.533	4.203	3.912	3.780	3.656	3.427	3.223	2.799	2.468	2.204	1.990
14	13.004	12.106	10.563	9.295	8.244	7.367	6.628	6.002	5.724	5.468	5.008	4.611	4.265	3.962	3.824	3.695	3.459	3.249	2.814	2.477	2.210	1.993
15	13.865	12.849	11.118	9.712	8.559	7.606	6.811	6.142	5.847	5.575	5.092	4.675	4.315	4.001	3.859	3.726	3.483	3.268	2.825	2.484	2.214	1.995
16	14.718	13.578	11.652	10.106	8.851	7.824	6.974	6.265	5.954	5.669	5.162	4.730	4.357	4.033	3.887	3.751	3.503	3.283	2.834	2.489	2.216	1.997
17	15.562	14.292	12.166	10.477	9.122	8.022	7.120	6.373	6.047	5.749	5.222	4.775	4.391	4.059	3.910	3.771	3.518	3.295	2.840	2.492	2.218	1.998
18	16.398	14.992	12.659	10.828	9.372	8.201	7.250	6.467	6.128	5.818	5.273	4.812	4.419	4.080	3.928	3.786	3.529	3.304	2.844	2.494	2.219	1.999
19	17.226	15.678	13.134	11.158	9.604	8.365	7.366	6.550	6.198	5.877	5.316	4.844	4.442	4.097	3.942	3.799	3.539	3.311	2.848	2.496	2.220	1.999
20	18.046	16.351	13.590	11.470	9.818	8.514	7.469	6.623	6.259	5.929	5.353	4.870	4.460	4.110	3.954	3.808	3.546	3.316	2.850	2.497	2.221	1.999
21	18.857	17.011	14.029	11.764	10.017	8.649	7.562	6.687	6.312	5.973	5.384	4.891	4.476	4.121	3.963	3.816	3.551	3.320	2.852	2.498	2.221	2.000
22	19.660	17.658	14.451	12.042	10.201	8.772	7.645	6.743	6.359	6.011	5.410	4.909	4.488	4.130	3.970	3.822	3.556	3.323	2.853	2.498	2.222	2.000
23	20.456	18.292	14.857	12.303	10.371	8.883	7.718	6.792	6.399	6.044	5.432	4.925	4.499	4.137	3.976	3.827	3.559	3.325	2.854	2.499	2.222	2.000
24	21.243	18.914	15.247	12.550	10.529	8.985	7.784	6.835	6.434	6.073	5.451	4.937	4.507	4.143	3.981	3.831	3.562	3.327	2.855	2.499	2.222	2.000
25	22.023	19.523	15.622	12.783	10.675	9.077	7.843	6.873	6.464	6.097	5.467	4.948	4.514	4.147	3.985	3.834	3.564	3.329	2.856	2.499	2.222	2.000
26	22.795	20.121	15.983	13.003	10.810	9.161	7.896	6.906	6.491	6.118	5.480	4.956	4.520	4.151	3.988	3.837	3.566	3.330	2.856	2.500	2.222	2.000
27	23.560	20.707	16.330	13.211	10.935	9.237	7.943	6.935	6.514	6.136	5.492	4.964	4.524	4.154	3.990	3.839	3.567	3.331	2.856	2.500	2.222	2.000
28	24.316	21.281	16.663	13.406	11.051	9.307	7.984	6.961	6.534	6.152	5.502	4.970	4.528	4.157	3.992	3.840	3.568	3.331	2.857	2.500	2.222	2.000
29	25.066	21.844	16.984	13.591	11.158	9.370	8.022	6.983	6.551	6.166	5.510	4.975	4.531	4.159	3.994	3.841	3.569	3.332	2.857	2.500	2.222	2.000
30	25.808	22.396	17.292	13.765	11.258	9.427	8.055	7.003	6.566	6.177	5.517	4.979	4.534	4.160	3.995	3.842	3.569	3.332	2.857	2.500	2.222	2.000
40	32.835	27.355	19.793	15.046	11.925	9.779	8.244	7.105	6.642	6.234	5.548	4.997	4.544	4.166	3.999	3.846	3.571	3.333	2.857	2.500	2.222	2.000
50	39.196	31.424	21.482	15.762	12.234	9.915	8.304	7.133	6.661	6.246	5.554	4.999	4.545	4.167	4.000	3.846	3.571	3.333	2.857	2.500	2.222	2.000

Source: Adapted from Norman Barish, Economic Analysis for Engineering and Management Decision Making (New York: McGraw-Hill, 1962).

623

TABLE B   Present Value of a Single Payment: PVSP

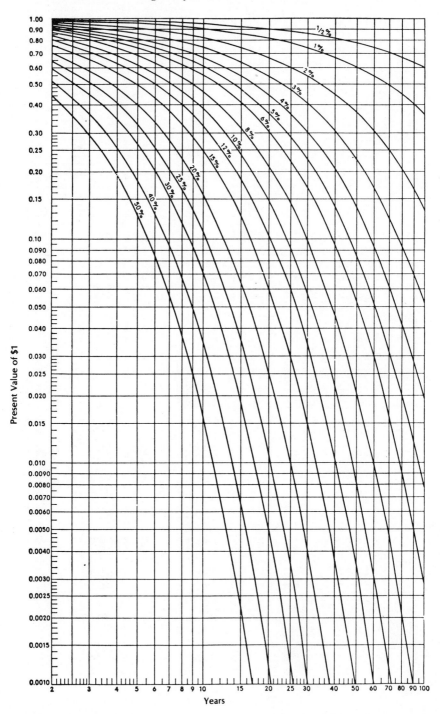

Years

TABLE B (concluded)   Present Value of $1

$$PV = (1 + k)^{-N}$$

Years Hence	1%	2%	4%	6%	8%	10%	12%	14%	15%	16%	18%	20%	22%	24%	25%	26%	28%	30%	35%	40%	45%	50%
1	0.990	0.980	0.962	0.943	0.926	0.909	0.893	0.877	0.870	0.862	0.847	0.833	0.820	0.806	0.800	0.794	0.781	0.769	0.741	0.714	0.690	0.667
2	0.980	0.961	0.925	0.890	0.857	0.826	0.797	0.769	0.756	0.743	0.718	0.694	0.672	0.650	0.640	0.630	0.610	0.592	0.549	0.510	0.476	0.444
3	0.971	0.942	0.889	0.840	0.794	0.751	0.712	0.675	0.658	0.641	0.609	0.579	0.551	0.524	0.512	0.500	0.477	0.455	0.406	0.364	0.328	0.296
4	0.961	0.924	0.855	0.792	0.735	0.683	0.636	0.592	0.572	0.552	0.516	0.482	0.451	0.423	0.410	0.397	0.373	0.350	0.301	0.260	0.226	0.198
5	0.951	0.906	0.822	0.747	0.681	0.621	0.567	0.519	0.497	0.476	0.437	0.402	0.370	0.341	0.328	0.315	0.291	0.269	0.223	0.186	0.156	0.132
6	0.942	0.888	0.790	0.705	0.630	0.564	0.507	0.456	0.432	0.410	0.370	0.335	0.303	0.275	0.262	0.250	0.227	0.207	0.165	0.133	0.108	0.088
7	0.933	0.871	0.760	0.665	0.583	0.513	0.452	0.400	0.376	0.354	0.314	0.279	0.249	0.222	0.210	0.198	0.178	0.159	0.122	0.095	0.074	0.059
8	0.923	0.853	0.731	0.627	0.540	0.467	0.404	0.351	0.327	0.305	0.266	0.233	0.204	0.179	0.168	0.157	0.139	0.123	0.091	0.068	0.051	0.039
9	0.914	0.837	0.703	0.592	0.500	0.424	0.361	0.308	0.284	0.263	0.225	0.194	0.167	0.144	0.134	0.125	0.108	0.094	0.067	0.048	0.035	0.026
10	0.905	0.820	0.676	0.558	0.463	0.386	0.322	0.270	0.247	0.227	0.191	0.162	0.137	0.116	0.107	0.099	0.085	0.073	0.050	0.035	0.024	0.017
11	0.896	0.804	0.650	0.527	0.429	0.350-	0.287	0.237	0.215	0.195	0.162	0.135	0.112	0.094	0.086	0.079	0.066	0.056	0.037	0.025	0.017	0.012
12	0.887	0.788	0.625	0.497	0.397	0.319	0.257	0.208	0.187	0.168	0.137	0.112	0.092	0.076	0.069	0.062	0.052	0.043	0.027	0.018	0.012	0.008
13	0.879	0.773	0.601	0.469	0.368	0.290	0.229	0.182	0.163	0.145	0.116	0.093	0.075	0.061	0.055	0.050	0.040	0.033	0.020	0.013	0.008	0.005
14	0.870	0.758	0.577	0.442	0.340	0.263	0.205	0.160	0.141	0.125	0.099	0.078	0.062	0.049	0.044	0.039	0.032	0.025	0.015	0.009	0.006	0.003
15	0.861	0.743	0.555	0.417	0.315	0.239	0.183	0.140	0.123	0.108	0.084	0.065	0.051	0.040	0.035	0.031	0.025	0.020	0.011	0.006	0.004	0.002
16	0.853	0.728	0.534	0.394	0.292	0.218	0.163	0.123	0.107	0.093	0.071	0.054	0.042	0.032	0.028	0.025	0.019	0.015	0.008	0.005	0.003	0.002
17	0.844	0.714	0.513	0.371	0.270	0.198	0.146	0.108	0.093	0.080	0.060	0.045	0.034	0.026	0.023	0.020	0.015	0.012	0.006	0.003	0.002	0.001
18	0.836	0.700	0.494	0.350	0.250	0.180	0.130	0.095	0.081	0.069	0.051	0.038	0.028	0.021	0.018	0.016	0.012	0.009	0.005	0.002	0.001	0.001
19	0.828	0.686	0.475	0.331	0.232	0.164	0.116	0.083	0.070	0.060	0.043	0.031	0.023	0.017	0.014	0.012	0.009	0.007	0.003	0.002	0.001	
20	0.820	0.673	0.456	0.312	0.215	0.149	0.104	0.073	0.061	0.051	0.037	0.026	0.019	0.014	0.012	0.010	0.007	0.005	0.002	0.001		
21	0.811	0.660	0.439	0.294	0.199	0.135	0.093	0.064	0.053	0.044	0.031	0.022	0.015	0.011	0.009	0.008	0.006	0.004	0.002	0.001		
22	0.803	0.647	0.422	0.278	0.184	0.123	0.083	0.056	0.046	0.038	0.026	0.018	0.013	0.009	0.007	0.006	0.004	0.003	0.001	0.001		
23	0.795	0.634	0.406	0.262	0.170	0.112	0.074	0.049	0.040	0.033	0.022	0.015	0.010	0.007	0.006	0.005	0.003	0.002	0.001			
24	0.788	0.622	0.390	0.247	0.158	0.102	0.066	0.043	0.035	0.028	0.019	0.013	0.008	0.006	0.005	0.004	0.003	0.002	0.001			
25	0.780	0.610	0.375	0.233	0.146	0.092	0.059	0.038	0.030	0.024	0.016	0.010	0.007	0.005	0.004	0.003	0.002	0.001	0.001			
26	0.772	0.598	0.361	0.220	0.135	0.084	0.053	0.033	0.026	0.021	0.014	0.009	0.006	0.004	0.003	0.002	0.002	0.001				
27	0.764	0.586	0.347	0.207	0.125	0.076	0.047	0.029	0.023	0.018	0.011	0.007	0.005	0.003	0.002	0.002	0.001	0.001				
28	0.757	0.574	0.333	0.196	0.116	0.069	0.042	0.026	0.020	0.016	0.010	0.006	0.004	0.002	0.002	0.002	0.001	0.001				
29	0.749	0.563	0.321	0.185	0.107	0.063	0.037	0.022	0.017	0.014	0.008	0.005	0.003	0.002	0.002	0.001	0.001	0.001				
30	0.742	0.552	0.308	0.174	0.099	0.057	0.033	0.020	0.015	0.012	0.007	0.004	0.003	0.002	0.001	0.001	0.001	0.001				
40	0.672	0.453	0.208	0.097	0.046	0.022	0.011	0.005	0.004	0.003	0.001	0.001										
50	0.608	0.372	0.141	0.054	0.021	0.009	0.003	0.001	0.001	0.001												

TABLE C   Mantissas for Four-Place Common Logarithms

N	0	1	2	3	4	5	6	7	8	9
10	0000	0043	0086	0128	0170	0212	0253	0294	0334	0374
11	0414	0453	0492	0531	0569	0607	0645	0682	0719	0755
12	0792	0828	0864	0899	0934	0969	1004	1038	1072	1106
13	1139	1173	1206	1239	1271	1303	1335	1367	1399	1430
14	1461	1492	1523	1553	1584	1614	1644	1673	1703	1732
15	1761	1790	1818	1847	1875	1903	1931	1959	1987	2014
16	2041	2068	2095	2122	2148	2175	2201	2227	2253	2279
17	2304	2330	2355	2380	2405	2430	2455	2480	2504	2529
18	2553	2577	2601	2625	2648	2672	2695	2718	2742	2765
19	2788	2810	2833	2856	2878	2900	2923	2945	2967	2989
20	3010	3032	3054	3075	3096	3118	3139	3160	3181	3201
21	3222	3243	3263	3284	3304	3324	3345	3365	3385	3404
22	3424	3444	3464	3483	3502	3522	3541	3560	3579	3598
23	3617	3636	3655	3674	3692	3711	3729	3747	3766	3784
24	3802	3820	3838	3856	3874	3892	3909	3927	3945	3962
25	3979	3997	4014	4031	4048	4065	4082	4099	4116	4133
26	4150	4166	4183	4200	4216	4232	4249	4265	4281	4298
27	4314	4330	4346	4362	4378	4393	4409	4425	4440	4456
28	4472	4487	4502	4518	4533	4548	4564	4579	4594	4609
29	4624	4639	4654	4669	4683	4698	4713	4728	4742	4757
30	4771	4786	4800	4814	4829	4843	4857	4871	4886	4900
31	4914	4928	4942	4955	4969	4983	4997	5011	5024	5038
32	5051	5065	5079	5092	5105	5119	5132	5145	5159	5172
33	5185	5198	5211	5224	5237	5250	5263	5276	5289	5302
34	5315	5328	5340	5353	5366	5378	5391	5403	5416	5428
35	5441	5453	5465	5478	5490	5502	5514	5527	5539	5551
36	5563	5575	5587	5599	5611	5623	5635	5647	5658	5670
37	5682	5694	5705	5717	5729	5740	5752	5763	5775	5786
38	5798	5809	5821	5832	5843	5855	5866	5877	5888	5899
39	5911	5922	5933	5944	5955	5966	5977	5988	5999	6010
40	6021	6031	6042	6053	6064	6075	6085	6096	6107	6117
41	6128	6138	6149	6160	6170	6180	6191	6201	6212	6222
42	6232	6243	6253	6263	6274	6284	6294	6304	6314	6325
43	6335	6345	6355	6365	6375	6385	6395	6405	6415	6425
44	6435	6444	6454	6464	6474	6484	6493	6503	6513	6522
45	6532	6542	6551	6561	6571	6580	6590	6599	6609	6618
46	6628	6637	6646	6656	6665	6675	6684	6693	6702	6712
47	6721	6730	6739	6749	6758	6767	6776	6785	6794	6803
48	6812	6821	6830	6839	6848	6857	6866	6875	6884	6893
49	6902	6911	6920	6928	6937	6946	6955	6964	6972	6981
50	6990	6998	7007	7016	7024	7033	7042	7050	7059	7067
51	7076	7084	7093	7101	7110	7118	7126	7135	7143	7152
52	7160	7168	7177	7185	7193	7202	7210	7218	7226	7235
53	7243	7251	7259	7267	7275	7284	7292	7300	7308	7316
54	7324	7332	7340	7348	7356	7364	7372	7380	7388	7396

TABLE C *(concluded)*

N	0	1	2	3	4	5	6	7	8	9
55	7404	7412	7419	7427	7435	7443	7451	7459	7466	7474
56	7482	7490	7497	7505	7513	7520	7528	7536	7543	7551
57	7559	7566	7574	7582	7589	7597	7604	7612	7619	7627
58	7634	7642	7649	7657	7664	7672	7679	7686	7694	7701
59	7709	7716	7723	7731	7738	7745	7752	7760	7767	7774
60	7782	7789	7796	7803	7810	7818	7825	7832	7839	7846
61	7853	7860	7868	7875	7882	7889	7896	7903	7910	7917
62	7924	7931	7938	7945	7952	7959	7966	7973	7980	7987
63	7993	8000	8007	8014	8021	8028	8035	8041	8048	8055
64	8062	8069	8075	8082	8089	8096	8102	8109	8116	8122
65	8129	8136	8142	8149	8156	8162	8169	8176	8182	8189
66	8195	8202	8209	8215	8222	8228	8235	8241	8248	8254
67	8261	8267	8274	8280	8287	8293	8299	8306	8312	8319
68	8325	8331	8338	8344	8351	8357	8363	8370	8376	8382
69	8388	8395	8401	8407	8414	8420	8426	8432	8439	8445
70	8451	8457	8463	8470	8476	8482	8488	8494	8500	8506
71	8513	8519	8525	8531	8537	8543	8549	8555	8561	8567
72	8573	8579	8585	8591	8597	8603	8609	8615	8621	8627
73	8633	8639	8645	8651	8657	8663	8669	8675	8681	8686
74	8692	8698	8704	8710	8716	8722	8727	8733	8739	8745
75	8751	8756	8762	8768	8774	8779	8785	8791	8797	8802
76	8808	8814	8820	8825	8831	8837	8842	8848	8854	8859
77	8865	8871	8876	8882	8887	8893	8899	8904	8910	8915
78	8921	8927	8932	8938	8943	8949	8954	8960	8965	8971
79	8976	8982	8987	8993	8998	9004	9009	9015	9020	9025
80	9031	9036	9042	9047	9053	9058	9063	9069	9074	9079
81	9085	9090	9096	9101	9106	9112	9117	9122	9128	9133
82	9138	9143	9149	9154	9159	9165	9170	9175	9180	9186
83	9191	9196	9201	9206	9212	9217	9222	9227	9232	9238
84	9243	9248	9253	9258	9263	9269	9274	9279	9284	9289
85	9294	9299	9304	9309	9315	9320	9325	9330	9335	9340
86	9345	9350	9355	9360	9365	9370	9375	9380	9385	9390
87	9395	9400	9405	9410	9415	9420	9425	9430	9435	9440
88	9445	9450	9455	9460	9465	9469	9474	9479	9484	9489
89	9494	9499	9504	9509	9513	9518	9523	9528	9533	9538
90	9542	9547	9552	9557	9562	9566	9571	9576	9581	9586
91	9590	9595	9600	9605	9609	9614	9619	9624	9628	9633
92	9638	9643	9647	9652	9657	9661	9666	9671	9675	9680
93	9685	9689	9694	9699	9703	9708	9713	9717	9722	9727
94	9731	9736	9741	9745	9750	9754	9759	9763	9768	9773
95	9777	9782	9786	9791	9795	9800	9805	9809	9814	9818
96	9823	9827	9832	9836	9841	9845	9850	9854	9859	9863
97	9868	9872	9877	9881	9886	9890	9894	9899	9903	9908
98	9912	9917	9921	9926	9930	9934	9939	9943	9948	9952
99	9956	9961	9965	9969	9974	9978	9983	9987	9991	9996

TABLE D   Binomial Coefficients

n	$\binom{n}{0}$	$\binom{n}{1}$	$\binom{n}{2}$	$\binom{n}{3}$	$\binom{n}{4}$	$\binom{n}{5}$	$\binom{n}{6}$	$\binom{n}{7}$	$\binom{n}{8}$	$\binom{n}{9}$	$\binom{n}{10}$
0	1										
1	1	1									
2	1	2	1								
3	1	3	3	1							
4	1	4	6	4	1						
5	1	5	10	10	5	1					
6	1	6	15	20	15	6	1				
7	1	7	21	35	35	21	7	1			
8	1	8	28	56	70	56	28	8	1		
9	1	9	36	84	126	126	84	36	9	1	
10	1	10	45	120	210	252	210	120	45	10	1
11	1	11	55	165	330	462	462	330	165	55	11
12	1	12	66	220	495	792	924	792	495	220	66
13	1	13	78	286	715	1287	1716	1716	1287	715	286
14	1	14	91	364	1001	2002	3003	3432	3003	2002	1001
15	1	15	105	455	1365	3003	5005	6435	6435	5005	3003
16	1	16	120	560	1820	4368	8008	11440	12870	11440	8008
17	1	17	136	680	2380	6188	12376	19448	24310	24310	19448
18	1	18	153	816	3060	8568	18564	31824	43758	48620	43758
19	1	19	171	969	3876	11628	27132	50388	75582	92378	92378
20	1	20	190	1140	4845	15504	38760	77520	125970	167960	184756

NOTE: $\binom{n}{m} = \dfrac{n(n-1)(n-2)\cdots(n-m+1)}{m(m-1)(m-2)\cdots 3\cdot 2\cdot 1}$; $\binom{n}{0} = 1$; $\binom{n}{1} = n$.

For coefficients missing from the above table, use the relation

$$\binom{n}{m} = \binom{n}{n-m}; \text{ e.g. } \binom{20}{11} = \binom{20}{9} = 167960.$$

TABLE E   Areas under the Standard Normal Curve

This table shows the area between zero (the mean of a standard normal variable) and z. For example, if $z = 1.50$, this is the shaded area shown below which equals .4332.

z	.00	.01	.02	.03	.04	.05	.06	.07	.08	.09
0.0	.0000	.0040	.0080	.0120	.0160	.0199	.0239	.0279	.0319	.0359
0.1	.0398	.0438	.0478	.0517	.0557	.0596	.0636	.0675	.0714	.0753
0.2	.0793	.0832	.0871	.0910	.0948	.0987	.1026	.1064	.1103	.1141
0.3	.1179	.1217	.1255	.1293	.1331	.1368	.1406	.1443	.1480	.1517
0.4	.1554	.1591	.1628	.1664	.1700	.1736	.1772	.1808	.1844	.1879
0.5	.1915	.1950	.1985	.2019	.2054	.2088	.2123	.2157	.2190	.2224
0.6	.2257	.2291	.2324	.2357	.2389	.2422	.2454	.2486	.2517	.2549
0.7	.2580	.2611	.2642	.2673	.2704	.2734	.2764	.2794	.2823	.2852
0.8	.2881	.2910	.2939	.2967	.2995	.3023	.3051	.3078	.3106	.3133
0.9	.3159	.3186	.3212	.3238	.3264	.3289	.3315	.3340	.3365	.3389
1.0	.3413	.3438	.3461	.3485	.3508	.3531	.3554	.3577	.3599	.3621
1.1	.3643	.3665	.3686	.3708	.3729	.3749	.3770	.3790	.3810	.3830
1.2	.3849	.3869	.3888	.3907	.3925	.3944	.3962	.3980	.3997	.4015
1.3	.4032	.4049	.4066	.4082	.4099	.4115	.4131	.4147	.4162	.4177
1.4	.4192	.4207	.4222	.4236	.4251	.4265	.4279	.4292	.4306	.4319
1.5	.4332	.4345	.4357	.4370	.4382	.4394	.4406	.4418	.4429	.4441
1.6	.4452	.4463	.4474	.4484	.4495	.4505	.4515	.4525	.4535	.4545
1.7	.4554	.4564	.4573	.4582	.4591	.4599	.4608	.4616	.4625	.4633
1.8	.4641	.4649	.4656	.4664	.4671	.4678	.4686	.4693	.4699	.4706
1.9	.4713	.4719	.4726	.4732	.4738	.4744	.4750	.4756	.4761	.4767
2.0	.4772	.4778	.4783	.4788	.4793	.4798	.4803	.4808	.4812	.4817
2.1	.4821	.4826	.4830	.4834	.4838	.4842	.4846	.4850	.4854	.4857
2.2	.4861	.4864	.4868	.4871	.4875	.4878	.4881	.4884	.4887	.4890
2.3	.4893	.4896	.4898	.4901	.4904	.4906	.4909	.4911	.4913	.4916
2.4	.4918	.4920	.4922	.4925	.4927	.4929	.4931	.4932	.4934	.4936
2.5	.4938	.4940	.4941	.4943	.4945	.4946	.4948	.4949	.4951	.4952
2.6	.4953	.4955	.4956	.4957	.4959	.4960	.4961	.4962	.4963	.4964
2.7	.4965	.4966	.4967	.4968	.4969	.4970	.4971	.4972	.4973	.4974
2.8	.4974	.4975	.4976	.4977	.4977	.4978	.4979	.4979	.4980	.4981
2.9	.4981	.4982	.4982	.4983	.4984	.4984	.4985	.4985	.4986	.4986
3.0	.4987	.4987	.4987	.4988	.4988	.4989	.4989	.4989	.4990	.4990

Source: Adapted from National Bureau of Standards, *Tables of Normal Probability Functions,* Applied Mathematics Series 23 (U.S. Department of Commerce, 1953).

TABLE F Percentage Points of the *t* Distribution

Example
Pr $(t > 2.086) = 0.025$
Pr $(t > 1.725) = 0.05$ for df = 20
Pr $(|t| > 1.725) = 0.10$

Pr df	0.25 0.50	0.10 0.20	0.05 0.10	0.025 0.05	0.01 0.02	0.005 0.010	0.001 0.002
1	1.000	3.078	6.314	12.706	31.821	63.657	318.31
2	0.816	1.886	2.920	4.303	6.965	9.925	22.327
3	0.765	1.638	2.353	3.182	4.541	5.841	10.214
4	0.741	1.533	2.132	2.776	3.747	4.604	7.173
5	0.727	1.476	2.015	2.571	3.365	4.032	5.893
6	0.718	1.440	1.943	2.447	3.143	3.707	5.208
7	0.711	1.415	1.895	2.365	2.998	3.499	4.785
8	0.706	1.397	1.860	2.306	2.896	3.355	4.501
9	0.703	1.383	1.833	2.262	2.821	3.250	4.297
10	0.700	1.372	1.812	2.228	2.764	3.169	4.144
11	0.697	1.363	1.796	2.201	2.718	3.106	4.025
12	0.695	1.356	1.782	2.179	2.681	3.055	3.930
13	0.694	1.350	1.771	2.160	2.650	3.012	3.852
14	0.692	1.345	1.761	2.145	2.624	2.977	3.787
15	0.691	1.341	1.753	2.131	2.602	2.947	3.733
16	0.690	1.337	1.746	2.120	2.583	2.921	3.686
17	0.689	1.333	1.740	2.110	2.567	2.898	3.646
18	0.688	1.330	1.734	2.101	2.552	2.878	3.610
19	0.688	1.328	1.729	2.093	2.539	2.861	3.579
20	0.687	1.325	1.725	2.086	2.528	2.845	3.552
21	0.686	1.323	1.721	2.080	2.518	2.831	3.527
22	0.686	1.321	1.717	2.074	2.508	2.819	3.505
23	0.685	1.319	1.714	2.069	2.500	2.807	3.485
24	0.685	1.318	1.711	2.064	2.492	2.797	3.467
25	0.684	1.316	1.708	2.060	2.485	2.787	3.450
26	0.684	1.315	1.706	2.056	2.479	2.779	3.435
27	0.684	1.314	1.703	2.052	2.473	2.771	3.421
28	0.683	1.313	1.701	2.048	2.467	2.763	3.408
29	0.683	1.311	1.699	2.045	2.462	2.756	3.396
30	0.683	1.310	1.697	2.042	2.457	2.750	3.385
40	0.681	1.303	1.684	2.021	2.423	2.704	3.307
60	0.679	1.296	1.671	2.000	2.390	2.660	3.232
120	0.677	1.289	1.658	1.980	2.358	2.167	3.160
∞	0.674	1.282	1.645	1.960	2.326	2.576	3.090

Note: The smaller probability shown at the head of each column is the area in one tail; the larger probability is the area in both tails.

Source: From E.S. Pearson and H.O. Hartley, eds., *Biometrika Tables for Statisticians,* vol. 1, 3d ed., table 12, Cambridge University Press, 1966.

TABLE G   **Values of the *F*-Ratio Where the Probability of a Larger Value = to .05**

Degrees of freedom for numerator

	1	2	3	4	5	6	7	8	9
1	161.4	199.5	215.7	224.6	230.2	234.0	236.8	238.9	240.5
2	18.51	19.00	19.16	19.25	19.30	19.33	19.35	19.37	19.38
3	10.13	9.55	9.28	9.12	9.01	8.94	8.89	8.85	8.81
4	7.71	6.94	6.59	6.39	6.26	6.16	6.09	6.04	6.00
5	6.61	5.79	5.41	5.19	5.05	4.95	4.88	4.82	4.77
6	5.99	5.14	4.76	4.53	4.39	4.28	4.21	4.15	4.10
7	5.59	4.74	4.35	4.12	3.97	3.87	3.79	3.73	3.68
8	5.32	4.46	4.07	3.84	3.69	3.58	3.50	3.44	3.39
9	5.12	4.26	3.86	3.63	3.48	3.37	3.29	3.23	3.18
10	4.96	4.10	3.71	3.48	3.33	3.22	3.14	3.07	3.02
11	4.84	3.98	3.59	3.36	3.20	3.09	3.01	2.95	2.90
12	4.75	3.89	3.49	3.26	3.11	3.00	2.91	2.85	2.80
13	4.67	3.81	3.41	3.18	3.03	2.92	2.83	2.77	2.71
14	4.60	3.74	3.34	3.11	2.96	2.85	2.76	2.70	2.65
15	4.54	3.68	3.29	3.06	2.90	2.79	2.71	2.64	2.59
16	4.49	3.63	3.24	3.01	2.85	2.74	2.66	2.59	2.54
17	4.45	3.59	3.20	2.96	2.81	2.70	2.61	2.55	2.49
18	4.41	3.55	3.16	2.93	2.77	2.66	2.58	2.51	2.46
19	4.38	3.52	3.13	2.90	2.74	2.63	2.54	2.48	2.42
20	4.35	3.49	3.10	2.87	2.71	2.60	2.51	2.45	2.39
21	4.32	3.47	3.07	2.84	2.68	2.57	2.49	2.42	2.37
22	4.30	3.44	3.05	2.82	2.66	2.55	2.46	2.40	2.34
23	4.28	3.42	3.03	2.80	2.64	2.53	2.44	2.37	2.32
24	4.26	3.40	3.01	2.78	2.62	2.51	2.42	2.36	2.30
25	4.24	3.39	2.99	2.76	2.60	2.49	2.40	2.34	2.28
26	4.23	3.37	2.98	2.74	2.59	2.47	2.39	2.32	2.27
27	4.21	3.35	2.96	2.73	2.57	2.46	2.37	2.31	2.25
28	4.20	3.34	2.95	2.71	2.56	2.45	2.36	2.29	2.24
29	4.18	3.33	2.93	2.70	2.55	2.43	2.35	2.28	2.22
30	4.17	3.32	2.92	2.69	2.53	2.42	2.33	2.27	2.21
40	4.08	3.23	2.84	2.61	2.45	2.34	2.25	2.18	2.12
60	4.00	3.15	2.76	2.53	2.37	2.25	2.17	2.10	2.04
120	3.92	3.07	2.68	2.45	2.29	2.17	2.09	2.02	1.96
∞	3.84	3.00	2.60	2.37	2.21	2.10	2.01	1.94	1.88

Degrees of freedom for denominator

TABLE G *(continued)*   **Values of the *F*-Ratio Where the Probability of a Larger Value = to .05**

Degrees of freedom for numerator

		10	12	15	20	24	30	40	60	120	∞
	1	241.9	243.9	245.9	248.0	249.1	250.1	251.1	252.2	253.3	254.3
	2	19.40	19.41	19.43	19.45	19.45	19.46	19.47	19.48	19.49	19.50
	3	8.79	8.74	8.70	8.66	8.64	8.62	8.59	8.57	8.55	8.53
	4	5.96	5.91	5.86	5.80	5.77	5.75	5.72	5.69	5.66	5.63
	5	4.74	4.68	4.62	4.56	4.53	4.50	4.46	4.43	4.40	4.36
	6	4.06	4.00	3.94	3.87	3.84	3.81	3.77	3.74	3.70	3.67
	7	3.64	3.57	3.51	3.44	3.41	3.38	3.34	3.30	3.27	3.23
	8	3.35	3.28	3.22	3.15	3.12	3.08	3.04	3.01	2.97	2.93
	9	3.14	3.07	3.01	2.94	2.90	2.86	2.83	2.79	2.75	2.71
	10	2.98	2.91	2.85	2.77	2.74	2.70	2.66	2.62	2.58	2.54
	11	2.85	2.79	2.72	2.65	2.61	2.57	2.53	2.49	2.45	2.40
	12	2.75	2.69	2.62	2.54	2.51	2.47	2.43	2.38	2.34	2.30
	13	2.67	2.60	2.53	2.46	2.42	2.38	2.34	2.30	2.25	2.21
	14	2.60	2.53	2.46	2.39	2.35	2.31	2.27	2.22	2.18	2.13
	15	2.54	2.48	2.40	2.33	2.29	2.25	2.20	2.16	2.11	2.07
	16	2.49	2.42	2.35	2.28	2.24	2.19	2.15	2.11	2.06	2.01
	17	2.45	2.38	2.31	2.23	2.19	2.15	2.10	2.06	2.01	1.96
	18	2.41	2.34	2.27	2.19	2.15	2.11	2.06	2.02	1.97	1.92
	19	2.38	2.31	2.23	2.16	2.11	2.07	2.03	1.98	1.93	1.88
	20	2.35	2.28	2.20	2.12	2.08	2.04	1.99	1.95	1.90	1.84
	21	2.32	2.25	2.18	2.10	2.05	2.01	1.96	1.92	1.87	1.81
	22	2.30	2.23	2.15	2.07	2.03	1.98	1.94	1.89	1.84	1.78
	23	2.27	2.20	2.13	2.05	2.01	1.96	1.91	1.86	1.81	1.76
	24	2.25	2.18	2.11	2.03	1.98	1.94	1.89	1.84	1.79	1.73
	25	2.24	2.16	2.09	2.01	1.96	1.92	1.87	1.82	1.77	1.71
	26	2.22	2.15	2.07	1.99	1.95	1.90	1.85	1.80	1.75	1.69
	27	2.20	2.13	2.06	1.97	1.93	1.88	1.84	1.79	1.73	1.67
	28	2.19	2.12	2.04	1.96	1.91	1.87	1.82	1.77	1.71	1.65
	29	2.18	2.10	2.03	1.94	1.90	1.85	1.81	1.75	1.70	1.64
	30	2.16	2.09	2.01	1.93	1.89	1.84	1.79	1.74	1.68	1.62
	40	2.08	2.00	1.92	1.84	1.79	1.74	1.69	1.64	1.58	1.51
	60	1.99	1.92	1.84	1.75	1.70	1.65	1.59	1.53	1.47	1.39
	120	1.91	1.83	1.75	1.66	1.61	1.55	1.50	1.43	1.35	1.25
	∞	1.83	1.75	1.67	1.57	1.52	1.46	1.39	1.32	1.22	1.00

Degrees of freedom for denominator

TABLE G *(continued)*   **Values of the *F*-Ratio Where the Probability of a Larger Value = to .01**

Degrees of freedom for numerator

		1	2	3	4	5	6	7	8	9
	1	4052	4999.5	5403	5625	5764	5859	5928	5982	6022
	2	98.50	99.00	99.17	99.25	99.30	99.33	99.36	99.37	99.39
	3	34.12	30.82	29.46	28.71	28.24	27.91	27.67	27.49	27.35
	4	21.20	18.00	16.69	15.98	15.52	15.21	14.98	14.80	14.66
	5	16.26	13.27	12.06	11.39	10.97	10.67	10.46	10.29	10.16
	6	13.75	10.92	9.78	9.15	8.75	8.47	8.26	8.10	7.98
	7	12.25	9.55	8.45	7.85	7.46	7.19	6.99	6.84	6.72
	8	11.26	8.65	7.59	7.01	6.63	6.37	6.18	6.03	5.91
	9	10.56	8.02	6.99	6.42	6.06	5.80	5.61	5.47	5.35
	10	10.04	7.56	6.55	5.99	5.64	5.39	5.20	5.06	4.94
	11	9.65	7.21	6.22	5.67	5.32	5.07	4.89	4.74	4.63
Degrees of freedom for denominator	12	9.33	6.93	5.95	5.41	5.06	4.82	4.64	4.50	4.39
	13	9.07	6.70	5.74	5.21	4.86	4.62	4.44	4.30	4.19
	14	8.86	6.51	5.56	5.04	4.69	4.46	4.28	4.14	4.03
	15	8.68	6.36	5.42	4.89	4.56	4.32	4.14	4.00	3.89
	16	8.53	6.23	5.29	4.77	4.44	4.20	4.03	3.89	3.78
	17	8.40	6.11	5.18	4.67	4.34	4.10	3.93	3.79	3.68
	18	8.29	6.01	5.09	4.58	4.25	4.01	3.84	3.71	3.60
	19	8.18	5.93	5.01	4.50	4.17	3.94	3.77	3.63	3.52
	20	8.10	5.85	4.94	4.43	4.10	3.87	3.70	3.56	3.46
	21	8.02	5.78	4.87	4.37	4.04	3.81	3.64	3.51	3.40
	22	7.95	5.72	4.82	4.31	3.99	3.76	3.59	3.45	3.35
	23	7.88	5.66	4.76	4.26	3.94	3.71	3.54	3.41	3.30
	24	7.82	5.61	4.72	4.22	3.90	3.67	3.50	3.36	3.26
	25	7.77	5.57	4.68	4.18	3.85	3.63	3.46	3.32	3.22
	26	7.72	5.53	4.64	4.14	3.82	3.59	3.42	3.29	3.18
	27	7.68	5.49	4.60	4.11	3.78	3.56	3.39	3.26	3.15
	28	7.64	5.45	4.57	4.07	3.75	3.53	3.36	3.23	3.12
	29	7.60	5.42	4.54	4.04	3.73	3.50	3.33	3.20	3.09
	30	7.56	5.39	4.51	4.02	3.70	3.47	3.30	3.17	3.07
	40	7.31	5.18	4.31	3.83	3.51	3.29	3.12	2.99	2.89
	60	7.08	4.98	4.13	3.65	3.34	3.12	2.95	2.82	2.72
	120	6.85	4.79	3.95	3.48	3.17	2.96	2.79	2.66	2.56
	∞	6.63	4.61	3.78	3.32	3.02	2.80	2.64	2.51	2.41

TABLE G *(concluded)*   **Values of the *F*-Ratio Where the Probability of a Larger Value = to .01**

Degrees of freedom for numerator

	10	12	15	20	24	30	40	60	120	∞
1	6056	6106	6157	6209	6235	6261	6287	6313	6339	6366
2	99.40	99.42	99.43	99.45	99.46	99.47	99.47	99.48	99.49	99.50
3	27.23	27.05	26.87	26.69	26.60	26.50	26.41	26.32	26.22	26.13
4	14.55	14.37	14.20	14.02	13.93	13.84	13.75	13.65	13.56	13.46
5	10.05	9.89	9.72	9.55	9.47	9.38	9.29	9.20	9.11	9.02
6	7.87	7.72	7.56	7.40	7.31	7.23	7.14	7.06	6.97	6.88
7	6.62	6.47	6.31	6.16	6.07	5.99	5.91	5.82	5.74	5.65
8	5.81	5.67	5.52	5.36	5.28	5.20	5.12	5.03	4.95	4.86
9	5.26	5.11	4.96	4.81	4.73	4.65	4.57	4.48	4.40	4.31
10	4.85	4.71	4.56	4.41	4.33	4.25	4.17	4.08	4.00	3.91
11	4.54	4.40	4.25	4.10	4.02	3.94	3.86	3.78	3.69	3.60
12	4.30	4.16	4.01	3.86	3.78	3.70	3.62	3.54	3.45	3.36
13	4.10	3.96	3.82	3.66	3.59	3.51	3.43	3.34	3.25	3.17
14	3.94	3.80	3.66	3.51	3.43	3.35	3.27	3.18	3.09	3.00
15	3.80	3.67	3.52	3.37	3.29	3.21	3.13	3.05	2.96	2.87
16	3.69	3.55	3.41	3.26	3.18	3.10	3.02	2.93	2.84	2.75
17	3.59	3.46	3.31	3.16	3.08	3.00	2.92	2.83	2.75	2.65
18	3.51	3.37	3.23	3.08	3.00	2.92	2.84	2.75	2.66	2.57
19	3.43	3.30	3.15	3.00	2.92	2.84	2.76	2.67	2.58	2.49
20	3.37	3.23	3.09	2.94	2.86	2.78	2.69	2.61	2.52	2.42
21	3.31	3.17	3.03	2.88	2.80	2.72	2.64	2.55	2.46	2.36
22	3.26	3.12	2.98	2.83	2.75	2.67	2.58	2.50	2.40	2.31
23	3.21	3.07	2.93	2.78	2.70	2.62	2.54	2.45	2.35	2.26
24	3.17	3.03	2.89	2.74	2.66	2.58	2.49	2.40	2.31	2.21
25	3.13	2.99	2.85	2.70	2.62	2.54	2.45	2.36	2.27	2.17
26	3.09	2.96	2.81	2.66	2.58	2.50	2.42	2.33	2.23	2.13
27	3.06	2.93	2.78	2.63	2.55	2.47	2.38	2.29	2.20	2.10
28	3.03	2.90	2.75	2.60	2.52	2.44	2.35	2.26	2.17	2.06
29	3.00	2.87	2.73	2.57	2.49	2.41	2.33	2.23	2.14	2.03
30	2.98	2.84	2.70	2.55	2.47	2.39	2.30	2.21	2.11	2.01
40	2.80	2.66	2.52	2.37	2.29	2.20	2.11	2.02	1.92	1.80
60	2.63	2.50	2.35	2.20	2.12	2.03	1.94	1.84	1.73	1.60
120	2.47	2.34	2.19	2.03	1.95	1.86	1.76	1.66	1.53	1.38
∞	2.32	2.18	2.04	1.88	1.79	1.70	1.59	1.47	1.32	1.00

Degrees of freedom for denominator (row labels at left)

Source: From E. S. Pearson and H. O. Hartley, eds., *Biometrika Tables for Statisticians*, vol. 1, 3d ed., table 18, Cambridge University Press, 1966.

TABLE H   **Values of d_L and d_U for the Durbin-Watson Test ($\alpha = .05$)**

n	$k = 1$		$k = 2$		$k = 3$		$k = 4$		$k = 5$	
	d_L	d_U	d_L	d_U	d_L	d_U	d_L	d_U	d_L	d_U
15	1.08	1.36	0.95	1.54	0.82	1.75	0.69	1.97	0.56	2.21
16	1.10	1.37	0.98	1.54	0.86	1.73	0.74	1.93	0.62	2.15
17	1.13	1.38	1.02	1.54	0.90	1.71	0.78	1.90	0.67	2.10
18	1.16	1.39	1.05	1.53	0.93	1.69	0.82	1.87	0.71	2.06
19	1.18	1.40	1.08	1.53	0.97	1.68	0.86	1.85	0.75	2.02
20	1.20	1.41	1.10	1.54	1.00	1.68	0.90	1.83	0.79	1.99
21	1.22	1.42	1.13	1.54	1.03	1.67	0.93	1.81	0.83	1.96
22	1.24	1.43	1.15	1.54	1.05	1.66	0.96	1.80	0.86	1.94
23	1.26	1.44	1.17	1.54	1.08	1.66	0.99	1.79	0.90	1.92
24	1.27	1.45	1.19	1.55	1.10	1.66	1.01	1.78	0.93	1.90
25	1.29	1.45	1.21	1.55	1.12	1.66	1.04	1.77	0.95	1.89
26	1.30	1.46	1.22	1.55	1.14	1.65	1.06	1.76	0.98	1.88
27	1.32	1.47	1.24	1.56	1.16	1.65	1.08	1.76	1.01	1.86
28	1.33	1.48	1.26	1.56	1.18	1.65	1.10	1.75	1.03	1.85
29	1.34	1.48	1.27	1.56	1.20	1.65	1.12	1.74	1.05	1.84
30	1.35	1.49	1.28	1.57	1.21	1.65	1.14	1.74	1.07	1.83
31	1.36	1.50	1.30	1.57	1.23	1.65	1.16	1.74	1.09	1.83
32	1.37	1.50	1.31	1.57	1.24	1.65	1.18	1.73	1.11	1.82
33	1.38	1.51	1.32	1.58	1.26	1.65	1.19	1.73	1.13	1.81
34	1.39	1.51	1.33	1.58	1.27	1.65	1.21	1.73	1.15	1.81
35	1.40	1.52	1.34	1.58	1.28	1.65	1.22	1.73	1.16	1.80
36	1.41	1.52	1.35	1.59	1.29	1.65	1.24	1.73	1.18	1.80
37	1.42	1.53	1.36	1.59	1.31	1.66	1.25	1.72	1.19	1.80
38	1.43	1.54	1.37	1.59	1.32	1.66	1.26	1.72	1.21	1.79
39	1.43	1.54	1.38	1.60	1.33	1.66	1.27	1.72	1.22	1.79
40	1.44	1.54	1.39	1.60	1.34	1.66	1.29	1.72	1.23	1.79
45	1.48	1.57	1.43	1.62	1.38	1.67	1.34	1.72	1.29	1.78
50	1.50	1.59	1.46	1.63	1.42	1.67	1.38	1.72	1.34	1.77
55	1.53	1.60	1.49	1.64	1.45	1.68	1.41	1.72	1.38	1.77
60	1.55	1.62	1.51	1.65	1.48	1.69	1.44	1.73	1.41	1.77
65	1.57	1.63	1.54	1.66	1.50	1.70	1.47	1.73	1.44	1.77
70	1.58	1.64	1.55	1.67	1.52	1.70	1.49	1.74	1.46	1.77
75	1.60	1.65	1.57	1.68	1.54	1.71	1.51	1.74	1.49	1.77
80	1.61	1.66	1.59	1.69	1.56	1.72	1.53	1.74	1.51	1.77
85	1.62	1.67	1.60	1.70	1.57	1.72	1.55	1.75	1.52	1.77
90	1.63	1.68	1.61	1.70	1.59	1.73	1.57	1.75	1.54	1.78
95	1.64	1.69	1.62	1.71	1.60	1.73	1.58	1.75	1.56	1.78
100	1.65	1.69	1.63	1.72	1.61	1.74	1.59	1.76	1.57	1.78

TABLE H *(concluded)*   **Values of d_L and d_U for the Durbin-Watson Test ($\alpha = .01$)**

n	$k = 1$ d_L	$k = 1$ d_U	$k = 2$ d_L	$k = 2$ d_U	$k = 3$ d_L	$k = 3$ d_U	$k = 4$ d_L	$k = 4$ d_U	$k = 5$ d_L	$k = 5$ d_U
15	0.81	1.07	0.70	1.25	0.59	1.46	0.49	1.70	0.39	1.96
16	0.84	1.09	0.74	1.25	0.63	1.44	0.53	1.66	0.44	1.90
17	0.87	1.10	0.77	1.25	0.67	1.43	0.57	1.63	0.48	1.85
18	0.90	1.12	0.80	1.26	0.71	1.42	0.61	1.60	0.52	1.80
19	0.93	1.13	0.83	1.26	0.74	1.41	0.65	1.58	0.56	1.77
20	0.95	1.15	0.86	1.27	0.77	1.41	0.68	1.57	0.60	1.74
21	0.97	1.16	0.89	1.27	0.80	1.41	0.72	1.55	0.63	1.71
22	1.00	1.17	0.91	1.28	0.83	1.40	0.75	1.54	0.66	1.69
23	1.02	1.19	0.94	1.29	0.86	1.40	0.77	1.53	0.70	1.67
24	1.04	1.20	0.96	1.30	0.88	1.41	0.80	1.53	0.72	1.66
25	1.05	1.21	0.98	1.30	0.90	1.41	0.83	1.52	0.75	1.65
26	1.07	1.22	1.00	1.31	0.93	1.41	0.85	1.52	0.78	1.64
27	1.09	1.23	1.02	1.32	0.95	1.41	0.88	1.51	0.81	1.63
28	1.10	1.24	1.04	1.32	0.97	1.41	0.90	1.51	0.83	1.62
29	1.12	1.25	1.05	1.33	0.99	1.42	0.92	1.51	0.85	1.61
30	1.13	1.26	1.07	1.34	1.01	1.42	0.94	1.51	0.88	1.61
31	1.15	1.27	1.08	1.34	1.02	1.42	0.96	1.51	0.90	1.60
32	1.16	1.28	1.10	1.35	1.04	1.43	0.98	1.51	0.92	1.60
33	1.17	1.29	1.11	1.36	1.05	1.43	1.00	1.51	0.94	1.59
34	1.18	1.30	1.13	1.36	1.07	1.43	1.01	1.51	0.95	1.59
35	1.19	1.31	1.14	1.37	1.08	1.44	1.03	1.51	0.97	1.59
36	1.21	1.32	1.15	1.38	1.10	1.44	1.04	1.51	0.99	1.59
37	1.22	1.32	1.16	1.38	1.11	1.45	1.06	1.51	1.00	1.59
38	1.23	1.33	1.18	1.39	1.12	1.45	1.07	1.52	1.02	1.58
39	1.24	1.34	1.19	1.39	1.14	1.45	1.09	1.52	1.03	1.58
40	1.25	1.34	1.20	1.40	1.15	1.46	1.10	1.52	1.05	1.58
45	1.29	1.38	1.24	1.42	1.20	1.48	1.16	1.53	1.11	1.58
50	1.32	1.40	1.28	1.45	1.24	1.49	1.20	1.54	1.16	1.59
55	1.36	1.43	1.32	1.47	1.28	1.51	1.25	1.55	1.21	1.59
60	1.38	1.45	1.35	1.48	1.32	1.52	1.28	1.56	1.25	1.60
65	1.41	1.47	1.38	1.50	1.35	1.53	1.31	1.57	1.28	1.61
70	1.43	1.49	1.40	1.52	1.37	1.55	1.34	1.58	1.31	1.61
75	1.45	1.50	1.42	1.53	1.39	1.56	1.37	1.59	1.34	1.62
80	1.47	1.52	1.44	1.54	1.42	1.57	1.39	1.60	1.36	1.62
85	1.48	1.53	1.46	1.55	1.43	1.58	1.41	1.60	1.39	1.63
90	1.50	1.54	1.47	1.56	1.45	1.59	1.43	1.61	1.41	1.64
95	1.51	1.55	1.49	1.57	1.47	1.60	1.45	1.62	1.42	1.64
100	1.52	1.56	1.50	1.58	1.48	1.60	1.46	1.63	1.44	1.65

TABLE I **Formulas for Taking a Derivative**

1. The derivative of a constant is zero, and the derivative of x is one.

2. Derivative of a monomial in x:

$$\frac{d(cx^n)}{dx} = cnx^{n-1}$$

Example:

$$\frac{d(2x^3)}{dx} = 2(3)x^{(3-1)} = 6x^2$$

3. Derivative of a power of a polynomial in x where, $u = f(x)$:

$$\frac{d(cu^n)}{dx} = cnu^{n-1}\frac{du}{dx}$$

Example:

$$\frac{d(2x^3 - 4x^2)^3}{dx} = 3(2x^3 - 4x^2)^2(6x^2 - 8x)$$

4. Derivative of a sum of polynomials in x where, $u = f(x)$, $v = g(x)$, . . . , $z = h(x)$:

$$\frac{d(u + v + z)}{dx} = \frac{du}{dx} + \frac{dv}{dx} + \frac{dz}{dx}$$

Example:

$$\frac{d(3x^3 - 6x^2 + 5x - 10)}{dx} = 9x^2 - 12x + 5$$

5. Derivative of a product of two polynomials in x where, $u = f(x)$, $v = g(x)$:

$$\frac{d(uv)}{dx} = u\frac{dv}{dx} + v\frac{du}{dx}$$

Example:

$$\frac{d(x^2 + 2x)(x - 3)}{dx} = (x^2 + 2x)(1) + (x - 3)(2x + 2) = 3x^2 - 2x - 6$$

6. Derivative of a quotient of two polynomials in x where, $u = f(x)$, $v = g(x)$:

$$\frac{d\left(\frac{u}{v}\right)}{dx} = \frac{v\frac{du}{dx} - u\frac{dv}{dx}}{v^2}$$

Example:

$$\frac{d\left[\frac{x^3 - 1}{x^2 + 3}\right]}{dx} = \frac{(x^2 + 3)(3x^2) - (x^3 - 1)(2x)}{(x^2 + 3)^2}$$
$$= \frac{x^4 + 9x^2 + 2x}{(x^2 + 3)^2}$$

TABLE I *(concluded)*   **Formulas for Taking a Derivative**

7. To take the partial derivative with respect to a particular variable of a multivariate function, $Y = f(X_1, X_2, \ldots, X_n)$, use the formulas above while treating the other independent variables as constants.

Example:

$$w = 3x^2 + 2xy - 3z$$

$$\frac{\partial w}{\partial x} = 6x + 2y$$

$$\frac{\partial w}{\partial y} = 2x$$

$$\frac{\partial w}{\partial z} = -3$$

INDEX